HISTORY OF THE WELSH GUARDS

DEDICATED

BY PERMISSION

TO

HIS MAJESTY THE KING

COLONEL-IN-CHIEF OF THE REGIMENT

HISTORY OF THE WELSH GUARDS

BY C. H. DUDLEY WARD, D.S.O., M.C.

WITH AN INTRODUCTION BY
LIEUTENANT-GENERAL SIR FRANCIS LLOYD
G.C.V.O., K.C.B., D.S.O., etc.

LONDON
JOHN MURRAY, ALBEMARLE STREET, W.
1920

Vandyke, London.

COLONEL H.R.H. THE PRINCE OF WALES.

[*Frontispiece*

INTRODUCTION

IT is the lot of few regiments, as it is of few great men or women, to have the story of their birth and early years written by a contemporary hand. We all know how difficult it is to prove events even within our own times, and therefore the nearer we get to them the more unlikely it is that they recede into the realm of fiction.

The Welsh Guards have this advantage, and, seeing that their inception took place during a great war, it is all the more important that their advent should be set down clearly and by one who was present.

I had the advantage of being present and assisting at the birth, and no one can be better qualified than Major C. H. Dudley Ward, D.S.O., M.C., to carry on the story with its *baptême de feu* and glorious exploits in the subsequent years of war.

It had been the unanimous wish of the Welsh people— than whom none are more noted for their loyalty to the Crown—that the Principality should take its place among the nations of the British Isles in finding a regiment to assist in guarding the Throne.

King George V gave expression to this sentiment, and to his own wishes, on February 6th, 1915, by commanding Field-Marshal Earl Kitchener, K.G., then Secretary of State for War, to put His Majesty's orders into execution. Accordingly, as I was commanding the London District, I was sent for by the Field-Marshal and ordered to raise a battalion immediately. On my asking Lord Kitchener how soon he expected this to be done, he replied, in his usual abrupt manner: "In a week!" My answer was: "They shall go on guard on St. David's Day"—and they DID!

Haste being the order of the day, I asked the help of Col. Sir Henry Streatfeild, commanding the Grenadier Guards, who most generously gave me free access to my old regiment, which I was not slow to take advantage of, by calling upon all Welshmen to join the colours of the Welsh Guards.

A nucleus of some 300 men was thus formed. Officers quickly came in, and with non-commissioned officers who volunteered from the Grenadier and Scots Guards, the foundation of a great regiment was laid, and my promise redeemed, for on St. David's Day, to the strains of the Scots Guards band, the 1st Battalion, Welsh Guards, mounted guard over the King at Buckingham Palace.

Such was their beginning. Their history—is it not already writ large in letters of blood and gold worthy of the Land of our Fathers in the book of the Great War?

When future generations of Welsh Guardsmen look back on those dark but glorious days they will remember with pride the names of Murray Threipland and Douglas Gordon, of Palmer and Osmond Williams, of Bulkeley and the historic name of Clive, of Sergt. R. Bye, V.C., and Mathias, of Waddington and Ham, of Ulyatt and Hammond, and of many another unknown to history or fame who by dying, or living, won the great regiment through to its place of honour—a place which will be maintained so long as the British Army holds up the British Empire.

To all I recommend the ably written pages that follow. They contain what is known of the Welsh Guards during the past four years clearly set out, although, no doubt, as time rolls on and men's visions of the events of these times become clearer, more will be added.

FRANCIS LLOYD,
Lieutenant-General.

Aston Hall, Oswestry,
September 1919,

CONTENTS

CONTENTS

APPENDICES

LIST OF ILLUSTRATIONS

ix

MAPS

MAPS IN TEXT

HISTORY OF THE WELSH GUARDS

CHAPTER I

THE CREATION OF THE REGIMENT

THE character and temperament of the Welsh people cannot fail to produce great and valiant soldiers. A nation which, in spite of invasions by the sword, of enforced and of willing political union with a stronger neighbour, in spite of the more lasting and subtle erosions of nationality produced by close and intimate commercial ties and intercourse, retains its language, reveals an indomitable spirit, a power of endurance and reaction under reverse, a character which can never acknowledge defeat.

Amongst the people of Great Britain there is a feeling of romantic affection for Wales, an open admiration of her proved gallantry. The mind jumps at once to the special association of the country with the King's eldest son—probably to the legend of Edward I, which has so impressed itself on youthful imagination by the pictures in elementary history-books of the King holding a naked babe before a vast gathering of fierce warriors, and so introducing to them their new Prince—which appeals to the pride every man has in his national customs and traditions.

Wales and the Welsh are continually thrusting themselves into the everyday life of the people of Great Britain by commanding a leading position in sport, with their many great footballers and renowned "Fifteens,"

1

and their fiery and determined fighters in the " Ring " ; in art with their singers ; in commerce with their coal.

"Gallant little Wales " is no idle catch phrase. The Anglo-Saxon has absorbed many nationalities, but the Ancient Briton resists him to this day, though for centuries they have fought the common enemy side by side. The proud colours of the old Welsh Regiments carry but a small portion of the military history of their country. It is a glorious history. But the military position of the Welsh in the United Kingdom was not complete until His Majesty King George V ordered the formation of a Welsh Regiment of Foot Guards.

Now that each country of the United Kingdom is represented by a regiment of Foot Guards it may seem strange that Wales was not called upon earlier for this loyal and proud duty; but the representative idea was not general until a recent date. There has been no slight on Wales. The history of the old regiments shows that their foundation was of a haphazard nature. The loyalty of Wales was recognised by the Tudors, and the oldest Guards, the King's Bodyguard of the Yeomen of the Guard, was formed of the trusted Welsh friends of Henry VII, and retained its Welsh customs for a considerable period. Col. Sir Reginald Hennell, D.S.O., in his interesting history of this ancient corps, mentions feasting on St. David's Day in 1531, 1532, 1536, and in 1537 a grant of 40s. given to one of the Guards " towards St. David's Day Feast," and that " the Yeomen of the Guard present Princess Mary with a leek on St. David's Day."

The Yeomen of the Guard were the first troops of a standing army, the first permanent bodyguard of the King, and that they should have been Welsh is but natural when it is remembered that Henry VII was of Welsh descent, and that his most trusted support came from Wales. But in forming this first Guard after Bosworth Field, Henry, who had to rule over a country rent and devastated by civil war, did not for obvious reasons give it a title to suggest party favour. As it was the people did not view the establishment of a permanent Guard with enthusiasm; it was against all precedent, and household duties had to be given to the Guard, which nevertheless was a real fighting force. So the fact that Welsh Guards have not been known as such is due only to the accident of a name given at a time when ideas on the army in general, and the Foot Guards in particular, were in their infancy.

Of the three old regiments of Foot Guards only the Scots Guards bear a title of distinctive nationality. The claim of Wales became obvious with the formation of the Irish Guards. The question of who thought first of Welsh Guards is somewhat futile ; the Welsh are not a slow-witted people, and the gap was there for the whole nation to see. At that time, however, it was not easy to increase the army, and the Scots Guards actually lost their 3rd Battalion. The opportunity only occurred with the outbreak of the Great War. Letters appeared in the daily press, but it is certain that Lord Kitchener had strong opinions on the subject. He was very keen that the Brigade of Guards should be both comprehensive and characteristic of the very best types of British manhood, and he could not tolerate any exclusion of Wales. Knowing the hopes of his Welsh subjects, and their marvellous response to the call to arms, His Majesty never signed a document with greater pleasure than the one now put before him by his Minister for War.

On February 26th, 1915, His Majesty King George V authorised by Royal Warrant the creation of a Welsh Regiment of Foot Guards, to be known as the Welsh Guards. Lord Kitchener was then Secretary of State for War, and set about the task with characteristic energy. General Sir Francis Lloyd,[1] commanding the

---

[1] The order to raise the regiment was given by Lord Kitchener to Sir Francis Lloyd on February 6th. The actual conversation is so typical of both men that we give the note, made at the time by Sir Francis Lloyd :

LORD KITCHENER, very abruptly : " You have got to raise a regiment of Welsh Guards."

SIR FRANCIS LLOYD : " Sir, there are a great many difficulties in the way which I should like to point out first."

LORD KITCHENER, very rudely : " If you do not like to do it some one else will."

SIR FRANCIS LLOYD : " Sir, when do you want them ? "

London District, and the senior serving Welsh soldier of the day, was given power to proceed with the formation. Interviews were short. Major W. Murray Threipland, Grenadier Guards, was sent for by Sir Francis Lloyd, seen by Lord Kitchener, and finally by His Majesty the King, and was given command of the battalion about to be raised and also, as a temporary measure, of regimental headquarters.

To the stoutest-hearted man the raising of a new regiment of Foot Guards is no light task. The brigade of Guards have very naturally a standard of excellence which permits no adverse comparison, and human nature is such that anything new, with the inevitable and illogical reproach of having no customs or traditions, will, when associated with such a body, be subjected to searching and frequently irrational criticism from the older and more experienced formations. Some tangent thought must have been present in Lieut.-Col. Murray Threipland's mind from the moment of his appointment. The desire of every commanding officer that his battalion should be the best, and the burden of responsibility which rests with command would, with a new regiment of Foot Guards, have the additional weight of anxious, as distinct from friendly, rivalry. Lieut.-Col. Murray Threipland never shrank, however, from making a decision, or hesitated having once come to a decision.

The selection of the battalion staff involved far-reaching appointments—a mistake in sergeant-major, drill-sergeants, or company sergeant-majors is difficult to rectify when once these ranks are confirmed. An established battalion has the great advantage of watching each man from recruit stage upwards; a new battalion must take a number on trust, or at best on second-hand recommendation. To fill the more important warrant

LORD KITCHENER : " Immediately."

SIR FRANCIS LLOYD : " Very well, sir; they shall go on guard on St. David's Day."

It is not hard to imagine that the order to raise the Welsh Guards hit Sir Francis from two opposite directions. As a Welshman he was delighted, as a Grenadier he thought at once of the many fine men his regiment recruited from Cardiff.

and non-commissioned ranks, it was decided to call for
volunteers from the Grenadier, Coldstream, and Scots
Regiments of Guards, and also permission was obtained
from Sir Henry Streatfeild, commanding the Grenadier
Guards, to appeal to Welshmen who had joined the
Grenadier Guards and were at the recruit depot at
Caterham.   In answer to this appeal made by Sir Francis
Lloyd 303 men, including 40 non-commissioned officers,
transferred.   A similar appeal to recruits at Caterham
produced 200 Welshmen.

The Regimental Roll was started, and as Lieut.-Col.
Murray Threipland was the first officer to join the Welsh
Guards, so the Regtl. Sergt.-Major W. Stevenson (from
the Scots Guards), became No. 1.

The problem of where to house and assemble the new
regiment was solved by the allotment of a portion of
the White City—that garish collection of white plaster
buildings raised, by Imre Kïralfy, on some vacant ground
at Shepherd's Bush for the holding of a kind of annual
fair and exhibition.

The official date for assembly at this place is given as
February 27th, and we find two days later, on March 1st,
St. David's Day, the Welsh Guards mounted guard over
the King at Buckingham Palace.   Without detracting
from the Commanding Officer's fine record, the explanation of this unique feat lies in the fact that he was able
at this period to act a few days before official announcement.   He himself states that Lord Kitchener gave him
verbal orders which enabled him to " get ahead " at once
without waiting for papers to go through various depart-
ments at the War Office.   Also there was the leaven of
experience in the battalion—or what was already formed
of it.

The officers who carried out these duties of the guard
were :

King's Guard

Captain [1]	.	.	. Lieut.-Col. Murray Threipland.
Lieutenant	.	.	. Lieut. R. G. W. Williams-Bulkeley.
Ensign .	.	.	. 2/Lieut. P. L. M. Battye.

[1] This is the only instance in the history of the Brigade of Guards of a
Commanding Officer going on duty as Captain of the King's Guard.

Buckingham Palace Guard

Lieut. Viscount Clive.
Sergt. of the King's Guard C. S. M. Woodhouse.

The remaining non-commissioned officers and men of the different guards were found from serving Welshmen who had joined from the Grenadier, Coldstream, and Scots Guards (they wore the badges of their late regiments). The King watched the parade from the palace windows.

These proceedings excited the liveliest interest amongst the general public, as well as a large and critical gathering of past and present officers of the brigade. It was an anxious morning for the Commanding Officer, but Sir Francis Lloyd, who had not the reputation of mincing words on army matters, expressed his approval of the manner in which this first important parade had been carried out. That night was the first and only occasion when Lord Kitchener dined " on guard." There were also present : Major-Gen. Sir Francis Lloyd, K.C.B., C.V.O., D.S.O., Major-Gen. Viscount Falmouth, K.C.V.O., C.B., Commander Sir Richard Williams-Bulkeley, C.B., Brig.-Gen. R. Scott-Kerr, C.B., M.V.O., D.S.O., Col. Fludyer, C.V.O., Col. H. Lewis, Sir George Arthur, M.V.O., and many others.

Now began the real business of training men at the White City. Recruiting presented no difficulties. Stories of the hard winter the army had experienced and was still going through in France and Belgium had succeeded those of the retreat from Mons and the first battle of Ypres, and seemed to be an excellent reason for a continual stream of volunteers. While men were being medically examined and sent to Caterham, and passed from Caterham to the White City to continue their education in drill and the use of rifle—on the very ground where the populace used to " wiggle-woggle " and " water-chute " to the strains of brass bands and under the glow of a hundred thousand coloured electric lights— the bitter and costly battle of Neuve Chapelle was being fought (March 10th), resulting, after three days of fierce fighting in driving the enemy back to a depth of 1,000 yards on a front of 3,000 yards ; and Hill 60 was being wrested from the Hun (April 17th) by self-sacrifice and the use of " jam-tin " bombs.   Recruiting was easy, and the only advertisement required was such as would draw the Welshmen who wished to join the army into the new Welsh Guards.   With this object in view a recruiting campaign was started throughout Wales, in which Sir Francis Lloyd engaged himself and also Lieut. Rhys Williams, who had transferred from the Grenadier Guards, and was well equipped with the silver and persuasive tongue of a successful barrister and budding politician for a jaunt of this nature.

On April 28th, when the second battle of Ypres had been raging a week, the battalion consisted of 31 officers and 1,316 other ranks, and was transferred to Esher, where it was quartered in the racecourse stands at Sandown Park.

Meanwhile the King had approved (March 19th) of the King's Colour, the Regimental Colour, and the eight Company Colours.   He also conferred a further distinction on the regiment by sanctioning the title of " The Prince of Wales " Company, for the leading company of the 1st Battalion.

The details of the uniform were also settled.   Both officers and men wore the leek as cap badge, which national emblem was repeated on the button designed by Mr. Seymour Lucas, R.A.   The peace time forage-cap of officers and men was to have a black band ; the tunic was to have buttons in groups of five ; the collar badge to be the leek, repeated on the men's shoulders.   The bearskin cap would be the same as in the other regiments of Guards, but would have a distinctive plume of green and white.

The selection of the leek as a cap-badge started some foolish discussion about a daffodil.   Was it not Heine who suggested that, though it is expressly stated Nebuchadnezzar " did eat grass as oxen," it was probably salad he consumed ?   Some people will suggest an alternative to anything.   Whether it was St. David who

2

ordered the victorious soldiers of King Alfred to wear the leek in their caps so that all men might know them, or whether the Welsh wore the leek at Cressy and Agincourt we do not know. Shakespeare was a bad historian, and we learn nothing from him, although he is so often quoted in this respect, beyond that the leek was a well-known emblem of the Welsh. The origin of the leek is lost in antiquity. Some writers have gone so far as to drag mistletoe into the discussion, though why the Ancient Briton should wear the sacred mistletoe as an emblem, any more than the skin of the sacred hare, or why he should substitute for it the leek, is not apparent. The plant itself is a native of South Europe, and one might hazard a guess that it was introduced during the Roman period of our history. The well-known remark of Cæsar that the Britons were stained with woad probably refers to a system of tribal markings ; but they did not wear any distinctive emblems. The idea of an emblem or badge would come with the Romans ; but the necessity of wearing such a thing as a leek, or the occasion on which it might be introduced, does not suggest itself until a much later period. A hastily assumed distinction on account of similarity of attire, and on an occasion associated with victory, is the most probable reason for it and its survival. One imagines, too, that it must have been a national affair, and not a petty squabble amongst local chiefs. Such a time could have presented itself during the Saxon or Early Norman period. We will not commit ourselves any deeper than this.

While we may pass over the minor details of early training of the new regiment, it is as well to consider at this point whom the Commanding Officer had to help him in the training. It is obvious that given dragons—Welsh ones would be most appropriate—you may kill one, and, by planting its teeth in the ground, raise a ready-made battalion, with officers and men trained to the last ounce ; but, failing the dragon, you are, under such conditions as prevailed in 1915,. faced with some difficulty. A certain number of officers may be got from regular and territorial forces—that is to say, excellent men with varying experience—but to complete the Commanding Officer will frequently be faced with no other alternative than to give commissions to excellent men with no experience whatever. But through keenness, intelligence, and hard work, under the guiding hand of Lieut.-Col. Murray Threipland and a few experienced helpers, these men soon transformed themselves into most efficient officers. We give the following list in the order in which the officers joined, and the rank they were given :

W. Murray-Threipland . .	Temp. Major, R. of O. Grenadier Guards, to Lieut.-Col. commanding the 1st Battalion.
G. C. D. Gordon . .	Capt. S.R. Scots Guards, to Major and Adjutant.
W. B. Dabell . . .	Superintending Clerk, Grenadier Guards, to Lieut. and Quartermaster.
Hon. A. G. A. Hore-Ruthven, V.C.	Capt. K.D.G., Major and second in command.
A. P. Palmer, D.S.O. .	Lieut. R. of O., Captain of No. 4 Company.
G. W. Philipps . .	Capt. Durham L.I., Captain of No. 3 Company.
R. G. W. Williams-Bulkeley	Lieut. R. of O. Grenadier Guards, Captain of No. 2 Company.
O. T. D. Osmond Williams, D.S.O.	2/Lieut. Scots Greys, Captain of Prince of Wales's Company.
J. H. Bradney . . .	Lieut. D.C.L.I., to Captain and 2nd in command of Prince of Wales's Company.
Rhys Williams . .	2/Lieut. R. of O. Grenadier Guards, to Subaltern.
H. E. Allen . . .	Lieut. Royal Fusiliers, to Subaltern.
H. E. Wethered . .	R. of O. R.A., to Subaltern.
Viscount Clive . . .	Lieut. Scots Guards, to Subaltern.
P. L. M. Battye . .	2/Lieut. S.R. Grenadier Guards, to Subaltern.
W. H. L. Gough . .	Lieut. Monmouthshire Yeomanry, to Subaltern.
R. W. Lewis . . .	Capt. Glamorganshire Yeomanry, to Subaltern.
J. J. P. Evans . . .	Capt. Welsh Horse Yeomanry, to Subaltern.
Earl of Lisburne . .	2/Lieut. R. of O. Scots Guards, to Subaltern.
K. G. Menzies . . .	2/Lieut. S.R. 2nd Life Guards, to Subaltern.
B. T. V. Hambrough .	2/Lieut. Welsh Regiment, to Subaltern.
J. A. D. Perrins . .	Lieut. Seaforth Highlanders, to Subaltern.

H. T. Rice . . .	.	Lieut. East Yorks Yeo., to 2/Lieut.[1]
G. C. H. Crawshay .	.	. 2/Lieut. Welsh Regt., to 2/Lieut.
H. A. Evan Thomas .	.	. 2/Lieut. S.R. Coldstream Guards, to 2/Lieut.
W. A. F. L. Fox-Pitt	.	. 2/Lieut. Cheshire Regt., to 2/Lieut.
Hon. P. G. J. F. Howard	.	. Lieut. Leinster Regt., to 2/Lieut.
F. A. V. Copland-Griffiths .		. 2/Lieut. Rifle Brigade, to 2/Lieut.
G. C. L. Insole . . .		. To Subaltern.
E. G. Mawby . . .		. 2/Lieut. Royal Fusiliers, to 2/Lieut.
H. G. Sutton . . .		. 2/Lieut. London Regt., T.F., to 2/Lieut.
R. Smith . . .		. To 2/Lieut.

Of other ranks there were : W. Stevenson from the
Scots Guards as Regimental Sergeant-Major, I. M. Smith
from the Grenadier Guards as R.Q.M.S., W. Bland
from the Grenadier Guards as Drill-Sergeant, C.S.M's.
H. J. Pursey, A. Pearce, J. G. Harris, G. Woodhouse,
and C.Q.M.S's. R. J. Young, G. H. Thomas, J. Beardsmore, T. Orton.

The officers joined at the White City, Keith Menzies
with a large cavalry sword, Harry Rice with the spurs
of his Yorkshire Yeomanry (and a wonderful word of
command " Plat-toon ! "), Claud Insole in a pot hat and
lounge suit—there were all sorts of clothes. Drill-Sergt.
Bland put most of these gentlemen through squad drill,
and their weird assortment of costume gave way by
degrees, and at the will of obliging tailors, to correct
dress.

Much hard work was done at Esher, but there was an
amount of play as well. It was a curious phenomenon
of the Great War that England never ceased entirely to
amuse herself. Certainly at that time, besides the field-
sports which seemed natural to every British gathering,
those who obtained leave to go up to town found the night
attractions of London equal to peace-time standards.
The ball at Brussels, before Waterloo, had its parallel in
London in a perfect craze of dancing. Private houses,
hotels, and night clubs seemed to vie with each other
from 11 o'clock onwards. And although people drew

---

[1] The rank of ensign was done away with in 1870, but 2nd lieutenants in
the Brigade of Guards are still referred to as ensigns. It is occasionally
found in official documents, although not an army rank.

long faces at the loss of Hill 60 on May 5th, and muttered vengeance for the sinking of the *Lusitania* on May 7th, and were thoughtful after visiting friends in hospital from wounds received at the battle of Festubert-Richebourg (May 9th), still at Rome one does as the Romans—and Esher is not so far from London.

That the training at Esher was thorough the after-record of the battalion proves, that it was not too irksome stories of the younger and high-spirited members of the officers' mess clearly indicate.

Other officers joined at Esher : the Hon. E. F. Morgan, H. H. Bromfield, J. V. Taylor, A. E. Price, Lord Newborough, E. R. M. Smith, J. Randolph, N. G. Wells, F. W. E. Blake, C. C. L. Fitzwilliams, H. Dene. As the training progressed reputations grew as the snowball when rolled in snow, and occasionally melted as fast on a hot field-day. Osmond Williams and Palmer stood out as commanding figures, and their energy was boundless. Dick Bulkeley showed that, with all his good looks and amusing conversation, he had not forgotten his previous soldiering, and could train men and officers to some purpose. He was one of those gallant men who deserve all praise and honour. Everybody knew that he had contracted a bad form of tuberculosis and that there was no necessity for him to rejoin the army at all. But he rejoined, and fought, and was eventually beaten by the disease. Newborough was another man who knew the insurance value of his life. There were giants in the earth in those days.

On May 23rd Italy entered the war—on June 4th the battalion returned to London and took up quarters at Wellington Barracks. This change of quarters meant that the battalion now took up as a whole the routine and duties of a Guards Battalion in the West End of London. The Commanding Officer might well be proud of this record. The strength of the battalion, including the depot at Caterham, was then 47 officers and 1,610 other ranks.

On June 16th Lord Harlech, who was an old Coldstreamer, and had afterwards commanded the Shropshire

Yeomanry, was appointed temporary lieutenant-colonel of the regiment, a very necessary appointment, as the battalion was nearing the day when it must sail for France. R.Q.M.S. C. E. Woods, 1st Battalion Scots Guards, became sergeant-major and superintending clerk at headquarters.

There are a few official ceremonies to be noted at this time. During the month of June the Lord Mayor of Cardiff, Alderman J. Richards, inspected the battalion, after which he presented the lieutenant-colonel with a cheque from the City of Cardiff for the purpose of buying band instruments and drums, and, in the words of the Diary, "they were afterwards entertained by Lord Harlech at Prince's Restaurant!"

On August 3rd the battalion paraded in the gardens of Buckingham Palace. In front of a large gathering, graced by the presence of their Majesties the Queen and Queen Alexandra, the King inspected the battalion.

The colours were then consecrated by the Bishop of St. Asaph. The Welsh Guards Choir, under Pte. G. Williams, sang "Ton-y-botel," "Aberystwyth," and "Hen Wlad Fy Nhadau." The two senior subalterns, Allen and Wethered, kneeling before the King, received the colours, and, after presenting arms, the ceremony closed with the battalion marching past in a tremendous downpour of rain.[1]

A few days later, August 7th, the following announcement appeared in *The London Gazette* :

"His Majesty the King has been graciously pleased to confer on the Welsh Guards the honour of becoming Colonel-in-Chief of the Regiment."

In the early morning of the 17th the battalion left Waterloo Station for Southampton and France. One of the few civilians on the station to see them off was Mr. John Burns, who, though a man of peace, has ever been a friend of the soldier. No doubt as he watched them

---

[1] See Appendix A.

he asked himself the same question as Palmer when the
battalion was being photographed a few days before
leaving—when the " artist " had said " Thank you,"
Palmer turned round, and, thrusting his great jaw out at
the " group," said, " I wonder how many of us will be
alive in six months' time ? "

CHAPTER II

FIRST DAYS IN FRANCE—ST. OMER—TRAINING—THE
OFFICERS' MESS — SPORT — CONFERENCE ON THE
ATTACK—THE MARCH TO LOOS

THE battalion left Waterloo Station in three trains which
started at 4.30, 5.30, and 6.30 a.m., embarking the same
afternoon for France—headquarters, transport, and eight
officers, under Capt. Bradney, on the s.s. *Palm Branch*,
Lieut.-Col. Murray Threipland with the battalion on s.s.
St. Petersburg. Both ships sailed about six in the evening.

The officers and staff were as follows :

Headquarters :

Lieut.-Col. W. Murray Threipland ; Lieut. and Adjt.
J. A. D. Perrins ; Lieut. W. E. Picton Phillips, R.A.M.C. ;
Lieut. N. G. Wells (transport) ; Lieut. and Q.M. W. B.
Dabell ; 1898 Regtl.-Sergt.-Major E. Barnes ; 5 Regtl.
Q.M.S. H. Pursey ; 2 Drill-Sergt. W. Bland ; 297 Drill-
Sergt. G. Woodhouse ; 3 Orderly-Room-Sergt. A. Alder-
son ; 90 Pioneer-Sergt. C. Branch.

Prince of Wales's Company :

Capt. O. T. D. Osmond Williams, D.S.O. ; Capt. Rhys
Williams (machine guns) ; Lieuts. H. E. Wethered (sig-
naller), E. G. Mawby, G. C. H. Crawshay, Hon. P. G. J.
F. Howard, R. Smith ; Nos. 23 C.S.M. L. Hunter (act-
ing) ; 9 C.Q.M.S. R. Young ; Sergts. 14 W. Hearn, 377
A. J. Thomas, 24 O. Ashford, 34 I. T. Williams, 60 A. H.
Kirby, 663 N. Carter, 816 W. Lauder, 39 D. Relihan ;
L/Sergts. 253 E. A. Moss, 502 M. Owen, 374 I. C.
Roberts.

No. 2 Company :

Capt. R. G. Williams Bulkeley ; Capt. J. H. Bradney ; Lieuts. K. G. Menzies, R. W. Lewis, J. J. P. Evans, F. A. V. Copland-Griffiths ; No. 6 C.S.M. A. Pearce ; No. 21 C.Q.M.S. Owen (acting) ; Sergts. 193 W. Beazer, 37 T. Davies, 36 J. Duddridge, 53 S. Rendell, 136 J. Regan, 26 W. Stokes, 1359 R. Scott Kiddie (Master Boot-maker) ; L/Sergts. 330 O. Murphy, 761 C. A. Bonar, 345 B. Evans, 44 S. Hare, 38 E. Lewis, 143 F. Phillips, 254 T. W. Thomas, 57 S. Williams.

No. 3 Company :

Capt. G. W. F. Philipps ; Capt. M. O. Roberts ; Lieuts. W. H. J. Gough (machine gun), H. J. Sutton, H. T. Rice, J. Randolph ; No. 16 C.S.M. D. Cossey ; 11 C.Q.M.S. Beardsmore ; Sergts. 45 T. W. Thomas, 55 E. Foulkes, 274 C. Simpson, 46 F. J. Green, 354 C. Morris, 742 R. E. Parry, 170 J. Epstein, 1900 T. H. Haylock (transport), 125 E. J. Williams, 358 J. Norton,66 W. Keay ; L/Sergts. 346 F. Owen, 54 A. Peak, 279 J. Phillips, 324 C. H. Cory, 105 F. Starnes (drums), 64 I. Davies.

No. 4 Company :

Capt. A. P. Palmer, D.S.O. ; Capt. H. Dene ; Lieuts. B. T. V. Hambrough,G. C. L. Insole, H. A. Evan Thomas, W. A. F. L. Fox-Pitt ; No. 8 C.S.M. T. Orton ; 13 C.Q.M.S. W. J. Church ; Sergts. 819 T. Pearson, 28 B. Pottinger, 114 R. Mathias, 356 A. D. Davies, 62 R. J. Richards, 766 C. Maclachlan, 303 D. J. Beavan, 50 W. Trott ; L/Sergts. 283 E. Helson, 235 E. Wheatley, 318 E. Evans, 174 G. Shackleford, 397 L. Nicholson, 231 D. J. Lewis.

It will be noticed that the senior sergeant-major, Stevenson, did not leave England with the battalion. He had been severely wounded at Ypres with his late regiment, the Scots Guards, and, though he was doing duty in England, was not sufficiently recovered for active service. Sergt.-Major Barnes was from the Coldstream

Guards. The record of the 2nd (Reserve) Battalion will be found elsewhere.

At 7 a.m. on August 18th the battalion landed at Havre.

Havre was the big base for the British Army and throughout the war was as much English as French. Not only was the quay swarming with men in the British uniform, but the hotels as well ; every other house in the centre of the town seemed to be an office of the British Army ; it was not an uncommon thing to find a tram driven by a British soldier ; and at the back or northern side of the town vast camps were erected on the high ground.

All reinforcements and new formations arriving in Havre went to the camps, and accordingly the battalion marched about three miles to Rest Camp No. 5 (canvas), where it stayed the night.

The next day, at 5.30 p.m., the battalion left for the " Front," or what most of the men imagined was the front. Marshal Roberts, Sutton and Rice, with 125 men, had special work to do and were to follow later.

All through the fighting of 1914 and part of 1915 the Guards Battalions were not gathered together as one unit. The 4th Guards Brigade, which went out in August 1914, and was in the 2nd Division, was composed of the 2nd Battalion Grenadier, 2nd and 3rd Battalions Coldstream, and 1st Battalion Irish Guards ; the 1st Brigade in the 1st Division was formed of the 1st Battalion Coldstream, 1st Battalion Scots Guards, 1st Battalion Black Watch, and the 2nd Battalion Royal Munster Fusiliers ; in the 7th Division was the 20th Brigade, which included the 1st Battalion Grenadier, 2nd Battalion Scots Guards, 2nd Battalion Gordon Highlanders, and 2nd Battalion Border Regiment. It had been decided, however, to form a Guards Division, and to the Guards Battalions already in France and Belgium were added the new Welsh Guards, the 3rd Battalion Grenadier Guards, which had not yet been used, and an extra battalion above establishment from each of the Grenadier, Coldstream and Irish Regiments of Guards.

The brigades of the division were formed with as little alteration of existing arrangements as was possible : thus the old 4th Brigade became the 1st Guards Brigade ; to the 1st Battalion Coldstream and 1st Battalion Scots Guards were added the 3rd Battalion Grenadier and 2nd Battalion Irish Guards, which now became the 2nd Guards Brigade ; from the 20th Brigade came the 1st Battalion Grenadier and 2nd Battalion Scots Guards, to form, with the 4th Battalion Grenadier and 1st Battalion Welsh Guards, the 3rd Guards Brigade.

The 4th Battalion Coldstream Guards became the pioneer battalion to the division and did most excellent work.

The place of assembly for the new division was at G.H.Q., and at about 10.30 a.m. on August 20th the 1st Battalion Welsh Guards arrived at St. Omer. Here they were met by Major-Gen. Lord Cavan, who had commanded the old 4th Guards Brigade and had now been promoted to the command of the Guards Division. Lord Cavan then informed Lieut.-Col. Murray Threipland of the composition of the division, and that the 3rd Brigade was commanded by Brig.-Gen. H. J. Heyworth. The battalion marched to billets in the village of Arques, about three miles from St. Omer.

Everything in the move from Wellington Barracks to Arques had been as satisfactory as might be expected. A horse seems to have been injured at Waterloo Station, but another was " drawn " at Havre. A more serious loss, and one much regretted in the future, was the motor ambulance. Mrs. Murray Threipland had presented the battalion with a motor ambulance, which was loaded on a ship and safely transported to the quay-side at Boulogne. But the landing officer would have nothing to do with it—there had been an Army Order that units were not to bring such things into France, and neither prayers nor entreaties, nor jocular winks and sly digs in the ribs would move that official to allow the ambulance to be landed. Rhys Williams departed on a secret mission to see a mysterious person in high authority, but failed in his effort to get round the order. The car had to return to England and many a pleasant outing was lost thereby—which was no doubt the intention of the Order.

As to the journey, for some people no boat in the world can possibly be comfortable, and nothing was expected of the *Palm Branch* and *St. Petersburg* ; we will say no more of the train journey than that there were thirty-four men in each truck, buoyed up with the novelty of their situation, and calling on " Dai " or " Ianto " to witness some strange sight in this foreign land.

The immediate business at St. Omer was divisional training, and the battalion had an active but a very happy and comfortable time there. Arques lies at the junction of a river, called Aa, with the canal system which runs through St. Omer and Watten and branches to Calais and Dunkerque. On the right bank of the canal is the forest of Clairmarais, the scene of several field-days. On the left bank (the Arques side) the country is flat for some way and then gently undulating. But the whole district, with its tree-lined roads and many small villages and hamlets, is very pleasing.

Training never ceased during the war. The hardened veteran, out of the line for a rest, joined the young recruit, who had just arrived in France for the first time, and trained. Besides the contemplated field training there was special training in bombing, wiring and trench digging.

Many bombs had been tried since the " jam-tin " days. There was a thing like a bit of large-sized gas-pipe called the " Bethune," though whether that was its official name we do not know. The War Office had produced a bomb on a stick with a lot of white streamers to it ; there was a long and a short Hales Grenade ; there was a very light bomb like a medium-sized yellow vegetable marrow, with a string on the end which one pulled before throwing it ; and maybe there were many others. But the Mills Bomb was becoming the universal bomb. Keith Menzies, with a number of N.C.O.'s, went through a course and became bombing officer.

Snipers, of whom there were thirty, came under J. J. P.

Evans, more commonly known as Jimjack. There were
some good men among these snipers—Sergt. Bowles, then
a corporal, had wonderful eyesight, and did extraordinarily good work later on ; and Parker, an ex-gamekeeper,
was an excellent man, as were Sergt. Bonar and Pte.
Tanner.

The trench-digging was done at Clety and Avroult,
ten and twelve miles away. Capt. Heath, of the 55th
Company R.E., gave instruction in wiring.

At this time the machine guns were still part of the
battalion establishment, and Rhys Williams (now a captain), Wilfred Gough, and Fox-Pitt, with sixty-six men,
went through a course. The battalion received another
gun while at Arques to make up the full complement of
four. They now possessed two Maxims, one Nordenfelt
(converted), and a Vickers.

A sudden move was practised, and we find the Commanding Officer noting that the transport was late in
starting. " Too much stuff on wagons. Attempt had
been made to carry all drummers' kits and kits of thirty
snipers." So the transport repeated the practice next
day, with the result that " loading improved."

Nigel Wells, who commanded the transport, was a
hard old warrior from one of the South American Repub-
lics. His face was the colour of mahogany (he was called
" Teak "), and he wore an eyeglass and a small piece of
moustache about half the width of his mouth. He said
he was twenty-nine years of age, and was annoyed when
some of the younger officers, looking at his sun-scorched
face, suggested he might be a hundred—the truth lay
anywhere between the two.

The greatest keenness and good-humour prevailed in
the battalion during this training at Arques. Osmond
Williams and Palmer, commanders of the two flank companies, had a standing feud as to whose was the best
company. Dick Bulkeley would come into the mess and
pull both their legs by boasting about his own company.
Soon they were hard at it. One would claim to have
marched with full kit twenty miles in six hours, the other
would say he had done the same thing in five and three-

quarter hours. And so on. If Humphrey Dene was there the thing became a noisy " rag." But both Osmond Williams and Palmer were born commanders of men, and each could draw on valuable past experience. That the battalion was hard and at the top of its form at the end of these few weeks of extra training at Arques there can be no doubt.

The mess was a problem which occupied the attention of the officers at this time. Bradney (rejoicing in the plebeian name of " Ginger ") was Mess President. Dick Bulkeley, protesting that he " knew all about it from a pal," had bought, before leaving England, mess-boxes for headquarters and each of the companies. These were very well made, but remarkably heavy, containing slots and holes and trays for plates and cutlery. He had also ordered vast quantities of foodstuffs to be sent out from Fortnum & Mason. Grumbles began to be heard about the weight of these boxes and their uselessness, and about the sameness of the food. Dick Bulkeley notes in his Diary : " A certain amount of discontent about the officers' messing—very bad—no fresh food (August 24th) " ; " Dined with Grizzy Napier No. 3 Company 1st Bn. Grenadiers at Wizernes. . . . Quite a nice change to taste some well-cooked, good fresh food (August 28th)." Bradney set about changing the menu, and apparently made a " corner " in rabbits. Very few members of the mess liked rabbits, but they had to be eaten, and Bradney, though he had a healthy appetite, could not eat them all himself. The rabbits started an argument which gained in volume and ended in enquiry. A mess meeting was held.

There have been many systems of running a mess, but the Commanding Officer laid down at Arques certain principles which were of incalculable good and were in the main adhered to until he left the battalion.

He insisted that where it was possible there should always be a battalion mess. Company messes tend to separate the battalion into water-tight compartments, but with one mess all officers are brought together every day, which is good. It also levels expense, and the

Commanding Officer's remarks had the effect of so
reducing expense that during the first year in France
messing cost each officer just under forty pounds.
Bradney was deposed in sorrow, not in anger, and
Keith Menzies reigned in his stead.

Of sport, in the way of organised meetings, little was
done, but Claud Insole writes a delightful account of a
Gymkhana given by the 2nd Battalion Scots Guards:

" September 2nd.

" I have just come back from a Gymkhana given by
the 2nd Scots Guards. It was quite a good show, and
crowds of people there. We went over in a motor-lorry.
There were jumping competitions for the officers, and
tugs of war and pony-races for the men. Teams of four
officers entered for the jumping from different regiments,
but as several cavalry regiments, like the Greys and 12th
Lancers and 20th Hussars, entered, we could not expect
to do much on our transport animals. The feature of
our lot was Rupert (Lewis) who went slowly round on an
old pony knocking everything flat; but he was very clever
to get round at all. The Colonel of the Scots Guards
(Cator) came flat on his back in the water, which caused
huge merriment. There was a large tent of tea and
drinks, and the pipers of the Scots Guards performed,
and the whole thing was exactly like a small country
horse-show. To-night a few of us are dining at the little
estaminet I live at, as we get so tired of the mess. Some
go and dine at St. Omer, but I get plenty of walking to
do without walking unnecessarily, and I have only been
there once in a motor-lorry."

Brig.-Gen. Heyworth soon became popular with the
battalion. He was a very handsome man in face and
figure—very spick-and-span, with well-cut clothes, and
boots which were a triumph of polishing. His hair,
which was abundant, was snow-white, as was his moustache, and he generally wore almost white wash-leather
gloves. His first advice to the battalion was: " The

only way for us to win this war is to go on killing Germans like vermin " (Bulkeley Diary). He went on leave for a short time, when the brigade was commanded by Lieut.-Col. Murray Threipland—Palmer commanding the battalion meanwhile—but he inspected the battalion twice and addressed the officers and men, complimenting them on their work.

Sir Francis Lloyd paid a visit to France during this time, and was present when Lord Cavan inspected the division. Also General Haking addressed the officers on the principles of attack. He advocated that platoon commanders should lead on and not worry about their flanks ; reserves would be behind them to fill up gaps, reinforce, clear up the situation and make good what had been won. This was understood to be the pith of his argument, and in view of later events is worth remembering—as is much more which this general has written and said.

. . . . .

The period of training came to an end, and on September 22nd the battalion marched to Roquetoire, and from there to Norrent-Fontes. On the 24th the Commanding Officer attended a conference at Lillers.

We know that during the early part of 1915, while the Welsh Guards had been in process of formation, activity in France had consisted, on the British side, of engagements at Neuve Chapelle on March 10th, at Hill 60 on April 17th, and round Festubert on May 9th. The Germans had launched their big attack, known as the second battle of Ypres, on April 22nd, when, thanks to the use of gas, they did very well—and but for the gallantry of the Canadians would have done even better. And they recaptured Hill 60 on May 5th. But there had been little else, except a smart action by British troops round Hooge, and a period of comparative quiet had reigned throughout the summer.

A new phase of the war was about to commence. It must be remembered that England had to make an army for continental use, on a quite different basis to the small, highly trained force we had previously considered sufficient for our needs. Not only must we have masses of men, but the Germans had clearly shown us the need for volume of artillery fire. At Neuve Chapelle new artillery had come into action, and in this battle Sir John French had concentrated some 300 guns on a comparatively small front; and the same, as regards artillery, may be said of Festubert. It was the new artillery coming into action as it was formed.

In a similar way new formations of infantry kept arriving in France.

So, when we say that the effect of the new army was first felt by the Germans in the month of September, we do not mean that new units were not used before that date. The period of quiet through the summer had given time for them to accumulate, so that we had not only taken over a greater length of line but had made preparations for a bigger attack than had been dreamed of before.

The conference which the Commanding Officer attended at Lillers was addressed by Lieut.-Gen. Haking, who commanded the XI Corps (composed of the Guards Division and the 21st and 24th Divisions—two absolutely new formations of new army units).

The Commanding Officer notes that Gen. Haking made a fine speech, but spoke too low and too fast. He said an attack was on the point of being launched by the French and ourselves. It would stretch north as far as Ypres, but the big effort would be made by the First Army (of which the Guards Division was a part) under Sir Douglas Haig. The army would attack from the La Bassée Canal to a point south of Loos. The IV Corps (Rawlinson) would be on the right, and the I Corps (Gough) on the left. The French would attack south of Lens in co-operation with us, and the battle would start the next day (25th). In rear of the centre of the I and IV Corps would be the XI Corps, with the 21st and 24th Divisions in front and the Guards Division behind them. The objective of the XI Corps was Douai. The proposed plan was that the I and IV Corps would take the German system of defence. If they failed the XI Corps would

3

assist, but if they succeeded the cavalry would be put through and the XI Corps would follow behind the cavalry.

He further explained that the coming attack would develop into the greatest battle of the war and would go a long way to shorten, if not end it.

All this, being no longer secret, was afterwards repeated to the officers and men of the battalion.

The next day, the 25th, the march was resumed under the most trying conditions of war. The concentration of troops was such that the roads were blocked again and again—infantry, artillery, cavalry, ammunition columns, engineers' stores, all kinds of stores ; and odd carts, odd little bands of men, on the road, by the side of the road, cutting across country—the whole making a continuous sound punctuated by shouts and curses. This congestion meant continual halting, and nothing is more tiring for troops. The transport was cut in half by a cavalry brigade at Brouay, and Wells used to tell the story of how he cursed the brigadier under the impression that he was a junior officer. As a matter of fact, the cavalry had the right of way, and divisions had been ordered to give them the road. Wells, however, did not know this, although if he had he would probably have cursed just the same.

There was some confusion in orders and billeting arrangements. The battalion passed through Haillicourt, wandered about in the country beyond, and eventually returned to the village, which, being recognised by the men, although it was dark, was greeted with the song, " Here we are, here we are, here we are again ! "

This return to Haillicourt was at 11.30 p.m. and billeting was not too easy. Palmer, in a fit of rage at not being admitted by the inhabitants of one house, broke down the door. The transport did not arrive for a couple of hours, and the men had to turn in without their tea, the cookers being with the transport.

The Commanding Officer notes it was " a very long and tiring day—men were very cheery—good news kept coming in, most of it probably untrue—poured with rain

all afternoon and evening—march discipline very good
all day and night."

The march had been accompanied by the distant rumble of guns, which never ceased the next day when the
journey was continued to Vermelles.   The roads were if
possible even more congested.   The transport had been
brigaded, but Wells accompanied the battalion with two
tool-carts, two ammunition-carts, the doctor's cart, the
officers' mess cart, and the mules.   The brigaded transport was again cut off, and arrived some hours after the
battalion.

A big bombardment was going on on the left when the
battalion arrived at Vermelles.   The British guns round
about that village were active, and there was a continuous rattle of rifle-fire.   A few ruins, still able to give a
little shelter, existed, but they were already occupied by
troops, so, a convenient trench having been found on the
outskirts of the village, in case of shelling, a bivouac
camp was formed for the night.

What would have been looked upon as superhuman
effort before the war became very soon an ordinary
achievement. Could you have slept on a ploughed field in
the pouring rain ?   Could you even have marched all day,
gone without sleep, and marched again next day ?   Undoubtedly excitement gives powers of endurance beyond
those of normal belief.   And the Welsh Guards were
deeply stirred by their first approach to battle—the guns,
our own and the Germans', the rifle-fire, the star-lights,
all was new to them and they were filled with speculative
thought.   The hum of conversation was going on round
the bivouacs—there was not much sleep that night.

Breakfasts were served at 5 a.m. on the 27th as a
precaution against hunger in the event of sudden orders
to move.   At midday orders were received that the
brigade would march at 2 p.m. for Loos.

CHAPTER III

BEFORE we follow the fortunes of the battalion at Loos
we must determine how far the plan sketched out by Gen.
Haking succeeded. The divisions of the two attacking
corps in line were the 47th, 15th, 1st, 7th, 9th, and 2nd.
The main points to remember are that Loos was on the
right of the attack, and behind Loos was Hill 70, the
crest of the hill being about a mile from the village.
Over the crest of the hill runs a main road from Lens to
La Bassée, passing through Hulluch and Haisnes, that
is to say along the whole of the front attacked. If we
keep this road in mind we can get the relative positions
of places of importance by placing them on the near or
the far side of the road. From right to left of the line
we have Hill 70, with the crest practically on the road ;
Puis 14 on the far side ; Bois Hugo on the far side and
close to Puis 14 ; the Chalk Pit just on the near side and
close to Bois Hugo ; Hulluch on the far side ; Cité St.
Elie on the road ; Hohenzollern Redoubt a good mile on
the near side of the road ; Haisnes on the road ; Auchy
a mile on the near side of the road.

The 47th Division started off well on the right and
captured the ground south of Loos, making a strong
flank by seizing some slag-heaps ; they also captured the
south end of Loos. The 15th Division took Hill 70 and
Fosse 14. The 1st Division got up on the line of the
Lens—La Bassée Road. The 7th Division reached the
outskirts of Hulluch and St. Elie. The 9th Division had
a very difficult task. Their line of advance was in the
direction of Haisnes, but between them and this village

was the Hohenzollern Redoubt and Fosse 8. Their left
did not make any headway, but they took Fosse 8 and
the Hohenzollern Redoubt, and a few Highlanders on
their right even went as far as Haisnes. The 2nd Division
were unable to make any advance, and Auchy remained
in German hands.

All this happened on the 25th, and it will be seen that
the failure on the left of the line put all the other divisions
in an awkward position. Also the I and IV Corps had
failed to get through, and according to plan the XI Corps
was to assist.

The 21st and 24th Divisions were engaged on September 26th, but in the bitter and varying battle which raged
during that day, far from helping the other two corps to
get through, their aid was seriously wanted to hold what
had been gained. In this war of attrition, until the
enemy's reserves had vanished, it was always possible for
him to make most vigorous counter-attacks, and the
results of battles at this date cannot be judged by the
amount of ground gained or the ability or inability to
get through the German line. The British rush had spent
itself, and while so doing the Germans had massed troops
for counter-attack—as much to take their toll of lives
and prisoners as to restore the situation.

The success of a battle planned to break through the
enemy line when he is known to have large reserves must
depend very largely on surprise and time. The British
were making feints and demonstrations all the way up
to Ypres—Foch on the British right was attacking, and
there was a big French attack down in Champagne. But
the German could still mass his reserves, watch where
his troops held us, and where our forward rush had led
us into dangerous salients, and then strike back with
speed and vigour. It will be understood that the margin
of time for a possible break through the German defences
was very small. The success of the Germans in holding
the left of our attack had given us a very odd sort of
line, and, as we had failed to get through, it became of
necessity a ding-dong battle.

On the 27th the most advanced points of our attack

had been driven in. The men of the 15th Division who had pushed out over Hill 70 and Fosse 14 had found themselves in a solitary kind of position, with few friends and many enemies. They had already tried to make themselves more comfortable before the 21st Division went up to help them, but Fosse 14, Hill 70, and the Chalk Pit all went back to the enemy, and the net gain on the right of the British line was Loos.

At 12.30 p.m. Lieut.-Col. Murray-Threipland received orders [1] that the 3rd Brigade would march to Loos in the following order : 4th Battalion Grenadier Guards, 1st Battalion Welsh Guards, 2nd Battalion Scots Guards, and 1st Battalion Grenadier Guards. The 2nd Brigade were to attack the Chalk Pit and Fosse 14, and when the brigadier was satisfied that they had occupied or practically taken these places the 3rd Brigade would commence an attack on Hill 70. The attack would be made by the 4th Battalion Grenadier Guards with the Welsh Guards in support in Loos. If the attacking battalion suffered heavily the Welsh Guards would occupy the line taken by the Grenadiers.

The ruined village of Vermelles now presented a scene of activity that had never been equalled in its most prosperous days. From the very ruins came the short, sharp thunder-clap of guns. Troops were everywhere. The two days and two nights of battle had left obvious marks. A stream of wounded and weary, drawn-faced stragglers limped along the road mixed up with the more energetic traffic. A move had been ordered and the bivouac camps were busy.

At 2.30 p.m. the Welsh Guards, headed by the Commanding Officer, marched off to Loos.

Lieut.-Col. Murray-Threipland always walked in a determined, thrusting manner, with his head a little bit forward. Standing over six feet, with broad shoulders and hard, lean figure, he had a commanding presence. Walking by the Commanding Officer's side was Perrins, with high cheek-bones and eyes which seemed to slant upwards. He generally carried a large leather

[1] Appendix B1.

case full of papers slung round him, an electric lamp, a revolver, and was said to have once added to his equipment a Maläy knife of fearful shape and size. He had a springy sort of walk and generally looked on the ground.

The order of march was the Prince of Wales's Company, with Osmond Williams, Mawby, Geoffrey Crawshay, Smith and Philip Howard ; No. 2 with Dick Bulkeley, Rupert Lewis, Keith Menzies and Copland Griffiths ; No. 3 with George Philipps, Harry Rice, Randolph and Sutton ; No. 4 with Palmer, Claud Insole, Basil Hambrough and Evan Thomas. Humphrey Dene was sent as liaison officer between the battalion and the brigade, and Jimjack Evans was with headquarters as scouting officer and general utility. The rest were left behind with the transport, or near it.

There is a road between Vermelles and Loos, and after following this a little way the whole brigade turned off to the left and went across country. On leaving the road they proceeded in artillery formation.

Before coming to Loos there is a rise in the ground followed by a long gentle slope down to the village. When the 4th Battalion Grenadiers topped this rise they were immediately seen by the enemy, who promptly opened heavy artillery fire on them which grew in volume as succeeding platoons, in close column of fours, slowly rose at intervals over the sky-line and proceeded steadily towards Loos.

This approach on Loos has become historical. It was witnessed by many. What troops there were over a large stretch of the front line to the left could see right up this slope, and it has been described by many as a most thrilling sight. Shrapnel burst, making puffs of smoke overhead, high explosive shells sent up sudden fountains of mud and black smoke which completely obliterated, according to the view-point, now one, now another of those small squares of advancing men, who, however, slowly and steadily continued to advance, the brigade covering a large area of ground in this formation.

The battalion was to be in support in or about the village, and finding, just outside it, a German trench, the Commanding Officer ordered the battalion into it while he went forward to find the brigadier, who had sent word that he was in Loos.

An unarmed Highlander was wandering about these trenches. He refused to get in or take any sort of cover, but, constituting himself into a sort of guide and showman, first pointed out the best bits of trench to get into and then directed attention to places of interest—Hill 70, the Chalk Pit, Fosse 14, Hugo Wood. As he walked up and down amidst a hail of shells the men repeatedly urged him to get into the trench, but he would not, and spoke with the utmost contempt of German shells. Afterwards he went with the battalion into Loos, where he disappeared.

Meanwhile the Commanding Officer of the 4th Battalion Grenadiers had been gassed and the position of his battalion was for the moment unknown. The brigadier directed that the Welsh Guards should be brought into the main street of the town and wait there for orders.

And so the men of the battalion presently saw the thrusting figure of their Commanding Officer, with Perrins tripping beside him, come rapidly towards them. They were taken out of the trench and into Loos, where the gas shelling was so bad they had to put on their horrible slimy bags called H.P. Helmets.

Humphrey Dene, describing the scene, says : " There was the battalion standing about anyhow, and making noises like frogs and penny tin trumpets as they spat and blew down the tubes of their helmets, and shells crashed into houses, and Bill (the Commanding Officer) dashed about trying to see Brigade Headquarters through the dirty glass of his helmet, which was absolutely useless because he refused to tuck the ends into his coat."

But he did find the brigade and was shown a map and a point on it where some of the 4th Battalion Grenadiers were supposed to be, and was ordered to take his battalion to them and commence an attack on Hill 70.

He then told the company commanders to take their companies through the village and get shelter where they could while he went to find the Grenadiers,

He discovered Miles Ponsonby in a low trench on the south-east of the village. Ponsonby said he had not more than 200 men with him.

The Commanding Officer then made the following arrangements : The Prince of Wales's Company would advance on the right on a two platoon frontage, and Ponsonby with his Grenadiers on a similar frontage on the left. No. 2 Company Welsh Guards would support the Prince of Wales's and No. 3 the Grenadiers. He gave a clump of trees on the sky-line as a mark to advance on.

Returning once more to Loos, he collected his company commanders and issued his orders. As the Prince of Wales's advanced No. 2 moved into place and then No. 3 ; No. 4 and Battalion H.Q. remained in the village.

The time was noted as 6.2 p.m. about a quarter of an hour before dark.

Headquarters were installed in a convenient ruin. At 6.50 p.m. the first report was sent to the brigade : " A wounded corporal reports that the 4th Grenadier and 1st Welsh Guards have captured two lines of trenches. I have launched my last company. 2nd Scots Guards should come up handy. Can you give me any information about my right flank, as I am anxious about it ? "

Palmer, with No. 4 Company, had been sent up to the trench where the Grenadiers had been, at the commencement of the attack, with instructions to try and get in touch with companies in front and find out if they required any reinforcements, but not to go himself, and to send back any information he could get.

Rhys Williams, with two guns, was sent to some trenches on the right held by the 10th Hussars.

The waiting at Battalion H.Q. when an attack has been launched is the most appalling experience. A long time, or what seems a long time, elapses before any news of the success of companies, or their position, comes in. There is practically nothing to do but think, although an attempt is made to do some more active work. A map, a typewritten sheet of paper is clung to as a sort of life-buoy, though probably neither conveys anything to one's mind. A message, even the classical question of how many pots of raspberry jam have been issued, becomes important; in fact, any excuse for activity of mind or body is welcome.

The first message of importance came from Keith Menzies, who reported in person that No. 2 Company was held up and wanted reinforcements. He spoke of a bank on the top of the hill, and said that the company were some twenty or thirty yards beyond it and could get no farther.

Soon after Menzies came Rupert Lewis with a similar story. Lewis's glasses had got fogged and dirty, it was pitch dark, and he had fallen into a trench and bruised his head. He had been promptly jumped on by some cavalrymen who occupied the trench and thought he was a German. However, when he had recovered his wind and senses, he explained who he was and was allowed to go.

From what he said the Commanding Officer concluded that it was not a case of reinforcements but that the front line had gone far enough. The brigadier had been most emphatic that the line to be occupied was to be on the reverse slope only.

Keith Menzies was sent back to tell Dick Bulkeley to dig in where he was. Palmer was ordered to move farther up the hill in closer support, and his place was taken by one company of Scots Guards, which had just arrived. A message was also sent to the brigadier to the effect that the required point had been reached, that the Grenadier and Welsh Guards had been considerably knocked about, and that it was advisable to bring up all the Scots Guards to dig in near the new line and allow the attacking troops to reorganise.

The right flank was causing the Commanding Officer some anxiety, as it was obvious that a large gap must exist between the right of his new line and the nearest troops in the old line, the 10th Hussars. So he sent for Palmer and told him to take his company up and make good the gap. Palmer asked if he might go and reconnoitre the situation, but was told to send some one else and only in the event of it being absolutely necessary should he.go himself.

At the same time a message arrived from Rhys Williams, who was also anxious about this flank, asking for news of the advance and for two more guns. Gough was sent up with both.

It must be remembered that the time of the attack was just as night was falling, and that the difficulty of getting up the hill was not occasioned by shelling or rifle-fire but by the darkness. To keep direction and keep in touch was extremely hard, as it always is in any night operation.

At the commencement of the advance it was still possible to see the clump of trees on top of the hill, but they gradually disappeared. That company commanders were alive to the importance of knowing each other's positions is shown by Osmond Williams halting in dead ground, short of the crest, until Dick Bulkeley ran into him. No. 3 Company, however, lost touch with the Grenadiers, who apparently swerved away to the left. Having lost touch there was no time to go searching about in the darkness. Osmond Williams was satisfied he had No. 2 behind him, but in any case he would have attacked with one platoon.

To describe the exact movements of each company is impossible—no man could tell of the movements of the other platoons of his own company.

Osmond Williams advanced and the three companies were swallowed up in the night.

But they could tell they had reached the top of the hill. A star-light went up—one—one, two, three—six of them —a dozen—twenty—a little ripple of fire—night had given way to a blazing patch of light in which one could see holes, unevenness in the ground which showed in hard black clumps and lines, and clear-cut figures with rifle and glinting bayonet advancing into the light, running forward out of the farther darkness. And then the little ripple of rifle-fire increased in an excited way, and with the rattling crash of machine guns pandemonium reigned.

What happened ? In the daylight it is possible to reconstruct from the next moment, the moment one was able to look round and see what men were then doing, but at night——

The dead knew nothing. The wounded knew they were hit. The unwounded would probably first realise that they were lying on the ground—and the roar of the enemy fire never ceased. Copland Griffiths describes a tornado, a monsoon, something fearful in the nature of a storm going on just over his head as he lay flat on the ground, and a bullet ripped him straight down the back so that he tried to lie flatter yet.

Such a situation cannot last for ever, and the firing quieted down. Men scraped holes where they were, or rolled into shell-holes, and in spite of a constant fusillade, with an occasional burst of intense fire, officers began to crawl about endeavouring to clear up the situation and collect their men.

Some sort of line was formed and companies got into touch with each other.

The Prince of Wales's Company on the right was very scattered. All their officers had been hit—Osmond Williams was mortally wounded and died the next day, Mawby and Smith were killed, Crawshay and Howard wounded. The men were hanging on under any sort of cover. No. 2 had fared better in officer casualties, although they were right up against the enemy. Copland Griffiths was the only one hit, and he was determined to hang on. No. 3 was on the left and slightly behind the other companies, but Philipps was hit, Randolph and Sutton killed. Dick Bulkeley established himself behind the bank spoken of by Menzies and sent down messages on the situation. Palmer came up the hill and began to talk to Bulkeley about the gap on the right of the line, but was immediately killed.

Dick Bulkeley went down himself to consult with the Commanding Officer. He could only summarise the position by saying it was damnable, but he was told he must try and dig in where he was, and half the battalion tools were sent up for that purpose (the other half had

been blown up).   When he had gone Rhys Williams appeared, hit, but not too bad, and gave what information
he had.   The doctor (Picton Phillips) dressed his wound
and he went back to his guns, but was ordered to hospital
later on.

A message was sent to Claud Insole telling him Palmer
was killed, but he was to take No. 4 Company and carry
out the order given to Palmer.

The Commanding Officer was now quite clear that the
battalion was where it was meant to go, but had still
cause to be extremely anxious, as they were by no means
firmly established and were evidently somewhat disorganised—more especially the Prince of Wales's Company,
of which there was the vaguest news.   A company of the
4th Pioneer Battalion Coldstream Guards had reported
to help in the consolidating, but he held them back until
the other companies of the 2nd Battalion Scots Guards
arrived.   Eventually Lieut.-Col. Cator came and said
that he had not more than two companies, but that the
remainder of the 4th Battalion Grenadier Guards had
turned up and were being sent with his battalion to take
over from the Welsh Guards.

The two Commanding Officers, accompanied by Rupert
Lewis, who had been retained at headquarters, then went
to look over the ground, and Dene was sent to find a
place for the battalion when they were relieved.

On inspection it was considered impossible to dig in
on the line occupied, then a mere matter of shell-holes
and scrapes—but a little further back there was an old
German trench, mostly fallen in, and the relieving troops
with the Pioneer Company and some engineers for wiring
were sent up to make this trench secure.   When Colonel
Cator was satisfied with the work done the Welsh Guards
were withdrawn, though a few remained up there until
October 1st.

By daybreak on the 28th companies began to reform
in some trenches south of Loos.   The shelling of the
village was very heavy and accompanied by a lot of long-
range machine-gun fire and sniping.   Rupert Lewis, who
had been sent to command the remains of the Prince of

Wales's Company, got a bullet through his arm, but remained at duty (as did Copland Griffiths). Cookers came up, and the battalion stayed in support until 7 p.m. on the 29th, when they marched back to Vermelles, and on the 30th to Sailly-Labourse.

As stated in the original order, the attack on Hill 70 was to be subsequent to the success of the 2nd Brigade. The crest of the hill was a fearful place unless the Chalk

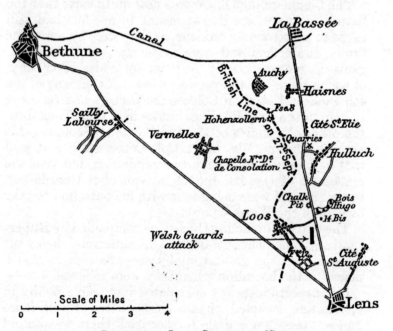

POSITION AT LOOS, SEPTEMBER 27TH.

Pit and Fosse 14, on the left, were taken. The brigadier was certainly under the impression that this had been done (at one time the 2nd Brigade had captured both these places, but were unable to hold Fosse 14), and when he heard that the Germans still held Fosse 14 it is stated, on good authority, that he commenced to write cancelling his orders of attack, when Col. Murray-Threipland's message to the effect that the attack had been launched was handed to him.

The satisfaction of the engagement, from the Welsh Guards' point of view, lay in the way the battalion had behaved and the fact that they had steadied the line. As has been explained, the attack was in the dark, and no one knew where the enemy was. Sir John French, writing of the previous day's action, says: "Reports regarding this portion of the action are very conflicting, and it is not possible to form an entirely just appreciation of what occurred in this part of the field." What remained of the 15th and 21st Divisions had been blown off the hill and down the slope, and so far as the battalion was concerned the attack started from the moment it came over the rise in the ground approaching Loos. The greatest credit is due to the new Welsh soldiers for their steadiness and determination.

Poor Osmond Williams was an able soldier and the impression he made on the battalion remains to this day. And he was a gallant gentleman. He was first gazetted to the 15th Hussars, but served in the South African War with the 19th Royal Hussars. Owing to a polo accident, he was subsequently invalided out of the army in 1908. Being refused a commission on the outbreak of war on the ground of health he enlisted in the Scots Greys, and, as personal orderly to Sir Philip Chetwode, carried the 5th Brigade Flag behind him throughout the retreat and subsequent advance to the Aisne. In November 1914 he was given a special commission by Sir John French as 2/Lieut. in the Scots Greys. In a dismounted attack at Wytschaete he killed eleven Germans with his own hand and won the D.S.O. It is a fine record of service to his country.

Palmer, who was the senior captain and acted as second in command, was a fanatical fighter, which showed itself in his face, in his actions and boundless energy, in his spoken word and in his record. In private life he was a mining engineer, and his military career started in 1899 in the 3rd Battalion East Surrey Regiment. When the South African War broke out he believed that his Militia would not be used, and resigned his commission to enlist as a trooper in the 34th Company of the Imperial Yeo-

manry. Bald official record shows that he was given a
commission in Africa, and rose to command this same
company, winning a D.S.O. and being twice mentioned
in despatches. At the end of that war he joined the
South African Constabulary, where he remained until
1907. He was a year in Zanzibar reorganising the police,
and was in Rhodesia when war was declared with Germany. But he managed to be at the first battle of Ypres
as a captain attached to the Royal Horse Guards. His
company, No. 4, or what is left of it, has never forgotten
him, and his photograph will be found in several houses
in Wales. He looked after the bodily comforts of his
men down to attending to their blistered feet himself,
but when one of them bobbed at something which
whizzed over his head in the streets of Loos Palmer
sprang at him and shook him like a rat.

Mawby, Randolph, Smith and Sutton have no military
record from which a paragraph can be made, but their
names must be handed down amongst those of the
gallant men who were the first Welsh Guardsmen to give
their lives for Great Britain.

Many were noted for outstanding gallantry in per-
forming their duty. Rhys Williams, Rupert Lewis and
Copland Griffiths carried on in spite of wounds of a painful and inconvenient nature, and Drill-Sergt. Bland, in
place of Sergt.-Major Barnes, who was sick, led the
ammunition-waggons and tool-carts through intensive
shelling in truly dramatic fashion. The action of Pte.
Grant, who with the help of Cpl. Hall, 4th Battalion
Grenadier Guards, succeeded in getting Osmond Williams
back from the advanced position where he had fallen,
and the efforts of C.S.M. Cossey, L/Sergt. F. Phillips, and
Pte. M. Jones to accomplish the same thing for George
Philipps, though acts of high courage, do not make such
good stories as that of Ptes. C. H. Witts, S. T. Harvard,
F. Perry and W. Bateman. These men succeeded in
getting very close to the enemy line in the charge and
jumped into a hole in which were built two shelters. In
one shelter was a dead German officer and in the other
two live German soldiers. They could not get back for

three days, and as a German sap from the main enemy line was only a few yards away, and was occupied, it was not quite clear to them whether they were to consider the two German privates their prisoners or their jailers. However, they did get away, and brought the two Germans with them, also the papers from the dead officer.

On October 2nd the first draft, 104 N.C.O.'s and men, arrived from England under Luxmoore Ball, a gigantic ex-Welsh Fusilier, who had come straight from the successful South-West African campaign and was burning to fight. The short time he had spent in England had been mostly in the orderly room asking to go out to France.

The rest at Sailly la Bourse was only for a few days, and the battle was still going on round about Loos. But during this rest Sir John French, Gen. Haking and Lord Cavan visited the various brigades and complimented all concerned on what they had done—Sir John French's remark to the assembled commanding officers was, "Magnificent work, gentlemen, magnificent."

On October 3rd the battalion marched back to Vermelles and relieved the 9th Battalion Highland Light Infantry in support trenches a mile east of the village. Battalion H.Q. was at Notre Dame de Consolation.

The Guards Division was now operating on the left of the great battle and was concerned with that mass of trenches and wire and machine guns called the Hohenzollern Redoubt. This place was thrust forward between the Quarries and Fosse 8, but nearest the latter. It had been taken in the first rush on September 25th, together with Fosse 8 and the Quarries. But on September 27th the Germans succeeded in regaining Fosse 8 and the Quarries and nearly the whole of the Hohenzollern Redoubt. The 85th Brigade (28th Division), under Gen. Pereira, restored the situation as regards the Redoubt (both he and his Brigade-Major John Flower being wounded in the fight); but, although some of them got on to Fosse 8, they could not hold it.

The Hohenzollern Redoubt, dominated by Fosse 8, was now a most unpleasant place. It was part of the

4

3rd German Line which included Fosse 8, so that British and Germans were not only within fifty yards of each other, but connected up by old communication trenches. Bombing attacks were fierce and frequent. By October 3rd the enemy had succeeded in getting into part of the Hohenzollern Redoubt. The Guards Division then took over from the 28th Division.

Much work was done by the battalion while in support at Notre Dame de Consolation connecting up the old British and German trenches. They went back to rest in Vermelles on the night of the 5th.

The billets in Vermelles were anything but comfortable. The gunners with their cheering weapons were all over the ruins, and, although one likes to hear the sound of British guns, no one wants to lie down by the side of them to rest. The Germans had a naval gun which fired armour-piercing shells with what seemed a retarded action, and they searched with this gun for the British batteries amongst the ruins. This went on all day and night, and there were a good few casualties.

There were several other reasons why Vermelles was not thought much of by the battalion, and the gas fatigue was one of them. This consisted of carrying cylinders of gas up to the front line. Gas was not very popular at that time, a feeling due no doubt to the many casualties caused by our own gas to the troops on September 25th. But, in any case, it was a dangerous fatigue. Three parties, of 184 men each, did this job under Bradney, Bulkeley and Roberts. Dene had the worst part of the business, having to direct the unloading and handing over of the stuff to the fatigue parties at the entrance of the communication trench. "Bullets," he said, "came flipping round the corner pretty frequently, and if one of them had punctured a heap of cylinders there was an end of me."

The maze of trenches, too, which led up to and round about the Hohenzollern Redoubt was most confusing, and several parties got lost in them. It is not pleasant to be lost with a cylinder of gas on your shoulder.

On October 8th the Germans launched a big attack

stretching from the Hohenzollern Redoubt to Loos, with a special effort against the former.   But the situation was " well in hand," and the Welsh Guards were not required and took no part in it.   As regards the line held by the Guards Division Lord Cavan wrote : " The battle ended in the complete repulse of three German battalions by handfuls of bombers of the Guards Division."

The night of the 12th saw the battalion back in billets at Sailly la Bourse, but on the 13th it was hurried into Lancashire Trench, on the north-east of Vermelles, to be in reserve to a fresh attack by a Line Division from the Hohenzollern Redoubt.   Humphrey Dene got a bit of a shell through the leg, and Claud Insole took over No. 4 Company.

The fighting was very severe.   The confused state of affairs may be gathered from the orders received on the 14th, which were that the 3rd Guards Brigade would take over the front line held by two brigades of the 46th Division, but when the 1st Battalion Grenadiers and the 2nd Battalion Scots Guards arrived they found that half the line they were supposed to take over was in the hands of the Germans.

The Welsh Guards did not move, but provided heavy fatigues digging in the front line and carrying material.

On the night of the 15th, 25 bombers from the 4th Battalion Grenadier and 25 from the Welsh Guards were rushed up under Keith Menzies to help a battalion of the Sherwood Foresters who had lost all their bombers. This party did well—being supplied with bombs night and day by another party under Luxmoore Ball—and returned on the night of the 16th.

But the German was not to have all the say in the matter of attack.   The Brigade H.Q. had been organising all the detonating and carrying of bombs, but this work was now handed over to the Welsh Guards   During the day the men detonated 9,000 bombs, and 7,200 were carried up to a reserve store between 10.45 a.m. and 5.30 p.m. ; each journey took one and a half hours, and a party of 25 men set out every quarter of an hour. Basil Hambrough was looking after the detonating and was sitting in a cellar with Charles Greville (4th Battalion Grenadier Guards) and a corporal when a shell hit the house and penetrated the cellar. The corporal was killed (Daniels)—Hambrough and Charles Greville got out. There were about 10,000 bombs in the cellar but none of them went off.

At 5 a.m. on the 18th a bombing attack by the 1st Battalion Grenadier and the 2nd Battalion Scots Guards commenced (in conjunction with the 2nd Brigade) with the idea of straightening out the line. The Welsh Guards H.Q. and No. 2 Company bombers went forward to support the 2nd Scots Guards. Together they won about 160 yards of " Big Willie." Sergt. Wheatley, one of the best battalion bombers, was wounded in the hand. The battalion was again thanked by Lieut.-Col. Cator.

Trenches were made to bring the part of Big Willie which had been gained into the system we held, and while engaged on this Claud Insole was approached by one of his men who told him there was a dead man in the shallow bit of trench he was working on. Insole, who knew that a lot of the men had a dislike of handling dead bodies, told him abruptly to throw this one out. He then overheard the following conversation :

" You heard what the officer said, Dai—we are to throw the man out."

Inaudible mumbles.

" Come on, Dai—you take the man's legs and I will take his shoulders. Now then. . . ."

" Oh, damn ! Ianto, the man has no legs ! What shall we do ? "

Inaudible conversation.

" The officer said so. Come on, now, take hold of him anywhere and let us throw him out."

Which was at last accomplished. This finer feeling, which was very prevalent when the battalion first arrived in France, soon disappeared.

The comparatively safe, if not comfortable, Lancashire Trench was left on the 19th, when the battalion went to Vermelles, and occupied, for the most part, cellars. The village was still a mark for German gunners, with their

infernal armour-piercing shells, mixed up with others, so
that, although they were called rest billets, it was prefer-
able to be nearer the front line.   During the four ensuing
days casualties crept up.   But another draft arrived on
the 20th.   Five officers—Capt. Aldridge, Lieut. Windsor
Lewis, Lieut. Williams Ellis, 2/Lieut. Crawford Wood and
2/Lieut. Dudley-Ward straight from England—and late
in the evening Capt. Allen with fifty men from the base
at Havre.

On the 23rd the battalion relieved the 1st Battalion
Coldstream Guards in the Hohenzollern Redoubt, of
which the following account was written at the time :

" We started in bright moonlight—a ghostly business,
especially when in a perfectly flat country of chalky soil
and rank grass, dug all over with trenches which appear
to be grey banks and mounds inhabited by men.   As one
walks along voices come from the ground, and lights glint
between cracks in so-called dugouts.   Now and then you
come across a group of men sitting silent on one of these
heaps and you realise, with a queer feeling, that they live
inside it.   We arrived at a hedge where there was an
entrance like a gateway sloping into a communication
trench.   Then in single file we started what seemed an
endless twisting and turning along a narrow deep ditch.
Finally we came to troops and dugouts—this was the
third line, they said.   And so we came to the second, and
so to the firing-line.   The men were posted without too
much confusion, relieving the Coldstream—and then followed a long, cold, and sleepless night. . . . The trenches
are good and bad mixed.   We hold about half new and
half old German.   The Hun trench stinks and has lots
of Hun bodies built into the parapet, and there are a
good many of our dead, men who took the place, lying
outside.   The chief method of warfare is bombs, which
we hurl at each other all night, fortunately with small
effect so far as we are concerned, but much fearful noise.
It seems to die away by mutual consent about four in
the morning, when the only regular sound is shelling from
our guns.   My job is chiefly to patrol the trench, which

I seem to have done ceaselessly—I have also inspected rifles. . . . When the early morning mist had cleared I peered at the German trench and the nasty ground in between through a periscope. The position is very odd, as we share one trench with the Hun and others face all sorts of ways. It is as though we had captured part of a maze. I wonder if we shall get the other part! There is at least some truth in describing the noise here as continual thunder.

"Oct. 25th.

" The Hun made a lively bomb display last night after dark, but of the many hundreds they threw only five fell in our trench and wounded two men slightly. They were more successful in other ways. Aldridge's company and some Grenadiers were sent out last night digging in front with the object of straightening our line and bringing it all close to the Hun. The Engineers went in front of them to put up wire and it was a good sight to see the Sappers work. The young fellow in charge led them down the trench and ' hoiked ' a few sandbags off the parapet to make a step, up which they all went over the top, strolling along as though there were no Huns there and laying out their wire as calmly as though they were demonstrating in a field. When they had nearly finished the Huns saw them and opened fire wildly. But they went on until machine guns started on them and were then ordered back. One fellow came lounging up to the traverse where I was, and, instead of jumping in as I expected, leaned over the sandbag parapet much as he would over a bar in a public-house. He jingled coins in his hand. ' That b—— Fritz out there,' said he, ' has only got tuppence in his pocket. Oh, I beg pardon, sir.' And he climbed in the trench. The Sappers lost three men. Aldridge and his men got under cover and were able to carry on till four this morning. Aldridge no casualties, Grenadiers one."—*Diary of C. H. D. W.*

But the Hohenzollern Redoubt cannot be adequately described. No. 2 Company held West Face, the sides of which were composed of dead men, equipment and a little loose earth. A brawny tattooed arm was found to belong to a Highlander of the gallant New Army, but most of these dead were Germans. Outside the trench were British dead on either side. On what was now the rear, formerly the German front, they clustered where the wire was uncut, and there was a nobility in the positions of these men which, unless it has been seen, cannot be communicated.

An enormous hand stuck out of the bottom of the trench at one place, and Dick Bulkeley was curious about it. " I wonder," said he, " who that hand belongs to ? " and tapped it with his stick. He had a portion uncovered and found it was a huge officer of the Prussian Guard. Everyone has a story of some fearful sight in the Hohenzollern Redoubt.

In spite of the heavy rain which fell on the night 24/25 the battalion did good digging work, connecting saps which had been thrown out. But soon the main trench began to fall in and their efforts had to be confined to clearing it.

The justifiable anxiety of the higher command proved to be unfounded, as the expected German attack did not develop ; indeed it was thought by the officers of the battalion that a relief was taking place in the enemy lines. The sniping and general truculence of the enemy seemed to die down and it required rifle grenades to stir them up.

On the night of the 26th the trench was handed over to the 6th Battalion Queen's and the battalion marched to Allouagne.

The relief was very slow and difficult. Men could not pass each other in the trench, and companies had to go out the same way as the Queen's were coming in. Men had to take off their packs and squeeze past the incoming troops. The way out was very long and wearisome, ankle deep in clay mud which went " chuck-chuck " as the men pulled their feet out of it. The battalion left at 6.30 p.m. and did not get out of the communication trench till about 9 p.m. Companies were very exhausted when they arrived at Bethune. A little farther on some intelligent person had posted sentries along the road so that battalions might not miss the way, but he put them on the wrong road. This was discovered by the Commanding Officer, who sent orderlies to try and stop his companies. The Prince of Wales's Company was warned and sent back ; the others, however, went on and eventually arrived at their correct destination, having done five miles too much. " The last four miles were the devil. We arrived at 4.30 a.m."

CHAPTER IV

ALLOUAGNE—MERVILLE—LAVENTIE

ALLOUAGNE was a scattered village in a corner of timbered country. The leaves were just beginning to turn
and rainy days were making the sun more welcome than
usual.

The companies were billeted in barns of farmhouses.
There was a sameness about these farms and outbuild-
ings, most of them being on the three sides of a square
plan with a pigeon-cot on a pole and a heap of evil refuse
in the centre. The sweet smell of the country may have
been there, but it was overpowered by the penetrating
odour from the unclean yards and sour beetroot pulp on
which the farmers fed their cattle. There was plenty of
straw, however, and men were learning that this is a
great comfort; a dry barn with plenty of clean straw
to lie on, two blankets and a waterproof sheet consti-
tuted a " good billet."

Changes and reinforcements to companies gave the
Prince of Wales's to Hugh Allen, with Luxmoore Ball,
Crawford Wood and Dudley Ward. No. 2 was still commanded by Dick Bulkeley, with Bradney and Keith
Menzies. Herbert Aldridge, with a slight limp and a
good-natured, shrewd face, with the complexion of a
dried apple, had No. 3, with Windsor Lewis and Harry
Rice. For the moment Claud Insole commanded No. 4
with Williams Ellis (who tried to learn Welsh and was
said to have accomplished the almost impossible feat of
marching from the Hohenzollern Redoubt dressed in
some patent armour which was then much advertised in
the daily papers).

47

Of the thirty officers who had left England with the battalion there were only eleven left. To the casualties on Hill 70 and Vermelles must be added Fox-Pitt and Hambrough wounded; Wethered, Evan Thomas and M. O. Roberts sick; Gough already away with the machine gunners who were brigaded and eventually formed into a corps apart. One new officer arrived at Allouagne, Battye, who was posted to No. 2 Company (The dates of all reinforcements will be found in the chapter dealing with the 2nd Battalion. The posting of officers to companies is not easy to follow, and we only propose to give them from time to time as the battalion went into action; they were frequently changed or lent by one company to another, and unless an incident of note occurred we will not weary the reader with a record of these temporary adjustments.)

"Jimjack" Evans remained at headquarters as "sniping" officer, and occupied a position which at various times was called "Intelligence," "Observation," and "Assistant Adjutant." Headquarters always required an officer other than the Adjutant, and was frequently the biggest company of the battalion. At this period there were not only snipers on headquarters, but thirty-four bombers as well—in fact, the bombing craze had gone so far as brigade bombers.

Headquarters was never organised as a company, although there were many who advocated that step. With drums, transport, signallers, shops, snipers, bombers, police and orderlies posted to companies, there were a number of men a company commander never saw except on pay day. There was no great difficulty in keeping the books, but it led to minor troubles whenever there was a sudden dispersal of headquarters to their own companies, which happened quite frequently. The principle of a company was, however, conceded by the appointment of an acting "Headquarter Quartermaster-Sergeant" wherever the billeting arrangements kept headquarters together. All through the war the battalion seemed to glide imperceptibly into further modifications of organisation.

Allouagne itself is not an interesting place, and the country round does not seem to have attracted much. It was possible to go to Bethune, but it was not a popular excursion.   Otherwise there were coal-pits—with the accompanying slag-heaps—and closely cultivated country.   The pits possessed baths, which the battalion was able to use with much benefit after a four-mile walk. Practically speaking this was the limit of exploration. But Allouagne seems to mark a definite period in the history of the Welsh Guards.   The battalion had fought its first fight and suffered heavy casualties.   Men came out somewhat dazed.   The game was new to them, and the comradeship of training at Esher is not the same as the comradeship of war.   They required a readjustment of ideas, both men and officers, and this readjustment would seem to have started at Allouagne.

The battalion was well trained and disciplined when it went into action, but such discipline is not second nature (the battalion was in France six months after the Royal Warrant for their formation was signed), and the few days, we may call it weeks, of fighting had confused them.

The tendency amongst all troops in war is to get dirty and slovenly.   A battle is a dirty business—you cannot shave, you cannot wash, you cannot clean your clothes, and you feed under conditions which are scarcely decent. Men come out of battle, and more especially their first battle, tired with a sort of nerve fatigue which brings lassitude, an inclination to remain dirty and live in an unclean manner long after their muscles have ceased to ache and their stiffness has worn off.   Experience shows that the only way to combat this evil is to establish rules and insist on their observance, whatever may chance. This lesson was speedily recognised at Allouagne.   Some things deemed impossible can be done, and others which would appear simple have to be modified.   When once digested, however, the experience becomes part of the life of the battalion, breeds a kind of instinct in those who follow, and the principle is not forgotten.

New and old, both ideas and men, became merged.

"You have no traditions," said a Grenadier, "no past!" It might have been true at Esher or at Arques, but the foundation of a big and glorious hall of fame was laid at Loos, and building commenced at Allouagne. It was a true regimental feeling. They had done something, they had a record.

The minds of men are governed and led by trivial matters. The big thing was that the Welsh Guards had been true as Welshmen to the fighting traditions of their race, but the fine reputation of a regiment may be lost to the public by a sparkling epigram levelled at a dull brass button.

The Welshman is not slow, and rose to the occasion. A precedent was established and will be carried on.

Probably, too, though no one realised it at the time, Allouagne marked the birth of the regimental soul, that fusion of the living and the dead which the new ensign describes when he speaks with pride of "The Regiment."

Leave was granted from Allouagne. The Commanding Officer went to Paris, Dick Bulkeley, Perrins and others went to England for seven days. Herbert Aldridge acted for the Commanding Officer, and Windsor Lewis for Perrins. A quiet, conscientious fellow was Windsor Lewis, and with a sense of humour. He had been through the South African War and was a thorough soldier.

Copland Griffiths and Rupert Lewis rejoined from hospital, and for ever after each accused the other of having been too warlike while in hospital and ruined every chance of a few weeks' leave at home. Rupert Lewis took command of No. 4 and Griffiths went back to No. 2. An unhappy accident occurred to His Majesty the King, who was in France, the day after the battalion arrived in this village. His horse fell with him, but fortunately he suffered no permanent injury, although badly bruised. It was doubly unhappy because he was to have inspected the division, and the opportunity never occurred again.

On November 9th the 3rd Brigade marched to billets around Merville. Nigel Newall joined the battalion the same day with eighty men. He had been in France before with the H.A.C., but declared that he was glad

to get back, as he had been bored to death with the
Tower, where the Reserve Battalion was now stationed.
He was an exceedingly keen young officer, with a most
happy disposition.

On the 14th the 3rd Brigade marched to billets near
Laventie.

Laventie is in the middle of a very flat country. La
Gorgue and the river Lys are to the west of it. In ordinary times this low-lying country is drained by means
of dykes and ditches, but even so the ground in the rainy
season would be sodden. The line the division was responsible for was about two miles north of Neuve
Chapelle. The village of Aubers and the celebrated
Aubers Ridge were in front of it, and looked down on the
swampy ground where the British were entrenched.

Claud Insole, who had been driving an ambulance at
the outbreak of war, had been up into Aubers and had
seen the open fighting which took place before the line
settled down. He used to describe how little scattered
bodies of troops tried to hold up the Germans, who out-
numbered them three to one. This front was also the
scene of the IV Corps (Rawlinson) effort on May 9th,
1915, part of the battle of Festubert; and during the
battle of Loos, Indian troops (Meerut Division) made a
demonstration and did well, but had no reserves to
maintain their advantage.

The first billets occupied were the scattered farms
round about Pont du Hem to the south of Laventie.

On the 15th company commanders went to the line to
spy out the nakedness of the land. They proceeded
straight up from the road which led to Aubers, and,
arriving at the cross roads at Fauquissart, found the
" trenches " just in front of them. They were not
trenches but breastworks, and lay about 150 yards east
of the road which runs from Neuve Chapelle to Fleurbaix,
and at the very bottom of the Aubers Ridge. As was
inevitable in such a position, great ponds and lakes had
formed at some places in the natural depressions of the
ground, at others where soil had been removed for building up the defences. The line had, however, the great

advantage of being open at the back, and so afforded, in spite of the accumulated water, plenty of room to move about in.

Behind the line was a series of forts, all on the breast-work plan, and there was a system of trolley railways running up to the back of this second defence.

The enemy, who were not aggressive, were at varying distances between 150 and 300 yards away.

The church at Fauquissart held out bravely against the assaults of the German artillery—the back wall, and a few remnants of the others, remained trying to hold up portions of the roof, which hung in disreputable festoons.

It was decided that the tour of duty would be two days in the front line, two days in support—support troops being billeted in the farms and at a later period in the town of Laventie—and after twelve days of this exchange the whole brigade would go back to La Gorgue in reserve.

On the night of the 16th the battalion relieved the 2nd Battalion Scots Guards in the line. It was held in a series of posts, some of them being a considerable distance apart. At night each post found double sentries, while the rest could sleep in the shelters, which were small dog-kennel arrangements built of mud-filled sand-bags and roofed over with bits of tin on which earth was piled. As shelters against anything but the mildest sort of weather these concoctions of tin and sandbags were absolutely useless, but the distance from the enemy, combined with his unenterprising disposition, permitted the use of fires to an extent never again encountered by the battalion. Not only did each shelter have its brazier, but the company cooks prepared and served hot dinners and teas in the line, frequently raising by their efforts clouds of smoke in the daytime and a blaze of light at night.

The work in this line was one long struggle against water, and the Welsh Guards spent weeks making water run uphill by "swishing" it along from one to another with spades.

The first few days in the line were very cold and the nights frosty. The enemy knew at once that a relief and change of troops had taken place. From the top of Aubers Ridge they could not fail to note unusual movement and draw their own conclusions. In the still frosty night a hail was heard—" O-o-oh, Tom-ee ! Who are you ? Who are you, Tom-ee ? " This went on for some time, when suddenly a high, Welsh voice replied, " Come over here, Fritz, and I will tell you." But Fritz went on with his " O-o-oh, Tomee-ee ! Who are you ? " and then the Welsh voice—" You —, —, —." Bang, bang, bang, when words failed to express his opinion of Fritz.

But the frost did not hold, and the only thing which seemed consistent was the wet. It snowed—and thawed. Sometimes the ponds were covered with ice, but it soon melted. There was one tour in the line when, as Claud Insole said, with his gentle voice and inability to pronounce the letter R, " It was so cold I could have scweamed with pain." He and Rupert Lewis took a brazier into their little mud hut and kept it there until the smoke got so bad they had to put their faces near the ground to breathe. Claud Insole wrapped himself up with fleece linings and mufflers, and was well served in this respect by his servant Jones, an old soldier and one of the best, who used to bring prodigious quantities of clothes into the trench. Rupert Lewis had a wonderful mackintosh cape, not issued by the Ordnance but bought somewhere in Cardiff, and with this thing covering two or three overcoats, his little figure bent nearly double under the weight, gum-boots reaching up to his waist, a shapeless cap, large, black-rimmed glasses, and large fingerless gloves, he looked like a little old witch. His physique was against him, but he resisted the conditions gallantly, as did Claud Insole, who was not of the strongest.

In a totally different fashion the huge Luxmoore Ball suffered from the cold and wet. After years in the West Indies and Rhodesia, to be plunged into a winter in Northern France is severe treatment. He got nasty doses of malaria.

Herbert Aldridge, another little man, had been a life-long sufferer from bronchitis, and had to fight this enemy as well as Germans.

No one knew if Dick Bulkeley suffered or not—he never said so. But he got a little bit of shell in his leg which, to a strong man, would have been nothing—it gave him a lot of trouble.

As has been explained, the system of defence consisted of the front line, held by three companies, and a series of strong points behind. The best place to be in was undoubtedly the headquarters of the company manning the strong points. You lived in a deserted farmhouse, which was at least weatherproof and enabled you to have a fire, and your duties included an inspection of the various posts held by your platoons. There was a nice walk from Wangerie down the Rue de Bacquerot and Rue Masselot to Felon's Post in Drury Lane, and the best way from there to Fauquissart Post was via the front line, where of course you would stop for a moment to see Herbert Aldridge. Perhaps Harry Rice would be in the headquarter dugout—his youth concealed beneath a bald head and a most impressive manner—busily engaged cutting out the pictures of prominent politicians from the *Sketch* or the *Tatler*, and French ladies from very French papers like the *Vie Parisienne*, and pasting them on the walls of the dugout, so that Mr. Balfour gazed with surprise at an undressed lady apparently trying to embrace Mr. Bonar Law, and Mr. Winston Churchill addressed a suffragette meeting—and this required many newspapers—Mr. Churchill in bathing-suit and quaint hat and the suffragettes arrayed in all those advertisements which one sees in the fashion pages of expensive periodicals.

Or Windsor Lewis would be there to discuss the war.

"I don't like this war—h'm, no. So wet and cold— h'm, frightfully cold—h'm, yes."

Perhaps you would hear him and Herbert Aldridge discuss company matters, and you would realise that they not only knew every man, but his private affairs and the condition of his family as well, and then you would begin to understand how it was the men loved both of them.

Young Leigh Pemberton, a Grenadier machine gunner, might drop in to this dugout for tea and keep every one laughing, and startle you with some such question as "Do you speak Boche?"

With plenty of time the journey could be prolonged, and from Keith Menzies information could be got of every unit within ten miles or so. Keith Menzies had a wonderful faculty for picking up this sort of information. He was, or affected to be, very short-sighted, and when he looked at anything more than fifty yards away would put his hand up to his right eye and pull the lids of the eye sideways—like an exaggerated Chinese eye But he noted every regimental badge that passed him and questioned men freely.

Percy Battye would talk of his future plans, social, military, commercial or sporting.

Dick Bulkeley would expound any subject.

Allen would be hospitable, and Luxmoore Ball reminiscent of West Indian life or enthusiastic about South Africa. Young Crawford Wood would want you to go ratting.

The way back lay through Fauquissart, where a visit might be paid to the gunners in the "Lounge"—a house filled with sandbags all but one small room, at the back, but in the end the German guns pounded it to pieces—and Road Bend, another post situated where the name implies.

Of course there was another sector with other forts, Église, Elgin, Erith, Grant's Post, Dreadnought, and farther back still, when the battalion was in support, Esquin, Epinette, la Flinque. And there was a rearrangement of the line which brought in Hougoumont and Masselot. But two or three people could always walk about at Laventie; in fact, at times there were so many little parties that they formed a stream of pedestrian traffic.

After twelve days in the forward area the brigade went back to La Gorgue, a well-populated town with a number of work-girls employed in normal times in the making of canvas. The Germans had occupied the place in their first advance and extracted fines. The billets were poor, but the people were hospitable.

An ante-room was established in one of the larger houses, but the mess was in another place—a long, narrow kind of passage-room with tiled floor, and no more recommendation than that it was big enough for all requirements. Keith Menzies, with the aid of Sergt. Marshall, still ran the messing, making local purchases of eggs and tinned stuff which, when the battalion was in the line, were equally divided between headquarters and companies. But the neighbouring town of Estaire provided attraction in the shape of a dining-place run by some women, and there were generally two or three absentees from the battalion mess.

Lord Cavan lectured officers of the division on staff work, but even that strenuous warrior could not make the subject attractive—the lecture has been described as dull.

La Gorgue saw the beginning of the divisional club. It was started by Sydney Jones, the Nonconformist minister. He secured a large shed and gave a general invitation to all ranks to attend. His ideas were vague, but he was searching for something which would be of use to the private soldier. This first meeting was an entertainment for school-children rather than an evening's amusement for men, and the very few who had attended were called upon to perform in a series of parlour sports such as " hunt the slipper " and racing cardboard frogs across the floor. It was a cold, cheerless evening. But Sydney Jones would not be beat. He would have other evenings and provide refreshment! He had the art of begging at his finger-tips, and was persistent in pushing forward ideas good and bad—the bad could always be dropped. At all events, a large organisation grew up slowly, supported by a canteen, which gave the men amusements and many comforts—and the officers too.

Officers who arrived in December were Capt. Gilead Smith, Lieut. Lord Newborough, 2/Lieuts. Jack Crawshay, Arthur Gibbs, Charles Dodd, Stephen Stokes, Maurice de Wiart, Pugh, and Lieut. Lord Clive. Clive, Arthur Gibbs and de Wiart went to the Prince of Wales's Company, Jack Crawshay to No. 2, Newborough and Pugh to No. 3, Dodd and Stokes to No. 4.

Newborough was a big, dark man with a gentle voice and manner. So long as he had plenty of cigarettes, which he smoked through a beautifully coloured meerschaum holder, he was, if not happy, at least filled with smoke and philosophic resignation.

" I shall never forget old Newborough's first experience of the line," said Copland Griffiths. " I found him in Elgin Fort, where he had gone with an advance party. The dugout was filled with water, and only a sandbag table rose like an island from the centre of it. Sitting on the table was Newborough, his feet in the water, a cigarette in his mouth, and over him an air of complete resignation, as though he was saying, " This is my home for two days, and it can't be helped."

What he liked was to sit quietly by a fire and yarn about old times—the men in the old Raleigh Club, his adventures in his yacht *Fedora* at Fiji and Singapore, and discuss the habits of the Chinese.

Clive was a keen soldier; it was the only thing which seemed to interest him in life. He loved parades and was a strict disciplinarian—woe to the man who appeared before him with a button undone or loose equipment; and yet he himself was a most untidy fellow. True, he had not a smart figure, but his clothes either could not or would not fit.

Jack Crawshay was a wise young man with the innocent, pink-complexioned face of a child. Arthur Gibbs a dark, solid, round-faced, full-lipped, bespectacled and competent officer, still very young. Stephen Stokes loved gardening, Charles Dodd could translate Greek like a professor and roll his R's like a Russian. Pugh knew something about the Lewis Gun, and de Wiart had a sense of humour. Gilead Smith was a painstaking soldier from the East Kent Regiment, and took command of No. 2 Company, Dick Bulkeley being sick.

Slightly before the advent of these officers came Rose Price, a tall, good-looking Indian cavalryman, as second in command.

Life was very cheery at La Gorgue. There were concerts—public ones in which Dick Bulkeley told some Welsh stories and Dabell sang "Killaloe"!—and private ones with Crawford Wood and Nigel Newall making a fiendish row singing duets. The most entertaining event of all was a boxing competition (January 10th), in which Thomas, cook of No. 4 Company, lost a fight but gained much renown.

The scattered support billets were changed on December 20th, the battalion going to the town of Laventie itself. A battalion mess was procured here for some time, and billets were very comfortable. There were even a few shops still open for trade. It was not shelled very often, but, considering it was well within field-gun range, the tenacity of the inhabitants was remarkable.

In the line there were rumours of battle, for news of what was said at conferences always trickled out by degrees and with many inaccuracies.

There was a scheme for the 2nd and 3rd Brigades to make a combined raid. Gas was to be let off for forty-five minutes, and after a five minutes' interval parties were to go over as far as the enemy second line, do as much damage as possible, and return with what they could carry or drive in front of them. For the 3rd Brigade it was settled that the Welsh Guards would do this. During the discussion of the scheme the Commanding Officer put in an objection to doing the attack with gas and at night. It would be, he said, impossible to see or hear while wearing the gas-bag, and the gas expert declared it would not be safe to enter the German lines without these bags on. The discussion continued, however, for some days. Details were arranged down to the carrying of red electric lights, and parties were selected, in all sixty-eight men. Then the scheme was altered to each brigade doing a raid by itself.

Patrols became very active. Luxmoore Ball, J. J. Evans, Crawford Wood, and Cpl. Bowles, the sniper, went over to the enemy line and threw messages over the parapet inviting them to give themselves up and come out of the wet! It had no result.

Amongst others Rupert Lewis had an amusing adventure. Jimjack Evans sent out a patrol of his snipers (Sergt. Bonar and two men) to cut German wire. A patrol also went out from No. 4 Company, knowing nothing about the Evans party, but when information of it was given him, Rupert Lewis and Broadwood, a Scots Guards machine-gun officer, went out to get the No. 4 patrol back. When they got near the German wire they saw what they supposed was four men coming towards them and began to move " home." The strange patrol followed, and Lewis and Broadwood began to run—so did the patrol. The sentries challenged and both pursued and pursuers replied. It was then discovered that Rupert had been chased back by his own men.

A raid was arranged eventually (December 27th), and Jimjack Evans, with Sergt. Gibbs, Sergt. Bonar, Cpl. Bartlett and Pte. Tanner, started to cut a way through the German wire. When they got up to the last strands, however, a sentry sent up a flare and they were seen. Bullets and bombs began to whistle through the air, and they had to go back. No further raid was possible that night.

Another raid was contemplated with a Bangalore Torpedo, an arrangement to blow up the wire; but an engineer went out to look at the enemy wire, got lost, was captured, and so it was thought best to abandon the scheme.

While at Laventie Lord Cavan left the division to take command of the XIV Corps, Gen. Feilding taking command of the Guards Division and Gen. Jeffreys of the 1st Brigade.

It is of interest to note that the Propping Company of 100 men (25 from each battalion) was started at Laventie. Percy Battye was given command, and his business was to work every night at strengthening the defences. The idea ensured continuity of work and plan and was very successful,

Casualties were not heavy, and only one officer, Nigel Newall, was hit. Hugh Allen went back to England sick, also Rupert Lewis; and Dick Bulkeley had to give up active campaigning and go to the base at Havre.

On February 15th the battalion marched back to Estaires, and on the 16th entrained at Lestrem for Calais.

The Laventie line was quiet and uneventful. Towards the end of January the artillery succeeded in stirring the enemy up, and there were occasions when his retaliation became warm. Topping, an excellent gunner, who was frequently behind the battalion with his battery, was shelled out of several positions, and the German gunner sometimes turned his attention to the forts; but, on the whole, the enemy confined his shelling for the most part to cross-roads and left the front line alone.

Some new formations, Welsh Fusiliers, a Scotch "Bantam" Battalion and some Yeomanry received instruction in trench duties from the battalion. Laventie was not a bad bit of the line.

CHAPTER V

It was said that the health of the troops had been so much considered that a trip to the sea had been arranged for them. Be this as it may, the troops enjoyed their stay at Calais. It was frightfully cold—it snowed—it froze—it snowed again, but there was a live town, with shops having something to sell, with restaurants having something to eat and drink, and with well-dressed, decent-looking women everywhere.

The battalion was under canvas, but no one minded except Luxmoore Ball and Herbert Aldridge, who could not stand it and went into houses. But when free from duty all men met in Calais, and mostly dined there every night.

There was, however, a great concentration of effort on bombing practice, a passion which lasted a long time. There had been some good bombing raids done by the Canadians, and of course the bombing of the Hohenzollern Redoubt was fresh in the memory of all, and so bombing became the *pièce de résistance*. All the morning fatigue parties worked with spades and sandbags, building a system of dummy trenches, with a huge sort of castle from which any practice could be viewed. The battalion was only at Calais for ten days, and most of the time was spent on this work. When it was finished each company had to do one attack with live bombs, which was amusing enough, while the brigadier looked on from

61

the castle. It was the commencement of an arrangement of bayonet-man, bomber, N.C.O., bomb-carrier, spade-man, wire-man, rifle grenade man, and so on, of which there were many variations. It seemed as though each time a successful raid was done the particular formation adopted for that raid became the standard for future practice.

On the sands there was an excellent range, but it was only used once, when each man fired five rounds rapid. To see some of the old Hythe-trained men like Sergt.-Major Bland and Pte. Sully slip five rounds into the target made one wish a prophet of the range would arise.

The battalion left on February 25th, by train to Bavinchove, the station for Cassel. They arrived at 7.30 p.m. in a snowstorm and with a seven-mile march before them. There was some difficulty in finding the road, as fields and road were all covered with a uniform depth of snow, and there had been no traffic. At 11.30 p.m. they arrived at Wormhoudt, where they found splendid billets, though scattered, and most hospitable people—the good French ladies had prepared hot coffee for the men and food for the officers.

On the 27th the officers had their first anniversary dinner at the Hotel de Kester. And on March 1st the whole battalion celebrated St. David's Day. These two dates are somewhat close together, and the February date was not always observed, even when it was possible. Major-Gen. Feilding, Brig.-Gen. Heyworth, and the senior officers of the other battalions of the brigade were present. The toasts were " The King " and the " Immortal memory of St. David." [1] A party of N.C.O.'s from the choir sang " Land of my Fathers," after which everyone had to sing something.

On March 2nd Humphrey Dene arrived cured of his wound and " fed up " with England. He took over command of No. 4 from Claud Insole, and his mercurial activity and boisterous good-humour soon communicated itself to the neighbouring messes (in Wormhoudt there was

[1] See Appendix C.

no room large enough for a battalion mess). He could, if he would, sit still for about an hour with a book and a pipe and his feet on the mantelpiece. Then suddenly the book would fly from his hand and his feet from the mantelpiece, and he would be engaged in a bear-fight with anyone who chanced to be in the room. Or he was off round the men's billets, or calling on another company, or going to see the horses at the transport and have his own horse saddled to ride five miles to call on a friend in the Scots or the Grenadier Guards.

He had as servant Dai Evans, a smart, good-looking Welsh boy, who was devoted to him. Humphrey Dene's voice would be heard roaring in his billet, "Evans! Evans!"

And at his elbow Evans would say, " Do you want me, sir ? "

" Evans, where have you been ? I have been calling you for half an hour ! Where are my breeches, Evans— where are my breeches ? Damn it ! you don't care if I live or die ! "

"They are on the chair, sir—you are sitting on them."

Anything to do with papers—orders or instructions— drove him distracted. "Look at this ! Who is the ass who wrote this? Who can understand what it means ? " and his thin face would flush and his eyes flash under a straight line of brows at the base of a round forehead.

Quite different was this energetic, quicksilver man, with thick hair of medium colour with hardly a white thread in it, and skimpy moustache, from Claud Insole, who was tall but with a slight stoop, thin, sandy hair and thick, closely-clipped moustache. Insole was short-sighted and wore glasses. He was gentle in manner and voice, and had a slight lisp—also he could not pronounce his R's. He could not shout, but he could, when occasion demanded, act swiftly, although there appeared a slow deliberation about him.

The one was an antidote to the other.

Wormhoudt was left on March 5th, when the battalion moved to a camp near St. Jan ter Biezen.

"We marched from Wormhoudt this morning at 8 o'clock after rather a scramble and the usual misadventure with the mess-cart—the horse bolted and the whole show got stuck in a hedge. The country we passed through was flat, with an occasional solitary and gentle rise with a village on top. The roads are very bad.

"The sun did its best, but there was snow and sleet in sharp showers. We crossed the Belgian frontier and arrived at our 'Camp.' Nothing I can write will describe the sort of place it is. We are in a mixture of tents and huts placed round a Hop Farm, but the hop-fields are now transformed into a sea of soft, sloshy mud. Small planks are laid down to walk on—they are sunk several inches in the mud and not too easy to find—and the whole battalion had to come into camp from the road, some 400 yards away, in single file. We roared when we saw it.

"The huts have tin roofs with gaps between the bits of tin, and the walls are partly mud and partly canvas. Each hut contains six small cubicles and one double-sized one for a two-company mess. Needless to say, they are cold as charity, though there is one stove ! The stove smokes and gives no heat, and only the language is really warm."—*Diary, C. H. D. W.*

Lieut. Picton Phillips left the battalion at this camp. He was exceedingly popular and an able doctor. His place was taken by "Mick" Rowlette, a most gallant young Irishman, who went through most of the worst engagements of the war, but was unfailingly cheerful, and had that great Irish quality of sympathetic encouragement for those in distress. His sturdy figure, round face, and kind eyes beaming through gold-rimmed pince-nez suggested his character. Sergt. Evans, who had been under Phillips, became Rowlette's right-hand man—the work of these two should never be forgotten by the regiment.

Newborough fell ill at St. Jan ter Biezen and returned to England. The battalion never saw him again—he died shortly after.

On March 15th a move was made to a camp in A.30 Wood on the other side—north-east—of Poperinghe. This was a much better camp. All the men were in good huts built in a wood—and there were excellent baths. The officers' baths, by the way, were apparently given by the Empress Club.

The whole country-side was alive with men, and here and there a monster gun stuck its ugly snout out of a wood or the side of a harmless-looking house. Altogether it was the busiest part of the British line. A constant stream of traffic went up and down the road, men on foot, men on horses, carts, waggons, motor-cars and lorries. Aeroplanes in numbers were buzzing round when the weather was decent—captive balloons appeared as steady black dots in the sky.

There were a lot of civilians who used to wander about—dirty-looking people who spoke a kind of pidgin English, and lived by selling chocolates and apples to the men.

In peace time no one would wish their worst enemy in Poperinghe—in war time, for those in the salient, it was the hub of the universe. It is a vile little town in the centre of a vile district.

All round Poperinghe were camps—their name is legion—but we are only concerned with those at St. Jan ter Biezen (where there were two together), one in the wood north-east of the town, A.30, and one on the road to Ypres not far from Vlamertinghe. In any of these camps the battalion was said to be at Poperinghe.

At one time or another most of the British army had been in this area. All have stories of Poperinghe —"The Fancies," "Ginger's Restaurant," and so on. They will speak of the long, wide *pavé* road leading straight east to Ypres, and of the semicircle the enemy had formed round that place from St. Eloi in the south through Hooge on the east, to Boesinghe on the north.

What one might call the south-eastern quarter of the circle was held by the Canadians. The XIV Corps, of which the Guards Division was now a part, held the north-eastern quarter of the circle—Hooge being the Canadian left.

CHAPTER VI

On March 16th the battalion moved by train to Ypres.

" To see a whole town in ruins is like being in an enormous churchyard. There is not a single house with a roof to it, and not a room with four whole walls. At the end of the town farthest from the Boche you can still follow the plan of the houses up to the top floors, but there are not many like that and only in two or three short streets. The only exception, I think, is the prison, which has been knocked about but has many good cells on the ground-floor and is, of course, untouched underground. As you get farther into the town the standing walls get shorter till they disappear in heaps of brick and dust. It is beyond description! No earthquake has ever devastated a town in such a fashion. The cathedral struggles valiantly to retain the title of ' ruin.' One side of the tower stands to a good height, with a corner turret almost perfect, and the entrance has an untouched Christ over the door. But in other places the ruined walls are half their original height, and in some are battered down into huge mounds of stone. Of the inside nothing remains— just broken pillars lying about and piles of powdered stone and smashed chairs. The same with the Cloth Hall. For the rest of the town the roads, cleared for traffic, run between what may be called banks of broken brick.

" There are some wonderful corners which have escaped, such as a small garden where no shell has fallen, or any bricks or rubbish, and where lilac bushes are budding and daffodils growing.

"At night—and there was a bright moon last night—
the town has a most weird appearance. No lights, no
sign of life, no sound from the ghostly ruins, but along
the roads parties of men, silhouettes shuffling over the
thick dust with just a little murmur of conversation.
And then will come a rumble in the distance, growing
into a crash and a jangle, and a line of artillery limbers,
each drawn by six horses, will come trotting through.
Then all will be quiet again except for the shuffling
silhouettes and the little murmur of conversation.

"This, of course, when there is no shelling."—*Diary,
C. H. D. W.*

Two places stand out on the Western Front above all
others—Ypres and Verdun. There is an interesting book
to be written, comparing the problems which had to be
solved and the blood that had to be shed in both places.
Ypres is the monument to the British Empire.

The salient was small and the position to be held was
villainous. The enemy looked down on the British lines
from every side. The Second Army (Plumer), which held
this line for so long, was always quoted at schools of
instruction as leading all the military arrangements of
the day, from signalling to artillery. One of the most
astounding things was the train from Poperinghe to
Ypres. It was a big effort to keep that train going, but
it must have saved thousands of lives.

The line, such of it as concerns us, held in March 1916
ran from just opposite Bellewaard Lake, through Rail-
way Wood, Gully Farm, Crump Farm (in front of
Potijze), Warwick Farm, Cross-roads Farm, Turco
Farm, to the canal about 700 yards south of Boesinghe.
This sector had three main roads leading from Ypres to
the enemy lines. From the north-east, from the Menin
Gate, came a southern road through Hooge to Menin,
and a northern road through Potijze to Zonnebeke.
From the north, the Dixmude Gate, was a road through
Weiltje to St. Julien, and so to Thourout. These three
roads stretched like three fingers through the sector
where the Guards Division operated.

With the first and second battles of Ypres we need not here concern ourselves, but, as a reminder of the general situation, and to enable us to understand the mood of the Germans, we must note a few of the principal events since the battle of Loos.

It is as well to bear in mind, even when following the fortunes of one battalion, that this war was fought, and the Welsh Guards were fighting, against the Central Powers of Europe, and not Germany alone. Germany was the leader and instigator of it all, but even as the Germans had to manipulate their reserves between the French, the Belgian, the Russian, the Rumanian, and to some extent the Austro-Russian and Austro-Italian fronts, so British troops, and amongst them the Welsh Guards, were affected by success or reverse on more distant fronts. A success of Austrians and Turks against the Russians was the cause of jubilation in Berlin and the German troops facing the British. Probably the average German recognised the magnitude of this war to a far greater extent than the average Englishman did.

The Central Powers had captured Poland, Serbia and Montenegro, the Russians had been driven out of Galicia, and Gen. Townshend had surrendered in Mesopotamia. The war was going well, the Huns had their " tails up," and Germany thought the time had come to turn her attention seriously to the Western Front. The Western Front became excessively lively. In February the big effort was made on Verdun, and it is interesting to note, in view of after-knowledge, the rumours which had circulated in the battalion about the French situation.

At the end of February the story was that the French were tremendously pleased with the way things were going, that they had made up their minds they would have to lose Verdun, and found that they were not only able to hold it but to inflict fearful losses on the enemy. Also that the Germans had made two mistakes—the first in attacking with the Alsatian Corps, and the second in not bringing up their guns to support their infantry.

But, apart from the battle of Verdun, the Germans became very aggressive round Ypres. In the middle of

February the enemy had captured six or seven hundred yards of trench near Hill 60—they had used a heavy bombardment and exploded five mines. This was re-taken in March, but it was the commencement of much severe fighting from Hooge to St. Eloi, and heavy bombardments of the salient in general.

The first sector taken over by the Guards Division was about 3,700 yards, and ran from a point about 250 yards north of the Menin Road to Wieltje, the actual left being on a trench called Pratt Street. This front was divided into a right and left sector by Duke Street.

So much has been said about the observation from enemy lines that the mental picture of Ypres, as imagined by those who have not been there, might very well be of a flat country surrounded by steep, frowning hills. Such is not the case. The ridges are very low. But in a flat country a thirty-metre rise is a matter of great importance. The ground just sloped very gently from the German positions down to the canal, and from thence to Poperinghe there was precious little in the way of a rise. For instance, the High Command Redoubt, which overlooked a large stretch of country, was on the twenty-five-metre contour. The trouble was that not only could the enemy overlook and enfilade our line, but all the country as far as Ypres was under observation and a great deal of it behind Ypres as well. All movement in day-time was most difficult.

The ground on the right of the division was very much cut up and wet. There was no protection there at all, and it was very weakly held. The most important point on the right was Railway Wood, where, although the trenches were barely " fair," there were shell-proof dugouts capable of holding 200 men. This was the highest ground we occupied, and the only possible ground for dugouts, being between the 35 and 40 metre contours, and with the Bellewaard Beke running only 200 yards to the west of it. Mining was going on there to a depth of 80 feet. The enemy were on the top of the ridge, which is just over 45 metres at Bellewaard Farm. From Railway Wood our line ran down the slope to the Ypres—

Zonnebeke Road, so that the retention of this high
ground was vital to our front line defences for over a
thousand yards.

The capture of Hooge would not seriously affect the
Guards Division, but would be troublesome for the
troops responsible for Sanctuary Wood, farther still on
the right.   In front of Potijze the defences were properly
described as " sketchy," and at Wieltje were bad.

The line the Welsh Guards took over had been allowed
to get out of repair, and consisted in most places of
trenches with an occasional breastwork.   It was difficult
to drain the surface water, as it would not percolate
through the clay; also there were many springs.   There
were no dugouts, and the enemy line at the farthest
point was 150 yards away.

The support line was in a bad state everywhere.

A further support line, the X line, which ran to Hell
Fire Corner, was well in view of the enemy, and could
be frightfully battered.   In fact, the front system would
have been untenable under a heavy and prolonged bombardment, and the intention was to withdraw to the
canal line if a big attack were made.

The battalion went into the line on March 20th, and
it was pitch dark—no moon till late and the sky was
overcast.   The march down the communication trench
was very slow (from Potijze).   Most of it was under water,
and the men fell about in the dark.   The line was really
a double line, one about fifty yards behind the other, and
the only shelters were in the rear line, and then not
sufficient for half the company.   No one had seen the
trench except at night, and it was impossible to know
what work should be done.   Probably all thought the
easiest thing was to make a new trench altogether.   But
the one evident job was to heighten the parapet.   For
this sandbags were necessary, and there were scarcely
100 in the trench.   And for any work spades were essential, and they had been left so scattered, and it was so
dark, that more than a dozen could not be found.
Fortunately the battalion had been late relieving, as
they were told to wait for gum-boots, but the two front

6

line companies stood in the trench after "taking over," wretchedly cold, and doing nothing, while officers and N.C.O.'s floundered about in the quagmire, trying to get some definite idea of the place and find necessary tools.

"We got a few men on to digging a drain, which seemed perhaps more wanted even than the parapet, and then, just before five o'clock, a party arrived with rations! We had a job to get them distributed before daylight. It was raining all the time, and very cold. We breakfasted about ten, and sat in a tiny shelter and dozed for a few minutes, only to wake up and laugh at our misery. Pa Heyworth (the brigadier) managed to get round, and found a box of rusty bombs and raised Cain. I wonder if he could suggest something for my rusty joints!"

The bit of line the battalion had taken over was from the left of the Railway Line to Duke Street. There were two companies in the front line and two companies in the X line, with Battalion H.Q. in the château grounds at Potijze.

The conditions were very bad, but work did progress. Spades were found, and the parapet heightened and strengthened. "The men were wonderful—cursing and blaspheming, but willing and cheery all through."

In the matter of casualties the first tour of duty was a lucky one; there were only 7. Ypres was a fearful drain on man-power. The casualties in Laventie were 15 in November, 11 in December, 8 in January, 5 in February. At Ypres they were 42 in April, 24 in May (11 days), 49 in June; and these were months when the battalion was not engaged in any enterprise against the enemy.

On the 24th they were all back at Ypres, and on the 25th went by train to Poperinghe. Meanwhile Gilead Smith had gone sick and Percy Battye took over No. 2 Company.

This was the first time the battalion was actually in Poperinghe. One of the immediate duties was to get the

men to the baths, and we find the Commanding Officer
notes that they are " not to my mind satisfactory.   Consist of two vats 10 feet by 10 feet and filled to a depth of
2 feet.   The water is changed every two hours, and only
one vat going at one time.   They take 120 men an hour,
so it means 240 men in same water—not sanitary or nice.
They say not sufficient hot water to do more.   I saw the
washing of clothes arrangement.   They first go through
a disinfector, and then are dipped in creosote, so they
should be all right."

The battalion being more or less clean, sought the
amusements of Poperinghe—the men at the canteens,
the officers at " Ginger's," or a place run, we think, by a
lady called " Kiki "; and everybody to the " Fancies."

In the morning there was drill, bombing practice, and
route marches—the afternoons were mostly free.   The
square in the centre of the town was a scene of much
movement both night and day.   There was " tremendous
traffic always going through, all military carts and limbers, and making a fearful clatter.   Horses of all kinds—
fierce ones, silly ones, and wise-looking ones with Roman
noses and hairy legs, and mules, absurdly like those in
Punch, having jokes on their own.   English soldiers in
crowds, and a good many French."

On April 3rd the Third Brigade went into the line
again, the Welsh Guards going in the Wieltje sector from
John Street to Buffs Road. (B9).   They were in the forward system for 16 days—4 days in the front line, then
4 days at Ypres, then again in the front line and again
at Ypres.   From the moment they arrived the enemy
started a steady bombardment of the front line.   By a
fortunate coincidence the divisional artillery, together
with the XIV and Canadian Corps' heavy guns, were to
start a bombardment on the 4th, and in order to thin
the line against retaliation a platoon from each of No. 2
and No. 3 Companies, with three officers, were left behind
in Poperinghe for four days.   The line then was very
thin—also very bad, being blown in in many places—and
very confusing.   The enemy bombardment increased to
" heavy fire " for two or three periods of half an hour

each every day, and it was practically continuous for the first four days in the line.

On April 11th, as the battalion were getting ready to relieve the Scots Guards, the enemy attacked the neighbouring division on the left, but were repulsed. The British artillery was also busy, and caused some annoyance to the German front line by searching it with 8-inch shells.

The 2nd Brigade had started the relief of the 3rd Brigade on the evening of April 19th, when the enemy increased their fire on Wieltje. It assumed such proportions that an attack was obvious, and the Welsh Guards, who were then in Ypres, took up their battle positions in the Kaai Salient (north-east side of the town). It was a bad place to get at, and the night was absolutely black. But beyond getting covered with mud, and using much strong language as they fell over heaps of brick and quantities of wire, they were not called upon to do anything further.

It was a lively night, as the enemy had attacked the Canadians on the right and the 6th Division on the left as well as the Scots and Grenadier Guards. A few got into a part of the line at Wieltje, but were killed or taken prisoners ; but they held some craters on the Canadian front, and some few hundred yards of trench on the 6th Division front. The 6th Division restored their line a few days later, but the Canadians were having a rough time on the right, and fighting there was incessant. It raged for a long time round some craters which were taken first by one side, then by the other, but the artillery fire on these occasions covered most of the salient.

During the ensuing eight days' rest at Poperinghe the whole battalion was inoculated against typhoid. "Mick" Rowlette presided with his needles and squirt, and beamed with delight at the abuse handed out to him. And the next tour of duty in the forward area was a strenuous one.

" On May 2nd there was some violent shelling on our front at midday and the early part of the afternoon,

and later the devil of a bombardment on the Canadians,
to which we only seemed to reply with a few whizzbangs—
as one of the men said, 'Another case of ninepence for
fourpence.' This was followed by heavy rifle-fire, so we
suppose the Boche has popped the parapet.

"We were listening to all this, and it had about finished, when Jack Crawshay came into the trench looking
very rosy and childlike, and announced he had been
ordered to crawl up to the Boches and listen to them
talking, he being acquainted with the Hun language.
He took Sergt. G. Davies and Sully with him. In about
an hour a bomb went off and the enemy sent up three or
four star-lights. We could then see three figures running
towards us, and the Hun saw them too, and began throwing bombs like mad and ripping off their machine guns.
But they all got back—Jacky out of breath and Sully
seemingly rather bored as he crossed his legs and lit a
cigarette. Jacky said they wandered about till they
heard some one talking, but could not quite place it.
Trying to find out where it was they bumped into a listening post. Someone said 'Wer Da,' and immediately
started to throw bombs. 'There was too much noise to
hear any more,' said Jacky, 'so I came back to report
what I had heard.'

"The battalion went back to Vlamertinghe instead of
Ypres, in quite a nice camp near the road, and we had
instruction in the management of a torpedo for blowing
up wire entanglements.

"We went back to Ypres by train on the 7th, and
found the Huns were shelling hard—the roads, the railway and the town. When we marched into the town we
found the roads blocked with traffic—a mass of transport
waggons and artillery limbers. The Hun was pumping
shells into the Square and the Menin Gate. Every now
and then an artillery limber would disentangle itself and
go galloping across, making a fiendish noise on the cobbles. Finally we got across the Square, and when we
reached the Menin Gate found the Hun was shelling the
road like mad. I don't know why we were not caught.
Our luck was that most of the shells fell by the side, and

those that fell on the road did not fall on us. This went on till the early hours of the morning, and started again at midday. They confined themselves mostly to the roads, but it was a heavy affair.

" No Man's Land is ours. Battye strolled over and put a flag on the enemy wire. Dene, Sergt. Mathias, and fifteen men strung themselves across and waited two nights running to catch a Hun patrol, but saw nothing. Crawford Wood did the same.

" In the early morning of the 9th the enemy started a heavy bombardment of Railway Wood. Our artillery seemed to be making good shooting too, especially their shrapnel, which burst about twenty feet from the ground. A devil of a lot of white and black smoke, and when the shooting was at its height the Hun let off a mine. The whole country shook, and a great column of smoke and earth rose slowly, like an enormous fountain. And then for a few seconds there was quiet, and then the welcome crackle of musketry, to show that all the Grenadiers were not blown up. Almost on top of it came a storm of shrapnel from our field-guns. It simmered down very quickly—some birds began to sing and some partridges called in the broken ground behind us. Later we heard that the brigadier had been killed by a stray bullet when going up to see the damage. It is very depressing, as he was a very gallant fellow and a very good sort—friendly with all his officers and knowing them all, and he always visited the line once in twenty-four hours, which is a great deal more than a good many do.

" The Hun attack failed miserably, but later on we got some shells and a lot of rain."

Officially life in the line was covered by the following order :

" All work will be done during the hours of darkness. There will be no moving about by day. Teas and rifle inspection will be carried out just before dark, work from dark to midnight—dinners at midnight—work to recommence at 1 a.m. until ' stand to arms,' which will

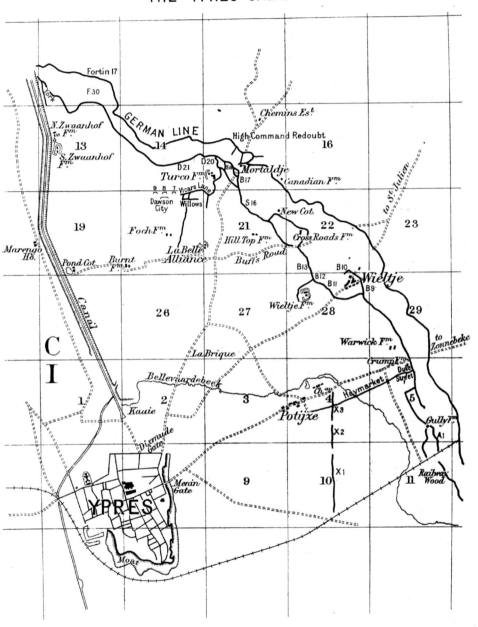

be for not less than twenty minutes.   Teas and inspection of arms, after which everyone will dismiss until
evening."

It sounds an easy life.

There was through all ranks the most genuine grief at
the death of " Pa " Heyworth—a brave and able soldier,
a good friend, and a picturesque figure.

The battalion came out of the line for two days in
brigade reserve at Camp A, near Vlamertinghe, and then
went into divisional reserve at Poperinghe for eight days.
There were fatigues on the new railway and the weather
was fine.   There were also some new officers—Kearton
and Goetz had joined on the 7th and Basil Hambrough
on May 11th.   But against that Keith Menzies had
gone home sick.

Under date May 19th there is an entry in the official
diary :

" Battalion marched at 8 a.m., arriving at Wormhoudt
at 1.15 p.m.—fourteen miles—under Major Price.   Very
hot day, and several men fell out."

This entry conceals an important fact noted by many
officers during the war.   Men do not get hard in trenches.
It is sometimes imagined that because the conditions are
bad, the weather vile, the fatigues heavy, that the men
must therefore be in excellent condition.   The very reverse is the case.   There was a sudden burst of fine
weather, of real summer heat, and the battalion had been
in the forward area since March 5th.   All went well until
they had gone about ten miles, and by that time the sun
was well up and the heat intense.   There was not a dry
coat in the battalion.   Then, going up a rise, the first man
collapsed.   There was nothing to be done ; the man was
in a faint.   And so it went on until they arrived at
Wormhoudt.   Out of twenty-five men who fell out
twenty-three fell down absolutely senseless, and the other
two were staggering about like drunken men, and would
have been down in another minute.   "'We left N.C.O.'s

to look after them, but it looked very bad to see some
forty men come in, half of them in an exhausted state,
a couple of hours or so after the battalion."

Such accidents are very annoying to the pride of a
regiment, but on the other hand they are a useful experience. The problem of how to keep men fit will vary
with the conditions prevailing at the moment. Practice
marching during the twelve or fourteen days in Ypres
and the front line (the period varied, see Appendix) was
out of the question; and while at Poperinghe in divisional reserve such hours of marching as could be done
between fatigues did not amount to many. There had,
however, been a tendency to do those few marches in
musketry order, with the idea of not unduly tiring the
men—a very questionable benefit under the circumstances.

At Wormhoudt Brig.-Gen. Charles Corkran arrived to
take command of the 3rd Brigade. He was probably the
most popular brigadier the brigade ever had. It is hard
to say, as the varying difficulties to be met would in all
probability reflect on the popularity of the brigadier—
popularity is not always based on reason. At all events,
for junior officers he had these qualities—that he was the
most approachable man, that he never forgot a name,
that when he knew something difficult was to be done
he always discussed fully with officers on the spot before
issuing his orders (when it was at all possible to do so),
and he created round him that atmosphere of benevolent
autocracy which induces men to obey orders for the sake
of those who give them, apart from a sense of duty, and
he had the absolute confidence of his brigade. The feeling was of whole-hearted support from the brigadier,
that he was helping you in a tight corner, and, whether
it was true or not is beside the point, that he would fight
the higher command to get everything that was asked
for when in action. As a fighter, too, he had up-to-date
ideas, and almost at once insisted on the value of trench
mortars.

Amongst the infantry there was generally a dislike of
trench mortars, which arose, we think, from the tentative

way they were first used. The little Vickers Gun, with
the stick-bomb, was very good in its way, but it was
annoying to the infantryman to see a few specialists
(total strangers) suddenly appear in the trench, set up a
little machine, fire half a dozen bombs, pack up their
machine, and go away; more especially as the time
necessary for the fulfilment of this action just about
coincided with the pause before the enemy retaliation.

The little Vickers Gun was used at Laventie—the
Stokes Gun first went into action with the division at
Ypres (when the battalion promptly lost the services of
Stephen Stokes for no other reason than that his name
was Stokes. But he was a good selection, and was an
excellent T.M. officer). Up to this date the Stokes Guns
had not been fired much.

Training never ceased at Wormhoudt. There was the
inevitable bombing practice, shooting at a small thirty-
yards range, wiring, and of course drill. And there were
sports as well.

The battalion sports took place on May 30th. Major-
Gen. Feilding and the brigadier attended, with a lot of
officers from all the battalions in reach, and some French
officers as well. It was a most cheery meeting. To
mention only a few of the outstanding characters, there
was C.Q.M.S. Hinton, with his red face, little pointed
moustache, and Herculean legs, winning the 100 yards'
race ; Sergt. Glover (then a private) outclassing everybody else in the walking race in full marching order, and
in his loud, cheery voice exchanging repartee with the
crowd ; C.Q.M.S. Hunter taking part in the tug-of-war,
the tattooed picture of the Virgin Mary on his chest ;
and Sergt. Pottinger, entering for every event and winning nothing, but enjoying himself hugely as he became
more and more exhausted. The Commanding Officer
won the officers' 100 yards' race, and the brigadier the
mule race—Dabell riding the celebrated beast, Isaac, and
getting a fearful toss. Sergt.-Major Bland and Drill-
Sergt. Dunkley marshalled the competitors. (Dunkley
had taken the place of Harris, who was wounded at
Wieltje.) It was a very successful meeting.

At these sports the battalion could always put in a fair number of entries for whom they need make no excuse. Rudge, the pioneer, and Manning were good class runners ; Drum-Major Herd was very fast on a 100 yards' sprint ; Watkins was quite a respectable high jumper until he was shot through the leg. C.S.M. Pearce, C.Q.M.S. Rendall, Pte. Davies (with a blue mark from a mine explosion on his nose), Pte. Young, Sergt. Owen, Sergt. Humphries, and many others were sportsmen against whom credit could be won.

On June 1st the battalion marched back to St. Jan ter Biezen, where they had L Camp, next to K, which they had formerly occupied.

The livening up which had been going on in the Ypres Salient now reached a high pitch. The struggle between French and German was still going on at Verdun, and the enemy knew of the preparations on the Somme Front. They decided to increase the pace at Ypres. On June 2nd they attacked the Canadians in force. The Welsh Guards were confined to camp, ready to move at a moment's notice, and from a distance watched the bursting shrapnel and the German artillery lights.

This attack was preceded by a hurricane bombardment and the explosion of mines, and was so far successful that the Canadians in the line were overwhelmed, and the enemy occupied Sanctuary Wood and Zouave Wood ; some few even got as far as Zillebeke. Bombardments then became incessant.

On June 4th Nos. 2 and 3 Companies, under Battye and Aldridge, and fifty men from No. 4, went up under Major Price to work on the defences of the canal bank and the L Line behind the canal.

"CANAL BANK,
"June 5th.

" The night was a bit noisy, not that we were shelled to any great extent, but we are working in front of some of our own batteries, and they were banging away in hearty fashion. Being a fatigue party in an area defended by other troops, we have to get shelter where we can. We were lucky last night in getting good dugouts,

but they are now wanted, and we go about a mile farther
back to-night.''

" June 6th.

" We had to clear at two this morning to make way
for incoming troops. The Canadians had launched an
attack about one, and the place was fairly warm, and a
heavy barrage round the back of the canal. There was
nothing for it and we had to go through. Lewis (Windsor
Lewis) had gone about midnight with the men who had
been working by day, so I sent my men off in small
parties, and by the grace of God they all got through,
with nothing more than a few chunks of mud blown at
them. I was very glad to reach the new quarters, which
are decent dugouts on either side of the Ypres—Elverdinghe Road. I put half of my men in the first lot and
took the other half over the road. Owing to the shelling
which still continued there was no one about, and I had
no idea which of the dugouts were for us; but, seeing a
man poke his head out of one, I asked him, and he directed
me to the back of a ruin. I then asked where Lewis was,
and he said he had been killed. It gave me a fearful
shock, and I could not believe it for a moment, but with
a hazy kind of idea that, after all, it was not so impossible
I managed to lead my men to the dugouts. Then the
man led me to another dugout, where I found poor Lewis
quite dead. A charming, kind, gentle man, of whom I
was very fond. He fussed and worried about his men
until he frequently made himself ill, and it was while
looking round to see that none of them were exposing
themselves that he got hit. I collected his personal
things and went to see Price. He was in a dugout about
half a mile down the road, with Percy Battye and No. 2
Company; quite a rotten place, too, with shells pitching
all round it. I then went back to my men dog-tired, and
slept for three hours.

" Lunched with Aldridge, who was very upset at the
news. And then another battle started, and the Hun
put down a barrage on the road. I got back to my place
about five, but the battle was still going on, and the road
not at all nice.''

" In the canal bank last night rumours were flying about in all directions—that we had lost some more trenches on the right, that we had retaken them, that we had not retaken them, that a ship with Kitchener and Robertson on board had been sunk, that it was only a ship called ' the Kitchener,' and Heaven knows what else."—*Diary, C. H. D. W.*

The evil fatigue was over, and the whole battalion was back in Wormhoudt on the 9th, the fatigue companies arriving the day after headquarters and the rest of the battalion. But the temper of the enemy may well be imagined. Verdun, it is true, was not going too well for him, but no doubt he was fed on stories of the masses of French soldiers he was killing, and in the death of Lord Kitchener he must have read an omen of the fall of Britain. But French and English, like the lady barber in Wormhoudt, went on with their business.

" The lady barber in the town cut my hair. She is a strong, stout body, taking the place of her husband, who is fighting. We talked of the war and of Verdun. I asked her how she would like it when the war was over and her husband came back—would she go on working ? She said all the women would continue to work and the men would rest all day. She also said women were lucky to be married now, as there would not be enough men to go round. I told her the women would have to share and share alike. She said, No ! a little sharing was all right during the war, but after each woman should have ' son bien ! ' "

On the 14th Major Price was called away from the battalion on a staff appointment. On the 15th a move was made back to St. Jan ter Biezen, L Camp ; on the same day the daylight-saving scheme was put into practice, and all watches were put back an hour.

The Commanding Officer and the company commanders went up to see the new line in the left sector, the

northern part of the salient, the scene of the enemy's
momentary success earlier in the year against the 6th
Division. It was reported to have some bad places in
it, and Luxmoore Ball, being told of an enemy sap about
fifty yards away, climbed out to have a look at it, and
was promptly shot through the shoulder. Clive then
took over the Prince of Wales's Company, having Crawford Wood and de Wiart under him.

The situation in the salient was that the Canadians
had re-established the whole of their line on June 13th,
but the fighting was still going on, and on the 17th we
find the battalion " standing to " all night, owing to a
German attack on Hooge and Railway Wood.

On the 18th they moved up to the canal bank.

The state of the companies was then as follows :

Prince of Wales's.	No. 2.	No. 3.	No. 4.
Lt. Lord Clive.	Capt. Battye.	Capt. Aldridge.	Capt. Dene.
2/Lt. Crawford Wood.	Lt. Copland-Griffiths.	Lt. Rice.	Lt. Insole.
2/Lt. De Wiart.	2/Lt. Crawshay.	2/Lt. Pugh.	Lt. Hambrough.
	2/Lt. Kearton.	2/Lt. Goetz.	2/Lt. Dudley Ward

Battalion bombers had been returned from headquarters to their companies after Laventie, but against that
companies were reduced by the Propping Company,
commanded up to this date by Copland Griffiths, and
now taken over by Arthur Gibbs.

Then there was a Tunnelling Company made up by
men from each battalion, which for a time was commanded by de Wiart. Also there were trench mortars
and machine guns to be supplied with men.

Snipers were becoming observers, and Jimjack Evans
left the battalion and went to brigade as O.C. Observers.

On June 18th the battalion took over from the 2/Yorks
and Lancs Regiment and the 8th Bedford Regiment.
The line was from B17 to D21, and there were two companies in support at Butt 7, Vicar's Lane, The Willows,
and La Belle Alliance (which was also headquarters).

All the right half of the line was under water to the
knees, and the trench and parapet only about four feet

high. The left was a straggling bit held by posts, with
no inter-communication by day.

From the start casualties were heavy. Battye was
hit, Cpl. Lawrence killed (the first man personally recruited by the Commanding Officer), and seven men
wounded.

Copland Griffiths now took over No. 2, and Kearton
immediately got hit (a slight head wound), but a few days
later, June 24th, Bagot and Evan Thomas joined the
battalion, and the former was posted to No. 2 Company
and the latter to No. 4.

The reason for these casualties, which were mostly
from rifle and machine-gun fire, was the state of the front
line trenches. It was possible to get up as far as Turco
Farm under cover, and then a choice had to be taken
between going over the top or wading through a trench
up to the waist in mud and water—and this in the month
of June! From the High Command Redoubt and
Mortaldje the enemy swept the whole of that front with
machine-gun fire which was kept up all through the night.

In the day-time he could see the slightest movement.
Two men were hit the first day trying to pass between
two posts which were not connected. Sergt. Mathias,
who scorned bullets, got them both in in a miraculous
way, as, so far as could be judged, the same German
machine gunner was still shooting.

The enemy had a fine position in the High Command
Redoubt. He could bring all he wanted right up without being in any way observed. Even from Hill Top
Farm (the highest point we held), which lay on the right
of the line held by the battalion, and slightly to the rear,
nothing of what was going on in the redoubt could be
seen. The ground was level and fell away gently from
the enemy lines—an excellent field for his machine guns
—and he had light trolley rails running into his front
line system.

Curiously enough, the trolleys used to betray him. He
made great use of his large Minenwerfen on this front,
and would wheel them up on the trolleys. They were
very powerful things, throwing a drum containing some

250 lb. of high explosives, and they would absolutely
destroy any trench.   Happily they could be seen coming
through the air—and also the wheels of the trolley
creaked.

The brigadier gave very definite orders to the artillery
about these things.   When the creak of wheels was heard
headquarters was promptly warned, and the suspected
position indicated.   If it was dark the first trailing spark
of light through the air confirmed the suspicion, and
almost before the bomb exploded a request for retaliation
was through.   The guns would then fire until the
" Minnie " had ceased, which was not as a rule very long.
The same policy was adopted with the machine-gun fire,
and with success.

CHAPTER VII

ON June 21st came the first indication of aggression from the Guards Division. Up to this time, beyond patrolling nothing had been undertaken against the enemy. But it was getting near the date of the big summer offensive on the Somme, and it was desired to keep as many of the enemy guns at Ypres as possible.

On all the front there was no more irritating point in the enemy organisation than Mortaldje Estaminet. It jutted out to between sixty and seventy yards of the British front line, and was the source of much machine-gun activity. On the 21st the Welsh Guards were ordered to prepare a minor enterprise against this organisation. The Commanding Officer notes : " From orders received the enterprise seems more than a minor one—no difficulty in taking it, but, to my mind, considerable big job consolidating and holding it."

There was nothing to be seen of the no doubt at one time welcome estaminet—a few bricks and a couple of iron girders, with their twisted ends sticking in the air, were the only indications of the cross-roads. Though it had melted into the general landscape of brown mud, broken stakes, and wire, there was just sufficient unevenness in the ground to indicate an excellent position for a machine gun ; but it was below the general German system.

Crawford Wood, de Wiart, and Sergt. Gibbs crawled about the outskirts, but the enemy were very watchful, and they were unable to learn much. They reported, however, two machine guns.

On the 23rd the battalion went into support at the Château Trois Tours, Brielen, where there were most delightful quarters. The château was untouched, or nearly so, and had round it a large moat where the men bathed and fished (Sergt.-Major Bland was very good at catching eels).

While the men enjoyed themselves the Commanding Officer and Humphrey Dene, now second in command, thrashed out the details of the attack on Mortaldje.

To the intense satisfaction of the Commanding Officer he found that the brigadier was in complete agreement with him as to not holding a trench on the enemy side of Mortaldje, and the brigadier announced that he had Major-Gen. Feilding's sanction to occupy instead a new trench to be made just in front of the existing line, and the estaminet would be denied to the enemy by means of two saps with bombing posts.

The first difficulty to tackle was that of space, of room to assemble in. The trenches, although much work had been done on them, were in an impossible condition, and the approaches to them worse still. Arthur Gibbs and his proppers were told to improve the communications, and the 2nd Battalion Scots Guards undertook the making of a new trench just in front of our old line.

Arthur Gibbs had a fearful job. Round Turco Farm there was a regular marsh, and for some days enormous parties carried down quantities of T-shaped frames and hundreds of sheets of tin to try and make some sort of a gutter through this marsh. It was, however, not a success, and was named by " Broncho " Dene " What a hope cut!" the official name being "Hope Cut." This annoyed Arthur Gibbs very much, as he had put in some very strenuous hours over the work.

The Scots Guards completed their trench with some few casualties.

It will be as well to keep in mind the whole of the XIV Corps' operations. The Guards Division were to undertake the following :

June 24th.—Wire cutting and bombardment on front of 1st Guards Brigade.

7

June 25th.—Digging of new trench by 3rd Guards Brigade between Forward Cottage (New Cot) and S16.

June 27th.—Wire cutting and bombardment in front of 1st and 3rd Guards Brigades.

June 28th.—Digging a new trench in conjunction with 20th Division between Wieltje and Cross-roads Farm.

July 1st.—Attack on Mortaldje Estaminet by Welsh Guards.

July 2nd.—Raid and gas discharge by 2nd Guards Brigade.

The 20th Division on the right was undertaking the following operations at the same time :

June 24th.—Wire cutting.

June 25th.—Raid on Salient C29.

June 26th.—Bombardment.

June 27th.—Wire cutting.

June 28th.—Bombardment.

June 28th.—Digging new trench from Wieltje to Cross-roads Farm.

June 29th.—Raid opposite Railway Wood.

June 30th.—Bombardment.

July 2nd.—Discharge of gas and smoke.

It will be seen that activity throughout the entire period was above normal.

Without going into details, the artillery preparation on the High Command Redoubt, and the trenches which in any way defended Mortaldje was to consist of : 20 rounds from a 12-inch howitzer, 130 rounds from 6-inch howitzers, 200 rounds from 4·5-inch howitzers, 30 rounds from 60-pounders, 600 rounds from 18-pounders, and big trench mortars were to fire 60 rounds to break up the wire round the estaminet. This was, of course, merely preparation, and does not include the covering fire for the attack itself.

Humphrey Dene was O.C. attack, which was to be carried out by No. 4 Company under Claud Insole.

The details of the attack were argued out and practised at the Château on ground marked out from aeroplane photographs. And finally Humphrey Dene got out these operation orders [1] :

"1. On the night of July 1/2, at 11.15 p.m., No. 4 Company, 1st Battalion Welsh Guards, will capture the Mortaldje Estaminet and approaches thereto.

"2. Object of attack.   To turn the enemy out of the estaminet and trench to the north thereof, and to prevent the future use of same by them for observing and offensive purposes, and to hold same for our observation and possible future advance.   The post will be held by two bombing posts, the position of which will be decided after its capture.

"3. The attack will be prepared and assisted by artillery, trench mortars, and Stokes Guns.   On the day fixed for the attack the artillery will bombard and knock in the three communication trenches running from German line to Mortaldje Estaminet.   The artillery will bombard certain selected points in the German front line and second line, from Canadian Farm to the road running from Turco Farm to Chemins Estaminet. An artillery barrage will commence and continue during the night of the attack round front of the Mortaldje Estaminet.

"4. The objective of the attack will be the trench running round the north of the estaminet.   The communication trenches running round the east and west sides of the estaminet will be blown up and blocked at C15c96 on the east side, and at $C15c8\frac{1}{2}6$ on the west side.

" During the operations two communication trenches will be dug from one or two selected bombing posts to our front line immediately south of the estaminet. The number and position of these posts will be decided after occupation of the estaminet.   These trenches will be wired on the outside.

"5. No. 4 Company, under Capt. Insole, will carry out the attack, and will have taken up positions as under by 11.5 p.m. on the night of 1/2 July :

[1] Appendix B 1.

" 1st *Line*.—No. 14 Platoon, with two bombing parties lying down in front of our new front line, the bombers on the flanks.

" 2nd *Line*.—No. 13 Platoon standing in the trench.

" 3rd *Line*.—No. 16 Platoon and part of No. 15 Platoon standing in S18 trench.

" *The Wiring Party* will stand in B17a trench, at the angle of the trench to the right of No. 16 Platoon.

" The 1st Line will be under Lieut. H. A. Evan Thomas, and will be composed as under :

" *Centre*.—Sergt. Mathias and eight men.

" *Right Flank Bombing Party*.—Cpl. Thomas and seven men.

" *Left Flank Bombing Party*.—Cpl. Blake and seven men.

" *Dress*.—The centre party full equipment less pack ; two bandoliers ; water-bottle to be filled ; each man to carry a wire-cutter, which will be attached either to his person or his rifle ; four men will carry six bombs each.

" Bombing parties will dress as above, except that bandoliers will not be carried. The carriers, with rifles slung, will carry two nosebags each holding ten bombs, remainder of these parties will each carry one nosebag holding ten bombs, with the exception of the N.C.O. and the two bayonet-men.

" The 2nd Line will be under 2/Lieut. C. H. Dudley-Ward, and will be composed as under :

" A centre party of Sergt. Pottinger and twenty-one men, and on either flank a party, which will be composed of one man carrying a roll of French wire, two men carrying spades, and one man carrying explosives for the right and left parties respectively. Two men of the 56th Company R.E. will accompany each of these last parties.

" The 3rd Line will consist of No. 15 Platoon, under Sergt. Nicholson, and No. 16 Platoon, under Sergt. Trott. Dress as for other parties, except that each man will carry a spade slung over his shoulder.

" The wiring party will be composed of sixteen men, under Sergt. Hyam. Six men will carry one roll of French wire each, nine men will carry two posts, screw, long, each, and every man will carry two staples stuck in his belt.

" All men will carry their emergency rations in the haversack.

" 6. At 11.15 p.m. the 1st Line will advance to the trench running round the north side of the estaminet. The four men with bombs will be detailed to drop out at the estaminet, to deal with any Huns that the 1st Line may have passed over, and to bomb possible dugouts. Upon entering the trench the right bombing party will work down the communication trench running from the right or east side of the estaminet, and will advance to a point ten yards beyond the entrance to a small sap which runs out of the trench on the right-hand side towards our line. The party will then commence to block the trench, and when the carrying party comes up will blow in the trench, assisted by the R.E., retire fifty yards, wiring the trench behind them, and hold the point until a permanent bombing post is selected.

" The left party will proceed down the left or western communication trench as far as a point five yards beyond the junction of the communication trench and the main trench. They will then proceed as for the right party. When the 1st Line have reached the trench running round the north side of the estaminet, a pre-arranged signal will be given for the 2nd Line to advance to this trench. The centre party, under Sergt. Pottinger, will reinforce the 1st Line in the trench, the working parties of bombers on the flanks and the two R.E. men will join their respective parties in the communication trenches, and proceed with the demolition of these trenches.

" 7. As soon as the post is taken the prisoners, if any, will be taken to the rear. Two bombing posts will be selected to secure the position, and communication trenches dug from them to our new front line. These communications will be wired on the outsides. This work will be performed by men of 15 and 16 Platoons in reserve in L and Y trench (S18).

" The platoon holding the captured German trench to

the north of the estaminet will reverse or destroy it at
the discretion of the officer in charge. The wiring party,
under Sergt. Hyam, will be sent up as soon as advisable
to wire the front and flanks of the new bombing posts.

" 8. One Lewis gun, under Pte. Murray, will remain
in support in our front line at C15c95. The second Lewis
Gun, under Pte. Evans, will operate under direct orders
of O.C. No. 4 Company, who, if he considers it necessary,
will send it up to assist in holding the captured position.

" 9. At 2.45 a.m., or earlier if considered advisable by
O.C. No. 4 Company, the company will, with the exception of the two bombing posts, retire and proceed in small
parties to their posts at Belle Alliance and the Willows.
The bombing posts will remain until relieved.

" Each post will be supplied with ten boxes of bombs,
two tins of water, one day's rations, 30 Mills adapter
bombs, and a sufficiency of tools.

" H. DENE,
Captain O.C. Attack,
" 29/6/16."

On June 28th the battalion left the Château Trois
Tours, crossed the canal, and wended their way up the
long communication trench to La Belle Alliance, and so
to the front line. It had rained the night before, and the
communications were very bad—and not improved by
Arthur Gibbs with a mass of men and material about
Turco Farm.

It was the 2nd Battalion Scots Guards that were being
relieved, but on arriving the trench was found to be
deserted—the whole garrison being out digging in front.
Howard, of the 2nd Battalion Scots Guards, worked hard
over this necessary but unpleasant task, and it was all
but finished that night. Crawford Wood and a party
from the Prince of Wales's Company came down from
Belle Alliance the next night and completed the work.
As he was going back again towards early morning the
gallant, cheery Sergt. Gibbs was killed by a bullet—an
unaimed shot fired at a venture into the darkness. The
following written at the time is of interest :

" *June 30th.*—There was the sound of fierce gunning down south yesterday, and Dene brought us the news that our people had popped the parapet—the result we do not know. There was also a small raiding affair near us last night, so it was fairly noisy. A lot of men came up to work in the trench; Bill came too, and was inclined to strafe Claud because our men were not doing enough work. When he had gone Claud murmured a complaint to me : ' Bill comes up here just as it is dark and we are detailing the men to work, keeps us talking for an hour, walks us up and down the twench till I'm dog-tired, and then says, " Why aren't the men working ? " Vewy unweasonable. Jones, bwing me a pear, or some fwuit.'

"We were relieved at 2 a.m. and went to Belle Alliance.

" *July 1st.*—I have been out with Dene, crawling on my hands and knees, to get a view of our bombardment for to-night. We sat in a hole which Jimjack had rigged up near Hill Top Farm. Up to now the artillery have made a bit of a mess in one or two places, but you really can't see much.

" *July 2nd.*—We took the position last night, but all is not yet well. When we filed into our places in the trench all was deathly quiet—much too quiet—and lights were going up in a jumpy manner, or so it seemed to me, from the estaminet. I think Evan Thomas started to get out slightly ahead of time, which was to be one minute before the artillery. At all events, they were seen immediately, and the Huns opened fire on them. I heard Sergt. Mathias yell out ' Come on,' and then our guns started with a swish and a roar, and I don't quite know what happened. I heard afterwards that Evan Thomas, Sergt. Mathias, Sergt. Jellyman, and a man called Lock, who used to be the C.O.'s servant, arrived far ahead of the rest. The Germans fled, though one stayed to fire point blank at Lock, who was killed. Sergt. Mathias had fallen into a shell-hole and lost his rifle, so had nothing but his bare hands, Sergt. Jellyman was loaded up with odds and ends, and Evan discharged his revolver to no purpose. The others then came up and chased the Huns up the trench to the right, but only

managed to catch and bayonet two.   Meanwhile Sergt.
Jellyman flashed his lamp, which was the signal for me
to start.   I arrived with a bunch of my fellows and found
men lying down and blazing away in front of them.
Pottinger immediately threw himself down and followed
suit.   I said, 'What the blank are you doing?' and
with some difficulty, owing to the noise, stopped them.
Then Cpl. Harris, who had apparently been up to the
right, came with a broad grin, and told me the enemy
had fled, but that he had managed to stick one of them.
I told him to come along with me and see what was going
on on the left, but some Engineers, who were to blow up
the trench, and had lost themselves, arrived at that
moment to enquire where they were to go, and while I
was questioning them Harris slipped away.   I took the
Engineers with me, and we ran on to the left.   There was
no sign of anybody, and we soon heard a hullabaloo in
front of us and came on Harris and a Pte. Jones having
an argument over two wretched Huns, who were scream-
ing and crouching by them, with their hands up and
yelling 'Mercy' in a hysterical, panting away.   Jones
wished to bayonet them, and Harris was hanging on to
him and explaining in forcible miner language that they
would take the —— —— back as prisoners.   I sent them
back with Harris, and then found Jones had wandered off
up the trench by himself, looking for more Germans.
When we came up to him he was plodding along in a
crouching attitude, and his bayonet flashing about in
front of him.   By this time we had gone about 100 yards
up the trench, which was not a good one, and arrived
at a deep place with a machine-gun emplacement.   I
told the Engineers to blow it up, and when we had
made a thorough mess of it with four or five lumps of
gun-cotton I went back to the main body, and arranged
for a few men to watch this left trench, which, being
shallow for a considerable way, did not worry me.

  "At the heap of bricks (the estaminet)—and there
were more than we imagined—men were arriving from
our own trench with bombs, wire, spades, and wanting
to know where to put them.   The noise was beyond

words. The Huns had started knocking the stuffing out
of our front line, but had not as yet found us.

"I established a dump for all stores, and set men to
work making a bombing post behind the pile of bricks.
Sergt. Jellyman and about twenty men were beyond this
point as a covering party.

"On the right I found Evan and Sergt. Mathias directing the blocking work. This was a very good trench,
quite dry, with boards down and beautifully arranged
sniping and bombing posts.

"The Huns were now plastering us with shrapnel
and H.E. Men were strung out trying to dig communication trenches to our front line, and they could be plainly
seen as the sky was bright with lights. Claud came
over, and I explained the situation to him. As there
was nothing for him to do he went back. Soon after I
got a note from him to say he had been hit, and would
I take charge ? The men were doing gallant work, but
the water-logged condition of the ground was against
them. Crawford Wood came out and asked if he could
do anything. He went back to bring up more wire.

"Little Cpl. James, who was in charge of the wiring
on the left, came up and told me his last man, Viggers,
had been killed, and could he have two or three more
men ! He had used up all his wire. My orderly, Cong-
don, was hit badly, and Lynch, who was also doing
orderly, got one through the arm, but said nothing about
it. I got a whack on the arm, and at the same moment
a man next me got a lump of shell in the stomach.

"We slaved on till two in the morning, and then I
withdrew the company, leaving two posts under Cpls.
Phillips and Thomas.

"The getting back was very trying. I had to go last,
and the men seemed an interminable time crawling back
through the scrape they had made. Evan Thomas had
gone on to lead the way, and Mathias was gathering up
wounded. The Huns were firing at us from all directions, and the gunners told me afterwards that they had
located five field-gun batteries which were pounding that
small bit of front.

"When I got in I found poor little Crawford Wood
had been killed while trying to bring more wire out to
me—a recklessly brave boy and a dashing platoon leader.
He had brains too.

"I explained all I could to Clive, and then hurried
back to the Willows with Mathias to arrange for more
stretchers to be sent down. Then back to Belle Alliance.

"Claud has a bit of shell in his foot. I saw him off
with a long cigar in his mouth and a broad grin. 'I
shan't be back for a vewy long time after this!' he said."

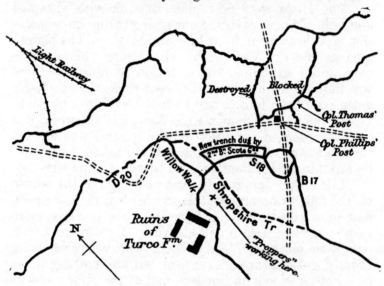

MORTALDJE—FROM AN AEROPLANE PHOTOGRAPH.

As the Commanding Officer had pointed out, it was
easy to take the place, but to consolidate and hold it
was a different matter. Jimjack Evans, from his observation post near Hill Top Farm, 500 yards away, reported
in the middle of the engagement the long lines of Welshmen calmly digging in the soft, mashy, pulpy ground,
with shrapnel bursting over them and high explosive
shells in their very midst.

The enemy guns quieted down. It was now broad
daylight. Suddenly a disreputable figure, Pte. Phillips,
arrived at La Belle Alliance, and said the enemy were

attacking. No sounds were heard, but Humphrey Dene
was at once sent down. He says when he arrived at Y
and L trench (S18) he found that the posts had been
attacked, but had repulsed the enemy. He sent a party
to strengthen them, but only one man, Ullyat, got there,
and found all of the first post wounded. Eventually
Dene got some bombs to the post, with reinforcements,
and the wounded away. The communication was very
bad—the shallow trench which had been made was
already full of water, and had also been knocked about
by enemy fire. He therefore put a small party on to
try to improve it. The enemy field-guns then opened
fire with shrapnel, and the big trench-destroying Minenwerfer was brought to bear on the unfortunate posts,
with the result that the old German trench was flattened
out and the garrison buried. Cpl. Thomas, with blood
streaming from his ears, succeeded in getting the men
out, with the exception of one, who was rescued by Cpl.
Hough. But the estaminet was untenable, as was also
most of our own front line, so a position was found for a
Lewis Gun which would keep the enemy out of any shell-
holes around the estaminet should he try to occupy them.

All day long the enemy kept up a trench-destroying
bombardment with their " Minnie." They worked on
No. 2 Company as well, up to D21 ; in the end Copland
Griffiths had the greatest difficulty in getting cover from
view for his men. The Germans attempted a cutting-
out enterprise against one of his posts, and attacked it
several times between Minenwerfer bombardments, but
Sergt. Beazer, in command of it, kept his men together
full of fight, and also, what was harder, kept his Lewis
Gun clean and drove them off with loss each time.

During the evening the local conditions were not improved by an Irish Guards' raid from the 2nd Brigade
front on the left, and Dene was not able to do anything
till 11 p.m. The artillery fire finally died down, and he
made a personal reconnaissance. He found nothing
round the estaminet but enormous craters, and was only
able to identify it by a few bricks and a sniper's loophole.
He put a Lewis Gun in one crater and some bombers in

another, and told Clive to get out a working-party to dig some sort of communication. Clive and his men were nearly dead beat, as he had only half of his company with him.

About 3 a.m. on the 3rd Dene was recalled by the Commanding Officer. That night Clive, having improved the craters, handed them over to the Scots Guards.

Dirty, tired, and reduced by ninety-six casualties, the battalion returned to the Château Trois Tours. Clive looked like an evil tramp, and absolutely beat to the world. Jack Crawshay and Copland Griffiths were not so tired, but were filthy, and roaring with laughter, having been all day successfully dodging Minnies. Nobody moved till very late the next day. Towards the evening there was an inspection of the ragged mobs which formed the two front line companies. There were hardly half a dozen men with whole suits. Jackets and trousers were torn to ribbons.

Crawford Wood was a great loss. He was a good-looking, most gallant and active youngster, and feared nothing in the way of a German or any of their weapons. De Wiart was blown up and carried away insensible. He did not recover for a long time. Mick Rowlette, the cheery doctor, went to the front line twice through the worst spasms of shelling and looked after the wounded. He was twice hit himself, but carried on till all was over. He was deservedly popular.

The prisoners proved to be from the 238 Reserve Infantry Regiment, 52nd Reserve Division, XXVI Reserve Corps. This Division held the line from Thourout Railway to a point slightly north of Canadian Farm; this regiment from the road Turco Farm—Five Chemins Estaminet to the left of their line. Mortaldje Estaminet was considered by the enemy as an important point. His plan was to join up the saps with the existing line and form a new front line in this sector; work was being steadily done on these saps with a view to this end. Major-Gen. v. Waldorf commanded the 52nd Reserve Division. The heavy British shelling, according to these prisoners, had affected the moral of their regiment.

The men had a canteen at the Château, and Sergts. Trott, Nicholson, Jellyman, Mathias, Ashford, Richards, Beazer, and many more could be heard exchanging their experiences over a mess-tin of beer. But good men had made the final sacrifice.

But it was not a period of rest, and the companies had to find heavy fatigues each night to help reconstruct the battered line, although, as Allie Boyd, of the 2nd Scots Guards, said, while wandering round amongst confused heaps and holes, " I am not looking for a line—there is none—but somewhere about there are some men at the bottom of shell-holes."

On July 6th the battalion went into divisional reserve at the camp in Wood A30.

On Sunday, July 9th, Major-Gen. Feilding paid a visit to the battalion, and, after congratulating them on the work done, gave ribbons in default of medals to Sergt. Mathias for the D.C.M. (this was for bringing men in under heavy fire some days previous to the attack on Mortaldje), and told him he would get a bar for the attack, and to Sergts. Bonar and Humphreys, L/Cpls. Harris and Thomas, Ptes. West and W. Jones for the Military Medal. At the same time Cpl. James was told his name had gone forward for a D.C.M., and well he deserved it; but unfortunately it was not so easy to present his action as a story which would appeal to any-one who had not been there, and in the end he got a Military Medal, as did Sergt. Beazer. However, there was to be a parade in Paris on the 14th, and these men left with others to attend with the Guards Divisional Contingent, so they all got a few days' holiday and amusement. The party consisted of : Lieut. and Adjt. J. A. D. Perrins, A/Sergt.-Major W. Bland, No. 29 Sergt. Humphreys, 557 L/Cpl. Bale, 1,245 L/Cpl. Trott, 758 Pte. West, 1,043 Pte. Ulyatt, 21 Sergt. Owen, 761 Sergt. Bonar, 196 Cpl. Churm, 861 Pte. Barker, 1,507 Pte. Walters, 59 Sergt. Hammonds, 229 Cpl. Thomas, 95 Pte. Buck, 278 Pte. Williams, 492 L/Cpl. Harris, 114 Sergt. Mathias, 613 L/Cpl. James, 798 L/Cpl. Thomas, 1,189 Pte. Jones.

Other awards granted under authority from the King were—Humphrey Dene and L. M. Rowlette the D.S.O. ; G. C. L. Insole and C. H. Dudley-Ward the Military Cross.

On the 14th the battalion was back in the canal bank and two days later in the front line. This tour of front-line duty was in the last segment of the salient, to the very north where the line curved round into the canal. The method of defence was peculiar. The front line proper seemed to stop abruptly opposite Fortin 17, where it straggled out into some dangerous and isolated bombing posts. Behind this came a line in echelon to the left curving round to the canal. Between these two lines there were a couple of posts ; but the whole arrangement left a wide bit of territory over which anyone might roam. There were remnants of a far more elaborate British system, linking up the whole of the sharp curve in the salient, but it had been found impossible to hold it owing to the lowness of the ground and the consequently water-logged condition of the trenches. An effort was being made to drain this flat expanse, and Engineers were busy with a deep boxed drain running roughly from the left of the front line—an isolated post F30—and passing to the right of the 2nd Line.

The Commanding Officer writes all the time that he " does not like it." But the difficulty was that, until the drain was completed and successful, nothing in the way of trenches in the abandoned area could be occupied after a little rain. In any case the sighting of new trenches must be a delicate matter, as, whichever way they were cut, the enemy could enfilade them.

There was very little wire, too, and as a first measure of precaution the Commanding Officer set about wiring from the north end of the echeloned trench (York Trench) to F30, and then proceeded to reclaim those parts of the old front line which could be linked up with the drain.

The work which was going on in this sector, together with the programme of raids and bombardments, undoubtedly worried the enemy. He bombarded night and day, and there is little doubt that he moved very few, if any, of his guns down south.

Once more we must point out that the fierce bombarding, the trench-digging, the series of raids, all designed to force the enemy to an artillery battle, besides killing him, were part of a far bigger movement—the battle of the Somme had started. It would not be such a wild stretch of imagination to say that the Guards Division first took part in the battle of the Somme while they were at Ypres. They were, at least, preventing troops and guns from taking part in that battle.

The first bombardment on the Somme had started on June 23rd, and the attack was planned to take place on the 28th, but, owing to bad weather, was put off till July 1st. Of the six corps engaged the three northern ones had failed to make any headway, but those to the south, together with the French, had broken through some fourteen miles of German lines, and were fighting hard to improve their gains. It was, therefore, of importance to continue the threat of attack at Ypres, even though the Germans must by then have suspected it was bluff.

Until the 26th the battalion held this line, and during the whole time was severely shelled. There was a little bombing scuffle round F30, with no result, but the enemy made no further attempt to come to grips.

Capt. Ashton, Rupert Lewis, Power, Wernher, Cazalet, and ninety-five other ranks joined the battalion at this period. Rupert Lewis took over No. 4 and Ashton No. 2. Power went to No. 4, Wernher to the Prince of Wales's, and Cazalet to No. 3 Company.

On July 27th the battalion left the Ypres area, marching from the camp in Wood A30 to the light railway to the north-east of Poperinghe, and entraining in two trains for Bolezeele. From that place they marched to Watten.

It is due to the transport to mention that they accomplished a march of thirty-two miles in the day to join the battalion at Watten. This is no mean performance when it is remembered that many of the men had to walk, and some take turn and turn about pushing Furbe stretchers loaded with Lewis Guns.

Lord Lisburne joined the battalion on the journey, and was posted to No. 2 Company.

This move was the first towards the Somme battle-field. Here and there a short halt of two or three days was made—as at this first stop, where the officers and men enjoyed themselves prodigiously by bathing in the canal, and where the half-clad Clive was chased by an infuriated old dame of seventy summers for undressing on her field ; but if any indication was wanted of what was happening, it was given by the Commanding Officer when he warned all ranks not to mention any changing of billets in letters written home.

CHAPTER VIII

MARCH TO THE SOMME—MAILLY-MAILLET—BEAUMONT
HAMEL—MÉRICOURT

THE situation on the Western Front may be very briefly summarised by saying that two battles were in progress —the one at Verdun, which had started in February, the other on the Somme, which started on July 1st. The enemy had made certain gains round Verdun, though the fortress still held; the French losses were great, but the German at least a third greater.

The July 1st attack had been over a front of about twenty-eight miles, but on the northern part of it, about the river Ancre, had come swiftly to a standstill. From Fricourt to the south, however, it still raged, with give and take fiercely contested. The general attack had changed to smaller, but no less bloody, engagements, with limited objectives. These battles were generally fought for woods and villages—there were Mametz Wood, the two Bazentin Woods, Bernafay Wood, Trônes Wood, Delville Wood, and, later, High Wood.

Local fighting went on for a month before, at the end of August, Delville Wood was in British hands. The first attack on Guillemont was launched on July 23rd, a date to be borne in mind. The first attack on Pozières was on July 22nd, and the matter was only finally settled on August 4th. The fierce attacks on High Wood lasted three weeks.

There is no doubt that the German infantry at that time was stubborn, and the big advance on a twenty-mile front and more was not repeated after July 1st, but the capture of definite areas was carried on slowly, on a

8   103

restricted front, and accompanied by tremendous bombardments from both sides. Each in itself was a battle, but the whole series must be considered as one.

Little of all this was known at Watten. Orders were of the briefest and given at the last moment. At 1 a.m. on July 30th the battalion started on a fifteen-mile march to Bavinchove—the station at which they detrained when moving from Calais. From here they proceeded by train at 6.30 a.m. to Frevent—crossing the path of their march from the Hohenzollern Redoubt to Allouagne. Arriving at Frevent at 11 a.m., they marched at once for Halloy. It was a fearfully hot day, and the Commanding Officer decided not to push right through, so a halt was called in a wood near Bouquemaison, where they rested under the trees from 2 till 6 p.m., with the result that the battalion marched into Halloy present to a man. They had marched a total of twenty-six miles, with a very tiring journey in an overcrowded train to split the distance in half.

The next move was to Bus les Artois, where the battalion stayed from August 1st to 6th, and from there to Arquèves till the 9th.

There is nothing of interest to record of these journeys, or of the halts. At Bus les Artois there was a battalion mess, but all was so arranged by this time—nearly a year's experience in France—that the comforts of both officers and men, so far as comforts could be obtained, were enjoyed and arranged for whatever the resources of village or camp might be. There was no necessity to fuss because of a sudden intimation on arrival at new billets that no battalion mess could be found. Sergt. Marshall, the "Universal Provider" of the battalion, issued food to company cooks, and in a very short time food was ready if wanted. The office of Mess President had by this time devolved on the second in command.

On the subject of cooks much could be written. Goodman, of the Prince of Wales's Company, was probably the best, at least he was thought so by Arthur Gibbs and Bob Bonsor, both gourmets; but this was at a much later period. Geoffries, of No. 3, and Thomas, of No. 4, were at this time the best-known characters. Geoffries was a man of many qualities, but no one could tell why or how he became a cook. Aldridge declared that he found him in the kitchen, a self-constituted cook ; how he got there Aldridge never dared enquire—he just came. But he always seemed to have food ready at a moment's notice, and some of it was well treated. Thomas, on the other hand, had started as a cook in the battalion mess, but had been found extravagant. He passed rapidly to No. 4. There never was a more devoted servant than Thomas, but the culinary art he acquired had not the lightness of touch which gives distinction to great artists, which raises them from scullions to *escoffiers*, which gives them the name of " genius," while they pass their own patronymic to a sauce. He was known to be in active correspondence with the *chef* of a Cardiff club, and had been seen taking lessons in the mysteries of omelette-making from a fat lady at Wormhoudt. But who taught him to make what he called " rimsoles," and why he boiled a galantine of chicken were two of those unsolved questions which disturb the soul of man.

On August 9th the battalion departed hurriedly for Mailly-Maillet—the Commanding Officer and Company Commanders went in motor-buses to see the new line they were to take over ; Humphrey Dene marched the battalion from Arquèves.

The line was between Beaumont Hamel and Serre, the front attacked by the 29th, 4th, and 31st Divisions on July 1st. The Welsh Guards were to be opposite a strong position known as the Quadrilateral (how many Quadrilaterals were there ?—and what an ominous name it seems to have been !). As usual the front line was down in a hollow, but the support lines were well up and with good observation.

The troops which so successfully resisted our onslaught on July 1st were of the XIV Corps, under Lieut.-Gen. v. Stein. The frontage of this corps was from just below Monchy au Bois to Fricourt. The northern sector was held by the 52nd Division, the centre by the 26th Reserve Division, and the southern by the 28th Division. As a result of the July fighting, the 28th Reserve Division, which held from Thiépval to Fricourt, was exhausted, and a new division took its place. But it was believed that the 26th Reserve and the 52nd Divisions were still in the line on a somewhat reduced front.

This XIV Corps, now opposite our XIV Corps, was a mixed formation, nominally raised in Baden, but containing also Würtemburgers, Prussians and Alsatians. It was, however, a good fighting corps, as the British VIII Corps had very good reason to know ; but its attitude since that big fight had been exceptionally passive, particularly in the matter of patrolling and sniping. The Welsh Guards were believed to be opposed by the 121st Reserve Infantry Regiment, recruited from Würtemburg.

As a matter of fact, despite the evil reputation of the line, Mailly-Maillet was at that time a charming little town, with delightful orchards and gardens round it, and was very little knocked about—but no one liked it. The battalion stayed there one night, and then moved into the line, relieving the 11/Lancashire Fusiliers—the Prince of Wales's on the right, with No. 3 in support, and No. 2 on the left, with No. 4 in support.

There was a lot of artillery between Mailly-Maillet and the line, and it did not seem as though many guns had been moved after the abortive attack. The Guards Divisional Artillery was up too, and Topping, an old friend of the battalion, had his field-battery in a very exposed position. As the battalion marched to the " Line," he was observed engaged in a duel with some enemy 4·2 " Hows." After each salvo from the 4.2 battery—and they were making good practice—Topping, perched on the top of a mound, would yell out orders, and his battery would loose off hard for a minute or so. A gallant fellow was Topping, and also his subaltern, who was of course known only by the name of Spindler.

The most conspicuous object on the right of the line was the huge mound that marked the crater of a monster mine fired on July 1st. The noted stronghold of Serre on the left was less conspicuous ; but, with the idea of an advance in mind, and possible danger-points to be

encountered, the eye was immediately attracted to the
innocent-looking left, and the imagination pictured the
German machine gunner squatting somewhere near the
top of that flat, gentle rise, and letting off a stream of
low-flying bullets—when once his gun was set he could
traverse the whole of that front.

The support lines and the communication trenches
showed what a tremendous lot of work had been done
prior to the attack ; and they were very little knocked
about.   But the front line system was absolutely flat.
At best the line was indicated by bits of shallow, wide-
open ditch, but mostly it was mounds and shell-holes,
broken bits of wood and splintered rifles, quantities of
torn equipment, and the half-decomposed dead.   On a
dark night you could smell your way into the front
line.

Patrols reported quantities of dead in No Man's Land,
and companies buried scores found in their own front
trenches.   Altogether no one liked this line, although it
was a good one.

The enemy was very active with small trench-mortars,
and he had a method of firing these which was new to
the battalion : he would fire a volley of them followed
by an irregular stream.   The first time he did this trick
he raised a report that a German bombing party was in
the trench.   Sergt. Ashford, of the Prince of Wales's
Company, gathered together three or four men, and some
boxes of bombs, and hurried to the spot, but found no
Germans, although one of their "Minnies" had killed
two men and wounded three others.   This was reported
to Clive as an attack, and he hearing, as he thought,
bombing going on in his front line, told Eddy Bagot to
send up the S.O.S., and went to see what was happening.
At battalion headquarters the sentry reported the S.O.S.,
and Humphrey Dene, rushing out of the dugout, was
knocked back again by a rocket whizzing in front of his
nose.   Picking himself up, he discovered Sergt.-Major
Bland cursing all rockets, and those who had invented
them, and explaining that one of the rockets had pre-
ferred a horizontal course to a vertical one.   But before

the guns had started a telephone message came through to say it was all an error.

The battalion was relieved by the 2nd Battalion Scots Guards on August 14th and went into a variety of rest-huts, ruins, and trenches round Collincamps. Major Bromfield, D.S.O., joined, and took over the Prince of Wales's Company from Clive; 2/Lieut. Hebert also joined, and was posted to No. 4.

On the 17th the battalion went in the line again, and were relieved by the 17th Royal Fusiliers on the 19th. During this last tour of duty the Commanding Officer lost his invaluable orderly, Beck, who was fatally wounded while standing by his side in the front line.

The experience in the Beaumont Hamel sector consisted entirely of burying dead and clearing out old trenches, and recollection of the line is generally an impression of unpleasantness. There is, however, one curious fact to be noticed: it was in the Beaumont Hamel line that the battalion first came across anything in the nature of underground dugouts. Deep dugouts were in process of construction, and shafts had been sunk, in some cases, too, the commencement of a gallery.

The novel situation stirred battalion headquarters to the issuing of special instructions. The corporals on duty were " not to enter dugouts "; the sergeant on duty was " forbidden to enter a dugout "; sentry groups were to remain as close to the sentries as possible and " not to enter dugouts."

The total casualties at Beaumont Hamel were twenty-one.

The battalion returned to their old camp at Bus les Artois, and on August 20th to Vauchelles les Authies; from thence to Gézaincourt on the 22nd (the men were able to visit the estaminets of Doullens and the officers to dine at the Trois Fils Inn), and to Vignacourt on the 24th.

This ended the marching for some time, as the last stage of the journey to Méricourt l'Abbé was made on the 25th by train.

The division was now in position behind the battle of

the Somme. Méricourt is on the River Ancre, a few miles to the east of the junction of that river with the Somme, and about twelve miles behind the front line.

Kearton rejoined on the day the battalion arrived at Méricourt, and the officers then were :—

Prince of Wales's Coy.	No. 2 Coy.	No. 3 Coy.	No. 4. Coy.
Major Bromfield.	Capt. Ashton.	Capt. Aldridge.	Capt. R. W. Lewis.
Capt. Lord Clive.	Lieut. Lord Lisburne.	2/Lieut. Fox-Pitt.	Lieut. Rice.
2/Lieut. Pugh.	Lieut. Evan Thomas.	2/Lieut. J. Crawshay.	Lieut. Power.
2/Lieut. Bagot.	2/Lieut. Goetz.	2/Lieut. Cazalet.	2/Lieut. Dudley Ward.
2/Lieut. Wernher.	2/Lieut. Dickens.	2/Lieut. Kearton.	2/Lieut. Hebert.
2/Lieut. Gibbs with Proppers.			

Also while at Méricourt " Mick " Rowlette returned as medical officer. Lees, an Edinburgh man, had been acting for him, and had now to return to the Field Ambulance ; but he was eventually posted to the 2nd Battalion Irish Guards, and won a D.S.O. in 1917 for great gallantry at Ypres. A most energetic and fearless fellow was Lees.

The battalion was accommodated in a large farm in the centre of the village, with the exception of one platoon and a few officers. But billets were good, and the situation of Méricourt very pleasant both for training and amusement.

The training took the direction of open fighting ; there were several battalion field-days and one brigade day. On the whole the training was not too successful, as the country was much cut up with growing crops, and no one was allowed to cross them ; it resulted in the troops passing these obstacles by going in file round the sides of them, a proceeding which destroyed all possible realism.

For recreation there was the river Ancre to bathe in, and company sports were held, also a concert.

Concerts by the battalion always caused a lot of amusement. There were some good " turns." Sergt. Price, the orderly room sergeant, was an artist of no mean merit, and used to do lightning sketches of various Welsh Guardsmen, accompanied by some funny " patter " ; C.Q.M.S. Rendall sang soulful songs in a soulful baritone voice ; Drill-Sergt. Dunkley was a popular favourite with " Old King Cole " ; Sergt.-Major Bland did not perhaps give the pathetic expression required to " A Broken Doll," but it was the only song he knew ; and Sergt. " Bob " Richards used to recite " Mad Carew " with much dramatic expression ; and there was always a choir.

And while these things were going on the sound of the battle was being continually wafted to the ears of the battalion, and all night the flash of the guns could be seen lighting up the whole of the distant horizon.

Guillemont, which had been attacked for the first time on July 23rd, at last fell to the 20th Division of the XIV Corps on September 3rd. Ginchy on the left of it was attacked by the XV Corps on the 3rd and 4th without success.

CHAPTER IX

THE BATTLE OF THE SOMME

On September 7th the battalion moved, and from that day until the morning of the 9th were billeted in the small village of Ville sur Ancre. It is interesting in view of future events to note that the Commanding Officer practised the battalion in an outpost scheme and night attack.

On the 8th the Commanding Officer was given some idea of what he would be expected to do. The XIV Corps now consisted of the Guards, the 20th, the 6th, the 56th, the 16th, and the 5th Divisions. The 5th and 20th had been engaged from September 3rd in the capture of Guillemont, and an advance in the direction of Leuze Wood, the left flank of the corps being south of Ginchy. On the evening of the 4th the 16th Division relieved the 20th on the left, and during the night 7th/8th took over the line opposite Ginchy from the 7th Division, XV Corps.

On the 9th the 16th Division, with the 56th on their right (they had relieved the 5th Division), were to attack in conjunction with the XV Corps. The Welsh Guards would relieve the left brigade of the 16th Division when it had captured Ginchy.

The Commanding Officer notes in the diary of September 8th that, although the left brigade was said to be a weak one, he does not think the relief " will be a picnic."

At 9 a.m. on September 9th the battalion marched to Carnoi. The roads were much congested, but, as the ground was hard, the infantry were able to take a parallel

111

course by the fields. Interest in the animated scene was added to by the accumulation of guns, which was enormous—they were in clumps and in rows. At Carnoi a halt was called, and the battalion stayed on the side of a hill, where dinners, and later teas, were served.

Packs on this occasion were carried up by lorries and dumped with the transport near a place called the Citadel.

The Commanding Officer then went to Bernafay Wood to see the Brigadier of the 49th Brigade, who was apparently in command of the 48th, and arrange details for taking over the line that night from the 48th Brigade. The intention had been for the battalion to stay in Carnoi until the result of the attack was known, but the brigadier asked that the relieving troops might be moved up at once. At 8 p.m. the battalion left for Ginchy, with two days' rations.

The officers who went in were:

Headquarters.—Lieut.-Col. Murray Threipland, D.S.O., Adjt. Lieut. J. A. D. Perrins, Asst.-Adjt. J. W. L. Crawshay.

Prince of Wales's Company.—Major Bromfield, D.S.O., 2/Lieut. Pugh, 2/Lieut. Bagot, 2/Lieut. Wernher.

No. 2 Company.—Capt. Ashton, 2/Lieut. Dickens, 2/Lieut. Goetz.

No. 3 Company.—2/Lieut. Fox-Pitt, 2/Lieut. Cazalet, 2/Lieut. Kearton.

No. 4 Company.—Capt. R. W. Lewis, M.C., Lieut. Power, 2/Lieut. Hebert.

2/Lieut. Gibbs with the Proppers.

Aldridge was ill, and had gone to Boulogne a few days before, and Evan Thomas was also sick. Dene, Clive, Lisburne, and Dudley Ward were left behind with the transport.

Guides met the battalion at Bernafay Wood, and led companies via Guillemont to Ginchy.

The orders were that the Prince of Wales's Company and No. 2 Company should take over from the 48th Brigade a line on the north of Ginchy and facing northeast. No. 3 Company was to move in on the left, and

fill up the gap between No. 2 and the XV Corps.   The
4th Battalion Grenadier Guards were to come in on the
right of the Prince of Wales's Company, and take over
a line facing due east from the 47th Brigade.[1]

The night was very dark, and on arriving at Ginchy

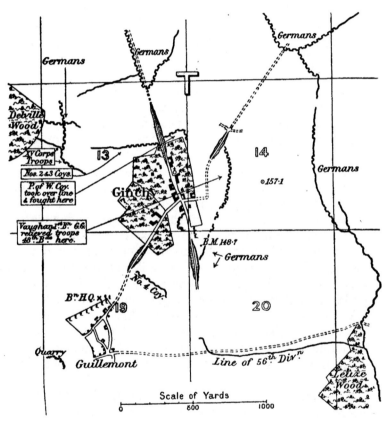

THE POSITIONS ROUND GINCHY.

much rifle-fire was encountered : also as the platoons
were being led through the ruins of that place they came
across small parties of Germans, who, however, surrendered at once.

About midnight the 48th Brigade commenced to file

[1] Appendix B 3.

past the Welsh Guards H.Q., which were on the outskirts of Guillemont, and a message arrived from Ashton : " Have taken over line—in places it is farther back than we thought. We took a lot of German prisoners, which went down with the relieved troops—herewith two more."

This was followed by a message timed 3.30 a.m. from Bromfield : " Have consolidated position T13b104 to T13b65. Unable to get in touch with the 4th Grenadiers on my right, so have had to throw back right flank while I have been engaged with the enemy."

In order to follow what happened it is as well to know where the companies actually were, rather than where they were imagined to be. Instead of facing north-east, which was the general direction of the enemy, they actually faced north-west ; they had taken over from the 48th Brigade a line along the outskirts of the wood at that end of Ginchy. Bromfield gives the position of his right with accuracy ; his left too far forward. This was shown by an examination of the ground some days later.

It must also be borne in mind that Bromfield, arriving on the heels of an attack, did not know what had happened. The situation on either flank of the 48th Brigade was that no advance had been made. No. 3 Company, under Fox-Pitt, was able to get connection with the XV Corps troops, but no doubt this would pull the left of the Welsh Guards' line back. The 4th Battalion Grenadiers were trying to relieve the 47th Brigade, but could not locate it, and there was no one on Bromfield's right.

All through the night Bromfield made exhaustive efforts to get in touch with the 4th Battalion Grenadier Guards, but found nothing but Germans, who fired and disappeared in the darkness, though a few were caught. No. 2 Company also rounded up a few small parties on their front.

It was a misty dawn, and at 7 o'clock there was very little light. Very rightly, Bromfield was still anxious about his flank, and had sent yet another patrol to try and get in touch with someone. Actually Sergt. Ashford,

in command of this patrol, had found troops: a mixed
company of some seventy men of the 48th Brigade, under
a gallant young officer who had been shot through the
neck, but, although he couldn't talk, was still active and
eager; these troops were in a trench near the sunken
road on the east of the village. Sergt. Ashford had just
returned to the right of the Prince of Wales's Company,
and was making his report there to Bromfield, when the
enemy attacked from the north-east.

It was a strong attack, and Bromfield seems to have
realised that he would be enveloped, for he gave an order
to the right of his company to fall back into the wood.
This they proceeded to do, but the enemy's left swept
round into the wood, and hand-to-hand fighting ensued.
Nos. 2 and 3 Companies were able to fire across the front
of the Prince of Wales's Company, and the right of the
German attack melted away; but the situation was very
serious.

This news was brought to the Commanding Officer
about 10 o'clock by Dickens, who was wounded in the
head, but he had already heard of an attack from Lieut.-
Col. Monck Mason, of the Royal Munster Fusiliers, who
was in touch with the mixed company of troops of the
48th Brigade (he asked, too, to be relieved, as his men
were without food or water), and had sent half of No. 4
Company to get in the gap between the 48th Brigade and
the Prince of Wales's Company. This half company,
however, became engaged in the trees just past the
church.

More than this he could not do, as the enemy was
reported to be on the south-east of Ginchy, and on the
right of the 48th Brigade troops. To meet any attack
from this quarter he had half of No. 4 Company in hand.

The lodgment the enemy had gained in the wood made
it very hard for Ashton to find out exactly what had
happened on his right. Fighting was continuous. The
ground immediately behind his company was clear, and
he knew the Prince of Wales's Company was still fighting
on his right, on the other side of the road through Ginchy.
Just before midday the young officer in charge of the

48th Brigade troops observed another enemy force, which
he estimated at a battalion, advancing through the mist,
and undoubtedly he did much to help break up this
second attack. But more of the enemy reached the
wood, and Ashton sent Goetz for reinforcements. Goetz
returned with Power and the other half of No. 4, they
being made up to seventy rifles by men from a Grenadier
carrying party, which had arrived at Battalion H.Q.,
and had been retained by the Commanding Officer as a
further reserve.

Meanwhile Capt. N. M. Vaughan had reported at
Battalion H.Q. with No. 3 Company, 1st Battalion
Grenadier Guards, and had been ordered to relieve the
48th Brigade troops. This he did at 12.30 p.m., but the
situation there was not good, as his left platoon shared
a trench with the enemy, and there was no one on his
right.

The critical nature of the situation does not seem to
have been quite clear to the enemy, who twice attacked
Vaughan with fury, but he beat them off, and at 3.30 p.m.
was able to report his trench and immediate front clear.

Slowly Ashton was getting news of his right. Bromfield, Bagot, Wernher were killed, and Pugh had been
carried out by Sergt. Ashford with a broken leg. A few
of the men of the Prince of Wales's Company had joined
No. 2—others were still in the shell-holes over the road,
and Sergt. Nicholson and a few men had joined the half
of No. 4 near the church.

With the arrival of Power and the other half of No. 4
Company, Ashton determined to try and cross the road,
and drive the enemy from the eastern side of it. The
task was given to Power, who tried to rush the road and
was at once killed.

It must be understood that this wood was a mass of
deep shell-holes—it had been bombarded by the British
heavy guns for some weeks—and there were heaps of
brick from the demolished houses by the side of the road,
and large heaps of earth from German dugouts; there
were fallen trees, too, and a great number of standing
ones. It was a confused jumble, and the men taking

cover in one shell-hole could not possibly tell if anyone was in the next, or if it was friend or foe.

The situation after the second German attack, and soon after midday, seems to have been that Vaughan, with his company of 1st Battalion Grenadiers, had taken over the trench about 150 yards to the east of the village, but the enemy was in the northern end of it, and was being bombed out; half of No. 4 Company was in the village on the east of the road, and about 50 to 100 yards north of the ruins of the church; the other half of No. 4 was on the left of the road and facing east; Nos. 2 and 3 Companies held their original trenches. The enemy was in the trench from which the Prince of Wales's Company had tried to get back into the wood, and the north-east end of the wood was occupied by a number of the enemy and a few of the Prince of Wales's men. There was also a belief, which seems to be well founded, that some of the enemy, who had been hiding in dugouts in the village, had once more taken up their arms—runners passing on the western side of the village were being picked off in an unaccountable way, and men trying to move from one shell-hole to another were being shot in the back.

Ashton now tried to bomb his way forward with rifle-cup adaptors. He gained a little ground, and reoccupied the end of the old Prince of Wales's Company trench, but it was not an enviable position, as the enemy were in shell-holes on either side of it.

The losses in N.C.O.'s was very heavy—four well-known figures, Sergt. "Bob" Richards, Sergt. Williams, Sergt. G. Davies, and Sergt. Jellyman were killed in gallant attempts to clear the enemy out.

All the fighting was so close that the artillery could do very little to assist. They searched all the ground outside the wood, but could do nothing with the wood itself. German fire, however, which had been directed against the southern half of the village, was in the afternoon directed to the northern half; this was the first indication that they had given up hope of retaking the place.

As the day wore on the situation improved in other

ways; fifty men of the 2nd Battalion Scots Guards were sent to Ashton with 100 boxes of bombs, and remained as reinforcements. Two more companies of the 1st Battalion Grenadier Guards reported at headquarters about four in the afternoon, but were held back till night; and at 10 p.m. two companies of the 2nd Battalion Scots Guards arrived.

With the night there was further improvement, and the Germans began to surrender in small groups. At 11.30 p.m. Capt. Drury Lowe, with the King's Company 1st Battalion Grenadier Guards, filled up the gap on Vaughan's left; Capt. Jack Stirling, with G Company 2nd Battalion Scots Guards, came in on King's Company's left, and cleared the eastern side of the Ginchy road; Capt. Fisher Rowe, No. 4 Company 1st Battalion Grenadier Guards, relieved No. 2 Company Welsh Guards; and Left Flank Company 2nd Battalion Scots Guards relieved Fox-Pitt and his company. Two companies 1st Battalion Irish Guards also reported, and were put in position in support north-east of Guillemont. The Welsh Guards went into reserve trenches north-west of Guillemont.

Bromfield had a very difficult task. It was the first time he had been in action in the war, the night was dark, the attack by the 16th Division had only just taken place and no one knew rightly what the situation was: the 4th Battalion Grenadier Guards were led to the wrong line, somewhere on the east of Guillemont; the 47th Brigade seemed to have gained their first objective, but after that lost direction and really made no progress; the XV Corps attack had failed; and finally the repeated German attacks were strong and determined.

Eddy Bagot died gallantly by the side of Bromfield; Power as he was leading his men; Cazalet was killed by a shell; Wernher was hit first in the leg, and was being carried out, when a sniper killed him. Pugh, Dickens and Hebert were hit in the fight; Evan Thomas and Rice as they were going up to the line with officer reinforcements.

With all the officers of the Prince of Wales's Company

out of action, Sergt. Ashford took command of what was
left and kept the remnant together—fighting until the
battalion was relieved. He also undoubtedly saved
Pugh's life. Ptes. 1,037 F. Aspinall, 423 J. R. Evans,
and 1,360 D. J. Evans were conspicuous for their
gallantry in rescuing wounded.

It is not possible to see every brave act, but the
following names are recorded : 648 L/Cpl. J. Crumb,
980 L/Cpl. W. Thomas, 1,095 L/Cpl. Henry Barber,
Ptes. 2,307 H. Burch, 791 F. Cantwell, 350 Sergt. H.
Hunt, 278 L/Cpl. H. Williams, 1,869 J. Broom, 456 W.
T. Turner, 1,250 G. Taylor, 892 T. Williams, 21 Sergt.
S. Owen, 558 Sergt. W. Morgan, 194 Sergt. G. W.
Moreland.

As an example of endurance and determination, we
need only mention the action of L/Cpl. C. L. Glover, one
of the cheeriest and best-hearted fighters that ever lived.
He was blown up and sent to the dressing-station apparently stone deaf and terribly shaken ; but when he
arrived at the dressing-station he found his hearing returning, although his nerves were still twitching so that
he could not keep his hands quiet. It was, however, a
sufficient recovery for Glover, who, still twitching and
shaky, returned to the Prince of Wales's Company and
carried on as acting company sergeant-major.

As to how the men fought in the hand-to-hand fighting, they used their bayonets with great effect. 1,656
Pte. William Williams was seen to dispose of several of
the enemy, until with a furious thrust he completely
transfixed a German and was unable to free his bayonet.
He knocked another down with his fists, and seized
yet another by the throat, when they both fell into a
shell-hole. More Germans rushed up, and the gallant
Williams did not rise again.

The total casualties were 205.

September 11th was a quiet day ; Ginchy yielded from
its hidden and half-destroyed dugouts more prisoners,
but the enemy contented himself with long-range bombardment with heavy guns, and made no further effort
to regain the village. In the evening the Welsh Guards

9

moved to Bernafay Wood, and the next morning marched
to a camp in what was known as Happy Valley, not far
from Fricourt.

The weather had now broken up, and it began to rain
hard.   The battalion rested and refitted in this camp as
far as was possible.   A draft of 180 men arrived from the
Entrenching Battalion (an organisation of the division
which was kept up to work on roads and supply drafts
to the various regiments, and which had its H.Q. in that
area).

At 6 p.m. on the 14th the Commanding Officer attended a conference at the Brigade H.Q., and went over
the details of the divisional attack to take place the
next day.

The 15th was to be a big day.   The idea was that
the Fourth Army should capture Morval, Les Bœufs,
Gueudecourt and Flers, that the Reserve Army should
attack on the north and the French on the south.   The
Guards Division were to take Les Bœufs, and would
have the 6th Division on their right and the 14th
Division, XV Corps, on their left.

The Guards Division were to attack with the 2nd
Brigade on the right and the 1st on the left ; the 3rd
Brigade in support.

The advance was to be in three bounds, with a slight
complication, a swing to the right, to give a change of
front for the 1st Brigade after the first bound.   Each
bound was roughly 1,200 yards.

The day will be remembered as the first battle in
which tanks took part.   The division was to have ten
—one on the left flank of the 1st Brigade and the other
nine in three columns.   They were to start from their
positions forty minutes before zero, and were timed to
reach their first objective five minutes before the infantry.

Some of these weird inventions were parked near the
camp in Happy Valley, and moved off to selected
positions on the 14th, watched by a wondering crowd
of British and French soldiers.   They created some
excitement and a great deal of amusement.   The
French soldiers did not think much of them, but

agreed that in this coming battle they would be good—
" Vous comptez sur la surprise ! "

On the night of the 14th the battalion moved from
Happy Valley to trenches west of Trônes Wood.   It was
raining most of the time.

The 1st and 2nd Brigades attacked at 6.20 a.m., and
we must lay particular stress on the following points :
the forming-up ground and the situation on either flank.

To form up in a restricted area like Ginchy, and extend
to either flank as the advance progresses, is a most difficult operation.   The general line of the attack was north-
east, but to the north-west of Ginchy, just below Delville
Wood, there were two trenches called Ale Alley and
Hop Alley, and some part of these, or a post near them,
was in the possession of enemy machine gunners ; in
other words, when the 1st Brigade started, they were
immediately enfiladed from the left.   Due east of Ginchy,
in the 6th Division area, was a strong fortification known
as the Quadrilateral, in a position to enfilade the 2nd
Brigade from the right.   These two points were to be
dealt with by the new tanks, but in each case the tanks
failed to put in an appearance.

The enemy fought with desperation.   The two Guards
Brigades, debouching from the trees and ruins of Ginchy,
came immediately under a withering machine-gun fire.
The first objective was taken, but the assaulting troops
were disorganised and the casualties 'enormous.   They
stayed where they were.   The 14th Division then came
up on the left, but with a gap between them and the
Guards Division ; but the Quadrilateral defeated the 6th
Division, which failed to advance ; in fact, the place was
not taken until the 18th.   So nothing more was done
that day.

Being warned that he would have to attack the next
morning, Lieut.-Col. Murray Threipland moved the
battalion slightly nearer to Ginchy, and in the evening
sent forward to find out if there was any forming-up
ground with cover.   Every trench, however, was occupied.

At 1 a.m. on the 16th orders were given that the 1st

Battalion Grenadier and the Welsh Guards would attack the original second objective, in conjunction with the 61st Brigade on the right. It was a continuation of the previous plan of attack, the 61st Brigade taking the place of the 2nd Guards Brigade. The hour was to be 9.30 a.m.

But local conditions were so bad they could not be surmounted so easily. Orders arrived in pulp, a solid sheet of rain fell all night, and communication was fearful. The 4th Battalion Grenadier and 2nd Battalion Scots Guards, who were in immediate support to the 1st and 2nd Brigades, occupied the only possible trenches on the long forward slope where the attacking troops had to assemble. There was no time to dig others. And, rather than have daylight find the battalion in this unenviable position, the Commanding Officer, having tramped about vainly in all directions seeking non-existing trenches, ordered the companies back to Ginchy. The 3rd Brigade H.Q., however, confirmed the previous orders for attack, and soon after midday the attack started, with the 1st Battalion Grenadier Guards on the right and the Welsh Guards on the left—they advanced from behind the position occupied by the 4th Battalion Grenadier Guards.

No. 3 Company was in reserve, and the attack was carried out by the Prince of Wales's Company on the right and No. 2 on the left, each on a two platoon front-age ; No. 4 was in support.[1] But the engagement was a repetition of the day before. Casualties were heavy— Clive was hit, and Ashton. The advance had to be made in sectional rushes, and the assaulting troops got into standing crops, where they lost direction, and, mistaking Gueudecourt for Les Bœufs, swung round to the left. When this mistake was discovered they were in close touch with the enemy on the line of the Flers—Les Bœufs Road, and decided to dig in.

The 4th Battalion Grenadier Guards then came up and got connection on the right and the 3rd Coldstream Guards on the left. The line was then some 200 yards short of the second objective.

[1] Appendix B 4 and 5.

There were some good men who fell that day—old
heroes of Mortaldje ; Sergt. Pottinger, Cpl. James, and
Pte. W. Jones were killed, and 723 Cpl. James Jones,
after leading his platoon forward in an exceptional manner, was badly wounded, to mention only a few where
so many should be immortalised. It was all hard and
confused fighting.

That night the line was relieved by the 20th Division.
The total casualties were 144.

The weather conditions continued to be very bad, and
the area allotted for the few days' rest was on the slope
of a hill near Carnoi. In the valley was a line of 9·2
howitzers, and on the opposite slope were cavalry lines,
the horses being knee-deep in mud ; but the worst feature
of the place was a well with unlimited water, and all the
transport for miles came and watered their horses in the
Carnoi Valley. Such few trenches as existed were rivers
draining the high ground ; the high ground itself was
sodden and wind-swept. The battalion remained in this
spot till the 20th, when they moved to Trônes Wood.
But the exposure and cold had affected the Commanding
Officer, who had spent the five days of the last action for
the most part in shell-holes, and he had to remain at the
transport lines too ill to go into another fight ; Humphrey
Dene took command of the battalion.

Companies were now getting very weak : the Prince
of Wales's, under Arthur Gibbs, was 52 strong ; No. 2,
with Lisburne and Goetz, just under 100 ; No. 3, with
Aldridge and Kearton, near 150 ; and No. 4, with Lewis,
not 100. The reserve of officers was Fox-Pitt and
Dudley Ward.

In Trônes Wood conditions were decidedly better than
at Carnoi ; there were a few dugouts, and shelters could
be found in a jumble of trees and trenches. The 21st was
spent in carrying for the R.E.

On the 22nd the battalion relieved the 4th Battalion
Grenadier and the 2nd Battalion Scots Guards on the
left of the line, the position of companies being, in order
from the right, No. 3, Prince of Wales's, No. 4, No. 2.

Lisburne and his company were working all night

digging a trench to connect up with the King's Own
Yorkshire Light Infantry on his left.   He had a covering
party out, and during the night the K.O.Y.L.I. bombed
an enemy sap on Gas Alley to such effect that the Germans bolted.   Some fifty returned to the attack, but
unfortunately for them came under the fire of Lisburne's
covering party, which did great execution with a Lewis
Gun.

The division were to attack on the 23rd, but at the last
moment the attack was postponed.   The day passed
quietly, and in the evening patrols from No. 2, under
Goetz, and some from the Prince of Wales's Company
went out and remained in touch with the enemy all
night; there was no indication of any retirement, but
only of extreme watchfulness, bombs being thrown,
accompanied by jumpy rifle-fire, from every point approached.

The 25th was fixed for the day of attack, and on the
night of the 24th the leading assault troops relieved the
battalion in the front line.

The battle line of the division was the 1st Brigade on
the right, with the 2nd Battalion Grenadier and the 1st
Battalion Irish Guards leading, and the two Coldstream
battalions in support, and the 3rd Brigade on the left,
with two companies of the 2nd Battalion Scots and the
4th Battalion Grenadier Guards leading, and the 1st
Battalion Grenadier Guards and Welsh Guards in
support.

The advance was to be in three bounds, known as the
Green, the Brown, and the Blue Lines—the green being
Needle Trench, the brown the outskirts of Les Bœufs,
and the blue the far side of Les Bœufs.   The 6th Division
was on the right and the 21st on the left.

The 3rd Brigade plan of attack was that the 2nd
Battalion Scots and the 4th Battalion Grenadier Guards
should go to the Brown line; and when that was captured the 1st Battalion Grenadier Guards would go
through and take the Blue line, the Scots Guards looking
after their right flank and the 4th Battalion Grenadiers
their left.   Two companies of the Welsh Guards were

to move into the left of the Green line and two remain in rear of the left flank.[1]

The 4th Battalion Grenadier and the 2nd Battalion Scots Guards formed up in the X and Y Lines, the 1st Battalion Grenadier Guards in the Z Line, and the Welsh Guards in Gas Trench and Switch Trench (T7 and 8).

A long, steady bombardment of the German positions was being carried on—it had started on the 23rd—and on the night of the 24th the enemy retaliated heavily on Gas and Switch Trenches, and managed to get some direct hits, causing casualties.

At 12.35 p.m. on the 25th the British shrapnel barrage came down and crept forward at the rate of fifty yards a minute. By three o'clock the 1st Battalion Grenadier Guards were on the far side of Les Bœufs, and Nos. 3 and 4 Companies Welsh Guards had moved up to the Green Line to consolidate. But the 21st Division had not come up on the left, and the whole of the left flank of the XIV Corps was exposed. The Green Line was the main German Line, Gird and Needle Trenches (the former being a continuation of the latter), and the enemy still held Gird Trench and part of Needle Trench, in the 21st Division area, in force. Humphrey Dene was ordered to make good this flank.

There was much machine-gun fire and heavy shelling, but Dene started off in his impetuous way with the Prince of Wales's Company and No. 2, and rushed them over the open, shell-pounded country, to Gas Alley, where they had to get in the trench. Arthur Gibbs, in answer to Dene's repeated " Come on, Arthur—can't you move ? " arrived in a state of collapse, his round face pouring with perspiration, his eyeglasses dimmed, and his lungs working like wheezing bellows. There was great difficulty in getting along, as the trench was found to be full of wounded ; but, as they penetrated farther, it became out of the question to go over the top, as the machine-gun fire was stronger than ever. Eventually the Green Line was reached, and, taking advantage of every shell-hole and bit of bank by the roadside, a flank

[1] Appendix B 6.

was formed from the Green Line to the north of Les
Bœufs.

It was a mixed force Dene commanded in making this
flank ; it consisted of fifty details of the 62nd Brigade
who had come up by themselves, one small company of
the 4th Battalion Grenadier Guards, numbering forty
men, under 2/Lieut. C. Keith, No. 4, Prince of Wales's
and No. 2 Companies Welsh Guards, with No. 3 in support in Needle Trench, three machine guns, and the 3rd
Brigade Trench Mortar Battery.

It looked as though there might be trouble from Needle
Trench, as there were some 400 of the enemy and machine
guns holding a strong point in that trench close to the
junction with Gas Alley. But at 6 p.m. a company of
the 1st Battalion Scots Guards came up with water and
ammunition, and Dene kept them and put them in above
No. 2 Company, and joining on the 1st Battalion Grenadiers. The enemy evidently began to lose heart, and a
machine-gun crew tried to slip away, as it was getting
dark, but all were shot, with the exception of one man
who surrendered with the gun.

But with darkness everyone became busy digging, and
before dawn a trench had been made.

At 3 a.m. Dene received orders to prepare to attack
the strong point, but later this was altered to " co-
operation when the 62nd Brigade come up."

At 6.15 a.m. the battalion saw for the first time a tank
go into action. Amidst silence, except for an occasional
shot—so occasional that the report seemed timid and
diffident—it advanced on the strong point. There was
no need for it to do anything more, as the entire garrison
came rushing out with their hands up and gibbering
with fear.

The flank being now clear of any known danger, Cpl.
Hicks was sent out with a patrol from No. 4, and came
back about noon to report that the Leicesters were in
Gueudecourt.

The enemy could then be seen running in the direction
of Le Transloy. There were, however, a few snipers still
concealed in shell-holes, and Dene told his orderly, Sully,

not to follow him about, but to deal with them. Sully
was a crack shot, and, having made himself comfortable
in a position of vantage, and lighted a fresh cigarette, he
killed two in quick succession—after which odd men came
in with their hands up, and there was no more trouble
in that quarter. These scattered Germans were always
a nuisance. A single man would lie in a shell-hole and
be passed over, and then would calmly snipe runners, or
any single or couple of men who approached him. To a
bigger party he would surrender if in danger of being
discovered, and if it was not convenient to detach a
man to take the prisoner back he would often be told to
get back himself, but at the first opportunity he would
slip into another shell-hole and start sniping again.
During this battle Stephen Stokes, being alone and on
the way to visit one of his guns, had a bomb thrown at
him by such a man. The bomb failed to do him any
harm, and fortunately it was the last weapon the German
possessed. He then wished to surrender, but Stokes
refused to accept it, and without argument shot him.
It may be argued that it requires brave men to do these
deeds, but as brave men they must be prepared to accept
the logical consequences of their actions.

The 62nd Brigade had come up a bit, but were not
yet level with the Grenadiers, and for the rest of the
day, although everybody wanted to get on, nothing
happened.

At 11 p.m. the Northumberland Fusiliers arrived and
took up a position on the left of the Grenadiers, after
which the 1st Battalion Scots Guards relieved the whole
of the 3rd Brigade.

The battalion marched back to Trônes Wood.

43 Sergt. C. H. Wren, 403 L/Sergt. C. O. Bowles, 1,869
Pte. John Broom were conspicuously gallant.

Casualties were returned as 78, and one officer, Rupert
Lewis, wounded.

The last attack had been favoured with good weather,
but it now started to rain again, and although Dabell
worked like a Trojan, and brought down every bivouac
sheet and bit of canvas he could lay his hands on, the

shelter so obtained was useless against the water, which seemed to ooze up out of the ground.

Burying parties went out, and this gave a good opportunity of seeing what damage had been done to the enemy and finding out how he had been situated.

The wood at Ginchy showed what was known before, a number of German dead mixed with our own. Bromfield and Bagot fell by the side of the trench which they first occupied, and the dead of both sides were thick round here. The enemy attacks had come from the north-east. About twenty-five to thirty yards from the trench, and stretching away in a rough diagonal line, the ground was thick with Germans; Lewis Guns and rifle-fire had taken toll of them in that direction. And it was easy to see how the left wing of the first German attack had swept round the flank of the Prince of Wales's Company, and got behind them in the wood; there were the German bombs ready to hand on the lip of dugout shell-holes, and in some cases their still and silent occupants lying at the bottom. But there were no traces of the Germans having held more than the north-east corner of the wood.

Inspection of the ground to the north-east of Ginchy revealed the fearful effect of the enemy flank fire on the 15th, before the 1st and 2nd Brigades reached the trench which was their first objective. Several men who were missing since the 16th were found in the growing crops.

The story of the 25th was a better tale, and German dead predominated.

The part played by the Guards Division in the battle of the Somme is shown on the map by a small advance, but on the ground could be read the true history : an advance through heavy artillery barrages, and the ground swept by machine-gun fire from the front and either flank. Surveying the scene quietly one felt that these men were not dead : death suggests something horrible, something broken, something grotesque and empty, but here was a silent grandeur, a calm, overpowering dignity. There had been very little of that hand-to-hand fighting where a man becomes wild and fierce, and in the mad exultation of personal conflict can die if he must ; these

POSITIONS IN THE SOMME BATTLE ADVANCE.

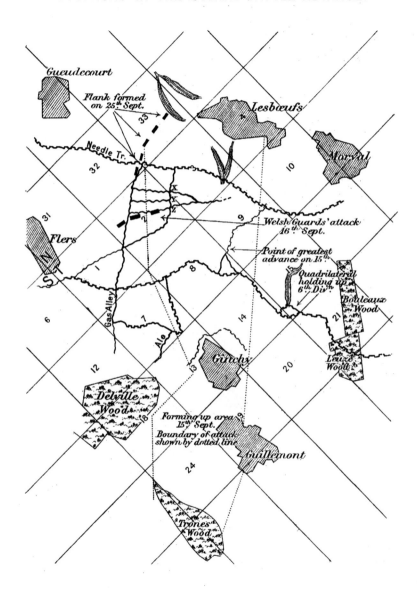

men, with the common names of Jones, Roberts and
Williams, had died walking steadily over soft, heavy
ground pitted with shell-craters, and carrying the heavy
load of modern war equipment, hearing the nerve-racking
crackle of machine guns, which became so intense that
it was one continuous sound punctuated by the loud
explosion of shells in quick succession—plodding on with
all these noises in their ears, round their heads—seeing
men fall all round them, but advancing stolidly until they
fell or " got there."   And they lay with rifle in hand and
load on their backs, face pressed against the crumbling
pounded ground.   But, even as the burying parties lifted
the fast decomposing bodies into the graves which had
been dug, one felt that the " life " which had controlled
these dignified remains of men was still in existence.

On the 29th the battalion moved to another camp near
Carnoi, on better ground and under canvas.   Luxmoore
Ball, more or less cured of his wound, Copland Griffiths, back from his rest at Havre, rejoined ; and with
them came Bird, Devas, Hargreaves, Upjohn, Dilberoglue.   Of these new officers Hargreaves was the only one
with any experience, he having already fought at Gallipoli, and proving himself later a most gallant and capable
officer.

From this camp to Fricourt, the Entrenching Battalion
Camp, on the 30th, the transport starting on this day
for St. Maulvis, for which place the battalion left on
October 1st, marching to Morlancourt, and from there
carried by the French in buses.

De Satge, the interpreter, arranged all the billets, and
food for the officers in a battalion mess.   De Satge was
well known in the division, having been for some years
previous to the war a master at Eton College.   Skavinski
was the first interpreter with the battalion at Arques in
1915, but he left in March 1916, when De Satge joined,
to remain until the early part of 1918.

The first order at St. Maulvis was that the men should
do nothing for three days.   Let them, said the Command-
manding Officer, eat and sleep as much as they like.
Billets were good, and Dabell was sent scouring the

country for vegetables, which were paid for out of the
Canteen Fund.

Ellis, Lascelles, and Downing joined, and there was a
general reposting of officers—Luxmoore Ball commanded
the Prince of Wales's Company, with Arthur Gibbs,
Lascelles, Devas and Bird; Jimjack Evans (returned
from the 3rd Brigade staff) had No. 2, with Lisburne,
Copland Griffiths and Ellis; Aldridge had No. 3 with
Fox-Pitt, Kearton and Downing, and, joining a few days
later, Wreford Brown; Dudley Ward, Upjohn, Hargreaves and Dilberoglue in No. 4. Nigel Wells, who had
done very good service, had been ill for some time, and
went home (where he was given employment in the more
congenial climate of Egypt), leaving the transport in the
hands of Goetz.

On October 4th the battalion was inspected and congratulated by the brigadier, and on the 7th by the major-
general.

Numbers were slightly made up by two drafts, 50 and
93, some old and some new men.

Most of the officers managed to get leave during this
month, but the leave for the men was very scanty, only
three and four passes issued per day, and there were still
138 men who had never been on leave since they arrived
in France with the battalion. At the end of October all
leave was again stopped.

On November 1st H.R.H. the Duke of Connaught inspected the division near Le Chaussey. Not being able
to talk to the whole of the division he addressed those
who had won decorations during the war. He said:

" It has given me the greatest pleasure to have been
able to see you here in France as a division, and to have
this opportunity of expressing to all those who have been
decorated for gallantry in the field my very great appreciation for what you have done during this great war to
uphold the traditions of the Guards.

" I appreciate very deeply the splendid spirit of
bravery which has been shown by all ranks in moments
of great trial and stress, and, while deeply regretting the
very serious losses you have sustained, I am very proud,

as Senior Colonel of the Brigade of Guards, of inspecting so distinguished a body of men.

" On all sides I hear of the splendid example set to the army by officers, non-commissioned officers, and men of the brigade.

" The parade I have just seen shows me that you have in no way abated the smartness of home service, and I consider that to-day's parade reflects very great credit on all ranks.

" I hope all those who have received these decorations may live long to enjoy them, and that your families at home may be as proud of you as I am."

CHAPTER X

THE battle of the Somme continued through the month of October, but with longer intervals between engagements. The weather, never good, had become vile, and the whole battle-field, pounded and smashed by months of shell-fire, churned up by troops and pack animals— wheeled traffic had to keep to the roads—was like a gigantic quagmire. Nevertheless, important gains in position were made on October 21st, with the capture of Regina Trench and Stuff Trench, two celebrated lines; and again on the 23rd to the east of Les Bœufs.

On November 11th a most successful engagement was fought in the neighbourhood of Beaumont Hamel, which resulted in the capture of 7,200 prisoners: this battle might be called the battle of the Ancre, but it is linked up with the Somme fighting, and a direct result of it, and marks the end of the big British operations of 1916.

Verdun, too, had been relieved, and the French declaration, " Ils ne passeront pas " was no idle boast.

The total number of prisoners taken by the British from July 1st to November 18th was 30,000, including over 800 officers; and of war material we captured 29 heavy guns, 96 field guns and howitzers, 136 trench-mortars, and 514 machine guns.

The greatest battle the world had seen up to that date appeared to have had no result. The gain of country was inconsiderable; the enemy moral may have sustained a rude shock, but he still fought strongly and well;

his losses in prisoners and casualties were great, but his
divisions still barred the way. That one battle should
last for months, and end with both sides stuck in the
mud, when a decision of some sort had in former wars
usually been reached in as many hours, was not an
encouraging thought to those soldiers who looked for a
speedy return to their homes.

On November 6th the battalion went back to the
Somme area by motor-bus, to Mansell Camp, near Carnoi.

Until the 14th they worked on roads and at a railway
siding near Trônes Wood.

The whole country had become one great heap of mud.
It had been fought over, it had been trampled on by
countless infantry, by horses—cavalry, artillery, all
manner of transport—it was covered with camps and
dumps. There were very few roads, the dry weather
tracks which had been constructed broke up with the
rain, and the dust which had accumulated on them only
served to make matters worse. All through the battle
only heavy traffic had been using the road between
Carnoi and Montauban, the lighter transport using the
tracks until the weather broke, so that now all traffic
used this road. It was no longer a road—it looked like
the bed of a mountain torrent. Horses splashing through
water two inches deep would fall into a hole with water
up to their bellies ; hundreds of men along the road
would be engaged, dodging in and out amongst the traffic,
trying to fill up the holes by throwing large stones into
them when the opportunity served ; and the traffic never
stopped, and the loose stones thrown into the holes were
as quickly ground into mud and washed away.

Three companies were put on to this road, with orders
to dig a drain, but, unfortunately, through some error,
it appeared that a bank was what was wanted, and so
they filled up the drain again.

This sisyphean task was left on the 14th, and the only
pleasant memory was of a Nissen hut occupied by Capt.
Heath, " Danny " Evans, and other merry engineers of
the division, who dispensed prolific hospitality.

When not engaged on this fatigue the men of the

battalion sat in, or stood by, their tents in Mansell Camp
and stared at the struggling mass of men and vehicles
on the road, or, turning the other way, viewed a wide
expanse of mud dotted over with horse-lines and
dumps.

Humphrey Dene was in command, as Lieut.-Col.
Murray Threipland was on extended leave, owing to
illness. Many were the discussions on the future.
"What is Fritz going to do?—tell me that," Dene would
challenge. No one could accept the idea of rounding up
several million German prisoners, or of doing anything
more than bend the enemy line. How, then, was it going
to end? The argument, repeated again and again,
always concluded in the same fashion—internal dissen-
sion would finish the war. "You mean," said Dene,
"Fritz will get bored with it. It bores me already ——.
This place bores me ——. You bore me, Dudley ——.
Oh, my God!"

Luxmoore Ball was laid up with rheumatism in his
wounded shoulder, and took little interest in anything
except how to keep warm. Lisburne and Jimjack Evans
were somewhat silent; Copland Griffiths read books and
smoked many cigarettes; Hargreaves tried to create
interest by yarning about Ceylon, and Upjohn by disser-
tations on old furniture and modern plays. The only
person in the officers' mess who seemed indifferent
these times, provided he got plenty of food, was Arthur
Gibbs. Arthur Gibbs's chief recollection and great
concern in the Somme fighting was the loss of a tin of
cherries.

The battalion moved for one night to Camp H, near
Montauban, and from there took over the line near
Gueudecourt from the 2nd Scots Guards.

We have said the condition of the Somme battle-field
was appalling. It was also confusing, having no landmarks, and at night one skyline looked exactly as any
other. Guides who could find their way about in day-
time invariably got lost at night. And to keep a
straight line in the mass of shell-holes and trenches was
impossible.

The battalion marched in by Longueval and Delville Wood, and the going at first was easy, as duckboards had been laid down for some 2,000 yards; but these came to an end, and then there were windings and twistings for no apparent reason in the dark until Needle Trench was reached. Headquarters was the German dugout in the strong point so closely watched on September 26th—a very large and deep affair. This dugout was due west of Les Bœufs, and the trenches to be occupied were due east of Gueudecourt, a distance of 2,000 yards; but it seemed like 20,000.

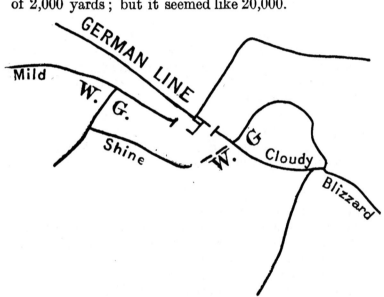

The Line at Gueudecourt. Note the German Post in the Centre.

It was freezing the night of the 15th, and the valley was hard as iron. The front line was a narrow trench hastily dug by the enemy. The commencement of dugouts existed in some parts, but nothing more advanced than seven-foot shafts. Dividing the two companies holding the front line (two were in Needle Trench) was a German strong point. The Welsh Guards held the left of the divisional line, and the Australians were on their left.

10

It was a nasty position, as supports were on the other
side of the valley, which was continually shelled by the
enemy, and in any event so far away that any assistance
was out of the question. The Germans, however, were
not disposed to make any raids or demonstrations, and
all that had to be contended with were the weather and
shelling.

On the 17th there was an inter-company relief, and at
the same time the weather broke. All through the day
it had been thawing, and with darkness came rain ; the
trench fell in, and the valley was a swamp. The relief
was made still harder by a heavy enemy barrage across
the valley. The outgoing platoons got lost in the pitch-
black night ; men fell into shell-holes and sunk to their
armpits in mud ; the companies in Needle Trench were
not present till long past daylight. And then it froze
again and then rained.

On the 19th the Prince of Wales's Company and No. 2
Company were relieved in the front line by the 1st Battalion Scots Guards, and on the 20th Nos. 3 and 4 Companies in Needle Trench by the 60th Australian Infantry
Brigade.

There were forty-three casualties in the Gueudecourt
Line, amongst them Hargreaves, hit in the shoulder,
and, what was more serious to the battalion, a lot of men
with trench feet—sixteen were evacuated on the 21st.

After a few hours' rest at H Camp the battalion
marched to Meault, a dreary ruin of a village, and there
a surprise was in store for them—the Welsh Guards Band,
which they had never seen or heard! The bandmaster,
Harris, waited a couple of miles outside Meault to play
the battalion in, and his intention was much appreciated,
although in effect he only led in the Prince of Wales's
company, marching in file ! This was the army order
for the congested roads, and also that there should be
200 yards' interval between companies. But he played
the regimental march for each company as it marched
into the village. Perhaps it was not such an undramatic
meeting as Harris thought at the moment.

Although any exercise of a military nature was not

possible in that mud-infested area, sport was attempted during the stay at Meault, and the Welsh Guards played a game of mud-larking football against the 1st Battalion Grenadier Guards, and beat them by two goals; there was also a concert and some boxing, in which Pte. Chamberlain once more proved himself a champion.

On November 29th Major Douglas Gordon joined, and on December 1st the Commanding Officer returned.

On December 2nd a move was made to Bromfay Camp, again in the Carnoi District, and the grim winter work in the Somme sector commenced.

The line was on the left of Sailly-Saillisel, and over against Le Transloy. The total distance from the camp to the line was about fifteen miles, and too far to march, so a triangle was arranged. From Bromfay Camp battalions marched to Maltzhorn Camp, near Montauban, and stayed there one night, and then on to the line. Outgoing troops marched from the line to the railway siding near Maltzhorn Camp, where they got into a train and were taken back to Bromfay Camp. The work in days and nights was as follows: three nights and three days in the line; then the relief, which was over as a rule about 7 p.m., and the march to the railway siding, which was reached about 11 p.m. (here the men had tea or cocoa and waited for the train, which started round about 1 a.m.); then the march at the other end, which brought troops into camp about 2.30 a.m. The first night's rest, therefore, did not start much before 4 a.m. The next day was spent in Bromfay Camp, and the following day troops marched to Maltzhorn Camp; one night at Maltzhorn and then a march to the line.

All through their part in the Somme Battle the Guards Division had been near the French, though not actually next to them, and the Transloy Line was taken over from the French. The French had started to make a good line, with deep trenches and good communication, and when first taken over in frosty weather it was easy to get about; but before anything in the way of revetting could be done a thaw set in and rain. The trenches fell to pieces, subsided within an hour. The whole country became a swamp, and from Haie Wood, between Combles and Morval, to the line, a distance of two and a half miles, each step forward was an effort. Everything possible was done to limit the traffic to the line—rations for the whole period were carried in by the relieving troops—but the absolutely necessary traffic cut up the soft muddy ground until men sank up to their knees in the puddled stuff. There was only one line along which anyone could move, and the track became wider and wider; but to leave the track altogether, especially as relief could only be done at night, meant a danger of getting lost in that bare, treeless country, with the even skyline. The march " in " was exhausting ; much more so the march " out," after three days in the mud without shelter of any sort or kind. A soup-kitchen was established by Sidney Jones, the padre, at Combles, and another at the railway siding, and they were great blessings. But the men arrived at Bromfay Camp wet to the skin.

Gen. Sir Francis Lloyd visited the Welsh Guards at Bromfay Camp during the month of December, and when his motor-car stopped in the muddy road opposite the entrance to the camp, he paused on the step. " By Jove," said he, " what a sea of mud ! "

And plunged boldly into the eighteen inches of " slush."

Maltzhorn Camp was the same.

It may be said that men were never dry, and the sick list in consequence was a big one. Some idea of the problems which had to be faced may be gathered from the story of overcoats. A young officer of one regiment of Guards was called before his brigadier to explain his reasons for giving orders to his company to leave their greatcoats in the line. His explanation that they were too heavy for the men to carry out was at first received as frivolous, not to say impertinent; but a coat, fresh from the line, was weighed and found to be over 70 lb. He was absolved.

The proppers had been brigaded, and Lascelles, in charge of the Welsh Guards section, struggled valiantly,

COLONEL W. MURRAY THREIPLAND, D.S.O.

carrying trench boards and laying them down to sink in the mud. Towards the end of December he succeeded in getting a path to the line, but it was always heavily shelled by the enemy.

On the 14th, just before the battalion left Bromfay Farm on its usual round to the line, the Commanding Officer addressed the men, and his first words were as a bombshell in their midst.

He had not been well since the Somme battles, and now the doctor had ordered him home.

That the whole battalion was genuinely grieved there can be no doubt. He had lovable qualities, simple habits, determination of purpose, and dogged perseverance; he looked after his men and their comforts extraordinarily well; he fought fearlessly for the good of his battalion when occasion arose; he never spared himself. His officers and men knew all this, and he won their respect and admiration. They knew he was a good soldier and a straight-minded man.

Major Douglas Gordon then assumed command.

Of the line itself there is nothing more of interest to note. The enemy was in as bad a state as the British troops opposite him. Patrolling was a farce, and no real enterprise was undertaken in that direction beyond inspecting the barbed wire, which was scanty enough. All the fighting was confined to the artillery, which was exceedingly active on both sides.

There was one slight alteration in the arrangement of the division, so as to cut down the duties in the front line as much as possible—the three brigades were turned into two groups.

Officers were getting short—Aldridge and Fox-Pitt had to go away to hospital in December. Dudley Ward went sick in the middle of January, and was soon after followed by Devereux, who had only joined in December, and Jimjack Evans went back to the staff. But Lieut. Bonn and 2/Lieut. Roderick joined on December 18th, and 2/Lieut. Culverwell towards the end of December.

Christmas Day was celebrated at Bromfay Camp. The surroundings were less propitious for gaiety than those at Laventie; the camp was surrounded with the utmost dreariness and desolation. Narrow trench-boards, fixed on piles driven into the mud, led you between the rows of black wooden huts. The huts had been built by the French, and were larger than the usual British hut; they were placed on the bare earth, and the floors were either dusty or greasy as they were dry or wet—a trench round the outsides prevented them becoming soft mud, and the surface only got wet. No provision had been made for fires, and no material was available for constructing chimneys; coal and coke were scarce. To enable the men to dry their clothes and get some sort of warmth, Dabell used to scour the countryside for wood, and succeeded in accumulating large heaps of débris each time the battalion was in the line. This fuel being gathered from old trenches, broken dugouts, and ruined villages and buildings, was always wet, but the men cheerfully built enormous fires in the centre of each hut, which in a short time was transformed into a good representation of a corner in hell.

The upper portion of the huts was filled with thick, eye-stinging smoke, in the midst of which dripping, mud-smeared greatcoats were hung on wires stretching from side to side. The men lay on bits of tin roofing, boards, sacks, anything which would keep them off the damp ground, and managed to fill the lower and purer air with tobacco-smoke. It was hell without the general excessive heat usually associated with that place. If you lay close up against the fire when it eventually blazed, one side of you was scorched, and if you moved a little way off you found yourself in a damp, dank fog.

The officers' hut was the same—with furniture. A long table ran down the centre with fixed benches along the sides of it. Against the walls of the hut were rows of beds (wooden frames with rabbit-wire stretched across them). Instead of the wood fire they had braziers filled with coke and a handful of coal, which made a vile smoke, with large floating smuts, and filled the hut with choking fumes, but no heat. Round each brazier a little group of people huddled together with outstretched hands,

Aldridge and Dene nursing bronchitis, Luxmoore Ball
rheumatism, and the rest trying to warm their misery
into sufficient energy for the repetition of bitter jibes
and jokes to conceal their thoughts.

A good place for a merry Christmas.

Against these conditions the Welsh Guards band
worked with heroic vim and cheerfulness; their fingers
may have been frozen—their faces were certainly blue—
but they played lively tunes without rest.

For their Christmas dinner the men had a quarter of
a pound of plum pudding, a quart of beer, and two
packets of cigarettes, and the band played for them.
Perhaps a more cheery dinner was held by the officers
on New Year's Eve, when they were joined at the close
of dinner by Charles Greville, Bernard Burke, Churchill,
and a few festive souls from the Grenadier camp opposite.
Mick Rowlette and the Grenadier doctor raced across the
rafters of the hut, Charles Greville sang many songs out
of tune, aided and abetted by Bernard Burke, Luxmoore
Ball mixed hot rum and pepper and called it punch, and
a crowd of subalterns "produced" de Satge from his bed
arrayed in a gorgeous suit of pyjamas. Everyone knew
they were going back to Ville sur Ancre the next day,
and hoped it meant the last of the Somme.

But the respite from mud was not for long, and on
January 10th, 1917, the battalion left Ville and marched
back to Billon Farm Camp, quite close to Bromfay Camp.
From there to Maurépas Camp on the 11th, and to Priez
Farm, where there was a big dugout-making and cable-
burying fatigue, on the 13th (No. 4 Company had to
return to Maurépas that night, as there was no room in
Priez Farm Camp). On the night of the 14th the whole
battalion was back at Billon Farm. Here they remained
working on roads and improving the camp until the 24th,
when they returned once more to Maurépas. On the
25th they went into the Frégicourt sector on the right of
Sailly-Saillisel, and opposite St. Pierre Vaast Wood.

The line, a matter of a dozen posts, was on the forward
slope of a most important ridge, which had at all costs to
be denied to the enemy. These front posts were held by

one company; in close support on the reverse slope was another company, and 500 yards behind them the remaining two companies in reserve. The battalion were in for four days, and then went back to Maurépas; and in the line again on February 3rd for three days, and so to Maurépas. But there is nothing of interest except the intense cold through the latter part of January and the beginning of February, which caused a great deal of suffering. It must always be remembered, when appreciating the work of the Welsh Guards, that the men had to fight against the weather as well as the Germans, and resisted the one as stoutly as the other. A hole in the ground gave them a little shelter from shell, rifle and machine-gun fire, but none from the cold and wet. The endurance of these men passed all belief, and their cheerfulness was wonderful. What they went through may be gathered from an order which came down from the Higher Command, acknowledging the severity of the conditions, and recommending Commanding Officers to do all in their power to stop complaints and keep all ranks in good spirits! The order was unnecessary for the Welsh Guards.

On the 10th the battalion marched to the railway siding near Carnoi, and from thence by train to Méricourt. Here they remained till March 2nd.

New officers arrived from England about this period. 2/Lieut. Bonsor on February 6th, 2/Lieuts. Saunders, Shand, R. R. Jones, Arthur, Devereux (from hospital) on the 17th, 2/Lieut. Jenkins and a draft of ninety-two on the 20th. The battalion had no padre since Capt. Thursby-Pelham went to hospital prior to the Somme battles, and Capt. Oldham, soon to be given the name of "Mog," which, being interpreted, meant "Man of God," joined on February 13th.

Company Commanders now were—Prince of Wales's Luxmoore Ball, No. 2 Lisburne, No. 3 Copland Griffiths, No. 4 Upjohn.

We must note that on the 23rd Gen. Lyautey, the French Minister for War, inspected the 3rd Guards Brigade near Ville—only the Prince of Wales's and

No. 2 Companies were available for this inspection, the others being on fatigue.

The Commanding Officer, Lieut.-Col. Douglas Gordon, having gone on a senior officers' course at Flexicourt, the battalion moved to Bromfay Camp on March 2nd, and Combles on the 3rd, under Major Humphrey Dene.

All through the winter the Guards Division had merely been called upon to hold sectors of the line, while their artillery bombarded the enemy lines and communications. Life was bad for the British, but it must have been absolute hell for the Germans. On the left of the Fourth Army (Rawlinson), in which the division was still included, was the Fifth Army (Gough), and it had made several small advances during the months of January and February. On February 25th the enemy suddenly began to retire on that front, and the Fourth Army redoubled its artillery action and prepared for possibilities. It was the beginning of the German retreat to the Hindenburg Line.

It was a skilful retreat, and every means was employed to retard the pursuing troops—trees were cut down, wells blown up, roads mined, billets destroyed. But the line was moving, and moving just north of Sailly-Saillisel, which was the destination of the Welsh Guards.

On the evening of March 4th Humphrey Dene took over the line in the midst of heavy shell-fire. The Prince of Wales's and No. 2 Companies were in the front line, No. 3 on the flank, and No. 4 in reserve. After two days No. 4 Company relieved the Prince of Wales's and half No. 2 in the front line.

This was one of the hardest tours of duty the battalion ever had. Heavy guns, field-guns, and trench-mortars fired continuously at the British line ; the line was blown in, and the men occupied shell-holes where they could ; enemy snipers waited to catch men moving from one hole to another, and, until the divisional artillery found them with shrapnel, did some damage. Communication was almost impossible. Rowlands, the signaller, was twice blown up and buried and the men he was working with

killed, but he carried on, merely asking, as this was his
first experience in the line, if it was always like this.
Humphrey Dene stormed for retaliation and more retaliation, for counter-battery work and ever more, and
for four days a fierce artillery battle raged. In the midst
of all this C.S.M. Pearce did good sniping, and seemed on
the whole to be rather enjoying himself. Sergt. Ashford
was badly wounded in this action, and Cpl. Parker, an
excellent sniper, so injured that he afterwards died.
There is no greater test of discipline and determination
than a prolonged and furious bombardment. In the
four days there were one officer (Jenkins) and seventy-
nine other ranks as casualties. When the 2nd Battalion
Scots Guards relieved on the 8th the fire was dying down.

The reason for this bombardment became obvious—
the enemy was firing off his accumulated ammunition
before removing his guns.

The battalion stayed at Maurépas from March 8th to
12th, and worked hard at making and repairing roads
for the advance : they then went back to Billon Farm,
where the same work was carried on ; and to Combles
on the 15th, still working on the roads. Illness once
more depleted the officers and men—Copland Griffiths
and Devereux went to hospital and England.

On the 19th the battalion was back in the line, where
all was quiet, but so changed the place was unrecognis-
able—the orchard through which the line ran had been
blown to pieces, and St. Vaast Wood appeared to have
been uprooted as a whole. But there were no Germans,
and the British outpost line was in front of the position
the battalion held.

On the 21st, under the Commanding Officer, who had
returned the day before, they took over the outpost line
near Manancourt, which they held until relieved by the
2nd Battalion Lincolnshire Regiment, and then marched,
with one night at Maurépas, to a camp near Péronne.

This ended the fighting in the Somme area ; the fighting had been hard, the weather had been hard, and the
men had been hard. The total casualties in the battalion
were 625. During the winter there was not only a

change of Commanding Officer for the battalion, but for the brigade as well—Brig.-Gen. Charles Corkran went to England and Salonika, and was succeeded by Brig.-Gen. Lord Henry Seymour. But, though the fighting was over for the time, the battalion stayed on at the camp near Péronne, and at Marquaix (April 23rd), working on the railway.

Meanwhile, from April 9th onwards, was fought the successful battle of Arras, yielding 1,400 prisoners and 180 guns. The Allied cause, however, had suffered a blow elsewhere. The Revolution had started in Russia, which must have cheered the enemy very considerably ; but, on the other hand, there was an additional menace which he did not at first realise—America had entered the war (April 5th).

No doubt time will reveal many grave miscalculations made by the Germans which are not now known, and there will be much discussion on the retreat to the Hindenburg Line ; at the time the enemy hailed it as a great strategic and tactical move. That their defensive position in that sector of the front was greatly improved there can be little doubt, and maybe the retreat released a few troops ; but that the interference with British plans caused any great inconvenience is open to question. What the exchange of a further battle on the Somme would have yielded is idle speculation, but the swift blow of the battle of Arras, following as it did close on the retreat, does not on the present surface of knowledge suggest any dislocation of British schemes.

There is, however, one point in favour of German strategic claims : that the evacuation of that large tract of country, after careful and systematic destruction of roads and railways, made it imperative for us to divert energy and material in that direction. Even so, it was a questionable success for him. There may have been a greater scarcity of material than was apparent—we know that rails were being torn up from the permanent ways in England and shipped to France before the retreat, which suggests that the demand for rails could not be met by the manuafcturers—but it seemed as though this diversion of material could only have caused a momentary embarrassment, and may in effect have merely reduced a precautionary reserve. At all events, whether from their association with railways or from observation of actual fact, to those Welsh Guardsmen who survive the war, this period at Péronne seems to mark a change for the better in communication. The speed in making railways, and the construction and maintenance of roads improved ; and with the experience of the awful winter roads in the Somme area fresh in their minds, they noticed an extensive use of the light railway. If the German strategy kept the Guards Division working in that area, it also created an enthusiasm for railway building which later made the work of the Engineers, and particularly the Canadian battalions, appear miraculous, and contributed to the distress of the Germans themselves.

The work of the Welsh Guards was appreciated by Col. B. Ripler, commanding the 1st Battalion Canadian Troops, in a letter to the Commanding Officer, in which he says :

" During the past two months we have had the opportunity of coming together nearly every day, either on the railway work or elsewhere, and I must say that the spirit with which your officers, N.C.O.'s, and men at all times carried out the work assigned to them in connection with the construction of the railway was one that reflects nothing but credit on your whole organisation. There has been a marked absence of the usual rough language and talking among the men while at work, a noticeable spirit of obedience and respect from your men to their N.C.O.'s, of your N.C.O.'s to your officers, and of your officers to where their spirit of obedience and respect should go. A large amount of work has been carried out by your battalion, and it has most certainly been carried out in a quiet and efficient manner, which is known to everybody in the 1st Battalion Canadian Railway Troops, of which I have the honour to be in command. You might be good enough to thank your officers for the hearty co-operation they have given us, and accept my own hearty thanks to yourself."

Humphrey Dene fell ill and was sent to England on May 1st. Luxmoore Ball took his place as second in command.

On May 20th the battalion entrained, and, travelling over the railway they had just made, moved to Corbie, and were billeted at a small village joining the town—La Neuville.

After ten days devoted to training they left again by train for St. Omer, arriving on the 31st at 12.30 a.m., and marched through Arques to the village of Campagne.

A year and nine months had passed since they left Arques to engage in their first battle.

CHAPTER XI

CONCENTRATION and training for a new attack at Ypres
were taking place. Although bombing still played a
prominent part in all work carried out in the back areas,
the rifle, which was always in danger of being forgotten,
was now given a little attention. Ranges were very
small, but on June 16th, two days before the battalion
moved out of the area, long-range practice was carried
out at Zudausques. There were competitions for bayonet
fighting and for the transport, held on June 4th, and a
big Old Etonian dinner in the evening (Lord Cavan presided over 250 diners). Frequent conferences took place
about training and censorship.

From time to time the question of censorship was
brought up before the battalion, presumably the result
of a general order, but the officers of the Welsh Guards
were always rather bored by it. The opinion was expressed that the time given to these discussions was
wasted, as no one knew anything of future arrangements,
or indeed very much of what was happening at any
particular moment. This was perhaps a slight exaggera-
tion, but it was a fact that officers of the Guards Division
knew less of the so-called secret plans than any other unit
they met with. Any information they received came
from back areas, from strange officers casually encountered at some training-school or when taking over a new
line ; if the men wrote at all about military matters that
which they had concocted was more in the nature of an
imaginative exercise than the truth. As to conversa-

148

THE FRONT ATTACKED BY THE WELSH GUARDS, JULY 31ST, 1917.
Wood 15 is below and to the right of Wood 16.

tion amongst officers, it generally roamed round the
extreme limits—either purely local or family affairs, or
the great issues of the war, the power of nations, the map
of Europe. But they did not fail to notice that these
" censoring " discussions always seemed the prelude to
hard fighting.

The battle of Messines started on June 6th, and the
rumble of the guns was a strange accompaniment to the
Coldstream Band which played to the battalion on
the 7th.

The battalion marched to Zudausques for two days'
practice on the big range, and on the 18th left by buses
for farm billets about a mile from Houtkerque.

The attack, which was not to take place for over a
month, had already been thought out in all the essential
details, and only required to be practised and fitted
together. Such minute preparations as they were to go
through had never been seen before by either officers or
men, and they created the liveliest interest.

A large training-ground was laid out with a scale representation of the assembly trenches and the enemy lines
to be attacked ; orders were issued as for the real thing ;
the barrages were represented by flags ; artillery and
engineer officers took part. The brigade did the whole
attack no less than six times. The Corps Commander,
Lord Cavan, watched the practice, and some of his subsequent remarks may be quoted :

" The men questioned knew what they were doing and
what they were going to do. He emphasised the necessity of each Platoon Commander satisfying himself that
every man in the platoon knows his job from the time he
starts to his final objective. He emphasised the necessity
of the supporting and reserve troops being given a free
hand as to their route and stopping-places, provided they
are up to time at the place required. He considered the
attack to be highly creditable."

The polishing went on, however, under the energetic
brigadier, Lord Henry Seymour. Minutes, even seconds,

became the subject of vehement argument and parts of the attack were repeated until everyone knew his rôle.

Briefly, the obstacles which had to be overcome were the canal, with Baboon Trench on the far side of it; Baboon Support, some 400 yards farther on; Wood 15, a strongly fortified spot some 1,200 yards beyond Baboon Support; and 700 yards beyond the far edge of the wood was Peuplières Farm, the limit of the battalion advance. The 1st Battalion Grenadier Guards were to be on the right and the 201st Regiment (French) on the left.

It would be as well to consider the organisation of a battalion at this date.

When the British Army first landed in France the infantry soldier was armed with rifle and bayonet. In the handling of these weapons (one should really consider them as one weapon) he was second to none. We have seen that the first new weapon he was called upon to study was the bomb.

So far as the Welsh Guards were concerned they began to use yet another weapon in November 1915, when they received one Lewis Gun. They received a second gun in December 1915, six more in March 1916, and a further eight while at Mailly-Maillet in August 1916. These dates may not coincide with the issue of Lewis Guns to other units.

At first the Lewis Gun teams were looked upon as men replacing the machine-gun teams, as specialists (as we have pointed out, the machine guns were almost immediately taken away from battalion control). When the number of Lewis Guns increased it soon became apparent that a great number of men in a company must know how to manipulate them, so that casualties could be easily replaced. The number of guns was again increased in 1918 by eight in January and eight in April—in fact, there were so many they could not be manned, although by that time every man in the battalion knew all about the gun.

From the very first bombing practice the men were also instructed in the use of rifle grenades—the Hales and

a modification which was first used in 1917. These were
different in action from the Mills Bomb, and fired from the
rifle (without bayonet) without any extra fitting to the
barrel; and they could be used in no other manner. An
attempt was then made to standardise the various bombs
or grenades, and have one bomb which could either be
thrown by hand or discharged from the rifle. A hole
was bored in the base of the Mills Bomb, so that a short
rod could be screwed in, and a cup to fit on the end of
the rifle-barrel and hold the bomb in position was provided; four of these cups were issued to each company
on September 8th, 1916, and the number subsequently
increased to sixty-four per battalion.

A much better arrangement was introduced in 1918:
an improved cup and a plate to screw on the bomb—the
range was increased to about 250 yards.

The infantry now had four distinct weapons officially
characterised as follows:

(a) The rifle and bayonet, being the most efficient
offensive weapon of the soldier, are for assault, for repelling attack, or for obtaining superiority of fire.

(b) The bomb is the second weapon of every N.C.O.
and man, and is used either for dislodging the enemy
from behind cover or killing him below ground.

(c) The rifle-bomb is the " howitzer " of the infantry,
and used to dislodge the enemy from behind cover and
to obtain superiority of fire by driving him underground.

(d) The Lewis Gun is the weapon of opportunity.

The platoon was taken as the smallest unit capable
of combining these weapons—a section of Lewis gunners,
a section of bombers, a section of rifle bombers, and a
section of riflemen.

The battalion practised the attack organised in this
fashion.

But before this practice was put to the test the battalion had to go through a most uncomfortable month
of fatigues in the battle area. On July 2nd a move was
made to a camp about one and a half miles west of

11

Woesten, and the men worked night and day at burying
cables and carrying material up to the front line. Short
practices of crossing the canal were gone through, and
demonstrations given for the Army Commander (Gough)
and many French officers; also demonstrations of
wiring.

The casualties on these fatigues were very heavy,
especially from gas. The enemy would concentrate a
bombardment on roads and tracks, and on places where
he knew work was being done, and there was scarcely a
night fatigue when gas-helmets were not worn. As may
be imagined, this added to the exhausting nature of these
fatigues.

On the 15th the battalion took over the front
line by Boesinghe Château, the line they would
attack from.

The Prince of Wales and Gen. Gaythorne Hardy visited
the battalion in this line. The shelling all the time was
heavy. Pte. 2,361 J. O. Pritchard had a nasty adventure
during the relief on the 19th. The enemy shelling had
been continuous and severe, with frequent short, crashing
barrages on all approaches to the line. Pritchard was
to act as guide to one of the relieving platoons, and had
to meet it at a point some two miles away On his way
to the rendezvous he was wounded in fifteen places, but
he completed his task and fainted as he led the platoon
into the front line. He had walked three miles from the
time he was hit, and had to lead the platoon through one
of the enemy crashing barrages while passing Boesinghe
Château. A fine example of endurance.

The new camp was in Forest Area near Woesten. It
was shelled and bombed by aeroplanes. Fatigues were
still called for until the 29th; 1,063 L/Cpl. Hutchings
and 280 Pte. Bottcher did good work getting wounded
men away in the midst of severe shelling.

On July 29th the battalion marched into the line
again, but the 1st Guards Brigade had crossed the
canal on the 27th, and the new front line was now
Baboon Support and the Support Line was Baboon
Trench.

CANAL TRENCHES HELD BY WELSH GUARDS, BOESINGHE CHÂTEAU.

The arrows point to supposed German posts. A shell has burst in the Canal by the second arrow from the right.

152]

On the night of the 30th the Prince of Wales's and No. 4 Companies moved across the canal and took up their battle stations.

The first assaulting wave was composed of two platoons of No. 2 Company on the right, and two platoons of No. 3 on the left; these four platoons were followed by two platoons of No. 4 as " moppers up " (a clumsy but expressive term). The other half of Nos. 2 and 3 Companies made the second assaulting wave. The whole of the Prince of Wales's Company formed the third wave, followed by the remaining half of No. 4 Company as " moppers up." [1]

Baboon Trench and Support had already been gained in a bloodless advance (William Arthur, a smart young officer, took a patrol as far as Wood 14 that night), so there were only two objectives. The Blue Line, that is to say the far side of Wood 15, became the first objective to be taken by the first wave. The second and third waves were then to go on to the second objective (the Black Line), and in due course the 2nd Battalion Scots and the 4th Battalion Grenadier Guards would go through them and take the third objective (the Green Line). The second wave, two platoons of No. 2, and two platoons of No. 3 Companies would be reformed as a reserve to the 2nd Battalion Scots Guards.

There were more definite orders as to who should be left out in this battle, a point we will deal with later, and companies were officered as follows :

Prince of Wales's Company under 2/Lieut. Gwynne Jones, D.S.O., with 2/Lieuts. Shand and Bonsor. No. 2 Company under Capt. the Earl of Lisburne, with Lieut. Rice and 2/Lieut. Baness. No. 3 Company under Lieut. Menzies, with 2/Lieuts. Arthur and Fripp. No. 4 Company under Capt. Battye, with 2/Lieuts. R. R. Jones and Hebert. Headquarters consisted of the Commanding Officer, Lieut. Perrins, the adjutant, and Capt. Arthur Gibbs. Lieut. Lascelles was liaison officer to the French regiment on the left.

---

[1] See Appendix B 7.

Zero hour was 3.50 a.m., but owing to the advance of July 27th, which had been accomplished by the Guards Division and the French, these two units could not move until zero + thirty-eight minutes, so as to give the divisions on the right time to get up.

All through the night counter battery work with gas-shells was carried on. The morning was dark and inclined to be wet.

At 3.50 a.m. the barrage, excepting that of the Guards Division and the French, commenced. With the shrapnel and high explosive was mixed a new projectile in the shape of boiling oil, which was discharged in a drum. Arthur Gibbs writes that evening :

" I should think the guns could have been easily heard in England. The noise on the Somme was terrific, but the noise during to-day and all through last night was still more stupendous. I should like some of the munition makers to come over and see the results of their efforts at home. I have just been thinking of the millions of people who have been working day and night for months for a victory like this. It would do them good to see us here."

At 4.24 a.m. the Guards Division barrage came down some 200 yards in front of the first wave, which promptly moved up to within 50 yards of it. The barrage crept forward at the rate of 25 yards a minute, and no opposition was met with until Wood 15, and there the right of the line was held up by machine guns in a concrete blockhouse on which the barrage had no effect. The barrage passed, and the flanks began to creep round, but were losing distance from the barrage. It was then that Sergt. Bye, having crawled within a reasonable distance, rushed forward and succeeded in getting behind the blockhouse, where he proceeded to bomb the inmates. The first objective was then taken, and the second and third waves went through the Blue Line and advanced on the second objective. On the flank was Wood 16, and again machine guns were missed by the barrage; indeed, they fired through the barrage and held up the advance. Sergt. Bye, who was truly inspired that day, went forward at a steady amble, stumbling over the uneven ground, so that with each fall he was thought to be dead, and again got behind the blockhouse and bombed the machine gunners. Once more the line swept forward and took its final objective. Sergt. Bye either killed, wounded, or captured over seventy men in these blockhouses, and for these deeds he received the Victoria Cross.

It was the first time men or officers had encountered blockhouses, but the Welsh Guards were not wanting in leaders to tackle them. R. R. Jones rushed one of them, and fired a rifle through the loophole, killing the machine gunner, while his men dealt with those trying to escape from the rear ; and 1,209 Pte. Hughes led the way to another in Wood 16, and, having killed or captured the inmates, received the congratulations of the generous French troops on the left, who were then able to go forward.

For a short time Colonel's Farm hindered the advance of the French, and the platoons of Nos. 2 and 3 Companies, who were in reserve to the Scots Guards, formed a flank to the division, but at 2.45 p.m. the line was level.

Meanwhile a half-company of the 4th Battalion Grenadier Guards and of the Scots Guards, who formed a special brigade carrying party, rushed up material to the Grenadier Guards H.Q. in Scots House, and to the Welsh Guards H.Q. in Sauvage House, and two sections of the 55th Field Company R.E. started to wire the Green Line the moment it was captured—the Welsh Guards having already consolidated the line in front of Wood 15. A pack convoy, under 162 Cpl. D. Luker, was also rushed up with material.

Arthur Gibbs says :

" I am afraid that we have not killed many Huns, as they ran too fast for us long before we came up to them. . . . With the exception of the short check at Colonel's Farm the French went through each objective side by side with our troops, and farther to the left went considerably beyond their last objective. The artillery support throughout the battle was magnificent: the creeping barrage was a uniform and unmistakable line behind which our troops advanced at a distance of only fifty yards; the counter battery work was so effective that the Germans never put down an effective barrage. A smoke barrage put down to cover the forming up of the 4th Battalion Grenadier and 2nd Battalion Scots Guards behind the Black Line was most successful. Communications worked exceedingly well . . . the brigade forward party was a complete success. . . . The medical arrangements worked so well that the whole battle-field was cleared of wounded by 10 a.m."

By 3 p.m. the 1st Battalion Grenadier Guards had taken over the whole of the Blue Line, and the Welsh Guards had moved back to Elverdinghe.

The actual advance of the division was up to the banks of the Steenbeek. The total captures of the division were 750 prisoners, 30 machine guns, and 1 howitzer.

The casualties of the battalion were 138, and amongst them were the gallant Lieut. R. R. Jones, mortally wounded, Lieuts. Rice and Arthur slightly.

The battle was now well launched. It had started with over 6,000 prisoners and the gain of important ground—the Pilkem Ridge, which the Guards Division had looked at for some months the previous year; but it was only a commencement, and for some months the fighting was of a most severe nature.

In some respects this third battle of Ypres was very like the Somme. On July 1st, 1916, there was a big full parade attack, which was held up on the left; on July 31st, 1917, there was also a full parade attack, and it was held up on the right; in each case the first big battle was cut down to a series of bloody struggles for limited objectives, in which the British artillery, concentrated

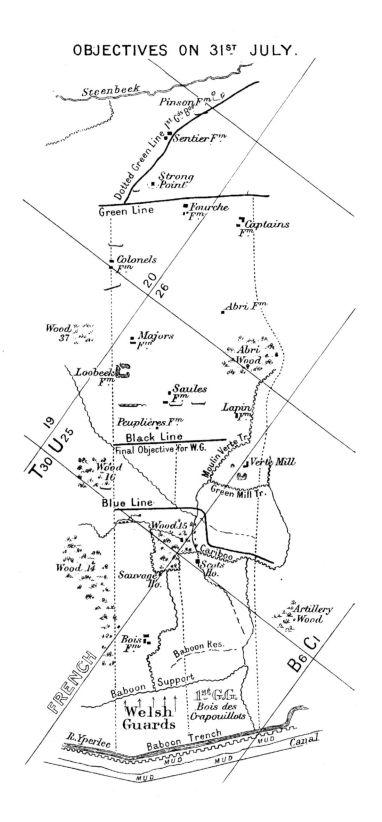

OBJECTIVES ON 31ST JULY.

to a greater extent than ever before, blew the handful of Germans who had remained in that small area to pieces, and enabled the British infantry to advance with very few casualties—except where a blockhouse occasionally gave trouble, or, what seemed more frequently to be the case, troops reached the point where the enemy knew the barrage would no longer be effective, and the German gunners would then concentrate on the British and blow them to pieces, and the German infantry would counter-attack. It was an artillery battle, and right gallantly did the artillery fight it. But the difficulties of Ypres were greater than those of the Somme, and the one great difficulty, as at the Somme, was the state of the ground. As ducks puddle a pond so did the artillery puddle this ground until the water could not sink, and, if it ran at all, did so from one shell-hole to another—and then apparently back again. Also, from the individual soldier's point of view, which had nothing to do with the larger tactical situation, the capture of one ridge always exposed another on which the enemy was firmly established.

In one important respect the experience of the division at the third battle of Ypres differed from the battle of the Somme—they did not see so many dead Germans, and Arthur Gibbs's lament was echoed throughout the battalion.

As at the battle of the Somme progress was slow, but the organisation to surmount the difficulties was extremely well thought out. A swarm of pioneers followed close on the heels of the assaulting troops, and roads of some sort were constructed, and guns and supplies got up to the line. The third battle of Ypres was a great effort.

The battalion rested after the attack in a camp near Zommerbloom Cabaret, on the south-west side of the Elverdinghe—Woesten Road, and before going into the line again on August 4th lost the services of Allan Perrins, who had been adjutant since the battalion arrived in France. A cheerful, active, hard-working fellow, who could keep his own counsel; he was a great loss to the battalion—but the staff is the road a successful adjutant generally takes, and so Perrins went to the XIV Corps. He was succeeded by Geoffrey Devas.

The Commanding Officer being on leave, Luxmoore Ball took the battalion into the line, which was along the bank of the Steenbeek to the west of Ruisseau Farm.

The line was not a trench, but rather a series of fortified shell-holes, which was perhaps fortunate, as the enemy's artillery fire was very severe; but he did not know the precise position of troops, and casualties were small—the best shooting was made on known spots such as Battalion H.Q. at Captain Farm, the Prince of Wales's and No. 2 Companies H.Q. at Signal Farm, and at Fourche Farm, where the other two companies had headquarters.

Some good patrol work was done by Battye and Bonn, who found some undamaged bridges across the Steenbeek; but otherwise there was nothing of note, and the 4th Battalion Grenadier Guards took over the line on the 6th.

The battalion marched to Elverdinghe—a heavy, tiring march through the lines of guns which had already crossed the canal—and entrained for Proven, arriving at 4.30 a.m. and finding quarters in Petworth Camp.

H.R.H. the Prince of Wales visited the camp on the 9th and went round his company lines, and on the 25th the 3rd Brigade was inspected by Gen. Antoine, commanding the First French Army, who presented the following with decorations: Lieut.-Col. Douglas Gordon, 2/Lieut. Lascelles, 2,254 Cpl. T. J. Evans, 2,270 Pte. T. L. Evans, 1,870 Pte. T. G. Hill with the Croix de Guerre, and Sergt.-Major Bland with the Médaille Militaire and the Croix de Guerre.

Strengthened by drafts of 150 men and Lieut. Hargreaves, 2/Lieuts. Ballard, Webb, and Tennant, the battalion went by train to Elverdinghe on the 27th and camped at Bleuet Farm; the 2nd Battalion Scots Guards were relieved in the front line, which was now to the left

WOOD 15 AFTER THE ATTACK.

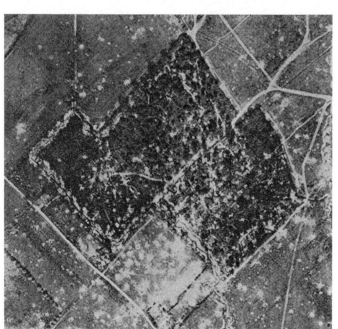

WOOD 15 BEFORE THE BOMBARDMENT.

158]

of Langemark and on the banks of the Broembeek, on the 31st.

It will be remembered that the XIV Corps was part of the Fifth Army (Gough), and on this army had fallen most of the fighting up to this date. In September the Second Army (Plumer—" Good old Plum," as the troops called him) took charge from the southern extremity of the attack to south of Langemark, and the series of fierce fights round and about Polygon Wood took place, winning ground all the time, but none of them planned to go to any great depth, and consisting for the most part of easy advances, immediately followed by bitter counter-attacks strongly pressed with strong forces.

Langemark therefore came in for some severe shelling, although no advance was attempted at that point. The line was held by shell-hole posts, and they were very scattered. The danger of enemy attack too was ever imminent. Ptes. 2,138 J. Lloyd Roberts, 2,661 J. Lewis, 2,759 T. Griffiths, and 2,851 T. Evans were names of men that were noted as having remained at duty though wounded (Lewis in seven places), and to remain at duty meant that they were squatting, wet to the skin, in mud-filled shell-holes.

The battalion was relieved by the 2nd Battalion Coldstream Guards on the 4th, and until September 21st worked on forward fatigues from the camp at De Wippe Cabaret and from Eton Camp. During this last tour of duty, however, the regiment lost a charming young officer, Tennant, a clever youngster who had shown in the few days he had been in action the greatest contempt for danger.

The next move was via Petworth Camp to Herzelle on the 22nd, and here, billeted in farm-houses amidst green trees, a programme of training for attack was carried out. The idea was open fighting, and the training ended in a brigade field day.

Some effort was made at this time to speed up the signalling section of the battalion. It was a difficult problem. Given highly trained men, it did not present insuperable difficulties, but many months of training are

required to get the ideal signaller, and he is as vulnerable
as any other man to wounds and sickness.   The problem
for the battalion in action was not one of laying wires
and shouting down a telephone; experience has shown
that wires do not stand two minutes through a bombardment; the alternative was visual signals.

Sergt. Hughes was in command of the signallers, and
was a good, hard-working signaller; Sergt. Thomas
and Sergt. Couch were also good men.   But they had
a difficult job.   It is curious that we never adopted
any system of rockets or Verey lights.   The problem
of communication in the barrage area has yet to be
solved.

On the 29th the battalion moved to Paddington Camp
near Proven, and heard they would attack again on
October 10th.

The activity of the " Forward Area " enveloped all
the country round Proven; the roads were thick with
traffic all the way up to the fighting lines, and enemy
aeroplanes were busy at night.

A great stride had been made by this time in anti-
aircraft measures.   Since 1916 searchlights abounded,
and at night, when the warning drone of an enemy
machine was heard, the sky would be lit up with criss-
cross shafts; when found, the aeroplane appeared as a
ghostly grey moth with a silver sheen on it.   Tracer
bullets were being used, and guns were plentiful.

As the war progressed it became more and more insisted upon that, when arrangements were once made, no
alteration or modification could be permitted even with
a battle in view.   Jack Crawshay had been dragged out
of the battle on the Somme to go on a Lewis Gun course,
and, trying to gallop across country in the dark, had fallen
from his horse and put his shoulder out, an accident
which took him home.   It had now been arranged that
Luxmoore Ball should go to England on a senior officers'
course at Aldershot, and, although the Commanding
Officer had gone to Paris on leave, and an action was
pending, Ball had to go.   He left on the 4th and Major
Jack Stirling, of the 2nd Battalion Scots Guards, com-

Langemarck.

Died 27.

Catalin
Farm.

A VIEW OF THE BATTLE-FIELD, THIRD BATTLE OF YPRES.

manded the battalion until Lieut.-Col. Douglas Gordon returned from Paris.

On the 5th a forward move was made to Cambridge Camp, near Elverdinghe, and on the 8th the battalion moved up to Wood 15, the brigade being in reserve for the attack.[1]

The attack was a short one, and had for its objective a line south of Houthulst Forest. The 1st Guards Brigade was on the right, and the 2nd Guards Brigade on the left; on the right of the division was the 86th Brigade of the 29th Division, and on the left the French.

Battalion H.Q. was in Saules Farm—or rather in a German pill-box near that farm, which was occupied by the brigade. Houthulst Forest was at the top of the usual sort of ridge found in the Ypres district, and quite a lot of the ridge could be seen from the top of the pill-box.

It was one of the few occasions when the battalion could sit as at a theatre and watch a battle in progress.

On the left of Battalion H.Q. was a row of other pill-boxes occupied by French artillery officers, who had their batteries just in front (the well-known advice not to camp near batteries was lost here, as the whole country was one vast gun-park), and at zero hour, 5.30 a.m., on October 9th the French and British guns opened with that volume of noise made new to the world by this war, and which was a continual fascination to all who heard it.

On the tops of the pill-boxes, of every mound of earth, even on stumps of trees, clustered little groups of interested watchers with field-glasses and telescopes. The French officers made themselves comfortable with chairs and tables for their maps, and all—guns, observers and spectators—were in full view of the enemy.

The French 75 mm. batteries put up a wonderful barrage, but there was little to choose between them and the British. Like a distant shower on the ocean the barrage crept forward, and behind it the brown line of

[1] Appendix B 8.

British soldiers and the blue line of French. They disappeared amongst the smoke and trees.

All objectives were captured and the battalion was not wanted that day ; but at 9 p.m. the following evening the battalion relieved the 2nd Battalion Grenadier and 1st Battalion Coldstream Guards, having to pass through a German barrage which was suddenly put down on the line of the Broembeek. The march up to the relief was fearful—the mud appalling, the ground so cut up that it was no longer possible to go round shell-holes, which had to be taken as they came, the men sliding in and clambering out.

Arthur Gibbs took over the right of the line, with Bonsor and Fripp ; and the left was taken by Battye and Taylor, Hebert and Newall. Roderick, with No. 3, and Bonn, with No. 2, took up shell-hole positions in support, but their lot was not enviable, as they were shelled from pillar to post, and were for ever moving backward and forward trying to avoid the enemy barrage.

Headquarters was in Louvois Farm, a dugout of fair proportions and doubtful strength, and was the point which everyone made for who had any business anywhere in the front line. Besides the headquarters staff under Drill-Sergt. Roberts, there were always several gunners or Engineers who dropped in to get a little shelter from the shells.

The 3rd Guards Brigade, which held the whole of the Divisional Front, and the 8th French Infantry Regiment on the left, were now in a pronounced salient, and the line had to be brought up level on the right. An attack was therefore ordered for October 12th, to pivot on the French, but it hardly affected the Welsh Guards, whose greatest advance, on the right, was only about 200 yards. This was carried out on the 11th, thanks to a patrol under 1,795 L/Sergt. Johnson—sent out by Arthur Gibbs as soon as he had taken over the line—who discovered that a blockhouse reported held by the enemy was vacant. Gibbs promptly occupied the post with a couple of Lewis Guns, and had several slight brushes with the enemy patrols, but no serious attempt was made by them

HOUTHULST FOREST. SCENE OF THE ATTACK ON OCTOBER 9TH.

162]

to retake the place.   So when the attack started on the
12th the Prince of Wales's Company were already in
position on their objective.

On the left Percy Battye joined the French.   For a
long time all was very quiet, and Battye came to the
conclusion that the enemy had retired on his front.   He
therefore sent out 2,169 L/Cpl. Davies, with Ptes. 859
Wallace, 2,849 Smith, and 2,259 Waddington to examine
the ground up to the forest.   It was broad daylight and
the men were armed with their rifles and apparently a
couple of bombs each.   After going about 200 yards Cpl.
Davies came across a trench which appeared unoccupied,
but on going nearer he discovered it to be full of the
enemy.   The first man who saw him held up his hands,
and he and his men threw in bombs.   Immediately
shouts and cries and a forest of hands went up from the
trench, and for a moment the small patrol must have
been thrilled with the idea that they were going to make
a big capture ; but a German down the line saw that
there were only four British in the patrol and began to
shoot, wounding Smith, and then the Germans took heart
and made the mistake of trying to capture the patrol.
A dozen or so climbed out of the trench and tried to lay
hands on the men who were attempting to get their
wounded comrade off.   Davies wisely decided to leave
him, and with his two remaining men ran for the company lines, but was himself hit on the way.   In the confusion the other two got off safely, and a French mitrail-
leuse caught the Germans and drove them back to their
trench with loss.   Waddington then went out alone and
brought in Cpl. Davies.   The enemy, however, got Smith
and their own wounded during the night, although Waddington and Wallace made further attempts with the
failing light of evening to get him.

The advance was made with no opposition, but the
battalion came in for all the enemy barrage and subsequent shell-fire when the rest of the brigade did attack
on the 12th, and until the relief by the 2nd Battalion
Coldstream Guards on the 13th the casualties were heavy.
Poor young Newall was killed while having a duel with

a German sniper, Taylor and Hebert were wounded by
shell-fire (Hebert while crossing the Broembeek, but led
his platoon into the line), and Fripp fell on a bayonet in
the dark and received a nasty gash. Bonn and Roderick
were at first driven from one lot of shell-holes to another,
but finally had to abandon all shell-holes owing to the
rain and had to sit about in the mud. First Bonn and
then Roderick came into headquarters and reported
moving their companies, and as they became more and
more tired Roderick became more gentle in manner and
Bonn got louder and drawled worse than ever.

One of the greatest annoyances came from a heavy
gun of our own which was firing short. Nothing could
apparently stop it, although it was causing casualties.
In desperation Jack Stirling loosed the pigeons to Corps
H.Q. with rude messages. Still it went on shooting the
battalion in the back. The Prince of Wales came up to
the line, and the gun started to drop shells all round him,
so that he and Gen. Gaythorne Hardy had to double
across to some pill-boxes in the Grenadier lines. With
great delight this incident was reported, but had no
result. Finally Col. Vickery, commanding the brigade of
field-artillery behind the battalion, was chased by this
gun all the way from the Broembeek to Louvois Farm.
His language was picturesque and profane. About two
hours after he had left the front line the gun, for some
reason or other, fired no more—or else confined its attention to the enemy.

The Commanding Officer returned from Paris on the
12th, and the battalion marched out in pitch darkness
and arrived at Larrie Camp, near Elverdinghe, in the
early morning of the 14th. They were wet to the skin
and covered with mud from head to foot. The camp was
bombed by aeroplanes during the morning. On the 16th
the battalion left for Watten, passing through a camp in
the forest area and Paddock Wood Camp at Proven,
whence the journey was completed by train. From
Watten—where Humphrey Dene, recovered from his
illness, met them—the battalion marched to Serques on
October 20th.

POSITIONS BEFORE HOUTHULST FOREST.

Houthulst Forest

P. of W. Coy. advance

Egypt Ho.

c
c
c
c
c
c
c
6
12
c
c
c
c
c

Faidherbe X Roads

No. 4 Coy.

Line taken over by W.G.

c
c
c
c
c
c
Louvois F.ᵐ

c
c c
c c
c c

U 4

10

Koekuit

c c
c

c c
c

16 17

29ᵗʰ Divⁿ

U 9

15

Cemetery

c
c c
c c
c

c
c

1ˢᵗ G.ᵈˢ B.ᵈᵉ

Ney Copse

Ney Wood

Broembeek

2ⁿᵈ G.ᵈˢ B.ᵈᵉ

French

Forming up Line

The losses of the battalion in the third battle of Ypres were far less than they had been in the Somme, and the total casualties of the period only came to 451. The battle went on till November, and the total number of captures by the British were 24,065 prisoners, 74 guns, 941 machine guns, 138 trench-mortars.

CHAPTER XII

THE battalion was quartered at Serques from October
20th to November 9th. St. Omer was within easy reach,
and nearer still was the small town of Watten, but, however small and insignificant the town, provided it was
not knocked about and was able to carry on something
like normal commerce, it always proved an irresistible
attraction for troops. It will be found that the Welshman
makes the smartest of soldiers—he has in him a natural
inclination for "cutting a dash"—and the moment he
arrived near any civilian-inhabited place he would take
an extra pride in his appearance. Consequently when
the Duke of Connaught paid a surprise visit on the 21st,
and the troops lined the streets of Serques, they presented a most creditable appearance, in spite of the fact
that they had only just come out of battle.

A few days later, the 25th, the Commander-in-Chief,
Sir Douglas Haig, inspected the whole division at Inglingham. These inspections were the occasions for ironic
cheers and laughter in the privacy of company messes.
There was always a fierce discussion whether such a thing
as quarter column still existed, or whether it was done
away with by the drill-book of 1914. By some it was
called quarter column, and by others column of half
companies—no one attempted to used the word "mass."
On this occasion companies were limited to 120 and 3
officers, and the parade was drawn up in a fashion which
was neither quarter column nor, strictly speaking, column
or close column of half companies. The march past was

on a rough field and a terrific gale of wind was blowing ;
it will therefore be appreciated that it was not too easy
as a parade.   However, the men did well, and for the
first time saw Sir Douglas Haig, who gave the impression
of being tired—his eyes were dull and his face a grey
colour.

Gen. Antoine, who was a great favourite in the division, was also to inspect the whole unit a few days later,
but, after marching to the parade ground the inspection
was cancelled owing to the bad weather; he did, however,
present decorations to officers, Percy Battye receiving
the Croix de Guerre.

The inhabitants of Serques were very hospitable people,
and made officers and men as comfortable as possible.
And at least the question so often asked in other towns—
" Where are all the pretty women of France ? "—did not
apply to Serques, where dwelt certainly one of the
prettiest girls in France.   Her mother kept an estaminet,
but, although the daughter attracted a number of people
to drink coffee, no payment was accepted.

The chief events at Serques were race meetings held
at Inglingham on October 28th and November 4th.
Humphrey Dene rode his horse " Ñato " and the Commanding Officer's horse " Charles," and Percy Battye
the No. 4 Company horse, a stiff-legged, hard-mouthed
brute called " Dick," but they were outclassed.   The
divisional train found some top-hats and frock-coats
and introduced the flourishing firm of " Pilckem and
Bilckem "; on this occasion they made money, but were
not always so fortunate.   Altogether two good days of
sport.

The billets were somewhat scattered.   Battye and his
company were away near Watten in some farmhouses,
and led a solitary though happy existence.   Roderick
and No. 3 were half a mile nearer, but even so a good
mile from headquarters.   The Prince of Wales's, No. 2,
and the transport under Goetz were in the village.

The battalion now consisted of : headquarters—Lieut.
Col. Douglas Gordon, Major Humphrey Dene, Capt.
Devas (Adjutant), Lieut. Martin Smith (Assistant Adju-

12

tant), Lieut. Dudley Ward (signalling officer) ; Prince of Wales's Company—Capt. Arthur Gibbs (on a month's leave), Lieut. Devereux, 2/Lieuts. Bonsor, E. J. Davies, and Llewellyn ; No. 2 Company—Capt. the Earl of Lisburne, Capt. Bonn, 2/Lieuts. Dickens, Webb, Borough; No. 3 Company—Capt. Roderick, Lieut. Menzies, 2/Lieuts. Kearton, Ballard, and Baness; No. 4 Company—Capt. Battye, 2/Lieuts. Hargreaves, Bowyer, Wreford Brown.

During the stay at Serques Lord Cavan was sent out to Italy, and for a time there was a rumour that the Guards Division would go too.

On November 9th the division left the XIV Corps and started on a march to the St. Pol district, the First Army area, where it would be in G.H.Q. reserve. The route was through Enguinegatte and Heuchin to Buneville—a fine country, well timbered, with beautiful autumn-tint vistas from the summits of the rolling hills. The journey was accomplished without incident beyond a farcical dispute at Heuchin—one of the most hospitable towns encountered—between one of the inhabitants and the Prince of Wales's Company :

" A somewhat prim young man came in with a formidable blue paper, and said a claim had been made against the men for taking straw and spoiling some grain. We went to the barn and the men admitted taking what seemed to them some used straw. The prim man became excited at once, said it was unthreshed straw, dived into a corner and produced a handful of grain and chaff, which he said was ruined, and claimed that the damage was great. He would bring the ' Adjoint ' next morning, he said, to value the stuff. The next morning there was a great meeting in the barn—Dene, the prim young man (who turned out to be the Mayor's nephew deputising for his uncle), the ' Garde Champêtre,' the ' Adjoint,' and the whole platoon who were in that barn. The prim young man began to state the claim, when suddenly the Adjoint, a sprightly old gentleman of some eighty summers, pounced on the straw with a scream of indignation, and, holding up a handful, asked six or seven times, regardless of any reply, if this was the straw ? Then threw it on the ground and called the claimant a dishonest thief, and announced that it was old straw and not worth anything. The claimant began to shout out a long story about his grain, but the old boy replied that as he had started to claim about old straw he would have nothing more to do with the case. He then walked out with gesticulations ! Claimant followed, Prim Young Man followed, Garde Champêtre followed, all talking and gesticulating, and so disappeared down the street. Complete victory for us ! Dene, puffing at a small and very foul pipe, his hands deep in his pockets, and his lean jaw stuck out, says : ' They are crazy. . . . Alphonse has gone crazy. . . . He has bats in the belfry. . . . Come on and see " Lizzie " ' (Lisburne)."

The battalion stayed a week at Buneville, training in open warfare and outposts. There was a secret conference at divisional headquarters, but the secret was very well kept, and in spite of excitement and rumours concerning numbers of tanks which·had been seen, no one seems to have suspected any further action for the division beyond taking over a new line from the French. The general feeling in the battalion at that moment seems to have been that the Italians were right out of the war, and that it would go on for years. To most people their next leave was the limit of their vision, and the most cheery men to talk to were Dene and Jack Stirling of the 2nd Battalion Scots Guards. Stirling never talked of the war in a local sense ; he was always full of news as to the condition of Germany, of troops drawn off the Western Front by some demonstration or other, and of French, British and American manpower. Dene was less interested in state-craft and strategy than fighting, and expressed himself emphatically : " For heaven's sake ! let us go forward and fight. . . . Let us finish the war. I don't want to live hoping for a billet behind the line—and what a billet ! —or leave every three months ! Give me discomfort, anything you like, for six or ten months, and let us finish the thing ! "

But the signs of something like active war were increasing. Buneville was to be left and orders were given to reduce kit, a dump for surplus kit being made at St. Pol.

The division moved on the 17th, and the battalion, marching via Grand Rullecourt, learned at Berles au Bois what the plan was. As at first explained, there were to be two attacks—the southern one (which did take place) and a northern one to cut in above Marquion—and the combined operations would, it was hoped, result in the fall of Cambrai. When the line had been pierced the division were to go through the gap with cavalry. No details were given ; it was just a broad indication, summed up in even more condensed fashion by Lisburne, who said, " We are supposed to capture Cambrai ! "

The battalion was now in the shell-devastated area. Berles au Bois was within a few hundred yards of the line which the enemy had evacuated in the spring, but there were still habitable houses, though most of them were scarred, and a few civilians.

The policy of limiting companies was again followed, and Bonsor, Llewellyn, and Ballard departed with 200 men to Bus les Artois. The battalion proceeded to Achiet le Petit, where it remained until the 22nd.

The march to Achiet le Petit was of the greatest interest to a battalion which had not been in that part of the country since the battle of the Somme. Already companies of coolies were clearing the wire and débris from the ground ; in many places the peasants were back on their reconquered farms, and had ploughed up their fields ; at Bienvillers and Bucquoy there were one or two lath-and-plaster cottages with red-tile roofs. The camp (canvas) was outside the village Achiet le Petit, of which very little remained.

The battle started on the 20th, and from that moment the battalion was under two hours' notice to move. All sorts of rumours came drifting in ; the first official news was on the 21st, when it was announced that Flesquières and Mœuvres were captured, and that the gallant 51st Division were moving to attack Bourlon Wood. The cavalry had crossed the Canal de L'Escaut, and the III Corps held the greater part of Gonnelieu Spur. On the 22nd the battalion marched about 2 a.m.

The approach to the battle was most confused. The first stage was by bus to Rocquigny, arriving there at 8.30 a.m., and leaving early on the 23rd for Beaumetz. But no very long halt was made there, and that night the brigade marched in single file across country via Doignies, Demicourt, and Graincourt to Flesquières, the division coming under the orders of the IV Corps. The night was dark and the track soft and heavy; no one knew where they were going, and the difficulties of keeping touch were enormous. The Welsh Guards were the rear battalion, and spent long periods either waiting by the side of the muddy track or doubling wildly after disappearing men in front of them. However, the battalion eventually took over German dugouts from some of the weary 51st Division in the early morning of the 24th.

The fighting on that part of the front which affects us was in the order of events as follows. The 51st Division had captured Flesquières on the 21st, and towards the evening had also taken the village of Fontaine Notre Dame, due east of Bourlon Wood. But the surprise of the British attack was over, and the enemy ready to counter-attack with strong forces. On the 22nd the 51st Division lost Fontaine; it attacked again on the 23rd without result. On the left of the 51st Division was the 40th Division, both being controlled by the IV Corps, and the latter operating against Bourlon Wood. The situation on the evening of the 23rd was not very clear, as a wire timed 7 p.m. states (to Third Army): "Situation indefinite, but R.F.C. are certain we hold Fontaine and Bourlon Village. Situation at Mœuvres still doubtful, but south position at least probably held by us"; and at 11.34 p.m. the Third Army instructs: "The success of to-day's operations must be assured at all costs, and if the leading brigade of the 40th Division have suffered heavily they should be relieved by their reserves or reinforced by part of the Guards Division."

The 40th Division was counter-attacked and driven from the high ground in Bourlon Wood. The operations which followed were of a piecemeal description. The 2nd Battalion Scots Guards were attached to the 40th Division ; the 4th Battalion Grenadier Guards were soon after placed under the orders of the 2nd Guards Brigade, and so were the Welsh Guards.

The scene round Flesquières was unbelievable. Companies were quartered round the cross-roads to the west of Flesquières, and headquarters was in a small quarry on the south of the village. Looking from the high ground towards Havrincourt Wood, the line of advance was revealed by the tank tracks, by the dead bodies of the enemy, and by abandoned equipment of all kinds. On the crest of the rise lay seven battered tanks, the work, it was said, of a German artillery major, who alone had remained with his guns (he is said to have put sixteen out of action). The brigadier gave orders that his body should be found and buried with honour, but although search was made all round the gun emplacements no trace of such a person could be discovered. Between Flesquières and Bourlon Wood was a plain or wide valley, and this was the scene of the most furious activity. With magnificent impertinence the gunners had drawn up their field-guns and lighter howitzers in rows, and all the work of batteries in action was going on in full view of the enemy.

The attack at Bourlon Wood by the 40th Division and 2nd Battalion Scots Guards took place and was successful, and one company of the Welsh Guards was ordered up in close support on the Graincourt—Marcoing Road. This fell to Roderick and No. 3 Company on the night of the 25th. On the night of the 26th the whole battalion moved up to the same road in support to the 2nd Guards Brigade attack—companies in sequence with the Prince of Wales on the right.

" The H.Q. Dugout is a small quarry in a little copse

and is part of the very strong support system of the
Boche. Our first look round in daylight was most interesting. The battle-field was all in front of us—the
smashed tanks, smashed German aeroplanes, the deep
German trenches, with the German dead and kit lying
about in the utmost confusion, and the tracks of the
tanks showing where they had cruised down the lines,
obliterating the wire and shooting down the trenches—
great work and a very fair advance. The ground is all
clean grass land with scarcely a shell-hole.

" At 5 p.m. on the 24th we were warned to go up to
the line—at 6 p.m. the order was cancelled, and Jack
Stirling went up with the 2nd Battalion Scots Guards.
It rained hard all night, but I heard this morning he had
done well (November 25th). . . . After a good night's
rest we again went forward (Douglas and I) on fresh
orders to prepare to move to another place just behind
the attacking troops. We rode there and trotted about
in full view of the Boche and within long rifle-range—
working parties and field-artillery men were doing the
same, and two tanks were worming around—but not a
shot was fired at us. Mick Rowlette has been talking
to a German doctor, who says they are purely on the
defensive. We found the people we were to relieve (the
4th Battalion Grenadier Guards) in a gorgeous though
unfinished dugout—a room about fourteen feet square,
underground and with thick concrete ceiling, and from
it a stairway leading to further underground galleries.
The place is furnished with cupboards, chairs, tables,
shelves for books, pigeon-holes for papers, looking-glasses
and a fireplace. Can't think why the Huns ran.

" We went back, and soon after Arthur Gibbs arrived
from leave. Then Calverly Bewicke to say orders had
again been cancelled."

The attack was launched at 6.20 a.m. on the 27th, and
the 2nd Brigade gained the village of Fontaine Notre
Dame, also the far edge of Bourlon Wood. The Prince
of Wales's and No. 2 Companies were at once moved to
Bourlon Wood, where they would be under the orders

of Viscount Gort, commanding the 4th Battalion Grenadier Guards. Arthur Gibbs and Lisburne had a most
unenviable task, having to cross wide open country in
full view of the enemy, who had already put down a
heavy barrage on their path. They suffered a few
casualties.

"We had orders to move on the 26th. The brigadier
wanted us to go early, so that Jack Stirling's battalion
could take our billets, but, as there was no place to go to
while we waited for zero hour, and as we had been lent
to another brigade, who did not want us to get on the
road at all until they had moved, Douglas managed to
avoid that evil. The whole business was very sudden—
just a short order that an attack would take place and
that we should be in support. D.G. took me to Brigade
H.Q., where a conference was going on, and we saw how
war is made. The conference was in a country house on
the outskirts of the village (Flesquières). There were no
doors, windows, or furniture, but a few shell-holes in the
walls. All the floors and passages were covered with wet
mud from the many people who were passing in and out.
One doorway was covered with bits of sacking and part
of a window-shutter, but the other rooms were open to
view from the passage, and seemed to be full of people
apparently engaged in making tea, or watching it being
made. Everyone was smoking and everyone looked
dirty.
"We pushed aside the sack-and-shutter door and found
a lot of people bending over a table on which were maps
and a number of candles in bottles or tins. These people
were the Brigadier (Brook) and the various Commanding
Officers discussing the attack. And here it was we received orders to move at five in the morning.
"We went back to our dugout and dined. Then
Jack Stirling arrived and told us of his experience as he
changed his clothes—it was snowing hard. He had been
ordered to take a wood of 600 acres with his 500 men. We
talked to him till 3.30 a.m. and then departed, picked up
the battalion, and marched down the track of a Boche

railway to a sunken road. It was raining. Some companies found shelter in old Boche dugouts, but mostly the men crouched under the bank.

" I hung on to D.G. like wax, having nothing else to do, and went with him to the new Brigade H.Q. in a farm (La Justice)—only to be told to return at 7 a.m.

" At 6.20 a.m. the battle started, and we should have had a good view but for the rain. D.G. and I were just behind the battalion in a gunner's dugout with a wire out to brigade. Very soon we had news that all objectives had been captured, and we thought that we should not be moved forward until the next day. But D.G. was sent for about 11 a.m. and I went too. Here was a repetition of the former brigade scene, only the brigadier was worried. He sat in a vaulted cellar with a small table, a map, a telephone, two smoking candles, and a blue pencil. The cellar was very stuffy, and was crowded with all sorts of people, who wrote on bits of paper, or ate bully beef, drank tea, or simply sat on the floor smoking cigarettes and waiting for orders. He said the situation was not too clear, and that two companies must go up to the wood at once. Then we had to race back and tell Arthur Gibbs and Lisburne to be off at once. They were practically ready, and we watched them going over a fold in the ground towards the distant wood and the Boche barrage. . . .

" In the gunner's dugout we waited for news. The gunners told us now and then what their fire orders were, so we were able to judge the progress, and gathered that all objectives had been taken. At about 3.30 we were up at brigade again. The brigadier, with the blue-pencilled map in front of him, was very busy with the telephone, reports coming in every few minutes. He was at least very concentrated, talking down the 'phone and pointing with his pencil to the map, as though the person at the other end of the wire was in front of him. ' By Jove!' he said, ' that is a funny-looking line! Go back!'

" Briefly he told us that, although objectives had been reached, casualties were very heavy, the front was exten-

sive, and he had ordered everyone back to their original
position. We were to go and relieve the 2nd Irish at
once. D.G. then told me to go straight up to the line
and find out what was happening. I took an orderly
with me, and had to go a long way round to avoid the
barrage which the Boche kept going. At last I reached
the wood and found the most frightful confusion. The
roads or tracks were filled with men and pack-horses—
shells were bursting all over the place and had a frightful
echo through the wood. The place we made for was a
small chalet in the centre, and round it were crowds of
men from every sort of unit and heaps of wounded. It
was so filled inside and out that I had to push my way
through. Alexander, of the Irish, was not there, having
moved his headquarters to his front line. It took me
much time and a lot of shouting to find someone who
knew where the line was—being somewhat old in war I
was not going to plunge about a wood at dusk while the
enemy were still in it. Alexander was on the high ground
in the wood, in a dugout just below a tall tree, with
observation platforms built amongst the branches. He
told me all there was to tell—how there was a strong
point filled with machine guns just inside the north-east
corner of the wood, and that it had defied all efforts to
capture it. He traced the line on a map for me and
gave me guides, and I departed. I dropped the guides
at their various companies—including Arthur Gibbs and
Lisburne, who had been held back in support on the near
edge of the wood—and returned to D.G. He had dined,
so I ate hastily as I told him of the situation, and off we
started. I was very tired with these three journeys, and
wet through, and, not having had a change for three days,
my feet were very sore. I was grateful for a fireplace
the Boche had made. We found the situation had become complicated by a belief that quite a number of men
had not been recalled and were still out beyond the
Boche strong point. Also no one seemed to know exactly
where the troops on our left were. D.G. was ordered by
the brigade to send out a patrol and find the missing men.
Kearton, from No. 3 Company, was selected. The relief

was completed, and, accompanied by Alexander, who refused to leave until he had heard the patrol report, we
started to visit the line.   But before we had gone more
than fifty yards through the trees a most furious fusillade
was started by someone on our left and was at once
answered by the Boche.   The air was filled with bullets,
and we jumped for shelter.   When it had stopped and
I got up from under a bank I found the others had gone,
so I returned to the dugout and found Alexander fast
asleep and D.G. brooding by the fire.   Before we made
a second attempt Kearton came back and reported being
shot at every time he tried to get round the wood.   The
enemy, he said, were right across the corner of the wood,
and had posts in the open too.   Alexander then went
back, and we round the line.   Nothing happened next
day (28th) except endless discussions with brigade as to
the exact position of our line.   So far as I know we were
not many yards out in our reports.

" In due course we were relieved and got out about
midnight.   The tracks were blocked with troops and
horses, and shelling was continuous.   To add to the
enjoyment, the Hun started gas-shelling, and I, as guide
to H.Q., fairly legged it, having lost my gas-bag—took
them across country and a bit off the line in the dark,
but we only went about a mile farther than we need have
done, and reached our billets about four in the morning."
—*Diary, C. H. D. W.*

Relieved by the 2/6th Battalion North Staffordshire
Regiment, the battalion marched to Ribecourt, and after
a short rest to a camp south of Trescault.

The rumour was that the division would remain in
the vicinity of Havrincourt Wood and work for a few
days on the roads, after which they would move out of
the sector altogether.

The camp was on a ploughed field which had been
churned up into a fearful state, and a move was made
to clear the wire from a corner of the wood, with the
object of pitching camp on cleaner ground, when at
9.30 a.m. on November 30th the Adjutant's (Geoffrey

Devas) rotund figure was seen plunging through the mud. He had an apologetic smile and a diffident manner as he announced that all companies would stand by to move at a moment's notice. "The Hun has broken through our line. . . . A hell of a mess up," said he.

Ammunition was hurriedly made up ; officers who were taking things easy, and had not yet breakfasted, found Sergt. Marshall packing up, but he provided them with a glass of port and a biscuit ; the drummers looked after the baggage and loaded it on the waggons.

One has only to look at the map and mark the bulge made in the German line to realise what he was doing. The hope of the Third Army was to capture the high ground of Bourlon and Fontaine, but troops had never been able to complete this operation, and the enemy succeeded in pinning the British effort to the apex of the salient. To hurry troops up and attack the long exposed right flank of the British, and follow the advance by a strong and main blow between Mœuvres and Fontaine would, provided they had sufficient troops, justify the hope of the German High Command to capture the whole of the British forces in the salient.

As the original attack from the line Gonnelieu—Hermies pushed north a right flank had been formed east of Banteaux, by Bois Lateau, and so to the east of Marcoing (where a crossing was established over the Escault Canal) to Noyelles, to the east of Cantaing, to Fontaine. The new line was not therefore a great distance from the old line north-east of Gonnelieu.

The right flank from Cantaing to Banteaux Ravine was held by five divisions ; from Banteaux Ravine to Vendhuille by one division. The German attack on this flank opened about 8 a.m. on November 30th, and was completely successful in its first stages. The British guns which had been moved close up to the line in order to cover the Masnières Line were taken. The deepest advance was to Gouzeaucourt.

Between 10 and 11 a.m. the Germans attacked in great force between Mœuvres and Bourlon Wood, and the VI Corps reported them to have broken through at a

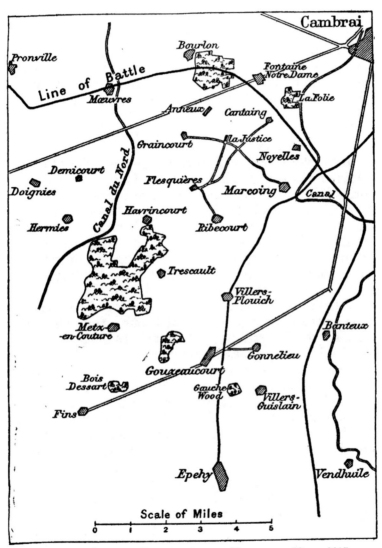

CAMBRAI. LINE OF BATTLE, 8 A.M., NOVEMBER 30TH, 1917.

point which would enable them to get between Grain-court and Mœuvres (the guns in Graincourt were ordered to have their teams up in readiness to withdraw). Other attacks were made from Fontaine, but the enemy seems to have suffered heavily from our guns at this point.

The position was extremely serious. The Guards Division were ordered to secure Gauche Wood and Gon-nelieu Spur; the 2nd Cavalry Division were to move on their right—no other troops were available immediately.

But the information in the hands of the 3rd Brigade was very meagre.

Just before midday the whole brigade marched through Metz-en-Couture and halted north of Bois Dessart. The brigadier then held a conference and viewed the country from the top of a hill. Horsemen could be seen galloping in an apparent aimless way, but otherwise nothing was visible. The news was scant; the Brigadier at the moment knew very little, and, referring to rumours, said a Labour Company was reported to be holding up the enemy, so that it did not look very serious.

Further curt orders came, and the brigade retraced its steps across country to a point about a thousand yards due south of Trescault. The 1st Brigade could then be seen advancing in assaulting lines over the skyline, and as they disappeared the crackle of musketry announced that they had got in touch with the enemy.

Looking back on Havrincourt Wood, where they had been quietly resting, the battalion realised that the position must be serious. Maps were scarce, but later in the day small scale-maps were procured and issued; the scale, however, was too small to give more than a very rough idea of what the country was like.

The 4th Battalion Grenadier Guards were ordered to go forward, and the rest of the brigade halted on the side of a bare hill and waited. It was bitterly cold, and the transport, with the men's food and cookers, had been left on the road.

The country was rolling, down-like hills. On the right and slightly in rear was Gouzeaucourt Wood; behind was Havrincourt Wood; on the left some tanks were moving into a long line.

Darkness came; the men huddled in little groups to keep warm; and still no news.

About 8 p.m. the Commanding Officer was sent for by the brigadier, whom he found squatting on the ground trying to read a map with a small torch. The situation as he then knew it was that the 1st Brigade (de Crespigny) had turned the enemy out of the village of Gouzeaucourt, and that for the moment the 3rd Brigade was not wanted. He had heard of the transport, which would soon be up.

Cheered by this news, the Commanding Officer returned to find the transport arriving with smoking cookers; very soon the men had some food.

And then came another period of waiting. It was a bright moonlight night, frosty and a bitter wind. No one could sleep or attempted to do so. Greatcoats, blankets and packs had been dumped at the camp; the cold was painful.

Just after midnight the brigadier again summoned the Commanding Officer.

Lord Henry Seymour, or Copper, as he was more generally called, was an extraordinary man. Nothing seemed to upset him, and if he was in any way worried he did not show it. Some sort of shelter had now been rigged up for him by means of a waggon tarpaulin, and he had been provided with a candle stuck on an old tin. His brigade-major, Fletcher, had gone on leave the day before, and Calverly Bewicke was doing Fletcher's work, with Cecil Keith to help him. The brigadier, smoking cigarettes, started the conversation by remarking that it was " a damned cold spot." He then announced his orders very briefly.[1]

The Welsh Guards were to attack with the 4th Battalion Grenadier Guards on their left and the 2nd Brigade on their right. The village of Gonnelieu was to be taken, and the ground to the south of it. The advance was not to be beyond the crest of the ridge on which the village

[1] Appendix B 9.

stood. The road from Gouzeaucourt to Gonnelieu would be the boundary between battalions ; the time of attack 6.30 a.m.—eleven tanks would co-operate.

Meanwhile the battalion had been ordered to move, and by the time this short conference was over was already in view. In the moonlight it streamed over the frozen hill to the sunken road just behind Gouzeaucourt. The 4th Battalion Grenadier Guards were there too, and the Commanding Officer went to consult with Lord Gort.

Gort said bluntly that he did not think the attack would succeed, as he had watched an abortive attempt by the 20th Division in the evening, and had never seen such a machine-gun barrage as the enemy put up. There was also a major of tank corps there, and he said he could not produce eleven tanks, as most of them would not " function."

Time was now getting on, and, hastily calling the Company Commanders together, the Commanding Officer ordered that No. 3, with Roderick, should advance on the right, and No. 4, with Hargreaves in command, on the left ; No. 2, with Dickens, would be a second " wave " in support, and the Prince of Wales's Company, with Arthur Gibbs, in reserve. Lisburne was very ill, and only at the very last moment was Dickens given command of No. 2 Company.

There was just time to reconnoitre the road and the forming-up point—a hurried walk through the village and a glimpse of the railway line.

The battalion then marched down to the railway line, where it formed up in two lines. It was then very dark and slightly misty.

No tanks were visible. The men had hardly extended when the order was given to advance, and the two assaulting lines climbed up the railway bank which faced them, and proceeded up the hill, disappearing in the darkness.

There was some wire half-way up the hill, which caused a certain bunching while the men got through the weak parts, and, what had not been known before, there was a false crest to the hill, or, to be more accurate, a deep re-entrant in the ridge from the north-west. The enemy occupied the slight depression which lay in front of the apparent crest, and as the first wave of men reached the first skyline star-lights went up from all sides and a perfect hurricane of machine-gun fire broke out. It was devastating. Officers and men fell in a line. On the left young Wreford Brown, in action for the first time, yelled to his men to lie down, which they did; No. 3 Company had no officers left and retired behind the crest of the hill; No. 2, with Baness alone untouched, were mixed up with No. 3.

The scene was beyond anything that had ever been met with. The ground was thick with dead and wounded men; curses and groans and shouts mingled with the hurricane crackle of the machine guns. And then in the weird light of star-lights in the foggy dawn a crowd of men began to stream down the hill. "What the hell is this?" said Broncho Dene. They were the wounded.

It was the most stupendous noise ever heard, and Dene and the Commanding Officer shouted in each other's ears. It was obvious that no human beings could hope to get through such a concentration of machine-gun fire; there were no field-guns, there were no tanks. Arthur Gibbs and the Prince of Wales's Company were sent for; and meanwhile the stream of dazed and blood-covered men was directed to the side of the railway bank where Mick Rowlette and Sergt. Evans were hard at work.

Arthur Gibbs was ordered to take up a position below the crest and send back any unwounded men there to reform on the railway. Finding some trenches near the spot he put his company in them.

Some little time was taken organising the few remaining stretcher-bearers to help Rowlette and Sergt. Evans; and also arranging for temporary bearers to clear the ground as much as possible.

Sergt. Hicks, of No. 4 Company, was brought in with a broken leg and smoking a cigarette while he calmly expressed the opinion that this was the hottest place he

13

had ever struck. Bowyer, with five bullets through
him, managed to gasp out that he hoped everybody
was not killed; and "Peggy" Kearton, walking between two men, replied with a smile, "Yes, I'm done
for—right through the stomach!" And there were
others.

The ghastly scene was made a field of triumphant
heroism by the men and officers of the three attacking
companies, and it is not detracting from the valour of the
Prince of Wales's Company to say that their courage
was uplifted by the gallant bearing of the shattered
companies they passed through on their way up the
hill.

There was sufficient light to see some 300 yards
through the morning mist when Dene went up the hill
to view the situation. He found Gibbs in some trenches
about sixty yards below the apparent crest of the hill,
and in his quick, energetic way asked, "What is over
there?" "Machine guns," said Gibbs. But Dene declared he was going to look, and crawled up and looked
over the top.

There was some shelling going on, and the first thing
he saw, just in view on the right, was a tank going very
slowly across the hollow between the false and the real
crest. Shells were falling all round it, and all sorts of
coloured lights were going up from the enemy lines
directing the fire. And then he saw Germans running
away.

He at once ordered Gibbs to bring two platoons close
up to the crest, and to watch the movements of the tank
and co-operate when he saw his chance. The running
enemy was making for a trench near the real summit of
the hill, and, from the rifle fire which he started to
direct against the tank, seemed in force. Dene then
went back to report.

The mist lifted and the enemy trench could be plainly
seen by the time the tank got there and turned to the
left, crossing Gibbs's front. It was fighting hard with its
light guns and Lewis Guns, and Gibbs decided it was the
moment for him to advance. He appears to have timed

the move to a second, as he and two platoons got across without a casualty, and relieved the tank of 200 of the enemy who were clustered in front of it with their hands up.

Young Wreford Brown, shot through the wrist, co-operated with him in this movement, with the remains of No. 4 Company, as though he had been on a field-day. The conduct of this youngster (he had been at the Entrenching Battalion for a year because he was under age) was most soldierly. He followed the instructions of the Training Manual in a cool and collected manner, lying down when he thought the machine-gun fire was intense, and advancing when he saw someone moving on his right, all the time with a nasty wound.

Gibbs manned the trench, deciding that he could go no farther with his two platoons, and sent down a report with a request for more men. He had got in touch with the Grenadier Guards on his left, but there was no one on his right. The tank, however, remained there until the Coldstream Guards got in touch on that flank.

To the skilful manœuvring of the tank the success of the advance must be given. Many of the enemy got away, but Gibbs collected no less than twenty-six machine guns in the trench, and there is no doubt, from ammunition-boxes found, that many were taken from the left of the line before the tank could close on it. The prisoners captured included some of the Jaeger Battalion No. 3 of the 2nd Machine Gun Corps, who said their company, with ten heavy machine guns, had reinforced the 1st Battalion of the 3rd Bavarian Ersatz Regiment and the 4th Sturm Battalion holding the line. To face such fire without barrage or the co-operation of tanks was impossible—and yet that is what the Welsh Guards set out to do.

The line was now held with the whole of the Prince of Wales's and No. 4 Companies, and twenty-five men from No. 2 were sent up to strengthen them. The brigadier, visiting the line about 11 a.m., decided that nothing more could be done.

All the wounded were brought in by midday, and only the line of dead remained to speak for the valour of the men. In front of the men were Webb, well ahead on the right, Borough, Roderick, and Hargreaves on the left, quiet, dignified figures lying with their faces to the enemy.

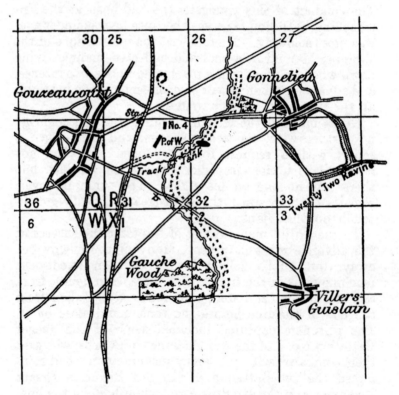

ATTACK ON THE GONNELIEU RIDGE.

Of the 370 men who started to storm the hill 248 were down in the first three minutes. Fifty-seven died where they fell.

Of the remaining officers, Kearton died the next day, but Bowyer recovered, as did Dickens, Devereux and Wreford Brown.

Two platoons of the King's Company 1st Battalion Grenadier Guards came up as reinforcements that night. Bitterly cold weather set in, and the battalion was relieved by the 1st Battalion Grenadier Guards (with the exception of the Prince of Wales's Company, which was left in support) on the night of December 2nd. The battalion marched back to bivouacs in Gouzeaucourt Wood.

By this time guns were beginning to arrive, replacing those captured by the enemy. A howitzer battery established itself in the wood, which became an unpleasant place for rest. It is interesting to note that the battalion recaptured one battery of field-guns between Gouzeaucourt and Gonnelieu, though whether the gunners ever succeeded in getting them out we do not know.

The Prince of Wales's Company was relieved on the 3rd ; and on the night of the 4th the whole battalion, being relieved by the 2nd Battalion Irish Guards, marched via Fins to Etricourt, where it spent the night. A camp had been pitched here on the side of a hill, and although they were tired no one was able to sleep owing to the cold. Search parties were sent out to find wood without success. In one tent Dene, Lisburne (very ill with bronchitis), Devas and Arthur Gibbs, having secured a mail-bag and a horse-rug, tried to keep warm by putting their feet in the bag and covering their shoulders with the rug ; but, although their efforts created a great deal of amusement, they did not result in any comfort.

Early the next morning the battalion entrained at Etricourt, and, arriving at Laherlière, marched to Gouy-en-Artois.

The line established by the Guards Division in this engagement was held, but a withdrawal was subsequently made from Bourlon Wood. The net gain of the battle of Cambrai is shown by a line from the western outskirts of Gonnelieu, La Vacquerie, north of Ribecourt and Flesquières to a point on the canal a mile or so north of Havrincourt, also by 11,100 prisoners and 145 guns either

taken or destroyed. The enemy, however, were in our
old front line between Vendhuille and Gonnelieu.

In this action at Gouzeaucourt the Guards Division
were under the orders of the III Corps, after passing for
about an hour into the VII Corps.

CHAPTER XIII

ARRAS—GAVRELLE—RŒUX

THE village of Gouy was dull and dirty. It was one of those places fitted up for troops, that is to say tiers of bunks had been built in the barns for the men, and officers' quarters were rooms stripped of every single piece of furniture, with the exception of the wooden frame covered with rabbit-wire which served as a bed. The few fields round the village which had not been under the plough were muddy and quite unsuitable for parades, which took place in the road.

The battalion occupied itself by refitting, and was joined by Ballard and Llewellyn with 160 men from the reinforcement battalion.

Bob Bonsor was in hospital, having put his knee out while trying to play football with some young officers, and Lisburne had to go to hospital, and did not return to France again during the war. But Bonn and Menzies, who had been on a musketry course, returned to the battalion. Lisburne was a great loss to the battalion—most sensible and gallant, and very good company.

After a week at Gouy the battalion moved to Arras, first to the prison and then into empty houses.

At the beginning of the year the enemy had been entrenched on the very outskirts of the town, but in the big battle of the spring he had been forced to retire some miles, and, except for long-range shelling, the place was now quite comfortable. Shops were open, a performance was given nightly at the theatre by a party of soldiers, who called themselves the " Jocks," and two hotels did a thriving business. These hotels had never closed throughout the war—another proof of the tenacity of our gallant Allies—although the " Commerce," near the railway station, had been hit several times (we believe they were forced to close later).

The condition of the town showed the fortitude which had been displayed by the civilians who had remained. The cathedral was a mass of ruins, and most houses bore the scars of at least one shell. What gave a more dilapidated appearance to the town in general was the absence of glass in the windows of private dwellings ; the shops in some marvellous way managed to renew a great many of their windows.

The optimism of the French was shown in other ways. Parties of well-dressed civilians would continually arrive in motors, and proceed with note-books and plans to discuss schemes for reconstruction.

The move to Arras was looked on with the greatest satisfaction by officers and men.

The battalion was now in the XVII Corps, under Lieut.-Gen. Sir C. Fergusson. The officers were : Prince of Wales's Company—Capt. Gibbs, with Llewellyn, Davies, Stokes; No. 2—Capt. Bonn, with Romer, Williams, Baness; No. 3—Capt. Dudley Ward, with Howard, Ballard; No. 4—Martin Smith (in command), Evan Thomas, D. B. Davies. When Bob Bonsor returned he acted for a time as quartermaster for Dabell, who was sick; eventually Bonsor took over the transport from Goetz, who went first to No. 2 Company and then to No. 4. Keith Menzies was on headquarters as assistant adjutant to Devas.

The river Scarpe runs north of Arras, flowing to the east. Following the course of the river the village of St. Laurent Blangy lies on the north bank, then Athies ; Feuchy is on the south bank ; Fampoux and Rœux on the north bank ; Pelves, within a few hundred yards of Rœux on the south bank, was held by the enemy—in fact, Rœux was a salient in the enemy line, the right flank being on the line of the river.

The Arras-Douai Railway crossed to the north of the

river after passing Fampoux, and was workable as far as Feuchy.

With the exception of one short tour of duty the battalion always held the line north of the river, and the system of holding the line from now onwards became very tiring for troops. The battalion was to hold the front line for three days, and then go into support trenches (Humid, Harry, Hussar) for three days, but, as the support trenches were if anything rather worse for comfort than the front line, the rest was one in name only ; and the first period of duty was for eighteen days.

As a position, however, the British line was very strong—the high ground was in our hands and the observation was extremely good. The first sector held by the battalion was between the Arras-Douai Railway and Civil Avenue, and it may be generally described as a bold spur running from the high ground in rear towards the enemy line.

The spur was strongly defended by machine guns in conjunction with deep dugouts made by the New Zealand Tunnelling Company. The general line ran north and south (including Gavrelle), and in front of this spur. The support trenches were some 1,200 yards in rear.

The battalion went up to the support line on January 1st, 1918, and relieved the 2nd Battalion Scots Guards on the 5th. (It seems that the Scots Guards worked off one day they were owing in the front line, but left with the battalion owing them a day.) The front line was found to be well dug and deep, but for the most part unrevetted. It was then cold, frosty weather, and the sides of the trench held together, but there was hardly any material to secure them in the event of a thaw. Gloomy prognostications were heard and soon were to be fulfilled. It started to rain, and then it snowed and became bitterly cold, and then it rained. The men worked like demons, but as fast as they threw the sloppy mud out of the trench it fell in again ; still they kept things fairly right until the 15th, when after a warm day a most fearful downpour of rain started as the 2nd Battalion Scots Guards were relieving. The trenches

simply melted away. They were half full of water to
start with, so, wherever the sides fell in, and that event
was universal, without any trampling a rich thick fluid
of the consistency of porridge was formed ; and of course
the relief made it worse. Nos. 2 and 3 Companies were
in a bad plight. Poor Bonn, with a cold that had deprived him of his voice, plunged about until he looked
like a gigantic newt fished out of some slime, and
Howard, having reached a telephone, wailed down it that
he must have men with ropes to pull his platoon out.
Men were actually above their knees in mud.

The Scots Guards started to relieve at 7 p.m. on the
15th, and the relief was not complete until 9.30 a.m. on
the 16th. And the support lines were just as bad. It
continued to rain until the battalion was relieved by the
1st Coldstream Guards on the 18th, when companies
entrained on the light railway which ran to Fampoux
on the north bank of the Scarpe, and were in Arras by
9 p.m.

We cannot leave this bit of line without mentioning
the work of the Y.M.C.A. This Association had a hut
in a sunken road near Humid Trench and sold the men
cigarettes and chocolates, and gave them hot cocoa and
tea. One of the members of the Association lived in
the hut and was always ready to provide anything he
had. The note we have on the subject is as follows :

" The man who runs the shanty is a Scot of about fifty
years of age—round, red face, scrubby moustache and
round tummy. He is fired up here all alone, and exists
and runs his place entirely on charity—that is to say, he
has to beg for parties to carry up what he wants, chop
his wood, and lend a hand generally. He sells cigarettes,
chocolate, writing-paper, and odds and ends, but gives
away tea and cocoa to all who want it. This is sound
and helpful work."

We regret that we do not know the name of this gentleman, but of the Association nothing can be said but
in praise. Its organisation reached the dreary village,

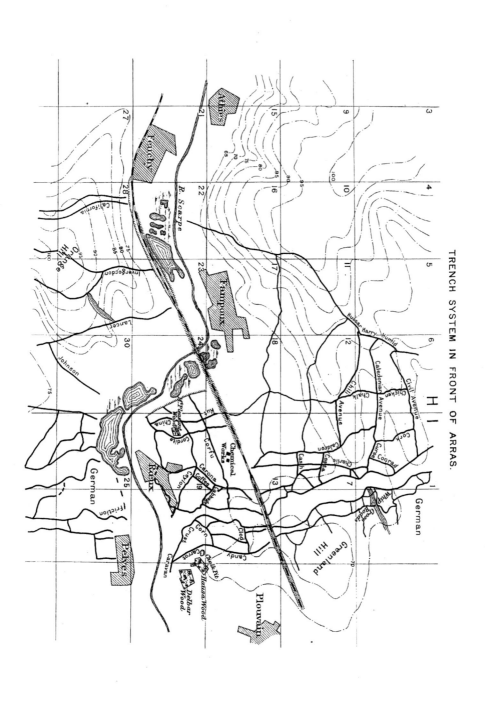

TRENCH SYSTEM IN FRONT OF ARRAS.

the bleak and lonely railway siding, and the exhausting swamp of the battle-field. It was not a charity but a friend, and the fighting soldier knew the Y.M.C.A. as a "pal."

An amusing situation arose about this time—Ball came back from his senior officers' course at Aldershot. He had left as second in command and was assured that he would retain the position, but now Dene was with the battalion and holding that acting rank. Luxmoore Ball only held the substantive rank of lieutenant, and Humphrey Dene was a captain and brevet-major. The difficulty was shelved for the moment by Ball being sent to the transport lines, "disguised," as Dene remarked, "as a nose-bag."

At the same time Arthur Gibbs was sent on a musketry course, and the battalion was getting short of officers. This raised the question, ever present in the minds of all troops, of leave. If Bob Bonsor came back and his knee held out, said Keith Menzies, there might be a chance of leave; but Walter Bonn, in the depths of depression with his sore throat and cold, shook his head sadly and whispered, "We can't even insure him!" But the dismal possibilities were relieved by dinners at the "Commerce" and the "Continental."

It was most extraordinary what the French managed to do in the way of food. Romer Williams, who loved entertaining and good living, and Keith Menzies gave a party at the "Continental"—hors d'œuvre, soup, fresh fish, duck, soufflé, savoury, coffee, and some excellent old rum; they found rare wines in the cellar, they produced cigars, and their guests had all the after discomforts of a Mansion House banquet.

On the 26th the battalion went into the line again, and held the sector from the Scarpe to the railway. This included the village of Rœux and the celebrated chemical works. Everybody felt satisfied with this bit of line; the trench was good, the position very strong, and the dugouts and the caves of Rœux gave plenty of shelter from shelling. The ruins of Rœux were described as a tricky bit of line; it was held by advance posts which were drawn in by daylight, and on the other side of the river was the enemy. That the enemy thought he might do something there was also fairly obvious, as he attempted to raid on the 27th, but found the posts too alert, so he contented himself with running about for a few seconds, uttering loud cries when fired at, and so disappeared.

This tour of duty and the succeeding ones for some time were shorter and, as different arrangements were made, of varying length. The battalion was relieved on the 30th, and returned to Arras by the broad-gauge railway.

During the next four days in Arras the Commanding Officer, who had been to Rouen, returned, but left the next day on leave to England. He was retained in England, and in due course assumed command of the Reserve Battalion.

Lieut.-Col. Gordon was a man of medium stature, and very energetic. He had commanded the battalion through some big engagements, and had carried out the complicated orders for the third battle of Ypres with minute care of detail. He was a disciplinarian, and kept the standard of smartness in the battalion at a high pitch; his Company Commanders, Arthur Gibbs, Lisburne, Roderick, Percy Battye, and for shorter periods, Upjohn and Bonn, had ably supported his efforts in this direction.

Of the officers who served under him Arthur Gibbs had proved himself a good company commander, popular with his men, cheerful, courageous and steady. Under Gibbs, though fifteen years his senior, was Bonsor, a man of much wisdom and of great administrative ability, but suffering under the physical disability of being very short-sighted; but a man who could command others and had their confidence, and by his example kept their spirits and courage high under the most distressing circumstances. And in that company were a lot of keen young men like Fripp, Gwynne Jones, Saunders, Shand, E. J. Davies and Llewellyn.

Lisburne was most gallant and painstaking, quiet and

Alice Hughes, Ebury St.

LT.-COLONEL DOUGLAS GORDON, D.S.O.

shrewd. Helping him was Walter Bonn, never out of temper, never, apparently, tired, and full of amusing conversation. Keith Menzies and Dickens were old members of No. 2 Company mess. Menzies was frequently taken away on headquarters, where he was most useful with his aptitude for finding out what was afoot.

Of Roderick we have written elsewhere ; he was a most painstaking officer, and served No. 3 Company well. Menzies was also in the company for a while. Rice, L. F. Ellis, Jenkins, Borough, Arthur and Webb were some of the younger men.

Percy Battye had done well with No. 4. He was cheerful, in spite of being lean, with a supreme contempt of the enemy and a slight flamboyant side to his character which endeared him to his men. Taylor, R. R. Jones, Hebert, Bowyer, and Wreford Brown were some of those who had helped him.

Dene assumed command of the battalion, and Luxmoore Ball was able to emerge from his "nosebag" condition.

When the new Commanding Officer took over, a new situation had arisen.

CHAPTER XIV

THE BIG GERMAN OFFENSIVE—PRELIMINARY RAIDS—
WARNINGS OF ATTACK

SINCE September 1917 the British Army had taken over
a further twenty-eight miles of front from the French, and
at the date we have now arrived at a total of 125 miles
of front was held.   But the fighting force of the British
Army was less in January 1918 than it had been in 1917.
When writing of divisions from this date onward it must
be borne in mind by the reader that in the month of
February they were reduced from thirteen battalions to
ten battalions, and that under this arrangement the
Guards Division lost the 4th Battalion Grenadier, the
3rd Battalion Coldstream, and the 2nd Battalion Irish
Guards, who were formed into a 4th Guards Brigade
and sent to the 31st Division.

Russia was no longer a belligerent, and the enemy
had now an enormous number of divisions and artillery
available from his Eastern Front.   By the middle of
February thirty-four divisions had been transferred from
other fronts to the Western Front, and the talk throughout
the whole army was of the coming German offensive.

Not only was there talk but a tremendous lot of work
so far as the Guards Division was concerned.   Whether
the battalion was in the line, or in support, large digging
fatigues went out every night, or were employed in
carrying up quantities of revetting material.   The men
never worked better, and the results of their labour were
no doubt felt by the troops who fought in that sector
later on.

Catch-words always crop up on these occasions, and the one most in use at that time was " defence in depth," but as battalions of the division held the line with three companies in the front line and one in close support, and were told that if the attack came the enemy would sweep over them, and in time utterly exterminate them, defence in depth did not appeal to them as a better personal condition of affairs than any other system.

Lieut.-Col. Dene, however, took all these things in a very cool manner, and, as his preoccupation had always been with the line and the fight whenever he had commanded the battalion before, so it was now. All the lugubrious preparations for an enemy advance were hailed by the battalion with shouts of laughter and much rough banter at the expense of the staff, who were accused of being " windy." But, in spite of laughter, it became quite a pastime to count divisions and try to arrive at some conclusion.

" Went to lunch with Jack Stirling. Vaneck was there and Jack began to count out divisions on the Western Front. Vaneck, from his real or pretended superior knowledge, contradicted him flat, and reminded him he had left out the Portuguese, to say nothing of odd little gangs like the Canadians, the Australians, and the Americans. Jack was somewhat taken aback, but then said we had none in reserve, whereupon Vaneck gave him figures to show that we had quite a respectable number, and with the French quite as many as the Boche. The promising and entertaining argument which had been indicated seemed to be deprived of its backbone, and the conversation trailed off into other spheres."—*Diary, C. H. D. W.*

On February 22nd the enemy again attempted to raid the battalion at a point north of Rœux, which was held by No. 2 Company. The night was dark and they had chosen the spot with care, between two posts. Walter Bonn was going round his line, followed by his orderly, Feely, a thin, red-faced, long-nosed Welshman, with a humorous twinkle in his eyes, when he thought he heard someone cough and looked over the parapet. Bonn could see nothing, but Feely declared he saw something move and started to fire. The first shot roused the " covey," as Bonn expressed it, and they both blazed away, Feely with his rifle and Bonn with his revolver. The posts on either side now saw the enemy and opened fire, and there was quite a lively chorus of sound, in the midst of which one of the Germans jumped over some last strands of wire and into the trench, to be immediately hurled to the ground by Bonn, who proceeded to pummel him unmercifully, while Feely implored him to get out of the way so that he might stick his bayonet into the fellow. The raiding party, carrying two wounded or dead, disappeared into the night, and Bonn, having secured his prisoner, sent out a patrol which came back with some half a dozen rifles and another prisoner.

From the prisoners it was learned that the party was composed of thirty-seven men under an officer and two non-commissioned officers, and that they had been promised two weeks' leave if they returned with identification.

As the battalion held some two thousand yards of front line with three companies, a raid of this kind had every chance of success. These prisoners had not been holding the line, but were special Sturm Truppen trained for the raid. One of the prisoners said the big offensive would start early the next month, the other professed to know nothing about it.

The enemy were very active with raids, and in a little over three months they attempted no less than 225 on the British Front. As the season progressed the British, who had been quiet, increased their raids, and throughout the month of February the division prepared a series of " minor operations " which took effect in March. Each brigade was to carry out one, and the 3rd Brigade raid fell to the Welsh Guards.

A point in the enemy's defences, where one of his communication trenches joined with his front line (Corn and Crust), was selected, and Paul Llewellyn, with thirty other ranks, was chosen to do it.   Claud Insole, who had rejoined the battalion a few days before, was in command of the arrangements.   As usual the raid was practised behind the lines, but it was a simple case of trying to get identification and was not a complicated manœuvre. The enemy's wire, however, was very strong.

For some days previous to the attempt the big trench-mortars (6-inch Newton) fired at various points besides the one selected for the raid, and blew gaps in the wire ; but the enemy was expecting this kind of enterprise, having been successfully raided by both the 1st and 2nd Brigades a few days before, and was in no way deceived.

At 4.58 a.m. on March 10th the artillery opened a protecting screen of fire, with the object of neutralising any machine guns which could affect the success of the raid, and at five o'clock Llewellyn and his men climbed over the parapet and dashed across.[1]   They reached the enemy trench without casualties, and in a few minutes had discovered a German, whom they made prisoner. But the enemy had cunningly occupied some shell-holes on the far side of the trench, and now proceeded to bomb them, causing a few casualties, amongst them Llewellyn, who had his thigh broken.   A few bombs in return caused the Huns to run, although apparently no damage was done.   Llewellyn then ordered his party to return to their lines, pluckily saw the last man out, and was carried behind them by his orderly, Duffy.   By this time the enemy had opened his S.O.S. barrage, and on the way back the prisoner was blown up, with two men who were taking him, and a dozen other men were hit.

Claud Insole at once organised search parties to get the wounded in.   They worked hard and fast, but it was getting light, and an enemy machine gun, which had been missed by the barrage, enfiladed the ground.   They brought in all the wounded they could see, but the roll was not complete.   Sergt. Glover, although himself wounded, set out again and brought in two ; Sergt. Ham and Pte. Duffy brought in two more ; there remained only the two dead men they knew of and Hughes, a

[1] Appendix B 11.

14

gallant company orderly. In spite of all efforts they
failed to find Hughes, and for the moment gave up
further attempts ; later in the day, however, he managed
to crawl in by himself. The raid had failed in its object,
for the prisoner was literally destroyed by a direct hit
from a shell, but the men of the Prince of Wales's Company had carried out their part with the greatest gallantry and coolness. They were quite ready to go and

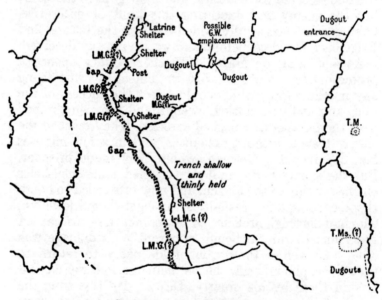

SKETCH OF GERMAN POSITION.
LLEWELLYN RAIDED THROUGH THE LOWER GAP.

get another prisoner, particularly Cpl. Meredith, who
had captured the man ; but that was out of the question.

The enemy artillery fire in this raid gave some foretaste
of the amount of guns he had accumulated. It spread
right back to Battalion H.Q., and caused casualties far
back from the front line. The gallant Ballard, watching
the shell-bursts and coloured lights from the mouth of his
dugout, was killed under the same circumstances as
Byrne a few days before, the shell striking the entrance
to the dugout.

Conditions had changed enormously since the battalion first went into the line. When company commanders had gone up to view the new trenches they had walked over Mount Pleasant Hill, to avoid the twists and turns of the communication trenches, and not a shot had been fired at them. The officers they had taken over from spoke well of the line, and the tameness of the enemy. But now the artillery had settled down to what was practically one continuous bombardment, broken only by convulsions of terrific, whirlwind fire.

From the staff came frequent warnings of impending attack. March 10th was confidently expected to be the day, and then the 13th. On the latter date the battalion was in reserve at Gordon Camp, just behind the railway on the east of Arras, and was reduced to battle numbers. The company sergeant-majors, with a percentage of men, were sent back under 2/Lieut. Mathew to Arras, the battalion slept in full equipment, and destructive artillery fire was rained on the enemy lines and back areas from midnight to daylight. No attack developed.

These continual warnings were somewhat trying to the nerves. A note under date March 7th reads :

"They tell us the Boche is going to attack on Sunday ! What evidence they have is kept locked in their bosoms. They cannot tell us definitely what to expect, although so precise in date and locality, and so every possible form of attack is solemnly enumerated. Orders for defence are changed with the greatest regularity—no wonder poor old Broncho [Commanding Officer] gets worried. And with it all, intentional or not, is ' wind,' by the side of which German frightfulness is mere child's play. Broncho said to me to-night : ' I don't know if we shall get out of this alive, but it is better to be dead than to be messed about indefinitely ! ' But the depths of his depression are not very profound, as he quickly added that he would make Fritz pay before he was finished. There is very little enemy preparation that one can see, but I have found one trench which seems to have no purpose beyond that of an assembly trench."

And on March 8th :

" Broncho came to see me and brought a map on which were marked all the new machine-gun positions, which seem extremely satisfactory. Personally I don't believe the entire **Boche Army** will get through this bit of line. He told me he had seen the Corps Commander (Fergusson) this morning, and that he was quite confident and wished the Boche would attack. To-day the policy is to encourage everyone, but I don't believe the remarks of the staff in general make the slightest difference to the spirits of the soldiery, who receive all warnings, whether of a confident or a depressing nature, with grins and laughter. The gunning to-day has been very active on both sides, but I think we have been more aggressive than the Boche. One thing is certain—if he comes in any strength my front line is bound to go, and I am making all the preparations I know of to fight in the support. . . . . It seems to me that the Boche has either moved up more guns or been forced to disclose silent batteries ; but hours of watching through a telescope reveal no further preparation or movement." —*Diary, C. H. D. W.*

The battalion went into the line again on the 15th and worked hard, digging and completing new trenches. On the night of the 19th the 2nd Battalion Seaforth Highlanders took over, and the battalion went by train to Bernaville for a month of rest and training. On the morning of the 21st the storm broke.

Between 4 a.m. and 5 a.m. the Fifth and Third Armies, holding from the Oise to the Scarpe Rivers, were engaged by a fierce and intense bombardment from the smallest trench-mortar to the long-range high-velocity guns,which bombarded as far back as St. Pol. The corps holding this front were : in the Fifth Army—the III (Butler), XVIII (Maxse), XIX (Watts), VII (Congreve) ; in the Third Army—V (Fanshawe), IV (Harper), VI (Haldane), XVII (Fergusson). The average front for each division in the Fifth Army was 6,750 yards, and in the Third

Army 4.700 yards. The number of divisions in each army was fourteen infantry and three cavalry in the Fifth Army, and fifteen infantry divisions in the Third Army; on March 21st sixty-four German divisions were launched against them.

It is only possible to give a bare outline of this great offensive, launched on a fifty-four mile front. Generally speaking, the defensive system was divided into an out-post area and a battle zone—the latter having two or three lines of defence according to the progress of work. By the end of the first day the enemy had reached the battle zone everywhere where he had pressed his attack (which did not extend seriously north of the Sensee River, and was not launched vigorously against the Flesquières salient). On the Third Army front Demicourt, Doignies, Lagnicourt, Bullecourt had fallen to the enemy.

Remembering the position where the Guards Division was, behind and slightly to the south of Arras, the enemy's advance of some 5,000 yards on the south of the Sensee to the outskirts of St. Leger and Croisilles made it obvious that it would soon be engaged. The following notes will indicate how the attack affected the battalion at the time :

" The great attack has apparently started. I think the cannonade began about one this morning, at least it seemed to me that I heard it most of the night, and at five it became absolutely furious. We lay in our beds and tried to sleep, but, as we all expected to be called out any moment, did no more than snooze. It went on well into the morning and only died down about eleven. . . . The attack at present just misses our old sector, and is apparently south of the Sensee River, but being in reserve we are liable to be sent anywhere. Of course it has meant much talk and speculation, and we have gathered together over maps in the mess, or in one of our huts—I share one with Bonn, Claud Insole, and ' Squiff ' (L. F.) Ellis—and tried to make out exactly what the Hun is trying to do. So far as we know he has bent our line on a small front of three miles ; but, as rumour has it that he is attacking on a fifty-mile front, it does not seem a great success. Everyone seems to think it is the real thing, and I believe there is a feeling of relief that it has come. . . .

" *March 22nd.*—The night was quiet, but now, midday, the battle rages. They say we are inflicting heavy losses with machine-gun fire, and have only lost a small fraction of ground, but all our news only applies to our own Army (Third). If we don't move off to battle today we play football with the Kiddies. . . . Scarcely had I written the above when an order came for the battalion to move at once. Broncho dashed off in a motor-bus to reconnoitre the line, but the work went on under Ball. Broncho returned at 2 p.m. and at 2.15 the battalion marched off for a mile or so, and then by bus. . . . The transport followed later—poor old Bob Bonsor fussing like a hen with ducklings, and being seriously impeded by his dog, which he led on a string and managed to entangle with people, horses, or carts."

The battalion arrived at Mercatel about four in the afternoon and took over a camp from the 1st Coldstream Guards. There had been no break-through in front of them, but the line was falling back.

That night the Third Army readjusted its front and withdrew from the Flesquières salient, and also swung back from the Scarpe, occupying the third line of the battle zone from Henin to Fampoux.

There was much night skirmishing and shelling during this readjustment, and the battalion passed an unsettled night, expecting to be called out at every minute.

The enemy success was to the right of where the division was holding the line, and in the early morning of the 23rd they broke through at Mory, a village some six miles away. It became clear that the division would have to swing back, and the Commanding Officer and Company Commanders reconnoitred the systems of defence behind them. But that evening the battalion moved up in close support to the front line, relieving the 2nd Battalion Scots Guards and details of the 31st and

3rd Divisions in the neighbourhood of Boyelles ; and the next day again relieved the Scots Guards in the front line east of Boiry Becquerelles.

Aeroplanes had reported that the enemy was massing between Henin and Croisilles, and the battalion stood to arms all night, but no attack developed.   When daylight broke on the 25th much enemy movement was seen in the neighbourhood of Henin, and the enemy was obviously bringing up more troops behind a ridge or fold of the ground about 800 yards away.   The system he employed was a lengthy one, but very effective : his troops trickled into the required position by threes and fours, offering visible but small and uncertain targets which approached over a wide front, and continued doing so the whole day.

But there was no cause for alarm.   The division had beaten off repeated attacks on the previous days, and this left wing of the Third Army was holding its ground, and was only forced to new positions by the enemy successes on its right.   Farther away still the Fifth Army was fearfully strung out, but since March 23rd the French were rapidly taking over the front south of Péronne.

The Guards Division had now been transferred from the XVII to the VI Corps, and on the right of the VI was the IV and then the V Corps.   On the morning of the 25th fierce fighting took place from Ervillers to the south, and, though Ervillers held, the enemy pressed forward to Grevillers in the afternoon.   Between Grevillers and Montauban was a gap separating the IV and V Corps, and by the evening of the 25th advanced troops of the enemy were near Puisieux-au-mont and Serre.   So during the night 25th/26th the IV Corps fell back on the line Bucquoy—Ablainzevelle, their left being in touch with the VI Corps at Boyelles.

The situation was so critical that at 2.30 a.m. on the 25th the Commanding Officer received a warning order that the Higher Command considered it might be necessary to withdraw some five miles to a line Adinfer—Ficheux—Blairville, which was called the Purple Line ;

but this was altered to an order to withdraw to a line Boisleux St. Marc—Mercatel.

The Welsh Guards were on the right of the divisional front, and the orders to withdraw were received at 11.30 p.m., although they mentioned the hour of 10 p.m.; but that something of the sort was happening the Commanding Officer was well aware, as the brigade on his right had started to go about 10 p.m. However, the movement was carried out in conjunction with the 1st Battalion Grenadier Guards, on the left.

No. 2 Company, under Bonn, held the line for twenty minutes after the Prince of Wales's and No. 3 Companies had gone, and then passed through No. 4 Company, who remained in the support line and covered the withdrawal of No. 2. Bonn had no easy task to perform, as before the twenty minutes were complete the enemy appeared on his wire—he was dispersed, but other patrols appeared as the last section were leaving the line. The enemy, however, was not unduly anxious to press on Bonn's heels, and No. 2 Company passed through No. 4, who in their turn left at the time appointed without seeing the enemy.

The whole battalion passed through the 2nd Battalion Scots Guards, who were in position just behind Boyelles, and remained in close support in front of Boisleux St. Marc.

March 26th was quiet, but farther south there was some confusion, and at the end of the day the right of the Third Army (which had assumed command of all troops north of the Somme on the 25th) had retired beyond the limits of necessity and rested on the Somme, about Sailly-le-Sec, while the left of the Fifth Army was five miles farther east. This was ground gained by the enemy with no effort, and on the 27th he attacked from Bucquoy to Boyelles.

The attack opened with heavy, destructive artillery fire in combination with sweeping machine-gun fire, from which the 2nd Battalion Scots Guards suffered severely. Before the enemy launched his infantry Nos. 2 and 4 Companies of the Welsh Guards moved up in extended formation close behind the 2nd Battalion Scots Guards, on to some high ground, and obtained an excellent view of the Germans being cut to pieces by the depleted ranks of the Scots Guards.   The enemy were unable to reach the wire.

But further on the right the enemy gained possession of Ablainzevelle and Ayette, although he was thrown out of the latter village a few days later.

On the night of the 27th the battalion relieved the 1st Battalion Grenadier Guards on the right of the divisional front.

The battalion held a front of some 2,000 yards with their right on Boyelles, and at 7 a.m. on the 28th the enemy commenced to bombard the trenches, and continued doing so with increased violence until 11.30 a.m. Companies on the right of the line reported the enemy massing in Boyelles, which was partly concealed by a rise in the ground.   The Commanding Officer put the artillery on to him, and the attack did not develop in that quarter.   On the left, however, the enemy drove back the division holding the hill north of Boiry Becquerelle on to the main Arras—Bapaume Road, and proceeded to attack the flank of the Prince of Wales's Company.   Claud Insole was not to be caught that way. He blocked his trench and held it with bombers, while his Lewis Guns cleared the open ground; 2/Lieut. E. J. Davies was killed while repelling this attack.

Later in the day the enemy could be seen bringing up guns on the distant ridge, but the rest of the day was quiet.   In the evening orders were given for the battalion to conform with the division on the left; the Switch Trench was abandoned, and the left of the battalion fell back on to the Green Line, a short distance in rear.

The attack on this day stretched from Puisieux to north of Arras, but the weight of it was directed against the 4th (Matheson) and the 56th (Dudgeon) Divisions on the north, and the 3rd and 15th Divisions on the south of the Scarpe River.   It is interesting to note that the 4th Division held the line immediately north of the river and inflicted a heavy defeat on the enemy; and that,

although the outpost line was overwhelmed, a party of
the 2nd Battalion Seaforth Highlanders, who had relieved
the Welsh Guards at Rœux, successfully held those ruins
all day.

The Commanding Officer was now relieved by Luxmoore Ball. Arthur Gibbs and L. F. Ellis went up from
the reinforcement camp the next day and joined their
companies. A few men also went up from the reinforcement camp to relieve an equal number of tired
men.

The 29th was a quiet day, but on the 30th the enemy
opened destructive fire at 8 a.m. on our front line
trenches, which he increased at 8.45 a.m. and spread to
the back areas. Luxmoore Ball had a very fair view of
the front line from his headquarters, situated in a sunken
road on the east side of Boisleux St. Marc, and with an
artillery officer watched the proceedings. The danger-
spot was Boyelles, half hidden by a rise in the ground,
and a spot where concentration could be effected without
being seen. An attack from this direction would involve
his right flank company, No. 4 Company, to which Claud
Insole had been moved on the return to the Prince of
Wales's Company of Arthur Gibbs.

At 10.20 a.m. the enemy thickened his artillery with
machine-gun fire, and a few minutes later our artillery
barrage came down across Boyelles.

At 10.45 a.m. the enemy artillery lifted off the front
line trenches to the supports, and was replaced with
intense machine-gun fire from the ridge north of Boiry
Becquerelle. At the same time fourteen aeroplanes came
over and dropped bombs, diving at intervals and firing
at the front line. Under cover of this overhead fire the
enemy debouched and advanced from Boyelles.

The attack was directed against the 1st Battalion
Grenadier Guards on the right and No. 4 Company Welsh
Guards, and was met with overwhelming rifle and Lewis
Gun fire. Luxmoore Ball had also caused two machine
guns to be placed on the bank above his headquarters,
and these, firing over the heads of the front line troops,
swept the ground before the advancing enemy.

A letter from Claud Insole throws light on the situation :

" I was relieved the night before last by Dudley Ward, and was sent to the transport for a rest. I arrived back about 3 a.m. and spent all yesterday, Easter Sunday, in bed. The day before yesterday we had a very exciting day, after a quiet night in which we did a lot of wiring, and getting up ammunition and bombs, etc., and digging ourselves deeper into the ground. The Huns started to shell us about 8 a.m., with every sort of shell from 8-inch, till the ground fairly rocked and the air was full of smoke. That lasted until about 10.30 a.m., when the barrage lifted and the Huns came over, mostly against the Grenadiers on my right and my company ; the rest of the battalion did not get attacked. We got off very lightly considering what a heavy shelling it was, and the relief when it lifted was so great that the men fairly cheered with delight when they saw the Huns coming, and some stood on the parapet and shouted to them to come on. They came on in twos and threes, running from shell-hole to shell-hole, and down hedges and ditches, but they never got nearer than our wire, which runs out for 250 yards, so the shooting was quite difficult. I think I got about four which I saw drop, but one cannot be certain ; but I took most careful aim."

The execution was very great. At one bad spot on the right a few of the enemy managed to reach the Grenadier Guards' trench, and were sent up to brigade as " souvenirs." These prisoners said two battalions had attacked, with one in support.

The rest of the day was quiet except that the hedges in front of No. 4 Company were still occupied by the enemy, who employed himself by shooting at stretcher-bearers carrying the wounded out of the line. The stretcher-bearers always declared that this was not generally done, and the risks they took seemed to bear out their contention, but on this occasion two were killed,

and there was no doubt as to what they were or what
they were doing.

The night was very dark, and patrols searching the
ground were fired at, and did not succeed in bringing
back any information.   But the next day, the 31st, after
carefully watching the hedges, Sergt. Waddington took
out a patrol of twelve men and a Lewis Gun and searched
the ground, but with orders not to become involved with
the enemy in Boyelles.   He counted and searched nineteen dead on the near side of the first hedge about five
hundred yards away, and reported many more on the far
side of it ; he also brought in two wounded Germans and
a machine gun.   The movement was observed by the
enemy artillery, which opened fire, and, as there was no
object in holding the line of the hedge, he came back
without casualties.

It is seldom possible to find out what actual damage
a battalion has inflicted on the enemy, but as this bit of
front was protected from the fire of the Grenadier Guards
through the formation of the ground, the battalion may
claim to be responsible for all the dead opposite the front
held by it, and the right wing of the German attack was
entirely dealt with by Nos. 4 and 2 Companies of the
Welsh Guards.

The battalion casualties were six killed and twelve
wounded.

On the night of the 31st the battalion was relieved by
the 26th Canadian Infantry Battalion, first-rate troops,
who not only had organisation and efficiency as watch-
words, but carried out the principles in a manner which
commanded the greatest admiration.   The Prince of
Wales's and No. 3 Companies went to a forward reserve
position in a railway bank and the remainder of the
battalion to Blairville.

The big German attack on the Somme battle area
ceased after April 5th for a while, and was not re-
newed at all on the Guards Divisional front.   Of
the total of fifty-eight British divisions on the Western
Front forty-six had been used in this battle, but
although the enemy had made a deep salient he had

THE BRITISH LINE AFTER THE GERMAN OFFENSIVE.

not reached Amiens, as he had hoped, or indeed any other vital point.

It was remarked during this trying time that the troops holding the front lines were far less excited than the organisation in rear. Rumour is ever a powerful enemy in war, and on this occasion it was perhaps more dangerous than the Germans.

" It was evident from the state of the roads, the behaviour of the military and civil population, and the rumours that seemed to be shouted about, that something very near a panic was going on. Early in the morning of the 26th all reinforcements were ordered to hold some roads a mile from Halloy on a story that the enemy had broken through. Two excitable brigadiers spread alarm by shouting to everyone they met to get to their posts, so 2,000 men were made to lie out in fields all day, and at five in the evening march five miles to repel an enemy probably ten miles away from that point, and then five miles back again. As a Frenchman told me : ' We see the military marching and countermarching in an undecided manner, and, not knowing what has happened, become alarmed.' "—*Diary, C. H. D. W.*

In the midst of all this turmoil Gen. Foch had assumed supreme command of all operations (March 26th).

On April 9th the enemy transferred his attentions to the Lys Valley, and for a while things hung in the balance, but he was eventually stopped. The 4th Guards Brigade did some gallant deeds in the northern fighting.

Note.—" In the short course of the German offensive our armies in France lost, either by capture or destruction, 1,000 guns, 70,000 tons of ammunition, 4,000 machine guns, 200,000 rifles, 250,000,000 rounds of small-arm ammunition, 700 trench-mortars, and 200 tanks. These losses were made good in a fortnight."—*Mr. Kellaway, House of Commons*, 25/6/19.

CHAPTER XV

BLAIRVILLE was on some high ground that fell away towards the north-east and gave a fine view of the country as far as Monchy. Looking towards the enemy (east) from Blairville, the outstanding feature was a spur running from the main ridge in a northern direction and curving to the east; from this spur all the country over Boyelles and in the direction of St. Leger was visible. The British undoubtedly held the superior position, although from some points the enemy could obtain very good observation over our forward positions.

From the point of view of comfort of troops, however, the situation was not so good. They were in the devastated area from which the Germans had retreated in the early part of 1917, and although since then vast hut-camps had been erected, the last battle had reduced these to a mass of charred and broken wood, and twisted, shrapnel-riddled bits of tin. The enemy completely destroyed everything in the nature of a camp within reach of his guns, and made most of the material useless. New material was almost impossible to get, and the only shelter for troops when out of the front line was in a few huts behind Blairville. These huts, besides being inadequate, were inconveniently situated, and eventually there was a readjustment which placed all troops in trenches to the south of Blairville. But for the time being two companies found shelter in the huts of Blairville and two in the " Purple Line " in front of Blairville. The usual rotation of reliefs went on.

212

On April 5th No. 3 Company, now under Claud Insole, captured a prisoner, who stated that no further attacks were to be made on this front ; but the enemy artillery were very busy, and the trenches became very bad owing to rain.

" Shelled all night, sometimes growing intense—at five this morning it was fairly fierce.   Claud got a prisoner, who says there is plenty of artillery in front of us but not many troops—he was a nasty, slimy man.   It rained all night, but the day is fine.   The trouble is that one cannot get dry, and one only sleeps when practically done in.   Toby Mathew is very amusing.   His trousers are caked with mud, his coat is one running sludge of mud, his respirator bag a " wodge " of crumpled muddy canvas round his neck, his face is streaked with dirt and his tin hat negligently hung on his head well over his right eye.   He is only nineteen, has a face like a baby, and a keen sense of humour."

The battalion was relieved at midnight, and two companies occupied the Purple Line for one night and then changed over with the other two in the huts at Blairville.

" We did not go back to billets, but to an open trench with no cover at all for the men.   It was so dark we had to wait till the morning, and then got broken bits of tin from shelled huts and made shelters.   It stopped raining and the men's spirits rose. . . .

" *April 8th.*—Rear organisation is getting better, but does not yet run to time, and everyone can still be said to be living from hand to mouth.   I have men now who are ragged about the trousers to the extent of indecency, and many have their bare toes sticking through their boots.   I wash on an average every other day, but the men are worse off, and only get a shower-bath and a change of clothing once a fortnight.   These small things count, as a clean man is always more refreshed than a dirty one.   Our hut for the one-day rest is a small two-roomed wooden shack, and has in it eight officers so closely packed that they cannot all get up at once. In the morning fried eggs and bacon are side by side with shaving soap and hair-brushes, and a man washes from one basin next to a similar one from which another eats porridge. . . . There is still a coming and going of troops both on our own and the enemy side, and all in full view of each other—and the cannonade is continuous. Broncho Dene and Claud hold out well, and indeed it is the younger men who crack. Stokes, a useful young officer about twenty-three years of age, has cracked, and Marshall Roberts is on the verge of it. Bonn and Romer Williams are both strong as horses. But the private soldier is a marvel, and my admiration for him is beyond bounds. . . . My two boys, Toby Mathew and Ben Davies, are splendid."—*Diary, C. H. D. W.*

During the next tour in the line the battalion suffered a great loss in the death of Claud Insole, on April 12th.

" Gentle, gallant Claud is dead. . . . It was a beautiful sunny day, and, after looking round for an hour or so, I returned to my dugout and Keith Menzies rang me up and told me Claud had been killed by a shell. ' I thought you would like to know,' said he, and I replied ' Thanks ! ' Speech means nothing. The divisional chaplain said to our chaplain, Mog, when the battle was on : ' What have you been doing, Mog ? '—' I called at the casualty clearing-station and buried eight men,' replied Mog. ' Good,' said the other man of God. . . ."

On April 14th the division was relieved by the 2nd Division. The Welsh Guards were relieved by the 17th Battalion Royal Fusiliers and marched back to Barly via Beaumetz, Monchiet and Gouy ; but the next day they moved to a camp at Fosseux. The division was now in Third Army reserve and under orders to move at three hours' notice.

The country round Fosseux and Barly was closely cultivated, and the usual restrictions as to growing crops were in force, so that field work could not be carried out

on any useful scale.   In any case, the peasants were very
sensitive at that time, as a camp of Chinamen lay between
Fosseux and Barly, and these strange labourers were
working all day completing new lines of defence in the
event of fresh attacks and the evacuation of more country, and the damage to growing crops was great.   But
there was a fair rifle-range, and the battalion profited by
it.   Also Romer Williams, who had been responsible for
Bob Bonsor's dog, a police dog from Paris, produced with
equal ease two good ponies.   The ponies were matched
against the 2nd Battalion Scots Guards " stable " with
excellent results.

Brig.-Gen. Follett took command of the brigade, which
since April 2nd had been under Lieut.-Col. Orr Ewing.
Lord Henry Seymour, " Copper," as he was universally
called, brave as a lion, and always cheery, was much
regretted when he left.   In the new brigadier the battalion welcomed a tried and courageous battalion commander with long service and experience in France.   He
was a tall, dark, strong-faced man with a quiet manner ;
there was a look of Lord Kitchener about him.   At times
he had a curious abbreviated manner of speaking, jerking
out single words separated by long pauses.   In the middle of the summer, one very hot day, when everybody
was sitting in their shirt-sleeves, he arrived at Battalion
H.Q. with his face streaming with perspiration.   " Drip-
ing ! " said he.   " Fearful," replied the Commanding
Officer, " can't move."   The brigadier looked at him
without a blink of his eyelid.   " No. . . . Meat fat . . .
bad return . . . see to it."   And it gradually dawned on
Lieut.-Col. Dene that it was the salvage of beef dripping
the brigadier was talking about.

At this time there was a general change of staff.
Aubrey Fletcher, who had been brigade major to the
3rd Guards Brigade, went to divisional staff, as did
Calverly Bewicke, the staff captain.   Both of them had
been good friends to the battalion.   And Cecil Keith, a
" learner," quite a youngster but remarkably able, who
had been with the brigade staff for a long time, also went
to the division.   Nesbit came as brigade major, and

15

Acland Hood as staff captain. There were other "learners" who came and went—Gregory, Simmonds and Buchanan, afterwards brigade major.

The battalion did not stay very long at Fosseux. On April 24th it marched to Berles au Bois, and on the 25th relieved the 15th Battalion Lancashire Fusiliers in the line between Ayette and Ablainzevelle. Details, under Luxmoore Ball, moved via Barly to Warlincourt.

We have not said much about "Details," which now began to assume an important position. When the battalion first arrived in France details were the "Drums" and "Shops." Sergt.-Major Bland and all the company sergeant-majors took part in the battle of Loos, and afterwards always went into the line ; the transport, the quartermaster and his staff, which, when the battalion was in the line, included the company quartermaster-sergeants, the drums, the master tailor, the master shoemaker, each with his staff, and generally the pioneer sergeant with part of his men, remained at the transport lines. A few officers were also left out of the battle of Loos.

At the battle of the Somme instructions were given to Commanding Officers, but the actual numbers to be left out of the battle were at their discretion. Lieut.-Col. Murray Threipland on this occasion added to the officers he had selected the sergeant-major, all the company sergeant-majors, and a selected number of N.C.O.'s. It was not a large party.

Definite orders were given at the third battle of Ypres, when it was laid down that the minimum to be left out of the engagement was :

From Battalion H.Q.—Either the Commanding Officer or the second in command.

From companies.—Either the Company Commander or the second in command. Not more than two Company Commanders to go in with their companies.

Not more than twenty officers, excluding the medical officer, to go in with the battalion.

N.C.O.'s. and riflemen.—Each company would leave out one sergeant, one corporal, and one lance-corporal.

Each platoon would leave three privates. In addition 33 per cent. of Lewis gunners, scouts, snipers, signallers and runners were left.

The sergeant-major and all company sergeant-majors were also left out.

These arrangements were made for and applied to battle formations. For the ordinary tour of duty in the line the battalion carried on as before, taking the sergeant-major or drill-sergeant and company sergeant-majors.

In a series of excellent pamphlets on the training of platoons it was further laid down that the minimum strength of that unit was twenty-eight, exclusive of Platoon H.Q. As battalions began to feel the strain of war, and reinforcements became less in number, this figure of twenty-eight became a vital one, and company commanders were ordered to reduce their platoons to that number.

Reduction in the course of ordinary duty in the line was started at Arras, although it was not always strictly carried out, and Company Headquarters would not bear too close an inspection (the period in the line at Ypres 1917 must be considered as part of the battle). A sort of rough rule was established that so long as sections were composed of an N.C.O. and six men an extra man or two on headquarters did not matter.

At first Company Commanders followed the mistaken but very natural policy of leaving out the sickly and least competent of their men. But after the German offensive the tour of duty in the line became a matter of six weeks, and they soon found it better to give their men a rest when they could. Every week there was an exchange of men with the Details, so that it became a matter of whose turn it was to go out of the line. When the battalion held the Ayette Line the Details were at Warlincourt; when on the Boyelles front at Berles au Bois.

The ridge on which Blairville stood ran in a general south-westerly direction through Adinfer Wood, and was defended by the Purple Line. This was the main battle position. The Ayette sector was on the right of the

position. The outpost line was on the road Ayette—
Ablainzevelle, sweeping round the village of Ayette so
as to include some five hundred yards of the Ayette—
Ablainzevelle Road.

The brigade held this front with two battalions in the
outpost line and one in the Purple system. This arrangement gave each battalion four days in the Outpost Line
and two in the Purple Line. When in the latter position
companies were able to march to Monchy and get shower
baths and clean clothing, but the change of clothing was
still at the rate of once a fortnight. Of other comforts
there were none, and officers and men lived in the dog-
kennel variety of shelter made of tin and a few sandbags.

There were frequent warnings of impending attack.
The warnings were received with equanimity by the
troops, who had seen the massed artillery behind Adinfer
Wood, and could also look over the top of their trenches
and see miles of enemy country which offered little protection to any attacking troops; Ablainzevelle, well
covered with trees, and standing on a spur which shot
out from the ridge the British were holding, was the only
dangerous spot. But catch-words began to be bandied
about, the result of the study of the German offensive.
"Infiltration" was the word, and "Hurricane Fire"
from trench-mortars was to set it loose. We are happy
to note that the Welsh Guards never indulged in this
kind of conversation, which seemed to admit tacitly the
enemy to be what he claimed, a superman. The Commanding Officer, who looked after his line with the utmost care, said, "They talk to me about infiltration!
If Fritz comes floating down these valleys, welcome 'Der
Tag!'" And the battalion, remembering Gen. Haking's
speech before Loos, saw that this was no new method of
attack. However, metaphorically, they dammed the
valleys with barbed wire, and one way and another the
defences on this front became formidable.

The arrangement in the outpost area was two companies in the front line of posts, one in support and one
in reserve.

At first the enemy was quiet and inclined to show

himself, and the battalion snipers had several good days
before he learned discretion.   And then he disappeared
so completely that it was difficult to find him at all.
Every night patrols tried to locate posts and sometimes
succeeded, but subsequent patrols would frequently report the disappearance of such posts.   Unfortunately
2/Lieut. C. D. Whitehouse, with eleven men, was caught
on one of these adventures, while trying to discover the
exact nature of one of these posts.   He got into the
place, but found it strongly held and had to fight to get
out.   Only four men of the party succeeded in getting
back, and, though other patrols worked for several hours
and brought in five wounded, they did not succeed in
finding Whitehouse and two men.   The wounded reported that the enemy had picked up some bodies and
carried them away, and it was thought that Whitehouse
had been killed by a bomb.

But No. 4 Company took vengeance on a party of
about thirty of the enemy who tried to raid one of their
posts after a preliminary bombardment.

A further loss during the month of May was Howard,
a promising young officer, who was approaching the
position of Company Commander.

On June 6th the battalion was relieved by the 1st
Battalion K.R.R. and proceeded to Barly.   The officers
of the battalion were now :

Commanding Officer	Humphrey Dene.
Second in Command	Luxmoore Ball.
Adjutant . .	Devas.
Assistant Adjutant.	Jack Crawshay.
Quartermaster .	Dabell.
Transport Officer .	Bonsor.
Prince of Wales's Company . .	Arthur Gibbs, Upjohn, J. Ellis, Hill, Spence Thomas, Harrop, Hawksley.
No. 2 Company .	Bonn, Brian Gibbs, Tatham, Stanier, Dilberoglue, Paton.
No. 3 Company .	R. Lewis, L. F. Ellis, Gloag, Trotter, Courtney, J. A. Davies.
No. 4 Company .	Dudley Ward, Goetz, Mathew, B. Davies, Holds-worth, Watson, Brawn.

Romer Williams and Keith Menzies were with the
French Army as liaison officers ; Marshall Roberts had

gone home sick. It is, however, almost impossible to place officers other than Company Commanders, as, although casualties were not heavy, army schools still arranged courses to which officers had to be sent, and there was special employment of all sorts, so that there was a continual reposting of officers.

Excellent weather prevailed while the battalion was at Barly, and quite a lot of useful training was carried out at a 300-yard range and field work. The Commanding Officer was especially keen on working up rapid fire, and that a spirit of optimism reigned with the Higher Command was shown by the field training, which consisted entirely of attack and pursuit, and the reintroduction of the old diamond formation when under artillery fire or for the " Approach March."

The Brigadier took a lot of trouble over field training, and worked out a company scheme which included all the latest ideas of " dribbling " men into positions. There were " two company schemes " and " battalion schemes," and a lot of discussion over outposts to villages. In all this practice the brigadier used to wander about, quiet, helpful, and encouraging, and the youngest and most nervous of officers soon found that his somewhat taciturn appearance was in no way reflected in his character.

The battalion was quartered in and around the château grounds—most of the men in tents under the trees in the park ; the younger officers also in tents, while Company Commanders had rooms in the château. There were double company messes, as no room big enough for a battalion mess could be found, and the headquarters mess shared the ground-floor of the château with the brigade.

The Division H.Q. were at Saulty, and on June 22nd a horse-show was held there, at which the battalion took first prize in officers' heavy-weight and light-weight chargers, second prize in officers' chargers jumping competition, and third prize for heavy draught-horses, which had been with the division since formation.

Brigade sports were held at Barly with some amusing

events. In the bare-backed mule-race the battalion
thought it had a certainty. The Commanding Officer
rode a fast beast provided it would make up its mind to
start, and Jack Crawshay rode its stable companion with
instructions to sit still on its back and it would follow
its " friend " !   Once they were started everyone felt all
would be well. But no one ever understood a mule.
They started all right, the Commanding Officer well
ahead, and Crawshay a good second, while the rest were
nowhere—most of the riders were on the ground. Unfortunately Simmonds (a Grenadier " learner " on the
brigade staff) kept his seat and pounded along in a zigzag
course 200 yards behind the leading two. Then, as the
Commanding Officer swept round the turn into the
straight, the Welsh Guards transport men, gathered
together in a bunch, yelled and cheered. Round whipped
the mule off the course, gallumphing in queer shapes in
any direction but the winning-post ; and Crawshay's
beast followed it. Simmonds zig-zagged along, every
tack bringing him nearer the post. Everybody shouted,
which made matters worse ; but the transport had seen
their mistake, and some of the men ran round the mules
waving their arms, and headed the animals back on to
the course, but Simmonds won by a head.

The race between transport officers was won by Bob
Bonsor, who, blind as a bat and no rider, mounted the
same mule as the Commanding Officer had ridden—by
this time most of the nonsense had been whacked out of
it—and bumped solidly round the course, while the fresher
animals of the Grenadier and Scots Guards Battalions
unseated their riders at every hundred yards or so.

There was also a blindfold drill competition won by
the Prince of Wales's Company.

The battalion easily scored the highest number of
points in the meeting.

Four days later, on June 30th, the Duke of Connaught visited the division and witnessed a comic football match, twenty-five a side and four balls, between
the Welsh Guards and the 1st Battalion Grenadier
Guards, and the latter had their revenge.

We have mentioned field practice, rifle practice and
sport, but the drill of the battalion was not forgotten.
Sergt.-Major Bland had been relieved by Sergt.-Major
Stevenson in May.   Bland had done a lot of exceedingly
good work with the battalion.   He was popular with
officers and men.   Although the only two battles he had
been allowed to take part in were Loos and Gouzeaucourt,
he had been in the line continually for two years.   No
one was more sorry than himself at the order to return
to England, but it was, on the other hand, rather hard
on Sergt.-Major Stevenson to be kept indefinitely with
the Reserve Battalion.

Stevenson had been badly wounded earlier in the war
while serving with the Scots Guards, the joint of his knee
being damaged, and active service was out of the question for him when the battalion left England.   He had,
however, been fit for some time, and Bland had had a
long and successful career, and so the change was effected.

One does not compare such men : the services of both
were of inestimable value to the regiment.

One other amusing incident occurred during this rest
at Barly—Capt. Smart, of the 2nd Canadian Division,
gave a series of clever demonstrations in patrolling and
stealth raids.   The major-general, all the brigadiers and
commanding officers assembled to witness one of these
demonstrations.   The Canadian party were to start
about three hundred yards away and creep as close as
they could to the audience.   The patrol was seen standing in the distance, and when Smart blew a whistle they
all lay down and disappeared in the long grass.

From time to time Smart asked if any could be seen ;
but, although officers consulted in whispers with each
other, no one committed himself except, for some unknown reason, Lord Gort.   "Yes," said he, "I can see
two . . . three."   Of course every one gathered around
Gort and asked to be shown.   He pointed to patches of
grass in the middle of the field.   "They are going," said
he, "at a tremendous pace."   A chorus of "Yes, yes—I
see," broke out.   Gusts of wind were moving the long
grass in many directions, but nothing like a crawling

man. The most any patrol could hope to do was to get
within a hundred yards of the audience, as the grass
became very thin, and there was nothing in the nature
of a ditch on the straight line of advance they could get
into. Suddenly Smart said : " There are four men
within ten yards of you ! " And there were. The men
had made a wide détour behind a bank, got well behind
the party of watchers, and approached them along the
side of a hedge to which they had all turned their backs.
Smart then blew a whistle, and the rest of the patrol
stood up—they had advanced about thirty yards in as
many minutes. After explaining how the four men had
worked round, Smart proceeded dryly to say that any
advance across the flat ground which was being watched
could only be done very slowly, and in this case it would
probably take several hours to reach the possible limit.
Everyone who thought he had discovered something and
not said so then felt very pleased.

On July 6th the battalion relieved the 15th Lancashire
Fusiliers in the left sector opposite Boyelles. The line
held on this occasion was practically the same as before,
the one alteration being that nothing was held north
the road Boisleux St. Marc—Boiry Becquerelle. The
front trench had been deepened and posts connected up
so that a tour of the line could be made in daylight.
Otherwise there was not much change.

In the method of holding the sector there had been
several changes. The brigade now held a one-battalion
front, with one battalion in support on Hill 115, the spur
which ran out from the main ridge (about S 1), and one
battalion in reserve in trenches south of Blairville.

The system of holding the outpost line was slightly
altered several times, but broadly speaking it was two
companies in the front line, one in support and one in
reserve. In the event of attack there were secret orders
that the front two companies should, if possible, fall back
on a line at the foot of Hill 115. The support company
would be left in advance of this line, but they had a
strong position, and the artillery arrangements gave
them good protection. It was a daring plan, and de-

pended for success on getting early knowledge of the enemy attack.

Meanwhile most active patrolling was carried on, but the enemy was never caught out of his defended lines.

While in this sector the battalion was drawn much closer to the artillery than ever before. Up to that time, but for a few exceptions, the artillery officers were only known to Battalion H.Q. and not to the Company Officers. Under Lieut.-Col. Murray Threipland the battalion mess had kept all officers in close touch with headquarters, so that they occasionally saw visitors, but, owing to force of circumstances, the battalion mess had gradually disappeared, and was quite impossible under the fighting scheme of this date. But Humphrey Dene and Charles Vickery, who commanded the 74th Artillery Brigade, were both men who loved society. Consequently the headquarter mess became a place where Company Officers dropped in to tea and dinner, and there they frequently met Col. Vickery and some of his officers, and were invited by them to their messes. This was made the more possible by the fact that all were gathered together in a small area at Blairville.

Great efforts had been made in these trenches to construct habitable sandbag cabins. The mess in both reserve and support headquarters was quite good—transplanted to an English garden either would be considered a quaint tool-shed. But many an amusing yarn was told after dinner in these places, Col. Vickery having a stock from Egypt and the East which were hard to cap.

At this time polo was played practically in sight of the enemy. On a clear day one could see the hill of Monchy from the polo-ground, and maybe the German artillery observer, when he turned his telescope that way, sometimes wondered what was happening. Col. Vickery was responsible for the ground, and the Commanding Officer and Keith Menzies were the chief players from the battalion—the brigadier played also.

The work was strenuous, but the fighting uneventful. Several times the brigadier complimented the battalion on patrol work and digging and wiring. But the enemy was hardly ever seen, and confined his aggressive efforts to shelling trench systems and roads. Casualties were steady, a continual loss, although never very great at any one time. The most severe loss was C.S.M. Orton.

Orton was a smart and most capable warrant officer. He had exceptional organising ability, and whatever he took in hand was done swiftly, quietly and well. He had been company sergeant-major to No. 4 Company until the end of 1916, when he was transferred to a base depot to train Canadian troops. He was away for some months, and when he returned was posted to the Prince of Wales's Company, much to Arthur Gibbs's satisfaction. No man ever deserved the meritorious medal more than he did. He was an excellent soldier.

The battalion had cause to be thankful it had not lost more of its warrant officers. C.S.M. Orton was by no means the first to be hit. Drill-Sergt. Woodhouse was hit at Vermelles, Drill Sergt. Harris at Ypres in the St. Jean sector—he came out again, was given a commission and left the battalion at Serques—and before many weeks Drill-Sergt. Roberts was to be hit. C.S.M. Pearce was a reckless man, and had some very narrow escapes, especially at Arras when he pursued an enemy patrol, was seen by an enemy machine gunner, and got a bullet through his steel helmet. Beardsmore was another stout fighter, and Jenkins and Coyne loved to engage in rifle grenade and sniping duels. C.S.M. Cossey was twice hit. Considering the length of time they had been in the front line, and the severity of the weather, changes had been remarkably few.

C.Q.M.S. Hunter had acted as company sergeant-major for the Prince of Wales's Company until Roberts arrived at Laventie. Pearce had been with No. 2 Company all through ; Cossey, of No. 3 Company, was hit at Loos, and his place taken by Beardsmore, who received a commission while at Arras, and was succeeded by Coyne, until then company quartermaster sergeant of No. 3 (Coyne had followed C.Q.M.S. Henton, No. 3 Company, who died of sickness) ; No. 4 had Jenkins after a short period of Wadeson, who had taken over from Orton when he went to the base.

Promotions had been few. Sergt.-Major Bland had been promoted to that position when Barnes left. Harris then came out in December 1916 as drill-sergeant. Roberts received a definite appointment as drill-sergeant at the end of 1916, Harris having been wounded, and Dunkley, who had joined the battalion at Ypres, having gone home sick. The vacancy in the Prince of Wales's Company caused by Roberts's appointment was filled first by Cossey for a very short time, and then by Sergt. Nicholson, who acted as sergeant-major for several months with great success, when he received a commission and Orton was called back from the base. Young was company quartermaster-sergeant of the Prince of Wales's Company, but had to go home on account of deafness, and, after several sergeants had held an acting appointment, Sergt. Hyam received the promotion.

C.S.M. Moseley was sent out from home to fill poor Orton's place. Freestone joined the battalion as drill-sergeant in the spring of 1918.

CHAPTER XVI

AMERICAN TROOPS—THE OPENING OF THE GREAT ADVANCE—ST. LEGER

IN trench warfare, and indeed in all warfare, any rain of greater proportions than a shower causes extra discomfort, and perhaps assumes more importance than it should—one remembers the mud, the days and nights in wet clothes, the trickle of water down the neck while peering over the parapet, the futile attempt to smoke a sodden cigarette, the state of the bread brought in by the ration parties, and the falls in the slime. Generally the summer was good, and, although the battalion spent long weeks in the trenches, their spirits were in no way affected. Except for the prevalence of boils, the health of the men was excellent.

Sergt. Manuel, of No. 4 Company, was out of the line with boils for some considerable time. He was a very gallant and cheerful fighter. Sergt. Trott had been in the line for six weeks on end, during which he had not seen Manuel. When the battalion went out to rest these two worthies met. " I have got something interesting to show you," said Trott, and produced an ordinary round of ammunition which he held up in front of Manuel's nose. " This," he explained, " is what we use in the line to kill Germans—we call it a ' round.' Want to keep it as a souvenir."

Looking back at the humdrum, matter-of-fact manner in which duties were performed, the days when there seemed nothing more to do but lie in the sun, and the only grumble was when enemy shells shifted you from one spot to another, the cheery evenings with the Com-

manding Officer, Luxmoore Ball, Walter Bonn, L. F.
Ellis, Geoffrey Devas, Upjohn, Toby Mathew, Ben
Davies, Paton and the " Boys," with visits from Vickery,
Rymer Jones, and the rest of the merry crew of the 74th
Brigade—and recalling the conversations on possible
German attacks, with the inevitable remark from someone that " I don't believe there are any Huns opposite
us at all," and the Commanding Officer's " I want to
have a cut at Fritz. . . . Are we asleep ?   Are we
wooden men to be stuck in these holes for Fritz to have
cock-shies at us ? "—it seems curious that no whisper
of possible future events reached the ears of the battalion.
And yet the possibility was indicated.

The enemy efforts on the Somme and the Lys Valley
had secured some result for him which a further success
might turn into disaster for the Allied Forces.   A gain
of mere territory does not mean much unless it includes
centres of vital importance.   The two great enemy
" drives " had placed the Germans within striking distance of much-used and valuable railway junctions at
Amiens, Bethune, and Hazebrouck.   St. Pol was within
range of his long guns.   He only required a little more
and British communications in Northern France would
be disorganised.

This was generally known and understood in the
battalion, but the foreigner's estimation of British character as " arrogant " would seem to be right in this one
respect, that the feeling of the British Army was not
one of dismay, but rather of assurance that " if the
damned railway is cut we will push up the stuff in hand-
carts."   Despondency was absolutely unknown, and
throughout the British Army repeated attacks strengthened the obstinate determination of all ranks to perse-
vere.   The Commanding Officer, arriving in the front
line, having passed through severe shelling, was typical
in his remarks.   ", What is this fool Fritz doing ?   What
is his game ?   Does he think he is going to stop me
going up the line.   What ? "

But while we emphasise the dull and unexciting nature
of the routine of duty, the pleasant weather and company

in the vicinity of Blairville, there were flashes of irritation caused by warnings of attack. Sir Douglas Haig indicates in his despatches that the Higher Command was discussing fresh enemy attacks up to the second week of July, and that one of the fronts considered to be threatened was Arras—Amiens—Montdidier. The British general staff considered that the enemy would first attack farther south, and their judgment proved sound. No doubt what came down through the Guards Division were precautionary warnings.

On July 15th the enemy launched an attack south of Reims and crossed the Marne. On the 18th Marshal Foch launched his counter-offensive from Château Thierry to Soissons.

American troops were in both these actions. American troops had been training at Warlincourt and the areas behind the Guards Division, as everyone knew, and on July 23rd American troops—15 officers and 85 N.C.O.'s and O.R.'s from the 80th Division U.S.A.—were attached to the battalion for forty-eight hours' instruction in trench duties. On August 5th the battalion, plus six platoons of the 1st Battalion 320th American Infantry Regiment, relieved the 1st Battalion Grenadier Guards in the front line, and the battalion began to think that the future might bring some change in the monotony.

" *August 6th*, 1918.—I relieved the Grenadier Company at 11 p.m. yesterday, but the Americans under me did not arrive till past one, and the line did not settle down till past three. The first wink of sleep I have had since 7 a.m. yesterday was at 12 noon to-day, and then the staff, having slept well in their beds all night, and desiring employment before 2 p.m. lunch, wakened me! However, the Americans seem good, keen men—they are fresh and interested. Toby Mathew is with me and Brawn—both good companions. The trenches are very muddy, but the weather is improving after last night's showers. There are rumours of leave being doubled. . . .

" *August 8th*.—More Yankees came in last night and the old lot departed. They make one laugh, they are so

green, but they are so devilish anxious not to be caught
napping they are positively dangerous to anyone going
round the line—every sentry you visit receives you with
a bayonet in your face. Some of them went out on
patrol last night, and, as usual with novices, thought
they saw an army of Huns in every row of stakes. I
ordered them to fire on everything they thought sus-
picious, and the result was a ripple of shots all night.
I wonder what the Huns think has happened. Broncho
came round this morning with the American major, a
southerner called Gordon. He was a long, hard-looking
fellow, and very thirsty. Without saying a word he took
hold of a bottle of diluted peroxide I used to clean my
teeth and had a long drink. ' Gee ! ' he said, ' that is
the strongest water I have had for some time ! ' I hope
it won't hurt him.

" *August 9th.*—One unfortunate American killed by
one of our own shells. There is a small percentage that
drop short and an occasional one of these hits. I have
straffed like the deuce about it. These Americans are not
bad. They are very keen, willing and good-tempered.
Everything goes wrong with them in the process of learning—they are starved for food or water and suffer infinite
annoyances, but they keep up their spirits well. Last
night must have been a weird experience for them. It
started with Brawn going out on patrol, which filled
them with excitement, and then worked up to a full
' harassing shoot.' The air was full of shells—field-guns,
medium, and heavies up to 12-inch, coming singly or in
salvoes, with fierce, long-drawn wails and whistlings—and
above them the drone of aeroplanes. The sky was cut
with searchlight rays, and then ' wumph, wumph, wumph,
wumph ! ' as each plane dropped its load of bombs.
Noisy, tiring night.

" *August 10th.*—Yesterday afternoon we amused ourselves by having a duel with the Hun—it is quite entertaining, and the men love it. The Hun starts it by firing
his Minenwerfers—which are numbered as far as we know
them—and the moment anyone sees where they are
coming from a runner dashes down to me, I 'phone the

artillery, giving the Minnie number, and also send runners in all directions to our trench-mortars. Yesterday the Hun, who had been quiet for some weeks, suddenly fired eight rounds and wounded an American, and within ten minutes a deluge descended on him till the air was thick with dust. The Yanks were delighted, but the funniest was Brawn. He kept on breaking from stolid contemplation of the scene with a ' By God ! Ha, ha, ha ! ' until his face became crimson—then as quickly became stolid, almost bovine again. After a quarter of an hour of this we stopped and waited—so did the Hun. But after two hours he fired again, and I sent the word ' repeat,' and every one duly repeated. Brawn had to go to a court-martial, and Toby and I conducted the relief, which was somewhat messed up by Walter Bonn forgetting, apparently, that we had Americans with us—it was not a good lesson for the Yanks. Poor Toby had a hard time, and we arrived in our new quarters, in close support, at one, and sat till two eating marmalade—Toby chatting in a clever, boyish, high-spirited manner—when we had a couple of hours' sleep and went out for ' stand to.' Five minutes after the Hun gave us a burst of hurricane shelling, and Toby and his orderly were hit—I fear both badly. They were very cheerful, and kept on asking each other how they were. Mags, the orderly, with a bit of his nose off, his hand smashed, and his kneecap torn off, observed that he was ' well cam-u-fladged.' "
—*Diary, C. H. D. W.*

The battalion was relieved and went to Saulty on the night of August 11th.

On July 23rd Marshal Foch had held a conference at which decisions of the first magnitude were arrived at. The opening move in the great Allied offensive was to free the railway communications, and French, American, and British armies were each to work on its own front with that object in view. The British army was to free the Paris—Amiens Railway by an attack on the Albert—Montdidier front. When the success of this general attack had been achieved the French and American

16

Armies would continue the advance, converging on
Mezières, while the British armies would cut the communication running through Maubeuge to Hirson and
Mezières, which was the sole line of supply for the German armies on the Champagne front. The success of
the British army in this direction would also be an
immediate threat to the German armies in Flanders.

This was a battle planned on a grand scale, and knowing what were at least the published limits of previous
efforts, one cannot but admire the confidence of the
Marshal in issuing such orders.

For the battle of Amiens Marshal Foch placed the
First French Army, commanded by Gen. Debeny, under
Sir Douglas Haig. The British Fourth Army, under
Rawlinson, was to open the attack. The Fourth Army
was composed of the Canadian Corps on the right, with
the 3rd, 1st, and 2nd Canadian Divisions in line, and the
4th Canadian Division in support; the Australian Corps,
with the 2nd and 3rd Australian Divisions in line, and
the 5th and 4th Australian Divisions in support; the
III Corps, with the 58th and 18th Divisions in line and
the 12th Division in support. The First French Army
attacked an hour after the British assault had been
delivered.

The battle opened at 4.20 a.m. on August 8th, and on
the first day the Fourth Army had advanced about seven
miles, and had captured 13,000 prisoners and between
300 and 400 guns, and by August 12th it had reached
the old German line of 1916, a total advance of twelve
miles, with a total capture of 22,000 prisoners and over
400 guns.

The French and Americans to the south had kept pace
with the British advance, and the elastic nature of the
Allied Forces is shown in this battle when it is noted that
a regiment of the 33rd American Division joined the
Fourth Army, and, on the 13th, the First French Army
ceased to be under Sir Douglas Haig.

The railways were free. There was still the Lys salient,
but the general advance south had forced the enemy to
alter his plans in the north, and already on the night

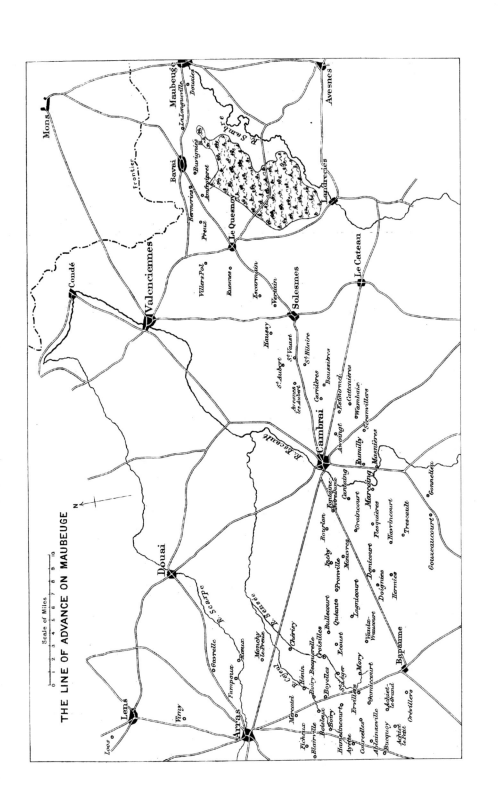

THE LINE OF ADVANCE ON MAUBEUGE

August 13/14th British patrols were pushing forward in that salient, and on the 18th and 19th the Second Army under Plumer advanced, capturing 900 prisoners and threatening disaster to the enemy.

On the 15th the Welsh Guards moved to the reserve area at Blairville, and on the 18th relieved the 1st Battalion 320th Regiment U.S.A.—who were in support on the right of the former positions occupied in the Purple Line and behind the 1st Battalion Irish Guards—and so for the moment came under the command of the 1st Brigade. On the 20th the battalion relieved the 2nd Battalion Scots Guards in the original support line, and on the 21st was relieved by the 16th Battalion Northumberland Fusiliers and moved back to some trenches to the east of Ransart and close to Adinfer Wood.

Opposition to the Fourth Army had stiffened. The moral of the German infantry had been rudely shaken, but the picked men of their machine-gun units found in the devastated area of the old Somme battle-field ideal ground for their arms and tactics. For miles the ground had been pounded into odd shapes and trenches crossed and recrossed in a bewildering fashion ; the whole was covered with a thick tangle of weeds effectively concealing shell-holes, trenches and remnants of wire. Though the advance slowed down pressure was not relaxed.

The time had come for the Third Army to move, not only on account of the resistance opposite the Fourth Army, but in order to take full advantage of ground which had been denied Sir Douglas Haig in the first battle of the Somme. The ridge which we have mentioned, and which was defended by the Purple Line, was held in 1916 by the enemy ; a successful attack between Albert and Arras would turn the old Somme positions now in front of the Fourth Army. So on August 21st the IV and VI Corps attacked from Miraumont to Moyenville. The line ran : 42nd, New Zealand, 37th, 2nd and Guards Divisions.

The attack pivoted on the Guards Division, consequently the advance of the division on this day was not very deep, but it rendered any further action on the part

of the division the more difficult, as surprise was then out
of the question. It must, however, be borne in mind
that any movement of troops and guns to oppose one
corps might materially help another corps, and that the
general advance on the St. Quentin—Cambrai line was
to be spread far to the left of the division, where difficult
tasks awaited the Canadian Corps and the XVII Corps
on August 25th ; so that part of the duty of the Guards
Division was to pin down troops and guns.

On the 23rd the 2nd Guards Brigade and the 1st
Battalion Grenadier Guards attacked from the line
Gomiecourt—Hamelincourt and advanced some 4,000
yards to a line west of St. Leger, and in the evening the
battalion relieved the 1st Battalion Coldstream and two
companies of the 1st Battalion Scots Guards in the
neighbourhood of Judas Farm.

At one o'clock in the morning of the 24th the Commanding Officer received orders to attack at 7 a.m. in
the direction of Ecoust, with the 2nd Battalion Scots
Guards on the right and troops of the 56th Division on
the left. St. Leger would not be entered but enveloped,
the Welsh Guards passing to the north and the Scots
Guards to the south.[1]

Orders were issued to companies at 3.15 a.m., No. 3
Company (L. F. Ellis) to lead the attack, followed by
Nos. 4 (Goetz), Prince of Wales's (Upjohn), and No. 2
(Bonn) Companies at 300 yards' interval, and each in
artillery formation.

At that time Battalion H.Q. were fixed as to area by
the brigade, and on this occasion were a long way from
the front line ; the companies, too, were very scattered.
The moment he had got his orders out the Commanding
Officer went round all companies to give final advice
and see that all was ready, for the time was short.
Unfortunately, while doing so he was wounded.

He had a fine record with the battalion. As second
in command he had taken part in the minor operation at
Mortaldje, had commanded the battalion on September
25th and subsequent days in the battle of the Somme

[1] Appendix B 11.

MAJOR (ACTING LT.-COLONEL) HUMPHREY DENE, D.S.O.

of 1916, and frequently in the line, notably in those
unpleasant places Gueudecourt and Sailly-Saillisel.
Under him the battalion was perhaps more aggressive
than it had ever been, for he was a fighter with an impetuous nature, and frequently led his troops in person.
His handling of the battalion through the anxious times
of March and April was admirable, and his high spirits
permeated all troops under him.   He had magnetism,
and was essentially a man of action.   To get work done
was all he cared about—the reporting of it bored him.
" Went to position ordered.   Held it till relieved " was
all he had to say of September 26th, 1916.   " Battalion
in line " is a frequent entry in his diary, followed still
more frequently with the one word " Ditto " on subsequent dates.   Occasionally one comes across a hastily
scrawled " Nothing Doing."   Col. Murray Threipland was
the best diary writer, Col. Dene the worst.   Col. Douglas
Gordon was colourless and not too illuminating, but he
wrote something.   Col. Luxmoore Ball was lucid, and
indulged in caustic comments.   The best diary is always
the most indiscreet.

Luxmoore Ball was in charge of Details at Berles au
Bois, and command fell for the moment to Walter
Bonn.

At 7 a.m. the artillery opened and No. 3 Company, led
by L. F. Ellis, advanced on a frontage of 875 yards.
They came under fire from the start—the element of surprise had passed, and the enemy had put in the line two
of his best divisions from reserve.   Paton led No. 11
Platoon on the left and managed to get round and surprise a machine gun in Bank Copse and bayonet the
team.   Keeping close behind the barrage, the company
entered the trench Windmill Lane and advanced along
the railway, where captures of a field-gun and prisoners
were made.   One of the unavoidable incidents of the
advance under barrage fire now occurred—the men
pushed on too fast and were caught in their own barrage.
This led to some confusion, but Ellis quickly reorganised
his company and the advance was continued.

St. Leger was passed, the outskirts yielding a few prisoners, but there was again a check from machine guns just behind the town. Ellis rearranged his company in line of sections in file, and in this formation reached the Leger Reserve Trench with few casualties.

The Scots Guards could now be seen on the right under heavy machine-gun fire. No. 4 Company had come up into Leger Reserve, and a platoon was sent to help clear the ridge on the right against which the Scots Guards were advancing. This platoon found the enemy inclined to stand along the railway embankment, and a hidden machine gun suddenly opened on them and half the party were hit. The situation was critical, but was saved by the swift action of a Lewis Gun crew which got into action on the enemy gun and enabled the rest of the platoon to get under cover. Orders were then received that no further advance would be made that day.

Gloag, who commanded No. 10 Platoon on the right of No. 3 Company, gives an account of the proceedings.

" We entered a shallow chalk-pit, lined with dugouts on its east bank, and were in full view of the village of St. Leger, which was apparently quite deserted. We could see nothing of the 2nd Scots Guards, who were supposed to be on our immediate right, and the village itself was empty. We waited in the chalk-pit for our barrage to move ahead ; there was no enemy shelling, only a few shots from the other side of the village. The barrage lifted, and, as Paton led his platoon forward, a shell dropped into the centre of it, killing two men, and wounding several, including the platoon sergeant (Jones). We pushed forward to the road running due north from St. Leger, and went through the northern part of the village, but had to halt owing to intense machine-gun fire from the east. Ellis ordered me to crawl forward and reconnoitre a trench that ran parallel with the road (from north to south) a little beyond the village. I did so and found the trench too shallow to afford any adequate cover, and it was badly knocked about and difficult to approach. Our barrage then came down on us again, and we withdrew to the road for about fifteen minutes.

Sergt. Jones was badly wounded shortly before this temporary withdrawal.

"When the barrage lifted we went forward some 80 yards until we reached a line of trenches called St. Leger Reserve. That was our objective, but there were no signs of the Scots Guards on our right; Ellis halted, and instructed me to take out a fighting patrol along the railway, and endeavour to work round to the rear of the machine guns that were very active south of the railway embankment. It was very difficult to climb over the embankment owing to the fire, and my intention was to have followed the embankment on the north side towards Croisilles, and cross it about 300 yards from the St. Leger Reserve Line. There was very little cover on my left (*i.e.* north of the embankment), and I had gone forward about 200 yards when a machine gun that had hitherto been silent opened fire, wounding several men. We took cover in shell-holes, and one of my Lewis gunners (Guardsman Spencer) succeeded in spotting the position of the German machine gun. We opened fire, and would have continued, but save for the shell-holes we were in there was no cover, the ground sloping evenly from the German machine-gun position to the embankment. It was extremely difficult to withdraw the patrol, but the two Lewis gunners gave us covering fire, retiring as they fired. It was entirely due to their coolness and excellent shooting that the patrol were able to return without further casualties. The sergeant who accompanied me (Davis) behaved with the greatest gallantry, and carried in one of the wounded under fire.

"Prior to this patrol going out, I had been a short way down the embankment with a corporal and one man, and five Germans surrendered to us. I think they were the crew of a trench-mortar, but am uncertain regarding this.

"After my unsuccessful patrol had returned I reported to Ellis. The St. Leger Reserve trench (which had now become the front line) was being shelled with gas-shells (mustard and tear-gas), and I found Holdsworth in the section of trench that lay between the road and the em-

bankment, for No. 4 Company had come up. I got
slightly gassed getting to Company H.Q., for it caught
me before I could adjust my respirator.

" Later in the afternoon I relieved Paton in the left
of the line. The trench was very shallow, barely two
feet deep, with deep slits in the bays, but very trying to
work along, for it was swept with machine-gun fire, and
Upjohn had been killed in trying to get along it to No. 3
Company H.Q."

During the night the line was reorganised, No. 2 Company relieving No. 3 in Leger Reserve Trench; Prince of
Wales's and No. 4 were in Leger Trench, and No. 3 in
reserve in a sunken road.

The advance was to continue at 4.30 a.m. with tanks.[1]
At the appointed hour a thick mist made it impossible
to see more than ten yards, and there was no sign of any
tanks. But No. 2 Company advanced and got in with
the bayonet on some advanced enemy posts, but soon
ran into thick wire and heavy fire from machine guns.
The situation was very confusing. It was so dark no
one could tell where he was with any degree of certitude.
Patrols tried to cut the wire, but found the enemy alert
and were unable to get through.

While the company lay down in the long grass attempts were made to get in touch with troops on either
flank, but none could be found. Small parties of the
enemy kept looming through the fog as though to attack,
but were easily driven off with considerable loss.

The Prince of Wales's Company followed the line of
the railway too far, and appeared on the left of No. 2
Company, where they also ran into wire and machine
guns and lost a number of men.

Meanwhile Hill (commanding No. 2 Company) had
managed to get messages back to Bonn, and Bonn, filled
with anxiety, started off with Pte. Hammond, the headquarters orderly, to view the situation for himself. He
got completely lost in the fog and penetrated the enemy
lines. Fortunately Hammond had good eyes, and, recog-

[1] Appendix B 12.

nising enemy troops, though dimly seen, they tried to
get back, only to discover more Germans behind them.
Bonn then spent an exciting hour, his greatest difficulty
being, he declared, to stop Hammond from shooting at
different parties of the enemy.   Hammond was one of
the coolest and most gallant of men.

Goetz, with No. 4 Company, had in the meantime
disposed his company with some skill on the right flank
and informed Ellis of the fact.   And, after an hour and
a half of probing about, Ellis decided to order all companies back into Leger Reserve Trench.   When this was
accomplished belated orders arrived that no advance
would be made east of Leger Reserve Trench.   Shortly
after Walter Bonn managed to return.

The two days' fighting is remarkable for the manner
in which the enemy stood to be bayoneted.   The advance was contested all the way.   The fog on the morning of the 25th, together with the fact that troops on the
right and left did not advance owing to some misunder-
standing about time, and the non-appearance of tanks—
which, indeed, would not have helped in keeping direction—gave Bonn and the officers under him a most
difficult task ; but he had cleared the ground in front
of him to a depth of 1,000 yards, and the enemy did not
come back.

The prisoners taken were 86 ; one field-gun and
seven heavy machine guns were also captured by the
battalion.

Casualties were 144.

From 1,215 Cpl. Drake, who was killed trying to rush
a machine gun by himself, to 2,333 Pte. Llewellyn
Edwards, who, having dropped his rifle while scrambling
over some wire, engaged in fisticuffs with the enemy, all
the men did well. 823 Sergt. E. Jones, 408 Sergt. Davies,
1,037 Sergt. Aspinall, 1,876 L/Sergt. Gilbert, 1,063
L/Sergt. Hutchings, 1,078 Cpl. Attfield, 216 L/Cpl. R.
Davies, 252 L/Cpl. Messer, 1,529 L/Cpl. G. Thomas, Ptes.
4,153 H. Crebben, 4,016 J. Cornelius, 144 S. G. Spencer,
and 2,111 H. G. Neale were a few whose names were
noted for good work.

Poor Upjohn was a very gallant fellow, with supreme contempt for the enemy.

The battalion was relieved on the night of the 25th by the 2nd Battalion Coldstream Guards, and marched back to trenches east of Boiry, and from there on the 27th to trenches south of Ransart. Major Luxmoore Ball then assumed command and the battalion refitted.

Luxmoore Ball stood 6 feet 4 inches, with a fine width of shoulder. He was a very dark man, with blue eyes, a fierce expression, quick temper, and the heart of a boy. He enjoyed life thoroughly. Like Humphrey Dene, he had had much experience in the trenches, and has the longest active service with the battalion of any officer in the regiment, with the exception of Dabell. He was the only Commanding Officer in the Brigade of Guards to wear the D.C.M.

For a few days the battalion trained and rested, and on September 2nd the 3rd Guards Brigade concentrated at a place called Maida Vale between Mory and Ecoust. The battalion bivouacked in old trenches west of Ecoust, and at 5.20 a.m. on the 3rd formed up on the line of the railway north of Ecoust to attack in the direction of Lagnicourt.[1] The 2nd Guards Brigade were on the right of the battalion and the 2nd Scots Guards on the left. This attack was again preceded by a barrage, which crept forward at the rate of 100 yards every four minutes, and at 6.45 a.m. an advance of 2,000 yards had been made with little opposition, although the battalion gathered in fourteen prisoners and a quantity of abandoned machine guns.

All this country was organised with lines of trenches, and was capable of vigorous defence; but the enemy was now near the Hindenburg Line, where he proposed to stand.

The leading companies, No. 4 and the Prince of Wales's (under Harrop) sent out patrols to the high ground to the east of Lagnicourt and found the ridges were not held, and at 1 p.m. the whole brigade continued the advance to about 3,000 yards from Mœuvres, when lead-

[1] Appendix B 13.

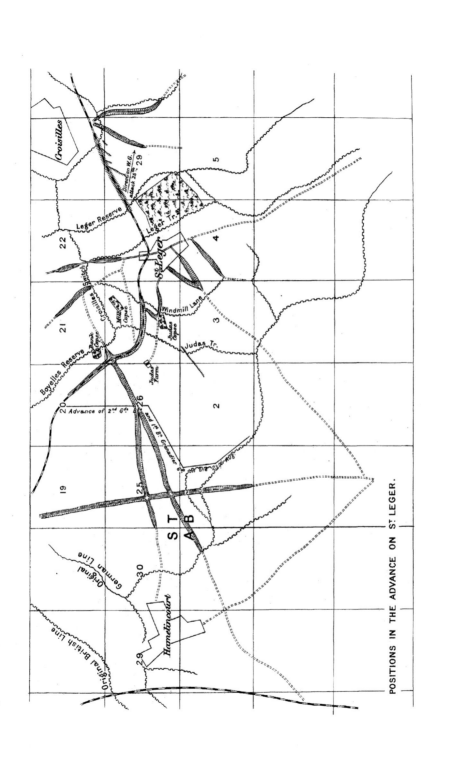

POSITIONS IN THE ADVANCE ON S⸌ LEGER.

ing companies formed an outpost line. No opposition was met with beyond long-range shelling.

The battalion was relieved at 1.30 a.m. on the 4th, and at 5.30 a.m. again passed through the outpost line with the 2nd Battalion Scots Guards on the left as advance guard to the division. The order was No. 3 Company on the right, No. 2 on the left, No. 4 in support, and the Prince of Wales's Company in reserve. The corps on the left were reported to hold Mœuvres, and the division was ordered to advance to the Hindenburg Support, but no serious attack was to be made if the enemy showed signs of resistance.

When the leading companies reached the ridge east of Boursies they were met with long-range machine-gun fire, and the enemy showed himself in numbers on the opposite ridge; it was therefore decided to consolidate on the ground occupied. A flank was formed, as the troops on the right were not in touch.

Twice during the day Trotter gallantly led patrols to try and cross the valley, but each time was driven back, he being mortally wounded in the last attempt. And so matters remained until 6.30 p.m., when the 2nd Scots Guards attacked under a barrage, and No. 3 Company Welsh Guards with strong patrols out in front advanced across the valley and gained the opposite ridge. Here they encountered heavy machine-gun fire from the Hindenburg Line, but they occupied Goat Trench and tried to work forward down communication trenches; they found, however, that all the trenches were blocked and held, and that the whole line was strongly defended with many machine guns.

It was now dark, and all through the night the enemy kept up a constant machine-gun fire. In spite of this patrols tested the possibility of further advance, but found the whole front heavily wired. The Scots Guards found the same strong defence on the left. Shelling was constant, and the reserve company was heavily gassed.

There was still a large gap on the right of the battalion, and at 3 p.m. orders were received that as this gap would not be filled by troops on the right the Welsh Guards must make it good. The battalion was now some 1,200 yards from the Canal du Nord, on the far side of which was a commanding rise crowned by Bourlon Wood, with direct observation over any movement. No. 2 Company succeeded in getting two platoons into Goat Trench, on the right of No. 3, but shelling then became so intense that the Commanding Officer directed that no further attempts should be made. It must be remembered that Goat Trench was an enemy trench, and protected by belts of wire, so that all approach to it was down a forward slope and over the wire. At night a way was cut through and the remaining two platoons of the company moved in on the right.

The 3rd Guards Brigade was relieved that night by the 2nd Guards Brigade, and the battalion went into trenches and dugouts east of Lagnicourt.

We are now at September 5th and in front of the Hindenburg Line. The advance from the positions Ayette—Boyelles had been merely pursuit of the enemy, who only stood when the battalion attacked at St. Leger on August 24th—we are speaking of the days when the battalion led the advance. But now the enemy was in his celebrated stronghold, the invincible Hindenburg Line, the place where he undoubtedly meant to stand and hold up the advance—a by no means impossible dream, as he was numerically stronger than the British forces before him. But, although he had scrambled back to the Hindenburg Line, its stability was already threatened.

The Canal du Nord is only an incident in the Hindenburg Line, which ran from St. Quentin in the south, by the Scheldt Canal, La Vacquerie, in front of Ribecourt and Havrincourt (on the east of the canal), then along the western bank of the canal to Mœuvres, where it turned west to Quéant. The Hindenburg Line ceased here, but was linked up to the strong Lens defences by a mass of trenches and wire known as the Drocourt—Quéant Line.

On September 2nd the 1st and 4th Canadian Divisions, the 4th, 52nd, 57th, and 63rd Divisions broke through the Drocourt—Quéant system and accelerated the enemy retreat behind the Hindenburg Line while threatening that line itself.

Ten days later the 62nd Division captured the village of Havrincourt.

Meanwhile, the battalion rested in trenches near Lagnicourt, and had baths which had been fixed in the ruins of that village. On the 12th it went back into the line in what was called the Mœuvres sector, immediately north of the Bapaume—Cambrai Road. Shelling was very severe, and the gallant Sergt. Evans, the sick sergeant, was mortally wounded on the 16th. His acts of courage and coolness while tending the wounded are beyond number—a quiet, smiling, smart man of medium height, with clear blue eyes and square jaw, with a cheery word for every stricken man, never weary, never flustered—he was a great loss.

The enemy was most active ; not only did he shell the line night and day and use a great deal of gas, but his patrols were adventurous. On the 17th No. 4 Company was attacked as the battalion was being relieved by the 2nd Battalion Coldstream Guards. The enemy selected the extreme left post, which was held by a platoon under Sergt. Waddington. An old communication-trench connected the British and enemy line at this point, and the enemy tried a bombing raid down this trench. Sergt. Waddington led his men out of the trench and bombed the enemy from the parapet. Foiled in this direction, they now tried to rush Waddington in the open, but he and his men met them there and drove them back. It was quite a brisk little fight.

After a rest near Noreuil the battalion went into the Demicourt sector, on the south of the Bapaume—Cambrai Road. Posts on the right of the battalion front were on the Canal Bank, and Adams, a new officer, succeeded in taking a small patrol across the canal in daylight. At night, however, the enemy was very aggressive, and twice made attempts on the right company (No. 3). The company was disposed in a series of posts and the ground was very broken and confused. The first raid

was a matter of a patrol getting between two posts and
being met by an orderly who, however, managed to escape
with a bayonet-wound.   The patrol was then chased out.
Encouraged no doubt by thinking it was easy to get
through, a more ambitious attempt was made the next
night, but was met with Lewis Guns.   Paton then went
out to get identification from the enemy dead, but as he

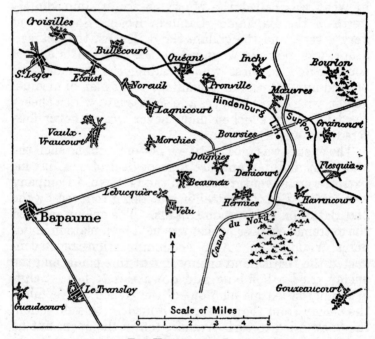

THE HINDENBURG LINE.

reached them the British barrage came down in No Man's
Land and wounded his orderly.   Paton hastily cut a
shoulder-strap from the nearest body and helped his
orderly back.   The battalion was at that moment being
relieved by the 2nd Battalion Coldstream Guards, and
only when he was back in the trenches near Lagnicourt,
and went to report, did Paton discover that the shoulder-
strap was blank.

The battalion rested from the 23rd to the 26th.

The country in front of the Hindenburg Line was most desolate.

" All the villages are flat, merely marked by heaps of white and brick-coloured dust, the trees are all cut down, and the series of ridges have no landmarks of any kind to distinguish one from the other.   Wandering about, one finds gun-pits and stacks of ammunition of all sizes— these are sometimes in sunken roads, but mostly dotted about the country, which is all overgrown with coarse grass.   It is good country for any sort of manœuvres, as it is criss-crossed with trenches, though they are over-grown and look like ditches."—*Diary, C. H. D. W.*

But during the pause of three weeks the desolation, without losing any of its frightful atmosphere of destruc-tion and ruin, became a most animated scene.   Marshal Foch, in consultation with Sir Douglas Haig and other Allied Commanders, had decided on four simultaneous offensives.   The Americans were to thrust west of the Meuse and in the direction of Mezières ; the French, to the west of the Argonne, were to advance in close co-operation with the Americans and with the same objec-tives ; the British would drive forward on the St. Quen-tin—Cambrai front in the direction of Maubeuge ; and the Belgian and Allied Forces would push forward in the direction of Ghent.

CHAPTER XVII

THROUGH THE HINDENBURG LINE

In front of the British Army was the last belt of prepared defences on which all the skill and ingenuity of the enemy, all the study of the past forty years, had been lavished. One felt "Der Tag" had arrived. There was a kind of eagerness, an expression of expectancy, a curious grin noticeable among the men. Every man was used to the whistle, wail, and crash of shells, to the drone of the night aeroplane, and the wumph, wumph, wumph of its bombs; but there seemed to be more bitterness, more determination in the shelling, and certainly enemy aeroplanes had never been chased as now.

The peculiar waving drone of the enemy aeroplane would be heard every night, and the dark vault of the sky would be cut by countless shafts of light searching for the adventurer of the air; one ray would catch him and at once all rays would concentrate on the large but ghostly night-moth. Aircraft and machine guns then opened fire, phosphorus bullets rising like a trail of sparks. Suddenly high up in the heavens a star would appear, blinking—dot dash dash dot, dot dash dash dot —and while an observer might wonder why a star should apparently signal, or if his eye had played him false, a little trail of sparks would come down from nowhere, and one seemingly settle on the silvery aircraft. Was it fancy, or could a long-drawn "A-ah" be heard? The settled spark grew and grew—the course of the aeroplane altered towards the earth—as it swept down it blazed, and, as a flame slanting from the sky, fell to the ground. And the star twinkled while a signaller read "Cheerio."

Before the division attacked again it lost its old tried
and trusted leader. Lord Cavan had the honour of first
commanding the division, and Major-Gen. Matheson that
of commanding in the very last phase of the Great War,
but Major-Gen. Feilding may be looked upon, from the
length of time he commanded and the number of engagements he went through, as the commander of the Guards
Division. He had sound common sense and was absolutely fearless—two good qualities for a soldier. Promotion is not always viewed by lower ranks with favour
—that is, promotion which cannot affect their own status
—and in this case it was generally wished that Geoffrey
Feilding's promotion might have been delayed.

To the battalion itself Percy Battye and Fox-Pitt
returned—Battye to No. 4 Company (Dudley Ward becoming second in command of the battalion), Fox-Pitt
to the Prince of Wales's Company. All was ready for
the attack. The Welsh Guards came out of the line of
organised trenches for the last time, and were billeted in
some German dugouts under a bank to the east of Lagnicourt.

" All days are much the same with the exception of
X and Y days. These lettered days are a product of
the war. Whenever anything is doing the two preceding
days are called X and Y, the day of action ' Z ' day—to-
day is the Y day. During the last ten days we have
been preparing for a big battle, though it only became
known five days ago. I believe it is to be the biggest
fight of the war, and is of absorbing interest. All plans
are laid up to a point, and then they cease, as that point
means success, and the catch word ' exploiting success '
is applied. My map is of all colours of the rainbow, each
colour meaning a different move. I have painted one for
each company commander, and for once I think each
officer knows what is being attempted on his flank to a
distance of a corps frontage on either side. I am not
quite clear how many corps will really attack, but rumour
has it that four armies are going. At any rate one feels
there is a plan, and that is very encouraging.

17

" Ball is doing things very well. He understands his
scheme, knows his map, and has explained everything
clearly to all concerned. It only remains to be seen if
he can apply what he knows to the ground, and I think
he will. Yesterday the major-general in his pow-wow
with officers and N.C.O.'s. gave a glimpse of the larger
movements which should extend over a good many days.
He also told us what troops we might expect to meet.

" I shall be left behind with Sergt.-Major Stevenson,
who is raging like a bull, and declaring, with many stut-
ters, ' I, sir, I—I am ab-ab-absolutely useless, sir ! '

" The guns we have in position are beyond counting,
and just lie about with no attempt at concealment. Ammunition the same. Tents are pitched in full view of the
enemy ; thousands of grazing horses crown every sky-
line ; at night the roads are impassable with the quantity
of horse, motor, and tank traffic ; and by day and night
the one continual noise is from aeroplanes buzzing about.
Cavalcades of officers, with maps waving in the air, ride
along tracks looking at the country—in fact, no one gives
a damn for the Boche, who, considering the vast preparations, is wonderfully quiet. He can't say we don't tell
him we are coming.

" *September 27th.*—Every one went to bed early last
night and about 10.30 p.m., just before going to sleep, I
heard a few drops of rain fall on the roof of my tin shelter.
Reveille was at 3 a.m., and it was then drizzling, very
fine like mist ; the ground, however, beyond being slimy
on the surface, was good. The first thing I heard was
Stevenson calling out, ' Get up, everybody—meet the
Germans at 4.30 ! ' Then there was a thud, and for the
first time I heard him swear good solid army oaths. But
his good spirits returned, and I heard him slide away
saying, ' Where is my valet ? Does he want me to bring
him a cup of tea ? '

" Breakfast at four, and everybody very cheerful while
they got ready without any fuss. At ten minutes to five
the battalion marched with an interval of 50 to 100 yards
between platoons, Ball and H.Q. going last. . . .

" Stevenson and I climbed to a high spot at 5.20, and

the barrage started to a second. It was still dark, but the misty rain had cleared and half a moon shone brightly ; a decent breeze was blowing patches of light clouds towards the Hun, and prevented us hearing the forward guns which had been moved up almost behind the front line. The whole horizon was lit up with a bright, yellow, flickering glow, like summer lightning, and then Hun lights, green and red, shot up in bunches, but not a great number of them.

" At six o'clock the first aeroplane went over—at 6.30 the first balloon went up. We walked leisurely forward with the growing light, and topping the next rise, found the distant battle was before us like a coloured print of such scenes. We were looking due east, and a low, dark cloud-bank hid the rising sun, but above the cloud-bank was a blaze of red and yellow light. We could see a succession of ridges and the silhouettes of two villages—a large one far off in the centre—and on the left high, commanding ground with Bourlon Wood. Smoke was drifting up and away from us, rising first in round, woolly puffs, then in feathery spirals ; but the view was vast and distant, so that these shell-bursts seemed puny things, making innumerable small streaks and blobs of white and light grey. Pin-point flashes scattered about the blue ridges showed where many enemy guns were firing, and, from a military point of view, I was surprised at the small number of enemy flashes, also, as far as one could make out at that distance, the poor reply to our fire.

" We were not allowed to look at the spectacle very long, as the sun shot out of the cloud-bank and effectively blinded us.

" As we strolled back we found balloons coming forward, floating high above the motor-lorries to which they were attached. Columns of artillery limbers, squads of Red Cross men, carts, mules, and a stream of men passed in an endless procession down the road.

" Soon after 10 a.m. Spence Thomas, who had been in charge of a party carrying Lewis Guns and ammunition so as to save the fighting men as much as possible, came back. He told me the battalion had crossed the canal

without casualties, and that the Hun barrage was nothing.　He had, however, lost eighteen killed and
wounded by a stray shell which pitched right into the
centre of his party just over the next rise.　I sent him
back to Details."—*Diary, C. H. D. W.*

To follow the movements of the battalion, we must
once more give a general idea of the big plan of battle.[1]
The IV, VI, and XVII and Canadian Corps were attacking in the direction of Cambrai on a thirteen-mile front
from Gouzeaucourt to Sauchy Lestyre.　Of the VI Corps
the 3rd Division was on the right and the Guards Division
on the left.　The 57th Division was to operate on the
left of the Guards.　Orders issued covered an advance
to the St. Quentin Canal.　On the right flank the 1st
Battalion Gordon Highlanders and a battalion of the
Suffolk Regiment were to accompany the 2nd and 1st
Guards Brigades to the east of Flesquières, when the
2/20th London Regiment would pass through and continue the advance to Marcoing.　On the left flank it was
hoped that the 9th Battalion King's Liverpool Regiment
would advance to the outskirts of Cantaing, which place
would be assaulted by the 1st Battalion Royal Munsters.
　Those were the orders.　Actually the 57th Division did
not advance till later in the day, and the 52nd Division
crossed the canal on the left of the Guards Division, but
were held up by the strong defences before Graincourt.
The point to be remembered, in following all the movements of the Guards Division, is that the division on their
left flank was stationary after crossing the canal, and
that the village of Graincourt was only captured by the
63rd Division late in the day.　The enemy resistance at
that point was of a most desperate nature.
　The line of advance for the Guards Division was to the
south of Graincourt, and north of Flesquières through
Orival Wood, Nine Wood to Noyelles sur l'Escaut.　On
the right flank everything went according to plan.
　The 2nd Guards Brigade opened the attack ; the 1st
Brigade were to go through them and advance to the

[1] Appendix B 14.

east of Flesquières, and the 3rd would carry on to
Noyelles sur l'Escaut.

The rôle of the 3rd Guards Brigade was to march
behind the two attacking brigades, and form up for the
assault four hours after zero on ground to the north-east
of Flesquières, when it would pass through the 1st
Brigade. The 1st Battalion Grenadier Guards marched
on the right, the 2nd Battalion Scots Guards on the left,
and the Welsh Guards were in support with No. 3, No. 2
and Prince of Wales's Company in rear of the Grenadiers,
No. 4 in rear of the Scots Guards.

The head of the column passed the Bapaume—Cambrai
Road at zero, having then some 5,000 yards to go before
reaching the canal. No inconvenience was caused by
enemy shelling until the canal was reached. The crossing had been arranged at Lock 7, which was an obvious
place on which the enemy had concentrated considerable
shell-fire, but the battalion halted in a sunken road and
crossed by sections, slithering down the steep bank and
climbing slowly up the opposite one, and they suffered
no casualties. At this point it was obvious that all was
not progressing according to plan.

The Grenadiers were halted, there was no sign of the
Scots Guards, machine-gun fire from the direction of
Graincourt was very heavy, and the air was alive with
hissing and whip-like sounds. The companies took cover
along a bank and in some trenches running parallel to the
canal. At 8.50 a.m. the Grenadiers started to advance,
and the Welsh Guards Companies took up their positions
in rear and followed. It was then seen that the 2nd
and 1st Brigades were forming a long flank in the old
British Line facing Graincourt (Shingler and Silver
Trenches).

Taking advantage of trenches running on the line of
his advance, L. F. Ellis, with No. 3 Company, led the way
to the outskirts of Flesquières, which was being heavily
shelled. Already the battalion had suffered considerable
casualties. No. 2 Company and the Prince of Wales's
Company had become involved in a trench occupied by
the 2nd Grenadier Guards (Shingler), and while Fox-Pitt

and Coleman (commanding No. 2) were trying to extricate them three tanks advanced across the line in a north-east direction. At once the enemy concentrated his guns on them and two were destroyed; the third turned and retired down the length of the trench to the discomfiture of the troops in it.

Eventually these two companies got out of the trench and followed Nos. 3 and 4 to the outskirts of Flesquières. Ellis led the way to the north and joined up with the Grenadiers in a sunken road and some trenches immediately to the east of that village.

It will be seen by a glance at the map that the 1st and 2nd Guards Brigades, having stormed the Canal and driven the enemy beyond Flesquières, were now strung out, forming a flank facing Graincourt, which was far behind the 3rd Brigade (it transpired that the 2nd Battalion Scots Guards had become involved in this flank). The valley to the east of Graincourt was held by a number of field-guns and field-batteries, which fired at the advancing Welsh Guards over open sights, and in any further advance beyond Flesquières troops meeting resistance would be in the uncomfortable position of being shot at from front and rear. As it was the battalion reached this point with some difficulty. Troops were somewhat bewildered by the situation, and persisted in trying to follow their natural inclination, which was to face the enemy they could see; moving under heavy shell-fire and machine-gun fire to what was apparently a flank was puzzling. Eventually Fox-Pitt and Coleman, aided by the Commanding Officer, who walked about under fire in the most inspiring way, succeeded in getting the rear half of the battalion to the east of Flesquières, and joined up with Nos. 3 and 4 Companies.

The Commanding Officer now found Lord Gort, commanding the 1st Battalion Grenadiers, in the sunken road on that side of the village. Lord Gort had been wounded in the face and arm, but said that he had two companies well on the way to Premy Chapel, a strong point on the east of the spur which runs in the direction Noyelles sur l'Escaut, and that he was going to push on,

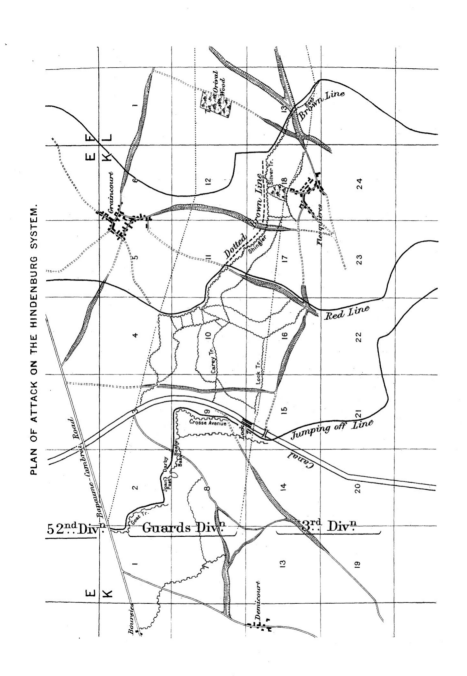

PLAN OF ATTACK ON THE HINDENBURG SYSTEM.

with King's Company on the right and No. 3 Company on the left. He asked the Commanding Officer to look after his flanks. Ellis was therefore told to follow the King's Company, and Coleman to follow No. 3 Company of the Grenadiers, Fox-Pitt to take his company to a position about 1,200 yards to the north-east of Flesquières. Meanwhile No. 3 Company of the Grenadiers had started to move, and Battye had taken up a position with his company on the flank facing Orival Wood; when the Commanding Officer heard of this he ordered Battye to move to the east of Fox-Pitt and hold the spur which runs in the direction of Cantaing (L14 and 9).

The King's Company, advancing on the right, split into two; the right half was followed by a platoon of No. 3 Company, under Powell, the left half was followed by Adams and his platoon. There seems to have been no officer with the King's Company, and the right half, coming across part of No. 4 Company of the Grenadiers, halted. Powell went forward and ordered the No. 4 Company to advance, and gave them the direction; the King's Company party he told to support No. 4. They advanced along a bank to within some fifty yards of the first defences of Premy Chapel Trench—where they came under such heavy fire that they sent back word they could get no farther. At this moment troops came up on the left and proved to be the other half of King's Company. The whole of King's Company now joined together, but could make no headway, and eventually fell back on Beet Trench.

Powell then decided to put No. 4 Company of the Grenadiers in a trench on his right, Nigger Trench, and Premy Support; Adams was strung out on his left.

Ellis now arrived with the rest of his company in Beet Trench, and, finding that the 2/20 London Regiment had come up on the right of the No. 4 Company of the Grenadiers, ordered Powell to withdraw his platoon as a reserve behind Beet Trench; with some difficulty he also withdrew Adams, placing three Lewis Guns on the line which his platoon had occupied.

Meanwhile Fox-Pitt had taken up a position astride the Flesquières—Cantaing Road to the north of the road from Premy Chapel. Battye and his company were cruising about in the direction of Orival Wood, and Ben Davies had penetrated the wood with a Lewis Gun team, and succeeded in surprising and annihilating an enemy machine-gun team before Battye received his orders to move to the east of Fox-Pitt. He tried to cross the ridge in front of Fox-Pitt, but the enemy, in the valley behind Graincourt and in the direction of Anneux, were fighting with desperate courage to keep the line of retreat for their infantry in Graincourt open, and directed such heavy fire on him with field-guns at close range that he had to retire in the direction of Flesquières. Nothing daunted, Battye tried, by passing behind Fox-Pitt, to reach the spur, and, by taking advantage of folds in the ground, made some progress, but the ground became unfavourable, and he came under fire from Premy Chapel on his right and the valley on his left. However, he clung on in the safer folds of the ground until he found the No. 2 and 3 Companies of the Grenadiers had given up hope of advancing in that direction, and were falling back on the line of trenches in rear, when he took up a position on the left of Fox-Pitt.

The Commanding Officer determined not to make any further attempt to gain Premy Chapel—Lord Gort had gone back and he was the senior officer on the spot. He was, moreover, without any artillery support, as the brigade had news that Premy Chapel was occupied by the Grenadiers, which information had been passed on to the Higher Command, and the artillery would not fire on Premy Chapel; it also seemed as though the Germans were massing in Premy Chapel for a counter-attack— troops were seen marching in that direction. To add to these difficulties he was being fired at by the guns in the valley and also a forward field-gun in Premy, supported by many machine guns. By the time he had convinced the brigade that the enemy held the east end of the ridge Graincourt had been entered by the 62nd Division, the enemy could be seen streaming away in the direction of

Cambrai, and he had order to stand fast for the night. Great credit is due to the Commanding Officer for the way in which he handled his battalion through a most confused action.

The battalion was relieved by units of the 2nd Division and marched back to rest in the trenches east of Lock 7.

In view of the position on the left it is extremely

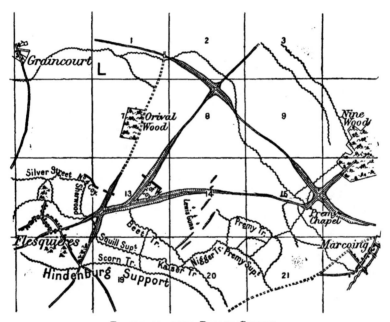

POSITION BEFORE PREMY CHAPEL.

doubtful whether Premy Chapel could have been taken. For the apex of the division to have reached the point it did was a feat of which it could be proud. We have laid more stress on the point than its importance deserves, but the inability to get the artillery on to Premy Chapel raised a certain amount of controversy at the time, and, as the Commanding Officer truly remarked a day or two later, " Your temper cannot be expected to be good when you are being shot at from front and behind ! "

The holding by the Guards Division of such a terrific flank after storming the Hindenburg Line was a wonderful performance.

Fox-Pitt and Willoughby were wounded, and eighty-seven other ranks killed and wounded.

CHAPTER XVIII

THE piercing of the Hindenburg Line completed the first phase of the great battle—for it must be considered as one battle, wherein the might of Germany was drawn up from the sea to Switzerland, and facing it was the might of France, Britain, and a strong but not a full-strength army of America.

Co-operating with the advance of the First, Third and Fourth Armies were the French and American Armies in the south, and an Allied Force of British, Belgian and French, under the King of the Belgians, in the north. The attack in the north opened on September 28th, the XIX and II Corps of the Second Army attacking on a four-and-a-half mile front south of the Ypres—Zonnebeke Road, with the Belgians on their left as far as Dixmude. At the end of the day the British had reached Kortiwilde, Zand Voorde, Kruiseecke, and Becelaere, far beyond the limits of the 1917 advance ; and the Belgians Zonnebeke, Poelcapelle, and Schaap Baillie, and had cleared the enemy from Houlthulst. The Lys front was again the scene of rapid enemy withdrawals.

The Hindenburg Line was the last and strongest of the enemy prepared positions. From the point of his farthest advance in the spring of 1918 to the Hindenburg Line the whole country was cut and recut by lines of trenches and dotted with strong points built by both sides. Between the trenches a growth of wild vegetation concealed a mass of shell-holes and barbed wire. Roads, bridges and railways had been blown up. The whole presented such an obstacle as could only be overcome

step by step.   Generally speaking, from the Hindenburg
Line onwards, fighting was of the open-country order,
where woods, rivers and a few hastily-dug defences were
the only obstacles.

When speaking of woods, rivers and a few trenches as
the only obstacles we must qualify that statement, and
confine it to obstacles which the fighting troops had to
meet.   There was another kind, and the most difficult
to|surmount of all—the roads and railways.   Whatever
may be said of the handling of enemy troops in this
retreat there is no doubt that his arrangements for
destroying roads and railways were excellent, and time
after time a halt had to be called lest assaulting troops
out-distanced their supplies.

The second phase of the offensive, so far as the Third
Army was concerned, started on October 8th.

The 3rd Guards Brigade was now under Brig.-Gen.
Hayward, for we have to record the death of Gen. Follett
on the 27th from a bullet which struck him down soon
after the battalion had crossed the canal.   He was a
good friend of the battalion, hard-working himself, and
considerate for others.   As a soldier he was very sound,
with long experience with his battalion before he was
promoted to the brigade.   When he approached Company Officers he knew what he was talking about, and
what they were talking about, two points greatly appreciated by those concerned.   He was, too, a charming,
kind-hearted man.   Everyone who knew him felt his
loss deeply.

Of all the energetic brigadiers the battalion served
under Gen. Hayward was the worst, or the best.   The
moment he arrived he started overhauling the organisation of battalions.   The battalion remained by the side
of the canal, living—

" In holes in the ground with bits of tin over them.
For miles there is not a house, a barn, a roof of any kind.
Piles of crumbling brick, mostly battered to dust, mark
the spots where villages once stood.   There is no sign of
cultivation—just waste—rusty shells that have not gone

off, bits of others that have, and confused heaps of some that have not been used ; then rusty barbed wire, bits of clothes, boots, broken rifles, bayonets, scabbards, old rusty bombs, caps, steel helmets, dead horses, mounds with little tumbledown crosses, old, half-fallen-in trenches, paper, rags, and over it all—to-night—the most glorious sunset."—*Diary, C. H. D. W., October 3rd.*

Reinforcements had ceased and it was necessary to husband the men battalions possessed. Instructions of a minute character had been issued, but there had always been given a certain latitude in their observance ; also the strength of the battalions had fallen to such a low state that it was impossible to carry them out to the letter. These instructions laid down definite numbers— that is, a minimum for Battalion H.Q. for companies and for details; but, as the total strength of the battalion was below the minimum laid down, the question of organisation raised much discussion.

The first point insisted on was that there should never be less than 10 officers and 50 other ranks at " Details " or " Reinforcements," and that figure was strictly adhered to as regards the N.C.O.'s and men. Then came the knotty problem of headquarters, divided into a fighting portion of 70 and an administrative portion of 66—the fighting portion never reached 70, and the administrative was generally over 66. Companies were cut down to three platoons. The fighting portion of Company H.Q. was laid down as nineteen, but, as it included five signallers, who could not be made up also, two scouts and two sanitary men, a Lewis Gun was generally taken into the battle, was manned by so-called scouts and sanitary men and signallers, and Company H.Q. became in effect a fourth platoon. This pamphlet of instruction was an admirable thing, provided battalions had a minimum available strength of 642 to go into battle. But such numbers were not available at that time.

The question of a battalion strength was always wrapt in mystery. We have before us a return of strength in October which shows on that particular day a *total strength* of 715, and yet the fighting strength, as understood by regimental officers, *i.e.* the number of men who marched into battle, was 399, including Battalion H.Q. Such headings as " employed " (at Division and Brigade H.Q.), " courses," " leave," and " sick " account for 104 ; at Details there were 72 (including the drums); the transport had then sunk to 60 (including the quartermaster and his administrative people). It was said at the time that everyone knew it was impossible to put a quart into a pint pot, and it should be equally obvious that a pint would never fill a quart pot.

The Commanding Officer spent hours over the organisation of the battalion, and ended with a sigh and the philosophical remark, " No one will ever parade the battalion in the middle of a battle, so it really does not matter."

While the battalion rested on the canal bank it was visited nearly every night by enemy aeroplanes which dropped bombs along the line of the canal; but there was very little shelling from long-range guns. Baths were fixed at Doignies, not far from Bonsor's transport lines. And on the whole the weather was fine, so the rest was real.

On the 7th the battalion marched to Flesquières and then to Masnières.

" We are off again to finish the war. We moved at 5.30 p.m. and are billeted in Flesquières, which is shelled at regular intervals. Dick Ball worried a good deal about his horse when we arrived, and we searched everywhere for a sheltered place for him, but in the end he had to be put with the others. Horses are getting valuable, and this one is as the apple of Ball's eye.

" The news to-day is scarce, but rumours are good. The latest is that the Boche Allies have asked for an Armistice ! As a shell has just pitched within a few yards, it seems too good to be true, and to-night as we rode forward in the dusk we could see Cambrai burning— not very like an Armistice. But something is going wrong with the Hun.

"*October 8th.*—Occasional shelling throughout the night which did no harm, but one of those odd things happened which make one believe in luck—one of the men died in his sleep! 'Heart,' so Pills says. (Lieut. Fuoss. Rowlette had gone home sick from Arras.)

"The leading division attacked this morning at 4.30 a.m. and the first lot of prisoners came through about 9 a.m.—they were the usual wretched, pale-faced lot. Attacks and counter-attacks seem to go on all day. Early in the proceedings we were at one hour's notice to move, and started off at 4 p.m.

"The traffic along the roads on these occasions is enormous—one long column fills the road. I suppose we marched about three miles, when we halted on a message that plans had been changed. The Huns shelled us and the village in front at that moment, so Ball left me and the transport to settle down where we could and went off with the battalion. We succeeded in finding a Hun dugout and were quite comfortable. The division attacks to-morrow morning at dawn—our brigade is in reserve.

"Our deep dugout kept us away from draughts, but in a thick fug. In the morning Bob Bonsor and I started off with the limbers about five—no need to be called, as the air was stifling and I could not sleep. The barrage for the 1st and 2nd Brigades attack started at 5.20 a.m. and was pretty heavy. The morning was bright and with a white frost. On the way we met Crawley de Crespigny (1st Brigade) moving up, and he told us he had attacked from the Red Line, as the farther one—where he should have been—Green—had not been taken yesterday.

"We found Dick Ball having breakfast and in very gay mood. He and his headquarters had slept in a door-less and windowless ruin—with a few extra holes in it as well. I had some coffee as he ate breakfast. Percy Battye came in to see us—he and his company had slept in some trenches and were fairly cold. After we had talked for a while a message came that the battalion must be ready to move at half an hour's notice. I went to

join the transport, and by ill luck ran into the new brigadier, who began to ask questions about where I was
staying, and eventually insisted on my going back to
Details. So Ellis, Bonn and I returned—as they were
being left out this time—to a wretched hole called
Labucquières, about twenty miles away."—*Diary,
C. H. D. W.*

The battalion moved at 10.45 a.m. and marched to
Seranvillers, where a halt was made for the night.

French troops were attacking from St. Quentin to
Sequehart, and the Fourth and Third British Armies from
thence to Cambrai. Considerable resistance was met
with at the opening of the attack, but on the 9th the
enemy were driven back rapidly. Farther south on this
same day, October 8th, French and American troops
made great progress east of the Meuse and in Champagne.

On the 10th the pursuit still continued, and the
battalion, still in reserve to the division, marched to
Estourmel. After attending a brigade conference the
Commanding Officer announced that the battalion would
again move at 2 a.m. on the 11th. The afternoon was
spent by the Commanding Officer and Company Commanders reconnoitring the road, and at 10 p.m. orders
were received [1] that the 3rd Guards Brigade would pass
through the Outpost Line held by the 1st and 2nd Brigades and continue the advance on a three-battalion
frontage—1st Battalion Grenadier Guards on the right,
2nd Battalion Scots Guards in the centre, and the Welsh
Guards on the left—each battalion would advance on a
two-company frontage. One battery R.F.A. would act
in close co-operation with each battalion, also one section
of the Machine Gun Company and two guns from the
Trench Mortar Company.

At 1 a.m. the battalion moved. The early morning
was quite quiet, and the forming-up position, a road
some 800 yards to the west of St. Hilaire, was reached
without incident.

The Commanding Officer's account of the events which

[1] Appendix B 15.

followed is amusing, and shows an amount of peevishness which was perhaps excusable. He says the "Artillery Liaison Officers and the machine-gun officer should have reported at this time, but did not do so—the officer in charge of trench-mortars reported but had left his guns at Boussières!"

The battalion, with the Prince of Wales's Company (under Goetz) on the right, No. 4 (Percy Battye) on the left, No. 2 (Coleman) in support, and No. 3 (Gwynne Jones) in reserve, passed through the Outpost Line at 5 a.m. The companies passed to the north of St. Hilaire and over a ridge which separated them from St. Vaast. Although it was not light the enemy was watchful and alert, and as troops began to descend into the valley they came under heavy machine gun and artillery fire. The enemy revealed himself holding a line along the railway to the north of St. Vaast.

All companies deployed, and the Prince of Wales's Company worked to the south-east to get round St. Vaast, while No. 4 advanced slowly towards the cross-roads on the west of the village. As the light improved machine-gun fire became more accurate, and the advance could only be carried on by small parties taking advantage of every bit of cover. A cavalry patrol rendered great assistance to No. 4 Company by moving rapidly down the valley with such determination that it actually reached the first houses of the village. Taking advantage of this diversion, No. 4 reached the road on the west side of St. Vaast.

All reports were to the effect that the railway and a malthouse to the north-west of the village were strongly held, and the machine-gun fire from these points was very heavy. Neither artillery nor trench-mortars were available to help companies by moving the enemy machine gunners, and the division on the left had failed to advance, so that there was a gap of over a thousand yards on the left of No. 4.

By 7 a.m. the Prince of Wales's Company had worked round to the east of St. Vaast, and a platoon of No. 2 Company entered the village, where they captured a

18

number of prisoners. But the railway bank, with a number of sidings at a detraining point to the north-east, was a formidable obstacle, and strongly held, and the Scots Guards on the right had met with considerable resistance, so could give no effective aid; in view of the situation the Prince of Wales's Company decided to dig in.

About 9.30 a.m. a second cavalry patrol tried to repeat the manœuvre of earlier in the morning by passing round the south of the village, but machine-gun fire was now very accurate, and they had to retire.

And so the situation remained until 10.30 a.m. when, to the relief of the Commanding Officer and all concerned, the artillery battery arrived and opened on the railway. No. 4 and No. 2 Companies were then able to advance and complete the line on the far side of St. Vaast.

Any further advance with the enemy holding St. Aubert was out of the question. The Commanding Officer of the 3rd Battalion London Rifle Brigade proposed to attack St. Aubert from the south, and sent an officer to arrange how the Welsh Guards could best assist them. Col. Luxmoore Ball, while promising all help with covering fire, expressed the opinion that such an attack would be courting disaster. This message brought up Gen. Hayward with the Commanding Officer of the London Rifle Brigade Battalion, and they agreed that some other solution should be tried.

A caustic note by the Commanding Officer reads :

" About this time hostile machine-gun and shell fire on our leading troops was greatly assisted by our corps heavies, who commenced to shell our support and reserve companies heavily. The enemy also gassed the valley and the village."

During the night repeated patrols were sent out under Powell, Foot, Adams and Wiseman, but in each case they found the enemy still holding the line of the railway. About eight in the morning, however, an aeroplane re-

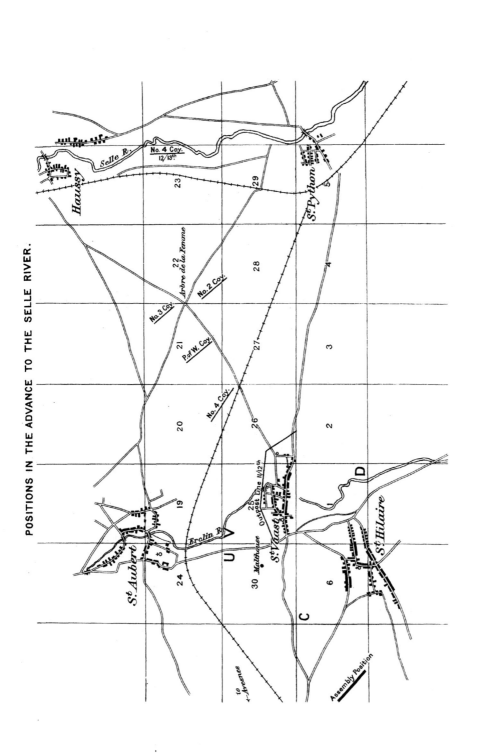

POSITIONS IN THE ADVANCE TO THE SELLE RIVER.

ported that St. Aubert did not appear to be occupied, and a patrol was again sent out, to find that the enemy had retired from the railway, but the Prince of Wales's Company reported them on the ridge " Arbre de la Femme."

The XVII Corps on the left then began to move, and at 3 p.m., after a preparatory bombardment, the battalion occupied the " Arbre de la Femme " ridge. Patrols in advance reported that the enemy was holding the east of the river Selle in force.

At midnight Battye took No. 4 Company forward, with Watson and his platoon in advance. Watson encountered an enemy patrol of six men near the river, and succeeded in killing three—the rest escaped. A light bridge had been provided, and Battye's orders were to place it across the river ; but he found that the river was some twenty feet wide and the bridge only sixteen ; there was, however, an enemy bridge in good condition. He also found that the river was fordable.

Just before daybreak he passed half his company to the eastern bank, and for some time the enemy did not discover their presence. Later in the morning machine-gun fire and shelling became so bad he withdrew them to a more favourable position on the western bank. But he established the fact that the enemy held a sunken road half-way up the opposite ridge, and that he was holding the crest of the ridge strongly ; also that there was a considerable force in Haussey. He himself was slightly wounded and gassed and went down to the hospital.

On the night of the 13th the battalion was relieved by the 1st Battalion Scots Guards and marched back to St. Hilaire.

Considering that the country was most favourable to the enemy, the battalion did not suffer heavy loss. Of officers, Battye, Fleming, Holdsworth and Adams were wounded, and the casualties among the men were thirty-seven. All the usual difficulties of an exposed flank were encountered. But the enemy resistance stiffened everywhere as he crossed the Selle, and to have a flank in the air was by no means a new situation for the Welsh Guards.

To advance in this open country in the face of opposition required not only courage but initiative on the part of N.C.O.'s. and men. 153 Cpl. P. Jones, 776 Cpl. G. Winter, 2,478 L/Cpl. E. Boyle, 2,708 L/Cpl. T. M. Jones, 1,010 L/Cpl. F. Cosford, Ptes. 1,972 W. A. Harris, 872 E. Gordon, 2,881 J. E. Vaughan, 1,522 E. Roberts, 2,251 D. O. Jones, 2,763 T. D. Clancy, 2,627 E. L. Jones, 3,417 E. R. Owen, 3,850 W. Garnett, 263 H. J. Matthew, 1,254 S. T. Baldwin, were conspicuous in these qualities.

On the 17th the battalion moved to Carnières for a short rest. On the 19th the division was ordered to attack at 2 p.m. on the 20th—1st Guards Brigade on the right, 3rd on the left and 2nd in reserve. Of the 3rd Brigade the 1st Battalion Grenadier Guards would open the attack and capture the first objective; the Welsh Guards on the right, and the 2nd Battalion Scots Guards on the left, would then pass through the Grenadier Guards and capture and consolidate on the final objective, which was the ridge commanding the Harpies River.

The Commanding Officer went on leave and the battalion was taken into action by the second in command.

" On the 19th Details were in process of moving from the unspeakable hole of Labucquières, in fact, L. F. Ellis had already gone with half, when about three in the afternoon a note was brought me from Guy Darrell to say I was to get ready to join the battalion at once. This was followed in a few minutes by Guy himself, who told me Dick Ball was going on leave, and that I was to take over command. I said, ' This is all very well, but I hear there is to be a battle to-night ! ' Guy mumbled that he would tell me all about it later, and was so obviously discreet I thought something had happened. In due course we left in the motor, and I found he could tell me very little. He said the attack had been decided on very hurriedly, and that there was no word of Ball leaving till that morning, the 19th. He knew nothing of the arrangements.

" He dropped me at St. Hilaire at 5 p.m. where I found Dick Ball, who was able to give me half an hour before going to catch his train. It was to be a night attack over ground which no one had seen, except Battye, for the space of an hour or so, and he (Ball) had done all he could to prepare the battalion. It appears he was only told that morning he was to be left out, and rather than go back to the Details he applied for special leave. The thing was not his fault. Tiny Buchanan then came to fetch him with a car, and said how sorry he was I had such short notice—and so they both left.

" I was without a map. I knew I was at a place called St. Hilaire, but had no idea where the battalion was, but a guide was to fetch me. Willie Arthur was there and talked of places I had never heard of—he also had no map and was staying with the transport—and he could tell me nothing about the orders of attack except that he thought it started at 2 a.m., and that the battalion would have to move about 10 p.m. Finally the guide arrived and I reached the battalion at St. Vaast about 8.30 p.m.

" Had some dinner and Company Commanders to see me and tell me what they had been ordered to do—Devas had not even got a copy of brigade orders, which apparently Dick Ball had taken with him, so that at the moment I was, as Humphrey Dene would say, ' a wooden man.[1] '

" The battalion marched at 10.50 p.m. in drizzling rain, through which an invisible moon gave a faint light. All was very quiet, and only the Hun shelled some cross-roads with one long-range gun. We reached the first assembly place just before midnight, on the road from St. Vaast to Haussy and about midway between the villages. I put the battalion on the right of the road in the order of advance—Bonn (No. 2) on the right, and Gwynne Jones (No. 3) on his left ; Ronnie Goetz (P. of W.) behind Bonn, and Coleman (No. 4) behind Gwynne Jones ; headquarters in rear.

[1] Appendix B 16.

" Jack Stirling arrived and put his battalion on the left of the road.

" The battle was to start at 2 a.m. with the Grenadiers in front (they were already on their jumping-off place, which was a railway cutting), and they were to cross the railway at 2.10 a.m. There was only one order for me to give, and that was the time we should leave our assembly place. Settled this for 1 a.m. Jack Stirling put his starting time back a quarter of an hour to agree with me, and we set our watches.

" At ten minutes to two the leading companies arrived at a spot about 300 yards behind the railway ; my instructions were that they should move from there at 2.5 a.m.

" The very devil of a shoot started at two, and as I, with headquarters, found myself a couple of hundred yards in front of a line of field-guns, it was most unpleasant.

" As to my command there seemed to be nothing to command, I could see no one and could not go to them— in fact one's interest seemed to slip away in a curious fashion. Vaguely I wondered if the leading companies had crossed the railway. After crossing the railway they would have to cross the river Selle, which would take some time—so we sat on the side of a trench and waited till 2.30 a.m.

" By that time I thought we might as well be moving. The barrage was still going on in a furious fashion, and old Geof. Devas and I stumbled over coarse grass clumps and into shell-holes, followed by young Evans and headquarters. My old friend Sergt. Mathias was doing sergeant-major, and was full of his usual quips.

" When we reached the railway we found Coleman climbing out of the cutting, and he told me Goetz's last platoon had just gone. There was no Hun shelling at all—nothing to disturb us but the noise of our own 18-pounders, and rain.

" The Grenadiers were to take a sunken road and stop. We were to go through them and continue advancing to a ridge overlooking another stream. By the time Coleman had his first platoon across the Selle it was a quarter

to three, and the Grenadiers were timed to reach the road
at 3.10. It was some way off, and I felt a bit anxious
about companies getting lost, so went ahead with Devas
and three orderlies. Crossing a river is a slow business ;
those who have crossed always hurry on, and so the
whole force gets scattered. The ground was fearfully
heavy, all plough and uphill from the river. Devas and
I were wet through with heat and rain before we caught
Coleman's first platoon. I halted them and told them
to wait for the rest of the company, and then chased after
Goetz. He had no notion where he was, and could only
say he was sure the other companies ' were in front.' I
was certain he was too far to the left, but it was no use
trying to correct him till we had found the other companies. Eventually we came across some Scots Guards
and I knew I was right, as they were supposed to be on
our left. We made a cast to the right and found the
sunken road, but no sign of the Grenadiers. Chased still
farther to the right, and met someone brandishing a revolver, who said he was a Grenadier. Then we found
Gwynne Jones and Bonn, and Goetz was sent back to
bring up his company and correct the direction of the
reserve company.

" Walter Bonn was very worried by not finding anyone on his right—the Irish should have been there. I
told him to carry on and I would see to his flank by
means of Goetz. Gwynne Jones and Bonn then started
after the barrage, which was about seventy yards in front
of them.

" When Goetz arrived I sent him echeloned to the right
in rear of Bonn. Coleman I kept with me behind the
road. Meanwhile I got in touch with Jack Stirling, who
was too far to the left, and also asked Bill Bailey to send
some of his Grenadiers out to the right and try to get in
touch with the Irish.

" The next thing was a message from Bonn that he
was held up by machine-gun fire—and a similar one from
Jones. Went with Goetz to see Bonn and found him
digging in a ploughed field. It was about 4.30 and the
light very bad—thick misty rain. You could see very

dimly the tree-tops of an avenue. It appeared that the enemy could see us, as we were fired at as we walked about. Bonn said there were three or four guns in front of him—all I could make out was that the ground in front was very flat and exposed—but he said he had sent a message to the Scots Guards to try and work forward on his left. I hesitated to order him forward, as if he was right there was little chance of doing any good, and yet we, as we moved about, had only drawn rifle fire. I decided to try a sweep round to the right, and sent Goetz back to instruct one of his platoons; but I was still uncertain until we walked to the left of Bonn's line, when a machine gun ripped out from a house one could just see on the left.

" Went back and got Jack Stirling on the wire. He told me he had reached his objective on the left, but that his right was stuck, and could I shift the Hun from the house ? He seemed a bit annoyed and peevish about something, and indeed the impression I had was that the attack was sticky for no very great reason. However, I told him what I was doing, and that if he could help I would tell Gwynne Jones to try and work round the house. He said he had some trench-mortars and would use them.

" Went off again to see Gwynne Jones, but before I had gone very far saw little groups of men advancing from his company. Bonn's company then started to advance and, it being lighter, I could see a few Huns running from the line of trees. About that time Coleman reported that he had found the Irish Guards about 1,000 yards on our right, and that they were going forward rapidly. I then got the whole battalion moving, and we advanced with only a few shots against us to the far ridge.

" Coleman's company caught some Huns with Red Cross armlets, and in possession of a machine gun—they killed them all—but they took some twenty prisoners in other places.

" The right still seemed to me in a funny state, but I told Bonn to dig in and send forward a patrol at once.

Two machine guns fired at us intermittently, which was
not astonishing, as we all stood about on the sky-line.
Put Goetz in position in support and Coleman in reserve,
then returned to the sunken road."—*Diary, C. H. D. W.*

This night attack was quite a big affair, being carried
out by the 38th, 17th, 5th, 42nd, 62nd, Guards, and 19th
Divisions of the Third Army, and the 4th Division of the
First Army. On some parts of the front tanks were
used, and stout resistance had to be overcome. On the
Guards Division front, except for the anxiety natural to
an appreciable advance in the dark, there was really little
resistance, and nothing in the nature of real fighting ; the
enemy merely retired to the heights on the far side of
the river Harpies.

The patrol which Bonn sent to reconnoitre the river
was under Stanier, who had every man hit and a bullet
through his steel helmet before he returned. He showed
great tenacity of purpose, measured the depth and width
of the stream and took notes of wire on the opposite
bank, and succeeded in getting all his men back—a
very creditable performance.

All through the day the enemy shelled the area between the two rivers heavily, and used a lot of gas.
During the night of the 20/21st Coleman took No. 4
Company down to the line of the Harpies River, and
established posts there, otherwise the situation remained
the same until the battalion was relieved on the night
of the 21st and marched back to St. Hilaire.

The total casualties in this advance were thirty.

Since passing to the east of the Hindenburg defences
a rest had some meaning for the battalion.   Villages had
scarcely been touched by shell fire—there were a few
houses wrecked in each one, but by comparison with the
devastated area they seemed in good repair—and the
men had billets with a whole roof, and a board floor to
sleep on.   Dirt and filth were there in quantities, but
that could be cleared away.   St. Hilaire was a very comfortable little village, and the battalion stayed there
until November 2nd.

Training for the attack was carried on with the idea of getting round strong positions held with few troops; and there was the usual despair in the battalion over O.B.1919, the instructions on organisation.

Gen. Matheson inspected the battalion on October 26th, drawn up according to the pamphlet O.B.1919, and the numbers were: Prince of Wales's Company, 78; No. 2 Company, 81; No. 3 Company, 73; No. 4 Company, 93; headquarters (includes stretcher-bearers), 50; At the Details were 31; on leave and employed away, 69.

To the great regret of the battalion the Adjutant, Geoffrey Devas, was taken on the staff of the 3rd Guards Brigade. He had carried on well since Perrins left, and during the very worst moments his cherub face never ceased to beam with good-nature and confidence. Jack Crawshay took his place.

CHAPTER XIX

THE LAST FIGHT—THE ARMISTICE

On November 2nd the battalion marched to Vertain. The last stage of the battle had started, and on the line of the Fourth, Third and First Armies opened with an attack by the XVII Corps, of the Third Army, and the XXII and Canadian Corps, of the First Army, at 5.15 on November 1st. After two days' fighting Valenciennes was captured and a more general advance could be made. A big attack was launched on November 4th by the Fourth, Third and First Armies on a thirty-mile front. The battalion left Vertain on November 3rd.

" *November 2nd.*—In view of the move which was to take place ' after dinners,' the battalion did nothing this morning beyond get ready. At 12 o'clock there was a conference at brigade, and the Brigadier explained in the loosest way the plans, for there are two. In the first plan the 1st and 2nd Brigades attack to a depth of about three miles, and we go through them and carry on a further three or four miles. The second plan is for the 1st and 2nd Brigades to go for seven miles, and we go on from there—very ambitious. Anyway, we were given orders to move forward at 5 p.m. to Escarmain. It seems strange to come out of the line, as we did ten days ago, to a place which was only a short way behind, and within that short space of time find yourself so far from the battle front that you can march eight miles forward and still be about five miles away from the front line.

" We started then at 5 p.m. and proceeded in pitch

dark. The stillness of the night was broken by the sound of music—brass bands and bugle bands—and we soon realised we were not the only people marching forward, but that there were troops on parallel roads right and left of us. It is more cheering than the approach to the Somme battle in 1916. I never thought we should march forward with bands!

After two and a half hours of marching we reached a village (Vertain) three miles from our destination, and there found old Courtney in a state of physical and mental collapse. He had been arranging billets all day, and all forward villages were so packed with troops that there was no room for us. But tents had been pitched quite close to where we were. Switching a battalion off the line of march at night when it is marching with 100 yards' interval between platoons, and in the midst of countless other traffic, is dangerous work. In the attempt the cookers and two limbers evaded us and went wrong—they turned up, however, at 10.30 p.m.

" We found the tents pitched on muddy ground, but, thank goodness, a large supply of unthreshed wheat!

" We all turned in by eleven.

" *November 3rd.*—Orders have come round that the second plan will be adopted.

" Have been to a brigade conference, and the final arrangements are not very complicated so far as we are concerned. The attack (1st and 2nd Brigades) is to start at 5.30 a.m. and we are to march from here at 6.30 a.m. We halt just behind the place where our present line is and wait for orders. On our left a whole brigade has gone forward with cavalry in front of them. . . . Night is coming on and it is beginning to rain.

" *November 4th.*—A disturbed night, with messages from the brigade altering plans,[1] and the time of attack from 5.30 to 6 a.m. The battalion was wakened at 4.30, and after breakfast marched at 7.30 a.m. in misty sunrise. The roads were packed with traffic moving forward, and we did not reach our assembly place—Mortry Farm, some distance beyond Capelle—owing to bad

[1] Appendix B 17.

blocks in the rotten roads, till 10.20 p.m. There we stuck in a field, watching the traffic going by, and also a large quantity of propaganda balloons letting loose leaflets over the Hun country. We then had a fiddling march with many stops, owing to traffic crossing a small bridge—I had eventually to take the battalion across country—to the village of Villers Pol, which was in the hands of the Boche this morning. The billets were good. Another conference at 6 p.m. The 3rd Brigade are to attack, passing through the 1st and 2nd Brigades at 6 a.m. to-morrow. This battalion is in reserve.

" I saw Dick Ball during the evening. He had secured a car from G.H.Q. and come right through, and was furious at being ordered back to Details by the brigadier. I am bound to say I should have been angry too.

" *November 5th.*—We had to be in position at 5.30,[1] so I marched at 4.30 a.m. It was not more than two miles, but so dark that I had to leave a margin of time. The opening barrage was very little. It began to rain, but we found the place all right and stuck there, on the side of a hill, till soon after 9 a.m., when we set out for Preux au Sart. Brigade H.Q. had moved ahead of us, and we got stuck in the mud on the side of a hill for twenty minutes, so we did not make good time. The brigadier met me in Preux and said the people on our left were a bit sticky, but he was not going to wait for them, and ordered me to keep pushing forward just behind the Scots Guards and Grenadiers. There was no question of losing the way, so I rode forward to see what was doing. Found Jack Stirling in a roadside house writing dozens of messages, which he gave to an army of orderlies. Told him what I was doing, and he gave me the position of his companies. ' I see,' he told me, ' if it flows you will keep close behind.' New word, ' flows ! '

" The battalion came up and got into barns while I and Jack Crawshay pushed on to Amfroipret to see Bill Bailey (1st Battalion Grenadier Guards). The Huns had blown up all the road junctions, and we had to climb through hedges to the far side of the town. We did not

[1] Appendix B 18.

find Bill, but bullets were flying about pretty freely, and we discovered we were in the front of the battle with some small tanks which were on the point of attacking. Regardless of the poor quality of our horsemanship, Jack and I galloped back over cobbles and holes. The next move was an order to go into Amfroipret with the battalion, which I did. I was also told to be ready to advance at any moment. This state of uncertainty continued until late in the afternoon, when definite information was given that we were to attack in the morning. By the time I knew what was required it was dusk, and I had only time to send the first two company commanders, Battye and Coleman, to have a look at the ground before it was dark. They did not see much.

" The brigadier did not know what the division would do in the morning, but wanted me to be ready with a plan to capture the first high ground in conjunction with Bill Bailey.[1] Saw Bill, who seemed very bored with the whole proceedings, but we fixed up a boundary along a railway, and arranged with Vickery for artillery. Then Jack Crawshay and Willie Arthur helped me to work out a plan and orders to start on a one-company front, and develop to two. This I explained fully to Battye and Coleman, who were to do it.

" At 8 p.m. definite orders arrived—very short and sketchy—with a marked map. They practically said, ' You will be on the left and work according to map." The map took us further than the arranged plan, so company commanders were called up again and they marked their maps.[2]

" About 10.30 p.m. the Hun, who had been shooting steadily at the village, began to bombard it. The streets were full of flying bricks and glass, and one could not move. This went on till 2 a.m. and then eased a bit, and we thought we might get an hour or two of sleep, but a message came from Battye asking for stretcher-bearers, as he had some thirty casualties. Sent up all the stretchers, and a dozen men, and had the unfortunate fellows brought into a barn next door for the doctor to

[1] Appendix B 19. [2] Appendix B 20.

work on. It appeared that a shell had pitched in the middle of the barn occupied by the company and done in the best part of two platoons, and Battye, like the other companies, had only three.

" Everyone was tired, and I did not want to detail a fresh company for the attack, and have all the N.C.O.'s. awake while it was explained to them, so I told Battye he must carry out the first part of the attack and take the village of Buvignies, and that I would arrange for Ellis to go through him and take his place from there onward.

" There was no sleep for us at all. At 5 a.m. the battalion was moving. No. 2 Company under Coleman opened the attack from the Grenadier Line, and No. 4 followed them. Battalion H.Q. had moved forward to the east of the village, and at 6 a.m. No. 3 joined head-quarters just as the attack started. At 6.30 No. 3 followed the assaulting companies, and the Prince of Wales's Company moved up to their place. As the battle progressed the Prince of Wales's Company, Battalion H.Q., machine-gun and trench-mortar sections went forward, but, owing to the shelling, these moves were half an hour late. Jack Crawshay and I rode forward and left Willie Arthur to whip up.

" We found that Battye had taken the village without much trouble—Ben Davies missed a Hun five times with his revolver, and the fellow got away, but they secured several prisoners. The village streets were swept with bullets from Bavai, and were also being shelled by two light field guns from the east of Bavai. Vickery's boys attached to me, with two field-guns and a howitzer, were up in wonderful quick time—the fat little How in the middle of the street, and the two field-guns just off the street in a field—and got to work searching for the Hun field-guns and machine guns.

" The village was on the top of a rise with a perfectly straight road running through it to Bavai, and there followed some picture-book fighting. The machine gun-ner arrived with his limbers and pack mules, and un-loaded before coming up the rise into the centre of the

village. German machine guns were firing straight up
this road, and I ordered him to engage them from a
favourable house. Soon he had two guns blazing through
two windows, the field-guns and the How were going
all the time, a man was hit in the street, a Frenchman
dragged me into his house and his wife fell on my neck
and kissed me—it was some minutes before I could settle
down and get things in order.

"This village of Buvignies is to the south-west of
Bavai, and our attack was due east. The 24th Division
was by way of being on our left, but I had no news of
them at all. The Scots Guards were immediately behind
me, round the village called Bermeries, and seemed
already to be protecting the flank of the advance. On
my right was Bill Bailey with the 1st Battalion Grenadier
Guards.

"I put Battye with his weak company astride the road
on the Bavai side of the village, and kept J. Ellis with
the Prince of Wales's Company resting in some barns.
And then we had to wait for some news of No. 3 Company, which Battye reported as having gone on in the
right direction, and of No. 2 on the right. I knew Coleman must have reached his first line all right, and sent
two runners to look for him and find out what he was
doing.

"Vickery arrived in tremendous form. He gave me
another section of guns and told his officers to ' put in
some of your snappiest and keep on firing. . . . You are
young, my boy ! . . . Work does you good.'

"And then came a note from Coleman to say he was
digging in and word from L. F. Ellis to say he was getting
on ! Gwynne Jones was hanging about doing liaison
with the brigade, so I sent him with orders to Coleman
to push his company well forward on the right of No. 3,
and not to think of his flank, as Bill Bailey was on his
right. Bavai, half hidden in the mist, was the rotten
spot, and L. F. Ellis seemed to be advancing boldly with
his flank exposed to Bavai, so I sent J. Ellis with the
Prince of Wales's Company to keep in close support
and look after the flank, with particular instructions

to hold the railway line with one platoon until it
was relieved.

"All the time we worked at this left flank. No. 4
Company went forward and relieved the Prince of Wales's
platoon on the railway, while headquarters held the
Buvignies—Bavai Road. I also sent forward a trench-
mortar and two machine guns. Eventually we held the
cross roads south-east of Bavai with a flank of 3,000
yards. There was never a word of the 24th Division,
and I dared not try and press on any farther with the
unknown quantity, Bavai, on my left.

"During the night the Hun started blowing up things
in Bavai. It was dark as pitch, but, after smelling round
for some time, patrols entered the town about two in
the morning—to Cpl. White, I think, belongs the honour
of being the first to enter Bavai. . . .

"For L. F. Ellis I have nothing but the highest praise.
He ran the whole battle in the front line, and showed
the most extraordinary courage and determination all
through—quite a little tiger.

"By the time the 2nd Brigade had assembled to go
through the outpost line a platoon of the Prince of
Wales's Company was in the southern part of the town
holding the roads.

"Immediately after six I decided to have a look at
Bavai, so that I could withdraw my people, who had
been ordered to hold the flank of the 3rd Grenadiers until
the 24th Division came up. I took Percy Battye, Jack
Crawshay, and six men with me, and we had a most
amusing morning. We were hand-shaken, we were
kissed, we were cried over—a fearful business. Finally,
working our way down a side-street, there was a commo-
tion. Women began to scream and run about, a clear
way was made down the street, and we saw some civilians
pointing—and then half a dozen Huns seemed to bound
out into the middle of the street. The men dashed forward—Percy brandishing an empty rifle he had picked
up—and then the crowd closed round again and everyone
began to talk. The Huns were having their packs pulled
off by the civilians, who were calling them brutes, rob-

19

bers, etc. I got hold of Sergt. Ham and told him to have the Huns fall in, which he did, and we continued our journey. On the western side of the town we met troops of the 24th Division and I told an officer he could get on. About two hours later I withdrew companies into billets in Buvignies—the poor fellows were wet to the skin and deserved a rest.

"Jack Stirling, acting for Hayward, who had been wounded, came to see me and told me Dick Ball was on his way up, and to get out a report about Bavai. There was other writing required, and I was kept busy until the evening.

"*November 8th.*—There was a brigade funeral at 11.30 a.m. for men killed at Amfroipret—including six of ours. At 2.30 p.m. we had another funeral at Buvignies. Poor young Powell was amongst the killed, and Pte. Hammond, the H.Q. orderly, a first-rate fellow. When Mog had finished I announced to the battalion over the graves of the dead that the result of their gallant efforts and the supreme sacrifice of their comrades was at hand; that German Plenipotentiaries had come through the French line under a flag of truce to ask for terms.

"Later in the day Dick Ball arrived and assumed command."—*Diary, C. H. D. W.*

This engagement near Bavai was entirely L. F. Ellis's and No. 3 Company's fight. At the start from Amfroipret, Coleman had advanced, with his company extended, through the hedges dividing the country on the left of the railway. Battye, following Coleman, had attacked Buvignies from the south, and had found but a few of the enemy there. Ellis then arrived, and, forming up his company on the east of the village, advanced in the direction of Prehert Farm.

Visibility was extremely bad owing to the fine, misty rain which continued all day. Working through the hedges—the boundaries of the fields in this part of the country were partly wire but mostly hedges—he soon got in touch with the enemy on the railway.

Ellis was a little man who indulged at times in quick,

fretful outbursts of temper. All previous conversations and instructions indicated a quick advance, a hustling of the enemy. The railway was not a long way from Buvignies, and when Ellis found the leading platoon of his company checked he went forward to see what was happening. There was a lot of noise going on from enemy machine guns firing out of the mist in front of him and from Bavai on his left, but at the moment nothing from the railway, some fifty yards in front of the bank and hedge behind which his platoons were lying. He found a consultation going on as to what should be done, and was informed that the railway cutting was held. Immediately he lost his temper and began to fume. " Nonsense ! there is no one there," said he, and pushing through the hedge, ran across the intervening fifty yards, and jumped into the cutting. He found himself in the middle of about thirty Germans. He had nothing but his walking-stick, which he flourished. At that moment there was a loud report over his head and a German fell. Another report, then several more in quick succession. L/Cpl. E. Gordon and L/Sergt. W. Jones had, fortunately for Ellis, followed him as soon as they had seen what he was doing, and from the top of the bank were firing at the enemy.

Gordon was one of the best shots in the battalion, and Jones, though not so good, could scarcely miss at such close range. The Germans were startled, confused, and ran, but Jones accounted for five and Gordon for six before they reached the protection of an adjacent hedge and the favouring mist.

The whole company were now streaming into the cutting, and Ellis was stamping up and down telling them not to bunch. Without giving them breathing-time he led the way over the opposite bank and through the first hedge. Facing him was a long, gentle slope with wire fencing to the fields. Almost at the top of the rise the enemy were entrenched in " slits," and to gain this ground there was a lot of fighting of an exciting character. Ellis had fired his men, and they advanced up the slope in short rushes. A lot of ammunition was expended, but the casualties were surprisingly few. Ellis personally led a Lewis Gun team, and when the No. 1 was shot through the neck, worked the gun himself. Powell was killed trying to rush a light machine gun, and at his heels Pte. Hammond, who for a long time had been Humphrey Dene's orderly. L/Cpl. Gordon was shot through the leg, but lay on his back firing over his feet like a Bisley marksman—Gordon's shooting undoubtedly did much to shake the enemy. He was a very cool man, and claims twelve " kills " that day. Pte. Arthur Thomas, too, though wounded in the face, continued firing his Lewis Gun. The enemy were either killed or they ran, and Prehert Farm was reached.

Ellis then proceeded to clear the immediate neighbourhood of the farm, and quite a game of hide-and-seek went on amongst the small orchards and hedged paddocks surrounding the place. It could almost be said that the men " enjoyed " this fighting.

With Bavai held, the position of the company had to be considered. Coleman, with No. 2 Company, should have been forwarded on Ellis's right, but Coleman was searching for the Grenadiers on his right and waiting for them to advance. The whole original scheme of attack was based on the right of the line keeping forward, whereas the left had shot away well in advance.

J. Ellis, who had been sent up with the Prince of Wales's Company, now got in touch with L. F. Ellis (Squiff) and relieved his anxiety as to his Bavai flank.

In due course Gwynne Jones reached Coleman, and No. 2 Company advanced on the right.

From the farm to the main road the advance was slow—a matter of working steadily from hedge to hedge in face of stiffer resistance. The left flank was fed until only headquarters held the surroundings of Buvignies. In the patrol work to his front and towards Bavai " Squiff " Ellis showed the greatest skill. He had not enough men to risk further adventure, and was ordered to stand fast; but he marked each enemy post and each retirement was known to him at once. He first got in touch with a French civilian on the very outskirts of Bavai

THE LAST ACTION.

soon after midnight, and the town was entered about 2 a.m. the following day.

We have mentioned 872 L/Cpl. E. Gordon, 756 L/Sergt. W. M. Jones, and 3,093 Pte. A. Thomas. Others who led were—1,465 L/Cpl. S. White, Ptes. 3,275 R. F. Charnley, 3,861 G. W. Snell, 624 L/Cpl. A. Raisley, 834 L/Cpl. W. C. Gardener, Ptes. 3,555 I. H. Owen, 974 C. Thomas, and 3,069 C. G. Sendy, and there were many more.

Casualties were one officer, ninety-three other ranks.

The advance was carried on by the 1st and 2nd Brigades at a great rate (the 3rd Brigade advance had been carried out on the whole width of front of the 1st and 2nd Brigades). After two nights' rest in Buvignies the Welsh Guards marched, on the 9th, to Longueville. To say the army was moving gives no conception of the scene. For miles the roads were packed tight with traffic, and were being rapidly churned up into mud and loose stones, and ended abruptly, at such points as cross roads, forked roads and level crossings, in huge craters where the retreating Germans had blown up a mine. Traffic had then to turn off into soft fields where horses plunged, jibbed and became bogged. Through this congestion the infantry threaded its way in single file, or at most in file. Platoons were broken into and scattered, but by this time the men were wise in war, and officers knew when to shout and when to be quiet; the men arrived at their destination. On the same day the 3rd Battalion Grenadier Guards entered Maubeuge.

On November 10th the battalion marched to Douzies.

The last great battle was nearing its end. The Fourth, Third and First Armies were advancing rapidly, the Fifth Army had captured Peruwelz, Antoins and Tournai, the Second Army had reached Renaix; cavalry were nearing Ath, and troops were approaching Grammont. Early on the morning of the 11th the 3rd Canadian Division killed or captured the whole of the German garrison of Mons, and the *Diary of the Welsh Guards* has this bald entry on that date : " News reached the battalion that an Armistice had been signed to take effect at 11.00 hours

to-day." In the same quiet way was the conclusion of
hostilities celebrated by the Welsh Guards at Douzies.
There was some mild kind of junketting amongst the
divisional staff at Maubeuge, but otherwise the soldiers
rested or cleaned their kit.

The order posted outside Battalion H.Q. was :

" Hostilities will cease on the whole front as from
November 11th at 11 o'clock (French time).

" The Allied troops will not, until a further order, go
beyond the line reached on that date and at that hour.

" (*Signed*) MARSHAL FOCH."

. . . . .

We feel we have not done justice to the valour of those
men who formed and fought The Battalion of Welsh
Guards. Amongst the fallen are officers, from Randolph, Mawby and Smith, who were the first, to Powell,
who was the last, whose names are merely mentioned ;
there are hundreds of private soldiers who are not mentioned at all. To tuck the names of gallant men who
made history into an Appendix is an expedient which
raises bitter reflections. Has a man who gave his life
no better reward than that ? Not one of them ever
sought such miserable recompense as a paragraph in a
book. If such is needed, remember he was a Welsh
Guardsman, and each time the words " Welsh Guards "
or " Battalion " occur it is he, it is his effort which is
meant. Beyond this every soldier who fought and fell
in the Great War has his reward in the memory of his
friends; but an adequate monument, worthy of his sacrifice, can only be erected by the future action of his
countrymen—men whom he never saw.

While writing of gallantry we have the deeds of some
men at Mortaldje always in our mind. It was easy on
this occasion to describe, we will say, 1,189 Pte. W. Jones
advancing alone with only the flickering, shadow-raising
flare from Verey lights dispersing the dark of a moonless
night. We can see him stumbling along the strange
trench, we can see the walls of earth on either side of

him, his bayonet flashing, the sharp turn in the trench
and the jumping light throwing a shadow like a black
wall from the angle of the turn. We appreciate the
courage which led him through the shadow and round
the turn in the trench. We realise that he knew he might
meet the enemy at any moment, and was deliberately
seeking him—he was a determined man looking for his
enemy. But what are we to say of Cpl. David James?
He was not looking for Germans. He grasped no
weapon, his mind was not worked up to the frenzy of
killing. He slipped into treacherous shell-holes, tripped
over unseen stakes, tore his clothes on rusty bits of wire
that rose out of the earth like brambles, and over his
shoulders was a coil of the same kind of wire, scratching
his face and hands, clinging to his legs, his coat, his
sleeve, catching at everything he passed and jerking him
back. He led his party of men into the open and commenced to lay out his wire.

Mud, mud, mud comes as a kind of chant through
every account of the war. Slimy mud, green mud, blue
mud, brown mud, black mud, hiding sharp bits of tin,
old bayonets, rifles, caps, clothes, dead men. Shell-holes
one can understand; they are just holes of varying sizes—
and the mud at the bottom of them. There are lots of
shell-holes; the ground is pitted with them, like small-
pox—bad small-pox; and the ridges of earth, separating
one from the other, are ridges of soft, crumbling earth
into which your feet sink, and it sticks to your boots.
There is no grass. The whole thing is destruction—the
earth is destroyed, pounded, smashed, blown up for miles,
making a long belt of devastation where the two great
armies face each other. This is the open.

At any time you would hate to walk over the open;
you would hestitate to touch an open, bleeding wound,
how much more would you hesitate to touch this
wounded, festering, putrid earth? Cpl. James did not
think about it. All he thought about was laying out
his entanglement of barbed wire.

But we have not yet finished with the " open." In
the open you are exposed—you might as well be naked—

you feel so naked.   And you seem to tower above everything, you are gigantic, and the only covering you think
of is a small, deep shell-hole in the ground.   It is because
you hear sounds all round you which you know may kill
or maim.

A man was blown up at Mortaldje, flung twisting in
the air amongst a shower of mud.   He began to run
about in an aimless manner, with short pauses to take
off some portion of his garments.   After a while he ran
about naked until another shell killed him.   He was mad
and felt naked.   This is the open.

Cpl. James worked at his wire in the open.   Something
infinitely more vicious in sound than thunder was crashing all round him.   The explosions cut one another like
the shell-holes in the ground.   But Cpl. James made a
good job of his wire.   He had six men with him.   One
was smashed—then another.   He worked with Pte.
Viggers.   Viggers was smashed, and Cpl. James was alone.
All his men were broken and scattered like bits of old
stakes, and mixed with other shattered fragments in the
mud.   This was the result of the sound all round him,
crashing sound and flashes of light.   The sound was still
there, shaking the air, and making the earth stagger.
Cpl. James had put out all his wire.   There was more to
be got out, but he had no men to fetch it.   If he had
more men could he put up more wire, or would they all
be killed too ?   No one was supervising his work ; he
was all alone.   The Verey lights enabled him to see that
everyone else in the open was apparently engaged on
some work, so it was extremely unlikely that he could
get more men to carry wire.   Cpl. James asked for more
men ; said his job was unfinished.

Of course he was only doing his duty.   He was not
supposed to be killing Germans, and there is no story of
valour attached to him.   He was killed at the battle of
the Somme.

In a dim kind of manner these acts were sometimes
recognised, and Cpl. James received a Military Medal ;
he might well have been given more.   On the other hand,
the conditions of fatigues at the battle of the Somme

and the third battle of Ypres were very similar to this incident at Mortaldje and differ principally as to the proportion of casualties—also the casualties were picked up and the fatigue carried out—yet no one received even a Military Medal, and no one is mentioned for carrying out these fatigues in this account of the war.   Hard as it is to raise a thrill over Cpl. James's duty while a minor operation is in progress, it is still harder where the every-day duty of the battalion is concerned.

What are we to say of a man like G. E. Randall, who, rather than fall out when the battalion was on the march because the sole of his boot came off, tramped into billets with a track of blood behind him ?   He might be called a gallant fellow.   We can feel for Randall—many people have suffered from a sore foot, and imagination can supply the muddy, cut-up road and maybe the shell-pounded track.   But can many people, without the experience, imagine the sentry in the trench ?

The sentry has marched there, four or five miles, carrying his rifle, a hundred and twenty rounds of ammunition, a heavy pack, a spade and a bag of rations. It is cold and it is raining, but he is sweating under his load. And he arrives at the trench. The trench is perhaps six feet deep, and he cannot see over the top, but, as he tramps along it, he brushes the muddy sides with his sleeves.   If there are no trench-boards his feet sink over the tops of his boots in thick, glue-like mud.   His post is a step cut in the side of the trench, a step which will allow seven or eight men to sit on it. He stands on the step, his rifle in hand, his bayonet fixed, and his head over the top of the parapet and about eighteen inches above the level of the ground.   He stares into the night, and each bump in the ground, each tuft of grass, each stake holding the barbed wire in front of him looks big and moves.   His eyes are always playing tricks.   At times he gets dazed, so that he sees nothing at all.   He hears movements of rats, or birds, or the wind. He gets cold and is relieved after one hour, and then sits cold and drowsy for two hours—or perhaps he has to work at

digging or revetting. Bullets crack about his ears like
whips. Sometimes the shells blow up the trench near
him. Everyone stands to arms an hour before daylight,
and then he eats his breakfast. During the day he gets
longer intervals for rest on his muddy fire-step, as, of the
six men in his post, one only is on sentry by day and two
at night. It rains all the time. His feet are wet, his
clothes are wet, he is blue with cold. This goes on for
two or four nights, and on the third or fifth, as the case
may be, he is relieved by another unit and marches back
to billets with his load, minus the rations, but plus a
considerable weight of mud and water. He rests in a
dilapidated barn with holes in the roof, and frequently
water on the earth floor, or else he rests in another trench
with the added luxury of several bits of tin as a roof.
He is probably bombed or shelled during the nights and
days that follow, but possibly does one hour only each
night as sentry. And then he goes back to the " Line "
again. And this goes on for months. He has only one
suit of clothes at a time and one pair of boots at a time.
There is no story of valour, but what are we to say of
the man who did it, and sang while he did it ?

But, it will be said, certain men mentioned have done
all this and more—they have been noted as having done
more than their duty ! For all we know, so has every
other man. The nominal roll of the Welsh Guards is the
list we give of gallant men, and the deeds of the battalion
are their deeds.

Thos. Fall, Baker St.

CAPTAIN (ACTING LT.-COL.) R. E. C. LUXMOORE BALL, D.S.O., D.C.M.

CHAPTER XX

THE quiet manner in which troops received the news of an Armistice was most remarkable. Their attitude, their conversation, expressed the question, "And what happens now?"

Military routine continued without any change so far as hours were concerned. The battalion might well have thought itself in rest billets ten miles behind the line. There was actually a slight alteration in the nature of the work. All parades were of a more strictly ceremonial nature, and greater attention was given to dress and smartness. There was no more musketry and bombing practice; drill took place every day without the variation of field work, with battalion schemes, company schemes, and platoon schemes; there was squad drill, company drill, and battalion parades.

It must not be thought that such drill had been banished during the war. The change was in degree in the matter of drill, and complete only in abandonment of field practice. In spite of all the difficulties which attend smartness while active war is in progress, it had been maintained. But, although free from rust, there had not been the time to keep a permanent polish, a peace-time polish, on the battalion. The work was now directed to levelling up the men, to bringing the backward man up to standard.

The new brigadier appointed to the 3rd Brigade was John Campbell, of the Coldstream Guards. Most people knew him; all had heard of him on the Somme battle-

field, where he won a V.C. on September 15th, 1916.
But he had been away from the division for some time
in command of a Line Brigade. He arrived in a bad
temper. He wanted to command a Brigade of Guards
in action, and the fighting was over; he was very sore.
He soon settled down, however, and a better, kinder-
hearted man never walked. He would do anything for
an officer or man in his brigade—all he asked for in
return was efficiency, and he got it.

The question of guards became a prominent one.
They were to be as the King's Guard for smartness.
This brought up the further question of clothes, of
shoulder-titles, of caps and badges. On the one side was
the Ordnance Department complaining of extravagant
demands for clothing, on the other the brigadier storming
because a man on guard had his trousers patched.

The battalion was fairly well off for shoulder-titles.
When the shortage of brass became serious they had been
withdrawn, and worsted badges with "Welsh Guards"
in white on a black ground had been issued, to be sewn
on the shoulder-seams of the sleeve. These were a regimental expense, and it was not too easy to renew them.
The brass leeks were now reissued as well, and gradually
all these difficulties were overcome.

On November 14th there was a thanksgiving service
of a public nature in the Roman Catholic Church at
Maubeuge.

The mayor and town officials, the divisional staff, commanding officers, and seconds in command attended.
And after the service the major-general was given a flag
by the mayor—this ceremony taking place in the square.
The one disappointment amongst the onlookers was that
the mayor did not kiss the major-general (we believe bets
had been made on the subject). It was thought a pity
that no one had suggested it to the mayor, not so much
because money was at stake but to see what the major-
general would do. Willie Arthur had been assaulted in
this fashion by a French peasant, and "I hit him in the
stomach, d— him." But our Allies, with their thoughts
on their devastated country, and the years of bitterness

through which they had passed, were in no mood for
jokes of this description.

The next day the battalion was paraded to hear a
lecture on demobilisation, delivered by Valentine
Williams of the Irish Guards.

On the 16th there was an open-air Protestant Thanksgiving at Maubeuge ; 25 per cent. of all units in the
division attended.

These were austere festivities.   Maubeuge did its best
to be gay, but it had not the wherewithal to be festive.
The Coldstream Guards band played in the square, and
the populace seemed pleased with the music, but there
was a grim correctness covering their actions.

During these few days preparations for the advance
to the Rhine were in progress.   Men who were not fit
for a strenuous march were weeded out, and on the 18th
the division marched for Villers-sire-Nicole.   The Details
moved by bus to Solesmes.

We do not propose to follow the movements of the
battalion step by step over the 212 miles to Cologne.
The strictest march discipline was observed all the way.
Full regulation kit was carried by each man, and the
transport had its regulation load.   Not a single man fell
out on this march.   The roads were bad, the marching
at times was hard ; many men had their toes through
their boots before reaching Cologne, and soap could no
more be supplied than shoe-leather ; the supply of fresh
meat failed, as did forage for the horses.   It was a great
march, and the battalion deserves all praise for the way
it was accomplished.

It was in the nature of a parade march, with much
fussing and worrying over details.   And there were
amusing efforts by units to secure points.   The brigadier
found Lieut.-Col. Luxmoore Ball riding along the line
one morning.   " Well, Ball," said he, " everything all
right ? "   " Splendid," replied Dick Ball, " except the
under carriages of the brigade transport, which have not
been cleaned."   The brigadier rode on in silence and
passed the battalion.   Presently he came cantering up
to the Commanding Officer—" I say, Ball, your battalion

is disgraceful! Two men going about like poets! You must see they get their hair cut!"—and afterwards he told Geoffrey Devas, with great glee, that "Ball took my name over the transport this morning, but I got back on him!"

One town will always be remembered on this march— Monceau-sur-Sambre. The battalion arrived there on November 20th, and was met by the municipal band. The burgomaster delivered an oration of welcome, and the officers were banqueted and the men treated to the "Wine of Victory."

The wine of victory was a levy on the inhabitants. Treasure and wine had been concealed from the rapacious Germans under the foundations of houses, in the gardens, in the fields, and now every Belgian who had possessed anything of the kind found a spade and dug it up. Burgundy flowed. Here was real feasting and mad rejoicing. Laughing girls danced with the men in the square—no Belgian at Monceau-sur-Sambre could do enough for a Welsh Guardsman. And it was all well done, a genuine welcome, a heartfelt expression of thanks for deliverance.

The rejoicings continued for four days and ended with a banquet to officers on the evening of the 23rd. The next morning the march was continued to Chatalet.

The battalion crossed the German frontier at Poteau at 8.39 a.m. on December 13th. The weather was bad, with heavy rain and a high wind, and the roads in a fearful condition. The inhabitants were surly or servile. Cologne was entered during the afternoon of the 20th.

All Details had arrived in Cologne by train on the 19th, so the whole battalion was assembled in a large school in Redwitz Strasse in Sulz, a suburb of Cologne.

Explicit orders were issued against any form of fraternising, a condition which most Germans in Cologne seemed only too anxious to foster. Certain restaurants were allocated for the exclusive use of civilians, but otherwise there were few restrictions for troops.

The behaviour of the Welsh Guards in Cologne was, as it had always been, exemplary. They had, no doubt,

many temptations, cunningly offered by the Germans;
but their attitude was always correct, and in all respects
they proved themselves the smartest battalion in the
Guards Division.

A party composed of 2/Lieuts. Stanier and Paton,
Drill-Sergt. Pearce, and Sergts. Grant and Pates left for
England on the 23rd to bring out the Colours.

On the 28th demobilisation commenced with the
despatch of 8 policemen and 5 miners, and on the next
day of 213 miners and 4 policemen; but after a time the
hasty dispersal of the Army of Occupation became serious
and had to be stopped. The battalion was then reduced
to little more than half strength, and the last draft,
which joined the Details at Solesmes, and was composed
largely of young miners, had gone home again within a
few weeks of their arrival.

Christmas dinners were eaten on the 29th, and,
although good, owing to the congestion on the railways
the men did not get all that had been sent out to them
from Regimental H.Q. However, the sergeants' mess
had a good spread on New Year's Day, and after dinner
entertained the officers.

There was, of course, great excitement amongst the
inhabitants when the Colours arrived on January 7th.
A platoon from each battalion in the division (with the
exception of the new Grenadier, Coldstream, and Irish
War Battalions, who had rejoined the division prior to
the march into Germany) were drawn up in front of the
railway station. Enormous crowds assembled to watch
the ceremony.

It was a fine sight when the Colours marched out of
the station and took their places in the centre of each
platoon while the massed drums played in rear. Each
brigade party then marched to its own area. Many
Germans both round the Station Square and on the line
of march had to be ordered to salute the Colours.

There were no inspection parades while the battalion
was at Cologne, but barracks were visited by Gen. Sir
Herbert Plumer on January 8th, by H.R.H. the Prince of
Wales on January 15th, and by Gen. Sir H. S. Rawlinson

on February 14th. Sir Herbert Plumer brushed aside all the surface work, and in a few minutes was asking questions in a quiet, charming, courteous manner which went right to the heart of good management. Lieut.-Col. Luxmoore Ball, however, had worked the battalion up to a state of perfection second to none; the material he had could not have been better used. There was, on that occasion, one amusing incident. A scheme of education for the men had been ordered, and the Welsh Guards' scheme had been started a few days before the Army Commander's visit, but was not quite in an easy groove—the lecturers, drawn from the officers of the battalion, had not become fluent. Lieut. Saunders was just opening his first lecture on history when Sir Herbert Plumer and a crowd of senior officers entered the hall. Saunders, naturally enough, was thrown into confusion, but before he could make up his mind what to do Sir Herbert Plumer told him to go on. He did. He did not know what he was saying, but as though he was reading from a dictionary words flowed from him. At one moment the word " astronomy " echoed through the hall, then a list of rivers and lakes, followed by some allusion to the wheat-producing plains of North America, which bordered on an agricultural discussion. History is an all-embracing subject; he afterwards argued he was trying to make the point clear.

A slight epidemic of influenza broke out at Cologne. The battalion had not been absolutely free from it since they left St. Hilaire—2/Lieut. Foote had died of it. The astonishing thing about the whole campaign was the absence of serious epidemic.

On March 1st the battalion celebrated St. David's Day. The men had a special dinner—Cecil Keith, now on the divisional staff, had always shown the greatest good-will towards the battalion, and in this emergency once more came to the rescue with a light lorry in which Sergt. Marshall was despatched to Belgium to buy pigs. There was also a concert; the Scots Guards band not only played, but provided some good comic singers.

The officers' dinner was held in a room in a small

restaurant at the corner of Zulpicher Strasse and Franz Joseph Strasse. Col. Vickery, of the 74th R.F.A., Col. Pilcher, Major Charles Greville, Grenadier Guards, and Lieut. Rymer Jones, R.F.A., were invited. The toast was "Wales and the Regiment," given by the Commanding Officer, everyone standing, while the Welsh National Anthem was sung by 2/Lieut. Walters and the choir.

It was the last event on foreign soil. Early in the morning of March 6th the battalion marched out of barracks for the station at Ehrenfeldt. The Major-General, Brig.-Gen. Campbell, and the French Commandant of Maubeuge attended at the station to see the battalion off, and amidst cheers the train streamed out of Cologne soon after 9 a.m.

It was a slow journey. The men were in closed trucks and the weather was bad, but not too severe. Food was plentifully provided by canteens on the way. The battalion (with the cadre of the 4th Battalion Grenadier Guards) detrained at Dunkerque on the morning of the 8th. Before going to camp the men were all medically examined—one case of scabies was found.

On March 11th the battalion embarked on the ss. *North-West Miller*, and sailed from Dunkerque. The ship had to lie off Calais all night, no night sailing being allowed, and was met by Col. Murray Threipland at Tilbury Docks on the afternoon of the 12th—from there the battalion was carried to Barnes Station by train, and arrived at Ranelagh Club soon after 4 p.m. A number of the friends of officers and men had assembled to welcome them.

The following warrant officers, non-commissioned officers, and men are those who went out with the battalion and returned with it, having served the entire period with the battalion : 6 C.S.M. A Pearce, 23 C.Q.M.S. L. Hunter, 5 Q.M.S. H. J. Pursey, 50 C.Q.M.S. W. J. Trott, 374 Sergt. J. C. Roberts, 1,037 Sergt. F. Aspinall, 496 Sergt. G. Winter, 1,429 L/Sergt. B. Stone, 1,428 L/Sergt. J. Hughes, 1,359 Sergt. R. Scott-Kiddie, 1,036 Dr. L. Coley, 1,551 Dr. G. Denby, 152 Gdsm. T. J. Rees.

20

CHAPTER XXI

THE SECOND (RESERVE) BATTALION

FROM time to time we have mentioned the arrival of
drafts of officers and men in Belgium and France. The
supply and training of these drafts was the business of
the 2nd (Reserve) Battalion.

With the departure of the 1st Battalion to France the
2nd Battalion came into being. Command was given to
Lieut.-Col. J. B. Stracey-Clitherow, Hon. Colonel East
Riding of Yorkshire Lancers, and formerly Major in the
Scots Guards, a tall, handsome, large-hearted sportsman,
who was justly proud of the men he eventually turned
out.

At the commencement the following warrant and non-
commissioned officers were appointed : R.S.M. W. Stevenson, R.Q.M.S. I. Smith, Drill-Sergt. S. J. Dunkley,
Drill-Sergt. J. G. Harris, C.S.M.'s Roberts, Wadeson, and
Jenkins, C.Q.M.S.'s Lawson and T. W. Davies. Some
of these names will be recognised as having served with
the 1st Battalion, and holding a rank which does not
coincide with the above. The whole question of rank
is extremely confusing both with officers and men.
Under the system of giving acting rank everyone was
sent sliding up or down the scale as he was or ceased to
be employed, either because he went to France, or came
back to England on account of wounds or sickness, or
because someone else with the substantive rank appeared
and reported for duty. There were also many occasions
when a man was given acting rank because he was the
best man for the job, but, owing to the establishment

F. A. Swaine, 146, New Bond Street.

LT.-COLONEL STRACEY CLITHEROW.

being complete, he could not be given substantive promotion. It frequently led to apparent unjust treatment, but no one was ever able to suggest a better method.

Lieut. E. R. Martin-Smith was appointed Adjutant of the 2nd Battalion, and Lieut. and Quartermaster W. Shipley, formerly Coldstream Guards, was appointed quartermaster.

On September 9th the 2nd Battalion left Wellington Barracks for training at the camp at Marlow, where they remained until October 18th. The first draft, consisting of Lieut. R. E. C. Luxmoore Ball and 100 other ranks, was sent from Marlow on September 16th.

The winter was spent at the Tower of London, where many German spies and the traitor Casement were guarded by the 2nd Battalion. A more cheerful incident was an inspection and the presentation of the first Distinguished Conduct Medal won by the Welsh Guards (Pte. G. C. Grant) by Major-Gen. Sir Francis Lloyd on January 10th, 1916.

Naturally enough, being essentially a draft-finding unit, the strength of the 2nd Battalion was very fluctuating, and it was not always easy to find the men necessary for London duties. As compared with the reserve battalions of other regiments of Guards the 2nd Battalion Welsh Guards was the worst off for men, the regiment having an establishment of only one battalion. Also there was bound to be an uneven state of training in the men under Lieut.-Col. Stracey-Clitherow's command —at times he would be strong in recruits just arrived from Caterham Depot, and at other times he would have a high percentage of trained men returned through hospitals from the 1st Battalion. But his difficulties were made easier from June 12th, 1916, onwards, when his battalion moved to Tadworth.

After the summer training at Tadworth they moved to Orpington in Kent, which was part of the London District, on October 24th. A brewery was turned into a barracks for the men, and the officers were billeted in houses.

On May 15th, 1917, they moved once more to Tadworth Camp, and on September 5th to Ranelagh Club, Barnes, where they remained for the rest of the war.

Major-Gen. Sir Francis Lloyd was continually visiting the battalion, and inspected them on June 28th, 1916, April 14th, 1917, October 2nd, 1917, March 13th, 1918. Field-Marshal H.R.H. the Duke of Connaught also inspected them on January 9th, 1917, when the strength on parade was 20 officers and 581 other ranks. The battalion in every case was found up to standard.

In the training of the men Lieut.-Col.Stracey-Clitherow had the assistance first of Major Blake, until his health broke down, and then of Major Fergusson. There was also Capt.A.E.Price,who did good work with the messing of the battalion. These three, and of course the quartermaster, were the only permanent officers he had. Fox-Pitt took the place of Martin Smith as Adjutant when the latter joined the 1st Battalion, and Fox-Pitt was in due course replaced by Stephen Stokes. Company Commanders varied in the same way. Marshall Roberts, who had never recovered from the wound he received early in the war, was with the 2nd Battalion a long time. He went to the 1st Battalion twice, but each time his health gave way. He did most excellent work in training the young officers and men, although bitterly disappointed that he could not serve abroad.

On February 27th, 1918, a Memorial Service was held at Holy Trinity, Sloane Street, London, for officers, warrant officers, non-commissioned officers and men of the Welsh Guards who had fallen in the war. H.R.H. the Prince of Wales was present, and the congregation included the Lord Mayor of Cardiff and Welsh members of Parliament. The Bishop of St. Asaph (the Right Rev. Alfred George Edwards, D.D.) preached. The Rev. John Williams, D.D., Chaplain to the Forces, Minister of Llwnidris, Llanfair, P.G., Anglesea, read the lessons, the first in English and the second in Welsh. The service was most impressive.

Major G. C. D. Gordon, D.S.O., assumed command of the battalion on March 2nd, 1918, Lieut.-Col. Stracey Clitherow having been placed on retired pay. The retirement of the Commanding Officer was not altogether unexpected, as he often chaffed about what he called his "Anno Domini," but whatever that may have been he was hale and vigorous, and won the very real affection and esteem of all who served under him—and his drafts were good.

Major Douglas Gordon was again given the Acting rank of lieutenant-colonel, and his experience with the 1st Battalion enabled him to modify the system of training in some directions; but the war was nearing its end, and he did not send out a great number of men.

Two Army Orders of interest were the one appearing on March 22nd, 1918, abolishing the left-hand salute, the other on August 6th, when chevrons were ordered to be worn, one for each year's service overseas.

On September 26th Lieut.-Gen. Sir Francis Lloyd, G.C.V.O., K.C.B., D.S.O., who had had so much to do with the raising and training of the regiment, addressed all ranks on parade at Ranelagh in a farewell speech on the termination of his period of command of the London District.

The Reserve Battalion disappeared on March 18th, 1919, becoming absorbed in the 1st Battalion, which had returned on the 12th. Everyone connected with the organisation had reason to be proud of the work they had done.

The following is a list of drafts sent out to the 1st Battalion:

No.	Date.	Officers.	Other Ranks.	Remarks.
1	17.8.15	30	1,018	Battalion.
2	16.9.15	1	100	Lieut. R. E. C. Luxmoore Ball.
3	15.10.15	2	50	Capt. H. E. Allen and Lieut. P.L.M. Battye.
4	19.10.15	5	—	Capt. H. H. Aldridge, Lieut. B. C. Williams Ellis, Lieut. J. W. Lewis, 2/Lieut. C. H. Dudley Ward, 2/Lieut. E. Crawford Wood.
5	4.11.15	1	70	2/Lieut. N. Newall.
6	18.12.15	5	—	Lieut. Lord Newborough, 2/Lieut. J. W. L. Crawshay, 2/Lieut. C.E.S. Dodd, 2/Lieut. H. S. Stokes, 2/Lieut. A. Gibbs.
7	20.12.15	—	2	C.S.M. J. Harris, 15 C.S.M. P. Roberts.

No.	Date.	Officers.	Other Ranks.	Remarks.
8	6.2.16	6	—	Capt. H. G. Smith, Lieut. Viscount Clive, Lieut. F. F. Barlow, 2/Lieut. F. B. W. Williams, 2/Lieut. J. A. Pugh, 2/Lieut. M. C. de Wiart.
9	21.2.16	1	110	Capt. H. Dene.
10	28.3.16	—	3	Machine Gunners.
11	2.5.16	3	—	Lieut. B. T. V. Hambrough, 2/Lieut. R. E. O. Goetz, 2/Lieut. J. L. G. Kearton.
12	4.5.16	1	100	Lieut. H. A. Evan-Thomas.
13	22.5.16	1	57	2/Lieut. E. H. L. Bagot.
14	7.6.16	—	7	Machine Gunners.
15	19.6.16	—	5	Machine Gunners.
16	9.7.16	1	95	2/Lieut. W. A. F. L. Fox-Pitt.
17	12.7.16	3	—	Capt. H. G. G. Ashton, Lieut. Earl of Lisburne, 2/Lieut. P. C. Dickens.
18	13.7.16	1	50	2/Lieut. B. T. M. Hebert.
19	15.7.16	2	—	Lieut. J. W. Power, 2/Lieut. E. Cazalet.
20	17.7.16	2	—	2/Lieut. A. P. Wernher, Lieut. R. W. Lewis, M.C.
21	22.7.16	1	56	2/Lieut. C. W. Duncan to conduct and return.
22	5.8.16	—	3	Machine Gunners.
23	9.8.16	2	80	Major H. H. Bromfield, D.S.O., 2/Lieut. J. L. G. Kearton.
24	26.8.16	—	100	
25	31.8.16	—	8	3 Signallers, 5 Machine Gunners.
26	12.9.16	1	—	2/Lieut. M. A. Hughes.
27	13.9.16	—	2	Machine Gunners.
28	19.9.16	—	4	Signallers.
29	22.9.16	1	—	Capt. C. C. L. Fitzwilliams.
30	23.9.16	—	6	Machine Gunners.
31	25.9.16	8	—	Lieut. R. E. C. Luxmoore Ball, 2/Lieut. G. C. Devas, 2/Lieut. W. M. Upjohn, 2/Lieut. O. Bird, 2/Lieut. R. W. Hargreaves, 2/Lieut. P. Dilberoglue, 2/Lieut. W. N. Downing, 2/Lieut. H. F. Lascelles.
32	25.9.16	1	53	2/Lieut. L. F. Ellis.
33	4.10.16	1	100	2/Lieut. M. C. de Wiart.
34	12.10.16	1	—	2/Lieut. H. P. Gould.
35	18.10.16	1	50	2/Lieut. R. L. Wreford Brown.
36	21.10.16	2	—	2/Lieut. V. G. North, 2/Lieut. A. W. W. Berg (Machine Gun Company).
37	2.11.16	1	33	2/Lieut. R. G. de B. Devereux (conducting and return).
38	17.11.16	—	15	
39	25.11.16	1	—	Major G. C. D. Gordon.
40	11.12.16	3	—	Lieut. W. L. B. Bonn, Lieut. H. B. Roderick, 2/Lieut. W. N. Culverwell.
41	12.12.16	1	50	2/Lieut. R. G. de B. Devereux.
42	22.12.16	1	70	2/Lieut. J. L. G. Kearton.

No.	Date.	Officers.	Other Ranks.	Remarks.
43	23.12.16	1	30	2/Lieut. F. B. W. Williams (conduct and return).
44	19.1.17	1	70	2/Lieut. R. C. Bonsor.
45	31.1.17	1	100	2/Lieut. H. A. St. G. Saunders.
46	10.2.17	4	—	2/Lieut. R. C. R. Shand, 2/Lieut. W. Arthur, 2/Lieut. R. R. Jones, 2/Lieut. J. C. Jenkins.
47	14.3.17	1	100	2/Lieut. A. C. H. Borough.
48	18.3.17	1	100	2/Lieut. A. Gwynne Jones, D.S.O.
49	27.3.17	3	50	Capt. Battye, Capt. H. E. Allen, 2/Lieut. R. W. Youngman.
50	24.4.17	1	50	2/Lieut. G. D. Manley.
51	5.5.17	2	—	2/Lieut. B. T. M. Hebert, 2/Lieut. F. D. S. Fripp.
52	25.5.17	—	7	
53	26.5.17	2	150	2/Lieut. T. E. Byrne, 2/Lieut. H. E. Baness.
54	2.6.17	2	—	Lieut. K. G. Menzies, Lieut. H. T. Rice.
55	9.6.17	—	22	2 corporals and 20 men to join the Divisional Labour Company.
56	13.6.17	1	—	Capt. J. V. Taylor.
57	19.6.17	—	2	Signallers.
58	23.6.17	1	—	Lieut. E. R. M. Smith.
59	26.6.17	1	100	Lieut. N. Newall.
60	31.7.17	2	—	Lieut. P. C. Dickens, 2/Lieut. A. F. M. Carlyon.
61	9.8.17	2	150	Lieut. R. W. Hargreaves, 2/Lieut. G. C. S. Tennant.
62	9.8.17	3	—	2/Lieut. T. H. B. Webb, 2/Lieut. C. P. Ballard, 2/Lieut. P. Llewellyn.
63	10.8.17	1	—	Lieut. R. G. de B. Devereux.
64	4.9.17	1	—	Lt. C. H. Dudley Ward, M.C.
65	18.9.17	1	104	Lieut. N.M.Harrop (conducting and return).
66	3.10.17	3	—	Lieut. N. M. Harrop, 2/Lieut. C. T. Bowyer, 2/Lieut. E. J. Davies.
67	11.10.17	—	9	
68	12.10.17	1	—	Major H. Dene, D.S.O.
69	22.10.17	1	100	2/Lieut. G. P. Gore (conduct and return).
70	14.11.17	—	4	Signallers.
71	15.11.17	1	—	2/Lieut. G. P. Gore.
72	3.12.17	—	4	Signallers.
73	12.12.17	6	—	Lieut. Hon. P. G. J. F. Howard, Lieut. C, Romer Williams, 2/Lieut. J. A. Wiseman, 2/Lieut. D. B. Davies, 2/Lieut. B. Stokes, Lieut. H. A. Evan Thomas.
74	2.1.18	2	190	Lieut. P. Dilberoglue (conducting and return).
75	4.2.18	—	11	Signallers.
76	6.2.18	—	15	(Retransferred from Machine Gun Guards).
77	7.2.18	3	—	Lieut. M. C. de Wiart, Lieut. L. F. Ellis, 2/Lieut. T. Mathew.

No.	Date.	Officers.	Other Ranks.	Remarks.
78	15.2.18	1	30	2/Lieut. T. E. Byrne.
79	19.2.18	1	—	Capt. G. C. L. Insole, M.C.
80	3.3.18	1	—	Cpt. M. O. Roberts.
81	19.3.18	—	1	Pioneer-Sergt. Hart.
82	30.3.18	1	50	2/Lieut. C. M. Fleming.
83	31.3.18	2	210	2/Lieut. H. C. N. Hill, 2/Lieut. R. R. D. Paton.
84	1.4.18	—	10	A/iv.
85	3.4.18	2	—	Lieut. P. Dilberoglue, 2/Lieut. C. E. Davies.
86	5.4.18	1	—	Capt. R. W. Lewis, M.C.
87	13.5.18	—	1	No. 1 R.S.M. W. Stevenson.
88	20.5.18	2	—	Lieut. (A/Capt.) W. M. Upjohn, Lieut. J. W. L. Crawshay.
89	25.5.18	4	—	2/Lieut. A. B. G. Stanier, 2/Lieut. E. B. Hawksley, 2/Lieut. J. E. Gloag, 2/Lieut. T. B. Watson.
90	3.6.18	6	—	2/Lieut. W. A. Courtney, 2/Lieut. W. Holdsworth, 2/Lieut. J. A. Davies, 2/Lieut. H. B. Trotter, M.M., 2/Lieut. H. A. Spence-Thomas, 2/Lieut. H. L. Tatham.
91	9.6.18	—	50	
92	16.6.18	1	21	2/Lieut. J. A. Wiseman.
93	20.7.18	1	34	2/Lieut. P. A. L. Evans.
94	30.7.18	—	5	Signallers.
95	30.7.18	—	29	
96	16.8.18	1	36	2/Lieut. W. E. G. P. Powell.
97	1.9.18	1	⌐	Capt. P. L. M. Battye, M.C.
98	5.9.18	5	⌐	Lieut. P. G. Coleman, D.S.O., 2/Lieut. C. J. Willoughby, 2/Lieut. C. H. Adams, 2/Lieut. V. E. Foot, 2/Lieut. P. F. Reid.
99	10.9.18	—	12	
100	17.9.18	2	—	Lieut. W. F. A. L. Fox-Pitt, Lieut. W. Arthur, M.C.
101	23.9.18	3	—	Lieut. A. Gwynne Jones, D.S.O., Lieut. H. A. St. G. Saunders, 2/Lieut. L. D. W. Mackinnon.
102	4.10.18	—	1	
103	11.10.18	—	35	
104	17.10.18	—	6	Signallers.
105	22.10.18	1	—	Lieut. E. R. M. Smith.
106	29.10.18	1	50	2/Lieut. R. W. Smith.
107	2.11.18	5	—	Lieut. F. A. V. Copland-Griffiths, M.C., 2/Lieut. H. B. Miller, 2/Lieut. P. G. Dyke-Dennis, 2/Lieut. T. G. Walters, 2/Lieut D. B. Morgan.
108	10.11.18	2	225	Lieut. B. T. M. Hebert, M.C., 2/Lieut. A. Wharton.
109	25.11.18	1	40	2/Lieut. C. G. Kemball.

On March 22nd, 1919, a year and a day after the open-ing of the big German offensive, the Guards Division marched through London. The two battalions of Welsh Guards were now merged into one, and this recon-structed battalion was commanded by the officers who had returned with the 1st Battalion from Cologne; other officers who had been overseas, but were with the 2nd Battalion when it was abolished, commanded the demo-bilised and discharged men who took part in the march. At the head of the Welsh Guards Col. Murray Threip-land, Lieut.-Col. Douglas Gordon, and Major Dene rode abreast as former Commanding Officers of the service battalion, the battalion itself being under Lieut.-Col. Luxmoore Ball.

The place of assembly was in Hyde Park, and the route followed was through Hyde Park Corner, Grosvenor Place, and Buckingham Gate, in and out of the Buck-ingham Palace Gates—His Majesty stood under the porch to take the salute—down the Mall through the Admiralty Arch, along the Strand, Fleet Street, Ludgate Hill, to the Mansion House, where the Lord Mayor took the salute, and so back to Hyde Park by Cheapside, Holborn, Shaftesbury Avenue and Piccadilly. The Colours were carried by 2/Lieuts. Paton and Stanier.

On May 1st Lieut.-Col. the Hon. A. G. A. Hore-Ruthven, V.C., C.B., C.M.G., D.S.O., assumed command of the battalion.

Peace was signed at Versailles on June 28th, and a Triumphal March took place in Paris on July 14th. The British Army was represented by the colours of its regiments and the whole contingent was under the command of Col. W. Murray Threipland, D.S.O. Capts. P. Battye, M.C., and Keith Menzies, M.C., had the honour of carrying the Welsh Guards Colours through the Arc de Triomphe. The escort consisted of 351 Drill-Sergt. S. J. Dunkley, 41 Sergt. J. Evans, and 25 L/Sergt. R. Lawson, M.M.

On July 19th representatives from the Navy, the Army, and contingents from all Allied Forces marched in triumph through London. On this occasion the

Colours were borne by Capt. Rice and Lieut. Copland-Griffiths, M.C., and were escorted by a platoon. The route from Hyde Park was through Albert Gate to Vauxhall Bridge Road, via Sloane Street and Belgrave Square, through Kennington and Lambeth, over Westminster Bridge, and so through the Admiralty Arch to the saluting point, which was in front of the Victoria Memorial.

COLONEL LORD HARLECH.

CHAPTER XXII

REGIMENTAL HEADQUARTERS

In the early stages of formation Lieut.-Col. Murray-Threipland, commanding the 1st Battalion, performed the duties of Lieutenant-Colonel of the regiment, but on June 16th, 1915, Lord Harlech was given the temporary appointment to that position.

Q.M.S. C. E. Woods, of the 1st Battalion Scots Guards, returned from France to become sergeant-major and superintending clerk.

The position of Regimental Adjutant was filled by a succession of officers, who in most cases held an acting appointment only. They were:

Capt. M. O. Roberts (acting) .	17.1.16	to 3. 2.16
Capt. B. T. V. Hambrough (acting)	4.2.16	to 3. 5.16
Capt. R. W. Lewis (acting) . .	3.5.16	to 12. 7.16
Capt. H. E. Allen (acting) . .	13.7.16	to 26.10.16
Capt. P. L. M. Battye (acting) .	26.10.17	to 17. 3.17
Major R. G. Williams-Bulkeley .	17.3.17	to 12. 2.18
Capt. J. W. L. Crawshay . .	12.2.18	to 13. 5.18
Capt. B. T. V. Hambrough (acting)	13.5.18	to 1. 6.18
Capt. the Earl of Lisburne . .	1.6.18	to 9. 5.19
Capt. J. J. P. Evans . . .	10.5.18	

On October 15th, 1917, Col. Lord Harlech retired, and was succeeded by Lieut.-Col. W. Murray Threipland, D.S.O., with the temporary rank of colonel while commanding the regiment and regimental district; this rank was confirmed in *The Gazette* on October 15th, 1917.

On June 3rd, 1919, the King's birthday, His Majesty was graciously pleased to appoint H.R.H. the Prince of Wales Colonel of the Regiment.

CHAPTER XXIII

THE BAND

THE Bandmaster (A. Harris) was appointed on Sept. 8th, 1915. The formation of the band started about October 9th, 1915. The first performance in public was a Grand Welsh Patriotic Meeting, held at the London Opera House on March 1st, 1916, the band wearing full peacetime uniform. Lord Harlech was in the chair, the speakers being the Rt. Hon. Lord Justice Bankes, Major-Gen. Sir Francis Lloyd, G.C.V.O., K.C.B., D.S.O., Major Robert Jones, Dr. Lynn Thomas, C.B.

The band did duty with the guard at Buckingham Palace that morning for the first time. Full dress with bearskin cap was worn.

On October 28th, 1916, the band proceeded to France on a tour of three months' duty with the Guards Division and a few weeks later met the 1st Battalion returning from the front line just outside Méault, and played them to their billets. The troops were so tired that the band had to play in slow march time.

The massed bands of the Guards Brigade visited Paris in May 1917, and gave concerts in the Trocadéro and the Tuileries Gardens in aid of French charities.

On February 18th, 1918, the massed bands were ordered to Italy.

DIARY OF THE VISIT OF THE MASSED BANDS, BRIGADE OF GUARDS, TO ITALY (*Lieut. A. Harris*)

" *Monday, February 18th*, 1918.—Special train from Victoria to Folkestone, leaving at 8.28 a.m. Arrived Folkestone 10.30. Boat did not put out till midday. Crossed in the *Invicta*. Arrived Boulogne 2 p.m. All the bandsmen taken off to a large rest billet. Officers had luncheon at the buffet. Train left Boulogne for Paris at 7.30 p.m. Picked up the Irish Guards Band in the night (all under the command of Lieut. Fitzgerald, Grenadier Guards) at Abbeville. Delay in the train, and did not reach Paris until 7 a.m. instead of 4.40.

" *Tuesday, February 19th*, 1918.—Went to the Hôtel Meurice. All the bandsmen were put up for the day at the Leave Club. Left the Gare du Lyon at 8.25 p.m. after meeting the band of the Garde Républicaine, which joined the train.

" *Wednesday, February 20th*, 1918.—Reached Chambéry about 8 a.m. American band joined the train in the middle of the night. Reached Modane about 12 (French time). Luncheon provided by the Italian authorities for all officers and men. Left Modane a little after 2 (Italian time). On arrival at Turin officers got out and had glasses of champagne. Large crowd. Band playing National Anthems; hearty reception. Stopped at a station near Genoa; large crowd on platform; given tea, flowers, flags and postcards. Arrived Genoa 10 p.m. Station decorated and enormous crowds both inside and outside. Marched to what had once been an exhibition. People very enthusiastic. Taken into a large hall and given a very good dinner. Speeches afterwards. Returned to the train afterwards. Train kept on stopping during the night and lost five hours.

" *Thursday, February 21st*, 1918.—Arrived Pisa 9 a.m. Stayed there about an hour, and saw the Leaning Tower. Arrived at Livorno about midday. No breakfast, only coffee. Reached Grosetto about 5 p.m. Everyone given a packet containing food and wine. Journey afterwards very tedious. Finally reached Rome at 11 p.m. Enormous crowd on platform. Very hearty reception. Went to the Grand Hotel. The bandsmen were taken to the Carabinieri Barracks.

" *Friday, February 22nd*, 1918.—Rehearsal for the concert. Concert at the Augusteo in the evening. Great success. Bands of Brigade of Guards receive splendid ovation. Concert over a little before midnight.

" *Saturday, February 23rd*, 1918.—Inspection by the Under-Secretary for War of the Massed Bands at the Carabinieri Barracks in the morning. Bands afterwards marched round the barrack square playing. Concert again at the Augusteo in the afternoon for the wounded, of whom there were a great number present. Very enthusiastic audience.

" *Sunday, February 24th*, 1918.—The British Ambassador visited the Carabinieri Barracks and saw the bandsmen. In the afternoon a concert was held in the Villa Borghese. Enormous crowds all round. Ideal place. At 5 o'clock started to march to the Victor Emmanuel Monument; but no arrangements were made by the police to keep the ground. During the march it was practically impossible to play. Reached the Monument at 7 o'clock, where the bands played the various National Anthems. Then quite dark.

" *Monday, February 25th*, 1918.—At 2.30 the Massed Bands marched into the Quirinal playing. Other bands already formed up. The Italian Band played National Anthem, and one other piece ; the American Band then played : then the Band of the Garde Républicaine ; and last of all the Massed Bands of the Brigade of Guards— the National Anthem and ' Tipperary.' Presentations were then made to the Queen, who gave everyone in the Massed Bands a silver cigarette-case. Refreshments were then given. Band formed up. Gave three cheers for the King and Queen. Bands then marched round the courtyard playing, and then outside. Band of the Grenadier Guards played at the opening of an Anglo-Italian Institute in the evening.

(The flowers which had been given to the Massed Bands while at the Quirinal in the afternoon were distributed among the wounded at the hospital, which was highly appreciated.)

" *Tuesday, February 26th*, 1918.—Photographs were taken at the Carabinieri Barracks in the morning of the whole of the Massed Bands and the officers ; groups of officers ; and each band separately. Officers taken into the officers' mess for refreshments.

" *Wednesday, February 27th*, 1918.—Roman Catholics in the Massed Bands were received by the Pope in the morning at the Vatican. Played at the hospital in the afternoon. In the afternoon Madame Tetrazzini gave a tea at the Grand Hotel. Madame Tetrazzini sang several songs, and then asked all the men to join in and sing ' Tipperary,' which they did. Three cheers were also given for Madame Tetrazzini.

" *Thursday, February 28th*, 1918.—Massed Bands of the Brigade of Guards marched through the streets of Rome. Started an hour late owing to a tram conveying part of the bands going wrong. Marched past the Grand Hotel, through the Via Nationale, and up to the Victor Emmanuel Monument. Bands played 'Rule, Britannia!' and the Italian National Anthem. Then marched back to the Carabinieri Barracks, first going round the hospital opposite playing. Went to the station in the evening, where it was raining slightly. Enormous crowds. Left Rome in the same train as we came in at 9.30 p.m.

" *Friday, March 1st*, 1918.—Arrived in Florence about 8.30 a.m. Went to the Grand Hotel and the Hôtel de Ville. Small breakfast. Luncheon at Gambino's Restaurant. Taken in motor ambulances, etc., to the Garden of the Royal Palace, where a concert was held. Did not start until 4 o'clock instead of 2.30. Band of the Carabinieri played extremely long pieces; then the American Band played; then the Band of the Garde Républicaine; and then the Massed Bands—' Aida ' and ' Tipperary,' followed by Garibaldi's Hymn. They wanted the Massed Bands to march back to the hotels. No arrangements for keeping back the crowds. Dinner at Gambino's Restaurant.

" *Saturday, March 2nd*, 1918.—Train started for Milan about 7 a.m. Stopped at Bologna, and everyone was given a packet containing food and wine. Reached Milan about 6.30 p.m.—very late. Raining hard on arrival. Station very dark. Mayor welcomed bands on arrival. Then went to the Hotel Cavour. Men housed in barracks which had once been a school before the war.

" *Sunday, March 3rd*, 1918.—Big concert at the Scala

Theatre in the afternoon. A fine sight. Both the Italian Band and the French Band played too long. Mademoiselle Roch, from Paris, recited. Massed Bands received great ovation—the success of the afternoon. Bands tried to march off afterwards, but no police arrangements had been made to keep back the crowds, and they had to break off.

" *Monday, March 4th*, 1918.—Very wet day. In the afternoon a concert was given at the Lyric Theatre. The house was full of wounded. As usual the Massed Bands had an enormous success. Played ' Carmen,' ' Tipperary,' and Garibaldi's Hymn. Tea afterwards at Cova's Restaurant."

On the conclusion of this visit the band remained in Paris and gave a few concerts to wounded and men on leave. It then joined the division for the second tour of duty which started in Arras March 10th, 1918. Several successful concerts were given up to March 21st, when the concerts ceased. The band was ordered out of Arras at a moment's notice and went to Doullens. The bandmaster only succeeded in getting the instruments away two days later. Four days later the band was sent to Havre, remaining there some weeks, giving concerts at the hospitals, etc.

The band rejoined the 1st Battalion at Warlincourt on May 5th, and gave some enjoyable concerts in the farmyard—Battalion H.Q.

On May 27th, 1918, at the request of the American Embassy, the band proceeded to Paris, played at the Memorial Service on May 30th, and also gave concerts at the Leave Club on the 31st. Capt. Dudley Ward was in command of this party.

The band returned to England on June 1st. Two other important engagements were the National Eisteddfod of 1918 and 1919 at Neath and Corwen. It was also detailed for duty with the British Contingent in Paris in connection with the Great Victory March on July 14th, 1919, and had the honour of playing the Colours of the British Army through the Arc de Triomphe.

CHAPTER XXIV

A HISTORY OF THE WELSH GUARDS' CHOIR

By Captain G. C. H. Crawshay

THE Welsh Guards, since the day of their formation on February 27th, 1915, have actively associated themselves with Wales and all things Welsh. Welsh by birth, they have in every way portrayed the social characteristics of their country. Singing, boxing, and Rugby football have ever been prominent pastimes in the regiment; but it is through the medium of the first-named that they have drawn nearest to the heart of Wales and established their right to the name they bear. They have sung at home and overseas; in the barrack-room and in the firing-line; in the light of life and in the shadow of death; of joy and sorrow, of hope and despair; of things earthly and of things heavenly. Song being the natural expression of the Welshman's feelings, they ofttimes have foregathered to extol their national heroes and sing of their country's freedom. Their voices have rejoiced Generals and others of God's humbler subjects, who have travelled far by motor and on foot to hear what will always be known as the Welsh Guards' Choir.

The overwhelming desire to sing which seems to possess every Welshman has been responsible for the formation of many Regimental Choirs, which through good organisation and training have attained a high standard. It is that natural outburst of Celtic temperament, combined with a natural gift of harmony, which gives Welsh part-singing its distinctive charm. The

21

chief incentive of each choir has been their love of singing, while warmth of tone and depth of colour have
always been outstanding characteristics.

The first two organised Welsh Guards' Choirs were
formed simultaneously early in May 1915, before the
1st Battalion left for France; the one with the 1st
Battalion at Sandown Park, Esher, the other with the
9th Company, Welsh Guards, at the Guards' Depot,
Caterham. The 1st Battalion Choir, which was organised by Capt. Wilfred Gough, and of which No. 53
C.Q.M.S. S. Rendel and No. 737 Guardsman G. Williams
(afterwards sergeant) acted as joint conductors, numbered
about forty voices. Their first performance was at a
regimental concert at Esher, attended by a large number
of local people. Such was their success that the choir
at once became an institution which was destined to be
permanently associated with the regiment. This choir
later sang at the Steinway Hall, Albert Hall, and many
private houses.

The Depot Choir, in which Capt. Osmond Williams,
D.S.O., took a great personal interest, and of which No.
1,651 Guardsman (afterwards Sergt.) W. T. Jones acted as
conductor, was the outcome of men spontaneously gathering together in the evening and singing the old Welsh
hymns, "Aberystwyth," "Ton-y-Botel," and "Cwm
Rhondda." Capt. Williams was enthusiastic, and after
four days of practice the choir, over a hundred strong,
gave their first public performance in the Drill Hall,
Caterham, their repertoire including "Cydgan-y-Mor-
wyr," "Comrades in Arms," "Harlech," and "The
Soldier's Farewell." They created such an impression
that it still survives in the memory of the residents of
Caterham Valley, most of whom had never previously
heard a Welsh Choir. On July 24th, 1915, fifty picked
voices of the same choir travelled to Cardiff, under the
command of Capt. Osmond Williams, D.S.O., and Capt.
Viscount Clive (both of whom later fell fighting for the
regiment), and there gave a concert in the Park Hall,
which was attended by the Lord Mayor, the Corporation,
and many local people. The choir not only greatly en-

hanced its reputation, but also did much to stimulate recruiting for the regiment.

From August 17th, 1915 (the date on which the battalion proceeded overseas), the regiment has possessed as a rule no less than three distinct choirs—the Depot Choir, the Reserve Battalion Choir and the 1st Battalion Choir. This system proved very satisfactory, for many men, after enlistment in the regiment, became members of each choir in turn, while the training which they received at home proved of the greatest help to the 1st Battalion Choir overseas, which for long periods was unable to practise. It is impossible, in so short a space, to write a detailed history, however brief, of the various regimental choirs; but the list and notes in the appendix will act as a guide to the work accomplished, while the names of the principal conductors, together with the more important engagements of their respective choirs, will enable many ex-Welsh Guardsmen to trace the choirs of which they were members. Hospital, church, battalion, and regimental concerts, which were of weekly occurrence, are not as a rule included, and the 1st Battalion, Reserve Battalion, and Depot Choirs are as far as possible kept distinct.

This history would not be complete without further mention of the first choir in the annals of the regiment to compete in the National Eisteddfod of Wales.

The choir, which was personally organised and supervised by Capt. G. C. H. Crawshay, and of which No. 3,707 Cpl. J. Davies and No. 2,928 Guardsman J. Witcomb, A.R.C.O., acted respectively as conductor and accompanist, was formed in April 1918 at the Guards' Depot, Caterham. Although it contained many old soldiers, its formation was made possible by the Government's final recruiting rally, when some thousands of miners throughout Great Britain were released for service in the Army. It was at once realised that with the material to hand, and with three or four clear months in which to practise before the men would be ready to leave the depot, opportunities presented themselves for the formation of a choir the standard and strength of which circumstances

had not previously permitted. The choir, during the
whole course of its training at Caterham, practised two
hours a day, Saturdays and Sundays included. Their
first big public performance was at a regimental concert
given at the Apollo Theatre, London, on June 11th, 1918,
which was the means of bringing £500 to the Regimental
Prisoners of War and Comforts' Fund. On August 5th,
1918, the choir, eighty strong, left for Neath, to compete
in the male voice competition at the National Eisteddfod.
On arrival they were met by some 3,000 people, and
amidst considerable excitement were played to their
quarters by the band of H.M. Welsh Guards, under
Lieut. Andrew Harris, L.R.A.M. On August 6th and
8th they took part in the Ceremony of the Gorsedd,
joining in the procession and forming a circle round the
Logan Stone (Maen Llog) to keep the ground while the
addresses were delivered. This action on the part of the
authorities in asking representatives of the Army to
guard the sacred Gorsedd Circle is without precedent in
the annals of Eisteddfodau. They could have paid no
greater compliment to the regiment. The Gorsedd has
from time immemorial been regarded as a purely civil
and religious ceremony, from which the military have
been rigorously excluded ; but in the Welsh Guards the
Druids saw not the old-time band of hired assassins, but
Welshmen of their own blood whose ideals, love of home,
and pride of race, were also theirs ; Welshmen fired with
all their ancient ardour, once more fighting for Hen Wlad,
led by the descendant of the Saxon King who gave his
eldest son to be their Prince.

On Thursday, August 8th, the choir competed in the
male voice competition. On mounting the platform they
received a welcome which will never be forgotten, the
vast audience of some 15,000 people rising to their feet,
and cheering again and again.

The result of the competition was not announced until
nearly 6 o'clock, by which time the audience were in a
state of the utmost excitement. Dr. Vaughan Thomas
gave the adjudication in the test piece, " Here's to
Admiral Death," of which he himself was the composer.

Of the fourteen competing choirs Williamstown was placed first with ninety-two marks, the Welsh Guards second with eighty-two. The result was received with acclamation, it being everywhere recognised that the Williamstown Choir had given the finest sustained rendering of the piece, while that of the Welsh Guards, with the exception of the opening phrases, was of equal merit. It is never wise to make excuses, more especially when everyone has cause to be satisfied, but if the opening phrases had been rendered as they hitherto had been at practices the Regimental Choir would certainly not have been ten marks behind the winners. Nervousness was largely responsible for this defect, while the first tenors suffered from the loss of their leader, No. 5,376 Guardsman S. Jenkins, who was suffering from a severe cold and was unable to sing. There can be no doubt that the choir, as it was, achieved a really remarkable success from a musical standpoint. The first practice of the test piece was not held until the end of June, and in two months they proved that they could hold their own with choirs in Wales that had practised for over six. Credit for their performance must be given, not only to the conductor, Cpl. Davies, whose natural genius and Celtic temperament enabled him to bring out in each individual member that sense of artistic interpretation with which Welshmen are born, but also to the choir as a body, who never failed to attend daily practices after parade hours, when most men were only too glad to rest.

Owing to the large number of competitors, a special prize was offered for the choir which proved to be the quickest and smartest in mounting and leaving the platform. Mr. Thomas Powell, Inspector of Schools, Neath, announced after the adjudication that the Welsh Guards had been awarded this prize.

In the past the various choirs have only been maintained with the greatest difficulty; casualties abroad and draft-finding at home constantly caused changes of membership, while heavy duties prevented practices. But, in spite of every obstacle and disadvantage, it has always been possible, both with the battalion at home and overseas, to produce at an hour's notice a choir of some thirty to fifty voices capable of satisfying the most critical of ears.   It was mainly owing to the perseverance of these choirs that Col. Sir Henry Webb, Bt., saw fit to endow the Welsh Guards Choir with the sum of £5,000, as a lasting memorial to his son, 2/Lieut. Basil Webb, Welsh Guards, who fell in action on the Somme.   Taking into consideration the difficulties surmounted in the past, a bright future for the choir may be confidently predicted, provided that the rank and file of the regiment be composed of Welshmen.   Throughout the war this has been the case—may it continue to be so in peace time, in order that the regiment may always be represented at the National Eisteddfod, and as in Wales a certain county is known as the " Little England within Wales," so may in England the regimental quarters be known as " The Little Wales within England," its inhabitants both in peace and war worthily justifying its motto—

"Y Draig Goch y ddyry Gychwyn."

APPENDIX A

PRESENTATION OF COLOURS BY HIS MAJESTY THE KING TO THE 1ST BATTALION WELSH GUARDS, AUGUST 3RD, 1915

[INSTRUCTIONS]

1. The battalion will be formed up in three sides of a square facing Buckingham Palace. Band in rear. Colours cased in rear of battalion in charge of the senior drill-sergeant and two colour-sergeants.

2. *Battalion : Order—Arms, Fix—Bayonets, Slope—Arms, Open Order—March.*

3. *Battalion : Royal Salute, Present—Arms, Slope—Arms, Order—Arms.*—On His Majesty arriving at the saluting point the royal salute will be given. On His Majesty advancing to make his inspection the battalion will Order Arms.

4. His Majesty inspects battalion.

5. *Drums and Colours to the Front.*—All the drummers pass through the centre of the line and pile their drums, turn about and march back to their original places. The colour party will lay the Colours on the pile of drums, the King's Colour being on the right and also on the top. They will then turn about and march back, taking up their position in the front rank in the centre of the line.

6. *Officers for Colours : Quick—March.*—The four officers detailed will return their swords, advance, uncase the Colours and replace them on the drums. The senior major and senior lieutenant will uncase the King's Colour, the junior major and junior lieutenant will uncase the Regimental Colour.

By Senior Major's command : *About—Turn, Quick—March, Halt, About—Turn.*—They will then fall in, facing

317

the pile of drums, at twelve paces from drums, seniors on the outer flanks. The Commanding Officer will take place in front of the centre of this line.

7. *Battalion Stand at Ease, Glee Singers to the Front.*

8. *Consecration.*—After the Consecration Prayer, " Ton y Botel " will be sung.

9. *Battalion : Attention, Glee Singers to your Companies, Quick—March.*—Immediately after the Dedication " Hen Wlad Fy Nhadau " (" Land of my Fathers ").

10. By Senior Major : *Officers for Colours, Quick—March.*—The two lieutenants will fall in in front of His Majesty and kneel on the right knee. The two majors will take the Colours, advance towards His Majesty, and face inwards. The senior major will hand the King's Colour to His Majesty, who will hand it to the senior lieutenant. The junior major will hand the Regimental Colour to His Majesty, who will hand it to the junior lieutenant. When both lieutenants have received the Colours they will rise, and the two majors will turn towards the drums.

11. By Senior Major : *Officers Quick—March.*—The lieutenants will step back to the pile of drums, the majors will place themselves in line with the two lieutenants, turn about and draw swords. The lieutenants will bring the Colours to the order. The Commanding Officer will place himself in front of the centre of this line.

12. His Majesty's address. The Commanding Officer's reply.

13. *Drummers and Escort to the Colours to the Front.*—The drummers will again pass through the line, removing the pile of drums, and return to their places. The two majors will turn outwards, step off in quick time, and return to their places. The two lieutenants will take one pace outwards and carry Colours. The escort to Colours will advance in quick time, placing themselves alongside the lieutenants with the Colours.

14. *Escort and Colours : About—Turn.*—They will turn about and Colours will be unfurled.

15. *General Salute : Present—Arms.*—Band plays the general salute.

16. *Colour Party : Slow—March.*—This command will be given by the Commanding Officer when band has finished the General Salute. Band plays National Anthem. The

colour party will halt at the place in line with the front rank in the centre of the battalion and turn about on the lieutenant's word of command.

17. *Battalion : Slope—Arms, Close Order—March.*

18. *Battalion : Form Fours—Right, Quick—March, Left— Wheel, At the Halt, facing left, Form close Column.*

19. *March Past by Companies by the Right.*—The Commander of the Prince of Wales's Company will give the command *Prince of Wales's Company—By the right quick march.* The remaining companies following in succession at forty paces distance.

20. *At the Halt Close Column.*—The commands will be given by senior major.

21. *In Succession Advance in Fours from the Right : Left —Wheel, Left—Wheel.*—The command will be given by senior major.

22. *Battalion : Left—Wheel, Mark Time in Front, Halt, Left—Turn, On Markers, Right—Dress.*—The battalion will now be in three sides of a square in original formation.

23. *Royal Salute : Present—Arms.*—The officers will salute and the Colours will be lowered

24. *Slope—Arms, Order—Arms, Caps—Off, Three Cheers for His Majesty the King, Unfix—Bayonets, Slope—Arms, Move to the Right in Fours, Form—Fours, Right, Quick— March, Left—Wheel.*—The last word of command (left wheel) will be given when the battalion reaches the gravel path in front of the Palace, the battalion passing His Majesty in column of route. As each company arrives within ten paces of His Majesty the command will be given Eyes—Right by the Platoon Commander, who will give Eyes—Front when the rear of the platoon has passed. The officers will carry swords until the command Eyes—Front is given. The drums will place themselves in front of the battalion on the command Unfix Bayonets. The band will remain standing in their place at the rear of the battalion when in line, and will march off in rear of the last company.

(Signed) W. MURRAY-THREIPLAND,
Lieutenant-Colonel Commanding 1st Battalion Welsh Guards.

APPENDIX B

OPERATION ORDERS

THE actual orders for the attack at Loos were verbal. We give the Brigade Operation Order :

3RD GUARDS' BRIGADE

(1)　　　　OPERATION ORDER NO. 5

Ref. Map Trench Map 36.c. N.W., Sheet 3 and part of 1.

1. The 2nd Guards Brigade is attacking at 4 p.m. with objectives (1) Chalk Pit, (2) Puits 14.b. (Keep).

2. If the 2nd Brigade is successful the 3rd Guards Brigade which will have previously moved to a place of readiness in Loos, will attack Hill 70, H.31.c. and d.

3. The brigade will march in the following order to the place of readiness—starting-point No. 3 Level Crossing—at 2 p.m., 500 yards between battalions :

    4th Grenadier Guards.

    1 sect. Machine Gun Company [to be detailed by B.M.G.O.].

    1st Welsh Guards.

    1 sect. Machine Gun Company [to be detailed by B.M.G.O.].

    Machine Gun Company [less two sections].

    2nd Scots Guards.

    1st Grenadier Guards.

    Brigade tool-carts.

    55th Company R.E. (less pontoon wagons).

4. Each battalion will detail an officer to march with 4th Grenadier Guards, who will reconnoitre a position of readiness for the battalion and lead it to that place.

5. Two small S.A.A. carts and tool-carts will accompany each battalion.

6. The Brigade Ammunition Reserve, under Lieut. Lambert, 4th Grenadier Guards, will be at 14.b. I.3, and will be moved forward to Loos, starting from the former place at 5.30 p.m.

7. The remainder of 1st Line Transport will remain at present billets under Lieut. Lord Stanley, 1st Grenadier Guards.

8. Reports to Fort Glatz G.39.c. at 3 p.m.

3rd Guards Brigade 1.50 p.m.

R. TEMPEST,
Brigade Major.

Secret.

1ST BATTALION WELSH GUARDS

(2)   OPERATION ORDERS

CHAU. TROIS TOURS,
June 24th, 1916.

Ref. Secret Trench Map St. Julien, Sheet 28, N.W. 2.

1. On the night of June 30th, July 1st, or July 1st/2nd, the battalion will capture the Mortaldje Estaminet and approaches thereto.

2. *Object of the Attack.*—To turn the enemy out of the Estaminet and prevent the future use of same by them for observing and offensive purposes ; and to hold same for our observation and possible future advance.

3. *Artillery.*—The attack will be prepared and assisted by artillery, trench mortar and Stokes guns. On the day fixed for the attack, the artillery will bombard and knock in the three communication-trenches running from German line to Mortaldje Estaminet. The artillery will also bombard certain selected points in German front line and second line ; from Canadian Farm to the road, running from Turco Farm to Chemins Estaminet. An artillery barrage will commence and continue during the night of the attack round the front of the Estaminet.

4. *Objective.*—The objective of the attack will be the trench running round the north side of the Estaminet Mortaldje Estaminet. The communication trenches running in at the east and west side of Estaminet will be blown up and blocked at a point fifty yards each side of Estaminet.

5. *Communication Trenches.*—During the operations two communication trenches will be dug from our front line immediately south of Estaminet, to connect to posts held at Estaminet. These will be wired on the outsides.

6. *Procedure after Attack.*—On attack succeeding, all troops will be withdrawn from Estaminet or trench north thereof before daylight, with the exception of two posts, position and strength of which will be decided upon by O.C. Attack, and which two posts will be held.

7. *O.C. Attack.*—Capt. H. Dene will be the O.C. Attack.

8. *Composition of Party.*—The attack will be carried out by No. 4 Company, under Capt. G. C. L. Insole. Half the company in garrison at Vicars Lane will be placed at disposal of O.C. Attack, and will come under his orders for the night of the attack.

9. *Consolidation.*—O.C. Attack will arrange not only for taking and holding Estaminet, but also for wiring, digging communications, and consolidating the position.

10. *Signalling.*—The Adjutant will be responsible for communications between O.C. Battalion and battle station of O.C. Attack. The O.C. Attack will be responsible for communications between him and O.C. No. 4 Company at Estaminet.

11. *Stores.*—Stores as per Appendix A will be available on the night of attack at place mentioned therein, which will be in one of the front-line trenches held by the battalion.

Copies issued :

O.C. Prince of Wales's Company   Copy No. 1.
„   No. 2 Company   .   .   „   „   2
„   No. 3   „   .   .   „   „   3
„   No. 4   „   .   .   „   „   4
H.Q. 3rd Guards Brigade .   .   „   „   5
Retained .   .   .   .   „   „ $\begin{cases} 6 \\ 7 \end{cases}$

J. A. DYSON PERRINS,
Lieutenant, Adjutant 1st Battalion Welsh Guards.

The following stores will be available at a dump to be chosen by the O.C. No. 4 Company by 2 a.m. July 1st, 1916 :

Wire, concertina, coils   50
Wire, French, rolls   12
Wire, barbed, rolls   20
Posts, screw, long   25

Posts, screw, short	.	.	.	.	50
Staples, box	.	.	.	.	1
Hedging-gloves	.	.	.	.	20
Wirecutters .	.	.	.	.	55
Sandbags .	.	.	.	.	1,000
Spades	.	.	.	.	60
Picks .	.	.	.	.	10
S.A.A. boxes	.	.	.	.	12
Mills grenades	.	.	.	.	960
Mills grenades adapted		.	.	.	120
Verey pistols	.	.	.	.	4

Verey lights, 1 inch and 1½ inch boxes,
each size 3

Rockets, spray . . . . .

Water-cans, filled		.	.	.	6
Rations, tinned .	.	.	.	.	20
Nosebags .	.	.	.	.	30
Tape, white	.	.	.	feet	800

J. A. DYSON PERRINS,
Lieutenant, Adjutant 1st Battalion Welsh Guards.

Secret.

ADDENDA TO OPERATION ORDERS D/24–6–16

1. If it is found by the leading unit that the machine guns are still in position and firing from the saps at the Estaminet the company is not to be put over our parapet, and must wait to carry out the operation until they are silenced either by the Stokes or a new bombardment.

2. The 3rd Guards Brigade Stokes Mortar Battery will act under the orders of Capt. H. Dene, and during and after the attack will engage enemy machine guns.

3. The garrisons of D.20, D.21 will co-operate with the attack by bringing rifle and Lewis-gun fire to bear on the High Command Redoubt. They will also be prepared to reply to hostile fire directed on to the Estaminet from these localities, but this fire will only be opened in retaliation for enemy activity or on receipt of "S.O.S.," and the importance of allowing consolidation to proceed in peace must be borne in mind.

4. The medical officer will establish his dressing-station at Butt. 7, the 9th Field Ambulance will establish a post at Belle Alliance. Wounded will be evacuated via Boundary

Road or Foch Lane and the Burnt Farm Road or Coney Street.

5. All watches will be set at 12 noon, 8 p.m. and 10 p.m., time being telephoned from Brigade H.Q.

6. Prisoners will be sent to Brigade H.Q. under escort. They will be searched as soon as possible.

7. Battalion H.Q. will be at Belle Alliance. The O.C. Attack will be at Butt. 7, the O.C. No. 4 Company will be junction of Y and L Trench and B. 17a. Coney Street will not be used after 9 p.m. except for the evacuation of wounded. Orderlies will proceed by Boundary Road or east of it.

8. In the event of an enemy counter attack during the night the "S.O.S." signal will be sent by wire and visual and a para rocket, emitting stars intermingled with gold and silver rain, will be sent up. This message will only be used if the enemy attacks and must not be employed to obtain retaliation. These rockets will be issued to O.C. No. 4 Company and will be sent up from his headquarters.

J. A. DYSON PERRINS,
Lieutenant, Adjutant 1st Battalion Welsh Guards.

June 30th, 1916.

1ST BATTALION WELSH GUARDS

(3)   OPERATION ORDERS

September 8th, 1916.

Secret.

Ref. Map, Sheet 57.c. S.W. Longueval.

1. The 16th Division will attack from a line approximately T.20.d.2.5.—T.19.s.5.5 at 4 p.m. the 9th inst., and capture a line T.13.b.5.8—Cross Roads T.14.s.5.5—T.14.c.5.5 —T.14.d.9.3.

The XIV Corps will co-operate in the attack and will advance its right to T.13.a.

The 16th Division will be relieved by the 3rd Guards Brigade in their new line on the night of September 9th/10th.

The 1st Battalion Welsh Guards will take over the sector T.13.b.5.8—T.14.a.5.4.

The 4th Battalion Grenadier Guards will take over the sector T.14.a.5.8—T.14.c.5.6—T.14.d.9.3.

The above dispositions are liable to alteration if the attack of the 16th Division does not reach its allotted objective.

2. Dispositions of companies will be given when the Commanding Officer returns from the line to-morrow afternoon.

The Prince of Wales's Company will be on the right; No. 2 Company on the left, with Nos. 3 and 4 Companies in support.

A section of machine guns will be told off to the battalion.

Two companies of R.E. will be engaged in building strong points, one in the north-west corner of Ginchy and two to the north of Ginchy, to-morrow night.

3. Officers Commanding Companies, both in front and support lines, will lose no time in siting trenches and digging themselves in.

4. *Organisation of Companies.*—One bombing squad of one N.C.O., eight men, and one Mills rifle grenade man will be organised in each platoon.

Twenty-three bomb-carrying bags and four cups Mills have been issued to companies to-day. They will be carried by their bombing squads.

Twelve Mills bomb pin extractors have also been issued per company.

All Lewis-gun magazines will be taken up filled.

Stretcher-bearers will accompany companies, except the new men in training, who will march with Battalion H.Q.

5. Companies will proceed to the trenches in " Fighting Order " :

Web equipment, less pack.

Cape or waterproof with jersey to be worn rolled, on belt at back.

Haversack to be worn between the shoulders and to contain emergency rations *and two days' rations.*

Two gas-helmets.

Two sandbags to be carried tied on to the braces.

Two bombs, one in each pocket.

Two bandoliers (which will be issued at Carnoy).

A proportion of picks and shovels (which will be issued at Carnoy).

Wirecutters, Verey lights, and Verey ammunition to be carried by those detailed.

Bombers. Same dress and equipment, except that twenty-three bombers per company will carry a canvas bag containing eighteen bombs or Mills adaptors instead of the extra bandoliers.

Packs will be dumped under arrangements to be notified later.

6. Two signallers will go with each company. A receiving-station (visual) will be established at Battalion H.Q. and two reading groups will be pushed forward to get into communication with companies.

Telephone communication will be established if possible.

A post for directing orderlies coming from the companies to Battalion H.Q. will be placed at Waterlot Farm.

7. A contact aeroplane will be up over the position from 5.30 a.m. to 8 a.m. on the morning of the 10th inst. Front line companies will indicate their position by flashing tin discs, and lighting flares at 6 a.m.

These flares will be issued to-morrow.

8. Nine S.O.S. rockets will be issued to companies in front line and six to companies in support before proceeding to the line.

The current S.O.S. signal is three red rockets.

9. Battalion H.Q. on the night September 9/10th will be at approximately S.18.c.1.1, but will probably be advanced nearer Ginchy the following day.

10. There is believed to be a dump of water at the north-west corner of Bernafay Wood and a dump of tools at the south-west corner of the same wood.

It is not known if there are any dumps of S.A.A. or bombs near Ginchy. Officers Commanding Companies will take steps to form reserves collected off casualties.

11. The propping party will reassemble under 2/Lieut. A. Gibbs to-morrow at a time and place to be notified later.

12. Arrangements will be made to pick up water by Bernafay Wood as companies pass. Water-bottles will be filled from the water-carts before going into trenches, and men are warned to use them sparingly. The water taken up may be all that is available for companies till Monday night.

J. A. DYSON PERRINS, *Lieutenant.*
Adjutant 1st Battalion Welsh Guards.

Secret.

1ST BATTALION WELSH GUARDS

(4)   OPERATION ORDERS

September 14th, 1916.

Ref. Map 57.c.S.W. 1/20,000.

1. The Fourth Army will attack the enemy's defences between Combles Ravine and Martinpuich on September 15th with the object of seizing Morval, Les Bœufs, Guedecourt and Flers.

The French are attacking on the south and Reserve Army in the north. The 6th Division are attacking on the right of the Guards Division and the 14th Division on the left.

The division is attacking with 2nd Guards Brigade on the right and the 1st Guards Brigade on the left.

2. The 3rd Guards Brigade will be in divisional reserve, and will be formed up on night September 14/15th in and east of Trones Wood.

The 1st Battalion Welsh Guards will be along west edge of the wood.

At zero plus 1 hour 30 minutes the brigade will advance, and the 1st Battalion Welsh Guards will move to a position north-west of the 1st Battalion Grenadier Guards, who will be in vicinity of Guillemont Station. The left of the battalion will be about Waterlot Farm.

. Separate orders for the march to Trones Wood will be issued.

3. Fighting order as under will be worn :

    1 day's rations.
    1 iron ration.
    1 ration of Oxo and chewing-gum.
    1 haversack ration.
    3 bombs.
    1 Mills rifle-bomb.
    200 rounds S.A.A.
    Pick or shovel.

Signallers, orderlies, and carrying parties will not carry bombs or full complement S.A.A.

4. Battalion Sapping Platoon under 2/Lieut. A. Gibbs will be held in brigade reserve, and will assemble in Trones Wood near the point where the railway enters the wood and will draw eighty boxes Mills rifle-bombs at the above point during the night 14/15th.

22

5. A dump of S.A.A., bombs, R.E. material has been established on the edge of Bernafay Wood. Forward dumps are at S.24.b.9.8 and T.19.c.2.4.

The battalion will draw 125 tins of water at the Cross Roads north-west corner of Bernafay Wood during night September 14/15th, and when the battalion moves forward will dump them at Guillemont Station.

6. A contact aeroplane will be up from zero to dark on the 15th inst., and from 6.30 a.m. to 9 a.m. on the 16th.

If the battalion is in the leading line of the attack at 12 noon or 5 p.m. the 15th, or 6.30 a.m. 16th, they will light flares and make every endeavour to indicate their position.

Red flares will be used by infantry; blue by cavalry.

7. *Pack Animals.*—Two S.A.A. limbers will be parked at the south end of Trones Wood under command of Lieut. Barlow.

8. Prisoners will be sent to Crater Post A.8.a.6.3.

J. A. DYSON PERRINS,
Lieutenant, Adjutant 1st Battalion Welsh Guards.

Copies issued to

O.C. Prince of Wales's Company	Copy No.	1
„ No. 2 Company . .	„ „	2
„ No. 3 „ . .	„ „	3
„ No. 4 „ . .	„ „	4
Quartermaster	„ „	5
Transport Officer . . .	„ „	6
Retained	„ „	7

1ST BATTALION WELSH GUARDS

(5)   OPERATION ORDER

September 16th, 1916.

1. The situation is reported as follows : Our troops holding approximately as shown in map forwarded already. Enemy holding portions of Blue Line with scattered parties west of it. Any of our troops who were in Blue Line have been withdrawn.

2. The Guards Division will attack to-morrow morning.

1st Objective : T.9.d.87 to N.33.c.20.

2nd Objective : Eastern edge of Les Bœufs—T.4.b.5.3 —along road to Cross Roads N.34.a.29.

3. The 61st Infantry Brigade will attack on the right and the 3rd Guards Brigade on the left; boundary line T.8.b.5.0 —T.3.d.27—N.34.a.82. The XV Corps will attack on the left of the 3rd Guards Brigade; boundary line T.8.a.26— N.33.b.20—N.34.a.29.

4. Creeping barrage will commence 250 yards south-west of the Blue Line at zero and will creep on at zero + 10 at rate of 50 yards per minute to 200 yards beyond the Blue Line. Infantry will advance to the attack of the second objective at zero + 35 minutes, at which hour creeping barrage will become intense and will advance at the same pace until it has reached 200 yards beyond the second objective. Standing barrages will lift as creeping barrages reach them.

5. Zero hour will be 9.25 a.m.

6. The battalion will attack the second objective simultaneously with the 1st Battalion Grenadier Guards, and will advance from the place of assembly in the following order: No. 4 Company on the right on a width of two platoons, two platoons in support. Prince of Wales's on the left in the same formation. No. 2 will support the two leading companies in line. The leading platoons of No. 4 and Prince of Wales's will reach 100 from the barrage at 9.35 a.m. On reaching the first objective companies will reorganise, and No. 2 Company will advance on the second objective at 10 a.m. following the creeping barrage. No. 4 on the right and Prince of Wales's on the left will follow No. 2 Company on width of two platoons at 50 paces interval, being followed by their other two platoons at again 50 yards interval.

8. No. 3 Company Welsh Guards, 4 guns Brigade Machine Gun Company, 4 guns Brigade T.M. Battery will be held in reserve south-west of Ginchy in their present position.

J. A. DYSON PERRINS,
Lieutenant, Adjutant 1st Battalion Welsh Guards.

[*Note.*—The actual attack was launched on the order of Lord Henry Seymour, Commanding Officer of 4th Battalion Grenadier Guards, which would account for the change of formation. The delay has already been explained. The situation was somewhat confusing for Company Commanders.]

Secret.

1ST BATTALION WELSH GUARDS

(6) OPERATION ORDER

Ref. Map 57.c.5.w 1/20,000.

1. The Fourth Army will renew the attack on September 25th in combination with attack by the French in the south and the Reserve Army in the north. The Guards Division will capture Les Bœufs. The 1st Guards Brigade will attack on the right and the 3rd Guards Brigade on the left. The 5th Division will attack Morval on the right and the 21st Division (62nd Brigade) will attack Gueudecourt on the left of the Guards Division.

2. Objectives, assembly trenches, and dividing lines between brigades and divisions are marked on secret map.

1st objective	. . .	Green
2nd objective	. . .	Brown
3rd objective	. . .	Blue

The 2nd Battalion Scots Guards and 4th Battalion Grenadier Guards will capture the first and second objectives, and will advance in two waves on a front of two companies each. 2nd Battalion Scots Guards will attack on the right and 4th Battalion Grenadier Guards on the left. The 1st Battalion Grenadier Guards will pass through the two leading battalions and capture the third objective. The 1st Battalion Welsh Guards, less Nos. 3 and 4 Companies, will be held in brigade reserve at T.8.a.

3. The 2nd Battalion Scots Guards and the 4th Battalion Grenadier Guards will be formed up in X and Y Trench. The 1st Battalion Grenadier Guards will be formed up in the Z Line. The 2nd Battalion Scots Guards and 4th Battalion Grenadier Guards will advance at zero hour. They will reorganise in the first objective and advance on the second objective at zero plus one hour.

The 1st Battalion Grenadier Guards will advance so as to reach the first objective at zero + one hour, and will further advance to the attack of the third objective so as to reach their barrage 200 yards beyond the second objective at zero + two hours.

Nos. 3 and 4 Companies 1st Battalion Welsh Guards on the right and left respectively will be formed up in Gap Trench after relief on night September 24/25th, and will move into the X Line as soon as the 1st Battalion Grenadier

Guards vacate it.   In moving forward these two companies
will seize any opportunities offered by a slackening of the
enemy's barrage.   The left flank of No. 3 Company will
direct.

The Prince of Wales's Company and No. 2 Company 1st
Battalion Welsh Guards on the right and left respectively
will be formed up in T.8.a in the Switch Trench to the east
of Battalion H.Q., in the sector now occupied by two companies 2nd Battalion Scots Guards, whom they will relieve
on night September 24/25th.

The Prince of Wales's Company will be held in readiness
to act as a carrying party for the R.E. on receipt of order.
No. 2 Company will remain in Brigade Reserve.

4. The 1st Battalion Grenadier Guards will consolidate
the third objective with strong points on the flanks.   The
4th Battalion Grenadier Guards and the 2nd Battalion Scots
Guards will consolidate the second objective.

Nos. 3 and 4 Companies 1st Battalion Welsh Guards will
consolidate the first objective.   The O.C. No. 4 Company
will make a strong point on the left flank of the objective
and another at H.32.d.8.3, and will maintain touch with the
62nd Infantry Brigade.   O.C. No. 3 Company will maintain
touch with the 1st Guards Brigade.   O.'s.C. Companies must
be prepared to form defensive flanks.

5. A deliberate bombardment of the enemy's position will
be carried out on September 24th and 25th.   There will be
no extensive fire before the hour of zero.   A barrage creeping
at the rate of 50 yards per minute will precede each advance.

6. O.'s.C. Companies will report when they have reached
their assembly positions after relief on night September
24th/25th.

7. Two machine guns will advance with the 4th Battalion
Grenadier Guards as far as the first objective, and will be
placed to guard the left flank ; these two guns will remain
in the first objective and assist the 1st Battalion Welsh
Guards to consolidate there.

8. The Sapping Platoon will remain in Brigade Reserve
with No. 2 Company.

9. A battle dump is established 100 yards to the right
rear of Battalion H.Q. at about T.8.a.6.4.

10. Prisoners will be sent to the Craters A.8.a.   Officers
will be searched and effects forwarded with the escort.
Other ranks will not be searched.

11. Battalion H.Q. will remain at T.8.a.6.4. Efforts will be made to push forward a telephone-line to the first objective. A contact aeroplane will be in the air from zero hour until 6.30 p.m.

12. Each man will carry one day's ration, one iron ration, 1 haversack ration, 4 bombs, 200 rounds S.A.A., 1 pick or shovel, 2 sandbags.

13. Dressing stations are at S.30.b.5.6 and T.13.c.8.8. Battalion stretcher-bearers will carry cases towards T.13.c.8., until touch is obtained with ambulance bearer squads. Walking wounded will be directed to A.14.c.6.1 near Carnoy.

14. O.'s.C. Companies will detail N.C.O.'s and men as under No. 4 Company, nine men for Trench Mortar Battery, two men for brigade orderlies ; No. 3 Company, nine men for Trench Mortar Battery, two men for brigade orderlies ; No. 2 Company, four men for Trench Mortar Battery, two men for brigade orderlies ; Prince of Wales's Company, three men for Trench Mortar Battery, two men for brigade orderlies.

O.'s.C. No. 3 and 4 Companies will detail two and one N.C.O.'s respectively for Trench Mortar Battery.

These men will report to the adjutant at Battalion H.Q. Men for brigade orderlies 7 p.m. 4th inst., men for Trench Mortar Battery 11 p.m. 24th inst.

15. Rations, water, and a rum issue will be issued at Battalion H.Q. to-morrow night at a time to be notified. There will be no issue of rations on September 25th.

J. A. DYSON PERRINS,
Lieutenant, Adjutant 1st Battalion Welsh Guards.

September 24th, 1916, 12 *noon.*

(*Note.*—In para. 1 the 5th Division is mentioned on the right. This is wrong. The 6th Division was between the Guards and 5th Division.)

Secret.

1st BATTALION WELSH GUARDS

(7) OPERATION ORDERS NO. 23/17

Copy No. 7.

Ref. T.M. Sheet Bixschoote, St. Julien, 1/10,000.

1.

(*a*) On " Z " day XIV Corps is to attack the enemy in conjunction with corps on our right and left. The date of " Z " day will be notified later.

(*b*) Zero will be at dawn ; the exact hour will be notified later.

(*c*) Guards Division is attacking with the 2nd Guards Brigade on the right and 3rd Guards Brigade on the left. Boundaries and objectives are shown on the attached map.

(*d*) The 38th Division is attacking on right of Guards Division and 1st French Division (201st Regiment) on the left.

2. *Plan.*—There will be no movement of troops between zero — 30 and zero.

3. *Plan.*—3rd Guards Brigade will attack as follows :

(*a*) 1st Battalion Grenadier Guards and 1st Battalion Welsh Guards on right and left respectively and on a frontage of two companies each, will capture first objective (Blue Line).

(*b*) The same two battalions will capture second objective (Black Line).

(*c*) 4th Battalion Grenadier Guards (less two platoons) and 2nd Battalion Scots Guards (less two platoons) on right and left respectively will capture third objective (Green Line).

(*d*) 1st Guards Brigade is to capture fourth objective (Dotted Green Line) and also, if opportunity offers, to gain ground up to, and including, Red Line.

4. *Battalion Plan.*

(*a*) The battalion will attack in three waves.

(*b*) The *first wave* (two platoons No. 2 Company on the right, two platoons No. 3 Company on the left) will be responsible for capturing the first objective (Blue Line), supported by the second wave.

(*c*) The *second wave* (two platoons No. 2 Company on the right and two platoons No. 3 Company on the left) will support the first wave in the attack on the Blue Line, and the third wave in the attack on the second objective (Black Line).

(d) The *third wave* (Prince of Wales's Company) will be responsible for capturing the Black Line, supported by the second wave.

(e) The *Mopping-up Company* (No. 4 Company) will be responsible for mopping up all ground from Baboon Trench (exclusive) to Black Line (exclusive). The action of this company is shown in para. 7.

(f) The second wave will come under the orders of the O.C. 2nd Battalion Scots Guards after the latter pass the Black Line (see para. 5, sub-para. c. 1).

5. *Detail of the assault.*

(a) At zero + 34 minutes—

1. A barrage will come down 200 yards east of Brown Line (Baboon Reserve).
2. The first wave will be kneeling down on the east side of Brown Line (Baboon Reserve).
3. The front platoons' Mopping-up Company will be formed up close behind the first wave.
4. Second wave will be formed up 60 yards behind front platoons' Mopping-up Company.
5. Third wave will be formed up behind the second wave.
6. Rear platoons' Mopping-up Company will be formed up behind the third wave.

(b) *At zero + 38 minutes.*

1. First wave, followed by front platoons' Mopping-up Company and second wave, will advance to the capture of the Blue Line. There will be an interval of 15 yards between first wave and front platoons' Mopping-up Company, and 60 yards between front platoons' Mopping-up Company and second wave.
2. Third wave will follow second wave.
3. When the first wave enters the Blue Line the second wave will close up to within 15 yards of the Blue Line to enable it to assist the first wave at the earliest possible moment if called upon to do so.

   The third wave will close up to within 70 yards of the second wave, *i.e.* 85 yards from the Blue Line (first objective).
4. Action of moppers-up is shown in para. 7.

(c) *At zero + 2 hours 2 minutes.*

1. The third wave (having passed through the second

wave) will meet the barrage 150 yards in front of the Blue Line and advance to the capture of the Black Line.

The rear platoons' Mopping-up Company will follow the third wave at 15 yards' interval; second wave will follow rear platoons' Mopping-up Company at 60 yards' interval.

2. The second wave will, when the third wave enters the Black Line, lie down 15 yards on the near side of the Black Line.

After the 2nd Battalion Scots Guards have passed through the Black Line it will come under the orders of the O.C. 2nd Battalion Scots Guards, and will, as soon as possible, be ordered by that officer to proceed to about Major's Farm, U.25.b.50.85, and there consolidate as battalion reserve of 2nd Battalion Scots Guards.

The route of the advance of the H.Q. 2nd Battalion Scots Guards will be notified later, and O.C. second wave will arrange to make his H.Q. on or near that route. The company, therefore, coming under the orders of the O.C. 2nd Battalion Scots Guards will be composed of two platoons No. 2 Company and two platoons No. 3 Company (see para. 44, sub-para. 3). If this composite company is reduced to less than 100 men it must be made up by men withdrawn from third wave in Black Line.

3. Action of moppers-up is shown in para. 7.

(d) *At zero* + 3 *hours* 24 *minutes.*

1. Fourth wave, followed by Mopping-up Company and fifth and sixth waves (all found by the 2nd Battalion Scots Guards) will advance to the capture of the Green Line.

6. *Movements of Supporting Battalion (2nd Battalion Scots Guards).*

At zero + 60 minutes. In front line area (4th Battalion Grenadier Guards in vicinity of Baboon Support). At zero + 1 hour 45 minutes, in vicinity of Wood 15. At zero + 2 hours 30 minutes, leading waves to have crossed line of Scots House—Sauvage House. At zero + 3 hours, to be in opposition behind barrage protecting Black Line.

7. *Mopping Up.*

The Mopping-up Company (No. 4 Company) is divided

into two parts, each consisting of two platoons. Two platoons commence the attack in rear of first wave ; these are referred to in these orders as front platoons' Mopping-up Company. Two platoons are in rear of the third wave ; these platoons are referred to as rear platoons' Mopping-up Company.

(*a*) When the attack advances, the rear platoons' Mopping-up Company will mop up all ground between Brown Line (exclusive), to Wood 15 (exclusive). Special attention will be paid to Baboon Avenue and Bois Farm.

When this ground is cleared of the enemy, the rear platoons will reform and lie down 15 yards in rear of the third wave.

(*b*) When the first wave enters Wood 15 the front platoons' Mopping-up Company proceed to mop up Wood 15. Particular attention will be paid to Sauvage House and Wood 15 Trench.

As soon as the wood is clear of the enemy the front platoons' Mopping-up Company will reform and assist in the consolidation of the Blue Line.

(*c*) The rear platoons' Mopping-up Company, which have reformed and come into position behind the third wave, will advance behind the third in the assault of the Black Line and will mop up all ground between the Blue Line and the Black Line (exclusive).

Special attention will be paid to Wood 15 Avenue.

(*d*) The O.C. Mopping-up Company will make his H.Q. with the rear platoons until arrival at Wood 15, when he will make his H.Q. with the front platoons.

(*e*) After the rear platoons' Mopping-up Company have completed the mopping-up of the ground between the Blue Line and the Black Line they will rejoin the front platoons and assist in the consolidation of the Blue Line.

This company will then form battalion reserve.

8. *Consolidation.*

(*a*) The Blue Line will be consolidated by the first wave in depth, front, support, and, if possible, reserve, lines being dug. A wire entanglement will be constructed in front of each line consolidated, gaps being left to allow passage of troops.

The Mopping-up Company will become available to assist in this consolidation ; *vide* para. 7, sub-paras. (*b*) and (*e*).

(*b*) The Black Line will not be consolidated, but the third wave will dig " islands " to give themselves cover.   It will not be wired.

(c) The French will consolidate the Black Line, but not the Blue Line.

9. *Strong Points.*

(a) The O.C. No. 3 company will detail a party to construct and garrison a strong point of the cruciform pattern at U.25.c.2.8.

(b) The O.C. troops of Prince of Wales's Company in the Black Line will detail—

(1) A party to construct and garrison a strong point at about U.25.a.5.3 on left flank of the Black Line.

(2) A party to construct and garrison a strong point at U.25.a.3.0.

(c) These strong points will be wired all round.

(d) The strong points will each be garrisoned by one platoon with a Lewis gun, to be detailed by the O.C. the company detailed to garrison them.

(e) When work is started on strong points the fact will be reported to Battalion H.Q.   A further report will be sent in when they are completed.

10. *Machine Guns.*

(a) Two machine guns, under command of 2/Lieut. Wilson, Scots Guards, will be attached to the battalion for the attack.   They will follow the third wave on the right and left of the line respectively to the Black Line.

(b) Company Commanders can call direct on the services of these guns if necessary.

(c) 2/Lieut. Wilson will advance with the left gun.

(d) When the strong points at U.25.a.5.3 and U.25.a.3.0 are consolidated, 2/Lieut. Wilson will detail one gun to take up a position in each.

11. *Trench Mortars (Stokes).*

(a) At zero all guns of the battery will take part in the bombardment under orders of the brigade.

(b) At zero + 10 minutes two guns will come under orders of the O.C. 1st Battalion Welsh Guards.   These guns will move up in rear of the second wave to Baboon Support. They will there wait till the moppers-up have passed through, and will go with them to the vicinity of Sauvage House, moving by trench junction B.6.a.6.2, thence up Baboon Avenue.   Any Company Commander requiring their assistance will find them in the above-mentioned trenches, till the

Blue Line is captured, when they will be in Sauvage House. Lieut. G. G. Walker will be in command.

12. *Liaison.*

(*a*) A party as per margin [2/Lieut. H. F. Lascelles, 2 orderlies, 1 N.C.O., 8 other ranks], commanded by 2/Lieut. H. F. Lascelles, will keep touch with the 201st French Regiment on the left.

(*b*) Contact will be established on " Y " night on the Brown Line.

Throughout the attack the Liaison Party will advance in line with the leading waves as far as eastern corner of Wood 16 (U.25.a.4.3).

From this point touch will be kept by the Liaison Party, 2nd Battalion Scots Guards.

(*c*) Liaison posts, each consisting of two men, will be dropped at the following points : south-east corner of Wood 14 (B.6.a.9.7.)—Pompadour Farm ; eastern corner of Wood 16 (U.25.a.4.3).

Posts will be marked with a green flag with letters L.P. in white.

Each post must know the way to nearest headquarters, brigade, battalion, company.

(*d*) One interpreter and two orderlies will be attached to No. 3 Company.

(*e*) One N.C.O. and four men for Liaison Posts will be detailed by O.C. No. 3 Company, four men by O.C. No. 2 Company.

13. *Action in case Flanks held up.*

In the event of a unit on either flank of the brigade, or within the brigade, being held up, adjoining units will on no account check their advance. They will drop small parties to form a defensive flank while continuing to form forward to their objectives.

It is of vital importance that the barrage be followed closely by the infantry.

14. *Counter-Attack.*

(*a*) In the event of an enemy counter-attack the Green Line will be held at all costs.

(*b*) Should the enemy penetrate our lines, the Reserve Companies of 4th Battalion Grenadier Guards and 2nd Battalion Scots Guards will be used for immediate counter-attack.

(c) Troops holding the Blue and Black Lines will not be used in this immediate counter-attack.

(d) Should the enemy succeed in capturing the Green Line in spite of the immediate counter-attack of the Green Line troops, a fresh bombardment of that line will be ordered and an organised counter-attack under a creeping barrage will be made by brigade arrangements.

15. *Artillery.*

(a) At zero + 34 minutes a barrage will come down 200 yards east of Brown Line.

(b) At zero + 38 this barrage will creep forward to Blue Line at rate of 100 yards in four minutes. It will lift off southern portion of Blue Line (right boundary) to south corner of Wood 15 (C.1.a.15.75) at + 46 minutes, and off the northern portion (east corner of Wood 15, U.25.c.35.15 to left boundary) at + 1 hour 2 minutes, forming in each case a protective barrage 200 yards beyond the objective.

(c) At + 1 hour 31 minutes the barrage will begin to lift back from southern portion of Blue Line till it reaches Green Mill Trench, where it will dwell till + 2 hours 2 minutes.

(d) At + 2 hours and 2 minutes the barrage will begin to lift back along the whole divisional front to Black Line.

It will lift off Black Line at + 2 hours 10 minutes, and will form a protective barrage 200 yards beyond.

(e) At + 3 hours 24 minutes the barrage will begin to lift back to Green Line.

It will lift off Green Line at + 4 hours 5 minutes, and will form a protective barrage 200 yards beyond.

16. *Artillery Notes.*

(a) A standing barrage will be placed on each objective. This will in all cases lift back when or before the creeping barrage reaches it.

(b) The creeping barrage, when moving, will lift 100 yards at a time, pausing four minutes beween each lift.

(c) Where trenches exist the creeping barrage has been so arranged that its four minutes' pause is in the trench.

(d) The creeping barrage, when lifting off Blue, Black and Green Lines, will lift back 100 yards, pause four minutes, and then lift back another 100 yards and form a protective barrage.

(e) The creeping barrage which during the halts on the Blue, Black and Green Lines will be temporarily stationary, will become intense for four minutes before it recommences to lift back.

This will enable leading infantry to get close up to the barrage.

(*f*) A machine-gun barrage will be put down beyond the stationary artillery barrages.

17. *Smoke Barrages.*

Smoke barrages will be made by barrage guns as follows :

In front of Black Line from + 2 hours 14 minutes to + 3 hours.

In front of Green Line from + 4 hours 21 minutes to + 4 hours 45 minutes.

18. *S.O.S.*

On zero day and subsequently, S.O.S. signal will be a rifle grenade bursting into two red and two green lights.

No other light signal will be employed except flares to show the position of infantry to contact patrols.

19. *Contact Patrol.*

(*a*) A contact patrol will fly over the corps front at—

> Zero + 1 hour.
> + 2 hours 25 minutes.
> + 4 hours 20 minutes.
> + 5 hours 40 minutes.
> 1.30 p.m.
> 4.00 p.m.
> 8.00 p.m.

(*b*) Leading troops will show their positions to contact aeroplanes when demanded :—

(1) By Klaxon Horn.

(2) By series of white lights.

(*c*) S.S. 135 Appendix " A " will be adhered to in all communication with contact aeroplane.

(*d*) Each contact aeroplane will be marked with two black rectangular flags (2 feet by 1 foot 3 inches) attached to and projecting from the lower plane on each side of the fuselage.

(*e*) Flares (white) will be lit only by leading lines of infantry and *only when called for.*

They should be lit in bunches of three at intervals of 50 yards.

Great care will be taken that none are lit unnecessarily, as the supply is limited.

20. *Movement of Battalion H.Q.*

(*a*) At zero, Battalion H.Q. will be established in the front line.   When situation permits, the Battalion Forward Party, under 2/Lieut. G. C. Devas, will proceed to Sauvage House and establish a Forward Battalion Command Post either there or in the vicinity.

The Battalion Forward Party will drop a chain of runners on the following route : Original Battalion H.Q.—Trench Junction B.6.a.7.2, thence follow line of Baboon Avenue—Sauvage House.

Battalion H.Q. will move to the forward Battalion H.Q. at probably about zero + 2 hours.

The route followed will be that of the runner chain.

21. *Communications.*

(*Brigade Arrangements*)

(*a*) A Brigade Forward Station will be opened at Scots House, C.1.a.$\frac{1}{2}$.6. by zero + 2 hours 30 minutes.

A final Brigade Forward Station will be opened at U.25.6.7.2 by zero + 4 hours 20 minutes.

(*b*) The Brigade Relay Posts are at—

No. 4 Post	B.6.c.8.6.
No. 5 Post	B.6.b.5$\frac{1}{2}$.3.
No. 6 Post	C.1.a.$\frac{1}{2}$.6, Scots House.
No. 7 Post	U.25.c.9.5.
No. 8 Post	U.25.6.7.2.

Messages can be handed in at any of these relay posts.

(*Battalion Arrangements*)

(*a*) As soon as the Battalion Forward Party reaches Sauvage House a receiving-station for messages will be established.

All messages will be sent to this station for transmission.

When the situation permits, a telephone station will be established in the Blue Line and another in the Black Line.

Visual stations will also be established if the ground is suitable.

The positions of the stations will be notified on the ground.

(*b*) *Visual.*—The Divisional Central Visual Station will be at B.11.d.4.1.

The Brigade Visual Station will be at B.11.a.9.2.

The Battalion Visual Station will be in the front line at Battalion H.Q.

23. *Medical Arrangements after Zero.*

(*a*) One stretcher-bearer will proceed with each platoon. These will not carry stretchers.

Sixteen stretcher-bearers will accompany the regimental medical officer.

The regimental medical officer will accompany Battalion H.Q.

(*b*) The regimental stretcher-bearers will not carry wounded back to the dressing-station, but will only tie up cases and put them into the nearest shelter, marking the spot by sticking a rifle into the ground butt uppermost or tying a piece of bandage to some conspicuous mark.

(*c*) Positions of Field Ambulance Units are :
> Advanced dressing-station—Boesinghe Village.
> Walking wounded collecting post—Bluet Farm.
> Main dressing-station—Canada Farm.

24. *Prisoners of War.*

(*a*) Divisional collecting-station will be at Boussat Farm, B.10.d.4.8.

(*b*) Prisoners will be sent straight to this station by units which capture them.

(*c*) (i) Escorts will not consist of more than 10 per cent. of the number of prisoners ; (ii) When possible, lightly wounded men, or returning carrying-parties, will be used for this duty.

(*d*) (i) Officers will be searched immediately, all documents being removed and sent back with the escort ; (ii) N.C.O.'s and men will not be searched except for arms and ammunition ; (iii) where possible, officers will be kept apart from men.

(*e*) Prisoners of war are not allowed to smoke or talk, and no one is allowed to converse with them except Provost Staff and General Staff Intelligence.

25. *Dumps.*

A dump will be made under brigade arrangements at Sauvage House of the following :
> R.E. Material.
> Ammunition.
> Lewis Gun drums filled.
> Rations and Water.

The first load of R.E. material may be expected at about zero + 2 hours.

Officers commanding companies should send empty Lewis

gun drums to the dump to be exchanged, and at the same time send notification of their other requirements.

26. *Synchronisation of Watches.*

(a) Watches will be synchronised on " Y " day from a watch brought round by a brigade staff officer, as soon as possible after 11.30 a.m. and 7.30 p.m. O.C. companies will send watches to Battalion H.Q. at these hours to receive correct time.

(b) In no circumstances will synchronisation of watches be carried out by telephone.

J. A. DYSON PERRINS,
Lieutenant, Adjutant.

Copies issued :

O.C. Prince of Wales's Company	Copy No.	1.
„ No. 2 Company	„	„	2.
„ No. 3 „	„	„	3.
„ No. 4 „	„	„	4.
Quartermaster .	„	„	5.
Transport Officer	„	„	6.
Intelligence Officer	„	„	7.
3rd Guards Brigade, M.G.C.	„	„	8.
3rd Guards Brigade, T.M. Batty.	„	„	9.
3rd Guards Brigade .	„	„	10.
1st Battalion Grenadier Guards .	„	„	11.
2nd Battalion Scots Guards	„	„	12.
201st French Regiment	„	„	13.
Major R.E. Reserve Battalion .	„	„	14.

Secret.   *Copy No.*   .

1ST BATTALION WELSH GUARDS

(8)   OPERATION ORDERS, NO. 33/17

October 7th, 1917.

BY MAJOR J. A. STIRLING, M.C., COMMANDING 1ST BATTALION WELSH GUARDS

Map Reference, Bixschoote, 20 S.W. 4 1/10,000.

1. The Guards Division (1st and 2nd Guards Brigades) will attack in the direction of Egypt House, Carre, Faidherbe.

3rd Guards Brigade, less one battalion, will be in support in area Wood 15, Abri Wood.

2. On the night October 8th/9th, 1st Battalion Welsh

23

Guards will hand over camp to 2nd Battalion Scots Guards, clearing camp by 8 p.m.

3. The head of battalion will pass White Hope Corner at 11 p.m. in the following order : Battalion H.Q., Prince of Wales's Company, No. 4 Company, No. 3 Company, No. 2 Company. Companies will march with 100 yards' interval between platoons to assembly positions already shown to Company Commanders. Battalion H.Q. to Saules Farm. Route : Clarges Street—or Crapouillot Pontoon and Bridge Street.

4. Order : Fighting order, with greatcoats and waterproof sheets.

5. Trench stores will be carried as follows :

Per Man.	Per Company.	To Bn. Forward Dump at Wood 13 near P. of W. Company.
1 Shovel.	16 haversacks with rifle Grenades.	50 Boxes Mills Bombs.
1 Mills Bomb.		35 Boxes Rifle Grenades
170 Rounds S.A.A.	250 Verey Lights.	(20 per box).
2 Water Bottles filled.	2 front Company's 5 tins.	
1 Day's ration and	4 Tins S.O.S.	1,100 Ground Flares.
Emergency Ration.	1 Day's Ration in bulk.	200 " P " Bombs.

6. Lewis Guns and 20 magazines per gun will be taken by companies from this camp.

7. Packs and blankets will be stored by companies in the orderly room hut before leaving camp. Officers' kits in the quartermaster's stores. When battalion leaves Wood 13 to advance, greatcoats will be stored under guard at Forward Battalion Dump.

8. Two cookers and water-carts will go to south-west of Wood 13. There will be a rum ration issued in Wood 13.

9. Officers' trench kits and Verey light boxes (para. 5) will be carried on pack-ponies, two per company and two per Battalion H.Q..

10. Regimental aid-post will be on Bridge Street near " G " in Sauvage House.
Stretcher-bearers will be with their companies.

11. Runners. Companies will each detail two runners for attachment to Battalion H.Q.
If the battalion moves forward, companies will detail a further two to remain with Battalion H.Q.

12. Lieut. E. Martin Smith will be acting transport officer.

13. 2/Lieut. H. F. Lascelles, company-sergeant-majors, company-quartermaster-sergeants and storemen will return to the transport lines if battalion goes forward from Wood 13 area.

J. C. DEVAS,
Captain, Adjutant 1st Battalion Welsh Guards.

Copies issued to:

Commanding Officer.
O.C. Prince of Wales's Company.
  „ No. 2 Company.
  „ No. 3   „
  „ No. 4   „
Quartermaster.
Lieut. E. Martin Smith.
2/Lieut. H. F. Lascelles.
Lieut. Dudley Ward.
Two copies retained.

(9)   OPERATION ORDER NO. 51

1. Guards Division will seize the ridge Gauche Wood—Gonnelied to secure observation in the Twenty-two Ravine.

2. 4th Battalion Grenadier Guards and 1st Battalion Welsh Guards will occupy the line Gonnelieu inclusive to R.32.c.3.2. Details of disposition for attack will be arranged direct between companies.

3. 1st Guards Brigade will hold from R.32.c.3.2 to south-east corner of Gauche Wood. Dividing line between brigades for forming up is R.31.c.4.7.

4. Tanks will take part in attack, moving slightly in advance of infantry.

5. 70th and 235th R.F.A. Brigades will open an intense barrage at zero on Twenty-two Ravine.

6. Zero hour will be 6.30 a.m.

7. Position will be consolidated when gained.

C. F. KEITH,
Captain, Acting Staff Captain Guards Brigade.

Acknowledge.

1st Battalion Welsh Guards

(10) ORDERS FOR RAID

By Lieut.-Col. H. Dene, D.S.O.

Battalion H.Q.,
March 6th, 1918.

1. The 1st Battalion Welsh Guards has been ordered to carry out a raid on the enemy's front line on the night March 8th/9th.

The point of entry will be I.20.a.85.75 (junction of Corn and Crust).

Zero hour will be 3.30 a.m.

2. *Objects of the Raid.*—To capture prisoners and material.

3. *Composition of Raiding Party.*—2/Lieut. P. Llewellyn will be O.C. Raiding Party, which will consist of three parties composed as under :

No. 1 *Party.*—2/Lieut. P. Llewellyn, Sergt. Glover and fifteen other ranks.

No. 2 *Party.*—Cpl. Facey and six men.

No. 3 *Party.*—Sergt. Meredith and six men.

The Raiding Party will be assembled in our front line from I.20.a.58.80 to I.20.a.65.50.

4. *Plan.*—At zero, No. 1 Party will advance in sectional blobs at 10 yards' interval, with No. 2 Party 5 yards in rear of the right flank of No. 1 Party, and No. 3 Party 5 yards directly in rear of No. 2 Party.

On arrival at enemy's trenches, No. 1 Party will turn left from point of entry up Crust, and clear the trench for about 100 yards, carrying out the objects of the raid, killing Huns and capturing prisoners.

2/Lieut. P. Llewellyn will remain at the point of entry with small party to enlarge gaps in wire and to take charge of prisoners.

No. 2 Party, moving on right of No. 1 Party, will turn right from point of entry, clear the trenches for about 40 yards and establish a block.

No. 3 Party, following close behind junction of Nos. 1 and 2 Parties, will bomb up Corn Trench about 40 yards, establish a block, keep up rifle grenade barrage on the trench in front of them and remain there until raiding party withdraws.

They will not attempt to penetrate more than 40 yards.

The object of these two parties is to prevent a bombing attack from the enemy, and to cover No. 1 Party whilst carrying out the objects of the raid.

5. *Artillery.*—Artillery barrages will be carried out as shown on attached sheet.

The barrages will come down at zero − 2.

The 4·5 howitzers on I.20.b.05.95 will lift at zero + 2 on to Carrot.

The 6-inch Newtons on trench to be raided will lift at zero to trench between I.20.b.05.95 and I.14.c.85.30.

6. *Stokes Mortars.*—3rd Guards Brigade Trench Mortar Battery will fire as follows :

    (i) *Two guns.*—From zero − 2 to zero on trenches to be raided. From zero to zero + 20 on to short trench leading from Corn at I.14.d.08.00 to I.14.d.06.06.

    (ii) *Two guns.*—From zero − 2 to zero + 20 on enemy front line about I.14.c.84.26.

Rate of fire from zero − 2 to zero will be rapid.

From zero onwards, normal.

The 1st Guards Brigade T.M. Battery have been asked to fire on salient in enemy front line about I.14.c.8.8.

7. *Machine Guns.*—Barrages will be fired as follows :

    (i) Down Caravan.

    (ii) On Carrot and Candy.

    (iii) On Hausa and Delbar Woods.

    (iv) On Friction (south of river).

8. *Lewis Guns.*—Nos. 2, 3 and 4 Companies 1st Battalion Welsh Guards will co-operate by bringing as many Lewis Guns as possible to open direct fire on the enemy on the flanks of the raid area.

This Lewis-gun fire will open at zero − 2 and will be kept up, firing intermittent bursts, until five minutes after Raiding Party has withdrawn.

9. *Order of Withdrawal.*—At zero + 20 minutes a signal for withdrawal will be given by the firing of white parachute Verey light by the O.C. Company.

On the firing of this signal, if he has not already withdrawn, the O.C. Raid will withdraw his parties in the following order, and will bring with him all prisoners and material captured during the raid.

Order of withdrawal :

    (1) No. 1 Party.

    (2) No. 2 Party.

    (3) No. 3 Party.

O.C. Raid will remain at point of entry with Sergt. Glover and small party until all parties are clear.

O.C. Raid will withdraw as above before the signal is given if he is satisfied that his work is complete.

All that is needed are one or two prisoners. As soon as these are obtained, O.C. Raid will withdraw.

N.C.O.'s in charge of parties or sectional blobs will be personally responsible that no wounded men are left.

10. *Action after Withdrawal.*—On reaching our front line, all parties will proceed by Cabbage or Ceylon to Malay Cave, where they will reassemble and be checked by 2/Lieut. D. I. B. Davies.

They will be checked at Company H.Q. in Cabbage by Sergt. Hawkesworth and at Company H.Q. in Ceylon by Sergt. Williams.

11. *Communications.*—O.C. Company will be responsible for keeping communication between himself and advanced Battalion H.Q. by runner.

O.C. Raiding Party will be responsible for keeping communication between himself and O.C. Company in like manner.

Advanced Battalion H.Q. will be in Malay Cave.

Advanced Company H.Q. will be in dug-out in Ceylon at I.20.a.3.6. O.C. 3rd Guards Brigade Signals will arrange communication with these H.Q. and between them and Brigade H.Q.

12. *Lights.*—Arrangements are being made for coloured lights to be sent up all along the front, and for Verey lights to be sent up 250 yards on either flank of attack.

O.'s.C. No. 2, 3, and 4 Companies will co-operate in this.

13. *Dress.*—Fatigue dress, puttees. Box respirators at the " alert " position. Welsh Guards buttons, shoulder titles, identity discs will be removed. No letters or pay-books will be carried.

Special identity discs will be issued. Faces will be blacked. All N.C.O.'s will carry electric torches.

No. 1 Party will carry rifle with bayonet fixed, 20 rounds

of ammunition and two bombs in the pockets, and will be armed with clubs and daggers.

Nos. 2 and 3 Parties as under :

One bayonet-man with rifle, bayonet, and bandolier.

One rifle-bomber with rifle and cup for Mills adapter and bag containing 10 Mills adapters.

Two bombers with clubs and two bags each containing ten bombs.

Two bomb-carriers with rifle and bandolier, each carrying two bags containing ten bombs.

Every man will carry a pair of wire-cutters.

14. *Gaps in Wire.*

(a) *Enemy.*—Orders have already been issued to those concerned.

(b) *Our Own.*—O.C. Prince of Wales's Company will ensure that at least four good gaps are made in our wire after dark on zero night, and that tapes are laid out for some distance in the direction of the point of entry, and will arrange for ladders to be placed in our trench.

15. *Medical Arrangements.*—Four stretcher-bearers will accompany the raiding party ; two will carry stretchers and the other two will carry trench-boards to facilitate the crossing of the enemy's wire.

Medical N.C.O. and four stretcher-bearers will remain with O.C. Company at advanced Company H.Q.

Advanced dressing-station will be in Malay Cave.

16. *Disposal of Captures.*—All prisoners and material captured will be forwarded immediately to Battalion H.Q. Nothing will be taken from prisoners except their arms.

The divisional intelligence officer will be at Battalion H.Q. to interview prisoners.

O.C. Prince of Wales's Company will detail an escort of one N.C.O. and six men to be in readiness at Malay Cave.

17. *Action of Raiding Party previous to Zero.*— Leave Baudimont Barracks by bus at 11 p.m. to H.17.c.3.5, where party will de-bus and march slowly to Malay Cave. Rum and tea at Malay Cave. Final synchronisation of watches. Leave Malay Cave at — 30 minutes.

Arrive at assembly area at — 15 minutes.

Greatcoats will be worn, but left in Malay Cave pending withdrawal.

18. *Action of Raiding Party after Raid.*—Party will re-assemble in Malay Cave and remain there until enemy retaliation has finished.

They will then proceed in small parties to de-bussing point, from whence they will be conveyed back to Arras.

H. DENE,
Lieutenant-Colonel Commanding 1st Battalion Welsh Guards.

(11)   OPERATION ORDER NO. 1

3rd Guards Brigade will continue the advance to-day directed on Ecoust St. Mein; 1st Battalion Welsh Guards will attack on the high ground north of St. Leger on a one-company front south of St. Leger; 1st Battalion Grenadier Guards on right and 2nd Battalion Scots Guards on left will co-operate at zero. No. 3 Company will advance in extended order, and will be followed at 300 yards' interval by No. 4 Company, who, on No. 3 Company leaving their trench, will move into it, and on No. 4 Company moving off Prince of Wales's will move to its left and will follow at 300 yards' interval. No. 4 and Prince of Wales's Companies will move forward in blob formation, should the enemy's artillery fire permit this. No. 2 Company will move off at 7 a.m. and endeavour to get within 300 yards of Prince of Wales's Company, and St. Leger will not be entered but will be mopped up from the south by one company of 2nd Battalion Scots Guards.

Advance will be made by successive bounds.

First bound, Leger Reserve; second bound, B.6b&d; third bound, track running through Ecoust Reserve; fourth bound, road in C.4.a.c.&d. All ground captured will be consolidated in great depth. Boundary on north Grid Line north of T.26.27.28 due east onwards. Ecoust and Longatte will not be entered but will be enveloped.

Machine guns will cover the western exit of St. Leger. The guns attached to battalions will move in depth to protect the flanks.

56th Division will attack at zero with a creeping barrage and will deal with Croisilles.

Advance on our left must be made to conform with the 56th Division, which with a creeping barrage will be slower.

Artillery will open with a crash at zero and after with five concentrations and will move forward in support of infantry.

Zero hour, 7 a.m.

Battalion H.Q. will remain in present position unless companies are advised to the contrary.

Reports on the battle will be sent to Battalion H.Q. as often as possible.

Aid-post is in railway cutting below Battalion H.Q.

G. C. Devas,
Captain, Adjutant, Q.O.M.I.

August 24th, 1918.
Issued at 2.45 *a.m.*

(12)   OPERATION ORDER NO. 2

August 28th, 1918.

3rd Guards Brigade will continue the attack to-day ; 1st Welsh Guards on left on one-company frontage, 2nd Scots Guards in centre on two-company frontage, 1st Grenadier Guards on right on one-company frontage. Flank battalions will be responsible for protecting flank of brigade.

Companies will be on frontage of 875 yards. At zero No. 2 Company will advance in extended order, followed at 300 yards' interval by Prince of Wales's Company, No. 4 and No. 3 Companies, which are in reserve, will advance at similar intervals.

Advance will be made by bounds. Frst bound, Banks Road ; second bound, trenches at T.30.a, T.30.c, B.6.a.c ; third bound, Ecoust T.R. ; fourth bound, Railway U.25.a.b, U.26.b, Ecoust Reserve.

Touch on flanks will be gained at each bound before further advance.

Villages will not be entered except by patrols, but will be dealt with by tanks. Special instructions given to tanks to deal with Leger Wood, Cross Roads in 5.d, Ecoust Longatte.

Two sections M.G. are allotted battalion. Artillery will co-operate.

Zero hour will be 4.30 a.m.

G. C. Devas,
Captain, Adjutant, Q.O.M.I.

N.B.—In all probability the 56th Division will get on better than 62rd Division on right, in which case 3rd Guards Brigade will form a protective flank between the two on ridges running north-east.

(13) OPERATION ORDERS 3RD GUARDS BRIGADE

(There is no copy of Battalion Orders. From this date Orders were written on any piece of paper, and the continual moving about was not conducive to keeping records.)

1. Advance will be continued to-morrow by 3rd G.B. with 2nd G.B. on right and 52nd Div. on left. 1st W.G. will be on the right, 2nd Scots Gds. on left, 1 G.G. in support; objective and boundaries shown on map already issued. Leading batts. will be on a two-company frontage distributed in great depth. Leading batts. will form up on line of railway C.16.a&b, C.11.c&d. Leading companies will cross line Macauley Av.—Bolton Alley at zero. Barrage will come down on a line C.17 central C12.d central at zero. At zero + 7 it will creep forward at 100 yds. every 4 minutes until 300 yds. beyond the objective, where it will rest for 15 minutes. 1 section No. 2.4 G.M.G. will be attached to each leading Bn. The guns will move with support and reserve companies and on a flank. 8th Inf. Bde. are withdrawing all troops east of line Macauley Av.—Bolton Alley to that line by 4.45 a.m. When objective is reached front line will be held by posts only. Patrols will be pushed out as barrage permits to keep touch with enemy. Zero will be at 5.20 a.m. T.M.B. will be prepared to move up 2 guns to each leading bn. with 100 rounds per gun AAA. Both leading batts. H.Q. will be at C.8.a.24 AAA. Acknowledge.

J. N. BUCHANAN,
Captain.

(14) OPERATION ORDERS NO. 85/13

Secret. . *Copy No.* .

Map Reference 57eN.E. Secret map attached.
1. *Information.*
(1) The Third Army will resume the attack. The date, the divisions and their tasks have been notified to all concerned.

(2) *Objectives of Guards Division.*

(*a*) The first object is the Red Line, which will be taken by the 2nd Guards Brigade, who will also be prepared to protect the left flank of the division until rendered secure by the division on our left.

(*b*) The second objective is the Brown Dotted Line and the Brown Line, which will be taken by the 1st Guards Brigade.

(*c*) The third objective is the Blue Dotted Line, which will be taken by the 3rd Guards Brigade in conjunction with the 1st Guards Brigade.

(*d*) The final objective is the Blue Line.

2. *Intention.—Action of the 3rd Guards Brigade.*

(*a*) On " Y " day the 3rd Guards Brigade will concentrate in area north-west of Boursies.

(*b*) On " Z " day at zero + 30 minutes the brigade will advance in fours, with 100 yards' interval between platoons, in the following order :

> 1st Battalion Grenadier Guards on the right.
> 2nd Battalion Scots Guards on the left.
> 1st Battalion Welsh Guards in rear of 1st Battalion Grenadier Guards.
> (The routes to be followed are shown on the attached map.)

(*c*) Before reaching the Brown Line the 1st Battalion Grenadier Guards and 2nd Battalion Scots Guards will deploy into approach. March formation, each with two companies in front line, one company in support, and one in reserve.

The 1st Battalion Welsh Guards will move in artillery formation, with three companies in rear of 1st Battalion Grenadier Guards and one company in rear of 2nd Battalion Scots Guards, and will be prepared to protect the right flank of the brigade.

(*d*) The leading troops of the 1st Battalion Grenadier Guards and the 2nd Battalion Scots Guards will pass through the 1st Guards Brigade on the Brown Line at zero + 4 hours 30 minutes.

The 1st Battalion Grenadier Guards will advance along the spur running towards L.16, and the 2nd Battalion Scots Guards will advance along the spur running towards L.9 in order to gain the Blue Dotted Line and capture the batteries in that area.

(e) After gaining the Blue Dotted Line the advance will be continued to the Blue Line in conformity with the 57th Division on Containg.

(f) From the Blue Line patrols will be pushed forward into Noyelles-sur-L'Escaut in order to hold the crossings over the Escaut and the Canal de St. Quentin, should they be found unoccupied, so as to assist the 6th Infantry Brigade, who will pass through the 3rd Guards Brigade at this period.

(g) When the 2nd Division have passed through, the 3rd Guards Brigade will be concentrated east of the Canal-du-Nord, under orders to be issued later.

3. *Troops on Flanks.*

(1) Right flank. The 76th Brigade is the left brigade of the 3rd Division, the left battalion will be the 1st Gordons up to the Ravine Avenue, Sherwood Switch and Suffolks to Brown Line.

(2) 185th Brigade is the left brigade of the 62nd Division. 2/20 London Regiment goes through the Brown Line at zero + 4½ hours, in touch with the 1st Grenadier Guards up to the western outskirts of Marcoing, where the 8th West Yorks go through the 2/20th London Regiment.

Left Flank.—(a) The right brigade of the 57th Division is 172nd Infantry Brigade ; 9th King's Liverpools will take trenches in L.3.c.

(b) 1st Royal Munsters take Containg and the Blue Line.

4. *Concentration.*—The 1st Battalion Welsh Guards will remain in their present position.

5. *Approach March.*

(a) At zero — 35 minutes the head of No. 3 Company will be on the Lagnicourt—Louverval Road opposite Battalion H.Q. with No. 4 Company, No. 2 Company and Prince of Wales's Company up the valley running south towards Prince of Wales's Company's present billets.

At zero — 30 minutes the head of the column will move and take up its position with 100 yards' interval between platoons, and 100 yards in rear of last platoon of 1st Grenadier Guards.

O.C. No. 3 Company will send out to reconnoitre the position where his leading platoon will rest.

(b) The battalion will conform to the advance of the column of the 1st Grenadier Guards, and be prepared to move off at zero.

(c) Battalion H.Q. will be in rear of the column.

(d) The 2nd Coldstream Guards is the Reserve Battalion of the 1st Guards Brigade, and it is probable that they will remain in the area just east of the canal. Care must be taken that this regiment does not impede the advance.

(e) The head of the column will pass the under-mentioned points as under :

Bapaume—Cambrai Road at zero.

Canal du Nord at zero + 2 hours.

Head of column arrives on forming-up ground at zero + 4 hours (for 1st Grenadier Guards Sunken Road in L.B.c.3.7 to Scull Support ; for 2nd Scots Guards Sherwood Switch with right on Sunken Road K.18.d.8.4).

The 1st Welsh Guards will take up artillery formation when passing Flesquières, and will see that distance is kept during the forming up of 1st Grenadier Guards and 2nd Scots Guards.

6. *Formation.*

At zero + $4\frac{1}{2}$ hours 1st Grenadier Guards and 1st Scots Guards will advance cross the Brown Line in the Approach March Formation.

The 1st Welsh Guards will conform to the movement in artillery formation, with No. 3 Company, No. 2 Company, and Prince of Wales's Company echeloned to the right with 300 yards' interval and 300 yards' depth from the rear platoon of the preceding company.

No. 2 Company's leading platoon will cover the left platoon of the Reserve Company of the 1st Grenadier Guards. No. 4 Company will cover the right rear platoon of 2nd Scots Guards, and be in line with the leading platoon of No. 2 Company.

(b) The rear platoon of the Prince of Wales's Company will act as a flank guard protecting the right of the battalion, and at the same time act as liaison between the troops on our right.

7. *Communications.*

(a) On the objectives being reached Battalion H.Q. will be established about L.13.b.3.1. An orderly will be at the forked roads at L.13.c.d. to show the position of Battalion H.Q.

(b) A Battalion Relay Runner Post will be established at L.13.6.4.0.

Battalion H.Q. 1st Grenadier Guards. L.15.d.1.6.
Battalion H.Q. 2nd Scots Guards. L.14.b.Central.

(c) *Aeroplanes.*—Leading troops will light flares on being called for by 'Contact Plane by the Klaxton Horn or firing a Verey light. Leading troops will also signal by flashing tin discs.

(d) Success rifle grenades will be fired by leading battalions on reaching the Blue Dotted Line and crossings of Canal de St. Quentin at Noyelles.

(e) On all objectives being gained, companies will endeavour to get in touch with Battalion H.Q. by flag and lamp.

8. *Machine Guns.*

Half section will be attached to No. 2 Company and half section to No. 4 Company.

Machine Gun Company H.Q. and one section with Battalion H.Q. in reserve.

9. *Action of Artillery.*

(a) The artillery barrage governing the advance of 1st Guards Brigade and 2nd Guards Brigade will cease when the Brown Line in L.13 has been reached.

(b) The 74th and 75th Brigades R.F.A. will be prepared to support the advance of the 3rd Guards Brigade to the Blue Line.

10. *3rd Guards Brigade Trench Mortar Battery.*

(a) 4 guns and 200 rounds of ammunition will move in limbers with 74th and 75th Brigades R.F.A.

(b) Two trench mortars will be placed under the tactical disposal of the O.C. leading battalions to assist the advance in the event of its being held up.

11. *Canal Crossings.*

The 2nd Guards Brigade will put up blue and white flags at zero + a few minutes at the places most suitable for crossing the canal.

12. *Medical Arrangements.*

The first-aid post will be with Battalion H.Q.

The advanced dressing-station before zero will be at Salmon Post. After zero it will be at Lock No. 7.

13. *Synchronisation of Watches.*

On the time being received from brigade all officers will synchronise their watches at Battalion H.Q.

14. *Dress.*—Battle order, with empty packs.

15. *Zero.*—Zero hour will be notified later.

Captain, Acting Adjutant 1st Battalion Welsh Guards.

Copies *issued to :*

O.C. Prince of Wales's Company	Copy No.	1.
,, No. 2 Company . .	,, ,,	2.
,, No. 3 ,, . .	,, ,,	3.
,, No. 4 ,, . .	,, ,,	4.
Quartermaster	,, ,,	5.
3rd Guards Brigade . .	,, ,,	6.
Major C. H. Dudley Ward, M.C.	,, ,,	7.
Commanding Officer . . .	,, ,,	8.
Retained	,, ,,	{ 9. 10.

Secret.

(15)   OPERATION ORDER

No. 89/18.d.10/10/18

1. *Situation.*

The leading troops of 1st and 2nd Guards Brigade are on the line C.30.b.5.0—C.18.central—C.12.a.3.2.—U.29.central, with patrols pushed farther forward.

The New Zealand Division on right hold Aulicourt Farm. The 24th Division on left hold Avesnes.

2. *Plan.*

(*a*) Guards Division in conjunction with troops on both flanks is to continue advance to-morrow (11th).

(*b*) 3rd Guards Brigade will carry out the advance and will pass the enemy rear-guards so as to gain ground as quickly as possible.

(*c*) 1st Battalion Grenadier Guards will be on right, 2nd Battalion Scots Guards in centre, and 1st Battalion Welsh Guards on left.

(*d*) Dividing lines, boundary and successive bounds to be captured are shown on attached map.

(*e*) 1st Battalion Welsh Guards will advance with two companies in front (Prince of Wales's Company on right and No. 4 Company on left), No. 2 Company in support and No. 3 Company in reserve.

(*f*) Front companies will pass through the outpost line mentioned in para. 1 at 0500 hours.

3. *Approach March.*

(*a*) The positions of deployment of battalions, which will be reached at 0400 hours, will be as follows :

1st Battalion Grenadier Guards.	C.24.c.5.8.
2nd Battalion Scots Guards.	C.11.d.central.
1st Battalion Welsh Guards.	C.5.d.o.0.

(*b*) 1st Battalion Welsh Guards will leave present billets and march in order as per margin to deployment area. The head of Prince of Wales's Company will pass cross-roads H.5.b.15.95 at 0045. Route : Carnières—Boussières.

Prince of Wales's Company.
No. 4 Company.
No. 2 Company.
No. 3 Company.
Battalion H.Q.

The battalion will march closed up unless coming under shell-fire, when 100 yards' interval will be maintained throughout the column.

(*c*) " A " Echelon (transport) will accompany the battalion.

4. *Instructions.*

(*a*) Villages will be cut out. O.C. Supports Company will send a platoon to mop up after leading companies have passed round them.

(*b*) Close liaison will be kept with troops on either flank.

(*c*) Lewis Guns will be conveyed by limber to the church in Boussières, where they will be unloaded and carried on the men.

(*d*) Dress—battle order. Greatcoats will be dumped at present Company H.Q. and left in charge of cooks.

5. *Artillery.*

One battery R.F.A. will act in close co-operation with the battalion. Two brigades R.F.A. less three batteries will also support the advance.

Machine Guns.

(*a*) One section 4th G.M.G. is attached to battalion.

(*b*) Three companies 4th G.M.G. (less three sections) will be available if required.

Trench Mortars.

Two guns with 50 rounds per gun are attached to the battalion.

6. *Cavalry.*

As soon as the infantry advance has reached the eastern outskirts of Quieuy and St. Vaast, cavalry patrols will be pushed forward.

7. *Communications.*

Every effort will be made to get into touch with Battalion H.Q. by visual. Frequent reports of progress made will be sent to Battalion H.Q. by runner.

Battalion H.Q. will move along approved routes:

C.5.b.—St. Vaast.

B.27.a.—V.22.c.

Companies will report their arrival at position of deployment.

G. C. DEVAS,
Captain, Adjutant 1st Battalion Welsh Guards.

October 10th, 1918.

Copies issued by runner 2315.

All Companies.
Transport Officer.
Quartermaster.
2nd Battalion Scots Guards.

Secret.

(16)   OPERATION ORDER

No. 101/18

1. *Plan.*

The division is to carry out an attack before dawn on October 20th in conjunction with troops on right and left.

1st Guards Brigade will attack on the right.

3rd Guards Brigade will attack on the left.

2nd Guards Brigade will be in reserve.

2. *Method of Attack.*—3rd Guards Brigade will attack as follows:

(*a*) 1st Battalion Grenadier Guards will capture and consolidate the Green Line (first objective), 1st Battalion Welsh Guards on the right and 2nd Battalion Scots Guards on the left will pass through 1st Battalion Grenadier Guards on the first objective and will capture and consolidate the Red Line (final objective).

(*b*) 1st Battalion Grenadier Guards will attack with three companies in front line and one company in support.

24

1st Battalion Welsh Guards and 2nd Battalion Scots Guards will attack with two companies in the front line, one company in S.11, and one company in battalion reserve.

1st Battalion Welsh Guards will attack as follows : No. 2 Company, right front ; No. 3 Company, left front ; Prince of Wales's Company, support ; No. 4 Company, reserve.

3. *Flanks.*

1st Battalion Irish Guards will be the left battalion of 1st Guards Brigade on the right, 3rd Battalion Worcestershire Regiment will be the right battalion of 57th Infantry Brigade on our left.

4. *Artillery.*

(*a*) The attack will be supported by a creeping barrage of field artillery and a barrage in depth of heavy artillery. Field artillery barrage will open on the line of the road from V.30.o.50 to V.18.c.3.9. at zero. At zero + 3 minutes it will lift to a line 200 yards east of the road, where it will remain until zero + 23 minutes. It will then advance by lifts of 100 yards every 4 minutes to a line 300 yards east of first objective. In the sector of 1st Guards Brigade it will remain stationary on this line until zero + 126 minutes. In the sector of 3rd Guards Brigade it will lift from this line at zero + 70 minutes, and will advance by lifts of 100 yards every four minutes to the line of Solesmes—Valenciennes Road, building itself upon this road from south to north as it reaches it. At zero + 126 minutes the barrage will advance on the whole divisional front by lifts of 100 yards every four minutes, to a line 300 yards east of second objective. It will remain upon this line for four minutes and will then cease.

(*b*) Barrage tables will be issued later.

(*c*) One field artillery brigade fire thermite on machine-gun nests east of creeping barrage during the advance.

(*d*) The field artillery barrage will be 50 per cent. shrapnel and 50 per cent. H.E.

(*e*) A section of field-guns will be pushed forward in close support of the brigade for anti-tank defence.

5. *Liaison Posts* will be established with 3rd Battalion Worcester Regiment as follows :

(1) In neighbourhood of Road Junction V.12.c.8.1. found by 1st Battalion Grenadier Guards.

(2) On road at W.7.a.2.1. found by 2nd Battalion Scots Guards.

(3) The neighbourhood of Maison Blanche W.1.d.5.3. found by 2nd Battalion Scots Guards.

6. *Compass Bearing.*
The general compass bearing of the advance is 50° true.

7. *Consolidation.*
1st Battalion Grenadier Guards will be prepared to send forward two companies under orders from Brigade H.Q. for deliberate counter-attack should the situation so demand after capture of second objective. 1st Battalion Welsh Guards and 2nd Battalion Scots Guards will consolidate second objective immediately it is captured.

O.C. No. 2 Company and O.C. No. 3 Company will each push forward one platoon to form an outpost line not less than 400 yards in front of second objective and sufficiently far forward to be able to bring fire to bear on the crossing over the River des Harpies.

O.C. Prince of Wales's Company will send forward a patrol to locate any enemy west of River des Harpies and to report on possibility of infantry crossing that stream.

Support Company (Prince of Wales's Company) of 1st Battalion Welsh Guards and 2nd Battalion Scots Guards will be dug in, in readiness for immediate counter-attack.

Reserve Companies of 1st Battalion Welsh Guards (No. 4 Company) and of 2nd Battalion Scots will be prepared to form defensive flanks if necessary.

8. *Mopping Up.*
Prince of Wales's Company will be responsible for mopping up area first objective (exclusive) to second objective (exclusive) within the battalion's boundary.

9. *Contact Patrols.*
(a) Success signals will be fired from each objective as soon as captured.

(b) Contact patrols will fly over divisional front at—
> Zero + 5 hours.
> Zero + 6 hours.
> Zero + 7 hours.

Contact patrols will be sent out at any other time required on demand to Battalion H.Q.

10. *Time.*
Zero hour and arrangements for synchronisation will be notified later.

11. *Communications.*

(*a*) (i) *Battalion H.Q.*—1st Battalion Grenadier Guards will move forward with Reserve Company, and will be established in the neighbourhood of V.24.b.1.9 ; (ii) H.Q. 1st Battalion Welsh Guards and 2nd Battalion Scots Guards will move approximately on the line V,18.d. central to W.13.0.8.5.

(*b*) *Brigade H.Q.* will close at present position at 1600 hours and open at St. Hilaire at 1700 hours 19th inst.

Advanced brigade report centre will be established at V.27.b.9.9. at zero less 3 hours.

Visual station will be about V.22.c.9.5.

(*c*) Companies will send frequent reports to Battalion H.Q. as to progress.

12. *Orders.*

Instructions as to assembly, march, movement of transport, bridges, action of M.G.'s, will be issued later.

G. C. DEVAS,
Captain, Adjutant 1st Battalion Welsh Guards.

October 19th, 1917, 11.15. *noon.*

Copies issued :

Commanding Officer.
Second in Command.
All Companies.
Transport Officer.
Quartermaster.
2nd Battalion Scots Guards.

(17) OPERATION ORDER 113

Ref. 51 A 51 1/4,300.

1. *Task of 3rd Guards Brigade.*

3rd Guards Brigade will to-morrow move to area west of Villers Pol, and will be prepared, on receipt of orders from the division, either to support attack of 2nd and 1st Guards Brigades on November 4th, or to pass through 2nd and 1st Guards Brigades on early morning of November 5th, and continue to advance.

2. *Move.*

No. 4 Company.	The battalion in order as per margin to be ready to march at 0630 hours.
No. 3 Company.	Reveille 0433 hours.
Prince of Wales's Company.	
No. 2 Company.	Blankets to be dumped at No. 124, officers' and valises to be dumped
Headquarters.	

at Battalion H.Q. before the march.

3. *Transport.*

A echelon will march in rear of the battalion.

Remainder of first line transport will move under brigade control.

4. *Distance.*

An interval of 100 yards will be maintained between companies, headquarters and A echelon transport.

5. *Communications.*

(*a*) Brigade H.Q. will close Escarmain at 0830 hours, and open at Mornay Farm at 0930.   An advanced brigade report centre will be established at Mornay Farm at 0830.

(*b*) On arrival at assembly area R.8.b. Lieut. Gwynne Jones, mounted, will report to Brigade H.Q. at Mornay Farm.

6. *Routes.*

2/Lieut. Foot (+ 1 orderly) will proceed at 0530 hours to bridge at Q.30.c.7.8.

He will return and meet the battalion at Cross-roads Q.36.a.central at (and not before) 0738 hours.

He will report if bridge is intact.

7. *Units on Flanks.*

In the advance from the Red Line 2/20th London Regiment, 185th Infantry Brigade, 62nd Division will be on right of Guards Division.

On the left 13th Battalion Middlesex capture Blue Line, 9th Battalion Sussex go through and capture Green Line, both of the 73rd Brigade.   On Green Line 17th Brigade pass through 73rd with 8th Battalion Queen's and 3rd Battalion R.B. in support, and will continue advance through Red Line in above order.

17th Brigade H.Q. intend moving along road Jenlain—Wargnies-le-Grand.

8. *Bombs and Tools.*

O.C. Companies will detail a party to report to the transport officer on arrival at assembly area R.8.b. for bombs and tools.

9. *Water-bottles.*

All water-bottles will be filled.

10. *Synchronisation.*

All watches will be synchronised by the adjutant this evening.

J. L. CRAWSHAY,
Lieutenant, Adjutant 1st Battalion Welsh Guards.

Copies:

Prince of Wales's Company	.	No. 1.
No. 2 Company	. . .	„ 2.
No. 3 „	. . .	„ 3.
No. 4 „	. . .	„ 4.
Lieut. Gwynne Jones	. .	„ 5.
Transport Officer	. . .	„ 6.
Quartermaster .	. . .	„ 7.
2/Lieut. Foot .	. . .	„ 8.
Retained . .	. . .	„ {8. 9.}

(18) OPERATION ORDER 114

Ref. 51, 1/40,000

1. The 3rd Guards Brigade will pass through the line held by the 1st and 2nd Guards Brigades and continue the attack at 0600 hours on the 5th.

   1st Grenadier Guards will attack on the right.
   2nd Scots Guards will attack on the left.
   1st Welsh Guards in reserve.

2. The battalion will assemble in area M.2.a, west of La Flaque Farm, at 0530 hours.

   Brigade H.Q. at La Flaque Farm.

3. The head of the battalion in order as per margin will pass the point L.34.d.95 at 0430 hours.

No. 4 Company.
No. 3 Company.
Prince of Wales's Company.
No. 2 Company.
Headquarters.

4. Lewis-gun limbers will accompany companies. S.A.A. mules will accompany H.Q. The remainder of the transport will be under brigade control.

5. *Bombs.*
O's.C. companies will arrange to draw six boxes No. 36 and six boxes No. 22, both complete, from Sergt. Mathias at H.Q. billets before marching off, and are responsible that these are distributed.

6. *Tools.*
O's.C. companies will arrange to draw forty shovels and 10 picks per company from billet where Prince of Wales's Company cooker is now situated, before marching.

Sergt. Mathias will draw twenty shovels and five picks for headquarters.

The transport officer will supervise the distribution of tools.

J. CRAWSHAY,
Lieutenant, Adjutant, B.I.D.O.

Copies issued at :

Prince of Wales's Company	.	No. 1.		
No. 2 Company	.	.	.	,, 2.
No. 3 ,,	.	.	.	,, 3.
No. 4 ,,	.	.	.	,, 4.
Transport Officer	.	.	.	,, 5.
Quartermaster .	.	.	.	,, 6.
Sergt. Mathias .	.	.	.	,, 7.
Retained .	.	.	.	,, {8. {9.

(19)   OPERATION ORDER 115

Ref. 51, 1/40,000.

1. *Plan of Attack.*
In the course of the operations to be carried out by the 3rd Guards Brigade to-morrow the 1st Battalion Welsh Guards will be called upon to capture the village of Buvignies, H.35.d. and H.36.c.

2. The attack will be carried out by Nos. 2 and 4 Companies with No. 3 in support and Prince of Wales's in reserve.

(a) O.C. No. 2 Company will form up for attack on ground now occupied by left platoon of 1st Grenadier Guards at

N.4.a.3.6, with his right on the road Amfroipret—Bavisieux on a front of two platoons. One platoon he will hold in reserve. O.C. No. 2 Company will attack at 0615 hours.

Task.—To clear the hedges north of railway (inclusive) and south of Grid Line running east and west, and occupy the road N.6.a from the railway to H.36.c.20..

(*b*) No. 4 Company, in approach formation, will follow No. 2 Company to road north of railway N.5.b, and will then attack the village of Buvignies astride the road.

Task.—To secure a line which will include both road junctions in H.36.c.

The 1st Grenadier Guards will co-operate on the right, 2nd Scots Guards on the left. Companies will get in touch with these units on roads in N.6 and about H.35 central.

(*c*) *No. 3 Company.*—By 0600 hours No. 3 Company will be at the fork roads N.3.b. sheltered behind the houses on south of road.

(*d*) O.C. Prince of Wales's Company will be ready to move from his billets from 0615 hours onwards.

3. *Artillery.*

At 0600 hours the 74th Brigade Artillery will bombard the hedges in N.5.a and b and H.35.d. for ten minutes, when they will lift to the north and east of the village for ten minutes. Two field-guns and one howitzer will move forward in support of the battalion. The 75th Brigade R.F.A. will deal with enemy position south of the railway.

4. *Communications.*

Battalion H.Q. will move to the fork-roads H.3.b. A short line will be run to the house at the cross-roads N.4.a, where No. 4 Company will provide an instrument and the operator.

5. *Aid-post.*

Regimental Aid-post will be at Battalion H.Q., the fork-roads, and N.3.b.

J. CRAWSHAY,
Lieutenant, Acting Adjutant B.I.D.O.

Copies

Prince of Wales's Company .	No. 1.
No. 2 Company . . .	,, 2.
No. 3 ,, . . .	,, 3.
No. 4 ,, . . .	,, 4.
Retained	,, 5.
,, ...	,, 6.

OPERATION ORDER 116

To O's.C. all companies.

The enemy still holds positions in N.5 and the Buvignies Spur. 185 Inf. Bde. on our right hold from N.17 central to N.11.c.60—N.11.d.53—N.11.b.43 and are pushing a coy. forward to N.5.c.61 to-night. 3 G.B. hold approx. lines, N.d.4.40 northwards round north-eastern outskirts of Bermeries H.34.a.58. Thence 17th Inf. Brigade hold line about 500 yds. E. of river Cambronne. They are endeavouring to secure high ground in H.28 to-night. 3 G.B. will to-morrow attack the enemy to seize the following objective: N.5.a.95—railway crossing. N.6.a.26—road junction H.36.c.37. 1 G.G. will attack on right, 1 W.G. will attack on left. Dividing line railway N.6.a.45 to N.4 central inclusive to 1 W.G. 2 S.G. will co-operate with this attack by pushing troops H.35.a.4.b. 1 G.G. will endeavour to carry out their attack during night. Success or otherwise of such operation will in no way alter the action of 1 W.G., and such portions of 1 G.G. attack that are not effected to-night will be undertaken by them at zero hour. After capture of first objective to-morrow advance will be pressed eastward on successive objectives as follows: 1st bound, railway I.31a&c; 2nd bound, I.31.a.30.98—I.31.d.91; 3rd bound, road running through I.32.a&d; 4th bound, I.32 central line of road to I.33.c.91; 5th bound, I.34.b.19—I.35.c.02; 6th bound, the road J.31a and c east of La Longueville by 1 W.G. with 1 G.G. conforming on right. Detailed orders for capture of Buvignies already issued. At 0615 hours P. of W. Coy. will move to fork-roads at H.3.b. Headquarters and attached transport will move under orders of Lieut. Arthur. Coys. will carry Lewis Guns and bombs. Coy. limbers will report at present battalion headquarters at 0630. After 0630 hours coys. will move on orders from battalion headquarters. Ends.

1022.

Adjutant, B.I.D.O.

APPENDIX C

ST. DAVID

WITHIN the period covered by this history the toast of "St. David" was only given twice : at dinner " On Guard " on St. David's Day, 1915, when the toast was drunk in silence, and at Wormhoudt in 1916. On the latter occasion there was also no speech on St. David, as no one was very sure of his record beyond that he " gave us the leek." Indeed he does not seem to have done very much except uphold the doctrine of original sin against an unbelieving Welshman called Pelagius, or Morgan. Being an eloquent man, he met with great success in opposing the Pelagian heresy. He founded a number of monasteries, to one of which, at Minevia, now called St. David's, he transferred his see on becoming Archbishop of Caerleon-upon-Usk. He does not seem to have been a martial prelate, and his saintliness was founded on eloquence, conversions and good works. He lived, however, in the time of King Arthur, and possibly his eloquence was used to encourage the ardour and fire the spirit of the Welsh soldiers of the day. He died about the middle of the sixth century.

APPENDIX D

THE ARMISTICE

A. Clauses relating to Western Front

I.—Cessation of operations by land and in the air six hours after the signature of the Armistice.

II.—Immediate evacuation of invaded countries—Belgium, France, Alsace-Lorraine, Luxemburg—so ordered as to be completed within fourteen days from the signature of the Armistice.

German troops which have not left the above-mentioned territories within the period fixed will become prisoners of war.

Occupation by the Allies and United States Forces jointly will keep pace with evacuation in these areas.

All movements of evacuation and occupation will be regulated in accordance with a Note (Annexure 1).

III.—Repatriation, beginning at once, to be completed within fourteen days, of all inhabitants of the countries above enumerated (including hostages, persons under trial, or convicted).

IV.—Surrender in good condition by the German Armies of the following equipment :

> 5,000 guns (2,500 heavy, 2,500 field).
> 3,000 machine guns.
> 3,000 *Minenwerfer*.
> 2,000 aeroplanes (fighters, bombers—firstly D.7's— and night-bombing machines).

The above to be delivered *in situ* to the Allied and United States troops in accordance with the detailed conditions laid down in the Note (Annexure 1).

V.—Evacuation by the German Armies of the countries on the left bank of the Rhine. These countries on the left bank of the Rhine shall be administered by the local authorities under the control of the Allied and United States Armies of occupation.

The occupation of these territories will be carried out by Allied and United States garrisons holding the principal crossings of the Rhine (Mayence, Coblenz, Cologne), together with bridgeheads at these points of a 30-kilometre [about 19 miles] radius on the right bank, and by garrisons similarly holding the strategic points of the regions.

A neutral zone shall be set up on the right bank of the Rhine between the river and a line drawn 10 kilometres [6¼ miles] distant, starting from the Dutch frontier to the Swiss frontier. In the case of inhabitants, no person shall be prosecuted for having taken part in any military measures previous to the signing of the Armistice.

No measure of a general or official character shall be taken which would have, as a consequence, the depreciation of industrial establishments or a reduction of their *personnel*.

Evacuation by the enemy of the Rhine-lands shall be so ordered as to be completed within a further period of sixteen days, in all 31 days after the signature of the Armistice.

All movements of evacuation and occupation will be regulated according to the Note (Annexure 1).

VI.—In all territory evacuated by the enemy there shall be no evacuation of inhabitants ; no damage or harm shall be done to the persons or property of the inhabitants.

No destruction of any kind to be committed.

Military establishments of all kinds shall be delivered intact, as well as military stores of food, munitions, equipment not removed during the periods fixed for evacuation.

Stores of all kinds for the civil population, cattle, etc., shall be left *in situ*.

Industrial establishments shall not be impaired in any way, and their *personnel* shall not be moved.

VII.—Roads and means of communication of every kind, railroads, waterways, main roads, bridges, telegraphs, telephones shall be in no manner impaired.

All civil and military *personnel* at present employed on them shall remain.

5,000 locomotives, 150,000 waggons, and 5,000 motor-lorries in good working order, with all necessary spare parts and fittings, shall be delivered to the Associated Powers within the period fixed for the evacuation of Belgium and Luxemburg.

The railways of Alsace-Lorraine shall be handed over within the same period, together with all pre-war *personnel* and material.

Further, material necessary for the working of railways in the country on the left bank of the Rhine shall be left *in situ*.

All stores of coal and material for upkeep of permanent way, signals, and repair shops shall be left *in situ* and kept in an efficient state by Germany, as far as the means of communication are concerned, during the whole period of the Armistice.

All barges taken from the Allies shall be restored to them. The Note appended as Annexure 2 regulates the detail of these measures.

VIII.—The German Command shall be responsible for revealing all mines or delay-action fuses disposed on territory evacuated by the German troops and shall assist in their discovery and destruction.

The German Command shall also reveal all destructive measures that may have been taken (such as poisoning or pollution of springs, wells, etc), under penalty of reprisals.

IX.—The right of requisition shall be exercised by the Allied and United States Armies in all occupied territory, save for settlement of accounts with authorised persons.

The upkeep of the troops of occupation in the Rhineland (excluding Alsace-Lorraine) shall be charged to the German Government.

X.—The immediate repatriation, without reciprocity, according to detailed conditions which shall be fixed, of all Allied and United States prisoners of war ; the Allied Powers and the United States of America shall be able to dispose of these prisoners as they wish. However, the return of German prisoners of war interned in Holland and Switzerland shall continue as heretofore. The return of German prisoners of war shall be settled at peace preliminaries.

XI.—Sick and wounded who cannot be removed from evacuated territory will be cared for by German *personnel*, who will be left on the spot, with the medical material required.

B. Clauses relating to the Eastern Frontiers of Germany

XII.—All German troops at present in any territory which before the war belonged to Russia, Rumania, or Turkey shall withdraw within the frontiers of Germany as they existed on August 1st, 1914, and all German troops at present in territories which before the war formed part of Russia must likewise return to within the frontiers of Germany as above defined as soon as the Allies shall think the moment suitable, having regard to the internal situation of these territories.

XIII.—Evacuation by German troops to begin at once ; and all German instructors, prisoners, and civilian as well as military agents now on the territory of Russia (as defined on August 1st, 1914) to be recalled.

XIV.—German troops to cease at once all requisitions and seizures, and any other undertaking with a view to obtaining supplies intended for Germany in Rumania and Russia, as defined on August 1st, 1914.

XV.—Abandonment of the Treaties of Bukarest and Brest-Litovsk and of the Supplementary Treaties.

XVI.—The Allies shall have free access to the territories evacuated by the Germans on their eastern frontier, either through Danzig or by the Vistula, in order to convey supplies to the populations of these territories or for the purpose of maintaining order.

C. Clause relating to East Africa

XVII.—Unconditional evacuation of all German forces operating in East Africa within one month.

D. General Clauses

XVIII.—Repatriation, without reciprocity, within a maximum period of one month, in accordance with detailed conditions hereafter to be fixed, of all civilians interned or deported who may be citizens of other Allied or Associated States than those mentioned in Clause III.

XIX.—With the reservation that any future claims and demands of the Allies and United States of America remain unaffected, the following financial conditions are required :

Reparation for damage done.

While the Armistice lasts no public securities shall be removed by the enemy which can serve as a pledge to the Allies for the recovery or reparation for war losses.

Immediate restitution of the cash deposit in the National Bank of Belgium and, in general, immediate return of all documents, specie, stock, shares, paper money, together with plant for the issue thereof, touching public or private interest in the invaded countries.

Restitution of the Russian and Rumanian gold yielded to Germany or taken by that Power.

This gold to be delivered in trust to the Allies until the signature of peace.

E. NAVAL CONDITIONS

XX. Immediate cessation of all hostilities at sea, and definite information to be given as to the location and movements of all German ships.

Notification to be given to neutrals that freedom of navigation in all territorial waters is given to the Naval and Mercantile Marines of the Allied and Associated Powers, all questions of neutrality being waived.

XXI.—All Naval and Mercantile Marine prisoners of war of the Allied and Associated Powers in German hands to be returned, without reciprocity.

XXII.—Handing over to the Allies and the United States of all submarines (including all submarine cruisers and mine-layers) which are present at the moment with full complement in the ports specified by the Allies and the United States. Those that cannot put to sea to be deprived of crews and supplies, and shall remain under the supervision of the Allies and the United States. Submarines ready to put to sea shall be prepared to leave German ports immediately on receipt of wireless order to sail to the port of surrender, the remainder to follow as early as possible. The conditions of this Article shall be carried [out] within fourteen days after the signing of the Armistice.

XXIII.—The following German surface warships, which shall be designated by the Allies and the United States of America, shall forthwith be disarmed and thereafter interned in neutral ports, or, failing them, Allied ports, to be designated by the Allies and the United States of America, and placed under the surveillance of the Allies and the United States of America, only caretakers being left on board, namely :

    6 Battle Cruisers.
  10 Battle-ships.
    8 Light Cruisers, including two mine-layers.
  50 Destroyers of the most modern types.

All other surface warships (including river craft) are to be concentrated in German naval bases to be designated by the Allies and the United States of America, and are to be paid off and completely disarmed and placed under the supervision of the Allies and the United States of America. All vessels of the Auxiliary fleet (trawlers, motor-vessels, etc.) are to be disarmed. All vessels specified for internment shall be ready to leave German ports seven days after the signing of the Armistice. Directions of the voyage will be given by wireless.

Note.—A declaration has been signed by the Allied Delegates and handed to the German Delegates to the effect that, in the event of ships not being handed over owing to the mutinous state of the Fleet, the Allies reserve the right to occupy Heligoland as an advanced base to enable them to enforce the terms of the Armistice. The German Delegates have on their part signed a Declaration that they will recommend the Chancellor to accept this.

XXIV.—The Allies and the United States of America shall have the right to sweep up all minefields and obstructions laid by Germany outside German territorial waters, and the positions of these are to be indicated.

XXV.—Freedom of access to and from the Baltic to be given to the Naval and Mercantile Marines of the Allied and Associated Powers. To secure this, the Allies and the United States of America shall be empowered to occupy all German forts, fortifications, batteries, and defence works of all kinds in all the entrances from the Kattegat into the Baltic, and to sweep up all mines and obstructions within and without German territorial waters without any questions of neutrality being raised, and the positions of all such mines and obstructions are to be indicated.

XXVI.—The existing blockade conditions set up by the Allied and Associated Powers are to remain unchanged, and all German merchant ships found at sea are to remain liable to capture. The Allies and United States contemplate the provisioning of Germany during the Armistice as shall be found necessary.

XXVII.—All naval aircraft are to be concentrated and immobilised in German bases to be specified by the Allies and the United States of America.

XXVIII.—In evacuating the Belgian coasts and forts Germany shall abandon all merchant ships, tugs, lighters, cranes, and all other harbour materials, all materials for inland navigation, all aircraft and air materials and stores, all arms and armaments, and all stores and apparatus of all kinds.

XXIX.—All Black Sea ports are to be evacuated by Germany ; all Russian warships of all descriptions seized by Germany in the Black Sea are to be handed over to the Allies and the United States of America ; all neutral merchant ships seized are to be released ; all warlike and other materials of all kinds seized in those ports are to be returned, and German materials as specified in Clause XXVIII are to be abandoned.

XXX.—All merchant ships in German hands belonging to the Allied and Associated Powers are to be restored in ports to be specified by the Allies and the United States of America without reciprocity.

XXXI.—No destruction of ships or of materials to be permitted before evacuation, surrender or restoration.

XXXII.—The German Government shall formally notify the neutral Governments of the world, and particularly the Governments of Norway, Sweden, Denmark and Holland, that all restrictions placed on the trading of their vessels with the Allied and Associated countries, whether by the German Government or by private German interests, and whether in return for specific concessions, such as the export of shipbuilding materials or not, are immediately cancelled.

25

XXXIII.—No transfers of German merchant shipping of any description to any neutral flag are to take place after signature of the Armistice.

F. Duration of Armistice

XXXIV.—The duration of the Armistice is to be thirty-six days, with option to extend. During this period, on failure of execution of any of the above clauses, the Armistice may be denounced by one of the contracting parties on forty-eight hours' previous notice.

G. Time Limit for Reply

XXXV.—This Armistice to be accepted or refused by Germany within seventy-two hours of notification.

APPENDIX E

ENEMY DIVISIONS MET BY THE WELSH GUARDS

Date.		Sector.	Enemy Unit.
1915.			
September 27th	.	Loos.	
October 23rd	.	Hohenzollern Redoubt.	
November 16th	.	Laventie.	
1916.			
March 20th. .	.	Ypres. Menin Road to Weiltje.	11 L.W. Bde. On March 31st the 26th Divn.
June 18th	.	Weiltje to the Canal—June 26th.	13th Ers. Bde. On June 21st the 51st R. Divn.
August 10th .	.	Mailly-Maillet. Serre-Beaumont-Hamel.	
September 9–12th.		Ginchy.	5 Bav. Divn. Relieved by 56th Divn. on 10th.
September 15–17th		Gueudecourt Lesbœufs.	185th or 21st Divn.
September 21–25th		Lesbœufs.	51st R. Divn.
November 16–20th		Gueudecourt.	30th or 185th Divn.
December 7th	.	Le Transloy.	27th or 185th Divn. On Dec. 27th the 5th Bav. R. Divn.
1917.			
March 4th	.	Sailly-Saillisel and St. Pierre Vaast.	14th Bav. or 26th Divn.
July 15th	.	Boesinghe.	49th R. Divn.
July 29th	.	Attack of 31st.	233rd Divn. On 30th the 235th Divn.
August 4–6th	.	Steenbeek.	79th R, Divn.
August 31st .	.	Langemark.	26th Divn.
October 10th	.	Houlthulst.	187th Divn.
November 27th	.	Bourlon Wood.	3rd Guards Divn.
December 1st	.	Gouzeaucourt.	9th Bav. R. Divn.
1918.			
January 1st .	.	Arras.	236th Divn.
January 26th	.	Fampoux.	5th Bav. R. Divn. On March 1st 185th Divn.

377

Date.	Sector.	Enemy Unit.
March 22nd .	. Mercatel to Boisleux St. Marc.	Enemy attacked with 185th Divn. on the right, then 236th and 6th Bav. Divn., the latter probably opposite us. On April 8th the 234th Divn.
April 25th .	. Ayette.	234th Divn. On May 1st the 111th Divn.
July 6th .	. Boyelles.	5th Bav. R. Divn. On Aug. 8th the 21st R. Divn.
August 23rd .	. St. Leger.	234th Divn. On Aug. 24th the 23rd Sax. Divn.
September 2nd	. Ecoust—Lagnicourt.	40th Sax. Divn.
September 4th	. Boursies.	1st Guards Regt. On September 16th the 20th Divn.
September 21st	. Demicourt.	6th Divn.
September 27th	. Hindenburg Line.	20th, 6th, and 113th Divns.
October 11th	. St. Vaast.	208th Divn.
October 20th	. Vertain.	9th R. Divn.
November 6th	. Buvignies.	206th, 21st R., and 12th R. Divns.

NOTE.—In November and December 1916, and in March 1917, the boundary between the Divisions was not definitely known. The advance in 1918 was on a diagonal line to that of the retreating enemy.

APPENDIX F

MOVEMENTS OF 1ST BATTALION WELSH GUARDS

Date.				Place.
1915.				
August 18th	.	.	.	Le Havre.
,, 20th	.	.	.	Abbeville.
,, ,,	.	.	.	St. Omer.
,, ,,	.	.	.	Arques.
September 21st		.	.	Roquetoire.
,, 23rd		.	.	Fontes.
,, 25th		.	.	Haillicourt.
,, 26th		.	.	Vermelles.
,, 27th		.	.	Loos.
,, 29th		.	.	Vermelles.
,, 30th		.	.	Sailly-la-Bourse.
October 3rd	.	.	.	Vermelles (Chapelle Notre Dame de Consolation).
,, 5th	.	.	.	Vermelles.
,, 12th	.	.	.	Sailly-la-Bourse.
,, 13th	.	.	.	Vermelles (Lancashire Trench).
,, 19th	.	.	.	Vermelles.
,, 23rd	.	.	.	Hohenzollern Redoubt.
,, 27th	.	.	.	Allouagne.
November 9th	.	.	.	Merville.
,, 14th	.	.	.	Laventie (Pont du Hem).
,, 16th	.	.	.	,, (Line).
,, 19th	.	.	.	,, (Pont du Hem).
,, 21st	.	.	.	,, (Line).
,, 22nd	.	.	.	,, (Pont du Hem).
,, 24th	.	.	.	,, (Line).
,, 26th	.	.	.	La Gorgue.
December 2nd	.	.	.	Laventie (Pont du Hem).
,, 4th	.	.	.	,, (Line).
,, 6th	.	.	.	,, (Farms round village).
,, 8th	.	.	.	,, (Line).
,, 10th	.	.	.	,, (Farms).
,, 12th	.	.	.	,, (Line).
,, 14th	.	.	.	La Gorgue.
,, 20th	.	.	.	Laventie (in village).
,, 22nd	.	.	.	,, (Line).

379

Date.				Place.
December 24th	.	.	.	Laventie (Village).
,, 26th	.	.	.	,, (Line).
,, 28th	.	.	.	,, (Village).
,, 30th	.	.	.	,, (Line).
1916.				
January 1st	.	.	.	La Gorgue.
,, 13th	.	.	.	Laventie (Village).
,, 15th	.	.	.	,, (Line).
,, 17th	.	.	.	,, (Village).
,, 19th	.	.	.	,, (Line).
,, 21st	.	.	.	,, (Village).
,, 23rd	.	.	.	,, (Line).
,, 26th	.	.	.	La Gorgue).
February 1st	.	.	.	Laventie (Village).
,, 3rd	.	.	.	,, (Line).
,, 5th	.	.	.	,, (Village).
,, 7th	.	.	.	,, (Line).
,, 9th	.	.	.	,, (Village).
,, 14th	.	.	.	,, (Line).
,, 15th	.	.	.	Estaires.
,, 16–17th	.	.	.	Lestrem to Calais.
,, 25th	.	.	.	Wormhoudt.
March 5th	.	.	.	St. Jan ter Biezen.
,, 14th	.	.	.	Poperinghe (D Camp).
,, 16th	.	.	.	Ypres (Billets).
,, 20th	.	.	.	,, (Potijze Line).
,, 24th	.	.	.	,, (Billets).
,, 25th	.	.	.	Poperinghe.
April 3rd	.	.	.	Ypres (St. Jean Line).
,, 7th	.	.	.	,, (Billets).
,, 11th	.	.	.	,, (St. Jean Line).
,, 15th	.	.	.	,, (Billets).
,, 19th	.	.	.	Poperinghe.
,, 27th	.	.	.	Ypres (Potijze Line).
May 1st	.	.	.	Vlamertinghe.
,, 6th	.	.	.	Ypres (Potijze Line).
,, 10th	.	.	.	Vlamertinghe.
,, 11th	.	.	.	Poperinghe.
,, 19th	.	.	.	Wormhoudt.
June 1st	.	.	.	St. Jan ter Biezen.
,, 8th	.	.	.	Wormhoudt.
,, 15th	.	.	.	St. Jan ter Biezen.
,, 17th	.	.	.	Ypres (Canal Bank).
,, 18th	.	.	.	,, (Line Mortaldje).
,, 22nd	.	.	.	,, (Château Trois Tours).
,, 28th	.	.	.	,, (Line).
July 3rd	.	.	.	,, (Château Trois Tours).
,, 6th	.	.	.	Poperinghe (Wood A 30).
,, 14th	.	.	.	Ypres (Line extreme left).
,, 18th	.	.	.	,, (Billets in Canal Bank).
,, 22nd	.	.	.	,, (Line).
,, 26th	.	.	.	Poperinghe (Wood A 30).

Date.	Place.
July 27th	Watten.
,, 30th	Halloy.
August 1st	Bus les Artois.
,, 6th	Arquèves.
,, 9th	Mailly-Maillet.
,, 10th	Beaumont Hamel (Line).
,, 14th	Colin Camps.
,, 17th	Beaumont Hamel (Line).
,, 19th	Bus les Artois.
,, 20th	Vauchelles.
,, 22nd	Gezaincourt.
,, 24th	Vignacourt.
,, 25th	Méricourt l'Abbé.
September 7th	Ville sur Ancre.
,, 9th	Ginchy.
,, 12th	Bernafay Wood and Happy Valley.
,, 14th	Trones Wood.
,, 16th	Flers—Gueudecourt.
,, 17th	Carnoy.
,, 20th	Trones Wood.
,, 25th	Lesbœufs.
,, 26th	Trones Wood.
,, 29th	Carnoy (Mansell Camp).
,, 30th	Fricourt (Entrenching Batt. Camp).
October 1st	St. Maulvis.
November 6th	Carnoy (Mansell Camp).
,, 14th	Montauban.
,, 16th	Gueudecourt).
,, 20th	Montauban (H. Camp).
,, 21st	Meault.
December 2nd	Bromfay Farm.
,, 6th	Montauban (Maltzhern Camp).
,, 7th	Le Transloy.
,, 10th	Maltzhorn Camp.
,, 11th	Bromfay Camp.
,, 14th	Maltzhorn Camp.
,, 15th	Transloy Line.
,, 18th	Bromfay Camp,
,, 21st	Maltzhorn Camp.
,, 22nd	Transloy Line.
,, 24th	Bromfay Camp.
,, 26th	Combles (Haie Wood).
,, 28th	Transloy Line.
,, 30th	Bromfay Camp.
1917.	
January 1st	Ville sur Ancre.
,, 10th	Maricourt (Billon Farm)
,, 11th	Maurepas.
,, 14th	Maricourt (Billon Farm).
,, 24th	Maurepas.
,, 25th	Fregicourt.

Date.				Place.
January 29th	.	.	.	Maurepas
February 2nd	.	.	.	Fregicourt.
,, 6th	.	.	.	Maurepas.
,, 10th	.	.	.	Méricourt.
March 4th	.	.	.	Sailly-Saillisel.
,, 8th	.	.	.	Maurepas.
,, 12th	.	.	.	Maricourt (Billon Farm).
,, 16th	.	.	.	Combles.
,, 19th	.	.	.	St. Pierre Vaast.
,, 21st	.	.	.	Manancourt.
,, 24th	.	.	.	Maurepas.
,, 25th	.	.	.	Péronne.
April 23rd	.	.	.	Marquaix.
May 20th	.	.	.	La Neuville.
,, 31st	.	.	.	Campagne.
June 16th	.	.	.	Zudausques.
,, 18th	.	.	.	Houdtkerque.
July 2nd	.	.	.	Woesten.
,, 13th	.	.	.	,, (De Wippe Cabaret).
,, 15th	.	.	.	Boesinghe (Line).
,, 19th	.	.	.	Woesten (De Wippe Cabaret).
,, 29th	.	.	.	Boesinghe (Line).
,, 31st	.	.	.	Boesinghe (Attack).
				Elverdinghe (Zommerbloom).
August 4th	.	.	.	Steenbeek (Line).
,, 6th	.	.	.	Proven (Petworth Camp).
,, 27th	.	.	.	Elverdinghe (Bluet Farm).
,, 31st	.	.	.	Langemark (Line).
September 4th	.	.	.	Woesten (De Wippe Cabaret).
,, 13th	.	.	.	Elverdinghe.
,, 21st	.	.	.	Proven (Petworth Camp).
,, 22nd	.	.	.	Herxeele.
,, 29th	.	.	.	Proven (Paddington Camp).
October 5th	.	.	.	Elverdinghe.
,, 8th	.	.	.	Pilkem (Wood 15).
,, 10th	.	.	.	Houthulst.
,, 13th	.	.	.	Elverdinghe (Larry Camp).
,, 16th	.	.	.	Woesten (Forest Area).
,, 17th	.	.	.	Proven (Paddock Wood).
,, 20th	.	.	.	Serques.
November 9th	.	.	.	Enquinegatte.
,, 10th	.	.	.	Heuchin.
,, 11th	.	.	.	Buneville.
,, 17th	.	.	.	Grand Rullecourt.
,, 18th	.	.	.	Berles au Bois.
,, 19th	.	.	.	Achiet le Petit.
,, 22nd	.	.	.	Rocquigny.
,, 23rd	.	.	.	Flesquières.
,, 27th	.	.	.	Bourlon Wood.
,, 29th	.	.	.	Ribecourt.
				Trescault.
December 1st	.	.	.	Gouzeaucourt.

Date.				Place.
December 4th	.	.	.	Etricourt.
,, 5th	.	.	.	Gouy en Artois.
,, 11th	.	.	.	Arras.
1918.				
January 1st	.	.	.	Gavrelle (Line).
,, 18th	.	.	.	Arras.
,, 26th	.	.	.	Fampoux (Line).
,, 30th	.	.	.	Arras.
February 3rd	.	.	.	Fampoux (Line).
,, 14th	.	.	.	Arras (Gordon Camp).
,, 18th	.	.	.	Fampoux (Line).
,, 26th	.	.	.	Arras.
March 1st	.	.	.	Fampoux (Line).
,, 11th	.	.	.	Arras (Gordon Camp).
,, 15th	.	.	.	Fampoux (Line).
,, 19th	.	.	.	Berneville.
,, 22nd	.	.	.	Mercatel.
,, 24th	.	.	.	Boisleux St. Marc.
,, 25th	.	.	.	Boyelles.
,, 26th	.	.	.	Boisleux St. Marc.
,, 31st	.	.	.	Blairville.
April 2nd	.	.	.	Boisleux St. Marc.
,, 6th	.	.	.	Blairville.
,, 8th	.	.	.	Boisleux St. Marc.
,, 12th	.	.	.	Blairville.
,, 14th	.	.	.	Barly.
,, 15th	.	.	.	Fosseux.
,, 24th	.	.	.	Berles au Bois.
,, 25th	.	.	.	Ayette.
June 7th	.	.	.	Barly.
July 6th	.	.	.	Boyelles.
,, 10th	.	.	.	Blairville.
,, 18th	.	.	.	Boyelles.
,, 24th	.	.	.	Blairville.
August 4th	.	.	.	Boyelles.
,, 11th	.	.	.	Saulty.
,, 15th	.	.	.	Blairville.
,, 21st	.	.	.	Ransart.
,, 23rd	.	.	.	Moyenville.
,, 24th	.	.	.	St. Leger (Action).
,, 25th	.	.	.	Boiry St. Martin.
,, 27th	.	.	.	Ransart.
September 2nd	.	.	.	Ecoust (Action).
,, 3rd	.	.	.	Lagnicourt.
,, 4th	.	.	.	Boursies (Line).
,, 5th	.	.	.	Lagnicourt.
,, 11th	.	.	.	Boursies (Line).
,, 17th	.	.	.	Lagnicourt.
,, 18th	.	.	.	Noreuil.
,, 21st	.	.	.	Demicourt (Line).
,, 23rd	.	.	.	Lagnicourt.
,, 27th	.	.	.	Flesquières (Action).

Date.			Place.
September 28th	.	.	Canal du Nord.
October 7th	.	.	Flesquières.
,, 8th	.	.	Maznières.
,, 9th	.	.	Seranvillers.
,, 10th	.	.	Estourmel.
,, 11th	.	.	St. Vaast (Action).
,, 13th	.	.	St. Hilaire.
,, 17th	.	.	Carnières.
,, 19th	.	.	St. Vaast.
,, 20th	.	.	Selle River (Action).
,, 21st	.	.	St. Hilaire.
November 2nd	.	.	Vertain.
,, 4th	.	.	Villers Pol.
,, 5th	.	.	Amfroipret.
,, 6th	.	.	Buvignies (Action).
,, 9th	.	.	La Longueville.
,, 10th	.	.	Douzies.
,, 18th	.	.	Villers sire Nicole.
,, 19th	.	.	Binche.
,, 20th	.	.	Monceau sur Sambre.
,, 24th	.	.	Chatelet.
,, 25th	.	.	Fosse.
,, 28th	.	.	Nannine.
,, 29th	.	.	Gesves.
December 5th	.	.	Vyle et Tharout.
,, 6th	.	.	Borlon.
,, 10th	.	.	Jehonheid.
,, 11th	.	.	Abrefontaine.
,, 12th	.	.	Ville du Bois.
,, 13th	.	.	Mirfeld.
,, 14th	.	.	Hollerath.
,, 15th	.	.	Keldenich.
,, 16th	.	.	Sinzenich.
,, 17th	.	.	Liblar.
,, 19th	.	.	Gleuel.
,, 20th	.	.	Cologne.

APPENDIX G

EVENTS OF THE WAR

This list of dates was compiled and published by *The Times* as a short "Diary of the War." We give it with the permission of the Editor.

1914

June 28.—Francis Ferdinand shot at Serajevo.
July   5.—Kaiser's War Council at Potsdam.
       23.—Austro-Hungarian Note to Serbia.
       28.—Austria declared war on Serbia.
       31.—State of war in Germany.
Aug.   1.—Germany declared war on Russia.
       2.—German ultimatum to Belgium.
       4.—Great Britain declared war on Germany.
     10.—France declared war on Austria.
     12.—Great Britain declared war on Austria.
     15.—Fall of Liége.
     16.—British Army landed in France.
     20.—Germans occupied Brussels.
     23.—Japan declared war on Germany.
     24.—Fall of Namur.
     25.—Sack of Louvain.
     26.—Battle of Tannenberg.
     28.—British victory in the Bight.
     29.—New Zealanders in Samoa.
Sept. 2.—Russians took Lemberg.
      3.—Paris Government at Bordeaux.
      5.—End of retreat from Mons.
      6.—First Marne Battle begun.
     15.—First Aisne Battle begun.
     16.—Russians evacuated East Prussia.
     23.—First British Air Raid in Germany.

Oct. 9.—Fall of Antwerp.
13.—Belgian Government at Havre.
20.—First Battle of Ypres begun.
Nov. 1.—Naval Action off Coronel.
5.—Great Britain declared war on Turkey.
7.—Fall of Tsingtau.
10.—*Emden* sunk.
21.—British occupied Basra.
Dec. 2.—Austrians in Belgrade.
8.—Naval Battle off the Falklands.
14.—Serbians retook Belgrade.
16.—Germans bombarded West Hartlepool.
18.—Hussein Kamel, Sultan of Egypt.
24.—First Air Raid on England.

1915

Jan. 24.—Naval Battle off Dogger Bank.
Feb. 2.—Turks defeated on Suez Canal.
18.—U-Boat " Blockade " of England.
25.—Allied Fleet attacked Dardanelles.
March 10.—British captured Neuve Chapelle.
22.—Russians took Przemysl.
April 22.—Second Battle of Ypres begun.
25.—Allied Landing in Gallipoli.
May 3.—Battle of the Dunajec.
6.—Battle at Krithia, Gallipoli.
7.—*Lusitania* torpedoed.
8.—Germans occupied Libau.
11.—German repulse at Ypres.
12.—General Botha occupied Windhuk.
16.—Russian retreat to the San.
23.—Italy declared war on Austria.
25.—Coalition Cabinet formed.
June 2.—Italians crossed Isonzo.
3.—Russians evacuated Przemysl.
22.—Austro-Germans recaptured Lemberg.
July 2.—*Pommern* sunk in Baltic.
9.—German South-West Africa conquered.
24.—Nasiriyeh, on Euphrates, taken.
Aug. 4.—Fall of Warsaw.
5.—Fall of Ivangorod.
6.—New landing at Suvla Bay.
8.—General Birdwood's advance at Anzac.

Aug. 9.—British success near Hooge.
15.—National Registration.
17.—Fall of Kovno.
18.—Russian victory in Riga Gulf.
19.—Fall of Novo-Georgievsk.
21.—Cotton declared contraband.
25.—Fall of Brest-Litovsk.
Sept. 1.—Gen. Alexeieff as Chief of Staff.
2.—Fall of Grodno.
5.—Tsar as Generalissimo.
7.—Russian victory near Tarnopol.
18.—Fall of Vilna.
21.—Russian retreat ended.
25.—Battle of Loos and in Champagne.
28.—Victory at Kut-el-Amara.
Oct. 4.—Russian ultimatum to Bulgaria.
5.—Allied landing at Salonika.
6.—Austro-German invasion of Serbia.
9.—Belgrade occupied.
14.—Bulgaria at war with Serbia.
17.—Allied Note to Greece.
19.—Lord Derby on the 46 Groups.
22.—Bulgarians occupy Uskub.
28.—M. Briand French Premier.
Nov. 5.—Fall of Nish.
22.—Battle of Ctesiphon.
29.—British withdrew from Ctesiphon.
Dec. 2.—Fall of Monastir.
3.—General Townshend at Kut.
9.—Allied retreat in Macedonia.
13.—Salonika lines fortified.
15.—Sir D. Haig C.-in-C. in France.
19.—Withdrawal from Gallipoli.
25.—Turkish defeat at Kut.

1916

Jan. 8.—Gallipoli evacuation complete.
13.—Fall of Cettigne.
Feb. 9.—General Smuts appointed to East Africa.
16.—Russians entered Erzerum.
18.—German Kamerun conquered.
21.—Battle of Verdun begun.
24.—Germans took Fort Douaumont.

March 16.—Admiral von Tirpitz dismissed.
April 9.—German assault at Verdun.
  17.—Russians entered Trebizond.
  24.—Rebellion in Ireland.
  29.—Fall of Kut-el-Amara.
May 24.—British Conscription Bill passed.
  31.—Battle of Jutland.
June 4.—General Brusiloff's offensive.
  5.—Lord Kitchener lost at sea.
  14.—Allied Economic Conference in Paris.
  21.—Mecca taken by Grand Sherif.
July 1.—Somme Battle begun.
  25.—Russians occupied Erznjan.
Aug. 6.—Italian offensive on Isonzo.
  10.—Russians at Stanislau.
  27.—Rumania entered the War.
  29.—Hindenburg Chief of Staff.
Sept. 3.—Zeppelin destroyed at Cuffley.
  26.—British took Thiepval and Combles.
Oct. 10.—Allied ultimatum to Grceee.
Nov. 1.—Italian advance on Carso.
  13.—British victory on the Ancre.
  18.—Serbians and French took Monastir.
  29.—Grand Fleet under Sir D. Beatty.
Dec. 1.—Anti-Allied Riot in Athens.
  5.—Resignation of Mr. Asquith.
  6.—Germans enter Bukarest.
  7.—Mr. Lloyd George Prime Minister.
  12.—German " Peace Proposals."
  15.—French victory at Verdun.
  20.—President Wilson's Peace Note.

1917

Jan. 1.—Turkey denounced Berlin Treaty.
Feb. 1.—" Unrestricted " U-Boat War begun.
  3.—America broke with Germany.
  6.—British captured Grandcourt.
  24.—British took Kut-el-Amara.
March 11.—British entered Baghdad.
  12.—Revolution in Russia.
  15.—Abdication of the Tsar.
  18.—British entered Péronne.
  21.—First British Imperial War Cabinet.

April 6.—America declared war on Germany.

9.—Battle of Vimy Ridge begun.

May 4.—French took Craonne.

14.—New Italian offensive.

15.—General Pétain French C.-in-C.

June 7.—British victory at Messines Ridge.

12.—Abdication of King Constantine.

26.—First American troops in France.

27.—Mesopotamia Report issued.

29.—General Allenby commander in Egypt.

July 1.—Last Russian offensive begun.

14.—Bethmann-Hollweg dismissed.

17.—British Royal House styled " Windsor."

19.—Reichstag " Peace " Resolution.

24.—Russian defeat in Galicia.

31.—Great Allied attack around Ypres.

Aug. 29.—President Wilson's Note to the Pope.

Sept. 4.—Germans occupied Riga.

15.—Russian Republic proclaimed.

28.—British victory at Ramadieh.

Oct. 9.—Allied attack in Flanders.

24.—Italian defeat at Caporetto.

29.—Fall of Udine.

30.—Chancellor Michaelis dismissed.

31.—British captured Beersheba.

Nov. 1.—German retreat on Chemin des Dames.

4.—British troops in Italy.

6.—British stormed Passchendaele Ridge.

7.—British captured Gaza.

8.—Bolshevist *coup d'état* in Russia.

9.—Italian stand on the Piave.

17.—British in Jaffa.

18.—Gen. Maude's death in Mesopotamia.

20.—British victory at Cambrai.

30.—German reaction at Cambrai.

Dec. 6.—Armistice on Russian Front.

9.—British captured Jerusalem.

22.—Brest Conference opened.

26.—Sir R. Wemyss First Sea Lord.

1918

Jan. 5.—Mr. Lloyd George on War Aims.

20.—*Breslau* sunk ; *Goeben* damaged.

Feb.　1.—Germany recognised Ukraine.
　　　9.—First Brest Treaty signed.
　　16.—General Wilson Chief of Staff.
　　18.—German invasion of Russia.
　　21.—British capture Jericho.
　　24.—Turks recovered Trebizond.
　　25.—Germans at Reval.
March　3.—Second Brest Treaty.
　　　7.—German peace with Finland.
　　11.—Turks recovered Erzerum.
　　13.—Germans at Odessa.
　　14.—Brest Treaty ratified at Moscow.
　　21.—German offensive in the West.
　　24.—Bapaume and Péronne lost.
April　5.—Allied landing at Vladivostok.
　　　9.—New Military Service Bill.
　　11.—Armentières lost.
　　13.—Turks occupied Batum.
　　14.—General Foch, Allied Generalissimo.
　　15.—Bailleul lost.
　　18.—Lord Milner War Secretary.
　　22.—Naval raid on Zeebrugge and Ostend.
　　26.—Kemmel Hill lost.
　　27.—Turks occupied Kars.
　　30.—Germans at Viborg.
May　1.—Germans at Sebastopol.
　　　9.—Second Raid on Ostend.
　　27.—Second German Offensive.
　　29.—Soissons lost ; Reims held.
　　31.—Germans reached Marne.
June　1.—Attacks towards Paris held.
　　　9.—New German assault.
　　15.—Austrian offensive in Italy.
　　23.—Great Austrian defeat.
July　2.—1,000,000 Americans shipped to France.
　　15.—Third German offensive.　Second Marne
　　　　　Battle begun.
　　16.—Ex-Tsar shot at Ekaterinburg.
　　18.—General Foch's counter-attack.
　　20.—Germans recrossed the Marne.
Aug.　2.—Soissons recovered.
　　　8.—British attack at Amiens.
　　29.—Bapaume and Noyon regained.

Sept. 1.—Péronne recovered.
     2.—Drocourt-Quéant line breached.
    12.—American attack at St. Mihiel.
    15.—Austrian Peace Note.
    17.—New Macedonian offensive.
    19.—British advance in Palestine.
Sept. 25.—Bulgaria proposed armistice.
    27.—Hindenburg Line broken.
    29.—Bulgaria surrendered.
    30.—Fall of Damascus.
         Chancellor Hertling resigns.
 Oct. 1.—St. Quentin regained.
     4.—Abdication of King Ferdinand.
     9.—Cambrai regained.
    10.—British took Le Cateau.
    13.—French recovered Laon.
    14.—British troops at Irtkutsk.
    15.—British in Homs.
    17.—Ostend, Lille, Douai regained.
    19.—Bruges reoccupied.
    20.—Belgian coast clear.
    25.—Ludendorff resigned.
    26.—Aleppo fell to the Allies.
    27.—Austria sued for peace.
    28.—Italians crossed Piave.
    29.—Serbians reached the Danube.
    30.—Turkey granted Armistice.
 Nov. 1.—Versailles Conference opened.
     2.—British at Valenciennes.
     3.—Austrian Surrender.—Kiel Mutiny.
     4.—Versailles Armistice Agreement.
     5.—Full powers for Marshal Foch. Mr. Wilson's
         Last Note to Germany.
     6.—Americans reached Sedan.
     7.—Bavarian Republic proclaimed.
     9.—Foch received German Envoys.
         Abdication of the Kaiser.
         Chancellor Prince Max resigned.
         Berlin revolution.
    10.—Kaiser's flight to Holland. British at Mons.
    11.—Armistice Terms accepted.

26

APPENDIX H

FIRST BATTALION CHOIRS

April 1915 to March 1919

Where Stationed.	*Joint Conductors.*
Sandown Park, Esher.	No. 53 C.Q.M.S. S. Rendel.
Wellington Barracks.	No. 737 Sergt. G. Williams.

Engagements

Battalion Concert at Esher.	(First in the Regiment.)
Steinway Hall.	(Recorded elsewhere.)
Albert Hall.	

Banquet at Princes' Restaurant, given by Col. Lord Harlech, Commanding the Welsh Guards, in honour of the Mayor and Corporation of Cardiff, who presented the regiment with a cheque for the purpose of band instruments. The choir supplied the whole of the musical programme, and afterwards marched back to Wellington Barracks, attracting a large crowd of people by their singing.

Presentation of the Colours by His Majesty King George V at Buckingham Palace. The choir, prior to the consecration of the Colours by the Bishop of St. Asaph, sang " Aberystwyth," " Ton-y-Botel," and " Hen Wlad Fy Nhadau."

France and Belgium

It is obvious that there could be nothing in the nature of " A Notable Concert " while on active service—all concerts were what is called " scratch " affairs, and were very frequently held. The first occasion on which the choir sang was perhaps at Wiznes on September 4th, 1915, at a concert given by the officers of the Machine Gun School, when the Prince of Wales was present. The choir must be considered in France and Belgium as the leaven of song in the battalion. The really effective singing did not come from the choir standing in a body on a rough platform, but from the heart of the battalion when going into battle or after the fight. " In the sweet bye and bye, we shall meet on the beautiful shore," after the bloody engagement at Gouzeaucourt, when the shattered battalion was withdrawn to a wood behind the village, brought a hush over the camp. The singers were hidden amongst the trees in the moonlight and the air was frosty and still. This was not a concert, but a message, a song of hope and faith. There were many similar dramatic moments.

Nos. 737 Sergt. Williams, 53 C.Q.M.S. Rendel, Sergt. Jones, and 1,483 Guardsman Houldsworth were the leaders at various times.

RESERVE BATTALION CHOIRS

July 1915 to March 1919

Where Stationed.	*Conductor.*
Marlow.	No. 1,993 Sergt. W. Jones.
Tower of London.	
Orpington, Kent.	

Engagements

Lady Astor's Hospital at Cliveden.—The choir were taken up the river in steam launches and gave a concert to a great number of patients.

French Flag Day at Marlow. They were responsible for raising a large sum of money for the fund.

Savoy Hotel (St. Dunstan's Day). They sang a great number of old Welsh airs to a most appreciative audience.

London Opera House on St. David's Day, 1916. They received a tremendous ovation from a huge Welsh audience.

The Alhambra, St. David's Day Matinee, 1917, organised by the Countess of Lisburne. They sang " Y Delyn Aur " and " Martyrs of the Arena."

In addition to the above the choir, while at Orpington, gave a great number of concerts in local churches and hospitals.

Where Stationed.   *Conductor.*

Tadworth.   No. 2,336 Cpl. H. Lewis.

Engagements

Concert held at 10, Downing Street, 1917, in aid of Welsh industries. In the presence of H.R.H. Princess Mary they sang " Comrades in Arms " and " O mor ber yn y man." Ciro's Y.M.C.A.

Where Stationed.   *Conductor.*

Ranelagh.   No. 2,466 Guardsman Davies.

Engagements

Memorial service for officers, N.C.O.'s and men who died in the service of their country since the formation of the regiment, February 27th, 1915, held at Holy Trinity Church, Sloane Street, February 27th, 1918. The choir rendered the entire choral portion of the service, and sang in Welsh " Bethel," " Huddersfield," " Aberystwyth," and " Hen Wlad Fy Nhadau." The service was attended by H.R.H. Prince of Wales, the Lord Mayor and Corporation of Cardiff, the Mayors of many Welsh towns, and a number of the Welsh Members of Parliament.

Where Stationed.   *Conductor.*

Ranelagh.   No. 3,707 Cpl. J. Davies.

Engagements

Ciro's Y.M.C.A. This choir, about sixty strong, practised continuously for three months, showing the greatest promise. They were only permitted to give one concert at Ciro's Y.M.C.A. before at least forty members were ordered overseas.

DEPOT CHOIR

April 1915, and onwards

Where Stationed.   *Conductor.*

Guards' Depot,   No. 1,993 Guardsman, later
Caterham.   Sergt. W. Jones.

Engagements

Drill Hall, Caterham.
Park Hall, Cardiff, July 24th, 1915.
The history of this Choir has already been recorded.

Where Stationed.	*Conductor.*
Guards' Depot,	No. 2,850 Guardsman
Caterham.	T. S. Ellis.

Engagements

This Choir, with many changes of membership, was in existence for a considerable period. It sang at all depot concerts, and proved to be invaluable in training men before they joined the Reserve Battalion.

Where Stationed.	*Conductor.*
Guards' Depot,	No. 3,707 Cpl. J. Davies.
Caterham.	

Engagements

Regimental concert in aid of Prisoners of War and Comforts' Fund at the Apollo Theatre, June 11th, 1918, whereby the funds in question benefited by £500.

Welsh Prisoners of War Fund. Service at Westminster Abbey, June 22nd, 1918. In conjunction with picked voices of the London Welsh Choirs, they sang eight Welsh hymns. The service was attended by H.M. Queen Alexandra, the Prime Minister and some 10,000 people.

National Eisteddfod of Wales at Neath, August 1918 (recorded elsewhere).

Lord Northcliffe's luncheon to *The Times*' staff, August 1918.

Drill Hall, Caterham. A large sum of money was raised for a local fund, the attendance being record for the hall.

Concert to American troops at Winchester, September 1918, under the auspices of the British Committee for Entertaining American Forces. The Choir received a tremendous ovation from some 4,000 Americans.

Several concerts at the Palladium, the Alhambra, and Queen's Hall, under the auspices of the National Sunday League.

Maesteg Semi-National Eisteddfod, where they shared

the first prize with the local choir, the test piece, "Here's to Admiral Death," being the same as at the National Eisteddfod.

Concert at Maesteg Town Hall in aid of Local Heroes' Fund, when the hall was filled to overflowing, some 700 people standing throughout the performance.

Concert in aid of Prisoners of War Fund, regimental and local, at the Town Hall, Newport, on October 9th, 1918. The Choir was previously entertained to tea by the Lord-Lieutenant of Monmouthshire, Major-Gen. Lord Treowen, C.B., C.M.G., Major J. W. Benyon and the Mayor of Newport.

Wood Street Congregational Church, Cardiff, October 11th, 1918. Concert in aid of the regimental and *The Western Mail* Prisoners of War Funds.

Concert at the School Hall, Eton College. One of the most successful that the Choir ever gave, due to the enthusiasm and appreciation shown by the audience.

APPENDIX I

NOMINAL ROLL OF W.O.'s, N.C.O.'s, AND MEN OF THE WELSH GUARDS WHO SERVED OVERSEAS WITH THE 1ST BATTALION

[The obelisks (†) indicate the number of wounds.]

Regtl. No.	Rank.	Name.	Casualties.	Decorations.
2506	Gdsn.	Abbott, G. W. (Cardiff) . . .	K. in A.	
2695	,,	Abel, E. (Swansea)	† †	
3267	,,	Ablett, F. (Accrington) . .	K. in A.	
4863	,,	Abraham, I. (Robertstown, Glam.) .		
3044	,,	Acornley, R. (Burnley) . .	†	
894	,,	Adams, W. (Cilfynydd, Glam.) .	D. of Wds.	
2475	,,	Adams, H. C. (Canton, Cardiff) .		
2904	,,	Adams, A. (Widnes, Lancs.) .		
4758	,,	Adams, E. L. (Merthyr Tydfil) .		
2874	,,	Adamson, H. (Ashton-in-Makerfield) .	†	
2616	,,	Addison, W. W. (London, S.E.) .	† †	
3383	,,	Adley, E. E. (Swansea) . .	K. in A.	
2530	,,	Adnitt, T. (Swansea) . .	† †	
2783	,,	Airey, J. (Ulverston, Lancs.) .		M.M
1635	,,	Aked, P. W. (Liverpool) . .		
3899	,,	Alderman, E. W. (Birmingham) .	D. of Wds.	
3	O.R.Q.M.S.	Alderson, A. (Appleby, Westmoreland).		
3957	Gdsn.	Alderson, J. (Bradford, Yorks.) .		
4210	Musn.	Alexandra, J. H. (London, S.W.) .		
4571	Gdsn.	Allan, W. (Pontnewydd, Mon.) .		
116	,,	Allen, T. W. (Haverfordwest, Pem.) .	†	
601	L/Cpl.	Allen, S. (Cardiff) . . .	†	
1089	Gdsn.	Allen, W. (Wolverhampton) .	†	
1158	,,	Allen, S. (Ammanford, Carm.) .	D. of Wds.	
1248	,,	Allen, W. (Penygraig, Glam.) .		
2471	,,	Allen, W. (Roch, Pem.) .	K. in A.	
2717	,,	Allen, G. E. (Newport, Mon.) .		M.M.
3966	,,	Allen, F. (Coventry) . .	†	
4142	,,	Allen, S. (Mexborough, Yorks.) .		
4293	,,	Almond, W. (Bolton, Lancs.) .		
3940	,,	Alvis, A. C. (Salisbury) . .	†	
3461	,,	Ames, F. B. (Prescot) . .	†	
3292	,,	Anderson, J. (S. Shields) . .		M.M.

Regtl. No.	Rank.	Name.	Casualties.	Decorations.
3816	Gdsn.	Anderson, T. (Newcastle-on-Tyne)	†	
4131	„	Anderson, T. E. (Gateshead)	†	
4146	„	Anderson, H. R. (Swansea)	†	
1420	„	Anstey, G. M. (London)	†	
2432	Musn.	Antoney, G. M. (London)		
4749	Gdsn.	Anthony, S. (Swansea)		
2930	„	Apps, R. F. G. (Brighton)		
1118	„	Archer, D. R. (Wrexham)		
1187	„	Archer, A. M. (Wrexham)	†	
1518	„	Arkwell, T. (Newport)		
743	„	Armstrong, G. (Uttoxeter)		
470	L/Cpl.	Arnold, T. R. (Merthyr)	†	
1112	Sergt.-Cook	Arnold, J. (Machynlleth)	†	
1164	Gdsn.	Arnold, C. H. (Pontypridd)		
3936	L/Cpl.	Arnold, A. S. (Dorchester)	†	
842	Gdsn.	Arrowsmith, H. (Aberdare)	D. of Wds.	
4726	„	Arthur, D. S. (Merthyr)		
24	Sergt.	Ashford, O. (Norwich)	†	D.C.M.
4046	Gdsn.	Ashley, G. (Welshpool)	K. in A.	
1998	„	Ashton, E. (Ystalyfera)		
1008	„	Ashurst, W. (Ashton-under-Lyne)		
2829	„	Ashworth, A. (Oldham)	† †	
4300	„	Askew, W. (Liverpool)		
1037	Sergt.	Aspinall, F. (Ruabon)		M.M. and Bar.
1670	Gdsn.	Aston, I. (Port Talbot)	† † † †	
4119	„	Atchinson, R. (Chesterfield)	†	
3971	„	Atkins, P. (London)	†	
3520	„	Atkinson, T. (Wrexham)	K. in A.	
3902	„	Atkinson, T. (Silsden)		
4147	„	Atkinson, H. G. (Ilkeston)		
142	„	Atkiss, G. H. (Hucknall)		
1078	L/Sergt.	Attfield, C. (London, N.W.)	K. in A.	M.M.
4576	Gdsn.	Atyeo, E. J. (Neath)		
1301	„	Aubrey, W. G. (Pontyberem)	K. in A.	
2328	„	Aubrey, D. I. (Swansea)	†	M.M.
2937	„	Austin, S. T. (Gower)		
3578	„	Austin, W. (Bridgend)	D. of Wds.	
3650	„	Austin, R. (Bridgend)		
1856	„	Aylesbury, F. W. (Bargoed)	† † †	
3434	„	Baggott, S. (Llandilo)		
1687	„	Bagley, E. (Brownhills)	K. in A.	
96	„	Baglow, G. (Swansea)		
986	„	Bailey, A. R. (Swansea)		
3144	„	Bailey, F. W. (Fleet)	K. in A.	
3262	L/Cpl.	Bailey, F. C. (Newport)	†	
3528	„	Bailey, H. H. (Portsmouth)	†	
3795	Gdsn.	Bailey, T. W. (Birmingham)	†	
3999	„	Bailey, H. (Caerphilly)	†	
1872	„	Bainbridge, J. E. (Carmarthen)	†	
1554	„	Baines, A. (Wrexham)		

Regtl. No.	Rank.	Name.	Casualties.	Decorations.
2217	Gdsn.	Baines, E. H. (Church)	†	
3432	,,	Baines, J. (St. Helen's)	† †	
224	,,	Baker, G. E. (Grantham)	†	
1182	,,	Baker, P. W. (Peterston-super-Ely)	† D. of Wds.	
1785	,,	Baker, J. (Handbridge)		
1819	,,	Baker, T. (Caerphilly)	†	
2343	,,	Baker, G. H. (London)	K. in A.	
3318	Cpl.	Baker, G. (Bury St. Edmunds)	†	
3465	Gdsn.	Baker, F. H. (Cardiff)		
3809	,,	Baker, H. (Birmingham)		
4301	,,	Baker, J. A. (Crowley)	†	
3839	,,	Balcombe, F. (Icklesham)		
1254	,,	Baldwin, S. T. (Aberdare)		M.M.
3160	,,	Baldwin, J. (Chelmsford)		
557	L/Cpl.	Bale, R. (Caerphilly)	†	
117	Gdsn.	Ball, S. L. (Neath)		
4506	Cpl.	Banks, K. L. (Cardiff)		
1337	Gdsn.	Bannister, C. J. (Cardiff)	†	
2383	L/Cpl.	Bannister, J. R. (Pontypridd)	†	
1095	L/Sergt.	Barber, H. (Cardiff)	† †	
1352	Gdsn.	Barber, J. R. (Newport)	†	
861	,,	Barker, F. L. (Swansea)		
1212	,,	Barker, R. C. (Cardiff)		
128	,,	Barlow, A. J. (Tredegar)	D. of S.	M.M.
1072	,,	Barlow, F. (London)	† †	
643	,,	Barnes, H. G. (Pentre)		
1898	R.S.M.	Barnes, E. (Street)		
2674	Gdsn.	Barnes, R. (Ystrad Mynach)	K. in A.	
2902	L/Cpl.	Barnes, J. E. (Accrington)	†	
3101	Gdsn.	Barnes, E. (Pwllheli)		
1183	L/Cpl.	Barnett, J. (Ammanford)	†	
3129	Gdsn.	Baron, J. (Liverpool)	†	
4309	,,	Barrett, G. (Amersham)		
1439	,,	Barther, H. J. (Penmaenmawr)	†	M.M.
364	Sergt.	Bartlett, C. W. F. (Bristol)	†	M.M.
4615	Gdsn.	Bartlett, F. W. (Gilfach Goch)		
3552	,,	Bartley, J. H. (Bodfari)		
3810	,,	Barton, R. H. (Birmingham)		
1387	,,	Basten, C. (Cardiff)	† †	
532	,,	Bate, J. C. (Wrexham)	†	
296	,,	Bateman, D. (Newport)		
390	,,	Bateman, W. E. (Bury)		
3937	,,	Bates, J. (Belford)	†	
3868	L/Cpl.	Batterby, J. (London)		
1902	,,	Battey, C. E. (Bridgend)	†	
4173	,,	Baxter, H. (Birmingham)	†	
1265	Gdsn.	Beach, B. (Llanover)	† K. in A.	
644	,,	Beale, D. R. (Cowbridge)	K. in A.	
3203	,,	Beard, M. R. (Flint)	†	
4739	,,	Beard, C. (Merthyr)		
11	C.S.M.	Beardsmore, J. (Ilkeston)		

Regtl. No.	Rank.	Name.			Casualties.	Decorations.
1273	Gdsn.	Beavan, E. T. (Ystalyfera)	.	.		
193	Sergt.	Beazer, W. C. (Resolven)	.	.	.	M.M.
4249	Gdsn.	Beazer, J. A. (Neath)		.	.	
443	Cpl.	Bebb, J. H. (Newport)	.	.	† D. of Wds.	
398	Gdsn.	Beck, F. P. (Swansea)	.	.	D. of Wds.	
3698	,,	Beck, A. E. (Wrexham)	.	.	†	
4126	,,	Beckett, S. (Middlewich)	.	.		
4542	,,	Beckett, E. J. (Bargoed)	.	.		
5321	,,	Beddoe, J. H. (Porth)	.	.		
2524	,,	Bedford, G. T. J. (Llanwenarth)	.	.		
2005	L/Cpl.	Beech, E. H. (Wrexham)	.	.	D. of Wds.	
2536	Gdsn.	Beer, J. R. (Cardiff)	.	.		
2325	,,	Belch, E. (Hengoed)	.	.	K. in A.	
2275	Musn.	Belding, T. (London)	.	.		
2465	Gdsn.	Bell, L. P. (Cardiff)	.	.		
306	,,	Bellison, B. (Stoke-on-Trent)		.		
4303	,,	Bellwood, O. (Normanton)	.	.	†	
3821	,,	Belton, A. P. (Brighton)	.	.		
2272	,,	Bendall, G. W. (Swansea)	.	.	†	
3915	,,	Bender, W. (London, S.E.)	.	.	†	
101	,,	Bendon, W. (Cardiff)	.	.		
2996	,,	Benham, J. (Swansea)	.	.	†	
1247	,,	Benjamin, T. (Abernant)	.	.	†	
1287	,,	Bennett, W. (Aberdare)	.	.	†	
1600	,,	Bennett, W. C. (Cardiff)	.	.		
2812	,,	Bennett, A. (Huddersfield)	.	.		
2886	,,	Bennett, T. (Neston)	.	.	†	
3188	,,	Bennett, B. A. (Clacton)	.	.	K. in A.	
4057	,,	Bennett, F. (Redditch)	.	.	†	
4846	,,	Bennett, W. J. (Llanmorlais)	.	.		
534	Cpl.	Bentley, T. (Ashbourne)	.	.	D. of Wds.	
2262	Gdsn.	Bernard, J. (Gnosall)	.	.	D. of Wds.	
4307	,,	Berry, M. (Little Lever)	.	.	† †	
4524	,,	Berry, H. (Hull)	.	.		
890	L/Cpl.	Beswick, J. (Bargoed)	.	.	†	
3819	Gdsn.	Betsworth, H. F. (Eastbourne)	.	.		
4591	,,	Bettley, H. (Newport)	.	.		
4143	,,	Betts, A. G. (Abertillery)	.	.	†	
303	C.Q.M.S.	Bevan, D. J. (Burry Port)	.	.		
3360	Gdsn.	Bevan, H. W. (Bristol)	.	.	†	
3854	,,	Bevan, T. (Syston)	.	.		
4680	,,	Bevan, H. A. (Cardiff)	.	.		
3329	,,	Bevins, F. (Ulverston)	.	.	†	
676	,,	Bevis, E. J. (Caerphilly)	.	.	†	
2931	,,	Beynon, J. (Merthyr)	.	.	† †	
4756	,,	Beynon, W. F. (Llantwit)	.	.		
2359	,,	Bibey, B. (Blaenavon)	.	.	K. in A.	
4428	,,	Bickley, A. R. (Worcester)	.	.		
638	,,	Biffen, H. (Bargoed)	.	.	† †	
639	,,	Biffen, F. (Bargoed)	.	.	†	
833		Biggs, J. (Aberdare)	.	.	† † †	

Regtl. No.	Rank.	Name.	Casualties.	Decorations.
4436	Gdsn.	Bilby, R. B. (London)		
3770	,,	Billingham, F. (Birmingham)	K. in A.	
243	L/Sergt.	Birch, J. R. (Swansea)	K. in A.	
1055	L/Cpl.	Birch, H.(Bewdley)		
4250	Sergt.-Drm.	Birch, C. E. (Windsor)		
1069	Gdsn.	Bird, A. (Birkenhead)	†	
1516	,,	Bird, G. (Llanfoist)	K. in A.	
2079	,,	Bird, H. (Cardiff)		
2443	,,	Bird, A. (Cardiff)	†	
2071	,,	Bishop, E. (Pontnewynydd)	D. of Wds.	
2654	,,	Bishop, E. H. (Cardiff)	†	
2669	,,	Bithell, W. (Denbigh)	† †	
2279	,,	Black, W. J. (Sittingbourne)	† †	
3038	,,	Blacklidge, S. (Darwen)	K. in A.	
580	,,	Blackmore, W. (Cardiff)	D. of Wds.	
5262	,,	Blackwell, J. (Cardiff)		
1666	,,	Blain, A. J. (Llanelly)	†	
509	Cpl.	Blake, N. T. (Newport)	†	
3509	Gdsn.	Blake, C. T. (Trealaw)	K. in A.	
1060	,,	Blakeley, T. T. (Eccles)	† K. in A.	
4124	,,	Blanchard, A. (Bath)		
2	R.S.M.	Bland, W. (Church Stretton)		M.C., Med. Mil., Croix-de-Guerre (Fr.).
1093	Gdsn..	Bland, S (Oswestry)	†	
4148	,,	Blatcher, F. E. (Crayford)		
3299	,,	Bleasdale, J. W. (Padiham)	†	
2500	,,	Blewett, G. C. (Pembrey)	†	
1278	,,	Blick, V. (Neath)		
4110	,,	Bloss, Z. (Badingham)		
1470	,,	Bodden, D. (Corwen)	† †	
2060	,,	Bodman, G. W. H. (Whitland)	K. in A.	
761	Sergt.	Bonar, C. A. (Cardiff)		M.M.
472	Gdsn.	Bond, F. (Cirencester)	†	
4264	,,	Bootes, A. (Tonbridge)		
338	Cpl.	Booth, J. (Pontymister)	K. in A.	
1574	Gdsn.	Booth, R. (Castleford)	† †	
1575	,,	Booth, R. (Wakefield)		
3405	,,	Booth, J. J. (Liverpool)	†	
1146	,,	Bosanquet, R. E. (Cardiff)		
3616	,,	Boswell, W. T. (Cardiff)	K. in A.	
4586	,,	Boswell, E. D. (Merthyr)		
280	,,	Bottcher, W. (St. Mary's)	† †	M.M.
2892	,,	Boulton, T. (Wigan)	†	
3801	,,	Boulton, M. W. (Birmingham)	K. in A.	
4823	,,	Bound, D. A. (Aberdare)		
1982	,,	Bourne, H. (Tenby)	K. in A.	
3448	,,	Bowcock, T. (Warrington)	K. in A.	
796	L/Cpl.	Bowden, A. H. (Newport)	K. in A.	
605	Gdsn.	Bowdler, A. (Pontypridd)		
5334	,,	Bowdler, D. R. (Cardiff)		
271	,,	Bowen, W. A. (Porth)	† D. of Wds.	

Regtl. No.	Rank.	Name.	Casualties.	Decorations.
404	L/Sergt.	Bowen, D. (Swansea)	D. of Wds.	
1162	Gdsn.	Bowen, F. T. (Aberystwyth)		
1788	Cpl.	Bowen, H. C. (Brynmawr)	†	
2483	Gdsn.	Bowen, J. T. (Kilgerran)	†	
3323	„	Bowen, W. T. (Cardiff)	K. in A.	
5798	„	Bowen, W. J. (Swansea)		
3531	L/Cpl.	Bowers, P. (Southsea)	†	
403	Sergt.	Bowles, C. O. (Haverfordwest)		M.M.
3445	Gdsn.	Bowley, P. T. (Andover)	†	
1053	„	Bown, S. (Carlton)	D. of Wds.	
2159	„	Bowyer, E. F. (Oswestry)		
5525	„	Boyatt, T. E. (Tenby)		
4740	„	Boyce, C. G. (Bridgwater)	†	
4897	„	Boyce, C. F. (Abertillery)		
4898	„	Boyce, W. (Newport)		
2478	„	Boyle, E. (Pontypridd)		M.M.
2750	„	Boyle, G. W. (London, S.E.)	K. in A.	
1602	„	Brabyn, S. J. (Cardiff)	†	
4305	„	Brackpool, S. J. (Gillingham)	†	
3619	L/Cpl.	Bradley, G. (Cardiff)		
4616	Gdsn.	Bradley, A. E. (Rogerstone)		
2632	Musn.	Brain, A. H. (London)		
3143	Gdsn.	Braithwaite, J. G. (Liverpool)	†	
528	„	Brake, J. (Cross Keys)	†	
4308	„	Bramley, J. (Alfreton)		
90	Pnr. Sergt.	Branch, C. (Cardiff)		
2039	Gdsn.	Branch, T. (Blaenrhondda)		
4306	„	Branstone, F. E. (Coventry)		
3290	„	Brant, R. J. (Bracknell)		
4028	„	Bratton, C. C. (Welshpool)	†	
799	„	Brazell, G. L. (Swansea)	† D. of Wds.	
3847	„	Brealey, A. C. G. (Luton)	†	
4175	„	Bree, H. (Leicester)	†	
2396	„	Breeze, J. T. (Ruabon)	† †	
3353	„	Brewer, G. H. (Bristol)	K. in A.	
3963	„	Brewer, A. (Wealdstone)	†	
308	„	Briant, W. (Chichester)	†	
2795	„	Bridge, W. (Warrington)	K. in A.	
2839	L/Sergt.	Bridge, J. (St. Helen's)	†	
4310	Gdsn.	Bridgeman, L. (Walford)	†	
256	„	Bridges, W. R. (Treharris)	K. in A.	
3278	L/Cpl.	Bridges, A. (Windsor)	†	
56	Gdsn.	Bright, P. (Abergavenny)	†	
4424	„	Brint, L. (Gloucester)		
958	„	Britten, A. (Llanelly)	†	
171	„	Britton, D. (Swansea)	†	
3981	„	Broad, A. L. (Gravesend)		
4053	„	Brocklehurst, H. (Appleton)	K. in A.	
2104	Musn.	Brook, F. (London)		
2636	Gdsn.	Brookman, T. (Cardiff)	†	
3778	„	Brooks, L. (Oxford)	†	

Regtl. No.	Rank.	Name.	Casualties.	Decorations.
4304	Gdsn.	Brooks, S. (Bolton) . . .		
1869	Cpl.	Broom, J. (Barry) . . .	K. in A.	M.M.
2294	Gdsn.	Broome, A. (Airdrie) . . .	† †	
2295	,,	Broome, T. (Welshpool) . .	†	
891	Sergt.	Brothers, C. H. (Bridgend) . .		
285	Gdsn.	Brown, A. (Cardiff) . . .	†	
595	,,	Brown, F. W. (Cardiff) . .	† †	
1342	,,	Brown, E. S. (Cardiff) . .	† †	
1661	,,	Brown, W. (Cardiff) . . .	D. of Wds.	
2220	,,	Brown, D. (Neath) . . .	†	M.M.
2946	,,	Brown, J. W. (London, S.E.) .	D. of Wds.	
3541	,,	Brown. R. E. (Bristol) . .		
3774	,,	Brown, F. C. (Bournemouth) .	K. in A.	
3884	,,	Brown, G. H. (Ashton Keynes) .	† †	
3891	,,	Brown, J. E. (Mold) . . .	†	
4282	,,	Brown, S. D. (Caerphilly) . .		
4684	,,	Brown, L. (Mynyddislwyn) . .		
1772	L/Sergt.	Brumwell, T. L. (Llansantffraid)		
1372	Gdsn.	Bryan, A. A. (Cardiff) . .		
3789	,,	Bryan, J. (Birmingham) . .	K. in A	
940	,,	Bryant, H. (Bridgend) . .		
1460	,,	Bryant, T. G. (Cardiff) . .		
1789	L/Sergt.	Bryant, H. (Cardiff) . .	†	
95	L/Cpl.	Buck, P. (Penarth) . . .	† K. in A.	
2514	Gdsn.	Buckfield, S. (London) . .	K. in A.	
1810	L/Sergt.	Buckland, J. C. (Ruthin) . .	†	
2153	Gdsn.	Budd, G. (Cardiff) . . .		
2938	,,	Budworth, S. (London, W.) .	†	
3221	,,	Bugler, F. (Witchampton) . .	†	
1080	,,	Bull, S. S. (Derby) . . .	†	
4847	,,	Bullock, W. (Cardiff) . .		
129	,,	Bunce, H. C. (Kidderminster) .	† †	
4574	,,	Bundy, D. (Caerphilly) . .		
1611	,,	Bunkham, H. (Cardiff) . .	K. in A.	
2307	,,	Burch, H. (Newport) . . .		
2196	Musn.	Burditt, F. (Kettering) . .		
1509	Gdsn.	Burfitt, T. A. (Cardiff) . .	†	
913	,,	Burford, T. H. (Aberdare) . .	†	
164	,,	Burge, J. (Bristol) . . .		
425	L/Sergt.	Burge, C. (Cardiff) . . .	† †	
1029	,,	Burke, J. (Tyldesley) . .	† †	
2984	Gdsn.	Burke, C. (Newport) . . .	† D. of Wds.	
1136	,,	Burleigh, G. H. (Belbroughton) .	†	
882	L/Sergt.	Burman, G. W. (Cardiff) . .	† †	M.M.
2484	Cpl.	Burman, W. (Swanea) . .	†	
849	Gdsn.	Burridge, J. (Ogmore Vale) .	D. of Wds.	
230	,,	Burrows, J. (Golborne) . .	† K. in A.	
255	L/Cpl.	Burrows, L. (Brecon) . .	†	
2200	Gdsn.	Burt, V. C. (Cardiff) . .	† † †	M.M.
589	,,	Burton, W. C. (Barry) . .	† †	M.M.
4302	,,	Burton, C. (Wakefield) . .	†	

Regtl. No.	Rank.	Name.	Casualties.	Decorations.
478	L/Cpl.	Bush, J. (Cardiff)	†	
2339	Cpl.	Bush, J. R. (London, N.E.) . .		
2819	Gdsn.	Bush, I. (Port Talbot) . . .	† K. in A.	
2226	L/Sergt.	Bushell, S. C. (Barry) . . .		
1288	Gdsn.	Butchers, G. (Whitebrook) . . .	K. in A.	
1048	,,	Butler, A. G. (London) . . .	K. in A.	
2553	,,	Butler, J. H. (Tredegar) . . .	†	
2558	,,	Butler, D. A. (Pengam) . . .	K. in A.	
3752	,,	Butler, F. A. (Wolverhampton) . .	†	
1690	,,	Butt, C. W. (Churchdown) . . .	K. in A.	
2653	,,	Butters, W. (London, N.W.) . .	† † †	
3089	,,	Butterworth, F. (Eagley) . . .		
3138	,,	Butterworth, H. (London, W.) . .		
3518	,,	Button, J. (Llanelly)		
3935	,,	Button, F. (Newton)	†	
4841	,,	Bwye, A. (Barry)		
939	Sergt.	Bye, R. (Llanwonno)		V.C.
3452	Gdsn.	Bye, L. (Cheltenham) . . .		
3423	,,	Byles, T. (London, N.E.) . . .	†	
133	,,	Byng, E. (Swansea)		
4023	Gdsn.	Caffrey, T. E. (Blackburn) . .		
3831	,,	Caines, C. J. (Lewes) . . .	†	
1527	,,	Calcutt, T. W. (Hayward's Heath)	K. in A.	
476	,,	Caldwell, J. (Haslingden) . . .	K. in A.	
2856	L/Sergt.	Caldwell, J. (St. Helen's) . .	† †	
42	Sergt.	Callaghan, T. (Cwmcarn) . . .	K. in A.	
3749	Gdsn.	Campbell, H. L. (Chailey) . . .	†	
4000	,,	Cannock, F. (Caerphilly) . . .	K. in A.	
3068	,,	Cannon, T. (Rawtenstall) . . .	†	
4202	,,	Cannon, R. H. (London, S.E.) . .	†	
791	,,	Cantwell, F. J. (Aberdare) . . .		
3539	,,	Capson, W. (Bristol)	†	
3788	,,	Cardwell, T. W. (Stonehouse) . .	†	
3087	,,	Carlisle, F. (Talysarn) . . .	K. in A.	
3895	,,	Carlisle, E. (Bolton)		
3753	,,	Carmouche, V. J. (Leeds) . . .		
947	,,	Carpenter, W. E. (Mountain Ash) .		
2948	L/Cpl.	Carroll, C. M. (London, S.E.) . .	†	
3760	Gdsn.	Carron, S. (Liverpool) . . .		
663	Sergt.	Carter, N. (Bangor)	† K. in A.	
1023	Gdsn.	Carter, J. L. (Tetbury) . . .	K. in A.	
1214	,,	Carter, W. H. (Bridgend) . . .	D. of Wds.	
2577	,,	Carter, C. (Maidstone) . . .	K. in A.	
3286	,,	Carter, W. (Andover)	†	
4164	,,	Carter, J. W. (Leigh)	K. in A.	
4311	,,	Carter, A. J. (Cambridge) . . .	†	
4312	,,	Carter, F. (Wootton)	†	
4313	,,	Carter, S. (Cambridge) . . .	†	
2807	,,	Cartwright, J. (Warrington) . .	K. in A.	
1497	L/Cpl.	Carver, J. (Brecon)		

Regtl. No.	Rank.	Name.	Casualties.	Decorations.
3849	Gdsn.	Cash, A. H. (Doncaster)		
1047	,,	Cashell, H. M. (Pontymister)	†	
3796	,,	Cass, F. (Birmingham)		
2976	L/Cpl.	Catchpole, A. H. (Penarth)	†	
2061	Gdsn.	Cavill, H. J. (Cardiff)	†	
2964	,,	Chadwick, M. H. (Bradford)		
757	,,	Chamberlain, E. (Rhondda)		
2770	,,	Chamberlain, J. E. (Middlewich)	D. of Wds.	
2337	,,	Chandler, C. E. (London)	K. in A.	
2342	,,	Chapman, J. (London)		
3829	,,	Chapman, F. C. (Brighton)		
4001	,,	Chapman, F. H. (Smarden)	†	
2527	,,	Charles, B. J. (Cardiff)	†	
3282	,,	Charlton, J. (Durham)	†	
2479	,,	Charman, W. (London, S.W.)	†	
3275	,,	Charnley, R. F. (Clitheroe)		M.M.
3092	,,	Chave, A. (Tiverton)	† †	
1863	L/Sergt.	Cheal, J. (Cardiff)	† † †	
1864	Gdsn.	Cheal, A. H. (Cardiff)	†	
3010	,,	Chester, H. (Pontypridd)	†	
2034	,,	Cheverton, C. E. (Llanybyther)	K. in A.	
2434	,,	Chilcott, J. (Port Talbot)		
1790	Cpl.	Chilton, S. (Brynmawr)	† †	
465	Gdsn.	Chirgwin, H. (Cardiff)	†	
2429	,,	Chivers, T. J. (Abertillery)	†	
3000	,,	Chivers, F. B. (Porth)		
3726	,,	Chivers, J. F. B. (Portsmouth)	† †	
4736	,,	Chivers, T. J. (Cymmer)		
4761	,,	Chivers, E. G. (Tonyrefail)		
3720	,,	Christiansen, G. B. (Liverpool)		
4314	,,	Christmas, J. N. (Hove)	†	
630	,,	Chubb, T. (Tonypandy)		
4013	,,	Chuck, F. (London, S.W.)	†	
13	C.S.M.	Church, W. J. (Cardiff)		
1831	Gdsn.	Church, F. W. (Llandinan)		
4010	,,	Churches, T. (Cardiff)	K. in A.	
196	Sergt.	Churm, S. (Bilston)	† † †	
357	L/Cpl.	Clack, A. (Witney)	† K. in A.	
2763	Gdsn.	Clancey, D. T. (Sully)	†	M.M. and Bar.
4478	,,	Clapp, J. T. (Merthyr)		
1759	,,	Clare, F. H. (Llangollen)		
3362	,,	Clark, W. (Oldbury)		
3692	,,	Clark, F. W. (Bradford-on-Avon)		
4007	,,	Clark, W. A. G. (Gloucester)	†	
474	,,	Clarke, J. (Walsall)		
598	,,	Clarke, A. E. (Barry Dock)	K. in A.	
1092	A/C.Q.M.S.	Clarke, W. J. (London, N.)	†	
1231	Gdsn.	Clarke, F. (Newport)	K. in A.	
1232	,,	Clarke, A. (Newport)		
1353	,,	Clarke, J. (Penarth)		
1823	,,	Clarke, T. H. (Tonypandy)		

Regtl. No.	Rank.	Name.	Casualties.	Decorations.
3173	Gdsn.	Clarke, H. F. (Colchester) . . .	†	
3289	,,	Clarke, W. (Didcot)		
3964	,,	Clarke, A. (Harrow)	† †	
4484	,,	Clarke, F. (Cardiff)		
5666	,,	Clarke, E. (Llanelly)		
3039	,,	Claxton, G. (Rawtenstall) . . .	†	
3426	,,	Clayton, E. F. (Basingstoke) . .		
1842	,,	Clee, W. E. (Ystalyfera) . . .	† K. in A.	
3685	,,	Clegg, J. (Burnley)	† †	
2281	Dmr.	Clement, A. W. (Swansea) . . .	†	
2298	L/Sergt.	Clement, H. W. (Cardiff) . . .	†	
1039	Gdsn.	Clements, W. F. (Bristol) . . .	K. in A.	
118	,,	Clifford, R. (Cardiff)		
1001	L/Cpl.	Clifford, J. W. (Middlesborough) . .	†	
4315	,,	Clifton, T. (Loughborough) . . .	†	
3643	,,	Clothier, A. C. (Cardiff) . . .		
3913	,,	Cloughton, C. (Fairstead) . . .	D. of Wds.	
2074	,,	Clucas, T. (Cardiff)		
3960	,,	Coad, W. E. (London, S.E.) . .		
75	Sergt.	Coates, S. A. (Newport) . . .	†	
4732	Gdsn.	Cobley, S. (Caerphilly) . . .		
3537	,,	Cockbaine, H. W. (Bristol) . .		
2995	,,	Cockerill, W. J. (York) . . .		
4763	,,	Cockram, G. T. (Aberaman) . .		
2968	,,	Cohen, J. (Cardiff)	†	
4848	,,	Colcombe, W. (Treharris) . . .		
3317	,,	Coldrick, C. (Colne)	K. in A.	
633	,,	Cole, G. (Pembroke)	†	
4274	,,	Cole, W. T. (Ferndale) . . .		
1202	,,	Coleman, I. (Aberavon) . . .		
78	Dmr.	Coles, T. H. (Newport) . . .		
1981	Gdsn.	Coles, F. (Bargoed) . . .		
2619	,,	Coles, C. J. (Newport) . . .	D. of Wds.	
1036	Dmr.	Coley, L. (Halesowen) . . .		
2780	Gdsn.	Collett, H. A. (Newport) . . .	K. in A.	
2093	,,	Collier, W. (Rhondda) . . .	†	
2557	,,	Collier, C. (London), E. . . .	†	
1034	,,	Collins, G. (Cheltenham) . . .		
2873	,,	Collins, W. J. J. (Swansea) . .		
3779	,,	Collins, W. (Penarth) . . .		
4288	,,	Collins, J. F. (Windsor) . . .		
4645	,,	Collins, G. S. (Porth) . . .		
3904	,,	Colton, W. H. (Liverpool) . . .	D. of Wds.	
879	,,	Comley, E. (Aberdare) . . .	†	
672	,,	Congdon, D. A. (Dunbar) . . .	†	
1014	,,	Connick, A. (Swansea) . . .		
4538	,,	Connolly, J. (Cardiff) . . .		
2699	,,	Conway, J. (Cardiff) . . .		
2959	,,	Conwil, G. H. (Sheffield) . . .		
1314	,,	Cook, R. A. (Neath)	†	
1995	,,	Cook, W. S. (Cardiff)	†	

Regtl. No.	Rank.	Name.	Casualties.	Decorations.
2146	Gdsn.	Cook, I. A. (Newport)	† †	
2988	,,	Cook, E. G. (London, S.E.)	K. in A.	
3961	,,	Cook, T. (Blyth)	K. in A.	
4316	L/Cpl.	Cook, A. E. (London, S.E.)		
700	Gdsn.	Cooke, F. H. (Swansea)	† K. in A.	
3009	,,	Cooke, F. G. (Farnham)	†	
4622	,,	Cooke, A. (Llantrisant)		
1258	,,	Cooksley, G. A. (Cardiff)	† †	
3361	,,	Cookson, J. (Crosby)		
2015	,,	Coombes, H. G. (Newport)	K. in A.	
2804	,,	Coombes, W. (London)	† †	
341	,,	Cooper, J. T. (Ellesmere Port)	†	
563	,,	Cooper, S. (London)		
2775	O.R.C.S.	Cooper, A. (Chertsey)		
4123	Gdsn.	Cooper, A. (Newcastle-on-Tyne)	D. of Wds.	
3326	,,	Cootes, S. J. (Brecon)		
2756	,,	Copley, W. T. (Tumble)		
4607	,,	Copp, W. (Mardy)		
2205	,,	Corbett, S. (Wrexham)	K. in A.	
3086	,,	Corbett, G. O. (Cardiff)	K. in A.	
560	,,	Corcoran, J. (Aberaman)	†	
4168	,,	Cordes, B. (Gateshead)	†	
3315	,,	Cornell, T. J. (Swansea)		
2390	,,	Cornish, F. H. (Pembroke)		
4016	,,	Cornelius, J. H. (London, S.E.)	† †	M.M.
324	Sergt.	Cory, C. H. (Newport)	† †	
1010	L/Cpl.	Cosford, F. E. H. (London, S.E.)		M.M. and Bar.
3564	Gdsn.	Cosh, C. (Cardiff)	K. in A.	
16	C.S.M.	Cossey, D. J. (Skewen)	† †	
3305	Gdsn.	Costello, J. (Bacup)		
479	Sergt.	Couch, D. (Merthyr)		
4605	Gdsn.	Couch, A. C. (Cardiff)		
3889	,,	Couldwell, A. W. (Cardiff)		
4041	,,	Coulson, C. (Goole)	D. of Wds.	
3478	,,	Cound, F. (Worcester)	K. in A.	
281	,,	Counsell, C. (Whitchurch)	†	
2555	Musn.	Coverley, W. (Penmaenmawr)		
1667	Gdsn.	Cowley, D. (Swansea)		
3934	,,	Cowley, A. H. (Wrexham)	†	
2188	,,	Cowlishaw, J. (Malvern)		
84	Sergt.	Cox, J. R. H. (Cardiff)		
504	Gdsn.	Cox, W. H. (Cardiff)		
869	,,	Cox, D. (Ystalyfera)	K. in A.	
3743	,,	Cox. W. M. (Brighton)	†	
3970	L/Cpl.	Cox, W. (Hoo)		
4002	,,	Cox, J. (Longnor)		
5785	Gdsn.	Cox, L. (Cwmcarn)		
1358	C.S.M.	Coyne, T. (Glasgow)		M.S.M.
585	Gdsn.	Crabtree, R. A. (Cardiff)		
516	,,	Craddock, J. (Newport)	K. in A.	
2433	Musn.	Craig, D. J. (Edinburgh)		

27

Regtl. No.	Rank.	Name.	Casualties.	Decorations.
2502	Gdsn.	Craig, W. (Fochriw)	† D. of Wds.	
3281	„	Cram, G. (Jarrow)		
223	„	Cramp, J. J. (Aberavon)	†	
576	„	Craven, W. (Llandudno)	†	
1255	„	Crawford, W. (Wrexham)		
4299	A/Sergt.	Crawshaw, A. T. (London, N.W.)		
1883	Gdsn.	Cray, W. (Llanelly)		
1532	„	Creasey, A. W. (Cardiff)		
4153	„	Crebbin, J. H. (Liverpool)	K. in A.	M.M.
1076	„	Criddle, G. A. (Cardiff)	†	
3883	„	Criddle, P. (Liverpool)	†	
2482	„	Crompton, J. H. (Swansea)	†	
3256	„	Crook, A. G. (Chepstow)	†	
3834	„	Crook, R. (Abertillery)	D. of Wds.	
2794	„	Crooks, J. W. (Bramhall)		
149	Sergt.	Cross, C. H. (Bristol)	†	
428	Gdsn.	Cross, W. J. (Cardiff)	K. in A.	
3450	„	Cross, S. (Warrington)	†	
3277	„	Crossley, J. (Preston)	K. in A.	
1324	Sergt.	Crowley, W. (Cardiff)	†	
247	Gdsn.	Crumb, W. (Aberdare)		
648	Cpl.	Crumb, J. T. (Aberdare)	D. of Wds.	M.M.
2152	Gdsn.	Culley, G. H. (Cardiff)	†	
481	„	Cullis, W. (Gloucester)	K. in A.	
3738	„	Culshaw, H. (Liverpool)	K. in A.	
4186	„	Culver, W. G. (Ramsgate)		
3154	„	Cumberledge, J. (Stanley)		
1938	Cpl.	Cummings, J. H. (Merthyr)	† †	M.M.
3071	Gdsn.	Cunliffe, A. (Nelson)		
795	„	Curds, E. J. (Swansea)	†	
1137	„	Curtis, F. (Trealaw)		
1606	„	Curtis, F. H. (Neath)		
2045	„	Curtis, R. W. (Ruthin)	†	
3367	„	Curtis, F. (Maidstone)	K. in A.	
3457	„	Curtis, T. (Dursley)		
77	L/Sergt.	Cutler, F. J. (Pontllanfraith)	† †	
3699	Gdsn.	Dadding, W. J. (Stourbridge)	†	
3628	„	Dale, F. W. (Birmingham)		
2926	„	Dalton, C. W. (Cardiff)	† †	
2660	„	Dane, S. (Caerphilly)	†	
287	L/Cpl.	Daniel, A. R. (Oystermouth)	K. in A.	
1608	Gdsn.	Daniel, D. J. (Llanelly)		
1933	„	Daniel, T. B. (Nantgaredig)	K. in A.	
1066	„	Daniels, J. (Tunstall)	†	
1573	„	Daniels, T. A. (Cardiff)	† †	M.M.
3546	„	Dare, W. (Cardiff)		
4811	„	Davage, G. (Cross Keys)		
1057	„	Davenport, J. (Thornton)	† †	
4855	„	Davey, W. E. (Newport)		
2531	„	David, R. (Cardiff)	†	

Regtl. No.	Rank.	Name.	Casualties.	Decorations.
2645	Gdsn.	David, C. M. (Whitland)	† †	
4370	,,	David, W. J. (Cowbridge)		
970	,,	Davidge, H. E. (Blandford)	D. of Wds.	
1957	L/Cpl.	Davidson, J. W. (Pembroke)	†	
2358	Gdsn.	Davidson, J. H. (Newbiggin)		
3148	,,	Davidson, J. H. (Blackburn)		
5721	,,	Davidson, B. (Colchester)		
22	Sergt.	Davies, G. (Swansea)	† K. in A.	
37	,,	Davies, T. H. (Chalford)	†	
64	,, ·	Davies, I. (Flint)	† † †	
106	Gdsn.	Davies, R. (London)		
108	,,	Davies, I. (Ammanford)	†	
169	,,	Davies, W. (Neath)	† †	
185	,,	Davies, T. (Llanelly)	D. of Wds.	
216	,,	Davies, R. (Llanelly)		M.M.
240	,,	Davies, C. (Merthyr)	†	
245	L/Cpl.	Davies, R. H. (Caldicott)		
258	Gdsn.	Davies, S. (Neath)		
307	,,	Davies, A. A. (Merthyr)	†	
348	,,	Davies, G. (London)	†	
349	,,	Davies, T. (Newport)	†	
356	,,	Davies, A. D. (Haverfordwest)		
386	L/Cpl.	Davies, R. H. (Derby)	†	
394	Gdsn.	Davies, W. (Leigh)	†	
408	Sergt.	Davies, S. E. (Stockport)	†	D.C.M.
421	Gdsn.	Davies, G. (Hanley)	†	
426	L/Cpl.	Davies, H. C. (Llandaff)	D. of Wds.	
521	Gdsn.	Davies, F. (Castleford)	† †	
537	,,	Davies, D. H. (Porthcawl)	K. in A.	
564	,,	Davies, J. D. (Pontypridd)	†	
627	Dmr.	Davies, J. C. (Landore)		
658	Gdsn.	Davies, G. A. (Llanelly)	K. in A.	
759	,,	Davies, J. (Ferndale)	†	
760	,,	Davies, H. (Hull)	†	
779	,,	Davies, J. E. (Ammanford)		
784	Sergt.	Davies, J. (Oswestry)	†	
811	Gdsn.	Davies, R. (Anglesey)	†	
815	L/Sergt.	Davies, J. E. (Gwersyllt)		
835	Gdsn.	Davies, W. J. (Dowlais)	K. in A.	
836	Sergt.	Davies, T. (Blaenrhondda)		
841	Gdsn.	Davies, J. (Aberdare)		
843	L/Cpl.	Davies, S. (Rhondda)		
895	Gdsn.	Davies, E. (Pontypridd)	† †	
904	,,	Davies, E. (Gelli)	†	
949	,,	Davies, J. W. (Cardiff)	†	
983	,,	Davies, R. R. (Llanelly)	†	
989	,,	Davies, W. J. (Swansea)	†	
1142	,,	Davies, J. E. (Aberangell)	†	
1149	,,	Davies, T. J. (Llanelly)	K. in A.	
1169	,,	Davies, T. J. (Barry)		
1199	,,	Davies, B. (Merthyr)	D. of Wds.	

Regtl. No.	Rank.	Name.	Casualties.	Decorations.
1286	Gdsn.	Davies, R. (Aberdare) . . .		
1315	,,	Davies, T. (Aberystwyth) . . .	†	
1328	,,	Davies, A. (Pontypridd) . .		
1393	,,	Davies, E. (Swansea) . . .	† †	
1436	,,	Davies, D. W. (Mountain Ash) . .	†	
1438	L/Cpl.	Davies, W. (Bargoed) . .		
1446	Gdsn.	Davies, T. (Llandyssul) . .	D. of Wds.	
1448	,,	Davies, D. V. (Cardiff) . .	† †	
1487	,,	Davies, D. O. (Bettws-y-coed) . .	† †	
1599	,,	Davies, D. T. (Cwmdu) . .	†	
1614	,,	Davies, T. (Tenby) . . .		
1628	L/Cpl.	Davies, J. (Llandilo) . .	K. in A.	
1645	Gdsn.	Davies, J. (Ammanford) . . .	† †	
1668	,,	Davies, B. (Newport) . . .	K. in A.	
1683	L/Cpl.	Davies, F. J. W. (Cardiff) . .		
1694	Gdsn.	Davies, W. N. (Tonyrefail) . .	D. of Wds.	
1696	,,	Davies, J. (Tonyrefail) . .		
1703	L/Cpl.	Davies, E. J. (Aberystwyth) . .	†	
1747	L/Cpl.	Davies, G. (Swansea) . . .	†	
1753	Gdsn.	Davies, E. H. (Carmarthen) . .	D. of Wds.	
1776	,,	Davies, G. M. (Abergavenny) . .	†	
1844	,,	Davies, E. (Llansamlet) . .	†	
1892	,,	Davies, A. P. (Aberystwyth) . .		
1905	,,	Davies, C. C. (Shrewsbury) . .		
1989	,,	Davies, G. F. (Mountain Ash) . .		
1997	,,	Davies, O. (Carmarthen) . .	†	
2007	,,	Davies, S. C. (Llandilo) . .		
2024	,,	Davies, E. W. (Coedfranc) . .		
2028	,,	Davies, A. (Lydbury North) . .	K. in A.	
2042	,,	Davies, T. (Pontyberem) . .	D. of Wds.	
2043	L/Cpl.	Davies, T. M. (Lampeter) . . .	†	
2073	Gdsn.	Davies, E. D. (Tredegar) . .	† D. of Wds.	
2085	,,	Davies, W. J. (Skewen) . .		
2087	,,	Davies, R. W. (Cwmavon) . .		
2157	,,	Davies, D. C. (Pentre) . .		
2169	,,	Davies, E. S. (Denbigh) . .	† † † †	M.M.
2349	,,	Davies, H. F. (Llanymynech) . .	†	
2392	,,	Davies, E. (Abercarn) . .		
2402	,,	Davies, W. T. (Llangollen) . .	K. in A.	
2417	,,	Davies, H. (Crickhowell) . .	†	
2431	,,	Davies, H. G. (Presteigne) . .	†	
2439	L/Cpl.	Davies, D. J. (Abergwili) . .		
2489	Gdsn.	Davies, B. (Morriston) . .	K. in A.	
2564	,,	Davies, W. G. (Holywell) . .	K. in A.	
2571	,,	Davies, E. T. (Bodfari) . .		
2585	L/Cpl.	Davies, G. (Clarbeston) . .	†	
2587	Gdsn.	Davies, A. (Rhyl) . . .	†	
2611	,,	Davies, W. J. (Morriston) . .	† K. in A.	
2624	,,	Davies, W. (Cardiff) . . .	K. in A.	
2641	,,	Davies, J. (Boneath) . .		
2650	,,	Davies, S. F. (Oswestry) . .	† †	

Regtl. No.	Rank.	Name.	Casualties.	Decorations.
2657	Gdsn.	Davies, W. G. (Bridell) . . .	† †	
2691	,,	Davies, J. R. (Swansea) . .		
2737	L/Cpl.	Davies, D. (Llangunnock) . .		
2813	Gdsn.	Davies, F. J. (Oswestry) . .		
2837	,,	Davies, T. (Llanelly) . . .		
2866	L/Cpl.	Davies, A. (Flint) . . .		
2885	Gdsn.	Davies, C. (Wrexham) . .	†	M.M.
2888	,,	Davies, F. V. (Shrewsbury) .	†	
2916	,,	Davies, W. (Begelly) . . .	K. in A.	
2955	,,	Davies, D. (Cardiff) . .	D. of Wds.	
2957	,,	Davies, S. (Tranmere) . .		
3003	,,	Davies, D. H. (Talyllyn) . .		
3029	,,	Davies, J. (Wrexham) . .	†	
3030	,,	Davies, J. (Connah's Quay) .	†	
3091	,,	Davies, D. J. (Ferryside) . .	K. in A.	
3151	,,	Davies, D. J. (New Quay) .		
3152	,,	Davies, L. (Llangollen) . .	†	
3223	,,	Davies, W. (Bangor) . . .		
3244	L/Cpl.	Davies, W. (Llanfihangel) . .	D. of Wds.	
3341	Gdsn.	Davies, B. G. (Swansea) . .	†	
3342	,,	Davies, R. F. (Swansea) . .	K. in A.	
3346	,,	Davies, J. C. (Pontypridd) .	K. in A.	
3419	,,	Davies, C. W. (Wrexham) . .	†	
3451	,,	Davies, E. (Rhyl) . . .	†	
3559	,,	Davies, A. (Cardiff) . .	† D. of Wds.	
3589	,,	Davies, T. J. H. (Carmarthen)		
3655	,,	Davies, J. O. (New Quay) .		
3668	,,	Davies, E. T. (Lampeter) . .	†	
3673	L/Cpl.	Davies, T. (Oswestry) . .		
3708	Gdsn.	Davies, J. H. (Llandilo) . .		
3767	,,	Davies, H. (Ludlow) . .		
3835	,,	Davies, L. C. (London, N.) .		
3997	,,	Davies, A. G. (Usk) . .		
4020	,,	Davies, J. T. (Llanwrda) . .	† D. of Wds.	M.M.
4066	,,	Davies, H. W. (Mold) . .		
4072	,,	Davies, D. T. (Ynysbwl) . .	†	
4093	L/Cpl.	Davies, S. (Cardiff) . .		
4095	Gdsn.	Davies, T. (Llanidloes) . .	†	
4096	,,	Davies, D. W. (Talsarn) . .	†	
4107	,,	Davies, R. J. (Llangefni) . .	†	
4283	,,	Davies, J. (Gwnnws) . . .	K. in A.	
4318	,,	Davies, F. (Ellesmere) . .	K. in A.	
4319	,,	Davies, T. A. (Liverpool) . .	†	
4485	,,	Davies, W. A. (Cardiff) . .		
4510	,,	Davies, F. S. (Windsor) . .	†	
4518	,,	Davies, J. J. (Bognor) . .		
4553	,,	Davies, E. (Newport) . .		
4560	,,	Davies, D. R. (Cwmparc) . .		
4588	,,	Davies, W. (Merthyr) . .		
4597	,,	Davies, E. (Neath) . . .		
4634	,,	Davies, J. L. (Cymmer) . .		

Regtl. No.	Rank.	Name.	Casualties.	Decorations.
4637	Gdsn.	Davies, W. (Cardiff) .		
4650	,,	Davies, J. (Carmarthen)		
4662	,,	Davies, H. (Carmarthen)		
4664	,,	Davies, W. O. (Bridgend) .		
4748	,,	Davies, C. (Swansea) .		
4769	,,	Davies, T. M. (Fochriw)		
4772	,,	Davies, W. R. (Aberdare) .		
4810	,,	Davies, T. H. (Merthyr)		
4814	,,	Davies, R. (Aberaman)		
4856	,,	Davies, W. D. (Neath)		
4884	,,	Davies, H. G. (Newport)		
5190	,,	Davies, T. (Merthyr) .		
5322	,,	Davies, H. (Aberdare)		
5808	,,	Davies, J. S. (Cardiff)		
1208	,,	Davis, W. J. (Newport)	†	
1571	L/Cpl.	Davis, J. (Aberystwyth)	†	
1885	L/Sergt.	Davis, J. R. (Cardiff)		
3929	Gdsn.	Davis, E. C. (Drybrook)	†	
3979	,,	Dawes, P. (Newcastle)	K. in A.	
2120	,,	Dawkins, W. G. (Lamphey)	K. in A.	
3334	L/Cpl.	Dawson, A. E. (Northampton)		
4611	Gdsn.	Dawson, W. J. (Newport)		
359	,,	Day, A. (Llanhilleth) .	D. of Wds.	
1423	,,	Day. W. H. (Abertillery)	† D. of S.	
1743	,,	Day, F. (Mountain Ash)		
2831	,,	Day, E. (Ashton-under-Lyne)	†	
2338	,,	Dayer, J. C. (London)	† †	
2195	,,	Dean, E. (Swansea) .	†	
3620	,,	Dean, G. E. (Wrexham)		
863	,,	Deane, C. (Brynmawr)		
3890	,,	Dear, F. (Stotfold) .	† †	
1077	,,	Death, S. J. (London)	†	
4183	,,	Deeming, A. G. (London, S.W.) .	†	
1541	,,	Delaney, M. (Cardiff) .	K. in A.	
1551	,,	Denby, G. V. (Copthorne) .		
257	,,	Denman, A. (Yeovil) .		
1016	,,	Denman, S. A. T. (London, S.W.)		
5531	,,	Dennick, W. (Carmarthen) .		
3688	,,	Denning, G. A. (Cardiff)		
2214	,,	Denny, J. A. (Flint) .		
2266	,,	Dessent, W. (Pontypridd) .	K. in A.	
3473	,,	Dettmar, A. H. (Portsmouth)		
2869	Cpl.	De Wit, W. H. (Swansea) .		
27	Sergt.	Dexter, W. (Peterborough) .	†	
3325	Gdsn.	Dey, H. (Wakefield) .	†	
1401	L/Cpl.	Dickenson, C. H. (Castleford)	†	
1617	Gdsn.	Dickinson, W. H. (Cardiff) .		
131	,,	Dickman, J. H. (Tonypandy)		
1781	,,	Dimelow, A. (Sandycroft) .	†	
3489	,,	Dimery, V. L. (Cardiff)	D. of Wds.	
2513	,,	Dingle, F. C. (Cardiff)	† †	

Regtl. No.	Rank.	Name.	Casualties.	Decorations.
1002	Gdsn.	Dobby, R. (Middlesborough)	† †	
3885	,,	Doble, H. (Ilminster) .	K. in A.	
127	,,	Dobson, A. (Burton-on-Trent)	†	
952	,,	Dobson, E. I. (Cardiff)	†	
4154	,,	Dodge, A. D. (Manchester) .	†	
3181	,,	Dolan, J. W. (Ashton)	†	
615	,,	Donnelly, J. (Neath) .	†	
2678	,,	Donovan, P. (Cardiff)	D. of Wds.	
3251	,,	Domoney. A. (Blandford) .	†	
2723	,,	Dorgan, T. (Merthyr) .	†	
3197	,,	Dowell, J. R. (Rhyl) .	†	
4562	,,	Dowen, J. (Newport) .		
3622	,,	Dowling, A. T. (Cwmtillery)		
1021	,,	Downing, M. (Aberdare)	† †	
3577	,,	Downs, S. (Llangoed)		
3639	,,	Downton, E. W. (Holton) .		
1215	Cpl.	Drake, I. E. (Cardiff) .	† K. in A.	
2606	Gdsn.	Drake, A. J. (Bridgend)	† K. in A.	
3893	,,	Draper, A. H. (Bristol)	K. in A.	
1022	,,	Drew, H. (Clare)		
1230	,,	Driscoll, H. (Cardiff) .	† †	
2801	,,	Driver, H. T. (Shrewsbury)	† †	
3073	,,	Driver, J. (Nelson)	D. of Wds.	
3390	,,	Dryden, J. (Cardiff) .		
2855	,,	Duckworth, E. (St. Helen's)		
36	Sergt.	Duddridge, J. M. (Newport)	† †	
668	Gdsn.	Duffy, J. (Cardiff)	†	D.C.M.
669	,,	Duffy, J. (Neath)	†	
3269	,,	Dugdale, T. (Clitheroe)		
429	,,	Duggan, G. H. (Bargoed) .	† †	
1303	,,	Duggan, T. (Pontyberem) .	† † †	
2212	,,	Duncombe, T. (Cardiff)	†	
1073	,,	Dunford, H. D. (Evercreech)	K. in A.	
351	D/Sergt.	Dunkley, S. J. (Northampton)		
4255	L/Cpl.	Dunkley, D. (London, S.W.)		
484	Gdsn.	Dunn, W. A. (Cilfynydd)		
1163	,,	Dunn, T. W. (Swansea)		
3880	,,	Dunn, T. (Birmingham)	†	
249	L/Cpl.	Du Pree, D. A. (Swansea) .	D. of Wds.	
2194	Gdsn.	Dyer, W. (Airdrie)		
3910	,,	Dyer, M. (Cirencester)		
4659	Gdsn.	Eagles, C. (Newtown)		
1330	,,	East, W. (Bridgend) .	K. in A.	
4140	,,	East, A. (Ripley)		
4155	,,	East, H. J. (Manchester)		
3061	,,	Easthorpe, F. (Liverpool) .	†	
3911	,,	Eatwell, W. B. (Bath)		
3764	,,	Ecclestone, F. (Liverpool) .	K. in A.	
543	,,	Edge, E. (Liverpool) .	K. in A.	
2709	,,	Edney, A. (Cardiff) .	†	

Regtl. No.	Rank.	Name.	Casualties.	Decorations.
1264	L/Cpl.	Edmunds, B. (Cardiff)		
1482	,,	Edmunds, J. (Bridgend)	†	
158	Gdsn.	Edwards, J. (Gower)	†	
288	,,	Edwards, D. L. (Aberdare)		
459	L/Cpl.	Edwards, D. (Aberdare)		
675	Gdsn.	Edwards, J. S. (Ystalyfera)	K. in A.	
781	,,	Edwards, C. (Abercarn)		
801	,,	Edwards, E. J. (Trecynon)	K. in A.	
1106	,,	Edwards, J. H. (Aberystwyth)	†	
1148	,,	Edwards, W. H. (Deri)		
1207	,,	Edwards, T. A. L. (Pembroke Dock)		
1236	,,	Edwards, E. H. (Cwmaman)	† † †	
1356	,,	Edwards, L. (Bedwelty)		
1367	,,	Edwards, R. (Aberavon)	†	
1435	,,	Edwards, J. (Wrexham)	† K. in A.	
1514	,,	Edwards, D. J. (Llanelly)	D. of Wds.	
1618	,,	Edwards, R. H. (Aberystwyth)		
1646	L/Sergt.	Edwards, D. B. (Haverfordwest)	†	
1750	Gdsn.	Edwards, W. (Pembroke)	K. in A.	
1908	,,	Edwards, W. (Blackwood)	†	
1964	,,	Edwards, T. (Bargoed)		
2136	,,	Edwards, J. H. (Welshpool)		
2333	,,	Edwards, L. (Wrexham)	†	M.M.
2400	,,	Edwards, D. (Holywell)	K. in A.	
2510	,,	Edwards, S. (Queensferry)	†	
2818	L/Cpl.	Edwards, W. H. (Swansea)	†	
2863	Gdsn.	Edwards, I. W. (Wrexham)		
2967	Musn.	Edwards, J. (Wigan)		
3002	Gdsn.	Edwards, J. (Swansea)	K. in A.	
3005	,,	Edwards, J. (Dolgelly)	†	
3123	,,	Edwards, D. (Flint)		
3170	,,	Edwards, A. (Pontypool)		
3303	,,	Edwards, A. E. (Abergavenny)	K. in A.	
4050	,,	Edwards, G. B. (St. Asaph)		
4083	,,	Edwards, H. (Dolgelly)		
4321	,,	Edwards, A. (Horsham)	K. in A.	
4322	,,	Edwards, A. H. (Bristol)	†	
4642	,,	Edwards, G. (Merthyr Vale)		
4741	,,	Edwards, S. (Chesterfield)		
4747	,,	Edwards, S. H. (Neath)		
4776	,,	Edwards, A. M. (Bridgend)		
4873	,,	Edwards, G. J. (Cardiff)		
3923	,,	Elder, O. J. (London, S.E.)	†	
3264	,,	Ellicott, F. (Liverpool)	D. of Wds.	
2508	,,	Elliott, S. (Cardiff)		
2618	,,	Elliott, A. D. (Cardiff)	†	
2889	,,	Elliott, J. (Wrexham)	D. of Wds.	
3266	,,	Elliott, R. (Nelson)	†	
4857	,,	Elliott, W. J. (Neath)		
74	,,	Ellis, R. (Dinas)		
906	,,	Ellis, H. (Abergavenny)	K. in A.	

Regtl. No.	Rank.	Name.	Casualties.	Decorations.
1129	Gdsn.	Ellis, E. (Cardiff)	K. in A.	
1991	L/Cpl.	Ellis, E. (Holyhead) . . .	†	
2128	L/Sergt.	Ellis, C. E. (Carnarvon) .		
2066	L/Cpl.	Ellis, R. S. (Aberystwyth) . .	†	
2368	Gdsn.	Ellis, W. H. (Newport) . .	•	
2533	,,	Ellis, J. (Cardiff) . . .	†	M.M.
2850	,,	Ellis, P. H. (London, S.W.) .	•	
3167	,,	Ellis, T. E. (Liverpool) . .	†	
3954	,,	Ellis, R. (Newcastle-on-Tyne) .	K. in A.	
4742	,,	Ellis, J. W. (Nottingham) . .	•	
4804	,,	Ellis, B. C. (Briton Ferry) . .	•	
5825	,,	Ellis, C. (Manchester) . . .	•	
275	L/Cpl.	Emanuel, I. (Kidwelly) . .	K. in A.	
1802	,,	Emanuel, J. (Llanelly) . .	† †	M.M.
1816	Gdsn.	Embleton, T. J. (London) . .	•	
2517	,,	Emblin, W. H. (Neath) . .	•	
1879	,,	Emery, R. L. (Cardiff) . .	•	
2727	L/Cpl.	Emery, A. J. (Cardiff) . .	†	
2998	Gdsn.	Emmerson, R. E. (Harrogate) .	†	
1296	L/Cpl.	Enderby, H. A. (Menai Bridge) .	†	
2923	Gdsn.	English, J. (Oldham) . . .	†	
170	L/Cpl.	Epstein. J. (Cardiff) . . .	†	
2319	Gdsn.	Erasmus, E. E. (Swansea) . .	•	
3162	,,	Erskine, J. S. (Cardiff) . .	†	
1832	,,	Esmond, T. H. (Bridgend) . .	†	
3927	Cpl.	Eteson, E. (Preston) . .	•	
41	Sergt.	Evans, J. (Cardiff) . . .	•	
97	Gdsn.	Evans, D. J. (Swansea) . .	†	
197	,,	Evans, E. H. (Penarth) . .	D. of S.	
198	,,	Evans, S. (Swansea) . . .	†	
199	L/Cpl.	Evans, A. (Treorchy) . .	•	
220	Gdsn.	Evans, D. J. (Pontardulais) .	K. in A.	
294	,,	Evans, R. D. (Aberdare) . .	•	
302	,,	Evans, P. D. (Aberdare) . .	K. in A.	
318	Sergt.	Evans, E. (Newport) . .	•	
345	,,	Evans, B. (Denbigh) . . .	† †	
355	T/C.Q.M.S.	Evans, W. (Cardiff) . .	•	
361	,,	Evans, J. (Macclesfield) . .	†	
369	Gdsn.	Evans, E. (Aberystwyth) . .	† †	
423	,,	Evans, J. R. (Walsall) . .	†	M.M.
451	L/Cpl.	Evans, A. N. (Merthyr) . .	†	
515	Gdsn.	Evans, M. D. (Swansea) . .	•	
680	,,	Evans, J. (Aberdare) . .	•	
710	,,	Evans, M. (Aberdare) . .	† †	
729	,,	Evans, E. T. (Bargoed) . .	•	
751	,,	Evans, R. (Rhondda) . . .	†	
765	,,	Evans, A. A. (London) . .	†	
769	,,	Evans, W. L. P. (Cardiff) . .	† K. in A.	
772	,,	Evans, D. (Aberdare) . .	†	
778	,,	Evans, D. W. (Rhymney) . .	† D. of S.	
780	,,	Evans, D. G. (Llandovery) . ,	† K. in A,	

Regtl. No.	Rank.	Name.	Casualties.	Decorations.
800	Gdsn.	Evans, W. B. (Morriston) . . .	K. in A.	
839	,,	Evans, J. T. (Llanelly) . . .	† †	
883	,,	Evans, R. (Cardiff) . . .	†	
1103	,,	Evans, L. (Wolf's Castle) . . .		
1113	,,	Evans, J. (Rhymney) . . .		
1131	,,	Evans, D. L. (Aberdare) . . .	†	
1229	Sergt.	Evans, A. H. (Marshfield) . . .	D. of Wds.	D.C.M.
1243	L/Cpl.	Evans, J. T. (Knighton) . . .	†	
1270	Gdsn.	Evans, D. W. (Llanwrda) . . .	K. in A.	
1302	,,	Evans, I. (Whitland) . . .		
1348	,,	Evans, B. (Llanover) . . .	K. in A.	
1360	Cpl.	Evans, D. J. (Cardiff) . . .		M.M.
1362	Gdsn.	Evans, W. G. (Bargoed) . . .		
1398	,,	Evans, E. (Trecynon) . . .	K. in A.	
1432	,,	Evans, W. (Trealaw) . . .	K. in A.	
1478	,,	Evans, D. (Treherbert) . . .	† † †	
1484	,,	Evans, J. I. (Cockett) . . .	†	
1536	,,	Evans, E. (Bridgend) . . .		
1543	,,	Evans, W. A. (Kidwelly) . . .	†	
1563	,,	Evans, E. J. (Aberystwyth) . . .	† †	
1587	,,	Evans, J. H. (Cwmavon) . . .	†	
1649	,,	Evans, T. (Pontypridd) . . .		
1709	,,	Evans, W. (Ystalyfera) . . .		
1726	,,	Evans, D. (Llanelly) . . .	†	
1794	Sergt.	Evans, W. R. (Resolven) . . .	†	
1805	Gdsn.	Evans, J. W. L. (Penarth) . . .	†	
1814	,,	Evans, J. (Cardiff) . . .	†	
1822	,,	Evans, D. T. (Neath) . . .	K. in A.	
1867	,,	Evans, T. A. (Glyncorwg) . . .	K. in A.	
1936	,,	Evans, D. (Tonypandy) . . .		
1937	,,	Evans, A. (Tonyrefail) . . .	K. in A.	
1968	,,	Evans, D. R. (Clarbeston) . . .	D. of Wds.	
2012	L/Cpl.	Evans, J. (Llanarth) . . .	†	
2100	Gdsn.	Evans, P. J. (Swansea) . . .	† †	
2211	,,	Evans, R. W. (Conway) . . .		
2254	Sergt.	Evans, T. J. (Swansea) . . .	† †	Croix-de-Guerre (Fr.).
2267	L/Cpl.	Evans, W. L. (Llandrindod Wells) .	†	
2270	Gdsn.	Evans, T. L. (Treherbert) . . .	† † †	Croix-de-Guerre (Fr.).
2327	,,	Evans, E. (Dinas Mawddwy) . . .	†	
2348	,,	Evans, R. (Bodorgan) . . .	K. in A.	
2350	,,	Evans, J. (Guilsfield) . . .	†	
2404	,,	Evans, M. (Kenfig Hill) . . .	K. in A.	
2412	,,	Evans, H. (Llandudno) . . .	† †	
2459	L/Cpl.	Evans, D. J. (St. Clears) . . .	K. in A.	
2504	Gdsn.	Evans, D. L. (Blaengarw) . . .	† † †	
2566	,,	Evans, W. (Mold) . . .	† †	
2574	,,	Evans, H. (Cardiff) . . .		
2579	,,	Evans, H. (Bangor) . . .	K. in A.	
2610	,,	Evans, W. (Aberdare) . . .	K. in A.	

Regtl. No.	Rank.	Name.	Casualties.	Decorations.
2633	Gdsn.	Evans, C. J. (Bridgend)	K. in A.	
2754	L/Cpl.	Evans, A. (Llanycrwys)	† D. of S.	
2762	Gdsn.	Evans, C. W. (Reynoldstone)		
2851	,,	Evans, T. (Flint)	D. of Wds.	M.M.
2865	,,	Evans, W. O. (Flint)	†	
2871	L/Cpl.	Evans, C. (Swansea)		
2961	Gdsn.	Evans, R. (Cardiff)	K. in A.	
2992	,,	Evans, L. (Cardiff)	†	
3014	,,	Evans, G. (Shrewsbury)		
3016	,,	Evans, R. (Dolgelly)		
3020	,,	Evans, T. E. (Trefnant)	†	
3102	,,	Evans, T. (Neath)	†	
3207	,,	Evans, D. J. (Kidwelly)	†	
3227	,,	Evans, E. E. (Llanfair)	†	
3263	,,	Evans, T. R. (Merthyr)	K. in A.	
3399	,,	Evans, W. (Cefn)		
3464	,,	Evans, J. (Treorchy)		
3530	,,	Evans, W. C. (Pontardulais)	†	
3532	,,	Evans, J. (Swansea)	†	
3634	,,	Evans, D. J. (Llangollen)	† †	
3652	,,	Evans, W. G. (Cardiff)	†	
3660	,,	Evans, H. (Carnarvon)	D. of Wds.	
3694	,,	Evans, W. (Blaenpenal)		
3704	,,	Evans, E. P. (Hereford)	D. of Wds.	
4054	,,	Evans, T. (Conwil)	† †	
4105	,,	Evans, C. J. (Garndiffaith)		
4149	,,	Evans, D. L. (Bridgend)		
4222	Sergt.	Evans, H. C. (Llanelly)		
4269	Gdsn.	Evans, V. H. A. (Windsor)		
4320	,,	Evans, G. W. (Leicester)	D. of Wds.	
4392	,,	Evans, J. (Bolton)		
4397	,,	Evans, E. (Liverpool)		
4406	,,	Evans, D. (Wrexham)		
4471	,,	Evans, E. R. (Aberdare)		
4474	,,	Evans, O. J. (Pontypridd)		
4539	,,	Evans, W. (Clydach Vale)		
4580	,,	Evans, W. (Aberdare)		
4652	,,	Evans, A. L. (Abercynon)		
4656	,,	Evans, J. J. (Porth)		
4760	,,	Evans, D. R. (Newport)		
4773	,,	Evans, T. I. M. (Fochriw)		
4830	,,	Evans, W. G. (Ystalyfera)		
4858	,,	Evans, E. O. (Mountain Ash)		
1259	,,	Everett, C. V. (London)	†	
2096	,,	Everett, T. (Tonyrefail)	D. of Wds.	
1552	,,	Everitt, A. (Bargoed)	†	
4570	,,	Eves, A. J. (Aberaman)		
213	,,	Everson, L. (Machen)	K. in A.	
3516	,,	Ewert, A. (Newport)		
1252	,,	Exton, G. (Cardiff)	†	
4482	,,	Eynon, J. B. (Llanelly)		

Regtl. No.	Rank.	Name.	Casualties.	Decorations.
102	Gdsn.	Eyre, J. E. (Newport)		
52	L/Cpl.	Facey, F. (Hanley)	†	
311	„	Fairbanks, E. (Alton)	† †	M.M.
1110	Gdsn.	Fairchild, J. H. (Neath)	†	
719	L/Cpl.	Farley, J. (Aberdare)	D. of Wds.	
2287	Gdsn.	Farmer, G. (Welshpool)	†	
2834	„	Farmer, F. (Llandudno)	†	
786	„	Farrell, M. (Cardiff)	†	
4196	„	Faulkener, W. (Birmingham)		
2943	„	Fawcett, J. A. (Kendall)	D. of Wds.	
3793	„	Fear, R. F. (Anderford)	† †	
4228	„	Fearn, A. (Portsmouth)	†	
4121	„	Fearnley, C. (Halifax)		
3744	„	Fearon, G. H. (Liverpool)		
2782	„	Feely, J. (Ruthin)	†	M.M.
2929	„	Fehrenbach, E. J. (Cardiff)	K. in A.	
4593	„	Fellows, A. (Newport)		
107	„	Fender, S. (Swansea)	D. of Wds.	
3239	„	Fender, H. (Bolton)	†	
1445	„	Fenn, W. (Bangor)	† K. in A.	
604	„	Fennell, E. (Cardiff)	†	
3892	„	Fennell, R. J. (Bristol)		
4523	„	Fenner, R. T. (Derby)		
3041	„	Ferrall, W. J. (Manchester)		
2354	L/Cpl.	Field, F. E. (London)	†	
3028	„	Field, F. (Morling)	† D. of Wds.	
2786	Gdsn.	Fielding, C. (Glossop)	†	
4251	Cpl.	Filbee, W. (Aylesbury)		
4415	Gdsn.	Filet, A. (Pontypool)		
2838	„	Finch, J. (Earlestown)		
944	„	Fincham, H. (Neath)	†	
123	„	Fisher, L. W. (Stroud)	K. in A.	
977	L/Cpl.	Fisher, T. G. (Abertridwr)		
1343	„	Fisher, H. J. (Cardiff)	K. in A.	
3307	Gdsn.	Fisher, G. W. (Eccles)	† †	
629	„	Fitzgerald, D. (Pontypridd)	D. of S.	
2164	„	Fitzgerald, E. (Cardiff)	K. in A.	M.M.
3381	„	Flanagan, C. (Bolton)	D. of Wds.	
4162	„	Fleming, D. (Windermere)		
4324	„	Fletcher, S. W. (Northwich)		
1075	„	Flood, G. (Middlesborough)		
2114	L/Cpl.	Flynn, M. (London, W.)		
415	L/Sergt.	Fogg, G. E. (Liverpool)	†	
1381	Gdsn.	Folland, W. G. (Bridgend)		
3733	„	Foote, T. (Swansea)	†	
70	Cpl.	Ford, E. (Aberdare)	†	
702	Gdsn.	Ford, T. (Cockett)		
752	„	Ford, T. (Rhondda)	† † †	
2751	Musn.	Ford, C. (London, S.W.)		
3374	Gdsn.	Ford, A. (Leicester)		
2468	A/Sergt.	Forsdike, J. W. (London)		

Regtl. No.	Rank.	Name.	Casualties.	Decorations.
3198	Gdsn.	Forth, W. (Thirsk)	†	
2335	,,	Foster, F. (Swansea)	D. of Wds.	
2547	,,	Foster, D. L. (Mumbles)	K. in A.	
55	Sergt.	Foulkes, E. A. G. (Shrewsbury)	†	
182	Gdsn.	Fowler, W. T. (Cadoxton)		
353	Sergt.	Fowler, W. H. (Cardiff)	† †	
4369	Gdsn.	Fox, E. J. (Windsor)	†	
513	,,	Foxton, H. (Buxton)	† † †	
4198	,,	Fozard, J. E. (Pannal)	K. in A.	
299	L/Cpl.	Francis, S. (Llanelly)	†	
2461	Gdsn.	Francis, W. H. (London)		
2685	,,	Francis, B. (Swansea)	K. in A.	
3343	,,	Francis, G. (Liverpool)	†	
1777	,,	Franklin, A. (London)	† †	
2464	,,	Franklin, G. (London, N.)	†	
2876	,,	Franklin, A. (Swansea)	† †	
3098	,,	Franklin, T. P. (Cardiff)	†	
3441	,,	Franklin, A. (Blaenavon)	†	
3681	,,	Franklin, H. J. (Reading)	†	
2424	,,	Freeman, J. A. (Newtown)		
3870	,,	Freeman, F. C. (London, S.W.)		
4257	,,	Freeman, C. (Sheffield)		
17	C.S.M.	Freestone, A. H. (Stockerston)		M.S.M.
3886	Gdsn.	Freestone, R. W. (St. Albans)	†	
4547	,,	French, O. (Aberfan)		
4135	,,	Friday, J. E. (Coventry)	D. of Wds.	
3946	,,	Frost, H. (Crediton)	D. of S.	
4323	,,	Frost, J. W. (Enfield)		
1716	,,	Fry, L. E. O. (Pontypridd)		
2112	,,	Fry, J. (Pontnewydd)		
3998	,,	Fry, F. G. (Ferndale)	K. in A.	
1605	,,	Fudge, G. E. (Shrewsbury)	†	
3351	,,	Fudge, W. C. (Barrow)	†	
2962	,,	Fuller, J. (London, N.E.)	†	
2950	L/Sergt.	Furzer, H. (Cardiff)	†	
2965	L/Cpl.	Fyfe, M. (Bristol)		
1090	Gdsn.	Gall, C. H. (Dewsbury)	†	
4325	,,	Galloway, W. (Kingsley)		
3322	,,	Gamble, A. (Warrington)	D. of Wds.	
2285	Cpl.	Gammon, W. G. (Merthyr)	† †	
4037	Gdsn.	Garbutt, J. W. (Bushby)		
834	L/Sergt.	Gardiner, W. C. (Dinas)	†	M.M.
2241	L/Cpl.	Gardner, R. (Bangor)	†	
1424	Gdsn.	Garn, W. E. (Cardiff)	† † †	
3850	,,	Garnett, W. (Lancaster)	†	M.M.
1987	,,	Gaunt, A. A. (Ammanford)	†	
4329	,,	Gelsthorpe, A. H. (Mansfield)		
119	,,	George, S. (Pontypridd)		
1391	,,	George, E. (Porth)	† † †	
1594	L/Cpl.	George, T. H. (Cardiff)	K. in A.	

Regtl. No.	Rank.	Name.	Casualties.	Decorations.
2515	Gdsn.	George, F. D. (Cardiff)	† †	
2687	,,	George, E. (Swansea) .		
4144	,,	George, J. (Barrow)		
4328	,,	George, J. N. (Amble)	K. in A.	
956	,,	Gibbins, J. M. (Pontypridd)	D. of S.	
868	,,	Gibbon, E. (Porth) .		
4598	,,	Gibbon, R. (Merthyr)		
3781	,,	Gibbons, A. J. (Port Talbot)	†	
32	Sergt.	Gibbs, E. J. (London)	D. of Wds.	M.M.
618	Gdsn.	Gibbs, T. (Swansea) .		
2144	,,	Gibbs, T. (Newport) .	† D. of Wds.	M.M.
3279	,,	Gibbs, W. A. (Gateshead)	†	
3505	,,	Gibbs, W. F. (Swansea)		
4262	,,	Gibbs, H. W. (Croydon)		
2447	L/Cpl.	Gidden, E. (Southampton) .		
1437	,,	Giddings, A. (Newport)		
1876	,,	Gilbert, H. (Gloucester)	† †	M.M.
3076	,,	Gilbert, I. (Accrington)		
3283	,,	Giles, G. (Cardiff)	K. in A.	
305	,,	Gill, A. (Caerphilly) .	K. in A.	
1505	,,	Gillard, F. (Barry) .		
4239	Musn.	Gilligan, J. (Manchester)		
3731	Gdsn.	Gillman, A. (London, N.)	† †	
72	,,	Girling, G. (Nottingham)		
916	,,	Gittings, D. (Newtown)		
4536	,,	Gittins, E. (Bedlinog)		
652	,,	Glanville, A. (Cardiff)	†	
2659	Cpl.	Gleeson, J. (Cardiff) .	†	
1228	Sergt.	Glover, C. L. (Cardiff)	†	D.C.M.
1091	Gdsn.	Godding, W. R. (Portsmouth)	K. in A.	
1409	,,	Godfrey, D. (Cardiff) .	†	
2006	,,	Godfrey, C. (Cogan)	†	
432	Cpl.	Golding, C. (Barry) .	† K. in A.	
5818	Gdsn.	Golledge, W. T. (Ebbw Vale)		
3140	,,	Goodall, T. (Beaconsfield) .		
2480	,,	Goode, V. G. (Ogmore Vale)	K. in A.	
3477	,,	Goode, A. E. (Halesowen)		
3958	,,	Goodhind, W. C. (Bristol) .	†	
656	L/Cpl.	Goodger, S. (Cardiff) .		
1058	Gdsn.	Goodman, A. S. (London, S.W.) .	†	
2110	,,	Goodman, A. H. (Nantyglo)	†	
4326	,,	Goodman, A. (London, S.E.)	D. of Wds.	
3481	Cpl.	Goodrich, A. (Leicester)		
4127	Gdsn.	Goodwin, J. F. (Birchvale)		
872	L/Cpl.	Gordon, E. W. (Bridgend) .	† †	D.C.M., M.M. and Bar.
1634	Gdsn.	Gordon, D. (Barry)		
547	,,	Gornall, P. (Leigh)		
4075	,,	Gosney, D. P. (Aberdare)		
420	Sergt.	Gough, J. (Aberbeeg) .		M.M.
1570	L/Cpl.	Gough, R. (Newport) .	† †	
4278	Gdsn.	Gould, W. T. (Maesteg)		

Regtl. No.	Rank.	Name.	Casualties.	Decorations.
2556	Gdsn.	Gover, A. H. (Abertillery) . . .	†	
4508	L/Cpl.	Graham, A. (London, E.) . . .		
48	Sergt.	Grant, G. C. (Altrincham) . . .	† †	D.C.M.
1331	Gdsn.	Grant, D. C. (Barry)	K. in A.	
2680	„	Grant, W. (Cardiff)	†	
3371	„	Grant, H (Leicester)	†	
3814	„	Grant, M. E. (Wadhurst) . . .	D. of S.	
4799	„	Gravell, D. W. (Kidwelly) . . .		
3784	„	Gray, D. A. (Cirencester) . . .	†	
46	Sergt.	Green, F. J. (Cardiff) . . .	† †	
632	Gdsn.	Green, T. (Bargoed) . . .	K. in A.	
750	L/Cpl.	Green, J. (Treherbert) . . .	† K. in A.	
1074	Gdsn.	Green, G. E. J. (Abertridwr) . .	† †	
2320	„	Green, E. G. (Cardiff) . . .	D. of Wds.	
3430	„	Green, J. E. (Rawtenstall) . . .		
3612	„	Green, W. J. (Wrexham) . . .	K. in A.	
3740	„	Green, F. (Bilston)	† †	
1665	„	Greenfield, E. (Castleford) . . .	† †	
3873	„	Greenhough, C. E. (Wednesbury)		
4038	„	Greenland, J. E. (Newport) . .	D. of Wds.	
3192	„	Greenley, D. B. (Colwyn Bay) . .	†	
3057	„	Greenwood, E. J. (Cardiff) . . .	† † †	
4327	„	Greenwood, V. (Eastbourne) . .		
1592	„	Gregg, W. G. (Llansamlet) . . .	† †	
3815	„	Gregg, R. N. (Newcastle) . . .		
430	„	Gregory, A. (Madeley) . . .	†	
546	„	Gregory, J. (Cheltenham) . . .		
2299	Sergt.	Gregory, J. H. (Carnarvon) . .	†	
2757	Musn.	Gregory, H. (London) . . .		
3231	L/Cpl.	Gregory, F. W. (Liverpool) . . .		
1028	L/Sergt.	Griffen, T. (Hendon) . . .		
3359	L/Cpl.	Griffin, F. (Stourbridge) . . .	†	
3867	Gdsn.	Griffin, R. M. (Flaxbolton) . . .		
2243	„	Griffith, J. (Llanbedr) . . .	†	
31	A/C.Q.M.S.	Griffiths, W. (Birkenhead) . .	†	
530	Gdsn.	Griffiths, D. J. (Carmarthen) . .		
544	„	Griffiths, W. (Birmingham) . . .	† D. of Wds.	
908	„	Griffiths, W. J. (New Tredegar) . .	†	
937	„	Griffiths, D. J. (Llanbeia) . . .	† K. in A.	
1157	„	Griffiths, E. (St. Clears) . . .	†	
1253	„	Griffiths, W. (Cardiff) . . .	† †	
1319	L/Cpl.	Griffiths, A. A. (Hay) . . .	K. in A.	
1682	Gdsn.	Griffiths, W. M. (Neath) . . .		
1713	„	Griffiths, L. E. (Llandrindod) . .	†	
1748	„	Griffiths, D. (Swansea) . . .	†	
1782	„	Griffiths, A. (Shotton) . . .		
1792	Sergt.	Griffiths, R. (Wrexham) . . .	†	
1953	L/Cpl.	Griffiths, R. (Anglesey) . . .	†	
1971	Gdsn.	Griffiths, W. (Carmarthen) . . .	† †	
2049	„	Griffiths, O. (Mountain Ash)		
2056	„	Griffiths, W. J. (Swansea) . .		

Regtl. No.	Rank.	Name.	Casualties.	Decorations.
2058	L/Sergt.	Griffiths, T. (Bridgend) . . .		
2089	Gdsn.	Griffiths, H. (Llandyssul) . . .		
2141	„	Griffiths, W. (Begelly) . .	K. in A.	
2204	L/Cpl.	Griffiths, W. H. (Swansea) . . .		
2322	Gdsn.	Griffiths, A. (Welshpool) . .	K. in A.	
2371	L/Sergt.	Griffiths, H. (Llanfair) . . .		
2667	Gdsn.	Griffiths, E. T. (Liverpool) . .		
2759	„	Griffiths, T. (Blaenporth) . .	† K. in A.	M.M.
2836	„	Griffiths, S. (Llannon) . .	†	
2919	„	Griffiths, R. W. (Cardiff) . .	†	
3497	„	Griffiths, L. (Aberystwyth) . .	†	
3498	Dmr.	Griffiths, W. (Mold) . . .	†	
3576	Gdsn.	Griffiths, R. (Swansea) . .		
3590	„	Griffiths, R. W. (Welshpool) .	K. in A.	
3843	„	Griffiths, W. G. (Aberystwyth) .	†	
4785	„	Griffiths, D. J. (Melin Court) .		
4859	„	Griffiths, E. (Aberdare) . .		
1621	L/Cpl.	Grigg, W. T. (Tonypandy) . .	†	
3142	Gdsn.	Griggs, A. (Grays) . . .	†	
3184	„	Grimshaw, T. H. (Barrowford) .	K. in A.	
609	„	Gronow, E. G. (Tonyrefail) . .		
1006	„	Groom, J. (Birmingham) . .	† †	
1693	„	Grother, R. (Tonypandy) . .	†	
4208	„	Groves, E. G. (Cheltenham) .		
4860	„	Groves, G. E. (Pontypridd) .		
282	L/Sergt.	Gubb, C. (Swansea) . .	†	
1510	Gdsn.	Guest, C. (Wrexham) . . .		
1664	„	Gully, J. I. (Porth) . . .		
701	„	Guppy, E. J. (Swansea) . .	K. in A.	
2477	Cpl.	Gupwell, C. H. (Pontypridd) .	† †	
2529	Gdsn.	Gupwell, W. (Swansea) . .	† D. of Wds.	
3812	L/Cpl.	Gurney, R. E. (Gloucester) . .	†	
2022	Gdsn.	Guy, A. T. (Monmouth) . .	K. in A.	
1958	Sergt.	Gwilliam, J. (Abertillery) . .	†	
2797	Gdsn.	Gwilt, C. R. (Broseley) . .	K. in A.	
4784	„	Gwyn, J. (Cardiff) . . .		
3095	„	Gyles, A. W. (Cardiff) . .	K. in A.	
4330	Gdsn.	Habgood, F. J. (London, S.W.) .		
3941	„	Haddon, E. A. W. (London, S.E.)		
4042	„	Haggas, W. (Bradford) . .	D. of Wds.	
1616	„	Hagley, W. H. (Swansea) . .	K. in A.	
3845	„	Haig, F. J. (Aberlady) . .	K. in A.	
3149	„	Haigh, J. (Haslingden) . .	K. in A.	
1578	„	Haines, F. (Cardiff) . . .		
2253	„	Haines, E. (Newport) . .		
2649	„	Hake, F. W. (Cardiff) . .		
3642	„	Hale, C. (Cwmbran) . . .	D. of Wds.	
1185	L/Sergt.	Hall, F. (Cardiff) . . .		D.C.M.
3728	Gdsn.	Hall, T. (Liverpool) . . .	K. in A.	
3782	„	Hall, P. J. (Tonypandy) . . .		

Regtl. No.	Rank.	Name.	Casualties.	Decorations.
3804	Gdsn.	Hall, W. L. (Birmingham) .		
4134	„	Hall, W. (Prudhoe) .	† †	
771	L/Sergt.	Halladay, W. E. (Pontypridd) .		
3220	Gdsn.	Hallett, F. G. (Llanelly)	K. in A.	
3236	„	Hallworth, A. W. (Heckfield)	K. in A.	
1663	Sergt.	Ham, A. G. (Barry) .		D.C.M., M.M.
99	L/Cpl.	Hambleton, F. W. (Barry) .	†	
1128	„	Hamby, A. (Deptford)	K. in A.	
1672	„	Hamer, R. (Abernant)	D. of Wds.	
1770	„	Hamer, C. (Llanfyllin)	D. of Wds.	
2638	„	Hamer, J. (Rhayader)	† †	
2640	Gdsn.	Hamer, P. H. (Cwmdeuddwr)		
3785	„	Hamilton, P. G. (Petworth)	†	
1168	„	Hamm, S. (Pontypridd)	†	
1392	„	Hammond, J. (Pontypridd)	K. in A.	M.M. and Bar.
3200	„	Hammond, A. (Scarborough)	†	
3983	„	Hammond, G. (Sullington) .		
59	Sergt.	Hammonds, H. (London) .		
1549	Gdsn.	Hampshire, H. C. (Swansea)		
3103	„	Hampton, N. T. (Nelson) .	†	
969	Sergt.	Hanbury, J. (Aberavon)	† † †	
486	Gdsn.	Hannaford, W. H. (Newport)	K. in A.	
1197	L/Cpl.	Hansen, F. (Newport)	D. of Wds.	
4414	Gdsn.	Hardacre, E. G. (Pontypool)		
2981	„	Harden, J. R. (Cardiff)		
1327	„	Harding, F. (Cardiff) .	D. of Wds.	
2027	„	Harding, W. J. (Cardiff)	†	
2373	Musn.	Harding, F. (London)		
5783	Gdsn.	Harding, E. (Bridgend)		
3099	„	Hardwick, E. (Ledbury)	K. in A.	
2512	„	Hardy, G. (London, S.E.) .	† † K. in A.	
44	Sergt.	Hare, S. (Saundersfoot)		
2002	Gdsn.	Hargest, J. R. (Brecon)	†	
2436	„	Hargreaves, F. W. T. (Bradford)		
2117	„	Harley, S. F. (London)		
3499	„	Harley, J. (Knighton)	†	
1553	L/Cpl.	Harper, J. C. (Cardiff)		
1160	Gdsn.	Harries, J. G. (Haverfordwest)		
1972	L/Cpl.	Harries, W. A. (Haverfordwest) .	† †	M.M. and Bar.
4089	Gdsn.	Harries, D. L. (Swansea) .	†	
540	„	Harriman, R. (Ilkeston)		
7	D/Sergt.	Harris, J. G. (Swansea) .	†	
91	Gdsn.	Harris, W. (Rumney) .	D. of Wds.	
313	„	Harris, W. H. (Swansea)		
327	„	Harris, O. (Merthyr) .		
427	Cpl.	Harris, E. E. (Ely, Glam.) .		
492	L/Sergt.	Harris, J. (Newport)		M.M.
876	Gdsn.	Harris, T. (Tonypandy)	†	
1184	L/Cpl.	Harris, A. (Machen) .	D. of Wds.	
1818	Gdsn.	Harris, W. H. (Dorchester) .	†	
2055	Bdmr.	Harris, A. (London) .		

28

Regtl. No.	Rank.	Name.	Casualties.	Decorations.
2537	Gdsn.	Harris, R. A. (Aberkenfig)	†	
2559	,,	Harris, D. (Pontyberem)	K. in A.	
2740	L/Cpl.	Harris, W. J. (Cardiff)	†	
2951	Gdsn.	Harris, B. W. (Birmingham)		
3027	,,	Harris, P. (Stratford-on-Avon)	†	
3126	,,	Harris, S. (Cardiff)		
3600	,,	Harris, W. R. (Pontypridd)	†	
3768	,,	Harris, F. J. (Birmingham)		
4034	,,	Harris, J. (Cross Keys)		
4861	,,	Harris, D. W. (Dowlais)		
5324	,,	Harris, H. (Monmouth)		
437	L/Sergt.	Harrison, T. W. (Neath)	†	
1390	Gdsn.	Harrison, T. H. (Cardiff)	K. in A.	
2777	,,	Harrison, J. (Ulverston)	†	
3248	,,	Harrison, H. (Nelson)		
3636	L/Cpl.	Harrison, H. (Queensferry)	†	
4435	Gdsn.	Harrison, F. (Willaston)		
5196	,,	Harrison, I. (Caerphilly)		
200	Sergt.	Hart, A. (Newport)		
1500	L/Cpl.	Hart, T. H. (Cardiff)		
2487	Gdsn.	Hart, R. W. (London, E.)	† †	
2847	,,	Hart, W. (Warrington)		
828	,,	Hartland, H. (Stockton)		
4201	,,	Hartman, A. T. (London, E.)	K. in A.	
3968	,,	Hartnell, J. (London, N.)	D. of Wds.	
1926	,,	Harvey, A. T. (Hanley)	† †	
4528	,,	Harvey, W. (Porth)		
1321	,,	Hatcher, E. (Brecon)	K. in A.	
3328	,,	Hatcher, S. H. (Bournemouth)	†	
413	L/Cpl.	Hatton, W. (Mountain Ash)	† †	
2767	Gdsn.	Hatton, A. S. (Market Weighton)		
1268	Cpl.	Havard, S. T. (Pontypridd)		
2496	Gdsn.	Hawken, G. B. (Oystermouth)	K. in A.	
3355	,,	Hawker, C. W. (Bristol)	†	
998	Sergt.	Hawkesworth, W. (Newark)		
2135	Gdsn.	Hawkins, A. G. (Newport)		
3449	L/Cpl.	Hay, A. S. (Rhyl)	†	
552	Gdsn.	Hayes, T. (Llanelly)	†	
1239	,,	Hayes, G. H. (Cardiff)	†	
1334	Cpl.	Hayes, D. M. (Pontypridd)	†	
3128	Gdsn.	Hayes, J. (Flint)	K. in A.	
1900	Sergt.	Haylock, T. H. (London)		M.M.
1545	Gdsn.	Hayman, J. H. (Bridgend)		
2124	,,	Haynes, S. (Pontypool)		
2224	,,	Haynes, B. (Cowbridge)	†	
789	,,	Haywood, W. (Bargoed)	† †	
3536	,,	Hazell, W. (Bristol)		
498	,,	Headon, R. (Barry)		
3475	,,	Healey, H. (Wolverhampton)	†	
4561	,,	Healey, E. (Rogerstone)		
14	Sergt.	Hearn, W. (Manchester)	†	

Regtl. No.	Rank.	Name.	Casualties.	Decorations.
745	Gdsn.	Heath, H. (Rhondda)	K. in A.	
2702	„	Hecks, W. G. (Cardiff)	K. in A.	
246	„	Heddon, W. J. (Swansea)		
283	Sergt.	Helson, E. (Soanton)	D. of Wds.	
3711	Gdsn.	Hemmings. H. (Bristol)		
2448	„	Hems, G. J. F. (London, N.E.)	†	
617	L/Cpl.	Henderson, W. E. (Llanelly)	K. in A.	
3190	Gdsn.	Henderson, W. H. (Liverpool)	K. in A.	
3233	„	Henderson, T. G. (Kilkenny)	† †	
177	„	Henebery, T. (Cardiff)		
696	„	Henry, J. R. (Llanelly)		
2802	„	Henry, E. T. (Newport)	†	
113	C.Q.M.S.	Henton, J. L. (Lampeter)	D. of S.	
886	Gdsn.	Henwood, W. T. (Ystalyfera)	K. in A.	
491	„	Herbert, D. (Merthyr)	†	
1217	L/Cpl.	Herbert, T. D. C. (Aberavon)		
3048	Gdsn.	Herbert, G. H. (Burnley)	K. in A.	
1143	A/C.Q.M.S.	Herd, W. (London)		
3308	Gdsn.	Herdson, W. J.. (Manchester)	†	
4587	„	Heritage, W. W. (Treforest)		
3735	„	Herrington, J. (Brierley Hill)	†	
579	„	Hesketh, R. H. (Penmaenmawr)	† †	
3857	„	Hewett, D. R. (Cowbridge)	†	
2906	L/Cpl.	Hewitt, L. B. (Stockport)	†	
1322	Gdsn.	Hibbert, G. A. D. (Brecon)		
2771	„	Hibbert, J. (Western Point)	† K. in A.	
2193	Musn.	Hickey, H. (Crowthorne)		
3368	Gdsn.	Hickmott, C. T. (Maidstone)	K. in A.	
744	L/Sergt.	Hicks, A. (Tonypandy)	† † †	M.M.
2222	Gdsn.	Hicks, T. (Maesteg)	†	
2655	„	Hicks, S. (Barry)	†	
1444	Sergt.	Higgins, J. (Ammanford)	†	
4171	Gdsn.	Higgins, H. W. (London)	†	
402	„	Higgs, W. G. (Swansea)	†	
2894	„	Higham, H. (Padgate)	D. of Wds.	
555	„	Hill, T. (Newport)	†	
967	„	Hill, W. (Hereford)		
1870	„	Hill, T. G. (Barry)	† K. in A.	Croix-de-Guerre (Fr.).
2615	Musn.	Hill, W. R. (Brighton)		
2690	Gdsn.	Hill, E. T. (Pontypridd)	†	
3683	„	Hill, A. S. (Bristol)	†	M.M.
4733	„	Hill, H. (Cardiff)		
683	„	Hillman, E. A. (Cardiff)	†	
3484	„	Hills, J. (Ely, Cambs.)		
3802	„	Hinton, S. C. W. (Birmingham)	†	
4472	„	Hiscock, A. F. (Barry)		
4768	„	Hiscox, W. J. (Dowlais)		
3297	„	Hitchcock, F. (Abingdon)	†	
2170	„	Hitchcox, G. (Newport)		
3228	„	Hitchman, C. (Souldern)	† †	

Regtl. No.	Rank.	Name.	Casualties.	Decorations.
1609	Gdsn.	Hobbs, E. J. (Cardiff)		
2505	,,	Hobby, W. J. (Merthyr)	†	
2973	,,	Hobday, H. H. (Pontyclun)	K. in A.	
3820	,,	Hobden, G. (Eastbourne)	†	
2697	,,	Hocking, P. (Swansea)		
4087	,,	Hockridge, J. A. (Cardiff)	†	
877	,,	Hodges, F. (Tonypandy)	†	
1046	,,	Hodgson, J. D. (Workington)	†	
2046	,,	Hodgson, F. W. (Talybont)	†	
768	Dmr.	Hoffman, F. (Cardiff)		
3096	Gdsn.	Hoggarth, J. C. (Blackburn)	K. in A.	
832	,,	Holbrook. H. (Rhondda)	†	M.M.
3615	,,	Holding, F. (Blaenavon)	†	
104	,,	Hole, G. S. (Bristol)		
2230	L/Cpl.	Holland, H. (Crumlin)		
1400	,,	Holloway, J. H. (West Bromwich)	K. in A.	
2334	Gdsn.	Holloway, W. (Carmarthen)		
103	,,	Hollyman, A. (Cardiff)	D. of S.	
130	A/C.S.M.	Holme, G. H. (Liverpool)	†	M.M., M.S.M.
3825	Gdsn.	Holmes, J. L. (Nuneaton)		
4261	,,	Holmes, J. S. (London, W.)	†	
2963	,,	Holt, F. (Birkenhead)	† D. of Wds.	
3097	,,	Holt, A. (Hinckley)	† †	
4332	,,	Holt, W. J. (Bletchley)	†	
1848	L/Cpl.	Hone, G. H. (Cardiff.	†	
686	Gdsn.	Hookway, A. E. (Neath)		
326	Sergt.	Hooper, E. (Stockton)		
1153	L/Cpl.	Hooper, A. J. (Cardiff)	K. in A.	
3832	Gdsn.	Hooper, W. (South Molton).		
3617	,,	Hooson, A. (Mold)	†	
1377	,,	Hope, D. (Merthyr)	† D. of Wds.	
2162	,,	Hope, S. (Worcester)		
3261	,,	Hope, H. (Liverpool)	K. in A.	
483	,,	Hopkin, S. (Hanley)	K. in A.	
2676	,,	Hopkin, J. R. (Swansea)		
436	L/Cpl.	Hopkins, W. S. (Newport)	†	Croix-de-Guerre (Fr.).
917	Gdsn.	Hopkins, C. (Pontypridd)	†	
1102	,,	Hopkins, C. H. (Treforest)		
1249	L/Cpl.	Hopkins, W. (Cardiff)	†	
1418	Gdsn.	Hopkins, W. (Blaenrhondda)		
1613	,,	Hopkins, A. G. (Swansea)	†	
1811	,,	Hopkins, T. (Aberdare)	† K. in A.	
2374	,,	Hopkins, D. (Swansea)		
3571	,,	Hopkins, D. (Cardiff)		
4646	,,	Hopkins, E. J. (Aberdare)		
4877	L/Cpl.	Hopkins, D. J. (Cardiff)		
3730	Gdsn.	Hopkinson, W. T. (London, E.)		
3493	,,	Hopper, G. H. (Aberdare)		
5797	,,	Horn, C. (Bristol)		
3932	,,	Hornby, R. (Broughton)		

Regtl. No.	Rank.	Name.	Casualties.	Decorations.
4333	Gdsn.	Horne, J. T. (Ilkeston) . . .	K. in A.	
2386	,,	Horner, J. (Carmarthen) . . .	D. of Wds.	
2008	,,	Hotchkins, J. (Wrexham) . . .	†	
501	,,	Hough, F. (Newnham) . . .		
1512	L/Cpl.	Hough, O. (Cefn-y-Bedd) . . .	† †	
4331	Gdsn.	Houghton, A. (Melton Mowbray)	.	
1483	L/Cpl.	Houldsworth, W. N. (Hucknall) .	†	
1260	Gdsn.	House, E. J. (Swansea) . . .	K. in A.	
523	L/Cpl.	Howard, A. J. (Aberdare) . . .	†	
548	,,	Howard, P. (Leigh) . . .	†	
3268	,,	Howarth, J. (Blackburn) . . .	D. of Wds.	
3507	Gdsn.	Howarth, H. (Heath) . . .		
1686	,,	Howdle, T. (Walsall) . . .	†	
1191	,,	Howe, W. (Treherbert) . . .	†	
957	Sergt.	Howell, W. (Bristol) . . .	†	
1766	Gdsn.	Howell, E. L. (Newtown) . . .	†	
2548	L/Cpl.	Howell, W. J. (Swansea) . . .	† †	
134	,,	Howells, A. (Manchester) . . .		
650	,,	Howells, J. D. (Treharris) .		
1261	Cpl.	Howells, T. G. (Swansea) . . .	†	
1425	Gdsn.	Howells, T. (Cardiff) . . .	†	
2405	,,	Howells, T. (Merthyr) . . .		
619	,,	Hudson, J. (Treherbert) . . .		
4017	,,	Huggins, D. (Newcastle-on-Tyne) .	†	
68	,,	Hughes, R. D. (Abergele) . . .		
85	,,	Hughes, T. (Rhyl) . . .		
259	,,	Hughes, D. (Llangollen) . . .	K. in A.	
273	Sergt.	Hughes, T. A. (Newport) . . .		M.M.
385	,,	Hughes, J. O. (Cardiff) . . .	†	
454	Gdsn.	Hughes, J. (Newport) . . .	†	
457	,,	Hughes, J. W. (Burton-on-Trent)	†	
587	L/Cpl.	Hughes, P. E. (Barry) . . .		
667	Gdsn.	Hughes, A. (Delamere) . . .	D. of Wds.	
738	,,	Hughes, J. (Treharris) . . .		
747	,,	Hughes, C. S. (London, E.) . .	†	
748	,,	Hughes, C. S. (London, E.) . .		M.S.M.
825	,,	Hughes, R. J. (Henllan) . . .	K. in A.	
978	,,	Hughes, D. (Neath) . . .	† † †	
1209	,,	Hughes, W. (Bangor) . . .	† † †	D.C.M.
1283	,,	Hughes, S. (Porth) . . .	†	
1428	L/Sergt.	Hughes, T. E. (London) . .		
1481	Gdsn.	Hughes, H. O. (Abertridwr)		
1491	,,	Hughes, J. (Henllan) . . .	† K. in A.	
1660	,,	Hughes, J. (Carmarthen) . . .	†	
1751	,,	Hughes, W. T. (Wrexham) . . .	†	
2000	,,	Hughes, R. (Llangaffo) . . .		
2035	,,	Hughes, W. (Merthyr) . . .		
2057	,,	Hughes, T. (Liverpool) . . .		
2255	L/Cpl.	Hughes, J. (Narberth) . . .	†	
2511	Gdsn.	Hughes, R. H. (Cardiff) . . .	†	
2525	,,	Hughes, W. P. (Abergavenny) . .	† †	

Regtl. No.	Rank.	Name.	Casualties.	Decorations.
2668	L/Cpl.	Hughes, R. (Wrexham) . . .	†	
2811	Gdsn.	Hughes, T. (Trefnant) . . .	†	
2882	,,	Hughes, E. A. (Amlwch) . . .	†	
2914	,,	Hughes, R. H. (Llangedwyn) . .	†	
3106	,,	Hughes, H. R. (Llangedwyn) . .	†	
3155	,,	Hughes, R. (Holyhead) . . .	†	
3349	,,	Hughes, C. (Knottingley) . . .	†	
3388	,,	Hughes, H. (Holt)	† D. of Wds.	
3389	,,	Hughes, R. T. (Llangollen) . . .	†	
3427	,,	Hughes, F. (Rossett) . . .		
3453	,,	Hughes, P. (Flint) . . .	K. in A.	
3566	,,	Hughes, O. (Holyhead) . .		
3569	,,	Hughes, W. J. (Shrewsbury) . .	†	
3573	,,	Hughes, T. D. (Cardiff) . .		
3659	L/Sergt.	Hughes, H. (Liverpool) . . .	†	
3838	Gdsn.	Hughes, R. (Carnarvon) . .		
4049	,,	Hughes, J. O. (Abergele) . .		
4052	,,	Hughes, A. W. (Hawarden) . .		
4158	,,	Hughes, J. W. (Warrington) . .	†	
4197	,,	Hughes, M. (Ferndale) . .		
4260	,,	Hughes, W. J. (Waenfawr) . .		
4374	,,	Hughes, L. (Wrexham) . .		
4774	,,	Hughes, T. J. (Dowlais) . .		
4974	,,	Hughes, T. (Pentre) . . .		
5092	,,	Hughes, T. (Carmarthen) . .		
3492	,,	Hull, W. (Treharris) . . .	D. of Wds.	
3487	,,	Humphrey, C. F. (Sicklesmere) .	K. in A.	
29	Sergt.	Humphreys, A. J. O. (Darlaston) .	K. in A.	M.M.
1760	Gdsn.	Humphreys, J. H. (Llangollen) . .	†	
2050	L/Cpl.	Humphreys, W. A. (Nottingham) .	†	
2728	,,	Humphreys, C. E. (Birmingham) .	† †	
3606	,,	Humphreys, W. E. (Llandrindod Wells)	†	
4880	Gdsn.	Humphreys, R. J. (Cardiff) . .		
350	Sergt.	Hunt, H. C. (Merthyr) . . .	† † †	
1032	Cpl.	Hunt, F. C. (Portsmouth) . .	K. in A.	
2532	L/Cpl.	Hunt, B. (London)	†	
4516	Gdsn.	Hunt, C. A. (Birmingham) . .		
23	C.Q.M.S.	Hunter, L. (Bristol) . .		D.C.M.
4883	Gdsn.	Hunter, C. J. (Rogerstone) . .		
689	,,	Hurley, C. (Cardiff) . .	†	
2221	,,	Hurley, G. J. (Maesteg) . .	† †	
3737	,,	Huskinson, L. (Dewsbury) . .		
3714	,,	Hussey, H. J. (Bristol) . .		
1063	L/Sergt.	Hutchings, H. F. (Chesham) . .	†	M.M. and Bar.
3146	Gdsn.	Hutchinson, W. S. (Dyserth) . .		
239	,,	Hutton, W. (Swansea) . .	K. in A.	
160	L/Cpl.	Huxtable, W. J. (Cardiff) . .	K. in A.	
115	C.Q.M.S.	Hyam, S. A. (Gloucester) . .		
1416	Gdsn.	Hyatt, E. (Cardiff) . . .		
1787	,,	Hyatt, R. (Aberavon) . . .		
3083	,,	Hyde, A. (Blackburn) . . .		

Regtl. No.	Rank.	Name.	Casualties.	Decorations.
2182	L/Cpl.	Iles, P. (Newport)	†	
2960	Gdsn.	Imber, A. C. (Bethnal Green)		
987	,,	Inman, J. (Swansea)	† † K. in A.	
2714	,,	Ireland, J. (Cardiff)	† †	
4755	,,	Isaac, W. (Killay)		
1044	,,	Isum, G. (Portsmouth)		
1041	Gdsn.	Jackson, W. (Shelton)	D. of Wds.	
2823	,,	Jackson, O. (Royton)		
554	,,	Jacobs, H. (Llantrisant)	K. in A.	
3439	,,	Jacobs, W. L. (Portsmouth)	†	
4062	,,	Jacobson, A. (Barry)		
67	,,	James, W. (Newport)		
168	,,	James, C. (Tonyrefail)	K. in A.	
270	L/Sergt.	James, A. G. (Pembroke)	† †	
409	Gdsn.	James, W. S. (Pontypridd)		
600	L/Sergt.	James, A. (Llandaff)		
613	L/Cpl.	James, D. (Llanfrynach)	K. in A.	M.M.
641	L/Sergt.	James, A. (Pontypridd)	†	
657	Gdsn.	James, D. (Dowlais)	K. in A.	
775	,,	James, D. (Pentre)	†	
1192	,,	James, S. (Rhondda)	† †	
1213	,,	James, I. (Maesycwmmer)	†	
1368	,,	James, R. T. (Aberdare)	† †	
1454	,,	James, A. (Aberdare)	D. of Wds.	
1581	,,	James, H. (Llanwonno)	†	
1595	,,	James, J. (Bargoed)	† † †	
1847	L/Cpl.	James, J. G. (Haverfordwest)	† D. of Wds.	
1921	,,	James, W. N. (Bridgend)	†	
1934	Gdsn.	James, E. G. (Maesycwmmer)		
2133	,,	James, H. E. (Pembroke)		
2326	,,	James, J. (Cardiff)		
2722	,,	James, G. (Haverfordwest)	† K. in A.	
2933	,,	James, E. D. (Aberdare)		
3033	,,	James, W. (Llanerfyl)		
3125	,,	James, C. E. S. (Cardiff)	†	
3171	,,	James, A. (Hanley)	†	
3358	,,	James, B. (Swansea)	†	
3467	,,	James, W. J. (Llandovery)		
4592	,,	James, P. (Cross Keys)		
4644	,,	James, F. G. (Clydach Vale)		
4822	,,	James, W. C. (Pontypool)		
5696	,,	James, C. E. (Llanelly)		
1294	,,	Jasper, T. (Port Talbot)		
4334	,,	Jeacock. P. C. (London)		
1054	,,	Jeavons, W. (Tipton)	† †	
277	L/Sergt.	Jefferies, G. H. (Cardiff)	†	
4552	Gdsn.	Jeffkins, F. W. (Eastbourne)		
1277	,,	Jeffreys, A. (Tenby)	†	
1633	,,	Jeffries, C. (Pontypridd)	† K. in A.	
2623	,,	Jeffries, R. (Llandrindod Wells)	D. of Wds.	

Regtl. No.	Rank.	Name.	Casualties.	Decorations.
83	L/Sergt.	Jelleyman, F. (Gilfach Goch)	K. in A.	
20	C.Q.M.S.	Jenkins, W. (Cardiff)		M.S.M.
304	Gdsn.	Jenkins, T. (Nelson)	† D. of Wds.	
378	Dmr.	Jenkins, R. (Merthyr)		
424	L/Cpl.	Jenkins, J. A. (Merthyr)		
441	Gdsn.	Jenkins, W. J. (Llanbradach)	† K. in A.	
586	„	Jenkins, J. H. (Cardiff)		
763	„	Jenkins, W. J. (Carmarthen)		
855	L/Sergt.	Jenkins, I. (Llantrisant)	† †	
984	Gdsn.	Jenkins, R. (Neath)		
1280	„	Jenkins, A. T. (Gilfach)	† †	
1366	„	Jenkins, F. B. (Pontypridd)	†	
1427	„	Jenkins, D. H. (Llansantffraid)	K. in A.	
1700	„	Jenkins, T. A. (Builth Wells)		
1773	„	Jenkins, W. D. (Llanwenog)	† †	
1780	L/Cpl.	Jenkins, L. H. (Essex)	† K. in A.	
1825	Gdsn.	Jenkins, C. (Cardiff)	†	
1845	„	Jenkins, I. H. (London)		
2108	„	Jenkins, E. (St. Helen's)	†	
2181	„	Jenkins, J. (Pontypool)		
2258	„	Jenkins, D. (Merthyr)		
2341	„	Jenkins, H. E. (Pembroke Dock)	† †	
2406	„	Jenkins, T. M. (Merthyr)	†	
2441	„	Jenkins, H. (Swansea)	†	
2472	„	Jenkins, W. S. (Gower)	K. in A.	
2491	L/Sergt.	Jenkins, B. T. (Kilgerran)	†	
2495	Gdsn.	Jenkins, E. (Merthyr)		
2800	„	Jenkins, J. (Welshpool)	†	
3113	„	Jenkins, D. W. (Aberystwyth)		
3684	„	Jenkins, F. (Ludlow)		
3783	„	Jenkins, D. T. (Brecon)	†	
4011	„	Jenkins, W. S. (Merthyr)		
4640	„	Jenkins, W. H. (Brecon)		
4977	„	Jenkins, D. (Swansea)		
5201	„	Jenkins, J. (Swansea)		
4515	„	Jenkinson, H. (Halifax)		
1414	L/Cpl.	Jenner, V. J. (Newport)	† K. in A.	
1604	Gdsn.	Jennings, G. (Cardiff)		
1559	L/Cpl.	Jervis, H. (Caerphilly)	D. of Wds.	
3579	Gdsn.	Jervis, A. (Llangollen)		
2473	„	Jesty, G. (Cardiff)	K. in A.	
793	„	Jewell, A. (Swansea)	K. in A.	
3398	„	Jewell, F. (Newbury)	†	
3769	„	Jewers, R. A. C. (Birmingham)	†	
141	„	John, A. (Llansamlet)		M.M.
1326	„	John, E. (Caerphilly)		
1846	„	John, H. E. (Pembroke)		
2677	„	John, E. (Pontypridd)	†	
2679	„	John, R. (Penarth)	† D. of Wds.	
2713	„	John, S. (Cwmavon)		
2725	„	John, J. (Fishguard)	†	

Regtl. No.	Rank.	Name.	Casualties.	Decorations.
3512	Gdsn.	John, C. A. (Pembroke)		
3653	,,	John, R. (Pontypridd)		
3982	,,	John, D. P. (Aberdare)	†	
850	,,	Johns, F. G. (Briton Ferry)	†	
3145	,,	Johns, A. P. (Swansea)	K. in A.	
462	L/Cpl.	Johnson, F. C. (Meopham)		
938	Gdsn.	Johnson, W. (Mountain Ash)	†	
1568	,,	Johnson, W. T. (Newport)	† †	M.M.
1795	Sergt.	Johnson, A. E (Swansea)	†	M.M.
2203	Gdsn.	Johnson, H. C. (Llandovery)		
3060	,,	Johnson, E. W. (Cardiff)		
3182	,,	Johnson, F. (Nelson)	†	
3354	,,	Johnson, J. W. (Liverpool)	†	
3460	,,	Johnson, H. (Oakham)	K. in A.	
3649	L/Cpl.	Jonathan, J. H. (Pontypool)		
69	Cpl.	Jones, J. W. (Holywell)	†	
82	Gdsn.	Jones, M. (Treorchy)		M.M.
109	,,	Jones, J. (Rhayader)		
110	,,	Jones, R. (Welshpool)	K. in A.	
140	,,	Jones, J. (Flint)		
151	,,	Jones, D. T. (Bridgend)		
153	Cpl.	Jones, P. E. (Cardiff)		M.M.
166	Gdsn.	Jones, I. (Newport)		
201	,,	Jones, R. (Walsall)	K. in A.	
212	L/Sergt.	Jones, T. (Brecon)	K. in A.	
260	L/Sergt.	Jones, A. J. (Newport)		
272	Gdsn.	Jones, T. H. (Llanfechain)		
317	Sergt.	Jones, H. (Swansea)	D. of S.	
319	Gdsn.	Jones, W. (Gilfach Goch)	†	
328	Sergt.	Jones, T. (Kidsgrove)		
399	Gdsn.	Jones, D. (Preston)	†	
416	,,	Jones, S. (Hednesford)	†	
435	,,	Jones, D. (Bridgend)	K. in A.	
448	,,	Jones, W. J. (Swansea)	† D. of Wds.	
468	,,	Jones, A. (Aberfan)	D. of Wds.	M.M.
480	,,	Jones, W. (Rochdale)	† †	
511	,,	Jones, F. S. (Bury)	D. of Wds.	
526	,,	Jones, E. (Ammanford)	†	
561	Sergt.	Jones, W. (Aberdare)	†	
723	Cpl.	Jones, J. (Aberdare)	† †	M.M.
733	Gdsn.	Jones, R. E. (Pentre Broughton)		
753	,,	Jones, J. (Penygraig)	† K. in A.	
754	,,	Jones, D. (Aberystwyth)	K. in A.	
756	L/Sergt.	Jones, W. M. (Tonypandy)	†	M.M. and Bar.
785	Gdsn.	Jones, D. (Tonypandy)	†	
792	L/Cpl.	Jones. H. W. (Swansea)	†	
817	L/Sergt.	Jones, G. (Bangor)		
823	Sergt.	Jones, E. (Rhondda)	† † D.of Wds.	D.C.M.
871	Gdsn.	Jones, S. (Aberdare)	†	
921	,,	Jones, M. (Durham)	†	
964	,,	Jones, J. (Llanelly)		

Regtl. No.	Rank.	Name.	Casualties.	Decorations.
1005	Gdsn.	Jones, S. G. (Caerwent)	D. of Wds.	
1067	,,	Jones, J. (Llanelly)	K. in A.	
1100	,,	Jones, F. (Swinton)	K. in A.	
1123	,,	Jones, I. (Ruthin)	† K. in A.	
1124	L/Cpl.	Jones, H. J. (Wrexham)	†	
1132	Gdsn.	Jones, W. G. (Newport)		
1140	,,	Jones, G. F. (Haverfordwest)	† K. in A.	
1176	,,	Jones, W. G. (Builth Wells)		
1177	,,	Jones, E. (Pentre)	† †	
1189	,,	Jones, W. (Port Talbot)	D. of Wds.	M.M.
1219	,,	Jones, T. (Llwynypia)	†	
1237	,,	Jones, R. (Cwmavon)	† D. of Wds.	
1306	,,	Jones, R. E. (Llanfair)	†	
1371	,,	Jones, J. L. (Ammanford)		
1380	,,	Jones, H. M. (Aberystwyth)	K. in A.	
1383	,,	Jones, J. (Bridgend)	†	
1384	L/Cpl.	Jones, D. H. (Neath)	†	
1389	Gdsn.	Jones, J. (Llwynypia)	K. in A.	
1426	,,	Jones, G. H. P. (Newtown)		
1440	L/Cpl.	Jones, W. A. L. (Llangadock)		
1471	Gdsn.	Jones, I. (Llanfair)	†	
1479	,,	Jones, E. (Penrhyndeudraeth)	†	
1506	,,	Jones, W. (Wrexham)	†	
1511	L/Cpl.	Jones, B. (Wrexham)	† K. in A.	
1520	Gdsn.	Jones, D. O. (Colwyn Bay)	† † † †	
1523	,,	Jones, D. R. (Aberdare)	K. in A.	M.M.
1525	,,	Jones, I. (Llanelly)		
1530	,,	Jones, R. C. (Swansea)	†	
1558	,,	Jones, E. (Llantriant)	D. of Wds.	
1636	,,	Jones, E. (Pontypridd)		
1651	,,	Jones, W. T. (Cardiff)	† †	
1655	,,	Jones, D. (London, S.E.)	†	
1657	,,	Jones, B. (Carmarthen)	†	
1688	,,	Jones, S. G. (Bridgend)	†	
1695	,,	Jones, M. J. (Tonypandy)		
1705	L/Cpl.	Jones, R. O. (Liverpool)		
1712	Gdsn.	Jones, L. (Brithdir)	D. of Wds.	
1724	,,	Jones, D. L. (Mountain Ash)		
1729	,,	Jones, S. (Merthyr)		
1734	,,	Jones, H. W. (Rhyl)	†	
1756	,,	Jones, T. (Haverfordwest)	K. in A.	
1784	,,	Jones, J. G. (Mostyn)	K. in A.	
1826	L/Cpl.	Jones, W. E. (Trefnant)	†	
1835	Gdsn.	Jones, D. (Cardiff)	† † † K. in A.	
1914	,,	Jones, F. C. (Aberdare)	D. of Wds.	
1919	,,	Jones, J. (Aberavon)	†	
1961	,,	Jones, T. W. (Towyn)		
1969	,,	Jones, J. (Llandyssil)	† † † D. of Wds.	
1970	,,	Jones, D. (Aberdare)	†	
1975	,,	Jones, W. (Mountain Ash)		
1999	,,	Jones, W. (Llangaffo)	†	

Regtl. No.	Rank.	Name.	Casualties.	Decorations.
2017	Gdsn.	Jones, J. (Llanelly)	†	
2020	,,	Jones, T. J. (Wrexham) . . .	K. in A.	
2021	,,	Jones, J. (Monmouth) . . .	†	
2030	,,	Jones, E. (Lydbury)		
2041	,,	Jones, L. (Tycroes)	K. in A.	
2069	,,	Jones, B. (Cardiff)	†	
2075	,,	Jones, W. O. (Dolgelly) . . .		
2083	,,	Jones, D. H. (Newport) . . .		
2084	,,	Jones, D. O. (Colwyn Bay) . . .		
2086	,,	Jones, W. T. (Cwmavon) . . .	K. in A.	
2094	,,	Jones, E. T. (Cardiff) . . .		
2101	,,	Jones, D. (Corwen)	D. of S.	
2115	,,	Jones, E. H. (Aberystwyth) . .		
2122	L/Cpl.	Jones, W. (Penygroes) . . .	K. in A.	
2127	Gdsn.	Jones, J. W. (Llanfrothen) . .		
2139	L/Sergt.	Jones, R. (Denbigh) . . .	† † † † †	
2150	Gdsn.	Jones, D. T. (Cowbridge) . .		
2154	,,	Jones, J. D. (Brynmawr) . .	† †	
2176	,,	Jones, W. W. (Carmarthen) . .	†	
2179	Musn.	Jones, P. (London)		
2183	L/Cpl.	Jones, R. (Penrhyndeudraeth) . .	†	
2201	,,	Jones, E. (Aberystwyth) . . .	† †	
2240	Gdsn.	Jones, W. (Welshpool) . . .	†	
2246	,,	Jones, R. (Bangor)		
2251	,,	Jones, D. O. (Penbryn) . . .	† †	M.M.
2256	,,	Jones, G. R. (Abergavenny) . .		M.M.
2268	,,	Jones, H. A. (Brecon) . . .		
2284	,,	Jones, D. L. (Llandyrnog) . . .	D. of Wds.	
2290	,,	Jones, J. J. (Birkenhead) . .	D. of Wds.	
2291	,,	Jones, A. (Llansantffraid) . .	†	
2292	,,	Jones, D. (Menai Bridge) . . .		
2305	,,	Jones, T. (Llanwnen) . . .		
2315	,,	Jones, J. L. (Llangerniew) . .		
2387	,,	Jones, E. (Criccieth) . . .		
2398	,,	Jones, E. (Pwllheli) . . .		
2427	L/Cpl.	Jones, J. D. (Conway) . . .	† D. of Wds.	
2442	,,	Jones, E. C. (Llanbyther) . .		
2455	Gdsn.	Jones, W. G .(Aberdare) . .	† K. in A.	
2467	,,	Jones, D. W. (Merthyr) . . .	K. in A.	
2492	,,	Jones, E. (Llanelly) . . .	†	
2503	,,	Jones, D. M. (Porth) . . .	†	
2565	,,	Jones, W. (Rhyl)		
2582	,,	Jones, A. (Trealaw) . . .	K. in A.	
2603	,,	Jones, A. (Newport) . . .	†	
2627	,,	Jones, E. L. (Carmarthen) . .		M.M.
2629	,,	Jones, L. (Carmarthen) . . .		
2666	,,	Jones, O. C. (Pwllheli) . . .		
2675	Sergt.	Jones, J. (Llanarth) . . .	†	
2703	Gdsn.	Jones, T. (Swansea) . . .		
2708	,,	Jones, T. M. (Maesteg) . . .	†	M.M.
2738	,,	Jones, O. (Dolgelly) . . .	K. in A.	

Regtl. No.	Rank.	Name.	Casualties.	Decorations.
2743	Gdsn.	Jones, K. E. (Oswestry)		
2752	,,	Jones, E. O. (London)	†	
2792	,,	Jones, D. J. (Treherbert)		
2816	,,	Jones, D. (Denbigh)	†	
2820	,,	Jones, D. (Dolgelly)	K. in A.	
2828	L/Cpl.	Jones, I. (Llangenny)		
2841	Gdsn.	Jones, T. H. (St. Asaph)	D. of Wds.	
2864	,,	Jones, W. J. (Llandwrog)	†	
2877	L/Cpl.	Jones, A. E. (Bridgnorth)	†	
2898	Gdsn.	Jones, H. R. (Anglesey)		
2915	,,	Jones, H. W. (Wrexham)	†	
2952	,,	Jones, W. I. (Wrexham)	†	
3015	,,	Jones, D. E. (Llanbedarn)	D. of Wds.	M.M.
3017	,,	Jones, R. (Dolgelly)	† †	
3022	,,	Jones, R. R. (Dolgelly)	†	
3026	,,	Jones, W. T. (Rhyl)		
3043	,,	Jones, G. R. (Llanllyfni)	†	
3081	,,	Jones, H. P. (Barmouth)		
3082	,,	Jones, W. R. (Maentwrog)		
3084	,,	Jones, R. E. (Machynlleth)		
3110	,,	Jones, W. E. (Liverpool)	†	
3114	,,	Jones, W. (Talysarn)	† † †	
3131	,,	Jones, D. (Cardiff)	†	
3135	,,	Jones, W. (Bangor)		
3217	,,	Jones, D. T. (Kidwelly)	†	
3258	,,	Jones, A. (Neath)		
3270	,,	Jones, E. G. (Usk)	D. of Wds.	
3320	,,	Jones, J. J. (Cardiff)	†	
3385	,,	Jones, F. (Denbigh)		
3410	,,	Jones, T. (Leicester)	K. in A.	
3424	,,	Jones, W. A. (Prestatyn)	D. of S.	
3443	,,	Jones, D. (Brecon)	† †	
3444	,,	Jones, T. H. (Aberystwyth)	†	
3458	,,	Jones, L. (Llanasa)	K. in A.	
3472	,,	Jones, T. (Mold)	† †	
3501	,,	Jones, A. E. (Chirk)		
3511	,,	Jones, M. R. (Denbigh)		
3514	,,	Jones, H. (Trefdraeth)	†	
3519	,,	Jones, R. (Llangefni)	K. in A.	
3549	,,	Jones, D. T. (Wrexham)	†	
3550	,,	Jones, J. (Newtown)	K. in A.	
3551	,,	Jones, J. M. (Chester)		
3556	,,	Jones, J. (Cardiff)		
3558	,,	Jones, W. D. (Llandrillo)		M.M.
3560	,,	Jones, R. F. (Wrexham)	K. in A.	
3574	,,	Jones, T. L. (Llangollen)		
3575	,,	Jones, W. St. C. (Manchester)		
3587	,,	Jones, H. (Abergele)		
3593	,,	Jones, T. O. (Liverpool)	K. in A.	
3604	L/Cpl.	Jones, O. (Wrexham)		
3614	Gdsn.	Jones, W. O. (Conway)	D. of S.	

Regtl. No.	Rank.	Name.	Casualties.	Decorations.
3667	Gdsn.	Jones, W. (Hawarden)		
3671	„	Jones, D. (Caerphilly)	K. in A.	
3675	„	Jones, D. (Mydroilin) .		
3695	„	Jones, W. (Aberystwyth)		
3697	„	Jones, J. H. (Rhuddlan)	†	
3723	„	Jones, T. (Wolverhampton)	†	
3786	„	Jones, W. H. (Birmingham)	†	
3837	„	Jones, J. (Penygraig) .		
3853	„	Jones, J. H. (Llanrhaiadr) .		
3863	„	Jones, W. J. H. (London, S.E.) .		
3917	„	Jones, W. R. (Cwmavon) .		
4025	„	Jones, P. H. (Merthyr)	K. in A.	
4065	L/Cpl.	Jones, J. G. (Bangor)	†	
4068	Gdsn.	Jones, J. G. (Llantysilio)	D. of Wds.	M.M.
4100	„	Jones, W. R. (Caerphilly)		
4101	„	Jones, J. T. (Cardiff) .		
4245	Dmr.	Jones, E. (Ruthin)	†	
4290	Gdsn.	Jones, P. (Neath)		
4372	„	Jones, H. (Corwen)	†	
4382	„	Jones, W. (Manchester)		
4466	„	Jones, J. C. (Cardiff) .		
4476	„	Jones, C. (Dowlais)		
4490	„	Jones, G. J. (Pentre) .		
4565	„	Jones, B. (Cross Keys)		
4578	„	Jones, B. (Loughor)		
4594	„	Jones, G. A. (Pontypridd) .		
4599	„	Jones, D. (Merthyr)		
4628	„	Jones, J. (Abercynon)		
4673	„	Jones, J. T. (Morriston)		
4764	„	Jones, D. S. (Merthyr)		
5378	„	Jones, H. (Wrexham)		
5702	„	Jones, D. F. (Kidwelly)		
5837	„	Jones, J. (Cardiff)		
3510	„	Joslin, W. J. (Swansea)	†	
3967	„	Joyce, S. A. E. (Rochester)	†	
4919	„	Judd, H. (Cardiff)		
3630	„	Judge, H. (Birmingham)		
3011	„	Jukes, D. (Abertillery)	† †	
1923	L/Cpl.	Jury, A. (Bridgend) .	† K. in A.	
3680	Gdsn.	Justice, W. G. (Workingham)	†	
2070	Sergt.	Kealey, W. (London) .		
66	„	Keay, W. (Shrewsbury)	† †	
3676	Gdsn.	Keeble, C. V. (Bury St. Edmunds)	†	
3404	„	Keech, S. (Darlington)	†	
2769	„	Keeling, G. A. B. (Seacombe)	† †	
1538	„	Kellehar, B. (Hereford)	K. in A.	
1350	„	Kelloway, R. (Cardiff)	† †	
3976	„	Kelly, J. E. (Newcastle)	†	
473	Cpl.	Kemp, J. (Castleford)	† † †	
3807	Gdsn.	Kemp, H. A. (Birmingham)		

Regtl. No.	Rank.	Name.	Casualties.	Decorations.
527	Gdsn.	Kempson, A. J. (Cardiff)		
2384	L/Cpl.	Kennea, W. J. (Pembroke)		
625	„	Kennett, F. (Cardiff)	†	
3777	Gdsn.	Kenton, F. (Aldershot)		
3229	„	Kenyon, T. (Radcliffe)	†	
1566	L/Sergt.	Keoghane, D. (Cardiff)	† † †	
2206	Gdsn.	Kerton, C. (Newport)	K. in A.	
2329	„	Kerton, E. J. (Aberdare)	†	
1038	Cpl.	Kiernan, S. (Trefnant)	K. in A.	
2486	Gdsn.	Kiff, H. T. (Porth)	†	
3533	„	Kilford, J. (Bristol)	† †	
3799	„	Kindon, J. (Birmingham)	D. of Wds.	
1582	L/Sergt.	King, R. E. (Mountain Ash)		
1644	L/Cpl.	King, A. E. (Cardiff)	†	
2257	Gdsn.	King, W. J. (Cardiff)	K. in A.	
2288	„	King, W. C. (Porth)		
3291	„	King, W. R. (Clewer Green)		
3859	„	King, F. J. (Ystrad)	†	
4259	„	King, M. (Cardiff)		
60	Sergt.	Kirby, A. H. (Merthyr)	†	
3365	Gdsn.	Kirk, J. (Kenilworth)	†	
1122	L/Cpl.	Kitchen, R. T. (Aberavon)		
755	Gdsn.	Knight, A. J. (Rhondda)	†	
1557	„	Knight, G. L. (Tonypandy)	† †	
2191	„	Knight, W. H. (Foston)	†	
2286	Musn.	Knight, W. (Andover)		
2535	Gdsn.	Knight, R. (Abergavenny)	†	
1049	„	Knott, J. (West-Bromwich)	†	
3817	„	Knott, F. (Horsham)		
262	„	Knowles, W. E. (Aberaman)	D. of Wds.	
2833	„	Knowles, J. (St. Helen's)	K. in A.	
3626	Gdsn.	Labram, W. C. (Birmingham)		
3324	„	Lace, J. (Castleton)	†	
2271	L/Cpl.	Lacey, R. (Bridgend)	†	
3333	Gdsn.	Ladkin, H. (Leicester)	†	
3926	„	Laidlaw, M. W. (Holtwhistle)		
3906	„	Laight, C. H. (Birmingham)	†	
3245	„	Lake, W. (Cerne)		
3538	„	Lake, B. (Bristol)	†	
3888	„	Laken, W. H. (Birmingham)	†	
3336	„	Lambden, F. W. (Mitcheldean)		
2569	„	Lambert, A. (London, E.)	†	
2766	„	Lambert, F. (Eastbourne)	† †	
2746	L/Cpl.	Lambrick, J. (Swansea)	†	
2742	Gdsn.	Lane, W. J. (Cardiff)		
4031	„	Lane, T. H. (Ystrad)	†	
524	„	Langabeer, R. E. (Exeter)	D. of Wds.	
5824	„	Lange, H. N. (Swansea)		
979	„	Langford, A. (Neath)		
1809	Cpl.	Langford, L. (Tredegar)	D. of Wds.	

Regtl. No.	Rank.	Name.	Casualties.	Decorations.
2989	Gdsn.	Langley, G. (Cardiff)	†	
566	,,	Lanham, H. (Leicester) . . .	†	
1361	,,	Larcombe, F. (Newport) . . .	†	
2435	,,	Larcombe, P. (Pontypool) . .	†	
3088	,,	Larcombe, F. W. J. (Yeovil) .	†	
3209	,,	Lark, F. W. (Camberley) . .	†	
1857	Gdsn.	Laroche, D. (Cardiff) . . .	K. in A.	
2845		Latham, O. (Mold) . . .		
816	C.S.M.I.M.	Lauder, W. T. (Kelso) . .	†	
1489	Gdsn.	Law, A. J. (Bargoed) . . .		
3042	,,	Law, W. A. (Blackburn) . .	†	
4159	,,	Law, S. (Halesowen) . . .	†	
61	Cpl.	Lawless, A. (Frodsham) . .	K. in A.	
562	Gdsn.	Lawless, J. (Liverpool) . .		
1433	,,	Lawley, H. (Newport) . .	† K. in A.	
155	,,	Lawrence, A. (Cardiff) . .	K. in A.	
1498	L/Cpl.	Lawrence, H. (Trealaw) . .	K. in A.	
1779	Gdsn.	Lawrence, G. A. F. (Wilcoxon) .		
3169	,,	Lawrence, L. W. (London, N.) .		
4207	,,	Lawrence, F. (Mountain Ash) .	K. in A.	
25	L/Sergt.	Lawson, R. (Exeter) . . .		M.M.
614	Gdsn.	Lawson, C. (Neath) . . .	†	
4488	,,	Layzell, E. J. (Stretton) . .	† †	
2949	,,	Lea, A. C. (Little Budworth) .	†	
3875	,,	Leal, A. G. J. (London) . .		
3369	,,	Lee, N. (Leicester) . . .	† †	
3724	,,	Lee, W. (Wavertree) . . .	†	
3918	,,	Lee, H. G. (Hinckley) . .	† D. of Wds.	
4252	Cpl.	Lees, J. (Nottingham) . .		
2719	Gdsn.	Leftley. A. E. (Brockdish) .	†	
3703	,,	Leggatt, A. E. (Lipbrook) .	†	
4276	,,	Lehane, J. A. (Morriston) .		
2452	,,	Leigh, T. J. (Merthyr) . .		
5327	,,	Lemon, J. (Neath) . . .		
1746	,,	Leneham, J. (Preston) . .	†	
1791	,,	Leonard, J. W. (Wrexham) .	†	
3241	,,	Lester, R. (Pontypool) . .	†	
708	L/Cpl.	Letman, V. (Liverpool) . .	D. of Wds.	
874	Gdsn.	Leverton, A. N. (Swansea) .		
38	Sergt.	Lewis, E. (Aberystwyth) . .	† †	M.M.
139	Gdsn.	Lewis, G. A. L. (Bristol) . .	†	
231	Sergt.	Lewis, D. J. (Neath) . . .	†	
232	L/Cpl.	Lewis, A. (Neath) . . .	K. in A.	
339	Gdsn.	Lewis, W. B. (Merthyr) . .		
469	,,	Lewis, J. T. (Oswestry) . .	†	
529	,,	Lewis, W. J. (Milford Haven) .	†	M.M.
646	,,	Lewis, E. (Cwmbach) . . .	†	
682	,,	Lewis, E. J. (Cwmaman) . .	† D. of Wds.	
774	Dmr.	Lewis, T. (Brecon) . . .		
830	Gdsn.	Lewis, A. J. (Mountain Ash) .	†	
961	,,	Lewis, R. (Morriston) . .	D. of Wds.	

Regtl. No.	Rank.	Name.	Casualties.	Decorations.
1150	Dmr.	Lewis, D. T. (Aberystwyth)		
1173	Gdsn.	Lewis, A. C. (Cardiff)	†	
1476	,,	Lewis, D. (Bethesda)		
1579	,,	Lewis, T. (Trecastle)	†	
1584	,,	Lewis, E. W. (Aberdare)	†	
1627	Cpl.	Lewis, J. C. (Cardiff)	†	
1767	L/Sergt.	Lewis, G. (Machynlleth)	†	
1878	Gdsn.	Lewis, R. H. (Holyhead)		
1895	,,	Lewis, G. A. (Burry Port)	D. of Wds.	
1939	,,	Lewis, E. (Haverfordwest)		
1943	,,	Lewis, H. G. (Caerphilly)	†	
2001	,,	Lewis, R. I. (Llantrisant)	†	
2031	,,	Lewis, T. A. (Penclawdd)	K. in A.	
2145	L/Cpl.	Lewis, D. J. (Pontardawe)	† †	
2151	Gdsn.	Lewis, G. (Kerry)		
2172	,,	Lewis, H. (Aberystwyth)	† D. of S.	
2336	L/Cpl.	Lewis, H. (Clydach-on-Tawe)		
2344	Gdsn.	Lewis, L. (London)		
2401	,,	Lewis, T. M. (Aberdovey)	† †	
2413	,,	Lewis, E. H. (Talyllyn)	†	
2499	,,	Lewis, B. (Bridell)		
2614	,,	Lewis, B. (Merthyr)		
2656	,,	Lewis, F. R. (Narberth)		
2661	,,	Lewis, J. (Carmarthen)	† †	M.M.
2817	,,	Lewis, G. L. (Woolaston)	†	
2840	,,	Lewis, J. G. (Bangor)	†	
3045	,,	Lewis, T. J. (Llanelly)	K. in A.	
3066	,,	Lewis, G. (Aberystwyth)	†	
3136	,,	Lewis, H. J. (Tonypandy)	†	
3247	,,	Lewis, E. J. (Llwynypia)	D. of Wds.	
3321	,,	Lewis, H. W. (Newport)	†	
3446	,,	Lewis, D. (Llanllanfair)	K. in A.	
3594	,,	Lewis, W. E. (Pontardulais)		
3596	,,	Lewis, E. A. (Cardiff)	†	
3631	,,	Lewis, A. (Nottingham)		
3702	,,	Lewis, C. (Worcester)	†	
3876	,,	Lewis, J. (Llantrisant)	† D. of Wds.	
4090	,,	Lewis, S G. (Swansea)	†	
4097	,,	Lewis, W. (Pontypool)		
4129	,,	Lewis, I. (Swansea)	†	
4729	,,	Lewis, F. W. (Merthyr)		
4842	,,	Lewis, D. T. (Cardiff)		
5339	,,	Lewis, J. (Carmarthen)		
3402	,,	Ley, S. A. (Barnstaple)		
189	,,	Leyshon, G. J. (Llanelly)	D. of Wds.	
804	,,	Leyshon, F. E. (Burry Port)		
1365	,,	Leyshon, A. (Peterston)	K. in A.	
1935	,,	Leyshon, W. E. (Peterston)		
2450	,,	Leyshon, L. E. (Peterston)	†	
5720	Cpl.	Liebson, H. (S. Africa)		
1903	Gdsn.	Light, G. (Newport)		

Regtl. No.	Rank.	Name.	Casualties.	Decorations.
241	Gdsn.	Lilley, G. E. (Nuneaton) . . .		
1533	,,	Lindsell, J. F. W. (London) . .	†	
3758	,,	Line, W. (Wickham) . . .	†	
4335	,,	Lines, J. J. (Southery) . .		
2599	,,	Linnard, F. (Cardiff) . . .		
2184	,,	Linney, S. (Chesterfield) . .		
4338	,,	Linney, H. J. (Nuneaton) . .	†	
4339	,,	Lipscombe, A. M. (Staines) . .	†	
1042	,,	Llewellyn, E. (London) . .	K. in A.	
1120	,,	Llewellyn, D. (Bridgend) . .	† † † †	
1293	,,	Llewellyn, T. (Swansea) . .	D. of Wds.	
1442	,,	Llewellyn, A. (Cardiff) . .	† †	
1504	,,	Llewellyn, C. D. (Caerphilly) .		
2428	,,	Llewellyn, W. (Cardiff) . .		
2753	L/Cpl.	Llewellyn, G. H. (Swansea) . .	†	
2844	Gdsn.	Llewellyn, W. (Cardiff) . .		
2971	,,	Llewellyn, T. (Newport) . .		
3100	,,	Llewellyn, W. (Bridgend) . .	†	
3525	,,	Llewellyn, R. (Bristol) . .		
657	A/C.Q.M.S.	Lloyd, C. (Parkstone) . .	†	
87	Gdsn.	Lloyd, W. G. (Swansea) . .	†	
202	,,	Lloyd, J. (Cardiff) . .	†	M.M.
375	,,	Lloyd, R. (Llanfyllin) . .	†	
538	Cpl.	Lloyd, H. (West Bromwich) .	†	
731	L/Cpl.	Lloyd, W. G. Carmarthen) .	K. in A.	
932	,,	Lloyd, S. (Caerphilly) . .	† † †	
1623	Gdsn.	Lloyd, T. (Aberystwyth) . .	D. of Wds.	
1659	Cpl.	Lloyd, W. (Narberth) . .	†	
1710	Gdsn.	Lloyd, B. E. (Swansea) . .		
1925	,,	Lloyd, H. J. (Manchester) . .		
2332	,,	Lloyd, E. G. (Mold) . .	†	
2755	,,	Lloyd, A. E. (Southport) . .		
2822	,,	Lloyd, J. (Wrexham) . . .		
2842	,,	Lloyd, J. G. (Denbigh) . .		
2853	,,	Lloyd, O. (Pwllheli) . .		
3396	,,	Lloyd, W. S. (Pwllheli) . .		
3494	,,	Lloyd, J. W. (Welshpool) . .	K. in A.	
4074	,,	Lloyd, R. (Porth) . . .	†	
4281	,,	Lloyd, A. J. (Penarth) . .		
4766	,,	Lloyd, A. (Abercanaid) . .		
1347	,,	Lock, G. H. (Cardiff) . .	K. in A.	
1462	,,	Lock, J. (Pontypridd) . .	†	
2875	Cpl.	Lock, W. (Swansea) . .	†	
703	Gdsn.	Locke, J. (Rhondda) . .		
1680	,,	Locke, W. (Llanelly) . .		
4500	,,	Locke, W. G. (Merthyr) . .		
5280	,,	Locke, L. (Cardiff) . .		
2643	,,	Lockey, C. (London) . .	†	
4494	,,	Loder, W. J. (Cwmbran) . .		
573	L/Cpl.	Lodwick, T. J. (Llanelly) . .	† †	
1692	Gdsn.	Long, R. E. (Ammanford) . .		

Regtl. No.	Rank	Name.	Casualties.	Decorations.
2167	Musn.	Long, A. (London, S.W.)		
2601	Gdsn.	Long, B. G. (Cardiff)	†	
972	„	Longdon, I. I. (London)		
4337	„	Longmate, W. (Lincoln)		
3416	„	Loten, R. (Portsmouth)		
640	L/Cpl.	Lovall, G. (Bargoed)		
677	Gdsn.	Lovatt, A. E. (Cardiff)	†	
407	Sergt.	Lovell, A. W. (Pontypridd)	† †	
112	Gdsn.	Lovering, W. T. (Cardiff)	†	
2013	„	Lovis, R. (Dowlais)	K. in A.	
3364	„	Lowcock, A. (Barrowford)		
2809	L/Cpl.	Lowe, H. (Royton)	†	
329	„	Lucas, F. (Swansea)	†	
1631	Gdsn.	Lucas, T. G. (Cardiff)	†	M.M.
3654	L/Cpl.	Lucas, W. A. H. (Aberavon)	K. in A.	
3534	Gdsn.	Ludlow, E. W. (Bristol)		
461	„	Luen, L. (Barry)		
162	Cpl.	Luker, D. J. (Cardiff)		M.M. and
4922	Gdsn.	Lumber, E. H. (Landore)		[Bar.
2263	L/Sergt.	Lumley, A. (Sunderland)		
1906	L/Cpl.	Lund, H. (Cardiff)		
4063	Gdsn.	Lunn, G. (Llandudno)		
4336	„	Lunn, E. (Bognor)		
844	„	Lye, T. L. (Aberdare)	†	
1762	„	Lynch, J. (Cardiff)	†	
3535	„	Lyons, A. C. (Bristol)	†	
824	Gdsn.	Mabitt, D. T. (Radyr)	K. in A.	
1894	„	Machin, J. (Stoke-on-Trent)	† K. in A.	
2672	..	Mack, F. C. (Cardiff)		
766	Sergt.	Maclachlan, C. (Argyle)	†	
2798	Gdsn.	Maclean, J. F. (Penarth)		
3956	„	Madge, F. J. (Colebrook)		
694	„	Maggs, R. (Cardiff)	†	
2306	„	Maggs, J. (Pontypool)	† †	
4422	„	Maher, A. (Manchester)		
2642	„	Mainwaring, E. T. (Aberavon)	†	
923	„	Makings, W. (Brecon)	†	
3107	L/Cpl.	Malcolm, D. C. (Norham-on-Tweed)	† D. of Wds.	
3216	„	Maliphant, D. T. (Kidwelly)	†	
4224	Gdsn.	Mallaband, E. (Smallheath)	D. of Wds.	
3745	„	Malthouse, H. D. (Brighton)		
3479	L/Cpl.	Manfield, L. F. (Cardiff)	†	
1534	„	Mann, J. (Tonypandy)	† †	
4340	Gdsn.	Mann A. S. (Marden)	† †	
1238	„	Manning, J. (Brecon)		
3828	„	Manning, F. H. (Leamington)	† †	
463	„	Mansell, T. (Nelson)	† D. of Wds.	
4190	„	Mansell, J. (Oadley)	†	
1050	Sergt.	Manuel, W. (Middlesborough)	† †	M.M.
3215	Gdsn.	Mark, G. (Liverpool)	D. of Wds.	

Regtl No.	Rank.	Name.	Casualties.	Decorations.
3183	Gdsn.	Markland, W. (Manchester)	. .	
651	,,	Marklove, G. C. (Caerphilly)	. . K. in A.	
1345	L/Cpl.	Marks, P. J. (Cardiff)	. . K. in A.	
2824	Gdsn.	Markwick, J. (Oldham)	. .	
3754	,,	Marovich, T. H. (Cardiff)	. .	
3787	,,	Marris, G. H. (Birmingham)	. †	
191	Sergt.	Marsh, H. H. (Cardiff)	. †	
783	Gdsn.	Marsh, E. H. B. (Pengam)	. . D. of Wds.	
2901	,,	Marsh, P. (Golborne)	. . †	
161	L/Sergt.	Marshall, T. W. (Cardiff)	. . † †	
514	Gdsn.	Marshall, A. V. (London)	. . † †	
1024	Sergt.	Marshall, G. W. (London)	. .	
3153	,,	Marshall, E. J. (Ockenden)	. . K. in A.	
3345	,,	Marshall, J. F. (Liverpool)	. . †	
3375	,,	Marshall, F. (Netley Abbey)	. . D. of Wds.	
3878	,,	Marsters, C. E. (St. Ives)	. . K. in A.	
1830	Sergt.	Martin, G. F. W. (Bridgend)	. †	
2507	Gdsn.	Martin, W. B. (Port Talbot)	. . D. of Wds.	
4532	,,	Martin, T. C. (Bridgend)	. .	
4781	,,	Martin, F. R. (Cardiff)	. .	
3363	,,	Martindale, N. (Ulverston)	. . †	
4182	L/Cpl.	Martino, H. C. C. (London)	. .	
3288	Gdsn.	Maslin, R. (Reading)	. . †	
3638	,,	Mason, G. (Ferndale)	. .	
3078	,,	Massey, W. R. (Burnham)	. .	
2331	Musn.	Mason, E. (Glasgow)	. .	
47	Sergt.	Mathews, W. H. (Cardiff)	. .	
114	,,	Mathias, R. (Pontyrhyll)	. . †	D.C.M. and Bar.
1447	Gdsn.	Mathias, D. (Aberystwyth)	. . †	
263	,,	Matthews, H. J. (Pontypool)	. .	M.M.
885	L/Cpl.	Matthews, G. V. (Swansea)	. .	
1469	Gdsn.	Matthews, R. (Wrexham)	. . †	
1866	,,	Matthews, R. T. (Birmingham)	. . †	
3621	,,	Matthews, G. (Newtown)	. .	
4555	,,	Matthews, G. H. (Abertillery)	. .	
4730	,,	Matthews, C. (Llanharry)	. .	
2799	Sergt.	Mawdsley, R. H. (Prescot)	. . †	
1752	Gdsn.	May, R. (Bridgend)	. . K. in A.	
4342	,,	May, P. (Plymouth)	. . D. of Wds.	
1801	L/Cpl.	Mayer, R. (Smallthorne)	. . K. in A.	
4059	L/Sergt.	McCadden, D. A. (Queensferry)	.	
228	Gdsn.	McCarthy, J. (Swansea)	. . †	
1544	,,	McCarthy, J. (Cardiff)	. . †	
3049	,,	McConville, P. (Wrexham)	. . K. in A.	
3924	,,	McCormack, H. (Bradford)	. . †	
3772	,,	McCracken, A. S. (Wigton)	. . †	
2693	L/Cpl.	McDowell, J. (Cardiff)	. . K. in A.	
4122	Gdsn.	McGregor, C. H. (East Benton)	. . K. in A.	
2893	,,	Meadows, T. (Wigan)	. .	
2545	,,	Meehan, J. W. (London)	. . †	
264	,,	Megan, J. (Dowlais)	. .	

Regtl. No.	Rank.	Name.	Casualties.	Decorations.
2357	Gdsn.	Melhuish, A. G. (Llantwit Vardre)	†	
1758	„	Mellor, J. (Salford)	†	
1026	„	Mellows, G. (Nottingham)	† †	
3401	„	Melvin, A. (Padiham)		
3727	„	Mercer, T. H. (Chatham)	†	
244	L/Cpl.	Meredith, A. (Newport)		
503	Gdsn.	Meredith, A. E. (Monmouth)		
556	Sergt.	Meredith, J. W. (Newport)		
2399	Gdsn.	Meredith, J. (Cefnybedd)	K. in A.	
2604	„	Meredith, J. P. (Tredegar)	K. in A.	
2883	„	Meredith, I. (Trawsfynydd)	†	
4137	„	Merkin, J. (Derby)		
1227	L/Cpl.	Merrett, W. T. (Newport)		
2380	Cpl.	Merrett, R. (Bridgend)		M.M.
252	Gdsn.	Messer, G. (Hereford)	†	M.M.
1310	„	Metcalfe, W. (Carnarvon)		
2652	„	Metcalfe, G. (Gowerton)	K. in A.	
3056	„	Metcalfe, G. (Blackburn)	D. of Wds.	
3176	„	Metcalfe, W. V. (Sunderland)	†	
3554	„	Mewett, E. J. (Porth)		
2647	„	Michael, D. (Carmarthen)		
3595	„	Michael, S. (Neath)	†	
3306	„	Midgley, T. E. (Luddenden)	† †	
2283	„	Miles, E. J. (Cardiff)	† K. in A.	
4256	„	Miles, T. (Newport)		
471	„	Millard, T. H. (Maidenhead)	†	
2278	„	Millard, E. (Sittingbourne)	†	
4554	„	Millard, F. (Pontefract)		
1477	„	Millatt, H. (Mold)	† †	
3164	„	Millbourne, P. (Oxford)	†	
4109	„	Miller, R. E. (Bury St. Edmunds)	†	
4070	L/Cpl.	Millett, A. G. (Cardiff)		
919	Gdsn.	Millington, G. (Ebbw Vale)		
1567	L/Cpl.	Mills, H. P. (Stroud)	† †	
2980	Gdsn.	Mills, F. H. (Cardiff)	† † K. in A.	
3080	L/Cpl.	Mills, W. H. (Swansea)		M.M.
3969	Gdsn.	Mills, F. C. (Swansea)		
4150	„	Mills, W. D. (Kenfig Hill)		
433	„	Milson, B. J. (Ton Pentre)		
3191	„	Milton, J. D. J. (Cardiff)	K. in A.	
3257	„	Milton, G. (Caerphilly)	†	
3243	„	Minors, T. W. (London, E.)	† † †	
2340	L/Cpl.	Mitchell, L. T. (London, E.)		
2493	Gdsn.	Mitchell, W. R. (Port Talbot)		
2586	„	Mitchell, R. (Neath)	D. of Wds.	
3054	L/Cpl.	Mitchell, E. (Woolfold)		
3747	Gdsn.	Mitchell, A. (Brighton)	†	
649	L/Cpl.	Mizen, A. J. (Pontypridd)		
2939	Gdsn.	Mogg, E. T. (London)		
2917	„	Moline, A. (Cardiff)		
715	„	Monk, J. (Rhymney)	K. in A.	

Regtl. No.	Rank.	Name.	Casualties.	Decorations.
3158	Gdsn.	Montague, W. (Tranmere) . . .	†	
135	,,	Moody, D. R. (Wrexham) . . .		
3122	,,	Moon, R. (Liverpool)	†	
3980	,,	Mooney, T. (Newcastle)		
331	,,	Moore, A. G. (Newport) . . .		
2578	,,	Moore, P. J. (Bridgend) . . .	D. of Wds.	
2760	Sergt.	Moore, G. H. (Cardiff) . . .		M.M.
2815	Gdsn.	Moore, A. D. (Colwyn Bay) . .	†	
2970	,,	Moore, W. H. (Newport) . .	†	
3823	,,	Moore, T. J. (Nuneaton) . .	† K. in A.	
194	Sergt.	Moreland, G. W. (Cardiff) . . .	†	
4481	Gdsn.	Moreman, T. (Cardiff)		
126	,,	Morgan, H. H. (Bristol) . . .		
173	,,	Morgan, J. (Cardiff)		
176	,,	Morgan, J. (Cardiff) . . .	† †	
290	L/Cpl.	Morgan, M. J. (Lampeter) . . .	† †	M.M.
310	Gdsn.	Morgan, H. J. (Henxworth) . .		
558	L/Sergt.	Morgan, W. G. (Millom) . .	† †	
591	Sergt.	Morgan, I. T. (Gilfach Goch) .	D. of Wds.	
739	Gdsn.	Morgan, J. L. (Treharris) . . .		
897	,,	Morgan, T. (Ton Pentre) . . .	K. in A.	
951	,,	Morgan, T. V. (Troedyrhiw) . .	D. of Wds.	
954	Sergt.	Morgan, E. (Ton Pentre) . . .		M.M.
973	Gdsn.	Morgan, A. (Gilfach Bargoed) . .	K. in A.	
1096	,,	Morgan, D. R. (Abergavenny) . .	†	
1105	,,	Morgan, A. C. (Radnor) . . .		
1196	,,	Morgan, T. (Swansea). . . .		
1216	,,	Morgan, R. (Cilfynydd) . . .	K. in A.	
1336	L/Cpl.	Morgan, I. D. (Swansea) . . .	†	
1386	Gdsn.	Morgan, T. J. (Bridgend) . . .	†	
1451	,,	Morgan, J. (Brynaman) . . .		
1562	Cpl.	Morgan, I. O. G. (Aberystwyth) . .	†	
1589	Gdsn.	Morgan, H. (Bridgend) . . .	K. in A.	
1723	,,	Morgan, R. (Cardiff)	†	
1775	,,	Morgan, W. J. (Caerphilly) . .	†	
1929	,,	Morgan, W. (Llantwit Vardre) . .	†	
2032	,,	Morgan, J. (Cardiff)	D. of Wds.	
2068	,,	Morgan, G. V. (Aberdare) . .	† †	
2118	,,	Morgan, J. R. (Carmarthen) . .	K. in A.	
2171	,,	Morgan, J. (Newport) . . .		
2282	,,	Morgan, T. J. (Brecon) . . .		
2366	,,	Morgan, W. (Llangoedmor) . .	† †	
2546	L/Cpl.	Morgan, R. C. (Cardiff) . . .	†	
2592	Gdsn.	Morgan, G. A. (Hereford) . .	†	
2683	L/Cpl.	Morgan, E. J. (Cardiff) . . .	†	
2706	Gdsn.	Morgan, W. (Cwmllynfell) . .	D. of Wds.	
2735	,,	Morgan, E. E. (London) . . .	†	
2975	L/Cpl.	Morgan, F. R. (Ely, Glam.) . .	K. in A.	
3611	Gdsn.	Morgan, C. (Portsmouth) . . .		
3641	,,	Morgan, E. A. (Aberystwyth) . .		
3663	,,	Morgan, L. S. (Cardiff) . . .		

Regtl. No.	Rank.	Name.	Casualties.	Decorations.
4081	Gdsn.	Morgan, T. E. (Aberdare) . . .	D. of Wds.	
4626	„	Morgan, W. (Newport) . . .		
4728	„	Morgan, A. E. (Caerphilly) . . .		
4765	„	Morgan, W. J. (Neath) . . .		
4783	„	Morgan, J. P. (Crynant) . . .		
5018	„	Morgan, J. (Swansea) . . .		
5328	„	Morgan, W. (Llanelly) . . .		
525	„	Morgans, D. J. (Aberavon) . . .	† K. in A.	
2910	L/Cpl.	Morgans, J. (Aberystwyth) . . .	†	
1796	Gdsn.	Morice, R. G. (Swansea) . . .	† †	
81	L/Sergt.	Morisco, W. G. (Cardiff) . . .	† † † †	
4195	Gdsn.	Morphew, F. A. (Windy Nook) . .	†	
4496	„	Morrell, R. (Brynmawr) . . .		
3719	„	Morrey, H. (Liverpool) . . .	†	
100	„	Morris, J. (Cardiff) . . .	†	
354	Sergt.	Morris, C. (Nottingham) . . .	† †	
827	Gdsn.	Morris, J. S. (Aberdare) . . .	†	
925	„	Morris, A. (Cardiff) . . .	†	
934	„	Morris, R. (Swansea) . . .	†	
953	„	Morris, W. (Wrexham) . . .	K. in A.	
1490	„	Morris, S. (Rhymney) . . .		
1638	„	Morris, R. (Cwmyglo) . . .	K. in A.	
2106	„	Morris, J. (Neath) . . .	† †	
2116	L/Cpl.	Morris, E. L. (Ruabon) . . .	†	
2143	„	Morris, C. (Briton Ferry) . . .		
2247	Gdsn.	Morris, T. (Llangoed) . . .	†	
2303	„	Morris, G. T. (Swansea) . . .	†	
2593	„	Morris, T. E. (Carmarthen) . . .		
2835	„	Morris, H. (Newport) . . .	†	
2908	„	Morris, T. (Newport) . . .	†	
2913	„	Morris, R. (Abergele) . . .		
3196	„	Morris, E. H. (Wantage) . . .	†	
3483	„	Morris, J. E. (Llangadfan) . . .	†	
3485	„	Morris, T. W. (Cardiff) . . .	†	
3605	„	Morris, R. (Tredegar) . . .	K. in A.	
4114	„	Morris, W. H. (Barry) . . .	†	
4579	„	Morris, B. M. (Merthyr) . . .		
4734	„	Morris, M. J. (Cardiff) . . .		
4832	„	Morris, D. (Ystrad) . . .		
623	„	Morrisey, J. (Cardiff) . . .	†	M.M.
1121	„	Mort, D. T. (Aberdare) . . .	†	
30	C.S.M.	Moseley, V. H. (Pontypridd) . .		
3524	Gdsn.	Moseley, W. (Bristol) . . .		
4546	„	Moses, E. (Trelewis) . . .		
253	L/Sergt.	Moss, E. A. (Newport) . . .	†	
2681	Gdsn.	Moss, C. (Swansea) . . .	†	
3607	„	Moulsdale, R. V. B. (Llanrwst) .		
1978	L/Cpl.	Mountain, A. W. (Castleford) . .	† †	
848	Gdsn.	Mullane, D. (Cardiff) . . .	K. in A.	
1003	„	Mundy, W. J. (Guildford) . . .	† K. in A.	
5784	„	Munro, C. S. (Cardiff) . . .		

Regtl. No.	Rank.	Name.	Casualties.	Decorations.
3811	Gdsn.	Murfitt, F. H. (Cambridge) . . .	†	
330	Sergt.	Murphy, O. (Swansea) . . .	K. in A.	
1843	Gdsn.	Murphy, G. (Swansea) . . .		
3065	L/Cpl.	Murphy, J. (Ystalyfera) . . .	K. in A.	
1349	Sergt.	Murray, T. (Cardiff) . . .		
3157	Gdsn.	Murray, J. C. (Liverpool) . . .	†	
4341	,,	Murray, S. R. (Bolton) . . .	K. in A.	
3062	,,	Mustoe, A. C. (Cheltenham) . .		
2192	Musn.	Myatt, B. (Evesham)		
2219	Gdsn.	Myddleton, E. (Denbigh) . . .	†	
853	,,	Myers, A. J. (Cardiff) . . .	†	
1539	Gdsn.	Naish, A. C. (Caversham) . . .	K. in A.	
2166	Mnsn.	Nash, A. E. (Barnes)		
3990	Gdsn.	Nash. T. H. (Swansea) . . .		
692	,,	Neale, P. L. (Aberdare) . . .	K. in A.	
2111	L/Cpl.	Neale, H. G. (Barry)		M.M.
3741	Gdsn.	Neale, W. (Tipton)	†	
487	Cpl.	Needs, R. (Cardiff)	† †	M.M.
2905	Gdsn.	Needs. T. H. (Bristol) . . .		
363	,,	Nehemiah, J. H. (Swansea) . .	†	
4343	,,	Neighbour, H. H. (Leyton) . . .	†	
3715	,,	Neilson, A. E. (Wavertree) . . .	†	
3462	,,	Nevilles, J. (Murton) . . .	K. in A.	
1133	,,	Newall, T. N. (Widnes) . . .		
3459	,,	Newbold, H. J. (Chwilog) . . .	†	
2977	,,	Newbery, W. (Cardiff) . . .	† K. in A.	
3337	,,	Newman, F. G. (Caerphilly) . .	K. in A.	
3180	,,	Newport, J. (Oxford)	† † †	M.M.
2805	,,	Newton, J. (Spool) . . .	†	
373	,,	Nicholls, W. H. (Penrhiwceiber) .		
691	,,	Nicholls, J. (Aberdare) . . .		
1030	,,	Nicholls, J. J. (Penygraig) . . .	K. in A.	
2549	,,	Nicholls, W. (Swansea) . . .	†	
3515	,,	Nicholls, J. (Neath)	K. in A.	
3765	,,	Nicholls, A. (Birmingham) . .	K. in A.	
3792	,,	Nicholls, E. S. (Birmingham) . .		
397A	C.S.M.	Nicholson, L. H. (Liverpool) . .	†	
3130	Gdsn.	Nicholson, C. (Bristol) . . .		
3973	,,	Nicks, F. (Bramford) . . .		
2745	L/Sergt.	Nolte, P. (Cardiff)		
3480	Gdsn.	Noon, W. E. (Leicester) . . .	K. in A.	
150	,,	Noonan, E. (Manchester) . . .	†	
1757	Cpl.	Nordhoff, H. (Swansea) . . .		
1889	Gdsn.	Norgate, T. (Swansea) . . .	†	M.M.
343	L/Cpl.	Norman, J. E. (Swansea) . . .	† †	
3347	Gdsn.	Norman, W. (Ely, Cambs.) . . .	K. in A.	
4151	,,	Norman, W. S. (Southampton) .	† †	
3224	,,	Norris, P. (Padiham)	†	
358	L/Cpl.	Norton, J. (Bristol)	†	
2165	Musn.	Norton, E. W. (Penygraig) . . .		

Regtl. No.	Rank.	Name.	Casualties.	Decorations.
1715	Gdsn.	Nott, J. (Ludlow)	†	
5022	,,	Nott, W. H. (Swansea)		
120	,,	Nowell, L. (Llandaff)	D. of Wds.	
873	L/Sergt.	Noyes, D. (Swansea)		
3907	Gdsn.	Nutt, A. H. H. (Birmingham)		
3944	,,	Nuttall, W. B. (West Wycombe)		
2168	Musn.	Oakley, C. D. (Crawley)		
3139	Gdsn.	O'Brien, J. (Cardiff)	K. in A.	
2785	,,	O'Connell, G. (Denton)	†	
1833	,,	O'Connor, M. J. (Bridgend)	† K. in A.	
2308	L/Cpl.	Odell, F. J. (Cardiff)		
4887	Gdsn.	Ogborn, W. (Welshpool)		
1017	,,	Ogden, G. S. (Oldham)		
2457	L/Cpl.	O'Keefe, J. (Waterford)	K. in A.	
1339	Gdsn.	Okey, A. E. (Pontypridd)	†	
3974	,,	Oldham, H. (Worcester)		
3771	,,	Oliver, L. S. G. (Portslade)	†	
870	,,	Olsen, I. (Aberystwyth)		
3246	,,	Oram, E. (Newbridge)		
4344	,,	Orford, H. (Roydon)	D. of Wds.	
1088	,,	Ormrod, H. (Atherton)		
8	C.S.M.	Orton, T. E. (Wexford)	D. of Wds.	M.S.M.
2765	Gdsn.	Osborn, V. (Kettering)		
810	,,	Osborne, B. (Bargoed)	†	
1807	,,	Osborne, A. (Port Talbot)		
1610	,,	Osman, F. C. (Cardiff)	K. in A.	
2265	,,	Osman, G. A. (London, S.E.)	K. in A.	
4115	,,	Osmond, P. (Newport)		
2155	,,	Overson, A. E. (Llangollen)	†	
21	A/C.Q.M.S.	Owen, S. (Penmaenmawr)		M.M., M.S.M.
49	Sergt.	Owen, C. E. (Altrincham)	†	
332	Gdsn.	Owen, T. (Oswestry)		
346	Sergt.	Owen, F. W. (Maesteg)	K. in A.	
502	L/Sergt.	Owen, M. (Harlech)	K. in A.	
818	Gdsn.	Owen, J. R. (Amlwch)	†	
1292	,,	Owen, E. (Bargoed)	K. in A.	
1954	L/Cpl.	Owen, F. (Bridgend)	†	
2185	Gdsn.	Owen, O. S. (Holyhead)	†	
2250	,,	Owen, W. H. (Quaker's Yard)	† K. in A.	
2403	L/Cpl.	Owen, D. T. (Aberdovey)	†	
2534	Gdsn.	Owen, T. R. (Swansea)	K. in A.	
2726	,,	Owen, J. G. (Carmarthen)	†	
2734	,,	Owen, J. W. (Portmadoc)		
3127	,,	Owen, J. G. (Amlwch)		
3134	,,	Owen, W. W. (Llandwrog)	K. in A.	
3273	,,	Owen, J. (Llanfihangel-yn-Nhowyn)		
3417	,,	Owen, E. R. (Wrexham)		M.M.
3454	,,	Owen, J. (Denbigh)		
3555	,,	Owen, I. H. (Maesteg)	†	M.M.
3599	,,	Owen, W. (Llangattock)	†	
3610	,,	Owen, T. (Bangor)		

Regtl. No.	Rank.	Name.	Casualties.	Decorations.
4055	Gdsn.	Owen, J. L. (Denbigh) . . .		
4544	,,	Owen, I. (Dowlais)		
4585	,,	Owen, W. (Aberdare)		
4778	,,	Owen, C. (Treherbert) . . .		
4826	,,	Owen, G. J. (Bangor) . . .		
1109	,,	Owens, G. (Portmadoc) . . .	† † †	
2609	,,	Owens, O. D. (Ebbw Vale) . . .		
3124	Gdsn.	Padfield, R. (Manchester) . . .	†	
284	,,	Page, C. E. (Treharris) . . .	D. of Wds.	
1679	,,	Page, C. A. (Monmouth) . . .	D. of Wds.	
2048	,,	Page, R. (Newport)	†	
2426	,,	Page, H. H. (Kettering) . . .		
3658	,,	Page, S. (Bristol) . . .	K. in A.	
1379	Cpl.	Painter, J. (Cardiff)	†	
1407	Gdsn.	Palfrey, C. (Cardiff) . . .	D. of Wds.	
3662	,,	Palfrey, A. (Bristol) . . .		
344	Cpl.	Palmer, S. J. (Cadoxton) . . .	†	
1290	Gdsn.	Palmer, A. (Cardiff) . . .	K. in A.	
1317	,,	Palmer, J. C. (Monmouth) . . .	† † †	M.M.
1492	,,	Palmer, W. H. (Cardiff) . . .	†	
2394	,,	Palmer, W. (Tonypandy) . . .	†	
3339	,,	Palmer, A. (Fareham) . . .	† †	
4014	,,	Palmer, W. M. (Swansea) . . .		
2488	,,	Paradice, C. E. (Cardiff) . . .		
3693	,,	Pardoe, A. (Stourbridge) . . .	K. in A.	
1117	,,	Parfitt, A. (Porth)		
2130	,,	Parfitt, L. F. J. (Cardiff) . . .	†	
291	Sergt.	Parker, W. A. (Usk)	D. of Wds.	
1745	L/Cpl.	Parker, B. (Aberdare) . . .		
3040	Gdsn.	Parker, P. (Rawtenstall) . . .	†	
4081	,,	Parker, G. (Meopham) . . .		
4345	,,	Parker, P. W. (Brighton) . . .		
2696	Gdsn.	Parkhill, R. (Swansea) . . .	K. in A.	
802	Sergt.	Parkin, A. E. (Swansea) . . .	†	
4349	Gdsn.	Parlett, E. H. (Amberley) . . .	† †	
1004	,,	Parr, J. (Leigh)		
210	Cpl.	Parry, D. (Amlwch) . . .	† K. in A.	
266	L/Cpl.	Parry, F. (Treharris)	D. of Wds.	
445	Gdsn.	Parry, M. (Merthyr) . . .		
550	,,	Parry, C. A. (Aberdare) . . .		
742	Sergt.	Parry, R. E. (London, N.W.) . . .	†	
1084	Gdsn.	Parry, W. E. (Newport) . . .		
1630	,,	Parry, D. (Wrexham) . . .		
1769	Sergt.	Parry, T. (Churchstoke) . . .		
1783	L/Sergt.	Parry, N. E. (Connah's Quay) . . .	†	
1946	Gdsn.	Parry, G. H. (Birmingham) . . .	†	
2987	,,	Parry, T. W. (Aberdare) . . .		
3032	,,	Parry, R. H. (Llanllyfni) . . .		
3547	,,	Parry, S. H. (Liverpool) . . .		
4564	,,	Parry, H. A. H. (Cross Keys) . . .		

Regtl. No.	Rank.	Name.	Casualties.	Decorations.
4613	Gdsn.	Parry, S. (Welsh Hay)		
4737	,,	Parry, D. M. (Pendryn)		
4820	,	Parry, J. E. L. (Llandovery)		
551	,,	Parsons, W. (Caerphilly)		
1912	,,	Parsons, A. C. (Bridgend)	† † †	
2470	,,	Parsons, E. H. (London)	K. in A.	
3627	,,	Parsons, G. (Birmingham)		
4045	,,	Parsons, W. H. (Nant-y-derry)		
4541	,,	Parsons, W. N. (Cardiff)		
1521	,,	Partridge, T. (Cardiff)	K. in A.	
314	Sergt.	Pates, F. (Cardiff)		
1576	Gdsn.	Patrick, J. W. (Castleford)	† † † K. in A.	
4166	L/Cpl.	Patrick, H. (London, S.W.)		
2747	Gdsn.	Payne, W. A. (Trealaw)	K. in A.	
3679	,,	Payne, G. (Newmarket)	K. in A.	
4291	,,	Payne, G. H. (Leicester)	† †	
4347	,,	Payne, E. H. (High Wycombe)	D. of Wds.	
2174	,,	Peach, W. (Cardiff)		
3210	,,	Peake, W. E. (Birmingham)	D. of Wds.	
6	C.S.M.	Pearce, A. (Bedminster)		D.C.M.
488	Gdsn.	Pearce, W. (Cardiff)		
1282	,,	Pearce, H. (Aberdare)	†	
819	Sergt.	Pearson, T. (Kilmarnock)		
1517	Gdsn.	Pearson, J. (Cardiff)	† † D. of S.	
2416	,,	Pearson, S. (Caerphilly)		
3984	L/Cpl.	Pearson, A. W. (Newcastle)		
4156	Gdsn.	Peaty, W. E. (London)	†	
4106	,,	Pederson, F. (Penarth)		
2463	,,	Pedgeon, E. (Sully)	† †	
3506	,,	Pedgeon, W. J. (Penarth)		
54	A/C.S.M.	Peek, A. (Cardiff)	†	
3991	Gdsn.	Pemberton, J. (Newport)		
4088	,,	Pembridge, J. (Pontypool)		
2944	,,	Pennington, R. (St. Helen's)		
3914	,,	Penny, E. F. (Salisbury)		
4071	,,	Penny, G. (Pontlottyn)		
1615	,,	Peplow, J. (Shrewsbury)	†	
2945	,,	Percy, E. (St. Helen's)	† †	
1246	,,	Perkins, A. R. (Peterston)	K. in A.	
2848	,,	Perkins, W. (Wrexham)		
1827	L/Cpl.	Perrett, F. L. (Briton Ferry)		
382	Gdsn.	Perry, H. (Cardiff)	†	
1907	L/Cpl.	Perry, J. (Cardiff)	† D. of Wds.	
5664	Gdsn.	Perry, O. (Swansea)		
3490	,,	Petch, P. (Bury St. Edmunds)	†	
2595	,,	Peters, A. L. (Dunvant)	†	
3440	,,	Peterson, C. (Cardiff)	†	
3379	,,	Pettipiere, C. H. E. (London, S.E.)	† †	
1888	Cpl.	Phelps, S. A. (Cardiff)	K. in A.	
1950	L/Cpl.	Phelps, C. H. (Rhondda)		
2698	L/Sergt.	Phelps, F. (Aberdare)		

Regtl. No.	Rank.	Name.	Casualties.	Decorations.
4132	L/Cpl.	Philipson, R. (Elswick) . . .		
143	Sergt.	Phillips, F. (Cardiff)	D. of S.	
186	Gdsn.	Phillips, B. (Ferndale) . . .	† †	
188	,,	Phillips, L. (Ferry)	†	M.M.
192	,,	Phillips, E. W. (Aberdare) . . .	†	
279	L/Sergt.	Phillips, J. S. (Merthyr) . . .	† †	
608	Gdsn.	Phillips, W. J. (Mountain Ash) . .		
735	,,	Phillips, T. S. (Pembroke Dock) . .	†	
1104	,,	Phillips, B. (Burry Port) . . .		
1244	,,	Phillips, A. (Cardiff) . . .		
1320	,,	Phillips, W. (Oswestry) . . .	† †	M.M.
1355	,,	Phillips, G. (Abertillery) . . .	D. of Wds.	
1363	,,	Phillips, D. (Bargoed) . . .	† D. of Wds.	
1443	,,	Phillips, D. (Ammanford) . . .		
1453	,,	Phillips, B. J. (Brynaman) . . .		
1632	,,	Phillips, L. L. (Llanwonno) . .		
1674	,,	Phillips, C. C. (Gilfach Goch) .		
1803	C.S.M.	Phillips, E. A. (London) . . .		
1920	Gdsn.	Phillips, T. (Pembroke) . . .	†	
2018	,,	Phillips, F. (Liverpool) . . .		
2125	L/Cpl.	Phillips, E. A. (Swansea) . . .	†	
2425	Gdsn.	Phillips, H. W. (Merthyr Tydfil) .		
2733	,,	Phillips, H. (Gilfach Goch) . .		
2918	,,	Phillips, O. (Llansamlet) . . .	† †	
4085	,,	Phillips, W. J. (Haverfordwest) .	†	
4104	,,	Phillips, W. (Port Talbot) . . .	†	
4266	,,	Phillips, O. (Neath)		
4289	,,	Phillips, S. (Hengoed) . . .		
4489	,,	Phillips, W. J. (Pont-y-waun) . .		
4504	T/Sergt.	Phillips, F. W. (Mountain Ash) .		
4666	Gdsn.	Phillips, A. J. (Cardiff) . . .		
5819	,,	Phillips, A. H. (Merthyr) . . .		
251	L/Cpl.	Philo, S. P. (Aberdare) . . .	† † †	
1798	Cpl.	Philpin, J. W. (Ammanford) . .	†	
2663	Gdsn.	Philpot, E. C. (Cardiff) . . .		
3523	,,	Phipps, C. (Porth)		
2748	,,	Pickard, H. L. (Bargoed) . . .		
2796	,,	Pickersgill, E. (Cardiff) . . .	K. in A.	
422	L/Cpl.	Pickford, W. H. (Bargoed) . . .	†	
2189	Gdsn.	Picton, P. (Pembroke) . . .	D. of S.	
571	,,	Pierce, R. H. (Ruabon) . . .	†	
2215	,,	Pierce, C. H. (Flint)	K. in A.	
3382	L/Cpl.	Pierce, G. (Queen's Ferry) . . .	†	
3294	,,	Pilkington, E. (Darwen) . . .	†	
3225	,,	Pilling, W. (Burnley)		
4125	,,	Pilling, D. (Blackburn) . . .		
3717	,,	Pils, H. (Liverpool)	† †	
4178	Gdsn.	Pilsworth, A. J. (Cambridge) .	K. in A.	
1561	,,	Pimlett, W. G. (Haverfordwest) .		
146	Cpl.	Pink, J. H. (London)	†	
3425	Gdsn.	Pink, T. (Winchfield)	†	

Regtl. No.	Rank.	Name.	Casualties.	Decorations.
495	Cpl.	Pinkham, S. (Cardiff)	† † D. of Wds.	M.M.
4152	Gdsn.	Pitman, A. (London, E.)	†	
1318	„	Plaistow, H. A. (Monmouth)	K. in A.	
147	Cpl.	Plaster, S. R. (Blaenau)		
3748	Gdsn.	Plummer, T. G. (Hove)	K. in A.	
3204	L/Cpl.	Pole, J. W. W. (Oxford)		
862	Gdsn.	Pomford, A. F. (Swansea)	†	
2700	„	Pomroy, F. (Cardiff)		
411	„	Poole, A. S. (Tetbury)	† †	
3177	„	Poole, A. (Scarisbrook)	†	
3756	„	Pooler, L. S. (Tipton)		
3945	„	Pope, G. (Bristol)		
3661	„	Pople, E. G. (Bristol)		
1357	L/Cpl.	Porter, H. M. (Bedwelty)	D. of Wds.	
4348	Gdsn.	Porter, A. F. (Nottingham)		
3406	„	Potter, A. (Eye)		
3836	„	Potter, R. J. (Gravesend)	†	
28	Sergt.	Pottinger, B. (Brondesbury)	K. in A.	
204	Gdsn.	Pound, H. (Swansea)	K. in A.	
3645	„	Pounds, E. F. (Bournemouth)	K. in A.	
3468	„	Pountney, G. H. (Bournemouth)		
3471	„	Pountney, N. (Wolverhampton)	K. in A.	
156	„	Powell, J. (Cwmavon)		
265	„	Powell, S. G. (Chepstow)	† † †	M.M.
522	Cpl.	Powell, T. (Swansea)		
706	Gdsn.	Powell, W. (Cardiff)	†	M.M.
903	„	Powell, O. G. (Porth)	K. in A.	
1340	„	Powell, J. F. (Pontypridd)	†	
1413	„	Powell, A. J. (Neath)	†	
1841	„	Powell, J. (Mountain Ash)		
2107	„	Powell, M. (Neath)	† †	
2236	„	Powell, I. (Bridgend)		
3012	„	Powell, J. (Brecon)	D. of Wds.	
3386	„	Powell, R. H. (Liverpool)		
3629	„	Powell, A. H. (Abergavenny)	†	
4094	„	Powell, W. (Neath)		
4402	„	Powell, J. A. (Wrexham)		
4461	„	Powell, P. (Buckley)		
4676	„	Powell, G. (Darlington)		
4077	„	Power, M. J. (Cardiff)	D. of Wds.	
590	„	Powles, I. B. (Clydach Vale)		
3370	„	Prangnell, S. R. (West Cowes)		
1719	„	Pratt, T. E. (Barry)		
3826	„	Pratt, E. J. P. (Stroud)	†	
2787	„	Preece, G. (Ludlow)	†	
1824	L/Cpl.	Preen, H. J. (Pembroke Dock)	† K. in A.	
3920	Gdsn.	Presswood, H. (Worksop)	K. in A.	
221	„	Preston, J. (Newport)	†	
215	L/Cpl.	Price, T. J. (Blaenrhondda)	†	
414	„	Price, T. J. (Aberdare)		
588	„	Price, J. A. (Bedwelty)	† †	

Regtl. No.	Rank.	Name.	Casualties.	Decorations.
767	L/Cpl.	Price, J. (Tirphil) . . .	.	
864	,,	Price, P. L. (Tredegar) . .	. K. in A.	
907	,,	Price, R. (Port Talbot) . .	. † † †	
945	Sergt.	Price, J. C. (Cardiff) . .	.	
991	Gdsn.	Price, E. C. (Pengam) . .	. K. in A.	
1159	,,	Price, W. (Swansea) . . .	. †	
1417	,,	Price, D. T. (Velindre) . .	. K. in A.	
1486	,,	Price, T. (Merthyr) . . .	. † †	
1493	L/Cpl.	Price, W. (Flint) . . .	. † †	
1564	Gdsn.	Price, T. O. (Aberystwyth) . .	. †	
1711	,,	Price, A. G. (Corsygarnedd) .	. D. of Wds.	
1731	,,	Price, T. (Bedwas) . . .	. K. in A.	
2052	Cpl.	Price, W. (Abergwynfi) . .	. †	
2095	Gdsn.	Price, H. E. (Aberystwyth) .	. †	
2109	,,	Price, W. T. (Blaina) . .	. K. in A.	
2639	,,	Price, W. A. (Cwmdeuddwr) .	. †	
2978	,,	Price, W. H. (Penarth) . .	. †	
3242	,,	Price, O. (Merthyr) . .	.	
3470	,,	Price, T. W. (Mold) . .	.	
3701	,,	Price, W. T. (Halesowen) . .	. † †	
4346	,,	Price, W. E. (Buckley) . .	.	
4468	,,	Price, A. G. (Clydach Vale) .	.	
4795	,,	Price, G. (Dowlais) . . .	.	
1834	,,	Prickett, J. W. (Aberystwyth) .	. †	
2521	,,	Pridham, E. (Barry) . . .	. †	
1650	,,	Prince, J. (Castleford) . .	. K. in A.	
1284	Sergt.	Pring, E. (Newport) . . .	. K. in A.	
4169	Gdsn.	Pringle, J. (Hamble) . .	. †	
368	,,	Pritchard, A. (Abergavenny) .	.	
741	,,	Pritchard, W. (Shrewsbury) .	.	
889	,,	Pritchard, C. J. (New Tredegar) .	.	
1152	,,	Pritchard, L. (Llantrisant) . .	. †	
1364	,,	Pritchard, W. (Talsarnan) .	. K. in A.	
1800	,,	Pritchard, W. O. (Rhyl) . .	. K. in A.	
2293	,,	Pritchard, O. J. (Carnarvon) .	. D. of Wds.	
2361	,,	Pritchard, J. O. (Rhosgadfan) .	. † K. in A.	D.C.M.
2523	,,	Pritchard, B. T. (Newport) .	.	M.M.
3455	,,	Pritchard, G. (Llanelly) . .	.	
5803	,,	Pritchard, G. (St. Helen's) . .	.	
301	,,	Prosser, E. L. (Stockton) . .	.	
2375	,,	Prosser, D. J. (Pontypool) . .	.	
2707	,,	Prosser, G. (Porth) . . .	. †	
4731	,,	Protheroe, W. (Cardiff) . .	.	
920	,,	Prudhoe, J. R. (Ebbw Vale) . .	. †	
4051	,,	Pryce, J. (Welshpool) . .	. K. in A.	
2528	,,	Pugh, A. (Brithdir) . . .	. D. of Wds.	
2895	,,	Pugh, E. J. (Tonypandy) . .	.	
3021	,,	Pugh, H. B. (Dolgelly) . .	. †	
3691	,,	Pugh, J. T. (Aberystwyth) . .	.	
4403	,,	Pugh, W. E. (Wrexham) . .	.	
4420	,,	Pugh, R. (Ferryhill) . . .	.	

Regtl. No.	Rank.	Name.	Casualties.	Decorations.
622	Gdsn.	Pullen, W. H. (Cardiff)	†	
2540	,,	Purnell, H. S. (Cardiff)	† †	
58	Sergt.	Purse, W. J. (Sheffield)		
5	R.Q.M.S.	Pursey, H. J. (Street)		Croix-de-Guerre (Belgium).
2103	Musn.	Putt, G. (London)		
606	Gdsn.	Pyatt, F. J. (Pontypridd)	†	
3869	,,	Pyle, W. (Manchester)		
931	Gdsn.	Quartley, W. J. (Caerphilly)	†	
2927	,,	Quick, W. J. (Cardiff)	†	
3881	L/Cpl.	Quickenden, W. E. (Edenbridge)	†	
2907	Gdsn.	Quirk, H. (Birkenhead)	†	
3865	Gdsn.	Rackham, F. G. (Wrexham)		
570	L/Cpl.	Radford, W. (Congleton)		
624	,,	Raisey, A. (Bargoed)	† †	M.M.
3882	,,	Ramsden, E. J. (London, N.)	† D. of Wds.	
4047	Gdsn.	Ramsker, G. H. (Cadoxton)	K. in A.	
2612	,,	Randall, D. E. (Port Talbot)	†	
3205	L/Sergt.	Randall, G. E. (Bridport)	†	
2044	L/Cpl.	Ranson, C. W. (King's Lynn)	† D. of Wds.	
3007	Gdsn.	Ratcliffe, R. (Cardiff)	†	
3296	,,	Ratcliffe, R. (Bacup)	† K. in A.	
3624	,,	Ravenhall, F. (Birmingham)		
2175	,,	Ravenhill, G. A. (Chepstow)	†	
393	,,	Rawle, C. H. (Cwmbwrla)	†	
2982	,,	Rawlings, C. E. (Cardiff)	†	
3400	,,	Rawlings, W. D. (Llandudno)	† †	
4139	,,	Rawlinson, W. F. (Barrow-in-Furness)		
1430	,,	Read, W. T. (Tonypandy)	†	
4648	,,	Read, F. (Porth)	†	
4212	,,	Reading, J. (Chesham)		
2364	,,	Recke, T. (Swansea)		
466	L/Cpl.	Reed, A. (Talywain)	D. of Wds.	
971	Gdsn.	Reed, W. (Blandford)	K. in A.	
4317	,,	Reed, J. R. (Staines)		
86	L/Cpl.	Rees, S. B. (Aberaman)	K. in A.	
121	Cpl.	Rees, D. (Swansea)	D. of Wds.	
152	Gdsn.	Rees, T. J. (Llanelly)	†	
159	,,	Rees, E. (Llanelly)	† †	
172	Sergt.	Rees, W. H. (Llanelly)	†	
447	Gdsn.	Rees, W. D. (Swansea)	†	
896	,,	Rees, J. (Pontypridd)	† † †	
1382	,,	Rees, E. (Bridgend)	†	
1457	,,	Rees, W. (Haverfordwest)	D. of Wds.	
1671	,,	Rees, W. (Port Talbot)	†	
1673	,,	Rees, B. (Carmarthen)	†	
1763	,,	Rees, W. M. (Treorchy)		
1897	,,	Rees, T. J. (Sarn)	†	
1948	,,	Rees, W. (Rhayader)	K. in A.	

Regtl. No.	Rank.	Name.	Casualties.	Decorations.
2310	Gdsn.	Rees, T. L. (Bargoed) . . .	†	
2449	,,	Rees, C. (Porth) . . .		
2456	,,	Rees, W. (Porth) . . .		
2607	,,	Rees, G. (Aberdare) . . .		
2711	,,	Rees, S. J. (Tonypandy) . . .	†	
2720	,,	Rees, G. G. (St. Dogmaels) . .	D. of S.	
2788	,,	Rees, R. T. (Llangadfan) . .	D. of Wds.	
3195	,,	Rees, R. T. (Swansea) . .		
3218	,,	Rees, H. (Fishguard) . . .	†	
3557	,,	Rees, H. (Llandebie) . . .	†	
3672	,,	Rees, E. W. (Rhayader) . .	K. in A.	
4557	,,	Rees, T. (Glynneath) . . .		
4621	,,	Rees, D. (Dowlais) . . .		
4750	,,	Rees, A. (Swansea) . . .		
4829	,,	Rees, D. J. (Llansamlet) . .		
4881	L/Cpl.	Rees, H. E. (Bedwelty) . .		
1279	Gdsn.	Reeves, E. L. (Cardiff) . .	K. in A.	
136	Sergt.	Regan, J. H. (Swansea) . .		
39	,,	Relihan, D. (Newport) . .	†	
53	C.Q.M.S.	Rendell, S. (Swansea) . .		
2688	Gdsn.	Rendell, W. J. (Swansea) . .	D. of S.	
3376	,,	Renouf, J. F. (Southampton) .		
2444	,,	Reynish, T. (Llanstadwell) .		
857	,,	Reynolds, J. (Aberdare) . .	†	
1813	,,	Reynolds, H. (Ammanford) .		
4786	,,	Reynolds, H. J. (Blaina) . .		
3755	,,	Rhodes, A. (Wolverhampton) .	†	
3955	,,	Rhodes, G. (Alfreton) . .		
3665	,,	Rhydwen, A. (Wrexham) . .	K. in A.	
2410	,,	Rice, H. V. (Abergwile) . .	†	
62	Sergt.	Richards, R. J. (Gower) . .	K. in A.	
98	Gdsn.	Richards, H. (Cardiff) . .	†	
226	,,	Richards, W. (Merthyr) . .		
233	Sergt.	Richards, J. (Brynaman) . .		
440	Gdsn.	Richards, D. (Bargoed) . .	† †	
559	,,	Richards, W. (Llanelly) . .	†	
572	,,	Richards, T. (Pontmorlais) .	†	
732	,,	Richards, A. H. (Cardiff) . .	K. in A.	
992	L/Cpl.	Richards, E. J. (Bargoed) .		
1396	Sergt.	Richards, D. J. (Gorseinon) .		
1496	,,	Richards, I. (Brecon) . . .		
1965	Gdsn.	Richards, D. L. (Bargoed) .		
2208	,,	Richards, J. H. (Machen) . .	K. in A.	
2721	,,	Richards, J. T. (Ferndale) . .	†	M.M.
2781	,,	Richards, J. W. (Pembroke Dock)		
3393	,,	Richards, F. (Marazion) . .		
3502	L/Cpl.	Richards, E. T. (Rhos) . .	†	
3696	Gdsn.	Richards, E. (Aberystwyth) .	†	
4058	,,	Richards, W. D. (Porth) . .		
4595	,,	Richards, S. G. (Pontypridd) .		
4677	,,	Richards, T. (Gorseinon) . .		

Regtl. No.	Rank.	Name.	Casualties.	Decorations.
4790	Gdsn.	Richards, H. (Swansea) . . .	.	
1332	L/Sergt.	Richardson, W. H. (Bridgend)	.	Croix-de-Guerre (Fr.).
2498	Gdsn.	Richardson, T. R. (Cardiff) . .	†	
3052	„	Richardson, E. (Burnley) . . .	†	
3357	„	Richardson, W. (Lytham) . . .	†	
3916	„	Richardson, H. (Worcester) . .	†	
4176	„	Richardson, J. T. (Barrow-in-Furness) .	K. in A.	
2420	„	Rickeard, R. (Bristol) . . .	†	
3117	„	Riddiough, F. (Colne) . . .	.	
1013	L/Cpl.	Ridehalgh, F. (Manchester) . .	† K. in A.	
3409	Gdsn.	Ridley, A. J. (Gateshead) . . .	†	
2761	„	Rimmer, P. (Ashton) . . .	.	
3925	„	Rimmer, W. (Preston) . . .	†	
3871	„	Ringrose, G. J. (London, N.) . .	K. in A.	
2062	„	Rixon, R. R. (Cardiff) . . .	K. in A.	
697	„	Robbins, R. (Penrhiwfer) . .	K. in A.	
15	D/Sergt.	Roberts, P. H. (London) . .	†	M.S.M.
80	Gdsn.	Roberts, W. (Swansea) . . .	.	
222	„	Roberts, W. J. (Aberystwyth) . .	.	
333	Sergt.	Roberts, F. J. C. (Northwich) . .	K. in A.	
374	„	Roberts, I. C. (Llanllyfni) . .	.	
387	Gdsn.	Roberts, P. (Manchester) . . .	† †	
395	L/Sergt.	Roberts, W. (Brownhills) . .	†	D.C.M.
438	Gdsn.	Roberts, J. E. (Margate) . .	K. in A.	
512	„	Roberts, F. J. (Gloucester) . .	† †	
569	„	Roberts, A. J. (Ebbw Vale) . .	† †	
661	„	Roberts, T. (Conway) . . .	.	
688	„	Roberts, E. J. (Llandebie) . .	† K. in A.	
942	„	Roberts, J. (Wrexham) . . .	K. in A.	
1007	„	Roberts, J. (Bradford) . . .	K. in A.	
1165	„	Roberts, W. T. (Aberdare) . .	†	
1206	„	Roberts, J. (Anglesey) . . .	†	
1456	„	Roberts, W. (Holywell) . . .	†	
1466	„	Roberts, J. N. (Wrexham) . .	K. in A.	
1485	„	Roberts, T. (Swansea) . . .	†	
1519	„	Roberts, J. (Penmynydd) . .	.	
1522	„	Roberts, E. (Derwen) . . .	†	M.M.
1624	L/Sergt.	Roberts, H. J. (London, S.E.) . .	†	
1689	Gdsn.	Roberts, W. J. (Bridgend) . .	†	
1735	„	Roberts, H. D. F. (London) . .	†	
2023	„	Roberts, T. (Monmouth) . .	.	
2137	„	Roberts, W. T. (Welshpool) . .	†	
2138	„	Roberts, J. L. (Denbigh) . .	†	M.M.
2142	Musn.	Roberts, A. H. (London) . .	.	
2202	Gdsn.	Roberts, T. (Manchester) . .	†	
2314	„	Roberts, R. W. (Portmadoc) . .	†	
2367	„	Roberts, R. T. (Llanrwst) . .	†	
2411	„	Roberts, H. (Llandudno) . .	†	
2538	„	Roberts, D. (Blaengarw) . .	†	
2561	„	Roberts, C. (Rhyl) . . .	† †	

Regtl. No.	Rank.	Name.	Casualties.	Decorations.
2562	Gdsn.	Roberts, R. L. (Colwyn Bay)	K. in A.	
2563	Cpl.	Roberts, W. D. (Loughir)	† †	
2575	Gdsn.	Roberts, E. L. (Fishguard)		
2784	,,	Roberts, R. T. (Ruthin)	K. in A.	
2793	,,	Roberts, W. (Tremadoc)		
2827	,,	Roberts, W. (Holywell)	† †	
2884	,,	Roberts, J. (Welshpool)		
2887	,,	Roberts, G. (Dolgelly)	†	
2900	,,	Roberts, J. R. (Llandudno)		
3001	,,	Roberts, T. (Chwilog)	K. in A.	
3019	,,	Roberts, R. E. (Wrexham)		
3058	,,	Roberts, E. (Dolgelly)	D. of Wds.	
3185	,,	Roberts, E. M. (Bettws-y-coed)		
3214	,,	Roberts, D. (Menai Bridge)		
3254	,,	Roberts, R. W. (Flint)	D. of Wds.	
3407	,,	Roberts, A. E. (Wrexham)		
3421	,,	Roberts, H. (Flint)	K. in A.	
3433	,,	Roberts, J. (Liverpool)		
3486	,,	Roberts, T. W. (Cardiff)	K. in A.	
3491	L/Cpl.	Roberts, J. (Rhuddlan)		
3517	Gdsn.	Roberts, W. (Beaumaris)	K. in A.	
3581	,,	Roberts, H. (Anglesey)	†	
3582	,,	Roberts, J. (Pontardulais)	†	
3584	,,	Roberts, D. (Denbigh)		
3585	,,	Roberts, H. R. (Blaenau-Festiniog)		
3588	,,	Roberts, J. (Llaniestyn)		
3592	,,	Roberts, R. T. (Penmaenmawr)	†	
3597	Cpl.	Roberts, D. (Cardiff)	†	
3601	Gdsn.	Roberts, R. O. (Bettws-y-coed)	K. in A.	
3706	,,	Roberts, T. H. (Pwllheli)	†	
3718	,,	Roberts, W. (Liverpool)		
3848	,,	Roberts, W. W. (Liverpool)		
4048	,,	Roberts, T. W. (Llechylched)		
4084	,,	Roberts, P. (Ruabon)		
4103	,,	Roberts, J. (Penmynydd)	†	
4112	,,	Roberts, M. (Ferndale)	D. of Wds.	
4180	,,	Roberts, J. W. (Enderby)		
4350	,,	Roberts, H. A. (Birmingham)		
4413	,,	Roberts, H. (Cardiff)		
3420	,,	Robins, A. E. (Rhyl)		
1040	,,	Robinson, S. (Osset)	†	
4136	,,	Robinson, J. G. (Belper)	†	
3280	,,	Robson, L. (Walker)		
3670	,,	Rodd, J. (Cardiff)		
1263	,,	Roderick, D. H. (Merthyr)	D. of Wds.	
1542	,,	Rogers, J. H. (Pontypridd)	† †	
1815	,,	Rogers, J. J. (Bridgend)	†	
2454	,,	Rogers, W. J. (Llanwonno)	D. of Wds.	
2621	L/Cpl.	Rogers, H. (Barry)	†	
2704	Gdsn.	Rogers, H. (Cardiff)		
2911	L/Cpl.	Rogers, C. R. (Cardiff)	†	

30

Regtl. No.	Rank.	Name.	Casualties.	Decorations.
3094	Gdsn.	Rogers, S. (Chirk)	K. in A.	
4351	,,	Rogers, C. J. (Aston)	† D. of Wds.	
4411	,,	Rogers, D. J. (Neath)		
4661	,,	Rogers, W. J. (Llanelly)		
2705	,,	Roles, T. (Cardiff)	†	
3953	,,	Rolling, J. T. (Ompton)		
1467	,,	Rose, J. (Cardiff)	K. in A.	
2261	,,	Rose, J. T. (Stafford)		
4888	,,	Rosen, M. (Cardiff)	†	
762	,,	Rosser, J. T. (Carmarthen)	†	
3992	,,	Rosser, W. E. (Pontypool)		
4043	,,	Rossiter, F. A. (Porth)		
3120	,,	Rothwell, G. D. (Nelson)		
4287	,,	Rothwell, H. P. (Wigan)		
3175	,,	Roughley, J. (Ormskirk)	D. of Wds.	
3108	,,	Routledge, J. (Blackhill)	†	
148	,,	Row, H. D. (Newport)	K. in A.	
2518	,,	Rowe, H. (Merthyr)		
2941	L/Cpl.	Rowe, W. J. (Penygraig)	†	
3682	Gdsn.	Rowe, F. (Cardiff)	D. of Wds.	
1226	L/Cpl.	Rowitt, T. (Newport)		
1499	Gdsn.	Rowland, J. (Liscard)		
2581	,,	Rowland, S. (Porth)		
2940	,,	Rowland, C. E. (Wrexham)	†	
4743	,,	Rowland, D. (Bath)	†	
434	Dmr.	Rowlands, D. (Wrexham)		
583	Gdsn.	Rowlands, T. W. (Tredegar)		
829	,,	Rowlands, F. (Cadoxton)	K. in A.	
1116	,,	Rowlands, D. (Nantyglo)	K. in A.	
1307	,,	Rowlands, D. (Bangor)		
2186	,,	Rowlands, E. (Dolgelly)	D. of S.	
2229	,,	Rowlands, I. R. (Abergele)	† †	
2458	,,	Rowlands, A. I. (Merthyr)	D. of S.	
2954	,,	Rowlands, E. D. (Llanuwchllyn)	D. of Wds.	M.M.
3833	,,	Rowlands, F. (Ebbw Vale)	†	
3852	,,	Rowley, T. J. (Porth)		
3780	L/Cpl.	Rowney, G. (Wolverhampton)	†	
2011	Gdsn.	Rowse, W. G. (Cardiff)		
2197	Sergt.	Roxberry, H. (London)		
2868	Gdsn.	Roy, E. S. (Warrington)		
3951	,,	Roy, C. (Neath)		
1640	,,	Rudd, F. H. (Caerphilly)	†	
388	L/Cpl.	Rudge, J. A. (Manchester)	K. in A.	
2730	Gdsn.	Rudge, J. W. (Burton-on-Trent)		
1607	,,	Rudolph, T. (Cardiff)		
184	,,	Rumble, S. (Newport)		
2662	,,	Rumble, W. Caterham)	†	
968	L/Cpl.	Rumbles, J. (Monmouth)	D. of Wds.	
1281	Gdsn.	Russell, C. R. (Neath)		
2572	,,	Russell, S. (Cardiff)	K. in A.	
3447	Cpl.	Ruston, G. H. W. (Portsmouth)		

Regtl. No.	Rank.	Name.	Casualties.	Decorations.
3543	Gdsn.	Ryall, W. (Ryde) . . . ,	K. in A.	
3978	,,	Ryan, M. (Ayr)		
626	,,	Sadler, C. H. (Bargoed) .		
1548	,,	Sainsbury, G. (Swansea) .		
4120	,,	Salmon, H. (Derby) . .		
1262	,,	Salter, A. W. (Cardiff) .	†	
3972	,,	Salter, W. (Crediton) . .		
3977	,,	Sandel, C. H. (Birmingham)	†	
1329	,,	Sanders, J. (Cardiff) .	† †	
4206	,,	Sanders, G. H. (Barrow) .	†	
4234	,,	Sanders, J. (Cornwood) .		
1175	L/Cpl.	Sankey, A. S. (Merthyr) .		
3053	Gdsn.	Sandwell, B. J. (Scorton) .	†	
1335	L/Sergt.	Sansom, J. (Bridgend) .	† † †	
2519	Gdsn.	Sanson, B. J. (Cardiff) .	†	
1015	,,	Saunders, G. (Birmingham)	†	
1170	,,	Saunders, W. (Glyncorwg) .	† †	
988	,,	Savage, L. C. (Swansea) .		
3841	,,	Sayers, C. E. (Horsham) .		
1402	,,	Scott, A. (Castleford) .		
2710	,,	Scott, P. (Maesteg) .		
3051	,,	Scott, J. (Burnley) .	† †	
3059	,,	Scott, J. (Bacup) .	† † K. in A.	
3928	,,	Scott, P. A. (Aldershot) .	†	
1359	Sergt.	Scott-Kiddie, R. (Liverpool)		
2934	Gdsn.	Scully, T. G. (Wrexham) .		
3908	,,	Scully, W. H. (London, N.)		
1166	,,	Searle, A. E. (Barry) . .		
3874	,,	Seamans, H. (Wolverhampton)	†	
1642	L/Cpl.	Seaton, W. R. (Rugby) .	K. in A.	
4530	Gdsn.	Sedgbeer, S. (Bridgend) .		
3310	,,	Sedgwick, J. (Lr. Crumpsall)		
3276	,,	Self, G. H. (Clitheroe) .		
4353	,,	Sellors, S. (Derby) .		
2076	Musn.	Selwood, H. (London) .		
3069	Gdsn.	Sendey, C. G. (Exeter) .	† †	M.M.
1062	Cpl.	Sexton, G. (Pontypridd) .		
1256	Gdsn.	Seymour, J. (Barry) .	†	
174	L/Sergt.	Shackleford, G. (Swansea) .	†	
3436	Gdsn.	Shannon, A. (Newcastle) .	† †	
3897	L/Cpl.	Sharp, E. C. (London, S.E.)		
3488	,,	Sharpe, R. R. (Newton) .		
3070	Gdsn.	Sharples, A. (Trefnant) .	K. in A.	
3647	,,	Sharratt, A. (Bangor) .		
3238	,,	Shaw, A. W. (Malton) .	D. of S.	
4886	,,	Sheen, S. (Bedwelty) .		
76	,,	Sheeran, W. (Bangor) .		
660	Sergt,	Shehan, T. (Swansea) .	†	
89	Gdsn.	Shepherd, E. (Cardiff)		
845	,,	Sheppard, H. (Aberdare) .		M.M.

Regtl. No.	Rank.	Name.	Casualties.	Decora- tions.
3664	Gdsn.	Sheppard, H. (Bristol)		
1065	,,	Shergold, A. J. (Woburn)		
1200	,,	Shergold, R. C. (Bargoed)	†	
3105	,,	Sherwood, J. (Cardiff)	†	
698	,,	Shewry, W. J. A. (Neath)		
499	L/Cpl.	Shopland, W. (Cardiff)	† † †	
3202	Gdsn.	Shuttleworth, A. (Easingwold)	†	
4118	,,	Sibley, W. T. (Southampton)		
3648	,,	Sidney, W. J. (Newport)	K. in A.	
1082	L/Cpl.	Silcox, T. J. (Aberbeeg)	K. in A.	
1108	Gdsn.	Silver, A. J. (Neath)		
3163	,,	Simmonds, W. G. (Caversham)		
3986	,,	Simms, G. (Banbury)		
1421	L/Cpl.	Simons, T. J. (London)		
3037	Gdsn.	Simons, A. D. V. (Holywell)	K. in A.	
4744	,,	Simons, W. (Uxbridge)	K. in A.	
267	Cpl.	Simpson, W. (Bootle)	K. in A.	
274	Sergt.	Simpson, C. (Maindee)	†	
519	Gdsn.	Simpson, H. (Dewsbury)	†	
2460	,,	Simpson, W. (Merthyr)	†	
4128	,,	Simpson, E. (Birmingham)	†	
813	,,	Sims, W. E. (Ystrad)	† †	
2543	L/Cpl.	Sims, M. L. (Cardiff)	†	
3348	Gdsn.	Skinner, F. W. (Cranbrook)	†	
3201	,,	Skuse, R. (Abingdon)	† †	
3736	,,	Slater, L. H. (Dewsbury)		
749	,,	Slaughan, G. (Bridgend)	†	
3132	,,	Slawson, H. F. (Leeds)	†	
1654	,,	Slee, A. J. (Pontypridd)	K. in A.	
242	Sergt.	Smale, A. A. (Swansea)	D. of Wds.	
4405	Gdsn.	Smallman, E. C. (Cardiff)		
2345	L/Cpl.	Smart, F. E. (London, N.)	† †	
3572	Gdsn.	Smart, J. F. (Cardiff)		
541	L/Sergt.	Smith, E. H. (West Bromwich)	†	
1027	Gdsn.	Smith, T. (Merthyr Vale)	†	
1070	,,	Smith, F. W. (Long Eaton)		
1154	,,	Smith, R. (Pentre)	K. in A.	
1155	,,	Smith, F. (Swansea)	†	
1375	,,	Smith, W. J. (Penarth)	†	
1434	,,	Smith, J. (Garndiffaith)	†	
1901	,,	Smith, R. E. (Ely, Glam.)	K. in A.	
1977	,,	Smith, F. (Swansea)	†	
2199	L/Cpl.	Smith, V. (Cardiff)	†	
2658	Gdsn.	Smith, H. E. (Swansea)		
2671	,,	Smith, W. (Swansea)		
2724	,,	Smith, J. T. (Haverfordwest)		
2830	,,	Smith, A. H. (St. Helen's)	K. in A.	
2849	,,	Smith, H. E. (Cardiff)	K. in A.	
2985	,,	Smith, W. (Merthyr)	K. in A.	
2999	,,	Smith, W. E. (Tonypandy)	† †	
3050	,,	Smith, G. (Burnley)	†	

Regtl. No.	Rank.	Name.	Casualties.	Decorations.
3064	Gdsn.	Smith, F. (Nelson)	K. in A.	
3253	,,	Smith, J. H. (Cardiff) . . .		
3340	,,	Smith, B. (Leicester)	D. of Wds.	
3428	,,	Smith, W. (Nelson) . . .		
3646	,,	Smith, W. C. (Abertillery) . . .	† D. of Wds.	
3656	,,	Smith, A. (Cardiff)	†	
3734	,,	Smith, A. (Liverpool) . . .	†	
3790	,,	Smith, G. (Birmingham) . . .	†	
3840	,,	Smith, J. G. (Burgess Hill) . . .		
3898	,,	Smith, H. (Bradford)	†	
3943	,,	Smith, E. J. W. (Uxbridge) . .	†	
4080	,,	Smith, H. (Tredegar)	† D. of Wds.	
4787	,,	Smith, T. E. (Pencadr) . . .		
1820	Cpl.	Smyth, R. (London) . . .		
3861	Gdsn.	Snell, G. W. (Plymouth) . . .		M.M.
2953	L/Cpl.	Soffe, W. M. (Abertillery) . .		
634	Gdsn.	Solman, G. (Cardiff) . . .	K. in A.	
122	L/Cpl.	Soper, E. (Barry)		
178	Gdsn.	Soper, E. (Trealaw) . . .	† †	
927	Cpl.	Soper, H. (Newport) . . .	†	
2774	Gdsn.	Southern, G. R. (Earlstown) . .		
3373	,,	Southwell, E. E. (Southampton) .		
2758	L/Sergt.	Spargo, F. J. K. (London) . .		
1285	Gdsn.	Spark, E. (Ferndale) . . .	†	
2832	,,	Sparks, T. (St. Helen's) . . .	†	
3912	,,	Spary, C. A. (Plumstead) . .		
3156	,,	Spellman, J. (Liverpool) . .	K. in A.	
3137	,,	Spence, C. K. (Cardiff) . .	D. of Wds.	
144	,,	Spencer, S. G. (Berkhampstead) .	†	M.M.
2054	L/Cpl.	Spencer, C. (London) . . .		
4355	Gdsn.	Spensley, W. (Pontefract) . .	†	
924	,,	Spiller, E. J. (Cardiff) . . .		
1698	,,	Spillman, C. F. (Cardiff) . .		
3302	,,	Spinney, L. (Brighton) . . .		
3422	,,	Spoor, E. (Whickham) . . .	†	
718	,,	Spratling, J. (Trecynon) . .	K. in A.	
442	,,	Spuffard. E. (Neath) . . .	† † †	
2942	,,	Spurle, P. (Haverfordwest) . .	†	
419	,,	Stacey, W. J. (Cardiff) . .	D. of Wds.	
5222	,,	Stacey, S. G. (Aberdare) . .		
1225	,,	Standard, C. (Newport) . .		
3116	,,	Standing, W. (Burnley) . . .	†	
1218	,,	Stanley, R. J. (Cardiff) . .		
1836	,,	Stanley, W. (Pontypridd) . .	K. in A.	
4443	,,	Starkie, J. (Burnley) . . .		
105	Sergt.-Dmr.	Starnes, F. (Sussex) . . .		
3637	Gdsn.	Stay, W. H. (Frome) . . .	K. in A.	
3791	,,	Steel, A. W. (Birmingham) . .	D. of Wds.	
4354	,,	Steele, J. (London, N.E.) . .		
4373	,,	Steele, E. W. (Cardiff) . . .	†	
1577	,,	Steeples, J. (Bargoed) . . .	†	

Regtl. No.	Rank	Name.	Casualties.	Decorations.
2634	Gdsn.	Steer, W. G. (Pontypridd) . . .		
946	L/Cpl.	Stephens, T. (Cardiff) . . .		
1739	Cpl.	Stephens, E. (Manchester) . . .		
2378	Gdsn.	Stephens, F. (Cardiff) . . .	†	
2382	,,	Stephens, D. (Treharris) . . .	K. in A.	
4044	,,	Stephenson, C. E. (Keighley) . .	†	
3344	L/Cpl.	Steven, A. C. (Bedlington) . . .	†	
4237	Gdsn.	Stevens, W. (Pontypridd) . . .		
1	R.S.M.	Stevenson, W. (Caterham) . .		D.C.M. M.M., M.S.M.
1612	Gdsn.	Steward, F. J. (Swansea) . . .	K. in A.	
2225	Musn.	Stewart, P. P. (Dublin) . . .		
3391	,,	Stickley, H. (Wareham) . . .	D. of Wds.	
3394	,,	Stickley, C. (Wareham) . . .		
4352	,,	Stiles, F. (Harrow) . . .	†	
3121	,,	Stock, J. (Nelson) . . .	K. in A.	
2038	,,	Stocker, J. E. (Wrexham) . . .	† †	
26	Sergt.	Stokes, W. (Dover) . . .		
2516	Gdsn.	Stokes, W. G. (Cardiff) . . .		
4356	,,	Stokes, W. S. (Keighley) . . .		
1429	,,	Stone, B. J. (London) . . .		
2131	Musn.	Stone, W. (London. N.W.) . . .		
4789	Gdsn.	Stone, W. T. (Cwmavon) . . .		
3526	,,	Stonham, G. E. (Portsmouth) . .	†	
2362	,,	Storey, P. (Swansea)		
2909	,,	Storkey, F. L. (Pentre) . . .		
3800	,,	Strain, W. (Birmingham) . . .		
3300	,,	Strang, J. (Hebburn) . . .	†	
3287	,,	Strange, B. (Oxford) . . .		
2311	,,	Strathmere, L. G. (Cardiff) . . .	†	
3633	,,	Strawbridge, F. (Bridgend) . . .	†	
574	,,	Streeter, A. (Cardiff) . . .		
1850	L/Sergt.	Streeter, A. B. (Cardiff) . . .		
2846	Gdsn.	Strickland, D. A. (Apperley Bridge) .		
3529	,,	Stride, J. (Portsmouth) . . .		
4012	,,	Stride, H. G. (Cardiff) . . .	D. of Wds.	
1861	,,	Stroner, A. (Llanelly) . . .		
3284	,,	Strong, G. (Barrow) . . .		
2979	,,	Studley, W. J. (Cardiff) . . .	K. in A.	
3174	,,	Stunt, F. J. (Hastings) . . .		
3846	,,	Styles, H. L. (Levant) . . .		
250	L/Sergt.	Sullivan, J. (Cardiff) . . .	†	
2067	Gdsn.	Sullivan, W. (Cardiff) . . .		
2594	,,	Sullivan, J. (Cardiff) . . .		
92	,,	Sully, A. G. (Pontypridd) . . .	† †	M.M.
2670	,,	Sumner, E. (Denbigh) . . .		
3380	,,	Suter, S. G. (Birmingham) . . .	†	
3074	,,	Suter, C. A. (Accrington) . . .	†	
2896	,,	Sutton, A. M. (Ebbw Vale) . . .	†	
3739	,,	Sutton, G. W. (Middlewich) . .	D. of Wds.	
4407	,,	Sutton, A. E. (Wrexham) . . .		

Regtl. No.	Rank.	Name.	Casualties	Decorations.
1086	Gdsn.	Swain, J. E. (Ilkeston) . . .		
1910	,,	Swain, J. H. (Lydbury) . .		
2029	,,	Swain, S. (Lydbury) . . .	†	
2791	A/Sergt.	Swale, R. (Birkenhead) . .		
3965	Gdsn.	Swann, E. H. (Kenilworth) .	†	
389	,,	Swift, A. (Manchester) . .	†	
2180	Musn.	Swift, H. (London) . .		
3335	Gdsn.	Sykes, A. (Blackburn) . .	K. in A.	
3618	,,	Symes, O. (Cardiff) . .		
315	L/Cpl.	Symmonds, F. (Cardiff) .		
592	Dmr.	Symmonds, E. (Barry) . .		
594	Gdsn.	Symmonds, R. A. (Barry) . .	† †	
1625	,,	Symmonds, R. (Cardiff) . .	† † †	
2419	L/Cpl.	Talbot, T. (Swansea) . .	† †	
3827	Gdsn.	Tallett, A. C. (Coventry) .		
4061	,,	Tame, C. H. (Cardiff) .		
3856	,,	Tandy, W. G. (Bristol) . .	†	
145	,,	Tanner, E. (Swansea) . .		M.M.
1220	,,	Tanner, W. (Rhondda) . .		
1224	,,	Tanner, J. G. (Newport) . .	K. in A.	
4184	,,	Tansley, G. (Dolton) . .	†	
1033	,,	Tarbuck, M. (Wolverhampton) .	K. in A.	
2947	,,	Tarry, A. (London, S.E.) .	K. in A.	
211	L/Sergt.	Taylor, H. (Cardiff) . .	† †	
1250	L/Cpl.	Taylor, G. T. (Cardiff) .	† †	
1385	Gdsn.	Taylor, E. J. (Abergavenny) .	K. in A.	
1899	,,	Taylor, J. (Haverfordwest) .	†	
2825	,,	Taylor, F. (Oldham) . .	† †	
2870	,,	Taylor, E. (Bardsley) . .		
3008	,,	Taylor, G. (Cardiff) . .	†	
3067	,,	Taylor, R. H. (Waterford) .	†	
3750	,,	Taylor, F. A. (Brighton) .		
3798	,,	Taylor, J. C. (Birmingham) .	K. in A.	
3805	,,	Taylor, T. T. (Birmingham) .	K. in A.	
3851	,,	Taylor, T. G. (Morcombelake) .	K. in A.	
4022	,,	Taylor, W. J. (Pentre) .		
4357	,,	Taylor, L. (Burton) . .	†	
4440	,,	Taylor, H. (Preston) . .		
4133	,,	Taylor, E. (Lancaster) . .	†	
4589	,,	Taylor, G. (Neath) . .		
4885	,,	Taylor, G. M. (Cross Keys) .		
4015	,,	Teague, O. L. (Lydney) .		
5796	,,	Teague, W. (Neath) . .		
2789	,,	Temple, R. A. (Shrewsbury) .	†	
2826	,,	Thelwell, R. (Colwyn Bay) .		
1031	Cpl.	Thom, T. (Glasgow) . .		
10	L/Sergt.	Thomas, G. H. (London) .	†	
19	Sergt.	Thomas, C. (Pembroke) .	†	
45	,,	Thomas, T. W. (Bridgend) .	†	
163	Gdsn.	Thomas, W. D. (Cardiff) . .	†	

Regtl. No.	Rank.	Name.	Casualties.	Decorations.
217	Gdsn.	Thomas, E. (Ogmore Vale) . . .	†	
229	L/Cpl.	Thomas, J. (Briton Ferry) . . .	† †	
254	Sergt.	Thomas, T. W. (Cwmavon) .	† K. in A.	
334	Gdsn.	Thomas, S. (Merthyr) . .	†	
377	Sergt.	Thomas, A. J. (London) . .		
392	Gdsn.	Thomas, D. R. (Cwmbwrla) . .	†	
396	,,	Thomas, H. (Rochdale) . .	†	
405	,,	Thomas, R. (Hereford) . .	†	
507	,,	Thomas, H. M. (Alton, Bury) .	K. in A.	
674	,,	Thomas, T. L. (Ystalyfera) .	† †	
713	,,	Thomas, E. (Aberdare) .	K. in A.	
764	,,	Thomas, I. E. (Porth) . .	†	
798	L/Sergt.	Thomas, A. G. (Reading) . .		M.M.
808	Gdsn.	Thomas, D. J. (Neath) . .		
812	,,	Thomas, H. (Ynysddu) . .	†	
858	,,	Thomas, T. (Pontypridd) . .		D.C.M.
893	,,	Thomas, A. (Bargoed) . .		
915	,,	Thomas, J. (Pentre) . .	†	
926	,,	Thomas, G. R. (Merthyr) . .	†	
959	Cpl.	Thomas, W. (Senghenydd) . .	†	
974	Gdsn.	Thomas, C. (Swansea) . .	†	M.M.
980	Cpl.	Thomas, W. (Neath) . .	†	
982	Sergt.	Thomas, T. G. (Landore) . .		
1059	Gdsn.	Thomas, W. (Aberaman) . .	K. in A.	
1071	,,	Thomas, J. E. (Llanwrda) . .	K. in A.	
1097	,,	Thomas, W. J. (Pontypridd) .	†	
1107	,,	Thomas, F. (Newtown) . .	†	
1119	,,	Thomas, H. (Bangor) . .		
1125	,,	Thomas, T. H. (Aberdare) . .	†	M.M.
1134	,,	Thomas, I. (Brynmawr) . .	†	
1151	,,	Thomas, W. (Rhondda) . .	† D. of Wds.	
1171	,,	Thomas, J. (Barry) . .	† †	
1172	,,	Thomas, W. J. (Mountain Ash) .		
1201	L/Sergt.	Thomas, W. H. (Bedwas) . .	†	
1203	Gdsn.	Thomas, T. (Aberavon) . .	†	
1205	,,	Thomas, M. (Llangoed) . .		
1276	,,	Thomas, G. (Llanelly) . .	†	M.M.
1295	,,	Thomas, O. (Wrexham) . .	†	
1298	L/Cpl.	Thomas, W. (Llandilo) . .	D. of Wds.	
1311	Sergt.	Thomas, J. (Cardiff) . .	K. in A.	
1333	Gdsn.	Thomas, W. J. (Llanedarne) .	† D. of Wds.	
1373	,,	Thomas, W. H. (Chepstow) .	K. in A.	
1397	,,	Thomas, J. (Lahore) . .		
1422	,,	Thomas, E. L. (Holt) . .		
1431	,,	Thomas, T. O. (Treherbert) .		
1452	,,	Thomas, J. (Brynaman) . .	† K. in A.	
1472	,,	Thomas, D. R. (Briton Ferry) .	K. in A.	
1473	L/Cpl.	Thomas, W. (Abergwynfi) . .	†	
1495	Gdsn.	Thomas, G. (Brecon) . .		
1529	L/Cpl.	Thomas, G. (Cardiff) . .	† † † †	D.C.M.
1535	Gdsn.	Thomas, B. J. (Penarth) . .	D. of Wds.	

Regtl. No.	Rank.	Name.			Casualties.	Decorations.
1547	Gdsn.	Thomas, O. (Llanelly)	.	.	†	
1598	Cpl.	Thomas, H. W. (Cardiff)	.	.	D. of Wds.	
1684	,,	Thomas, W. (Wigan) .	.	.	† †	
1829	Gdsn.	Thomas, D. (Ammanford) .	.	.	†	
1838	,,	Thomas, J. (Nantymoel)	.	.	K. in A.	
1913	,,	Thomas, J. (Clynderwen)	.	.	K. in A.	
1918	L/Cpl.	Thomas, D. (Ystalyfera)	.	.	† †	
2014	Gdsn.	Thomas, C. (Pontardulais) .	.	.	†	
2063	,,	Thomas, J. (Manchester)	.	.		
2080	,,	Thomas, S. (Blaenavon)	.	.	K. in A.	
2134	,,	Thomas, M. (Tenby) .	.	.	†	
2210	,,	Thomas, G. (Conway)	.	.	†	
2213	,,	Thomas, A. J. P. (Llantrisant)	.	.	†	
2223	,,	Thomas, A. W. (Bridgend) .	.	.	† †	
2248	,,	Thomas, J. L. (Llanfairfechan)	.	.	K. in A.	
2312	,,	Thomas, T. (Hengoed)	.	.	†	
2318	,,	Thomas, E. (Swansea)	.	.	K. in A.	
2379	,,	Thomas, J. (Llanon) .	.	.	†	
2415	,,	Thomas, H. (Towyn) .	.	.	D. of Wds.	
2438	,,	Thomas, L. J. (Cwmdeuddwr)	.	.	D. of Wds.	
2481	,,	Thomas, R. (Port Talbot) .	.	.	†	
2494	,,	Thomas, B. W. (St. Clears)	.	.	† D. of Wds.	
2541	,,	Thomas, S. T. (Llangyfelach)	.	.		D.C.M.
2551	,,	Thomas, D. (Llandyssul) .	.	.	†	
2591	,,	Thomas, A. (Llandilo)	.	.	D. of Wds.	
2682	,,	Thomas, G. (Porth) .	.	.	.	
2689	,,	Thomas, H. (Neath) .	.	.	.	
2776	Cpl.	Thomas, T. R. (Pentre) .	.	.	.	
2860	Gdsn.	Thomas, J. (Penybont) .	.	.	K. in A.	
2862	,,	Thomas, A. E. (Shrewsbury)	.	.	†	
3093	,,	Thomas, A. (Rhostryfan) .	.	.	†	D.C.M.
3179	,,	Thomas, K. E. (Maldon) .	.	.	.	
3193	,,	Thomas, D. (Carnarvon) .	.	.	K. in A.	
3208	,,	Thomas, W. J. (Kidwelly) .	.	.	†	M.M.
3311	Dmr.	Thomas, W. H. (Helmshore)	.	.	.	
3313	Gdsn.	Thomas, J. (Haslingden)	.	.	K. in A.	
3495	,,	Thomas, T. I. (Aberystwyth)	.	.	† †	
3608	,,	Thomas, G. W. (Cardiff)	.	.	† K. in A.	
3609	,,	Thomas, R. J. (Cardiff)	.	.	†	
3644	,,	Thomas, W. O. (Llanon) .	.	.	†	
3742	,,	Thomas, G. H. (Bilston) .	.	.	.	
3989	,,	Thomas, W. (Cardiff) .	.	.	K. in A.	
4003	,,	Thomas, T. J. (Resolven) .	.	.	.	
4036	,,	Thomas, A. E. (Cardiff) .	.	.	.	
4079	,,	Thomas, J. M. (Tonypandy)	.	.	.	
4102	,,	Thomas, E. (Swansea) .	.	.	.	
4475	,,	Thomas, D. M. (Crynant) .	.	.	.	
4480	,,	Thomas, J. H. (Cardiff) .	.	.	.	
4550	,,	Thomas, E. A. (Nantymoel)	.	.	.	
4566	,,	Thomas, G. (Cwmgwrach) .	.	.	.	
4617	,,	Thomas, J. (Cardiff) .	.	.	.	

Regtl. No.	Rank.	Name.	Casualties.	Decorations.
4660	Gdsn.	Thomas, J. (Llanybri)		
4754	,,	Thomas, E. J. (Neath)		
4775	,,	Thomas, I. (Bridgend)		
4794	,,	Thomas, T. (Cardiff)		
4802	,,	Thomas, N. L. (Pontypridd)		
4806	,,	Thomas, I. (Neath)		
4828	,,	Thomas, E. (Penclawdd)		
5782	,,	Thomas, I. J. (Cardiff)		
518	,,	Thompson, J. J. (Middlesborough)	D. of Wds.	
3316	L/Cpl.	Thompson, J. G. (South Shields)	†	
3469	Gdsn.	Thompson, W. (Thirsk)		
4167	,,	Thompson, R. (Hull)		
500	,,	Thorley, H. (Endon)		
322	,,	Thorne, W. C. (Cardiff)	† K. in A.	
497	,,	Thorne, J. (Pontypridd)		
3988	,,	Thorne, T. (Penarth)	K. in A.	
3109	,,	Thornley, J. E. (Bolton)		
4358	,,	Thornton, A. (Bentley)		
214	,,	Thorpe, W. (Wigan)	† †	
1799	,,	Thorpe, W. E. C. (Cardiff)	†	
3866	,,	Thrift, S. S. (Bath)		
3072	,,	Throup, T. (Nelson)		
3806	,,	Tibbatts, J. (Birmingham)	K. in A.	
2105	L/Cpl.	Tilbrook, P. (London)		
3775	Gdsn.	Tiley, L. L. (Chipping Sodbury)	K. in A.	
35	Cpl.	Tilling, A. H. (Bristol)	† †	
2004	L/Cpl.	Timberlake, H. (Wrexham)	† K. in A.	
342	Gdsn.	Tinklin, C. (Cardiff)	K. in A.	
1622	,,	Tinklin, A. (Cardiff)	† K. in A.	
2972	,,	Tissington, F. W. C. (London, N.)	K. in A.	
3397	,,	Titley, P. (Shrewsbury)		
597	,,	Tittle, W. J. (Aberavon)	K. in A.	
410	,,	Tobin, J. (Merthyr)		
2857	L/Cpl.	Todd, H. J. (Suffield)		
3118	Gdsn.	Todd, R. H. (Morpeth)	†	
3372	,,	Toft, T. (Liverpool)	†	
124	,,	Tombs, R. (Cheltenham)	D. of Wds.	
1012	,,	Tomkins, W. (Wrexham)	†	
4141	,,	Tomkins, J. F. (Smethwick)	†	
45	,,	Tomlin, S. D. (London, S.W.)		
183	L/Cpl.	Tonge, D. J. (Llanelly)	†	
205	Gdsn.	Toombs, W. (Cardiff)		
3079	,,	Totman, S. W. (Colchester)	† K. in A.	
2969	,,	Townsend, J. (Cardiff)	† D. of Wds.	
3330	,,	Townson, W. (Ulverston)	†	
3700	L/Cpl.	Towse, E. (Storrington)		
4727	Gdsn.	Treadwell, G. (Neath)		
553	L/Cpl.	Treasure, J. E. (Cross Keys)	†	
5229	Gdsn.	Treharne, S. T. (Merthyr)		
2173	,,	Trehearn, E. T. (Ruthin)	K. in A.	
3553	,,	Trigg, P. (Llanelly)		

Regtl. No.	Rank.	Name.	Casualties.	Decora- tions.
4623	Gdsn.	Trigg, W. (Maesteg) . . .		
5230	,,	Tripp, T. W. L. (Caerphilly) . .		
50	C.Q.M.S.	Trott, W. J. (Cardiff) . . .		M.S.M.
1245	L/Sergt.	Trott, F. (Bridgend) . . .	D. of S.	
4612	Gdsn.	Trott, D. J. (Ogmore) . . .		
4404	,,	Trought, W. (Cardiff) . . .		
79	,,	Truman, I. (Swansea) . . .	K. in A.	
316	,,	Tucker, W. G. (Swansea) . . .	†	
1223	,,	Tucker, B. (Newport) . . .		
2598	,,	Tudball, A. W. (Swansea) . . .	†	
3545	,,	Tudor, S. O. (Trefeglwys) . . .		
1859	L/Sergt.	Tunley, W. (Hull)		
3312	Gdsn.	Tunnah, W. (Gateshead) . . .	K. in A.	
3931	,,	Turley, A. J. (Lydney) . . .	†	M.M.
320	,,	Turner, E. H. (Llanelly) . . .	†	
456	Cpl.	Turner, W. T. (Gloucester). . .	† † D. of Wds.	
582	L/Cpl.	Turner, J. N. L. (Merthyr Tydfil)		
610	Gdsn.	Turner, W. (Cardiff) . . .	D. of Wds.	
621	,,	Turner, C. (Cardiff) . . .	K. in A.	
806	,,	Turner, A. J. (Swansea) . . .	† †	
1992	,,	Turner, F. J. (Cardiff) . . .		
2123	L/Cpl.	Turner, B. (Swansea) . . .	†	
2198	Gdsn.	Turner, L. E. W. (Abergavenny) .	†	
2716	,,	Turner, T. J. (Cardiff) . . .	†	
5822	,,	Turner, W. (Newport) . . .	†	
2316	,,	Tuson, A. W. L. (Addlestone Hill) .	K. in A.	
3933	,,	Tweed, W. O. (Benwick) . . .		
3938	,,	Tweedy, H. (Alnwick) . . .	†	
1468	L/Cpl.	Tyler, B. (Cardiff) . . .	†	
3762	Gdsn.	Tyson, N. (Liverpool) . . .		
1043	Gdsn.	Ulyatt, J. (Chesterfield) . . .	†	M.M.
941	,,	Underhill, W. J. (Bridgend) . .	†	
1927	,,	Underwood, E. (Cardiff) . . .	†	
269	,,	Uren, A. (Newport) . . .	† †	
2126	Musn.	Urry, C. (London) . . .		
2388	,,	Urry, L. (London) . . .		
4446	Gdsn.	Uterus, A. (Manchester) . . .	†	
71	Gdsn.	Vaughan, D. (Penygroes) . . .		
654	,,	Vaughan, T. (Rhondda) . . .	†	
962	,,	Vaughan, D. (Treorchy) . . .	†	
2216	,,	Vaughan, R. (Monmouth) . . .	† K. in A.	
2302	,,	Vaughan, E. (Oswestry) . . .	†	
2437	,,	Vaughan, J. L. (Rhayader) . . .	†	
2462	,,	Vaughan, W. J. (Monkton) . .	K. in A.	
2881	,,	Vaughan, J. E. (Wrexham) . .		M.M.
2991	,,	Vaughan, J. (Mamhilad) . . .	K. in A.	
3265	,,	Veevers, W. (Nelson) . . .	K. in A.	
4517	,,	Venn, A. (Aberdare) . . .		
3975	,,	Vercoe, H. F. (Coventry) . . .		

Regtl. No.	Rank.	Name.	Casualties.	Decorations.
736	Gdsn.	Viggers, W. H. (Cardiff)	K. in A.	
1718	,,	Villeneuve, A. A. (Pontypridd)	K. in A.	
1441	,,	Vincent, C. (Ammanford)		
1374	Dmr.	Viner, R. (Talywain)		
2843	Gdsn.	Viney, G. H. (Wrexham)	† †	
599	,,	Vizard, R. (Cardiff)	D. of Wds.	
5234	,,	Vockman, A. (Swansea)		
2715	,,	Vokes, H. (Cardiff)	†	
2736	,,	Volk, R. C. (Cardigan)		
371	,,	Vowles, F. J. (Gilfach Goch)	†	M.M.
1736	L/Cpl.	Vowles, H. E. (Barry)	†	
2259	L/Cpl.	Waddington, O. F. (Pontypridd)		D.C.M. and Bar, M.M.
910	C.S.M.	Wadeson, R. (Preston)		
2790	Gdsn.	Wagstaff, H. H. (Leintwardine)	†	
505	,,	Walker, W. (Hereford)		
1494	,,	Walker, W. (Castleford)	†	
2631	L/Cpl.	Walker, W. G. (Bradford)		
2854	L/Sergt.	Walker, T. (Warrington)	†	M.M.
2993	Gdsn.	Walker, P. (Bedwelty)	†	
4130	,,	Walker, R. (London)		
859	,,	Wallace, J. R. (Rhondda)	†	M.M.
3732	,,	Waller, H. E. (Liverpool)	†	
138	,,	Walsh, D. M. (Cwmbwrla)	†	
237	,,	Walsh, P. (Newport)	†	
1415	L/Cpl.	Walsh, J. (Cardiff)		
2121	Musn.	Walsh, F. (Lichfield)		
336	,,	Walters, J. (Merthyr)	†	M.M.
431	,,	Walters, J. (Aberdare)		
899	,,	Walters, A. (Neath)	D. of Wds.	
1141	,,	Walters, J. (Llandebie)	†	
1507	L/Cpl.	Walters, H. H. (Marshfield)	†	
2026	Gdsn.	Walters, W. (Bridgend)	†	
4292	,,	Walters, W. J. (London, N.E.)	†	
911	,,	Walton, H. T. (Birmingham)		
3948	,,	Walton, P. C. (Kelvedon)	K. in A.	
2808	L/Cpl.	Warburton, W. (Warrington)	†	
4174	Gdsn.	Warby, A. S. (London, E.)	†	
1676	,,	Ward, H. H. (Aberystwyth)		
1737	L/Sgt.	Ward, J. R. (Aberystwyth)		
2684	Gdsn.	Ward, H. (Swansea)	K. in A.	
3366	,,	Ward, E. G. (Winchester)		M.M.
2445	L/Cpl.	Warlow, R. (Llanywern)	†	
777	Gdsn.	Warmington, A. P. (Cardiff)		
2925	,,	Warren, A. E. (Bangor)		
5305	,,	Warren, W. J. (Cardiff)		
337	,,	Waters, T. E. (Swansea)		
1222	Sergt.	Waters, A. (Newport)	†	
1862	Gdsn.	Waters, W. (Ammanford)		

Regtl. No.	Rank.	Name.	Casualties.	Decorations.
4620	Gdsn.	Waters, D. J. (Maesteg) . . .		
1079	,,	Wathen, E. (Gloucester) . . .		
292	,,	Watkins, D. T. (Maesteg) . . .		
401	L/Cpl.	Watkins, H. E. (Stroud) . . .	† †	
506	Gdsn.	Watkins, J. H. (Newport) . . .	†	
1555	,,	Watkins, T. D. (Cardiff) . . .		
1851	L/Sergt.	Watkins, I. J. (Brecon) . . .	†	
2242	L/Cpl.	Watkins, A. E. (Caerleon) . . .	K. in A.	
3013	Gdsn.	Watkins, A. (Brynmawr) . . .		
3237	,,	Watkins, L. (Pontypool) . . .	K. in A.	
4005	,,	Watkins, W. T. (Neath) . . .		
1966	,,	Watkiss, W. (Castleford) . . .	D. of Wds.	
695	,,	Watling, B. J. (Tonypandy) . .	† †	
2958	,,	Watmough, A. (Bradford) . . .		
533	,,	Watson, W. (Castleford) . . .	K. in A.	
1194	,,	Watson, S. (Llanelly)	†	
3212	,,	Watson, A. W. (Poole) . . .		
207	,,	Watts, W. C. (Newport) . . .		
1211	,,	Watts, W. (Abertillery) . . .	† †	
2589	,,	Watts, S. J. (Brawdy) . . .		
238	,,	Weaver, F. (Worcester) . . .	† †	
716	,,	Weaver, D. (Tredegar) . . .	† †	
1720	,,	Weaver, H. F. (Barry) . . .	K. in A.	
2686	,,	Webb, E. (Swansea)		
4191	,,	Webb, G. J. (London, N.W.) . .		
4361	,,	Webb, F. (Hastings)	†	
3625	,,	Webber, W. E. (Morriston) . .		
3377	,,	Webster, F. (Ely, Cambs.) . .	K. in A.	
3435	,,	Weedon, R. A. (London) . . .	†	
1697	,,	Weeks, A. J. (Mountain Ash) .	K. in A.	
1988	Sergt.	Weightman, J. F. (London) . .	†	
300	Gdsn.	Welch, W. J. (Newport) . . .	†	
993	,,	Welch, H. (Tonypandy) . . .	†	
3725	,,	Welch, A. (Portsmouth) . . .	†	
1508	L/Cpl.	Welford, A. W. (Stoke-on-Trent) .	†	
180	,,	Weller, C. (Swansea) . . .	†	
3580	,,	Wellings, A. J. (Cwmparc) . .		M.M.
520	Gdsn.	Welsby, G. (Salford) . . .	K. in A.	
3141	Cpl.	Went, J. (Grays)		
208	Sergt.	West, O. (Cardiff)		
758	Gdsn.	West. A. A. (Newport) . . .		M.M.
2088	,,	West, A. (Cwmavon) . . .		
3006	,,	Westcott, T. G. (Swansea) . .	†	
406	,,	Weston, W. S. (Aberdare) . .	† † †	
2694	,,	Weston, W. G. (Wolverhampton)	D. of S.	
3319	,,	Weston, B. (Caerphilly) . . .	K. in A.	
3112	,,	Whalley, C. (Burnley) . . .		
3250	,,	Whalley, F. (Nottingham) . .		
3035	,,	Whatmore, F. (Bath) . . .	† †	
577	L/Cpl.	Wheadon, S. (Tonyrefail) . .	†	
235	L/Sergt.	Wheatley, E. J. (Swansea) . .	† † †	M.M.

Regtl. No.	Rank.	Name.	Casualties.	Decorations.
453	L/Sergt.	Wheeler, E. (Tonypandy)	†	
3864	Gdsn.	Whetham, C. L. (Southampton)		
3763	,,	Whieldon, A. E. (Salisbury)		
2617	,,	While, T. G. (Burton)		
1403	,,	Whitby, D. W. (Abergavenny)	D. of Wds.	
2177	L/Cpl.	Whitcombe, H. (Pontypridd)	† †	
460	Gdsn.	White, C. J. (Pontypridd)		
930	,,	White, W. (Aberdare)	K. in A.	
1405	,,	White, A. (Reading)		
1465	Cpl.	White, S. (Cardiff)	† †	M.M.
1569	Gdsn.	White, G. (Stroud)	D. of Wds.	
2102	Musn.	White, P. E. (Hastings)		
2129	Gdsn.	White, E. (Bedwas)	K. in A.	
2158	,,	White, G. (Cardiff)	K. in A.	
2190	,,	White, V. H. (London)	†	
2729	,,	White, G. (Cardiff)		
3186	L/Cpl.	White, P. (Ton Pentre)	†	
3285	Gdsn.	White, H. C. (Blackburn)		
3666	,,	White, H. J. (Ystrad)		
3713	,,	White, E. (Newport)	D. of Wds.	
3766	,,	White, S. J. (Barry)	†	
3818	,,	White, C. G. K. (Batley)		
4138	,,	White, J. (Bristol)		
4533	,,	White, H. (Merthyr)		
928	,,	Whitehead, F. N. R. (Cardiff)	†	
2097	,,	Whitehead, W. (Carmarthen)	D. of Wds.	
4365	,,	Whitehead, J. (Chesterfield)	†	
5246	,,	Whitelock, A. W. (Neath)		
1643	L/Cpl.	Whiteman, F. J. (Merthyr)		
3168	Gdsn.	Whiteside, W. (Garstang)	†	
4364	,,	Whitlock, H. (Hucknall)	†	
3894	,,	Whittall, W. (London)	D. of Wds.	
3226	,,	Whittle, F. J. (Aberstone)		
1706	,,	Whitton, H. (Liverpool)		
3690	,,	Wicks, A. (Devizes)		
3722	,,	Wiggins, W. H. (Liverpool)	†	
4161	,,	Wigglesworth, F. (Barrow-in-Furness)		
4360	A/Cpl.	Wigman, W. T. (Ripley)	†	
4368	Gdsn.	Wilby, J. A. (Leeds)		
3378	,,	Wilcox, L. (Hoxne Eye)		
4610	,,	Wilcox, W. J. (Risca)		
1778	,,	Wilcoxon, J. O. (Wrexham)	K. in A.	
187	,,	Wilde, J. (Cardiff)		
2859	,,	Wilding, J. (Knighton)	†	
1061	,,	Wildman, A. (Liverpool)	† †	
489	,,	Wilkins, E. (Tredegar)		
2276	Musn.	Wilkins, F. (London)		
381	Gdsn.	Wilkinson, G. S. (Cardiff)	†	
2264	L/Cpl.	Wilkinson, W. E. (London, S.E.)	† †	
2924	Gdsn.	Wilkinson, G. (Burnley)	†	
3887	,,	Wilkinson, W. (Shipton)	†	

Regtl. No.	Rank.	Name.	Casualties.	Decorations.
679	Cpl.	Willcox, W. J. (Cardiff)		
3548	Gdsn.	Willett, C. H. (Cardiff)	† †	M.M.
34	C.Q.M.S.	Williams, I. T. (Abercarn)	†	
57	Sergt.	Williams, S. (London)	K. in A.	
93	Gdsn.	Williams, L. (Treharris)	†	
125	Sergt.	Williams, E. J. (Llangefni)	†	
154	Gdsn.	Williams, J. (Merthyr)		
195	„	Williams, E. (Pontypridd)	† †	
206	L/Cpl.	Williams, C. A. (Cardiff)	†	
248	„	Williams, R. (Pwllheli)		
276	Gdsn.	Williams, W. J. (St. Clears)	K. in A.	
278	„	Williams, H. (Bridgend)	†	
321	„	Williams, M. (Cardiff)	†	
347	„	Williams, T. (Wrexham)	D. of Wds.	
412	„	Williams, E. P. (Mold)	D. of Wds.	
455	„	Williams, B. E. (Cardiff)	†	
464	„	Williams, J. A. (Scarborough)		
467	„	Williams, E. J. (Dewsbury)	†	
485	Sergt.	Williams, L. (Swansea)		M.M.
510	Gdsn.	Williams, T. (Newport)		
545	„	Williams, H. J. (Malvern)		
596	„	Williams, J. (Pwllheli)		
637	„	Williams, T. C. (Cardiff)	K. in A.	
671	„	Williams, J. (Swansea)	K. in A.	
724	„	Williams, L. (Wrexham)		
737	Sergt.	Williams, G. (Aberystwyth)	†	
746	Gdsn.	Williams, A. (Rhondda)		M.M.
794	L/Cpl.	Williams, G. T. (Swansea)	†	
803	„	Williams, L. J. (Ystalyfera)	†	
807	Gdsn.	Williams, L. (Neath)	†	
846	„	Williams, D. J. (Caerphilly)	†	
854	„	Williams, D. (Cardiff)	† †	
875	„	Williams, T. P. (Dinas)		
880	„	Williams, G. (Aberdare)		
892	„	Williams, T. (Bargoed)	†	
901	„	Williams, E. L. (Neath)	D. of Wds.	
905	„	Williams, W. (Abercarn)	†	
935	„	Williams, J. (Swansea)	† †	
936	„	Williams, W. T. (Pantyffynnon)	K. in A.	
943	„	Williams, W. A. (Crook, Durham)		
1099	L/Cpl.	Williams, H. (Manchester)		
1101	„	Williams, W. J. (Abercynon)	K. in A.	
1114	Gdsn.	Williams, R. (Groeslon)	K. in A.	
1115	„	Williams, M. (Aberdare)	†	
1130	„	Williams, W. A. (Cardiff)		
1144	„	Williams, D. O. (Merthyr Tydfil)		
1188	„	Williams, J. (Bargoed)	†	
1190	„	Williams, J. (Llandebie)	†	
1233	„	Williams, E. (Brynteg)		
1257	„	Williams, F. (Barry)	†	
1266	„	Williams, F. F. J. (Cardiff)	†	

Regtl. No.	Rank.	Name.	Casualties.	Decorations.
1271	Gdsn.	Williams, C. O. (Carmarthen)	†	
1289	,,	Williams, E. (Caerphilly)		
1300	,,	Williams, J. (Pontyberem)	† † K. in A.	
1312	,,	Williams, T. M. (Aberystwyth)	†	
1338	,,	Williams, M. (Swansea)	† †	
1406	L/Cpl.	Williams, D. (Llanrystyd)		
1419	Gdsn.	Williams, S. R. (New Quay)	D. of Wds.	
1464	,,	Williams, J. (Brymbo)	†	
1474	,,	Williams, E. (Carnarvon)	D. of Wds.	
1475	L/Cpl.	Williams, T. (Carnarvon)	†	
1503	Gdsn.	Williams, R. (Caerphilly)		
1588	,,	Williams, J. (Rhondda)	† † †	
1652	,,	Williams, G. (Barry)	† †	
1653	,,	Williams, J. (Cardiff)		
1656	,,	Williams, W. (Porth)		
1821	,,	Williams, I. J. (Llandaff)		
1871	,,	Williams, J. (Bridgend)	†	
1911	,,	Williams, J. W. (Neath)	D. of Wds.	
1930	L/Cpl.	Williams, A. (Llantwit Fardre)	†	
1960	Gdsn.	Williams, T. (Llanwonno)		
1967	,,	Williams, A. (Swansea)	† K. in A.	
1986	Cpl.	Williams, A. H. (Llandebie)	†	
1996	Gdsn.	Williams, F. G. (Barmouth)	K. in A.	
2047	,,	Williams, W. P. (Brecon)	†	
2065	,,	Williams, R. (Pentre)		
2090	L/Cpl.	Williams, W. (Cardiff)	K. in A.	
2156	Gdsn.	Williams, R. P. (Ogmore Vale)	K. in A.	
2163	,,	Williams, J. (Cardiff)	†	M.M.
2209	L/Sergt.	Williams, F. (Newport)		
2227	Gdsn.	Williams, R. O. (Llanwrda)		
2239	,,	Williams, H. (Wrexham)		
2244	,,	Williams, R. E. (Llanfihangel)	† †	
2249	,,	Williams, J. H. (Bodfari)	D. of Wds.	
2297	,,	Williams, W. J. (Bethesda)	† †	
2351	,,	Williams, O. B. (Llanfairfechan)	K. in A.	
2352	,,	Williams, O. J. (Penmaenmawr)	† †	
2397	,,	Williams, C. (Treharris)	K. in A.	
2409	,,	Williams, J. T. (Llansantffraid)	K. in A.	
2414	,,	Williams, D. R. (Machynllyth)	D. of Wds.	
2418	L/Sergt.	Williams, V. (Griffithstown)		
2421	Gdsn.	Williams, E. D. (Brecon)		
2440	,,	Williams, R. (Llanddwywe)		
2526	,,	Williams, W. L. (Glyncorwg)	†	
2539	,,	Williams, M. (Merthyr)	†	
2560	,,	Williams, T. E. (Rhyl)	D. of Wds.	
2605	L/Cpl.	Williams, L. (Mountain Ash)		
2613	Sergt.	Williams, J. R. (Merthyr)		
2646	Cpl.	Williams, W. (Aberaman)	K. in A.	
2749	Gdsn.	Williams, J. R. (Nantlle)	K. in A.	
2779	,,	Williams, W. (Lamphey)	D. of Wds.	
2814	L/Cpl.	Williams, E. (Mostyn)	†	

Regtl. No.	Rank.	Name.	Casualties.	Decorations.
2852	Gdsn.	Williams, W. (Cardiff)	†	
2867	L/Cpl.	Williams, W. S. (Llanynis)	†	
2932	Gdsn.	Williams, J. E. (Welshpool)	†	
2990	,,	Williams, E. E. (Pontypool)		
3004	,,	Williams, W. H. (Wrexham)	† K. in A.	
3055	,,	Williams, U. V. (Llangyfelach)	K. in A.	
3085	L/Cpl.	Williams, T. (Barrow-in-Furness)	†	
3166	Gdsn.	Williams, J. (Liverpool)		
3206	,,	Williams, O. M. (Kidwelly)		
3211	,,	Williams, N. H. (Kidwelly)	K. in A.	
3219	,,	Williams, W. (Holywell)		
3293	,,	Williams, L. (Amlwch)		
3387	,,	Williams, H. (Carmarthen)	K. in A.	
3392	,,	Williams, R. M. (Corwen)		
3395	,,	Williams, O. R. (Llandegfan)	†	
3412	L/Cpl.	Williams, T. H. (Cardiff)	†	
3482	Gdsn.	Williams, W. (Carnarvon)	†	
3521	,,	Williams, J. G. (Blaenau-Festiniog)	†	
3544	,,	Williams, F. G. (Bristol)		
3561	,,	Williams, W. Cardiff)		
3583	,,	Williams, W. M. (Caerwys)	K. in A.	
3591	,,	Williams, J. H. (Holywell)		
3598	,,	Williams, W. J. (Monmouth)	K. in A.	
3613	,,	Williams, R. D. (Bangor)	†	
3623	,,	Williams, B. E. (Welshpool)		
3635	,,	Williams, J. M. (Penarth)		
3651	,,	Williams, H. (Barry)	K. in A.	
3687	,,	Williams, A. J. (Bristol)	K. in A.	
3773	,,	Williams, H. (Shrewsbury)	†	
3776	,,	Williams, S. (Tredegar)	†	
3813	,,	Williams, T. R. (Bargoed)		
4021	,,	Williams, H. (Porth)	†	
4069	,,	Williams, J. (Wrexham)	†	
4098	,,	Williams, C. (Port Talbot)	†	
4113	,,	Williams, G. J. (Port Talbot)	†	
4194	,,	Williams, W. F. (Birmingham)		
4410	,,	Williams, E. T. (Merthyr)		
4416	,,	Williams, H. (Newport)		
4445	,,	Williams, M. (Mountain Ash)	†	
4483	,,	Williams, J. (Cardiff)		
4548	,,	Williams, D. (Dowlais)		
4577	L/Cpl.	Williams, E. T. (Newport)		
4603	Gdsn.	Williams, T. C. (Ferndale)		
4636	,,	Williams, W. J. (Pontycymmer)		
4746	,,	Williams, F. W. E. (Stow-on-the-Wold)		
4751	,,	Williams, W. (Llandilo)		
4801	,,	Williams, E. (Llanspyddid)		
4835	,,	Williams, T. (Bangor)		
4843	,,	Williams, D. (Swansea)		
5333	,,	Williams, W. J. (Mountain Ash)		
2576	,,	Williamson, A. M. (London, N.E.)		

31

Regtl No.	Rank.	Name.	Casualties.	Decorations.
3761	Gdsn.	Williamson, H. (Carlisle) . . .	†	
167	L/Cpl.	Willis, H. G. (Bournemouth)		
1221	Gdsn.	Willis, F. (Newport) . . .	†	
3686	,,	Willis, S. (Bristol)	†	
782	Cpl.	Wills, C. (Bargoed) . . .		
2072	Gdsn.	Wills, J. (Brynmawr) . . .	K. in A.	
2625	,,	Wilmot, D. J. (Pontypridd) . .	†	
4563	,,	Wilmott, F. C. (Newport) . .		
1963	,,	Wilsdon, H. W. (Caerphilly) . .	†	
2665	,,	Wilson, A. (Swansea) . . .		
3075	,,	Wilson, T. (Askham) . . .		
3252	,,	Winkle, S. (Liverpool) . .	†	
3199	,,	Winkworth, E. (Hungerford) . .	† †	
446	L/Cpl.	Winn, R. (Tonypandy) . . .	† D. of Wds.	
4367	Gdsn.	Winn, A. H. (Shrewsbury) . .	†	
4708	,,	Winstone, B. G. (Cardiff) . .		
496	Sergt.	Winter, F. (Cardiff) . . .		M.M., M.S.M.
776	L/Sergt.	Winter, G. (Cardiff) . . .	† †	M.M.
3147	Gdsn.	Winter, C. T. (Darlington) . .	† †	
3640	,,	Wintle, C. E. (Chepstow) . .	†	
4363	Cpl.	Wise, F. (Eastbourne) . . .		
2928	Gdsn.	Witcomb, J. (Cardiff) . .	†	
1755	Sergt.	Witcombe, A. J. (Haverfordwest)		
888	Gdsn.	Witts, C. H. (London) . .	D. of Wds.	
1537	L/Cpl.	Witts, I. L. (London) . .	K. in A.	
286	Gdsn.	Wood, J. W. (London) . .	†	
831	,,	Wood, W. (Aberdare) . .	† † † †	
1316	L/Sergt.	Wood, R. D. (London) . .		
2313	,,	Wood, F. (London) . . .		
2501	L/Cpl.	Wood, A. (Glyn Neath) . .	†	
2879	,,	Wood, R. (Swansea) . . .	K. in A.	
2903	Gdsn.	Wood, H. A. (Glazebury) . .		
3413	,,	Wood, J. R. C. (Ryton-on-Tyne)	D. of Wds.	
4092	,,	Wood, G. E. (Leominster) . .		M.M.
4366	,,	Wood, W. H. (Raynes Park) .		
2673	,,	Woodberry, E. F. (Cardiff) .		
3314	,,	Woodcock, S. (Doncaster) .		
4145	,,	Woodgate, H. W. (Abertillery)		
297	D/Sergt.	Woodhouse, G. (Slough) . .	†	
4163	L/Cpl.	Woodhouse, F. (Hollingworth) .	†	
3710	Gdsn.	Woodland, A. G. (Bristol) . .	†	
2010	,,	Woodley, W. T. (Cardiff) . .	† K. in A.	
4203	,,	Woodmore, T. H. (Charlton) .	D. of Wds.	
3274	,,	Woodyatt, A. (Pontsticill) . .	D. of Wds.	
856	,,	Woolford, J. (Aberdare) . .	†	
3437	,,	Woolley, J. (Newtown) . .		
3586	,,	Woolley, J. L. (Connah's Quay) .		
3540	,,	Wootten, J. D. (Andover) . .	†	
4752	,,	Wordley, R. (Swansea) . .		
4078	,,	Workman, F. W. (Newport) .		
4362	,,	Wormald, J. (Wakefield) . .	† †	

Regtl. No.	Rank.	Name.	Casualties.	Decorations.
1556	Gdsn.	Worsfold, F. J. (Maidenhead)	K. in A.	
2485	,,	Worsfold, E. W. (London, E.)	K. in A.	
43	Sergt.	Wren, C. H. (Newport)		M.M.
2920	L/Sergt.	Wright, F. (Pentre)	† †	
3018	Gdsn.	Wright, W. H. (Wrexham)	†	
3031	,,	Wright, F. (Stafford)	†	
4359	,,	Wright, A. (Leeds)		
293	Sergt.	Wyatt, J. H. (Blackwood)	†	
662	Gdsn.	Wyatt, W. (Blaengarw)	D. of Wds.	
1873	,,	Wyatt, J. T. (Swansea)	K. in A.	
2300	,,	Wyman, A. F. (London, N.)		
2872	Gdsn.	Yardley, J. (Newport, Salop)	† †	
1009	,,	Yarnton, C. (London, S.E.)		
3429	,,	Yates, S. (Tipton)		
3844	,,	Yates, D. (Aberkenfig)		
1035	,,	Yearsley, J. (Denton)	D. of Wds.	
4026	,,	Yeates, V. J. (Pentre)	†	
4418	,,	Yeates, F. G. (Trowbridge)		
3194	,,	Yeldham, H. (Grays)		
1994	,,	Yemm, W. (Caerphilly)	†	
2773	L/Sergt.	Yonds, R. A. (Birkenhead)	†	
1274	L/Cpl.	York, H. G. F. (Ystalyfera)	† K. in A.	
1733	Gdsn.	York, S. (Northampton)		
9	C.Q.M.S.	Young, R. J. (Chalford)		
670	Gdsn.	Young, H. (Glyn Neath)	K. in A.	
1081	,,	Young, E. (Chesterfield)		
1583	,,	Young, G. E. (Pontypridd)	K. in A.	
1626	,,	Young, A. I. (Cardiff)	† †	
1658	,,	Young, A. E. (Llandyssul)	D. of Wds.	
2078	,,	Young, W. J. (Brecon)	†	
2997	,,	Young, H. (Poppleton)	† †	
3178	,,	Young, A. E. (Cardiff)	†	
3513	,,	Young, F. G. (Bourton)	†	
3922	,,	Young, H. G. (London, S.E.)	K. in A.	
5667	,,	Young, T. A. (Tonypandy)		

APPENDIX J

RECORDS OF OFFICERS OF THE WELSH GUARDS

(*Note*:—The B.E.F. service given is from the date of joining the Regiment.)

Name.	Date of joining Welsh Guards and former regiment and rank.	Rank on joining Welsh Guards.	Remarks.
Adams, C. H.	1918 From O. C. Bn.	2/Lieut.	Served with B.E.F. from 5.9.18 to 15.10.18. Wounded in action 12.10.18 and invalided to England on account of wounds. Promoted Lieut. 27.9.19.
Aldridge, H. H.	1915 From Temp. Captain R.F.A.	Captain	Served with B.E.F. 19.10.15 to 5.1.17. Invalided to England on account of sickness. To Egypt for employment on the Staff 6.10.17. Mentioned in Despatches.
Allen, H. E.	1915 From Lieut. Royal Fus.	Lieut.	Served with B.E.F. from 15.10.15 to 26.12.15 and from 27.3.17 to 19.5.17. Invalided to England on account of sickness. Promoted to Captain 9.6.15.
Arbuthnott, Hon. J. O.	1918 From O. C. Bn.	2/Lieut.	
Arthur, W.	1916 From O. C. Bn.	2/Lieut.	Served with B.E.F. from 10.2.17 to 3.8.17. Wounded in action 31.7.17 and invalided to England on account of wounds. B.E.F. 17.9.18 to 12.3.19. Awarded the Military Cross. Promoted Lieut. 22.5.18.
Ashton, H. G. G.	1915 From Lieut. Commdr. R.N.D.	Captain	Served with B.E.F. 12.7.16 to 22.9.16. Wounded in action 16.9.16 and invalided to England on account of wounds. Mentioned in Despatches and awarded the D.S.O.
Bagot, E. L. H.	1915 From R.M.C.	2/Lieut.	Served with B.E.F. 22.5.16 to 10.9.16. Killed in action 10.9.16.

Name.	Date of joining Welsh Guards and former regiment and rank.	Rank on joining Welsh Guards.	Remarks.
Ballard, C. P. .	1916	2/Lieut.	Served with B.E.F. from 9.8.17 to 10.3.18. Killed in action 10.3.18.
Baness, H. E. .	1916	2/Lieut.	Served with B.E.F. from 26.5.17 to 3.9.18. Transferred to Indian Army 25.9.18. Promoted Lieut. 26.6.18.
Barlow, F. L. T.	1915 From Lieut. E. Kent Yeo.	Lieut.	Served with B.E.F. 6.2.16 to 6.10.16. Invalided to England on account of sickness. B.E.F. 8.8.17 to 15.11.18. Awarded the Military Cross. Attached Guards M.G. Regt. Acting Captain from 19.2.18.
Battye, P. L. M.	1915 2/Lieut. S.R. Gren. Gds.	Lieut.	Served with B.E.F. 15.10.15 to 22.6.16. Wounded in action 19.6.16 and invalided to England on account of wounds. B.E.F. 27.3.17 to 26.1.18. Invalided to England on account of sickness. B.E.F. 31.8.18 to 12.3.19. Slightly wounded in action 13.10.18. Temporary Capt. 11.5.16 to 20.6.16. Promoted Capt. 14.10.16. Awarded the Military Cross, Croix de Guerre (French), and Legion of Honour (Chevalier).
Baxter, F. B. .	1918 From O. C. Bn.	2/Lieut.	
Berg, A. W. W. .	1916	2/Lieut.	Served with B.E.F. from 21.10.16 to 29.11.16. Attd. to Russian Govt. Committee 30.11.16 to 6.1.18. Mission to Siberia 7.1.18 to 17.8.18. Attd. to Foreign Office 18.8.18 to 7.6.19. Promoted Lieut. 30.4.17. Acting Captain from 7.1.18.
Bird, O. . .	1916	2/Lieut.	Served with B.E.F. from 25.9.16 to 18.3.19. Appointed Divisional Gas Officer 24.3.17. Awarded the Military Cross. Promoted Lieut. 30.4.17.
Blake, F. W. E. .	1915 From Lieut.-Col. 3rd Royal Sussex Regt.	Major	Served with B.E.F. 7.11.18 to 4.5.19. (Commandant P. of W. Camp.)
Bonn, W. B. L. .	1916 From Capt. Leicester Yeomanry (T.F.)	Lieut.	Served with B.E.F. from 11.12.16 to 26.1.19. Invalided to England on account of sickness. Acting Capt. from 20.7.17. Mentioned in Despatches and awarded the M.C. and D.S.O.

Name.	Date of joining Welsh Guards and former regiment and rank.	Rank on joining Welsh Guards.	Remarks.
Bonsor, R. C. .	1916	2/Lieut.	Served with B.E.F. from 19.1.17 to 13.1.19. Awarded the Military Cross. Promoted Lieut. 28.2.18.
Borough, A. C. H.	1916 From R.M.C.	2/Lieut.	Served with B.E.F. from 14.3.17 to 1.12.17. Killed in action 1.12.17. Promoted Lieut. 22.8.17.
Bowyer, C. T. .	1917 From O. C. Bn.	2/Lieut.	Served with B.E.F. from 3.10.17 to 10.12.17. Wounded in action 1.12.17 and invalided to England on account of wounds. Promoted 30.11.18.
Boyd, R. T. .	1918 From T/Lieut. Household Battalion.	Lieut.	Transferred at home from Household Battalion and placed on Retired List on account of ill-health caused by wounds 21.9.18.
Bradney, J. H. .	1915 From Lieut. D.C.L.I.	Captain	Served with B.E.F. from 17.8.15 to 19.4.19. On Staff from 11.5.16. Promoted Major 19.11.18.
Brawn, A. W. .	1918 From T/2/Lieut. Household Battalion.	Lieut.	Joined 1st Battalion in France 5.4.18. Invalided to England on account of sickness 13.9.18.
Bromfield, H. H. D.S.O. . .	1915 From T/Major S. Wales Bord.	Major	Served with B.E.F. from 9.8.16 to 10.9.16. Killed in action 10.9.16.
Burchell, J. P. T.	1918 From T/2/Lieut. Household Battalion	2/Lieut.	(Joined Battn. in France 18.3.18.) Attd. to Army Signal Service 12.8.18. Awarded the Military Cross. Promoted Lieut. 13.4.18.
Burrows, B. H. .	1918 From O. C. Bn.	2/Lieut.	Promoted Lieut. 26.12.19.
Byrne, T. E. .	1916 From O. C. Bn.	2/Lieut.	Served with B.E.F. from 26.5.17 to 22.9.17. Invalided to England on account of sickness. B.E.F. 15.2.18 to 9.3.18. Killed in action 9.3.18.
Carlyon, A. F. M.	1917 From O. C. Bn.	2/Lieut.	Served with B.E.F. 31.7.17 to 16.9.17. Invalided to England on account of sickness. Promoted Lieut. 1.9.18.
Carter, W. H. .	1918 From Lieut. Yeo. (T.F.)	Lieut.	

Name.	Date of joining Welsh Guards and former regiment and rank.	Rank on joining Welsh Guards.	Remarks.
Cazalet, E.	1916 From 2/Lieut. E. Kent Regt.	2/Lieut.	Served with B.E.F. 15.7.16 to 10.9.16. Killed in action 10.9.16.
Chamberlain, L. B.	1915 From Capt. Ret. Pay.	Captain	Relinquished Commission on account of ill-health, 19.7.15.
Clive, P. R., Viscount	1915 From Lieut. Scots Gds.	Lieut.	Served with B.E.F. from 6.2.16 to 21.9.16. Wounded in action 16.9.16 and invalided to England. Subsequently died in hospital at home on 13.10.16 of wounds received in action. Promoted Captain 11.5.16.
Coleman, P. G. D.S.O.	1917 From Lieut. N. Staffs Regt. (T.F.)	Lieut.	Served with B.E.F. from 5.9.18 to 12.3.19.
Copland-Griffiths, F. A. V.	1915 From 2/Lieut. S. Battalion Rifle Brigade	2/Lieut.	Served with B.E.F. 17.8.15 to 15.3.17. Invalided to England on account of sickness. Wounded in action slightly 27.9.15. B.E.F. 2.11.18 to 12.3.19. Mentioned in Despatches and awarded Military Cross. Temp. Lieut. 1.1.16. Promoted Lieut. 14.10.16. Acting Captain 19.1.17 to 11.4.19.
Courtney, W. A.	1918 From O. C. Bn.	2/Lieut.	Served with B.E.F. 3.6.18 to 12.3.19. Attd. Guards Division Reception Camp from 1.8.18. Acting Captain from 1.8.18 to 8.3.19. Promoted Lieut. 27.8.19.
Crawford-Wood, G.	1915 From Lieut. Royal Warwick Regt.	2/Lieut.	Served with B.E.F. 19.10.15 to 1.7.16. Wounded in action 8.4.16. Killed in action 1.7.16.
Crawshay, G. C. H.	1915 From 2/Lieut. Welsh Regt.	2/Lieut.	Served with B.E.F. 17.8.15 to 11.10.15. Wounded in action 27.9.15 and invalided to England on account of wounds. Promoted Lieut. 19.9.15. Promoted Captain 18.1.19.
Crawshay, J. W. L.	1915 From 2/Lieut. Scottish Horse, I.Y. (T.F.)	2/Lieut.	Served with B.E.F. 18.12.15 to 16.9.16. Invalided to England on account of sickness. B.E.F. 20.5.18 to 12.3.19. Awarded the Military Cross. Acting Adjutant 1st Battalion from 1.11.18 to 18.5.19. Promoted Lieut. 10.1.17. Attd. to

Name.	Date of joining Welsh Guards and former regiment and rank.	Rank on joining Welsh Guards.	Remarks.
Crawshay, J. W. L.—*continued* .			H.B. Officer Cadet Bn. 15.2.17 to 30.11.17 (Adjutant). Acting Regtl. Adjt. 29.3.18 to 19.5.18.
Crosse, W. W. R.	1918 From O. C. Bn.	2/Lieut.	
Culverwell, W. N.	1916 From Lieut. London Regt. (T.F.)	2/Lieut.	Served with B.E.F. from 11.12.16 to 16.2.19. 3rd Guards Brigade Trench Mortar Battery and Instructor School of Mortars. Promoted Lieut. 21.3.18. Acting Captain 27.4.17 to 17.2.19.
Cunliffe-Owen, A. R. . . .	1916 From T/Lieut. Royal Fusiliers	2/Lieut.	
Dabell, W. B. .	26.2.15 From W.O. Class I G. Gds.	Lieut. and Qrmr.	Appointed Quartermaster of 1st Battalion on its formation. Served with B.E.F. from 17.8.15 to 12.3.19. Mentioned in Despatches twice. Awarded the Military Cross. Promoted Captain 26.2.18. Awarded the M.B.E.
Daniels, A. C. .	1918 From R.M.C.	2/Lieut.	
Davies, C. E. .	1917 From O. C. Bn.	2/Lieut.	Served with B.E.F. from 3.4.18 to 20.7.18. Wounded in action (gas) 17.5.18 and invalided to England on account of wounds. Promoted Lieut 30.4.19.
Davies, D. A. .	1917 From O. C. Bn.	2/Lieut.	Served with B.E.F. from 23.10.17 to 26.5.18. Attached to Guards Machine Gun Regiment.
Davies, D. B. .	1917 From O. C. Bn.	2/Lieut.	Served with B.E.F. from 12.12.17 to 12.3.19. Awarded the Military Cross. Promoted Lieut. 1.2.19.
Davies, E. J. .	1917 From O. C. Bn.	2/Lieut.	Served with B.E.F. from 3.10.17 to 28.3.18. Killed in action 28.3.18.
Davies, J. A. .	1918 From O. C. Bn.	2/Lieut.	Served with B.E.F. from 3.6.18 to 12.3.19.
Davison, L. .	1918 From O. C. Bn.	2/Lieut.	

Name.	Date of joining Welsh Guards and former regiment and rank.	Rank on joining Welsh Guards.	Remarks.
Dene, H.	1915 Temp. 2/Lieut. Res. Regt. of Cavalry	Captain	Served with B.E.F. 17.8.15 to 16.10.15. Wounded 13.10.15 and invalided to England on account of wounds. B.E.F. 19.2.16 to 1.5.17 and invalided to England on account of sickness. B.E.F. 12.10.17 to 27.8.18. Wounded in action 24.8.18, and invalided to England on account of wounds. Mentioned in Despatches three times and awarded D.S.O. Temp. Major from 17.7.16 to 1.12.16. Promoted Bt.-Major 1.1.17. A/Major 25.1.17 to 1.5.17. Acting Lieut.-Col. while commanding 1st Bn. 27.2.18 to 25.8.18.
Devas, G. C.	1915	2/Lieut.	Served with B.E.F. 25.9.16 to 25.2.19. Adjutant 1st Bn. from 3.8.17 to 1.11.18. On Staff from 2.11.18. Mentioned in Despatches and awarded the Military Cross. Promoted Lieut. 30.4.17. Acting Captain from 3.8.17.
Devereux, R. G. de B.	1915	2/Lieut.	Served with B.E.F. 12.12.16 to 14.3.17. Invalided to England on account of sickness. B.E.F. 10.8.17 to 3.12.17. Wounded in action 1.12.17. Promoted Lieut. 5.3.17.
De Wiart, M.C.	1915 From 2/Lieut. Lancs. Fus. T.F.	2/Lieut.	Served with B.E.F. 6.2.16 to 4.7.16. B.E.F. 4.10.16 to 3.11.16. B.E.F. 7.2.18 to 1.5.18. Invalided to England on account of sickness. Placed on retired list on account of ill-health contracted on active service 4.7.18. Promoted Lieut. 5.3.17.
Dickens, P. C.	1915	2/Lieut.	Served with B.E.F. 12–7.16 to 15.9.16. Wounded in action 10.9.16 and invalided to England on account of wounds. B.E.F. 31.7.17 to 9.12.17. Wounded in action 1.12.17 and invalided to England on account of wounds. Placed on retired list on account of ill-health caused by wounds 14.6.19. Promoted Lieut. 5.3.17.
Dilberoglue, P.	1916 From R.M.C.	2/Lieut.	Served with B.E.F. from 25.9.16 to 8.11.16. Invalided to England on account of sickness. B.E.F. from 3.4.18 to 15.6.18. Promoted Lieut. 30.4.17.

Name.	Date of joining Welsh Guards and former regiment and rank.	Rank on joining Welsh Guards.	Remarks.
Dodd, C. E. S. .	1915	2/Lieut.	Served with B.E.F. from 18.12.15 to 4.9.19. On the Staff from 26.4.18. Promoted Lieut. 5.3.17. Acting Captain 20.9.18 to 15.8.19.
Downing, W. N.	1916 From O. C. Bn.	2/Lieut.	Served with B.E.F. 25.9.16 to 10.3.19. Attd. Base Depot from 27.11.16. Promoted Lieut. 5.2.18.
Dudley-Ward, C. H. . .	1915 From 2/Lieut. London Regt.	2/Lieut.	Served with B.E.F. 19.10.15 to 18.1.17. Invalided to England on account of sickness. B.E.F. 4.9.17 to 12.3.19. Mentioned in Despatches. Awarded the D.S.O. and M.C. Promoted Lieut. 10.1.17. Acting Captain 26.10.17 to 8.9.18. Acting Major 9.9.18 to 11.4.19.
Duncan, C. W. .	1916	2/Lieut.	Served with B.E.F. from 19.12.17 to 1.3.19. Attd. Guards M.G. Regt. Promoted Lieut. 30.4.17.
Dyke-Dennis, P. G. . . .	1918 From O. C. Bn.	2/Lieut.	Served with B.E.F. from 2.11.18 to 12.3.19.
Ellis, J. S. . .	1918 From T/Lieut. Household Battalion	Lieut.	Joined 1st Bn. in France 10.3.18. Returned to England 4.3.19. Wounded in action (slight) 8.11.18.
Ellis, L. F. .	1916 From Inns of Court O.T.C.	2/Lieut.	Served with B.E.F. from 25.9.16 to 20.7.17. Invalided to England on account of sickness. Wounded in action slightly 19.11.16. B.E.F. 7.2.18 to 28.2.19. Awarded the Military Cross and D.S.O. Promoted Lieut. 30.4.17. Acting Captain from 27.2.18.
Evans, J. J. P. .	1915 From Capt. Welsh Horse Yeomanry (T.F.)	Lieut.	Served with B.E.F. 17.8.15 to 21.4.19. On Staff from 13.4.17 to 9.5.19. Wounded in action 20.7.18. Mentioned in Despatches twice and awarded the Military Cross and Bar. Temp. Captain 1.1.16 to 6.1.17. Promoted Captain 5.3.19.
Evans, P. A. L. .	1918 From O. C. Bn.	2/Lieut.	Served with B.E.F. from 20.7.18 to 19.12.18. Invalided to England on account of sickness. Promoted Lieut. 27.8.19.
Evan-Thomas, H. A. . . .	1915 From 2/Lieut.	2/Lieut.	Served with B.E.F. 17.8.15 to 22.9.15. Invalided to England on account of sickness. B.E.F. 4.5.16

Name.	Date of joining Welsh Guards and former regiment and rank.	Rank on joining Welsh Guards.	Remarks.
Evan-Thomas, H. A.—*continued*.	S. R. Cold. Guards.		to 14.9.16. Invalided to England on account of shell shock. B.E.F. 12.12.17 to 23.4.18. Invalided to England on account of sickness. Promoted Lieut. 1.10.15.
Fergusson, H. C., C.M.G. . .	1916 From Lieut.-Col. A. & S.H. S.R.	Major	Senior Major Res. Bn. 2.4.16 to disbandment.
Fitzwilliams, C. C. L. . .	1915 From Temp. Captain A.S.C.	Captain	Served with B.E.F. 22.9.16 to 23.10.18. Attd. Machine Gun Corps. Awarded the Military Cross, Belgian Order of Leopold with Palm (Chevalier) and Belgian Croix de Guerre.
Fleming, C. M. .	1917 From O. C. Bn.	2/Lieut.	Served with B.E.F. from 30.3.18 to 6.11.18. Wounded in action 11.10.18. and invalided to England on account of wounds. Promoted Lieut. 28.2.19.
Foot, V. E. .	1918 From O. C. Bn.	2/Lieut.	Served with B.E.F. from 5.9.18 to 25.11.18. Died of sickness 25.11.18. Wounded in action (slight) 23.9.18.
Fox-Pitt, W. A. F. L. . .	1915 From 2/Lieut. Cheshire Regt.	2/Lieut.	Served with B.E.F. 17.8.15 to 20.10.15. Wounded in action 17.10.15 and invalided to England on account of wounds. B.E.F. 9.7.16 to 18.1.17, invalided to England on account of sickness. B.E.F. 17.9.18 to 30.9.18. Wounded in action 27.9.18 and invalided to England on account of wounds. Awarded the Military Cross. Adjutant Res. Bn. 18.6.17 to 15.9.18. Promoted Lieut. 27.12.15. Acting Captain 3.8.17 to 15.9.18 and from 21.9.18. Promoted Captain 19.5.19.
Fripp, F. D. S. .	1916	2/Lieut.	Served with B.E.F. 5.5.17 to 20.10.17. Wounded in action (accidentally) 12.10.17. Invalided to England on account of wound. Promoted Lieut. 30.4.17. Transferred to Indian Army 13.1.18.
Fripp, G. H. S. .	1918 From O. C. Bn.	2/Lieut.	
Gibbs, A. . .	1915	2/Lieut.	Served with B.E.F. 18.12.15 to 22.8.18. (Returned for tour of

Name.	Date of joining Welsh Guards and former regiment and rank.	Rank on joining Welsh Guards.	Remarks.
Gibbs, A.—*continued*			Home Duty.) Wounded in action 5.4.18. Awarded the Military Cross. Promoted Lieut. 5.3.17. Acting Captain 16.5.17 to 22.4.18.
Gibbs, B. N. .	1918 From T/2/Lieut. Household Battalion.	Lieut.	Joined 1st Bn. in France 2.4.18. Invalided to England on account of sickness 3.9.18.
Gloag, J. E. .	1918 From O. C. Bn.	2/Lieut.	Served with B.E.F. 25.5.18 to 31.8.18. Wounded in action (gassed) 25.8.18 and invalided to England on account of wounds. Promoted Lieut. 30.7.19.
Goetz, R. E. O. .	1915 From Lieut. Rifle Brigade.	2/Lieut.	Served with B.E.F. from 2.5.16 to 30.12.18. Mentioned in Despatches and awarded the Military Cross. Promoted Lieut. 5.3.17. Acting Captain from 6.9.18 to 10.1.19.
Gordon, G. C. D.	26.2.15 From Capt. S.R. Scots Guards.	Captain	Adjutant of 1st Bn. from 26.2.15 to 18.7.15. Commanded 1st Bn. with acting rank of Lieut.-Colonel from 10.1.17 to 12.2.18. Served with B.E.F. from 25.11.16 to 12.2.18. Mentioned in Despatches. Awarded D.S.O. Commanded Reserve Battalion from 2.3.18 to date of retirement on 15.6.19. Promoted Major 2.4.15.
Gore, G. P. .	1916	2/Lieut.	Served with B.E.F. from 15.11.17 to 26.1.19. Bombing Officer 3rd Guards Brigade and Instructor IV Corps Bombing School. Promoted Lieut. 15.3.18.
Gough, W. H. J.	1915 From Lieut. Mont. Yeo. (T.F.)	Lieut.	Served with B.E.F. 17.8.15 to 26.4.16. Invalided to England on account of sickness. Attd. to M.G. Company from 19.9.15. Promoted Captain 10.1.17. To half-pay list on account of ill-health 6.2.19.
Gould, H. P. .	1916	2/Lieut.	Served with B.E.F. from 12.10.16 to 30.4.17. Invalided to England on account of sickness. Attd. Gds. M.G. Regiment. Promoted Lieut. 30.4.17.
Greenacre, W. D. C. . .	1918 From O. C. Bn.	2/Lieut.	Promoted Lieut. 26.12.19.

Name.	Date of joining Welsh Guards and former regiment and rank.	Rank on joining Welsh Guards.	Remarks.
Gwynne-Jones, A., D.S.O.	1917 From Lieut. E. Surrey Regt.	2/Lieut.	Served with B.E.F. from 18.3.17 to 10.9.17. Wounded in action 21.7.17 and invalided to England on account of sickness. B.E.F. 23.9.18 to 13.2.19. Promoted Lieut. 30.4.17.
Halliwell, C. C.	1918 From T/2/Lieut. K.R.R.	2/Lieut.	Served with B.E.F. from 7.9.18 to 21.2.19. Attd. Guards M.G. Regiment.
Hambrough, B. T. V. B.	1915 From 2/Lieut. Welsh Regt.	2/Lieut.	Served with B.E.F. 17.8.15 to 22.10.15. Wounded in action 18.10.15 and invalided to England. B.E.F. 2.5.16 to 20.1.17. Invalided to England on account of sickness. Promoted Lieut. 16.6.15. Promoted Captain 20.5.18.
Hargreaves, R. W.	1916 From T/2/Lieut. Gen. List.	2/Lieut.	Served with B.E.F. from 25.9.16 to 30.11.16. Wounded in action 16.11.16 and invalided to England on account of wounds. B.E.F. from 9.8.17 to 1.12.17. Killed in action 1.12.17. Promoted Lieut. 30.4.17.
Harlech, G. R. C., Lord	1915 From Retired List Cold. Gds.	Colonel	Lieut.-Colonel Commanding the Regiment from 16.6.15 to 14.10.17.
Harrop, N. M.	1917 From Capt. Royal Welsh Fus. (T.F.)	Lieut.	Served with B.E.F. from 3.10.17 to 4.3.19.
Hawksley, E. B.	1918 From O. C. Bn.	2/Lieut.	Served with B.E.F. from 25.5.18 to 4.11.18.
Hebert, B. T. M.	1915 From 2/Lieut. Royal Sussex Regt.	2/Lieut.	Served with B.E.F. from 13.7.16 to 15.9.16. Wounded in action 10.9.16 and invalided to England on account of wounds. B.E.F. 5.5.17 to 15.10.17. Wounded in action 10.10.17 and invalided to England on account of wounds. B.E.F. 10.11.18 to 12.3.19. Awarded the Military Cross. Promoted Lieut. 5.3.17. Acting Captain 12.2.19 to 11.4.19.
Hill, H. C. N.	1917 From O. C. Bn.	2/Lieut.	Served with B.E.F. from 31.3.18 to 20.2.19. Awarded the Military Cross.

Name.	Date of joining Welsh Guards and former regiment and rank.	Rank on joining Welsh Guards.	Remarks.
Hoffgaard, G. A.	1918 From O. C. Bn.	2/Lieut.	
Holdsworth, W. .	1918 From O. C. Bn.	2/Lieut.	Served with B.E.F. from 3.6.18 to 14.10.18. Wounded in action 11.10.18 and invalided to England on account of wounds.
Hore-Ruthven, Hon. A. G. A., V.C., C.B., C.M.G., D.S.O.	1915 From Capt. K.D. Gds.	Major	On Staff July 1915 to August 1915. On Staff from January 1916 to May 1st, 1919. Brig.-General G.S. and Brigade Commander 26th Brigade. Assumed command 1st Bn. 1.5.19. Mentioned in Despatches three times and awarded C.B., C.M.G., D.S.O. with Bar, Croix de Guerre (French) and Croix de Guerre (Belgian). Promoted Lieut.-Col. 15.10.17.
Howard, Hon. P. G. J. F. .	1915 From Lieut. Leinster Regiment.	2/Lieut.	Served with B.E.F. from 17.8.15 to 2.10.15. Wounded in action 27.9.15 and invalided to England on account of wounds. B.E.F. 12.12.17. Wounded in action 24.5.18 and died of wounds. Promoted Lieut. 7.12.16.
Hubbard, E. W.	1918 From O. C. Bn.	2/Lieut.	Served with B.E.F. from 7.9.18 to 2.11.18. Wounded in action 24.10.18 and invalided to England on account of wounds. Attd. Gds. M.G. Regt. Promoted Lieut. 30.7.19.
Hughes, M. A. .	1916	2/Lieut.	Served with B.E.F. from 12.9.16 to 12.6.18. Attd. Guards M.G. Regt. Promoted Lieut. 30.4.17.
Hughes-Hughes, E. P. A. de B.	1916	2/Lieut.	Served with B.E.F. 17.3.17 to 23.7.17. Invalided to England on account of sickness. B.E.F. 23.7.18 to 17.2.19. Attd. Guards M.G. Regt. Promoted Lieut. 30.4.17.
Immelman, D. W. . .	1918 From O. C. Bn.	2/Lieut.	Promoted Lieut. 31.1.20.
Insole, G. C. L. .	1915	2/Lieut.	Served with B.E.F. 17.8.15 to 4.7.16. Wounded in action 1.7.16 and invalided to England on account of wounds. B.E.F. 19.2.18. Killed in action 12.4.18. Awarded the Military Cross. Promoted Lieut. 16.6.15. Temp. Captain 2.2.16.

Name.	Date of joining Welsh Guards and former regiment and rank.	Rank on joining Welsh Guards.	Remarks.
Ison, A. J.	1918 From Lieut. Northumberland Fus. (T.F.)	Lieut.	Served with B.E.F. from 7.8.18 to 1.2.19. Attd. Guards M.G. Regiment.
Jefferson, J.	1918 From R.M.C.	2/Lieut.	Promoted Lieut. 21.2.20.
Jenkins, J. C.	1916 From O. C. Bn.	2/Lieut.	Served with B.E.F. from 10.2.17 to 20.3.17. Wounded in action 8.3.17 and invalided to England on account of wounds. Promoted Lieut. 19.6.18.
Jones, R. R.	1916 From O. C. Bn.	2/Lieut.	Served with B.E.F. from 10.2.17 to 25.8.17. Wounded in action 31.7.17. Died of wounds 25.8.17. Mentioned in Despatches and awarded the D.S.O.
Kearton, J. L. G.	1916 From 2/Lieut. Royal Sussex Regt.	2/Lieut.	Served with B.E.F. from 2.5.16 to 26.6.16. Wounded in action 22.6.16 and invalided to England on account of wounds. B.E.F. 9.8.16 to 27.10.16. Invalided to England on account of sickness. B.E.F. 22.12.16 to 3.12.17. Died of wounds 3.12.17. Promoted Lieut. 30.4.17.
Kemball, C. G.	1918 From O. C. Bn.	2/Lieut.	
Knowling, H. W.	1918 From Lieut. A.S.C.	Lieut.	
Lascelles, H. F.	1916	2/Lieut.	Served with B.E.F. from 25.9.16 to 15.10.17. Invalided to England on account of sickness. Awarded Croix de Guerre (French). Promoted Lieut. 16.2.18.
Lewis, J. W.	1915 From Lieut. R. of O.	Lieut.	Served with B.E.F. from 19.10.15 to 6.6.16. Killed in action 6.6.16.
Lewis, R. W.	1915 From Capt. Glam. Yeo. (T.F.)	Lieut.	Served with B.E.F. from 17.8.15 to 26.1.16. Wounded in action slightly 27.9.15. Invalided to England on account of sickness. B.E.F. 17.7.16 to 29.9.16. Wounded in action 26.9.16 and invalided to

Name.	Date of joining Welsh Guards and former regiment and rank.	Rank on joining Welsh [Guards.	Remarks.
Lewis, R. W. —continued.			England. B.E.F. 5.4.18 to 23.8.18. (Returned to England for tour of duty at home.) Mentioned in Despatches and awarded the Military Cross. Temp. Captain from 16.11.15 to 1.2.16, 21.7.16 to 25.9.16. Promoted Captain 10.1.17.
Lisburne, E. E. H. M., Earl of .	1915 From 2/Lieut. R.O. Scots Guards.	Lieut.	Served with B.E.F. 12.7.16 to 11.12.17. Invalided to England on account of sickness. Wounded in action slightly 26.9.16. Acting Captain 21.1.17. Promoted Captain 30.4.17. Regtl. Adjt. 20.5.18. to 9.5.19.
Llewellyn, P. .	1917 From O. C. Bn.	2/Lieut.	Served with B.E.F. 9.8.17 to 23.3.18. Wounded in action 10.3.18 and invalided to England on account of wounds. Awarded the Military Cross. Promoted Lieut. 25.7.18.
Luxmoore-Ball, R. E. C. . .	1915 From Lieut. South African Forces.	Lieut.	Served with B.E.F. 16.9.15 to 18.6.16. Wounded in action 16.6.16 and invalided to England on account of wounds. B.E.F. 25.9.16 to 12.3.19. Commanded 1st Bn. from 8.9.18 to 12.3.19. Mentioned in Despatches three times. Awarded D.S.O., D.C.M., and Croix de Guerre (French). Temp. Captain from 1.1.16 to 16.6.16 and from 9.2.18 to 13.3.18. Acting Captain from 11.10.16 to 15.5.17. Acting Major from 16.5.17 to 10.1.18 and from 14.3.18 to 7.9.18. Acting Lieut.-Col. from 8.9.18 to 11.4.19. Promoted Captain 18.1.19.
Mackinnon, L. D. W. . .	1918 From T/2/Lieut. Household Battalion.	2/Lieut.	Joined 1st Bn. in France 7.4.18. Transferred to Res. Bn. at home 19.4.18. B.E.F. from 23.9.18 to 26.2.19.
Manley, G. D. .	1916 From O. C. Bn.	2/Lieut.	Served with B.E.F. 24.4.17 to 10.7.17. Invalided to England on account of sickness. Promoted Lieut. 19.6.18.
Martineau, H. M.	1915 From Lieut. Royal Berks Regt.	2/Lieut.	Resigned Commission on account of ill-health 19.9.15.

Name.	Date of joining Welsh Guards and former regiment and rank.	Rank on joining Welsh Guards.	Remarks.
Mason, F. R. .	1918 From O. C. Bn.	2/Lieut.	
Mathew, T. .	1917	2/Lieut.	Served with B.E.F. from 7.2.18 to 28.8.18. Wounded in action 10.8.18 and invalided to England on account of wounds. Promoted Lieut. 23.7.18.
Mawby, E. G. .	1915 From 2/Lieut. R. Fus.	2/Lieut.	Served with B.E.F. 17.8.15 to 27.9.15. Killed in action 27.9.15. Promoted Lieut. 28.4.15.
Menzies, K. G. .	1915 2/Lieut. S.R. 2nd Life Guards.	Lieut.	Served with B.E.F. 17.8.15 to 17.4.16. Invalided to England on account of sickness. B.E.F. 2.6.17 to 12.3.19. Awarded the Military Cross and Croix de Guerre (French). Temp. Captain 18.4.18 to 16.6.18. Promoted Captain 20.5.18.
Miller, H. B. .	1918 From O. C. Bn.	2/Lieut.	Served with B.E.F. from 2.11.18 to 12.3.19. Promoted Lieut. 29.11.19.
Morgan, D. B. .	1918 From O. C. Bn.	2/Lieut.	Served with B.E.F. from 2.11.18 to 12.3.19.
Morgan, Hon. E. F. . . .	1915	2/Lieut.	Promoted Lieut. 20.11.16. Resigned Commission on account of ill-health 1.5.19.
Morton, W. F. C.	1918 From O. C. Bn.	2/Lieut.	Promoted Lieut. 31.1.20.
Murray-Threipland, W. .	26.2.15 From Major R. of O. Gren. Gds.	Lieut.-Col.	Appointed to command the 1st Battalion on formation of the Regiment. Commanded the Battalion from 27.2.15 till 14.10.17. Served with B.E.F. from 17.8.15 to 16.12.16. Mentioned in Despatches three times. Awarded D.S.O. Appointed Lieut.-Col. of the Regiment on 15.10.17. Bt.-Col. 1.1.19. Colonel 26.2.19.
Newall, N. .	1915	2/Lieut.	Served with B.E.F. 4.11.15 to 25.1.16. Wounded in action 20.1.16 and invalided to England on account of wounds. B.E.F. 26.6.17 to 12.10.17. Killed in action 12.10.17. Promoted Lieut. 10.1.17.

32

Name.	Date of joining Welsh Guards and former regiment and rank.	Rank on joining Welsh Guards.	Remarks.
Newborough, W. C., Lord	1915 From Lieut. D.L.I.	Lieut.	Served with B.E.F 18.12.15 to 11.4.16. Invalided to England on account of sickness and died 19.7.16.
North, V. G.	1916 From 2/Lieut. K.R.R.	2/Lieut.	Served with B.E.F. from 21.10.16 to 19.12.16. Invalided to England on account of sickness. B.E.F. 3.10.17 to 25.9.18. Attd. Guards M.G. Regiment. Promoted Lieut. 30.4.17.
Osmond-Williams, O. T. D., D.S.O.	1915 From 2/Lieut. R. Scots Greys.	Captain	Served with B.E.F. from 17.8.15 to 30.9.15. Wounded in action 27.9.15 and died on 30.9.15 as the result of wounds.
Palmer, A. P., D.S.O.	1915 From Lieut. R. of O.	Captain	Served with B.E.F. from 17.8.15 to 27.9.15. Killed in action 27.9.15.
Paton, R. R. D.	1917 From O. C. Bn.	2/Lieut.	Served with B.E.F. from 31.3.18 to 12.3.19. Awarded the Military Cross.
Pell, L. H.	1918 From T/Lt. General List.	2/Lieut.	
Perrins, J. A. D.	1915 From Lieut. Seaforth High-landers.	2/Lieut.	Served with B.E.F. 17.8.15 to 15.3.19. Adj. of 1st Bn. 19.7.15 to 3.8.17. To Staff 3.8.17. Wounded in action slightly 15.9.16. Mentioned in Despatches and awarded the Military Cross and Bar, Croix de Guerre (French) and Order of the Crown of Italy. Acting Captain 5.4.18. Promoted Lieut. 16.6.15. Promoted Captain 20.5.18.
Philipps, G. W. F.	1915 From Capt. Durham L.I.	Captain	Served with B.E.F. 17.8.15 to 1.10.15. Invalided to England on account of wounds and subsequently placed on the half-pay list.
Pitchford, W. C.	1918 From O. C. Bn.	2/Lieut.	
Ponsonby, R. M. V.	1918 From O. C. Bn.	2/Lieut.	
Powell, W. E. G. P. W.	1917 From R.M.C.	2/Lieut.	Served with B.E.F. 16.8.18 to 6.11.18. Killed in action 6.11.18.
Power, J. W.	1915 From Lieut. Somerset L.I.	Lieut.	Served with B.E.F. 15.7.16 to 10.9.16. Killed in action 10.9.16.

Name.	Date of joining Welsh Guards and former regiment and rank.	Rank on joining Welsh Guards.	Remarks.
Prance, A. L. .	1918 From O. C. Bn.	2/Lieut.	
Price, A. E. .	1915	Lieut.	Promoted Captain 20.5.18.
Price, T. R. C. .	1915 From Major 11th Lan. (I.A.)	Major	Joined 1st Bn. in France on transfer 2.12.15. Returned to England 13.4.19. On Staff from 16.6.16 to 13.4.19. G.S.O. 46th Division. Brigade Commander 11th Brigade. Mentioned in Despatches three times and awarded the D.S.O., C.M.G., and Legion of Honour (Chevalier).
Pugh, J. A. .	1915 Ex.-Cadet O.T.C.	2/Lieut.	Served with B.E.F. 6.2.16 to 14.9.16. Wounded in action 10.9.16 and invalided to England. Promoted Lieut. 5.3.17.
Randolph, J. .	1915 From Lieut. Norfolk Regt. (T.F.)	Lieut.	Served with B.E.F. 17.8.15 to 27.9.15. Killed in action 27.9.15.
Read, A. B. .	1918 From O. C. Bn.	2/Lieut.	
Reid, P. F. .	1918 From O. C. Bn.	2/Lieut.	Served with B.E.F. from 5.9.18 to 7.1.19.
Rice, H. T. .	1915 Lieut. E. Yorks Yeo.	2/Lieut.	Served with B.E.F. 17.8.15 to 14.9.16. Wounded in action 19.6.16, 25.7.16, and 9.9.16. Invalided to England on account of wounds. B.E.F. 2.6.17 to 4.9.17. Wounded in action 31.7.17. Invalided to England on account of wounds. Promoted Lieut. 19.7.15. Promoted Captain 20.5.18.
Roberts, J. A. G. .	1918 From T/2/Lieut. Household Battalion.	Lieut.	Joined 1st Bn. in France 11.3.18. Invalided to England on account of sickness 21.8.18. Relinquished Commission on account of ill-health 8.2.19.
Roberts, M. O. .	1915 From Lieut. R. of O. Scots Guards.	Captain	Served with B.E.F. 17.8.15 to 31.10.15. B.E.F. 2.3.18 to 5.6.18. Invalided to England on account of sickness. Placed on half-pay list on account of ill-health caused by wounds 18.1.19.

Name.	Date of joining Welsh Guards and former regiment and rank.	Rank on joining Welsh Guards.	Remarks.
Roderick, H. B. .	1916 From Capt. Welsh Regt. (T.F.)	Lieut.	Served with B.E.F. from 11.12.16 to 1.12.17. Wounded in action 12.7.17. Killed in action 1.12.17. Acting Captain from 3.6.17.
Romer-Williams, C. . . .	1917 From T/Lieut. General List.	Lieut.	Served with B.E.F. from 12.12.17 to 1.1.19. Temp. Captain from 19.4.18 to 31.1.19. Awarded the Croix de Guerre (French).
Saunders, H. A. St. G. . .	1916	2/Lieut.	Served with B.E.F. from 31.1.17 to 7.7.17. Invalided to England on account of sickness. B.E.F. 23.9.18 to 12.3.19. Awarded the Military Cross. Promoted Lieut. 30.4.17.
Shand, R. C. R. .	1916 From O. C. Bn.	2/Lieut.	Served with B.E.F. from 10.2.17 to 12.3.19. Attd. 3rd Guards Brigade Trench Mortar Battery from 10.9.17 to 18.2.19. Awarded the Military Cross. Promoted Lieut. 22.5.18.
Shipley, W., D.C.M. . .	1915 From W.O. Cold. Gds.	Lieut. and Qmr.	Quartermaster Res. Bn. from 5.8.15 to date of disbandment. Promoted Captain 5.8.18.
Smith, E. R. M. .	1915	Lieut.	Adjt. Res. Bn. 17.8.15 to 17.6.17. Served with B.E.F. 23.6.17 to 27.2.18. With B.E.F. 22.10.18 to 10.12.18. Camp Commandant H.Q. Fifth Army. Promoted Captain 20.5.18.
Smith, H. G. .	1915 Temp. Capt. E. Kent Regt.	Captain	Served with B.E.F. 6.2.16 to 10.4.16. Re-transferred to E. Kent Regiment 23.8.16.
Smith, J. . .	1918 From O. C. Bn.	2/Lieut.	
Smith, R. . .	1915	2/Lieut.	Served with B.E.F. 17.8.15 to 27.9.15. Killed in action 27.9.15.
Smith, R. W. .	1918 From O. C. Bn.	2/Lieut.	Served with B.E.F. from 29.10.18 to 12.3.19. Promoted Lieut. 27.9.19.
Spence-Thomas, H. A. . .	1918 From O. C. Bn.	2/Lieut.	Served with B.E.F. from 3.6.18 to 12.3.19. Promoted Lieut. 27.8.19.
Stanier, A. B. G..	1917 From R.M.C.	2/Lieut.	Served with B.E.F. from 25.5.18 to 12.3.19. Wounded in action (slight) 20.10.18. Awarded the Military Cross. Promoted Lieut. 21.6.19.

Name.	Date of joining Welsh Guards and former regiment and rank.	Rank on joining Welsh Guards.	Remarks.
Stokes, B.	1917 From O. C. Bn.	2/Lieut.	Served with B.E.F. from 12.12.17 to 19.4.18. Invalided to England on account of shell shock. To retired list on account of ill-health 10.1.19.
Stokes, D. O. C. C.	1918 From O. C. Bn.	2/Lieut.	
Stokes, H. S.	1915	2/Lieut.	Served with B.E.F. 18.12.15 to 23.2.17. Attd. T.M. Battery from 8.4.16. Invalided to England on account of sickness. Awarded the Military Cross. Promoted to Lieut. 5.3.17. Acting Captain from 2.12.16. Adjutant Res. Bn. 15.9.18 to date of disbandment.
Storey, T. W.	1917 From 2/Lieut. M.G.C.	2/Lieut.	Served with B.E.F. from 27.11.17 to 6.3.19. Attd. Guards M.G. Regiment. Promoted Lieut. 11.5.19.
Stracey-Clitherow, J. B.	1915 From Ret. Pay Scots Guards.	Lieut.-Col.	Commanded Res. Bn. from 27.8.15 to 2.3.18.
Strang, W. F.	1918 From O. C. Bn.	2/Lieut.	
Sutton, H. J.	1915 From 2/Lieut. London Regt. (T.F.)	2/Lieut.	Served with B.E.F. 17.8.15 to 27.9.15. Killed in action 27.9.15. Promoted Lieut. 16.6.15.
Tatham, H. L.	1918 From O. C. Bn.	2/Lieut.	Served with B.E.F. from 2.6.18 to 12.3.19.
Taylor, J. V.	1915 From Capt. Welsh Regt.	Captain	Served with B.E.F. from 13.6.17 to 16.10.17. Wounded in action 11.10.17. Invalided to England on account of wounds.
Tennant, G. C. S.	1917 From R.M.C.	2/Lieut.	Served with B.E.F. from 9.8.17 to 3.9.17. Killed in action 3.9.17.
Thursby-Pelham, N. C.	1918 From Lieut. K.S.L.I. (T.F.).	Lieut.	
Trotter, H. B., M.M.	1918 From O. C. Bn.	2/Lieut.	Served with B.E.F. from 3.6.18 to 10.9.18. Wounded in action 4.9.18. Died of wounds 10.9.18.

Name.	Date of joining Welsh Guards and former regiment and rank.	Rank on joining Welsh Guards.	Remarks.
Trotter, P. C. .	1918 From T/Lieut. Res. H. Bn.	Lieut.	To Finland on Special Duty 18.5.19. Awarded the M.B.E.
Upjohn, W. M. .	1915	2/Lieut.	Served with B.E.F. 25.9.16 to 17.5.17. Invalided to England on account of sickness. B.E.F. 20.5.18 to 24.8.18. Killed in action 24.8.18. Promoted Lieut. 30.4.17. Acting Captain 31.1.17 to 20.5.18.
Vigor, G. St. V. J.	1918 From R.M.C.	2/Lieut.	
Walters, I. G. .	1918 From O. C. Bn.	2/Lieut.	
Walters, T. G. .	1918 From O. C. Bn.	2/Lieut.	Served with B.E.F. from 2.11.18 to 4.3.19.
Watson, T. B. .	1918 From O. C. Bn.	2/Lieut.	Served with B.E.F. from 25.5.18 to 12.3.19. Promoted Lieut. 30.7.19.
Webb, T. H. B. .	1916	2/Lieut.	Served with B.E.F. from 9.8.17 to 1.12.7. Killed in action 1.12.17.
Wells, N. G. .	1915	2/Lieut.	Served with B.E.F. 17.8.15 to 16.10.16. Invalided to England on account of sickness. To Egypt for employment on the Staff 21.5.17. Promoted Lieut. 20.11.16. Died of sickness in Jerusalem 9.10.19.
Wernher, A. P. .	1916 From 2/Lieut. R. Bucks Hussars.	2/Lieut.	Served with B.E.F. from 17.7.16 to 10.9.16. Killed in action 10.9.16.
Wethered, H. E.	1915 From Lieut. R. of O. R.A.	Lieut.	Served with B.E.F. from 17.8.15 to 10.10.15. Invalided to England on account of sickness. Attd. to British Legation at Athens from 10.4.16 to 23.7.16. To Staff, Egypt, 18.4.17, as G.S.O. Promoted Captain 1.10.15.
Wharton, A. .	1918 From O. C. Bn.	2/Lieut.	Served with B.E.F. from 10.11.18 to 12.3.19.

Name.	Date of joining Welsh Guards and former regiment and rank.	Rank on joining Welsh Guards.	Remarks.
Whitehouse, C. D.	1918 From T/2/Lieut. Household Battalion.	2/Lieut.	Joined 1st Bn. in France 13.3.18. Reported missing, believed killed, 27.5.18. Death accepted for official purposes as having occurred in action on 26.5.18.
Wickham, J. L. .	1915 From Lieut. S.R. Scots Guards.	Captain	Seconded for work under the Ministry of Munitions in June 1915. Promoted Major 29.3.18.
Wightwick, W. F. D. . . .	1916	2/Lieut.	Served with B.E.F. from 30.6.17 to 7.9.17. Attd. Guards M.G. Regiment. Promoted Lieut. 30.4.17.
Wilcock, P. J. C. .	1918 From O. C. Bn.	2/Lieut.	
Williams, Sir R., Bart. . .	1915 From 2/Lieut. Grenadier Guards. R. of O.	Captain	Served with B.E.F. from 17.8.15 to 2.10.15. Wounded in action 27.9.15 and invalided to England. Mentioned in Despatches and awarded the D.S.O. Asst. Military Attaché at Teheran from 20.11.15 to 23.11.16. Awarded the Russian Order of St. Vladimir (with Swords) and Persian Order of the Lion and the Sun (2nd Class). Subsequently employed on various Staff appointments.
Williams, E. H. I.	1915 From Temp. 2/Lieut. Welsh Regt.	2/Lieut.	Relinquished Commission on account of ill-health 29.2.16.
Williams-Bulkeley, R. G. W. .	1915 From Lieut. R. of O. Grenadier Guards.	Captain	Served with B.E.F. from 17.8.15 to 23.4.16. Wounded in action 8.12.15 and subsequently invalided to England and died as the result of wounds. Mentioned in Despatches and awarded the Military Cross. Promoted Major 2.5.17.
Williams-Ellis, B. C. . . .	1915 From Temp. Lieut. Royal Fusiliers.	Lieut.	Served with B.E.F. 19.10.15 to 25.11.18. On Staff from 13.4.16. Awarded the Military Cross. Promoted Captain 20.5.18.
Willoughby, C. J.	1918 From O. C. Bn.	2/Lieut.	Served with B.E.F. from 5.9.18 to 30.9.18. Wounded in action 27.9.18. Invalided to England on account of wounds. Promoted Lieut. 27.8.19.

Name.	Date of joining Welsh Guards and former regiment and rank.	Rank on joining Welsh Guards.	Remarks.
Wiseman, J. A.	1917 From O. C. Bn.	2/Lieut.	Served with B.E.F. from 12.12.17 to 22.4.18. B.E.F. 16.6.18 to 15.11.18. Invalided to England on account of sickness.
Wreford-Brown, R. L.	1916	2/Lieut.	Served with B.E.F. 18.10.16 to 6.12.17. Wounded in action 1.12.17 and invalided to England on account of wounds. Awarded the Military Cross. Promoted Lieut. 30.4.17.
Wynne-Williams, F. B.	1915 From 2/Lieut. London Regt. (T.F.)	2/Lieut.	Served with B.E.F. from 6.2.16 to 28.9.16. Invalided to England on account of sickness. B.E.F. 19.6.16 to 19.10.17. Gassed 12.10.17. B.E.F. 31.10.18 to 17.3.19. Attd. Guards M.G. Regiment. Awarded the Military Cross. Promoted Lieut. 5.3.17.
Wynn, A. R.	1916 From 2/Lieut. Mont. Yeo. (T.F.)	2/Lieut.	Promoted Lieut. 30.4.17. Attd. to Ministry of Munitions from 8.5.17.
Youngman, R. W.	1917 From O. C. Bn.	2/Lieut.	Served with B.E.F. from 27.3.17 to 13.8.17. Invalided to England on account of sickness. Promoted Lieut. 15.7.18.

APPENDIX K

COMPANY COLOURS

(BY THE REV. E. E. DORLING, M.A., F.S.A.)

PRINCE OF WALES'S COMPANY

Arms : *Gules three lions passant silver*

These are the arms attributed to Griffith ap Cynan, king of North Wales and founder of the First Royal Tribe, who flourished about the year 1079. Even if King Griffith displayed them (and there is no certainty that he did) they were not truly heraldic because they were not hereditary. The arms, however, came to be regarded in the middle ages as those of this king, and as specially emblematic of North Wales ; but it must be remembered that they were personal to King Griffith, and were not considered to have been borne by that monarch's eldest son and successor.

No. 2 COMPANY

Arms : *Vert three eagles gold set fessewise*

Owen Gwynedd, king of North Wales, eldest son of Griffith ap Cynan, is said to have borne these arms. They are now, as they have been for centuries, the coat-armour of Wynn of Gwydyr, who claims descent through Roderick, lord of Anglesea, from King Owen Gwynnedd.

No. 3 COMPANY

Arms : *Quarterly gold and gules with four leopards counter-coloured*

These arms were undoubtedly borne by Llewellin ap Griffith, prince of North Wales, and descendant of Owen Gwynedd. Llewellin did homage to Henry III for his principality of North Wales, but, having revolted against

Edward I, he was eventually defeated and killed at the battle of Builth on the Wye in 1248. His arms were assumed by Owen Glendower, who proclaimed himself king of all Wales in 1402. From that date this quartered shield, with the four counter-coloured leopards, has been regarded as the arms of Wales. As such they are borne in pretence and ensigned with his princely coronet upon the differenced royal arms by H.R.H. the Prince of Wales.

No. 4 COMPANY

Arms : *Gules a lion and a border indented gold*

These are the arms attributed to Rhys ap Tewdur, king of South Wales and founder of the Second Royal Tribe. This king was contemporary with William the Conqueror. Although it is not certain he bore these arms, they were attributed to him in after years and came to symbolise South Wales.

No. 5 COMPANY

Arms : *Gold a lion gules*

Attributed to Bleddyn ap Cynfyn, king of Powis and founder of the Third Royal Tribe. This prince ruled Powisland before the Norman Conquest, and, though it is open to doubt that King Bleddyn himself bore these arms, it is certain that a rampant lion, either red or black, came in process of time to be recognised as the heraldic emblem of Powis. King Bleddyn's son Meredith and his grandson Madoc are said to have borne a black lion in a silver field. Griffith Maelor (son of Madoc) differenced his father's arms by colouring the field with eight perpendicular stripes, alternately silver and red, and his descendants, the lords of Glyndwyn, bore the black lion of Powis upon the same paly field.

No. 6 COMPANY

Arms : *Paly of eight pieces silver and gules a lion sable*

These were the arms of the later princes of Powis, the last to bear them as such being Owen ap Griffith Vychan, lord of Glyndwyr (better known as Owen Glendower.) When this prince usurped the sovereignty of all Wales in 1402, he assumed the arms formerly borne by Llewellin.

No. 7 Company

Arms : *Silver, three boars' heads sable, quartered with Party bend sinister-wise ermine and erminois a lion gold*

These are said to be the arms of Ethylstan Glodrydd, prince of Ferlys (the land between Wye and Severn), and founder of the Fourth Royal Tribe . His own part of the device is the silver with black boars' heads ; the other arms with the golden lion are, it is said, those of his mother, Rhingor, daughter and heir of Gronwy ap Tewdwr-Trevor, lord of Whittington in Shropshire, which he assumed and quartered with his own.

No. 8 Company

Arms : *Gules three chevrons silver*

This coat is assigned to Jestyn ap Gwrgant, prince of Glamorgan, and founder of the Fifth Royal Tribe.

The eight Company Colours are designed and constructed on the model of the well-known flag called in the middle ages a standard.

This was a long, tapering flag having, for English bearers, next to the staff the peculiarly English emblem of the arms of St. George in a compartment slightly narrower than its height and occupying the whole width of the standard. The remainder consisted of two or more longitudinal strips of the livery colours of the bearer sewn together for the greater part of their length ; and its edges were richly fringed.

Upon the long parti-coloured portion were disposed the heraldic badges of the bearer, with two or more diagonal bands inscribed with his posy, or motto. At the extremity the material was slit for a short distance horizontally, and the two ends thus produced were rounded off.

It will be seen, from our illustrations, that these Company Colours follow this fashion precisely, except that the compartment next to the staff is in each case occupied by the arms of a Welsh king or prince instead of by those of the patron saint of England.

The longitudinal strips are the white and green of Wales, across which are thrown diagonally the motto bands proper to the respective companies. Two golden dragons are shewn as the badge of the Principality, and a like dragon appears upon the King's Colour. There is precedent for painting the dragon of Wales gold, since Mary Tudor and her sister Queen Elizabeth used a golden dragon as the sinister supporter of the royal arms ; but the far more usual tincture of the Welsh dragon is red. The three kings of the house of Tudor never displayed any but a red dragon, and for many centuries the red dragon has been considered to be the dragon of Wales.

The colouring of the fringes of each standard, it will be observed, follows the usual heraldic practice exemplified by the crest-wreath and mantling in an achievement of arms ; the tinctures are those of the principal colour and metal of the coat of arms with which they are respectively associated.

The mottoes on the Company Colours have, with the approval of His Majesty the King, been slightly modified. They are now as follows :

> (1) Y DDRAIG GOCH DDYRY CYCHWYN.
> The Red Dragon gives a lead.
> (2) GWYR YNYS Y CEDYRN.
> The men of the Island of the mighty.

(This, it will be seen, is an entirely new motto. The original, which might be given as " The valiant heroes of Wales," was a corrupt form of Welsh. " The Island of the Mighty " is Great Britain, and the Men of Britain, as opposed to Ireland, are the ancient Britons before the coming of the Saxons—in other words, the ancestors of the Cymry.)

> (3) FY NUW, FY NGWLAD, FY MRENIN.
> My God, my Land, my King.
> (4) GOREU ARF, CALON DDEWR.
> The best weapon is a brave heart.
> (5) OFNA DDUW, ANRHYDEDDA'R BRENIN.
> Fear God ; Honour the King.
> (6) NAC OFNA OND GWARTH.
> Fear nothing but disgrace.
> (7) Y GWIR YN ERBYN Y BYD.
> The truth against the world.
> (8) OFNER NA OFNO ANGAU.
> Feared be he who fears not death.

THE KING'S COLOUR

THE REGIMENTAL COLOUR

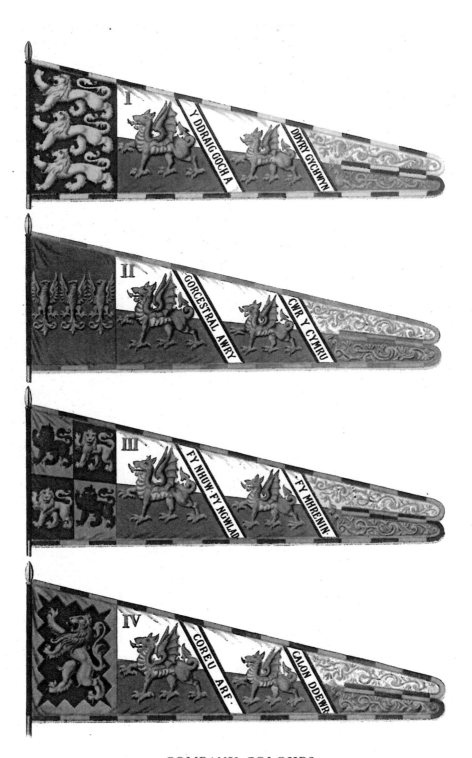

COMPANY COLOURS

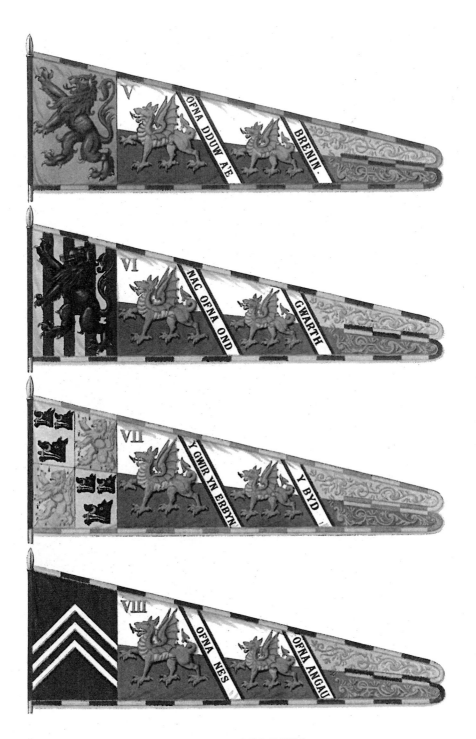

COMPANY COLOURS

INDEX

33

Lightning Source UK Ltd.
Milton Keynes UK
203f1450230913
UK00005B/120/A